to Rick
for a
encoura

Dave
March, 1993

*Alternative Paths*

# ALTERNATIVE PATHS

*Soviets and Americans,*
*1917–1920*

David W. McFadden

*New York    Oxford*
OXFORD UNIVERSITY PRESS
1993

Oxford University Press

Oxford   New York   Toronto
Delhi   Bombay   Calcutta   Madras   Karachi
Kuala Lumpur   Singapore   Hong Kong   Tokyo
Nairobi   Dar es Salaam   Cape Town
Melbourne   Auckland   Madrid

and associated companies in
Berlin   Ibadan

Copyright © 1993 by David W. McFadden

Published by Oxford University Press, Inc.,
200 Madison Avenue, New York, New York 10016

Oxford is a registered trademark of Oxford University Press

Library of Congress Cataloging-in-Publication Data
McFadden, David W.
Alternative paths : Soviets and Americans, 1917–1920 /
David W. McFadden
p. cm.   Includes bibliographical references and index.
ISBN 0-19-507187-5
1. United States—Foreign relations—Soviet Union.
2. Soviet Union—Foreign relations—United States.
3. Soviet Union—History—Revolution, 1917–1921.
4. United States—Foreign relations—1913–1921.   I. Title.
E183.8.S65M378   1993
327.47073—dc20   92-17949

1 3 5 7 9 8 6 4 2

Printed in the United States of America
on acid-free paper

*To the memory of my father, who never let me forget the reasons for my work.*

# ACKNOWLEDGEMENTS

The author gratefully acknowledges the assistance of the following individuals and institutions, without which the research and writing of this book would have been impossible:

Natalie Shiras, not only for living with this unfolding project in its various stages for more than six years, but for her careful help with syntax, grammar, and other problems a sprawling writer is subject to:

Alexander and Anne McShiras, for suffering their dad to spend far too long at the computer and have less time for reading, playing, and more exciting pursuits;

Diane Shaver Clemens, for untold hours of reading, writing, discussing, critiquing, probing and encouraging;

Leon Litwack, George Breslauer, Alexander Dallin, Jim Kettner, and Reggie Zelnik, for their encouragement, support, and numerous hours of critiquing draft material;

George F. Kennan, for his early encouragement of this project, and for sharing many boxes of private notes and other materials;

William Appleman Williams, Richard N. Debo, Alexander George, and Barton Bernstein, for their excellent research suggestions at early stages of the project;

Alan Greb, Jim Skelly, and the fellows of the Institute on Global Conflict and Cooperation of the University of California, for believing in me, assisting me, and holding me to a high standard of scholarship and instilling a sensitivity to other disciplines;

Mark Kleinman, Michael Bess, David Foglesong, Victor Silverman, Betty Dessants, and Alan Lawrence, for their willingness to spend hours discussing my work;

David Olsen, for his initial encouragement;

Jean-Luc Lebrun, for his assistance with French;

Krista Hanson, for her Russian tutoring and her calm insistence that I do new research in Moscow;

Alan Greb, Tair Tairov, A. O. Chubar'ian, Galina Androchnikova, Gennadi Alferenko, and the Foundation for Social Innovation, for making my research in Moscow possible;

Oleg Tumin, Anatoli Belyayev, Ivan Krasnov, Ludmilla Evgeneva, Sasha, and Tanya for assisting me so much during my stay in Moscow.

The Berlekey-Stanford Program on Soviet Studies; the Department of History of the University of California, Berkeley; and the Institute on Global Conflict and Cooperation, University of California; for support for research trips to Boston, Washington, Albany, London, and Moscow;

Rick DeAngelis, Bill Abbott, David Danahar, John Thiel, Betsy Hoagg, Egea Logan, the Research Committee of Fairfield University and the Humanities Institute of Fairfield University for their encouragement and support during the final stages of writing, editing, and revising;

Betty Unterberger, Lloyd Ambrosius, Linda Killen, Christine White, Katherine Siegel, and Fred Travis, for their thoughtful suggestions and encouragement;

The archivists and librarians at the Missouri State Historical Society, St. Louis; the Mudd Library, Princeton University; Sterling Library, Yale University; Harvard University Libraries; the Central Archive Administration of the Council of Ministers of the U.S.S.R., Moscow; the Bodleian Library, Oxford University; the House of Lords Records Office; the Public Records Office, Kew; National Archive Administration, Washington; the Library of Congress; Wisconsin State Historical Society, Madison; Bancroft Library, University of California, Berkeley; Hoover Institution on War, Revolution and Peace, Library and Archives; University of Chicago Library; Newberry Library, Chicago; Butler Library and Oral History Collection, Columbia University; New York Public Library; New York State Library and Archives, Albany.

Finally, many thanks to my editors at Oxford University Press, Sheldon Meyer, Karen Wolny, and Gail Cooper, for seeing this project to completion.

If I have omitted anyone through error or oversight, my deepest apologies. While I am fully cognizant of others' many contributions to this project, the final wording and thinking, including any errors, remain my own.

*Fairfield, Connecticut*                                                                                    D.W.M.
*July 10, 1992*

# CONTENTS

*Alternative Paths*

# INTRODUCTION

For four months I have been the link between the government of Russia and the government of the United States. I am still apparently trusted by both though we have had awful strains. . . . I am the best hated and best loved man of all the foreign leaders here. . . .

*—Raymond Robins to Wife, Margaret, April 14, 1918*[1]

It is most important and desirable to us that one of us should be able to officially go to the United States. This is the most important thing . . . nothing is more desirable to us than to get into friendly relations with the United States.

*—Soviet Foreign Minister Georgi Chicherin to Valentin Zorin, September 30, 1918*[2]

The origins of the complex and multifaceted relationship between Soviet Russia and the United States of America long predate the nuclear age and the conventional beginnings of the Cold War. The diverse dimensions of conflict, and efforts to resolve differences, date from the very beginnings of Bolshevik power: November 7, 1917. Far from there being a clear and unambiguous policy on either side, the first years of the relationship comprised a series of experimental attempts to come to terms with each other. These efforts occurred at a time of enormous pressure and change for both societies. Woodrow Wilson had only recently reversed course and committed the United States to the defeat of Germany in World War I, the first-ever commitment of American ground troops to a European war. Vladimir Lenin and the Bolsheviks looked into a totally unknown future, heading a government that they firmly believed could not survive without the assistance of revolutionary uprisings in Germany and elsewhere in Central Europe. In the course of the ensuing three years, the two leaders and their societies faced war, revolution, economic chaos, Red Terror, and Red Scare. And, in the process, a wide variety of people in both countries groped for means and ways to work out some relationship with each other, exploring opportunities in a bewildering array of on-the-spot diplomatic encounters, in Petrograd, Moscow, Stockholm, Paris, and New York.

3

These encounters, between military, economic, and political envoys with varying degrees of support from their governments, constituted the constantly changing reality of the earliest relationships between Americans and Bolsheviks. In a chaotic situation faced by policymakers in Washington and Moscow, these representatives proposed concrete responses to specific problems and advocated alternative approaches. Their story, far more than the policy debates in the White House, is the real story of the origins of Soviet-American relations.

The first efforts at a Bolshevik-American *modus operandi* occurred immediately after November 7, 1917, as American and Soviet representatives in Russia held specific discussions concerning possible military collaboration. These discussions were conducted by Lev Trotsky and Russian generals with the aim of deflecting an imminent German military advance. The U.S. representatives still hoped that German troops, supplies, or arms could be kept from being shifted to France, and that the Russian army might still be reconstituted as an effective fighting force.

These discussions were held primarily between American military representatives General William V. Judson, Captain Francis Riggs, and Colonel William Ruggles, and Bolshevik Foreign Commissar and later War Commissar Lev Trotsky. These talks concentrated on efforts to influence the terms of the armistice between Germany and Russia, and to transfer Russian army supplies to the Allies. The most important of these talks, between Judson and Trotsky, were also the first contacts between any U.S. official and representative authorities of the Soviet government. They in turn paved the way for months of other direct discussions. These discussions were never sanctioned by the U.S. War Department and were later halted by the U.S. State Department. Nevertheless, they saved military supplies for the Allies, kept German troops on the Russian front for several more weeks, and negotiated American military and engineering assistance for the new Red Army and the Soviet rail network.

These military discussions were expanded into economic and political issues by Raymond Robins of the American Red Cross Mission to Russia, from December 1917 to May 1918. Robins held at least weekly discussions with Lenin and Trotsky during these months. They reached agreements on a number of issues, which were accepted by both the American and Soviet governments. Robins concluded purchase agreements on behalf of the U.S. War Department for Russia's remaining supplies of strategic platinum, thus denying them to the German war effort. Lenin agreed, after numerous importunities by Robins, to an exemption from Bolshevik nationalization decrees for a number of United States corporations, including Singer, International Harvester, and Westinghouse. The critical operations of the American Red Cross in Russia were extended and expanded by the Robins-Lenin agreement, including the distribution of milk and surplus food, the provision of scarce farm implements and equipment, and the continued importation of medical supplies and devices.

Moreover, the fact of Robins' persistent negotiation on matters of political and economic importance had an impact. It kept alive the Soviet belief that some arrangement with the United States was possible, developed a degree of trust between the two parties for the first time, and kept proposals for constructive political and economic relations constantly before American policymakers. Although the U.S. State Department was opposed to Robins' efforts, and eventually forced his recall, Robins was supported for several months by U.S. Ambassador David Francis as a way to keep open a channel to the Bolsheviks. Robins' flood of reports reached Colonel House through the American Red Cross and the Director of the Committee on Public Information, George Creel. They were also relayed through British agent R. H. Bruce Lockhart to Sir William Wiseman and thence to House. Robins' direct talks impelled Arthur Bullard, Edgar Sisson, William V. Judson, and other American representatives to advocate *de facto* relations in the first critical months following November 7.

Robins and Lenin worked particularly hard to develop an economic proposal for the revival and stimulation of a Soviet-American trade. This comprehensive proposal, given by Lenin to Robins on May 14, 1918, presented an extensive analysis of Russia's economic situation and a detailed listing of materials and equipment that the Soviets needed from the United States and, in turn, Russian raw materials and resources available in exchange. It also suggested organizing Russian-American trade on the basis of credits and gold in order to sidestep the crucial question of currency inequalities. The document closed with the Soviet government's plea for permission to send an economic commission to the United States to negotiate the details of a trade agreement. While never adopted by the U.S. government, this plan served as a most important basis for Robins' advocacy of an alternative American policy toward Bolshevik Russia. It also provided the basis for Ludwig Martens' negotiation of contracts with American firms in 1919. Many of these contracts were prototypes for the Soviet-American trade of the 1920s.

Following Robins' departure in the spring of 1918, the specter of Allied intervention overshadowed efforts to achieve any working relationship. Yet Soviet foreign minister Georgi Chicherin and U.S. consul DeWitt Clinton Poole developed perhaps the best relationship between Soviet and American official representatives in the entire period. They succeeded in solving some practical problems and kept open a solid official channel of communication at their twice-weekly meetings from May to July of 1918. But their objectives were quite divergent. The imminence of Allied intervention prevented these men from moving any further toward a real working relationship. Poole hoped only to maintain the communication channel and work out practical matters. Chicherin desperately sought to forestall American participation in intervention, as well as to establish the basis for a firmer long-term relationship.

Specific agreements were reached, despite this disparity of objectives and the threat of Allied intervention. Expanded U.S. consular representation throughout Soviet Russia was grudgingly agreed to by the Soviet government, and American cipher access to its representatives maintained. U.S. railway engineers' assistance to the Bolsheviks was first offered, then later withdrawn.

In addition, economic discussions between American commercial attaché William C. Huntington and Bolshevik representative Jacob Bronski began the process of negotiation of a trade agreement, despite the unwillingness of the United States to make commitments.

Allied intervention in the summer of 1918 put an end to serious Soviet-American dialogue until December. Although the departure of American representatives and a tight Allied blockade effectively cut all contact, both sides groped for ways to resume their dialogue, even in the face of intervention, heightened civil war, and the Red Terror. In the United States and Soviet Russia, the struggle continued between those backing complete isolation and those favoring the search for a working relationship. Raymond Robins and Senator Hiram Johnson of California presented the case for an alternative policy to the Wilson administration and the Congress. At the same time, Maksim Litvinov and Lenin argued against Zinoviev and Trotsky that Soviet Russia should not acquiesce in the severing of relations with the United States, but should continue to pursue them to reduce the scope of intervention and to lay the groundwork for future diplomatic overtures.

The European armistice brought new efforts to reopen the dialogue. V. I. Lenin dispatched Litvinov as ambassador extraordinary to Stockholm in early December 1918, in an all-out effort to open up negotiations with Britain, the United States, and Scandinavia, in light of the coming peace conference. Litvinov appealed to President Wilson in a skillful Christmas Eve letter, which led to the dispatch of American attaché William H. Buckler to Stockholm for the first substantive discussions between an American and a Bolshevik representative since the Chicherin-Poole meetings. The proposals Litvinov made to Buckler, with specific provisions for ceasefire, economic relations, and debt settlement, laid the basis for subsequent negotations with William C. Bullitt in Moscow, and remained the heart of the Bolshevik position on a comprehensive settlement with the United States into the 1920s. Litvinov's initialing every page of the rather complete Buckler report makes this the only instance of a record of conversations agreed upon between the Bolsheviks and the United States in the Lenin-Wilson years.

The Paris Peace Conference marked a watershed in American and Allied policy toward Bolshevik Russia. The various schemes proposed at Paris all failed for one reason or another, partly because none had the full support of Britain, France, and the United States necessary for their implementation. There were three peace initiatives—Prinkipo, Bullitt, and Hoover-Nansen. Prinkipo, the Wilson-conceived effort to bring all the Russian parties together, failed because the French and most of the non-Bolshevik Russian representatives in Paris opposed it. Bullitt, the comprehensive plan with the greatest opportunity for success, was not pursued, largely because of altered political conditions in Britain and the lack of real support from Woodrow Wilson. The Bolsheviks rejected Hoover-Nansen food relief because it would have required them to give up substantial political and economic control over their own territory.

In both Moscow and Washington, intense political debate marked the consideration of various opportunities for dialogue at Paris. Trotsky and Zinoviev opposed positive Bolshevik response to both the Prinkipo and Bullitt proposals. Lenin, however, held to his decision to pursue peace and managed to override their objections. On the American side, William C. Bullitt commanded greater influence and support within the U.S. delegation than he is generally given credit for. An intense political struggle broke out over approaches to the Bolsheviks after the collapse of the Prinkipo Plan. Gordon Auchincloss and Vance McCormick put forward the Hoover-Nansen plan as an anti-Bolshevik alternative to the Bullit-Lenin agreement. Although Bullit still had enough influence to modify this initiative to make it less objectionable to Moscow, it was rejected by the Bolsheviks because of its stringent political conditions.

The collapse of the Bullitt proposals caused the Bolsheviks to renew their emphasis on economic diplomacy to achieve a political breakthrough with the United States. The centerpiece of this strategy in 1919 and 1920 was the mission of Ludwig C. A. K. Martens in New York to open up substantial discussions with American businessmen in order to build pressure to end the U.S. blockade and bring about recognition. This was accompanied by Soviet attempts to engage and then control *Tsentrosoyuz,* the Russian Union of Cooperatives, and various contacts with the West through the Commissariat of Foreign Trade missions to Copenhagen and London. Martens accomplished a great deal during his two years of work in New York. Substantial economic and technical contacts were established with American businesses that later resulted, in the 1920s, in the first blossoming of American scientific, technical, and economic interchange with Bolshevik Russia.

Martens worked hard, with the assistance of an able staff led by Santeri Nuorteva and Abraham Heller, to develop an array of serious contacts and discussions with American businessmen. Many meetings were held with such firms as Ford Motor Company, International Harvester, National City Bank, International Paper, and numerous American manufacturers of machinery, food, clothing, and chemicals. Nearly one hundred provisional contracts were signed between American firms and the Bolshevik government, pending the receipt of export permits. Martens also developed a technical and scientific support base, particularly of engineering talent for the assistance of Soviet Russia. Martens also insisted strenuously on remaining removed from American radicals' domestic squabbles. At times he even incurred the wrath of the left wing of American socialists, who tried to have him recalled, without success. But Martens' work with the American business community was serious enough to alarm the American-Russian Chamber of Commerce, the U.S. Commerce and State departments, and others strongly opposed to Bolshevik Russia, who mounted a strong political and economic counter-offensive against him.

Martens' mission and other Bolshevik economic initiatives met increasing hostility amid a worsening political and economic climate in the United States, finally getting caught up in what has become known as the Red Scare. Efforts of Bolsheviks to trade were continually stymied by the refusal of the United

States to lift economic restrictions, even after the Allied blockade had been officially ended. The Red Scare poisoned the political climate, and several of the government investigations launched as a part of it, particularly those of the Lusk and Moses committees and the U.S. Justice Department's Bureau of Investigation, seriously harassed the Martens bureau and eventually resulted in an order for Martens' deportation. Particularly important was the pivotal role, later denied, of Samuel N. Harper in providing information and analysis for J. Edgar Hoover's surveillance, investigation, and prosecution of Martens, journalist Isaac Don Levine, Albert Rhys Williams, and Raymond Robins, all of whom were advocating constructive *de facto* American relations with Bolshevik Russia.

At the same time, the Russia desk of the U.S. State Department increased its publication of detailed and sophisticated anti-Bolshevik material and assisted in the development, for the first time, of a comprehensive and detailed policy statement against the Bolshevik government. The final statement, the "Colby note," condemned Bolshevism in such an unqualified manner that it remained definitive government policy for both non-recognition and non-intercourse with Bolshevik Russia for three successive Republican administrations.

This book is a detailed investigation of all of these contacts: the successes, setbacks, and frustrations. The numerous encounters by these earliest practitioners of Soviet-American diplomacy and the process by which they struggled to find common ground to deal with common problems provide a revealing glimpse into a very different kind of diplomacy than is traditional. This is not the story of the meetings of two countries' ambassadors or of top-level discussions between foreign ministers: not that the individuals involved had no sanction from their governments. Soviet representatives like Maksim Litvinov or Ludwig Martens often had full powers to negotiate and settle political or military issues. Even Raymond Robins occasionally was empowered by Ambassador David Francis to settle certain issues. In other cases, such as those of DeWitt Clinton Poole or William H. Buckler, the brief was more tenuous, but they were still firmly embedded in the governmental chain of command. But none of these individuals relied primarily on policymakers to set the parameters of their interaction. Instead they made creative approaches and sought answers to at-times-intractable problems with the barest guidance from their principals. Sometimes, especially on the American side, they exceeded their instructions, and yet they were permitted, even encouraged, to continue their efforts.[3]

Several distinctive features of this interaction are apparent. First, most of those involved operated in a chaotic situation, with inadequate communication with their governments. Representatives and contacts were forced to take initiative in the absence of specific instructions. Second, they sought to build concrete and constructive relationships with their opposite parties, even when they disagreed with the other government's philosophy or objectives, in the belief that such attempt was important for the long-range benefit of the two societies and their relationship. Third, they persisted in their efforts to find positive approaches, even in the face of what appeared to be overwhelming setbacks.

A striking feature of this diplomacy on the American side is the habitual absence, except at certain points, of the guiding hand of President Woodrow Wilson or Secretary of State Robert Lansing. Wilson, despite his occasional preoccupation with Russia, was only another player, and not all that important a one, in the process of these three years of interaction. He did return periodically to "the ever-recurring question: How shall we deal with the Bolsheviki?"[4] But on only one occasion—the formulation of the Prinkipo proposal in Paris—did he become personally involved in the search for a solution. On other occasions he intervened, but usually laconically and spasmodically, never definitively. Wilson's persistent inability to settle it, and his preoccupation with other issues, simply left the door open for a variety of experimental interactions.

Sometimes it is assumed that the answer to the question of American policy toward the Bolsheviks was forthright and subject to no misinterpretation, or that it was decided once and for all, either in December 1917 when Lansing advised Wilson not to recognize the new government in Moscow, or certainly by the time of Wilson's decision to intervene in the Russian civil war in July 1918.[5] On the contrary, the Wilson administration was consumed with discussion and debate about the Bolsheviks. This debate, however, was sporadic and uncoordinated, and usually occurred within other, broader, contexts, such as conduct of the war, the settlement of the peace, or the prospects for stability and order in postwar Europe. Such policy as existed vacillated between a desire to find a workable arrangement and an intense moral antipathy to Bolshevism. This mirrored a political struggle in the broader society between those determined to strangle Bolshevism and those attempting to work with it and learn from it. Although recognition of the Bolsheviks was only briefly contemplated, and then only in the context of the breakdown of negotiations at Brest Litovsk early in 1918,[6] numerous efforts were made to come up with a policy that would enable informal contacts to go forward and some sort of working relationship to take hold. But the most fascinating thing about these discussions and debates is that they made very little difference for long stretches of interaction in Petrograd or Moscow. This book will seriously examine these episodes of policy debate and discussion, but in the context of the continuously evolving concrete relationship being formed on the spot in Petrograd, Moscow, Stockholm, and New York. For it was not the policy decisions in Washington that determined the interactions in Petrograd. Rather, the force and necessity of interaction constantly intruded on the policymakers.

Lenin and the Bolsheviks, on the other hand, were not only determined "to be reckoned with" and pursuing a more coherent strategy, but they were personally involved in carrying out that strategy. The Bolshevik policy toward the United States always made a pragmatic, working relationship a top priority. Lenin viewed the United States as a part of the capitalist world, and as a special, exceptional focus as well. He strove to divide and differentiate his

potential enemies, and he persistently believed that the United States could
be persuaded, through economic incentives, to recognize, or at least to work
with, Bolshevik Russia. In Moscow, early desires for recognition soon gave
way to more pragmatic hopes for a tacit working relationship.[7] Despite the
crucible of civil war and a certain degree of intraparty debate, Lenin's strategy
remained the pursuit of an opening with the United States, employing both
economic and diplomatic means.

Lenin's situation also differed radically from Wilson's in respect to these
early interactions not only because of the location of activity—from November 1917 until August 1918, the discussions all occurred in European Russia,
in Moscow, Petrograd, or Vologda—but because of his personal involvement.
Lenin, unlike Wilson, was not a detached policymaker. He was a full partici-
pant who based his strategy in part on the experience of his exchanges with
Raymond Robins, David Francis, and William C. Bullitt. Also, in stark contrast to Wilson's aloof unwillingness to interact personally with his Russian
envoys, Lenin discussed American interaction and policy with his envoys
Trotsky, Chicherin, Litvinov, Krasin, and Martens.

The encounters between Americans and Bolsheviks are detailed by an
astonishing array of written materials in American, British, and Soviet archives, many of which have been largely overlooked by previous historians.[8] To
the best of my knowledge, no Western study has been made of United States-
Soviet interaction in the 1917 to 1920 period, utilizing all sources and studying
them as a problem of both American and Soviet foreign policy and society.
There are, however, many excellent studies concerning some aspects of this
question, or that shed light on some particular negotiation or discussion.
George F. Kennan's groundbreaking two-volume work, *Soviet-American Relations, 1917–1920,* while crucial for a narrative of a portion of the early period,
remains unfinished, breaking off its discussion at mid-1918. Moreover, the
Kennan volumes do not treat United States-Soviet contacts other than the
Trotsky-Robins meetings in any depth, and place all discussions in the context
of World War I and the Allied decision to intervene in the civil war, a context
that seriously undervalues the importance of the interactions. Kennan also did
not have access to a number of new materials either from British or Soviet
archives when his study was finished in 1956.[9]

Several other studies, while useful in providing insight into some facets of
the questions at issue, do not look at the relationship between the United
States and Soviet Russia in this period as a whole. Arno Mayer's indispens-
able *Politics and Diplomacy of Peacemaking, 1918–1919* places the Prinkipo
and Bullitt missions squarely in the context of a swirling mix of political,
sociological, and cultural questions alive in European society, and provides a
model to which should be added the American and Soviet contexts.[10] Likewise, in this book, discussions between American and Bolshevik representatives cannot be considered apart from a serious look at two societies torn
asunder by revolution and reaction. American policy was set in the midst of a
society struggling between a fear of Bolshevism and an attraction to and hope
for the Russian revolution.[11] In Soviet Russia, contacts with the United States

took place against a backdrop of a Bolshevik Party nearly split over Brest Litovsk, the chaotic formative stages of the Comintern, civil war, famine, and Red Terror.

William Appleman Williams, Anne Meiburger, Neil Salzman, and James Libby have contributed monographs on the roles of Raymond Robins and Alexander Gumberg. Salzman's recent biography of Robins, while comprehensive on Robins' role, is based mostly on Robins' family papers and sometimes oversimplifies a complex story.[12] The best of Williams' work on Robins remains unpublished, and Libby's and Meiburger's works are limited in scope.[13] Recent work by Teddy Uldricks, Richard Debo, and Hugh Phillips has gone a long way toward a more in-depth understanding of early Soviet foreign policy, but they have not focused specifically on Lenin's discussion with, or policy toward, the United States.[14] Richard Ullman's three volumes on Anglo-Soviet relations in this period utilize for the first time new materials from the British Foreign Office archives, including Soviet cable intercepts, which are important for understanding the British relationship with the Bolsheviks, and, more important for our purposes, British influence on American policy and the specifics of American discussions with Bolshevik leaders.[15] Finally, despite the long years since its publication, Louis Fischer's two-volume study of early Soviet foreign policy remains essential, if only because of his personal acquaintance with Georgi Chicherin.[16]

Part I (Chapters 1 and 2) sets the Soviet-American context for the face-to-face exchanges that are to follow. Chapter 1 discusses Vladimir Lenin's and the Bolsheviks' American policy, following the evolution and development of a special approach to United States designed to parlay economic openings into political and diplomatic breakthroughs. This chapter highlights Lenin's personal role in the formuation and execution of Soviet diplomacy and examines his interaction with the United States and with his major advisers and envoys as well as the Bolshevik Party debates on the subject. Chapter 2 examines the American context, a far more confused and diffuse picture of ambiguity and contradiction. Rather than a coherent policy, it can be best characterized as reactive steps, endless discussions, and occasionally significant interchanges between Wilsonian advisers in Washington and envoys interacting with the Bolsheviks in Russia or Stockholm.

Part II (Chapters 3, 4, and 5) examines American-Bolshevik contacts in Soviet Russia after the Bolshevik revolution but before the final American decision to intervene in the Russian civil war and the departure of American representatives in August 1918. The first series of such discussions (Chapter 3) are those between American and Bolshevik military representatives. Chapter 4 considers the political and economic discussions of this period, initiated largely by Raymond Robins of the American Red Cross, between December 1917 and May 1918. In Chapter 5 the last effort to develop a working relationship prior to American intervention is examined. This effort consisted of the several discussions between Acting American Consul DeWitt Clinton Poole and Soviet Foreign Commissar Georgi Chicherin from May to July of 1918.

Part III explores the struggle to resume contact in the wake of intervention, blockade, and European armistice, and examines substantive interactions in the context of the Paris Peace Conference of 1919. Chapter 6 discusses the period from July to December 1918, an interlude marked by isolation, scattered overtures, and the struggle to resume dialogue, even in the face of intervention and Red Terror. On both sides, representatives groped for ways to get back in touch. The European armistice precipitated another series of discussions in 1918 and 1919, considered in Chapters 7, 8, 9, and 10. This range of meetings, discussions, and proposals in the space of four months explored various sides of what can be called the best hope for a real settlement between the Bolsheviks and the United States. These three Paris chapters cover material that is perhaps the best-known of all of the early story of Soviet-American diplomacy. They concentrate on three neglected areas of analysis: the critical nature of British-American cooperation and the breakdown of British support for certain American initiatives; a more complete consideration of Soviet debate and discussion; and the background struggles within the U.S. delegation concerning appropriate policy toward the Bolsheviks.

In Part IV (Chapters 11 and 12) a new and most significant Bolshevik economic approach to the United States in the wake of the failure of peace efforts in Paris is fully examined, followed by the American response. The centerpiece of this strategy was the mission of Ludwig C. A. K. Martens to New York to open up substantial discussions with American businessmen to build pressure to end the U.S. blockade and bring about diplomatic recognition. Although Lenin clearly miscalculated the prevailing power of politics and ideology in the Wilson administration, the Martens mission had more impact on subsequent American policy than has been generally appreciated. The full story of this detailed Bolshevik economic strategy is told here for the first time. New materials never before accessible to Westerners in the *Tsentral'nyi gosudarstvennyi arkhiv narodnogo khozhiaistva* (TsGANKh), the Soviet Archive of the National Economy, provide the sources for the heart of this story.

These Bolshevik initiatives met increasing hostility and a worsening political and economic climate in the United States, finally getting caught up in what has become known as the Red Scare. Chapter 12 will focus on the impact of the Red Scare on the Martens mission and the course of Bolshevik-American interaction.

All of the efforts to effect a working relationship between the United States and Bolshevik Russia between 1917 and 1920 did not result in any full or lasting cooperation. Yet the partial efforts, the limited collaboration, and the few serious negotiations did provide groundwork for the economic ties of the 1920s and were influential in the diplomatic breakthroughs of 1933. Moreover, an in-depth analysis of these attempts also reveals the character of political struggle in both societies behind the proposals and contacts, which is too often lost in a simplistic focus on the success or failure of the efforts themselves. Such an exploration can also enrich our understanding of the origins of Soviet and American fears, hopes, stereotypes, and admiration, which are essential underpinnings to the subsequent history of Soviet-American relations.

# I

# *The Soviet-American Context*

# 1

# Lenin's American Policy

No particular importance is attributed in Soviet circles to the stir which was caused by the press with regard to the question of the Soviet authority being recognized by the Allied powers. We have several times stated, says one of the most prominent representatives of the Soviet authority—that the formal recognition of the Soviet authority by England, France, America and Italy is not a question of primary importance to us. The Allied Powers are at liberty to recognize the Council of Commissars or not to recognize it. We require something different. We require to be reckoned with and that the diplomatic representatives of the Allied powers accredited to Russia, should not be the support of counter-revolution.[1]

Speaking American policy toward Russia QUOTE I told American Colonel Robins nineteen eighteen was to interest United States be friendly soviet russia long ago as that pointed desirability commercial relations both our viewpoint and American STOP we offered concession american capital STOP american businessmen new arriving Moscow agreed with us STOP outside all political questions simple fact remains america needs our raw material we need american goods STOP america gain nothing for herself by Wilsonian policy virtuous refusal deal with us because our government doesn't suit tastes. . . .
—*Lenin in Interview with Louise Bryant, October 1920*[2]

V.I. Lenin and the Bolshevik Party's policy toward the United States in the three years following the October Revolution remained remarkably consistent, yet reflected a maturing recognition of the realities of denied Bolshevik hopes for world revolution coupled with the continued survival and strengthened position of Soviet Russia. In its broad outlines, it meshed perfectly with the evolving policy of the Soviets toward the West in general and toward Britain and France in particular. But in some important respects, it diverged from this more general strategy by treating the United States as a special, and often favored, case.

The most basic element of Lenin's policy toward the United States was his insistence that the Bolshevik government "be reckoned with," in the words of the editorial in *Rodina*. Although always interested in formal recognition, the Bolsheviks soon abandoned efforts to bring this about, and instead unrelentingly pursued a strategy calling for some kind of *de facto* working relationship, in which it was hoped that economic contacts would lead to a growing political understanding. In this pursuit of a *modus operandi,* Lenin always coupled pleas for peace with the United States government with contacts and appeals to American workers and progressives. While under no illusions about the imminence of a workers' revolution in the United States, he did think that public pressure in America could assist in limiting America's role in intervention and also in achieving the breakthroughs he desired in economic relations and eventually, political recognition.[3] Lenin left no stone unturned, particularly in the pursuit of economic contacts with the United States, appealing not only to the United States government, but also to journalists, writers, radicals, businessmen; literally anyone who had any contacts in the United States.

Although it can be argued that Lenin's strategy failed to produce a breakthrough with the United States, in light of the ultimate refusal of the Wilson administration to "deal with" the Bolsheviks, politically or economically, the strategy did play its part in Bolshevik survival. It helped limit reluctant American participation in intervention. Moreover, the economic strategy began to pay off directly under the Republican administrations of the 1920s. Diplomatic hostility was maintained, but economic relations flourished, and played their role in the eventual recognition in 1933.[4]

This chapter will examine in more detail the dimensions of Lenin's strategy toward the United States. We will consider differences within the Bolshevik Party, Lenin's personal role, and the changes in policy from 1917 to 1920, focusing on key turning points in the overall effort to induce the United States to forego its opposition to the Bolsheviks in favor of a working relationship. For, as Lenin insisted to Louise Bryant in late 1920, "outside all political questions the simple fact remains America needs raw material."[5] This remained the essence of Lenin's approach to the United States.

Before looking in some greater detail at the evolution of Lenin's policy toward the United States, it might be well to address a prior general question: where and how was foreign policy made under Lenin? What was Lenin's personal role? What was the role of *Sovnarkom* (the Council of People's Commissars)? What was the role of the Commissariat for Foreign Affairs, its leadership, and its relationship to the Communist International (the Comintern)? What were the roles of Lenin's major advisers and assistants in foreign policy: Trotsky, Chicherin, Litvinov, Radek, Zinoviev, and others?

Lenin was undoubtedly his own foreign minister, and preeminent in foreign policy development and strategy at least from the time of Brest Litovsk. All evidence, including Lenin's own writings, published foreign policy documents, memoirs from Chicherin and other Bolsheviks, and memoirs of Western observers, points clearly to this conclusion, with which no historian disagrees.[6]

Clearly central to impressions of Lenin's direction of Bolshevik foreign policy was his calmness, clarity, and decisiveness, and the preeminence in all strategic discussions of his sure and primary concern for the survival of the

Bolshevik revolution and the Soviet state. Raymond Robins, often a partisan of Trotsky, told the story of Lenin's ability to turn around a mob of several hundred Red Guards, determined to rush off to the front to "save the revolution" in mid-February, 1918. Lenin, according to Robins, admitted forty or fifty leaders of this mob into his private office. He offered to prepare a special train for them to go to the front, but also said that he had the responsibility to tell them that his evaluation was that they did not have the troops or the firepower to overcome the Germans at the present time, and that if "they chose to force the Soviet Government into the channel of inevitable destruction he would resign, not being willing to be responsible for murdering his own child." The leaders listened, grumbled, and went out to calm their men and explain the necessity of the policy to make peace to save the revolution.[7]

Lenin was personally involved in the detail of every major Soviet foreign policy initiative, debate, or decision, from the time of the October Revolution until his incapacitation in 1923. He personally advised Trotsky, Chicherin, Litvinov, Krasin, and others on policy positions and diplomatic notes to the West, on many occasions specifying language for diplomatic notes.

Lenin made the key decisions on Brest Litovsk, supervised the details of negotiations with Estonia in 1919 and with Finland in 1920, directed the development of diplomatic approaches to Poland in 1920, and to Germany in 1918, and the beginnings of trade negotiations with Britain in 1920.[8] In key episodes of contact with the United States, Lenin personally discussed the possibility of accepting American military aid against the Germans in February 1918, met with Raymond Robins several times and personally drew up the Bolshevik economic relations proposal for the United States in May, discussed Chicherin's meetings with American consul DeWitt Clinton Poole in June 1918, critiqued Chicherin's and Litvinov's letters to President Wilson in October and December 1918, and made the basic decision about how to respond to Wilson's Prinkipo proposal in January 1919. He met with William C. Bullitt and negotiated the details of what became known as the Bullitt proposal in March 1919, and discussed in 1919 and 1920 (by mail and in person) Soviet policy toward the United States with Chicherin and L. C. A. K. Martens.

Lenin's preoccupation with foreign policy began even before the revolution. But he tended to neglect the details of foreign policy theory initially, in large part because of his conviction at that time that a European revolution would make foreign policy for any new Soviet state irrelevant. Lenin did have a number of ideas before the revolution that became working assumptions of early Soviet diplomacy. For example, he expected immediate hostility from capitalist Europe; he believed that sacrifices might have to be made to buy time for the development of the revolution; and, more important, he was absolutely convinced of the need to devote every waking moment to the stimulation of the revolution.[9] Unlike Trotsky, however, who had ascribed special significance to the spread of the revolution to Germany, Lenin did not feel that the very fate of the Russian revolution was tied completely to the revolution in Germany.[10]

Despite Lenin's preeminent role, it is important to point out that he rarely dictated Soviet policy. His views carried more weight because of the great respect he was held in by other Bolsheviks, but he consulted with top leadership on all important decisions, and he relied more on persuasion than coercion. He was even occasionally outvoted, and his ultimate sanction when he felt strongly about a line of policy was to threaten to resign.[11]

Although Lenin was personally involved in the establishment of both the People's Commissariat for Foreign Affairs (*Narkomindel*) and the Communist International, he was more directly involved in the policy of the former than the latter. Several historians have clearly documented the central role Lenin played in both policy and operations of the Narkomindel.[12] Lenin was involved to a lesser degree in the details of the Comintern. Adam Ulam notes that Lenin appointed Zinoviev to Comintern leadership partly as a way of removing him from day-to-day operations of the party leadership, and he is perplexed about why, after 1920, Lenin did not become more involved personally in the leadership of the International. Rather, just at the time it would have seemed he could have furthered the work of the International, he turned more and more to domestic policy. At the same time, however, he did not neglect the Narkomindel, consulting daily with Chicherin through the end of 1922.[13]

As effective head of both the Bolshevik party and the Council of People's Commissars (Sovnarkom), Lenin set policy in both bodies. Until recently, it has been almost universally assumed by Western historians that foreign policy was decided on in the Party, not in Sovnarkom.[14] T. H. Rigby, however, in his fine study of Lenin and Sovnarkom, shows that from the outset Lenin preferred to act through Sovnarkom, and that the Politburo (which was not even formed until 1919) and the Party did not become predominant until 1921 or 1922. In foreign policy, the close working relationship between Lenin and Foreign Commissar Chicherin preserved Sovnarkom's superiority until Lenin's incapacitation.[15]

The same debate about the overall nature of Lenin's foreign policy applies even more directly to the two agencies of that policy, the Comintern and the Narkomindel. Studies of the Comintern have tended to focus heavily on its success, or lack thereof, in instigating revolution in Europe.[16] Much more crucial in this book are the questions, To what degree was the Comintern an instrument of Soviet foreign policy under Lenin; did it conflict with the Narkomindel, and if so, how; and did this controversy ultimately affect Lenin's policy toward the United States?

The predominant interpretation, shared by most historians of the Comintern, is that the Comintern was more an arm of Soviet foreign policy than an association of Communist parties from different countries.[17] The major evidence for this conclusion is the activity of the Comintern and its frequent changes of policy in promoting world revolution, changes coinciding perfectly with changes in Soviet foreign policy. Some have taken issue with at least parts of this analysis. The early Comintern was plagued with considerable dissent and factionalism, and at least its formation was a purely voluntary coming-together of Communist parties, all enamored of the success of the Bolshevik revolution, but by no means bound slavishly to the decisions of its leaders. Moreover, contemporary evidence would seem to indicate that the Comintern was clearly seen as subsidiary, at least in the first several years, to the foreign policy decisions, strategy, and implementation of Sovnarkom and the Narkomindel.[18]

Regardless of the degree to which the Comintern was an instrument of Soviet foreign policy, its relationship to the Narkomindel remains important and deserves more analysis. In the beginning the functions of the Comintern (which was not founded until 1919) were actually carried out by the Narkomindel! The Bureau of Foreign Revolutionary Propaganda was set up under Trotsky and continued under Chicherin, operating always on the assumption that diplomatic relations were necessary, not only with governments, but with revolutionary socialist parties, and that these parties needed to be stimulated and supported. To that end, Sovnarkom allocated two million rubles in late December 1917, to support the international revolutionary movement, with decisions on its disbursal left to the Narkomindel.[19] When Lenin decided to issue the call for the formation of the Communist International in 1919 the work was carried on by Chicherin at the Narkomindel. Chicherin launched a wireless appeal for an international conference.[20] There is considerable evidence that one of the reasons for the formation of the Comintern was the increasing difficulty of maintaining both regular diplomatic relations and revolutionary appeals and propaganda in the same agency. Toward the end of 1918 and the beginning of 1919, it appears that Lenin and others in the Bolshevik leadership became convinced that the separation of traditional diplomacy from revolutionary propaganda was essential for the success of either.[21]

Evidence concerning the lack of Lenin's personal involvement in the day-to-day activities of the Comintern has already been noted. There is little doubt that, at least in his later years, Lenin de-emphasized the Comintern and its role. Ulam notes that Lenin's "intense internationalism that had characterized him between 1914 and 1918 really began to recede" after the establishment of the Comintern in 1919, except for a brief period of revolutionary enthusiasm during the Polish-Soviet War.[22] Louis Fischer cites an incident in mid-1920 that is quite illuminating. Lenin wrote a letter to Comintern chairman Zinoviev, insisting that Kuusinnen, a Finn, and not Béla Kun, the Hungarian Bolshevik leader, deliver the general report to the forthcoming Comintern Congress, because "he knows and thinks," and Lenin then added in German, "Was sehr selten ist unter den Revolutioneren." Fischer notes, "With this attitude he could not have expected much of the Comintern."[23]

The position of the Narkomindel, or People's Commissariat for Foreign Affairs, in the foreign policy–making process has been controversial among Western historians. Most traditional treatments of the Narkomindel deny any significant role to the People's Commissariat in Lenin's foreign policy. Theo Von Laue, for example, finds that "in the new dimensions of international relations opened up by the Bolsheviks, Chicherin and the Narkomindel could play only a limited part."[24] Robert Warth, Leonard Schapiro, Brancho Lazitch, Vernon Aspaturian, and Robert M. Slusser agree. Their essential argument is that the Bolshevik revolution marked a sharp break in Russian diplomatic practice, and that the stimulation of revolution through propaganda and subversion was henceforth the predominant aim of Soviet foreign policy. Traditional diplomacy, as practiced by the Narkomindel, played a clearly secondary role.[25]

Other historians writing more recently and with a broader array of primary sources to base their conclusions on, find the Narkomindel much more pivotal in Soviet foreign policy. Not only did Lenin play a major role in Soviet foreign policy formulation through the Narkomindel, but Georgi Chicherin probably possessed a greater degree of independence than later Soviet foreign ministers or their imperial Russian predecessors.[26] The Narkomindel was the first ministry to be put into operation after the revolution. It was almost completely staffed with Bolsheviks and other émigré socialists, who had acquired experience in skills, procedures, and techniques of foreign policy while carrying on socialist agitation abroad.[27] Lenin was quite clear in his praise for the organization and personnel of the Narkomindel, and his personal support for its work, asserting in 1922,

> this apparatus is an exceptional component of our state apparatus. We have not allowed a single influential person from the old tsarist apparatus into it. All sections with any authority are composed of Communists. That is why it has already won for itself (this may be said boldly) the name of a reliable Communist apparatus purged to an incomparably greater extent of the old tsarist, bourgeois, and petty-bourgeois elements than that which we have had to make do with in the other People's Commissariats.[28]

The key to this argument rests heavily on Lenin's role, because Chicherin was not made a member of the Central Committee of the Communist Party until 1925. Were Lenin not both head of state and head of the Party, as well as personally involved in Narkomindel formation and policy development, it is doubtful that Chicherin would have been able to hold his own against pressure from the Comintern. The truth of this can best be seen in the serious conflicts that developed between Narkomindel and Comintern in 1923 and 1924, when Lenin was incapacitated and Zinoviev asserted himself in foreign policy.[29]

Despite Lenin's undoubted preeminence in foreign policy, especially after Brest Litovsk, and the fact that Chicherin faithfully implemented his policies, certain conflicts among Bolshevik leaders concerning foreign policy and approaches to the United States did surface occasionally, usually reflecting wider fissures in the party over the central question highlighted in the Brest Litovsk treaty and its ratification: to what extent should Soviet Russia pursue a policy of compromise and conciliation with the capitalist West, and to what extent should a revolutionary policy be pursued? Lenin most often sided with the necessity of at least limited conciliation, with the notable exception of the opportunity created by the Soviet-Polish War. On all of the issues concerning the United States, Lenin and Chicherin pursued a conciliatory policy, but at times they had to persuade or coerce more reluctant colleagues. In an interview in *Novaya Zhizn*, published on March 29, 1918, Education Commissar

Lunacharsky revealed the existence of differences within the government on the question of utilization of aid and assistance from the United States, militarily against the Germans if necessary but also for economic development. Lunacharsky stated that both Bukharin and Zinoviev opposed any such contacts, but that Lenin was convinced that the United States should be approached.[30] By the time William C. Bullitt visited Petrograd and Moscow in March 1919, it appeared to him that virtually the same split regarding policy toward the United States remained. Trotsky had joined Bukharin and Zinoviev in arguing against making any agreement with the United States or the other Allies. Lenin, however, prevailed, and the Bullitt-Lenin proposals were sent to Paris.[31]

Lev Trotsky was appointed the first People's Commissar of Foreign Affairs, assuming the post with some reluctance, but convinced that it would take little of his time away from party affairs and the development of the revolution. To him is ascribed the famous phrase that he would "issue a few revolutionary proclamations and then shut up shop."[32] Trotsky spent little time with the administrative duties of the Narkomindel, preferring to use the position to conduct revolutionary propaganda, then to negotiate at Brest Litovsk. He left the day-to-day workings of the new commissariat to his lieutenants, I. A. Zalkind, E. D. Polivanov, and N. A. Markin, none of whom had the slightest notion of what diplomacy was all about, but who did manage to find and publish the Secret Treaties and issue revolutionary proclamations to Germany and the West.[33] In particular, Zalkind, Trotsky's Deputy Commissar, made a bad impression on all foreign diplomats he came into contact with.[34]

Trotsky's major role as Foreign Commissar was his pursuit of revolutionary diplomacy at Brest Litovsk. Following the decision to sign this distasteful treaty, Trotsky resigned as Foreign Commissar, taking up the reins as War Commissar some weeks later.[35] The change of portfolio, however, did not mean his exclusion from foreign policy debates and discussions. He continued to be centrally involved in key decisions until after Lenin's death, but his preeminent role in foreign policy ended with Brest Litovsk.[36]

Trotsky had far more contact with American and Allied representatives in Russia following the Bolshevik revolution than any other Bolshevik leader, even after his resignation as Foreign Commissar. The assessments by these representatives of Bolshevik attitudes and policies were often based on their reading of Trotsky's speeches and their recounting of their meetings with him. This continued to be the case until it was abundantly clear that no arrangement could be worked out between the Allies and the Bolsheviks to mutually oppose Germany, and that no agreement concerning Japanese intervention was possible.

Trotsky distinguished carefully among the various Allies from the beginning. He always viewed the United States (as did Lenin) as the most potentially friendly to (or at least tolerant of) Bolshevik power. He adopted a strategy designed to appeal to the United States, obtain assistance against the

Germans if necessary, and forestall full-scale American support for Allied intervention.[37]

U.S. and British representatives who met with Trotsky, including General William V. Judson, Raymond Robins, Arthur Bullard, and Bruce Lockhart, consistently assessed his overtures to the Allies as genuine, and his regard for the United States as sincere, and believed as late as late April 1918 that some "working arrangement" might be effected, and that Trotsky remained the most important link for the Allies to persuade the Bolsheviks to accept Allied intervention.[38] As British foreign secretary A. J. Balfour confided to Lord Reading on April 29, 1918:

> All witnesses returning from Russia . . . whether they like or dislike him, appear to agree in thinking that for the moment he holds an absolutely commanding position in Russia and in these circumstances we are obliged either to defy him, to work with him, or to do nothing . . . we are obliged to accept the second. . . .[39]

As the first few months of the revolution passed without a corresponding European revolution, both Trotsky and Lenin began to realize that someone else was needed to head up the Narkomindel and to develop a more traditional approach to foreign policy. When pressure on the British resulted in Chicherin's being released from prison and repatriated to Russia in January, Trotsky and Lenin discussed appointing him Deputy Foreign Commissar with the express intention of investing him with the responsibility of developing the Narkomindel as an institution and preparing its role in traditional diplomacy. Lenin may also have sent Trotsky to Brest Litovsk to remove him from the daily activities of the Narkomindel and to pave the way for his complete removal as Foreign Commissar. As Lenin became increasingly convinced of the necessity for signing the peace treaty with Germany, he likewise grew to see the need to put foreign policy under his direct control. Shifting Trotsky to War Commissar and elevating Chicherin to Foreign Commissar accomplished precisely that.[40]

The impact of Georgi Chicherin on the People's Commissariat of Foreign Affairs cannot be disputed. He served as Foreign Commissar from May (acting, from March) 1918 until 1930, and under his leadership the young Soviet state successfully emerged onto the world scene, signed treaties of trade and recognition with numerous states, and significantly strengthened its overall strategic position.[41]

Chicherin's major contribution was to put Soviet diplomacy and the Narkomindel as an institution on a sound, professional footing, and to separate it from the revolutionary propaganda of the Comintern. As Richard Debo has pointed out, upon Chicherin's elevation to the post of Foreign Commissar, standard diplomatic phrasing returned to the notes of the Foreign Commissariat.[42] Revolutionary propaganda lost its former importance, and the Narkomindel resumed its function as a foreign office. By the end of 1918 the transition was complete. Lenin called for the conference to form the Comintern, and revolutionary propaganda was functionally removed from the Narkomindel. Chicherin took steps to dissociate the Narkomindel and his own person from the new organization. He made only one contribution to the Comintern journal—discussing the different roles of Comintern and Narkomindel in Soviet foreign policy. From that time forward he was a tireless campaigner for traditional Soviet diplomacy.[43]

Chicherin was an unusual character. He was a brilliant linguist, well educated, and from an old Russian noble family. He began his career in the foreign service as an archivist in the old Ministry of Foreign Affairs in 1898, and became a socialist over the next several years, when he emigrated to England. Between the revolutions of 1905 and 1917 he worked as an agitator and organizer in England and was in prison at the time of the Bolshevik revolution. On returning to Russia in January 1918, he replaced Zalkind as Deputy Foreign Commissar and began immediately to reconstruct the ministry. He was his own hardest worker, concerning himself with every detail of diplomacy, and often working late into the night.[44]

Early in 1918, Chicherin and Lenin established what was to become the closest of working relationships. Chicherin faithfully followed every turn in Lenin's foreign policy, from Brest Litovsk to Genoa. He never acted in important matters without consulting with Lenin, but he also was given high praise by Lenin for his creative diplomacy within Lenin's guidelines. Chicherin's own world view, a blend of revolutionary idealism and traditional balance-of-power diplomacy, fit perfectly with Lenin's developing convictions about the necessary conditions for Soviet Russia's survival.[45]

Chicherin's close consultation with Lenin was to last five years, until Lenin's death. Chicherin, in his recollection, "Lenin and Foreign Policy," spoke of their close relationship in the following terms:

> during the period when Vladimir Ilyich took a most active part in all details of the life of the State, I was in almost constant contact with him in my field of work. During the first years of existence of our Republic I talked with him several times a day over the telephone, sometimes conducting long telephone conversations apart from direct meetings and not infrequent detailed discussions with him on current diplomatic matters of any importance.[46]

Chicherin was not without his critics within the Bolshevik Party and even within the Narkomindel, and Lenin was called upon several times to defend his leadership and his judgement. Chicherin was particularly under attack from the Soviet envoy to Berlin, A. A. Joffe, who resisted following his orders, as did V. V. Vorovsky in Stockholm. In both cases, Lenin admonished them that they were subordinate to Chicherin, as the People's Commissar for Foreign Affairs, and also impressed upon them Chicherin's virtues and Lenin's full backing for his work. In one classic letter to Joffe, Lenin laid out clearly his views of Chicherin's strengths and his problems, and why his work was critical to the Narkomindel:

> Dear Comrade Joffe, I am, to tell the truth, extremely angry with you . . .
> you write a lot on business matters in a personal letter to me . . . and insert a
> number of personal thrusts, attacks, pinpricks and so on against Chi-
> cherin. . . . Damn it, it's the frozen limit! . . . Chicherin is a splendid worker,
> most conscientious, shrewd, knowledgeable. such people should be highly
> appreciated. That his failing is lack of "commandership" does not matter.
> There are plenty of people in this world who have the opposite failing.
> Chicherin is a man you can work with, he is easy to work with. . . .[47]

On other occasions, Lenin was forced to defend Chicherin against Béla
Kun, Lev Karakhan, and Karl Radek, and he often wrote personal friends in
attempts to persuade Chicherin to take some time off and not kill himself with
work.[48]

Chicherin did not always agree with Lenin, despite their close coordination on major policy initiatives. There is some evidence that his attitude
toward the United States, his interest and willingness to conciliate, was even
stronger than Lenin's, and that he was sometimes open to taking steps that
Lenin was unwilling to approve. Chicherin strove to reassure American consul DeWitt Clinton Poole in July 1918, when Lenin had attacked the Allies in
a virtual declaration of war, that the United States "was not included" in the
attack, despite the known fact that Lenin was furious with the United States as
well.[49] And later, in early 1922, in consultation between the two in preparation for Chicherin's speeches and approaches at the Genoa conference,
Chicherin suggested that "a small change" be made in the Soviet Constitution,
enabling non-communist parties to put up candidates for office to meet the
American demand for "representative institutions" in Soviet Russia. Lenin
rejected this out of hand, lecturing Chicherin about the very nature of the
Bolshevik state.[50]

Although it is often argued that the thrust of Chicherin's foreign policy
was pro-German, while Litvinov's was pro-British,[51] Chicherin was central to
Lenin's strategy in 1918 to entice the United States into some kind of working
relationship and separate them from the British and French. After Raymond
Robins' departure and Trotsky's shift to the War Commissariat following
Brest Litovsk, Chicherin devoted much attention to cultivating a relationship
with American consul DeWitt Clinton Poole. This relationship, although only
lasting two months before intervention caused the departure of all Allied
representatives from Russia, did manage to solve a number of small practical
problems in the relationship, and Chicherin assisted Poole in the considerable
expansion of vice-consulates throughout Soviet Russia for the gathering of all
kinds of information. Chicherin insisted later that this was good strategy; he
also believed Vice-Consul Poole when he insisted that the American people
and the American government had "no desire to attempt to overthrow Soviet
Power." Therefore the United States deserved separate and unequal treatment from the British and French.[52]

Maksim Litvinov's major contribution to early Soviet foreign policy was as
diplomat extraordinary and Deputy Foreign Commissar. Although he dif-

fered with Chicherin over British and German policy in the 1920s, too much has been made of their disagreements under Lenin. From 1918 to 1920, Litvinov served in a staggering variety of posts throughout Europe, pursuing prisoner exchange, trade, and peace negotiations, primarily with the Allied powers. He served as a fitting symbol of the flexibility and seriousness of the new Narkomindel under Chicherin.[53]

Litvinov served Lenin in the West on a number of missions between 1917 and 1920, and became known for his pragmatic, no-nonsense approach and his general attitude that German imperialism was a bigger threat to Soviet Russia than the Western Allies. He also consistently argued within the Narkomindel against rhetorical and inflammatory diplomatic notes and in favor of conciliatory approaches, especially toward the United States and Britain. While in exile in Britain after the Bolshevik revolution, he was appointed People's Representative to Britain, and engineered the arrangement whereby R. H. Bruce Lockhart was accepted in a similar informal way as British representative to the Soviet government. Litvinov's contacts with Reginald Leeper of the Political Intelligence Department of the Foreign Office were characterized by pragmatic self-interest and strict diplomatic bargaining with a marked absence of abuse and propaganda. Lockhart and Litvinov parted from their one momentous meeting with considerable respect, which was to stand their governments in good stead until the total breakdown of relations in the summer of 1918.[54]

Litvinov maintained a keen interest in the United States. In June 1918, in the very critical period prior to the American decision to intervene, Litvinov became convinced that he could do more to assist in the campaign against intervention if he transferred to Washington. Lenin appointed him first diplomatic envoy to the United States but his credentials were refused, and he remained in London until exchanged for Lockhart in August.[55]

Following his return to Russia, Litvinov became Deputy Commissar to Chicherin, but was sent west again, this time to Stockholm, in late November 1918, in the hope of capitalizing on the Allies' armistice with Germany by opening up broad contacts with the West and securing a place for Soviet Russia at the Paris Peace Conference. Here he wrote notes to all the Western powers and had informal meetings with the various Scandinavian governments, the British, and finally the United States in the person of William H. Buckler. In the meeting with Buckler, Litvinov deplored the style of Chicherin's stinging note to Woodrow Wilson of October 1918, calling it "propagandistic journalism . . . calculated to repel rather than conciliate." In contrast, his famous Christmas Eve note to Wilson was a model of conciliation.[56]

With the help of these associates in planning and implementation. V. I. Lenin systematically put into operation a coherent strategy toward the United States from the time of the Bolshevik revolution until his death. This strategy was based first of all on a persistent effort to treat the United States differently from the other Western powers: to give it preferential treatment. The Bolsheviks believed that the United States was actually more sympathetic to the revolution than any other power; also that Soviet approaches to the United States would increase this already-existing reservoir of good will and would strengthen progressive forces in the United States in their efforts to prevent the U.S. government from joining in any attempts to strangle Bolshevism.[57]

The Bolshevik approach of positive differentiation of the United States from the other Western powers began with the revolution itself and persisted even in the face of what might appear to be evidence of American hostility. Trotsky, in a speech of November 24, 1917, emphasized the hostility of Britain and Germany toward Soviet power, but insisted that since America was not aiming at territorial acquisition in the war, "America can patiently receive the fact of Soviet Government. . . ."[58] Soon thereafter, in early December 1917, W. F. Sands, special assistant to the United States Embassy in Petrograd from 1916 to 1917, passing through Sweden en route to the United States, reported that "the other allies are not trusted as Americans are." Sands recommended strongly that the United States seize the advantageous position by refusing to side with either the Kerensky forces or the Bolsheviks.[59] At the same time, Trotsky gave yet another speech in which he was convinced that the American diplomats "have understood that they could not overcome the Russian revolution and therefore they desire to form with us 'friendly' relations considering that this will be an excellent means of competition with the Germans and particularly with the British capitalists after the war."[60]

After President Wilson's message to the Congress of Soviets, in which he again held out an olive branch to the Russian people but claimed that specific aid could not be granted, Soviet differentiation of the United States from the Allies became more marked. In a celebrated editorial in *Izvestia,* the Bolsheviks positioned the United States as the natural economic competitor of Germany, and in absolute opposition to Japan. Thus far, this was a familiar litany. But then the writer went on, in a most startling fashion:

> With the United States we may have friction, encounters, struggle, but there can also be an agreement . . . we can come to an understanding with the United States. . . . The United States is directly interested that Russia should politically and economically be strong and independent. In its own interests therefore it will and it must come to the aid of the Soviet government. . . . When they will become convinced that the Soviet rule is firmly established, the Americans will give us money and arms, locomotives and machines, instructors and engineers, etc. to do away with the economic disorganization and create a strong army. And, relying on their economic power, they will give it on better terms than other countries. . . .[61]

In *Novaya Zhizn,* on March 29, Commissar of Education and Culture Lunacharsky argued that the United States had already assisted the Soviets by putting pressure on Japan to restrain its interventionist impulses. The Bolshevik government, he said, recognized "the difference in the attitude of the United States toward Russia as compared with the attitude of other powers."[62]

Even after the ratification of the treaty of Brest Litovsk and the failure of the United States to respond to the last-minute appeal of Trotsky for aid, a friendly attitude toward the United States persisted. In May, Associated Press representative in Russia Louis Edgar Browne, assessing the state of affairs in the Bolshevik government, claimed that it "places more faith and confidence in America than in any other foreign power."[63] Another article in *Novaya Zhizn* on June 2 argued that the Bolshevik policy of maneuvering between the Germany and Allied powers depended in part upon enticing the United States into assistance against German encroachment, whether economic or military.[64]

Even in the face of the American decision to intervene in the civil war and the collapse of any pretense of friendly relations between the Allies and Bolshevik power in the summer of 1918, the Soviet government persisted in its determination to give special preference to the United States. When British and French diplomatic representatives were put under house arrest during the Socialist-Revolutionary uprising, American personnel were left alone; cause for a hurried exchange of cables between Consul Poole and Ambassador Francis, in respect to the "especially favorable situation which the American representatives occupy for the moment with respect to the Soviet authorities."[65] Chicherin, in an early September article in *Izvestia,* defended these special measures with regard to American citizens as necessary because, "although the United States Government was compelled by its Allies to agree to particpate in intervention . . . its decision is not regarded by us as irrevocable."[66]

The arrest of suspected American spy Xenophon Kalamatiano in conjunction with the Lockhart plot, however, did cause the Bolsheviks to have second thoughts about their tilt toward the United States. Peters and Dzherzhinsky of the Cheka were outraged, and Lenin took a temporarily harsher line, encouraging Chicherin in his vitriolic October 24 note to President Wilson.[67] By November, however, the Soviet tone had changed, even in discussing the specific Kalamatiano case. Chicherin reviewed the "entente conspiracies" in his survey of two years of Bolshevik foreign policy. While castigating Lockhart and Reilly, he ignored Kalamatiano's involvement despite the agent's continued imprisonment.[68] Only Litvinov continued to refer to Kalamatiano and American involvement in a caustic fashion, well into 1919 and 1920, perhaps because of his own imprisonment in Britain.[69]

By late September 1918, the Bolshevik desire to open up some contact with the United States reasserted itself and Chicherin tried to get word via Captain Webster of the American Red Cross, then on his way out of Russia, to Raymond Robins in Washington that every attempt should be made to get permission for an official Soviet representative to visit Washington, because "nothing is more desirable to us than to get into friendly relations with the United States" and that this had not proved possible despite all the attempts made with Consul Poole. "We most intensely wish to have another connection," Chicherin argued in an intercepted conversation with Zorin, chief of the Foreign Department of the Soviet of Petrograd.[70]

The same insistence on a special understanding with the United States was maintained following the end of the war with Germany in nearly every communication of the Bolshevik government in the context of negotiations in Paris. In Chicherin's note of response to the Prinkipo invitation, he pointedly separated the United States from the Allies, calling it "more friendly," and in an interview with Alfred Nagel, in March, 1919, he insisted that "America is most of all other countries interested in preserving one undivided Russian economic organization and is by no means interested in weakening Russia. . . . America is the first country from which peaceful notes reached us. . . . America is more in the spirit to make an agreement with Russia."[71]

While the possibility of an agreement along the lines of the Bullitt proposals remained, Chicherin even went so far as to omit the United States from a list of Entente countries to which he sent an appeal to the "Workmen of the Entente Countries" in late April, to put pressure on their governments to lift the blockade and to halt the supply of arms to the White forces.[72]

This desire to come to an agreement with the United States persisted. At the time of the Russo-Polish War, in response to questions from Internews Correspondent Frank Mason, Chicherin emphasized again that "a full agreement political and economic with the United States is one of the foremost desires of Soviet Russia and it would go to great lengths to enter into such an agreement."[73] And after the Wilson administration had made it clear, in the Colby note of August 1920, that it would have nothing to do with the Bolshevik government, Lenin and Chicherin turned their attention, both economic and political, to preparing the way for a hoped-for breakthrough with President-elect Warren G. Harding. The first official note to the new President and Congress, March 20, 1921, spoke almost exclusively of commercial and trade relations.[74]

Lenin's strategy for a breakthrough with the United States depended on a skillful integration of economic and political approaches designed to exploit every opening and seize any opportunity to breakdown capitalist and governmental resistance to contacts and weaken the interventionist forces.[75] Although many discussions with American representatives turned on political or military questions, such as the early discussions between Trotsky and Judson, most of the extended Robins-Trotsky-Lenin discussions, the Chicherin-Poole meetings, and the Buckler-Litvinov or Bullitt missions, contained economic elements. In addition, an entire range of discussions, probes, and proposals from the Bolsheviks to the Americans were exclusively or predominantly about economic questions.[76] The long-range political goal remained diplomatic recognition, but in the short run more pragmatic aims were the reduction of assistance to counterrevolution or intervention. In either case, the Soviets believed that economic ties would assist political breakthroughs.[77]

Lenin was vehement at times in his insistence that economic and political discussions needed to be separated for tactical reasons, and that the details of economic proposals needed to be pursued on their own merits, if there was any hope of achieving later political breakthroughs. For example, Lenin edited in great detail a proposed agreement with the American Corporation in June 1920, in which he urged that everything be "stipulated precisely: after delivery of their goods, delivery of ours or exchange at our port. No other way."[78]

Lenin also was alert for what he often saw as Allied attempts at sabotage, in the tying of political conditions to economic or aid proposals. He savagely attacked the Hoover-Nansen proposal linking humanitarian aid and economic relations to Allied control of railroads and a unilateral Bolshevik ceasefire in the civil war, insisting that economics and aid be kept separate from political conditions. The Bolsheviks would be open to any economic contacts and would accept aid, Lenin asserted, as long as there were no political strings attached. Politics had to be separately negotiated, and bargained on a political basis. As he advised Chicherin and Litvinov to respond to the Hoover-Nansen proposal in May, 1919: "If it's humanitarian aid, then do not bring politics into it, dear sir, but just start shipping (stress this). Just start shipping! We are even ready to pay through the nose for it and willingly admit you for control and give you every guarantee. . . . But if a truce, then this is politics . . . we are always ready for talks."[79]

Once economic contact, however tenuous, was established, it could be used to press for political talks. Not only could all of the individual business contacts be used to press the host government, but also trade representatives could be employed for that purpose. By the time the Soviet economic strategy with regard to the United States was fully implemented with the Martens mission in 1919 and 1920, enough experience had been gained with other such approaches (to Scandinavia in particular) that Litvinov could say confidently to Chicherin, "Exchange of goods is the only means of exerting pressure on governments for obtaining political relations."[80]

Although the majority of treatments of Soviet-American relations from 1917 to 1920 date the elaboration of Bolshevik proposals to the United States either from the Trotsky note to Raymond Robins seeking American aid to prevent the ratification of Brest Litvosk (February, 1918) or the full-scale Lenin economic proposal to Raymond Robins (May 1918),[81] extensive evidence exists of much earlier discussions and proposals. Trotsky even began proposing the services of American engineers to regulate the railroads and the expansion of economic relations with the United States as early as December 1917. He included such statements in the earliest military and political proposals to Judson and Robins.[82]

The most fully developed early Soviet proposal to the United States was conveyed to John Reed, an American radical, brilliant young journalist, and Bolshevik sympathizer, by a range of Bolsheviks, left Socialist Revolutionaries and newly appointed commissars, including those of agriculture, labor, welfare, and railroads. From Reed's discussions with these leaders in December and early January, there was unanimity that Russia needed foreign capital, not only "in supplying actual needs but also in developing new resources." The most detailed requests were from the Commissariat of Railroads, where locomotives, spare parts, and steel and iron pigs were requested. Simple tools were requested from Agriculture, together with tractors, metal-working machinery for labor, and clothing and food from the Welfare ministry. Reed argued, in his never-presented or -published report of these conversations that "there is absolutely no doubt that a policy of real material help to Russia would create a love for America in this country which it would be difficult to

alter. . . . A great many people here admit the necessity of American technical and intellectual participation in the development of Russia."[83]

At the same time, in the United States, former Provisional Government
Railroad Representative Yuri Lomonosov, on behalf of the All Russian Railway Union, declared his allegiance to the Soviet government. Lomonosov
continued his discussions with Americans on behalf of a comprehensive
American strategy for assistance and support for an expansion of Russian
railroads as a necessary part of building any resistance to the German occupation of Russia.[84]

Discussions concerning American assistance for the Russian railroads also
took place in early 1918 in Russia, between American railroad commissioner
Henry Emerson (who had come with the Railroad Commission under John
Frank Stevens in October 1917), and Soviet commissar Yuri Larin. The discussions ultimately broke down over the question of American control and Washington's inability to decide whether or not to proceed with any further discussions with the Bolsheviks under any conditions.[85]

In mid-February 1918, during the time of intense pressure on the Bolsheviks by the Germans, and the Bolshevik debate over the terms of the Brest
Litovsk treaty and whether to seek aid from the Americans and the British,
two serious Soviet-American economic discussions took place. Both of these
meetings involved American commercial attaché William C. Huntington.
One set of discussions was with Jacob Bronski, head of the Department of
Trade in the Commissariat of Trade, Industry and Labor, and the other was
with Yuri Larin, from the same department.

These two conversations would seem to indicate that at an early date,
Lenin and the Bolshevik government were willing to entertain the continuation of extensive trade relations with the United States, if only some kind of
agreement between the two governments could be negotiated. There is even
some indication that Lenin was willing (although it is doubtful that the United
States would agree) to honor the old commercial agreement between the
Provisional Government and Washington, were the United States, willing to
drop its recognition of that government in that agreement.[86]

Discussions between Bolshevik and American representatives in the month
of February 1918 were dominated by the ongoing drama at Brest Litovsk and
involved mostly questions of potential military aid should Russia resume the
war against Germany. But even here, Lenin's economic strategy played a part.
Trotsky's discussions with Robins concerning American aid always included a
proviso for economic cooperation, transportation assistance, and civilian supplies. One of the questions in the famous March 5 Soviet communication to the
United States read, "What kind of support could be furnished in the nearest
future, and on what conditions—military equipment, transportation supplies,
living necessities?"[87]

At the same time, the Bolsheviks began serious internal consideration of a
detailed economic proposal for presentation to the United States. Preliminary
discussions with Reed, Robins, Emerson, and Huntington were all useful in
gathering information. Staff in the Commissariat of Labor and Industry, For-

eign Trade, and the Council of the National Economy worked under Lenin's direction to formulate this proposal.[88]

The final proposal, presented to Robins on May 14 for transmission to the United States government, was an extensive analysis of Russia's economic condition and a specific, detailed listing of materials and equipment needed from the United States, and Russian raw materials and resources available in exchange. The document argued that "Germany will be compelled to surrender her leading place as a source for the economic life of Russia for the next few years to a country which has not been disorganized as much as Germany by the war. Only America can become that country."

Railroad supplies, agricultural machinery, electrical machinery, mining machinery, food, textile industry machinery, and all kinds of needs for the improvement of transportation were particularly and urgently requested. The document ended with a plea by the Soviet government for permission to send an economic commission to the United States to further elucidate and negotiate the details of any economic and trade agreement.[89] As if to underscore Soviet seriousness and commitment to progress on economic grounds with the United States, Lenin agreed, at Robins' urging, to exempt the major U.S. corporations then still operating in Russia, International Harvester, Singer, and Westinghouse Electric, from the Soviet decree nationalizing all industry.[90]

Although the late spring and early summer discussions between Foreign Minister Chicherin and Acting Consul Poole were dominated by Soviet concerns regarding growing Allied intervention, economic proposals from the Bolsheviks did not cease. Chicherin and Radek held one round of discussions with American vice-consul John Lehrs on economic concerns, and Chicherin asked Poole questions about the fate of the Lenin proposal to Raymond Robins on several occasions.[91]

Following the departure of Allied personnel from Bolshevik Russia in July and August 1918, the Bolsheviks renewed their appeals to the United States, beginning with the note from Chicherin to Wilson of October 24. While caustic in tone and holding Wilson and the Allies accountable for the tragedy of the civil war, it nonetheless held out an olive branch, and vociferously stressed the Soviet desire to meet any American economic demands:

> precisely what tribute do the Governments of the United States, England, and France demand of the Russian people? Do they demand concessions, do they want the railways, mines, gold deposits, etc., to be handed over to them on certain conditions, or do they demand territorial concessions? . . . We expect you, Mr. President, to state definitely what you and your allies demand. . . .[92]

By the time of Litvinov's telegram to Wilson in December, the vociferous and caustic tone had been replaced by a clear and polite appeal for a chance to be heard and a willingness to negotiate. But still the economic appeal remained: "help Russia retain her own sources of supply, and to give her technical advice how to exploit her natural richness in the most effective way, for the benefit of all countries badly in need of foodstuffs and raw materials. . . ."[93]

Soviet discussions with William H. Buckler, Ludwig Meyer of Denmark, and William C. Bullitt, and Chicherin's response to the Prinkipo invitation, while evolving politically in terms of the conditions under which the Bolsheviks would negotiate peace, remained consistent in their openness to, even their special pleading for, American trade, capital, and investment. Typical is the January 1919 letter to Ludwig Meyer: "Russia needs for her economic reconstruction and development all the technical skill, experience and material support which can be obtained. . . ."[94]

With the collapse of the Bullitt mission and the close of the Peace Conference, the Bolsheviks shifted their strategy to the United States itself. Ludwig C. A. K. Martens had been appointed in January 1919 as representative of the People's Commissariat for Foreign Affairs for the purpose of economic and diplomatic contacts with the United States, and he attempted to present his credentials to the State Department in late March, while the Bullitt proposals were actually pending.[95] Apart from this substantial initiative, Bolshevik contacts with the United States during the remainder of 1919 and 1920 were limited to occasional press interviews, radio and written appeals. Without exception, these uniformly called on the United States to normalize trade relations and raise the blockade, and promised substantial economic benefits in return. As Lenin emphasized to the *Chicago Daily News* at the height of Russia's isolation, October 1919, "We are decidedly for an economic understanding with America—with all countries but especially with America." And in 1920, in a discussion with Lincoln Eyre, correspondent of *The World,* Lenin noted: "we shall need American manufactures—locomotives, automobiles, etc.—more than those of any other country. . . . The world must come to us . . . in the end, Bolshevism or no Bolshevism."[96]

During the last year of the Wilson administration, especially the lameduck months in the fall and winter of 1920–1921, the Soviet government actually increased its emphasis on an economic strategy for the United States; only now, it devoted its attention to preparation for what it believed would be a new Republican administration, headed by Warren G. Harding. It hoped that the new administration would respond to the primacy of economic incentives over ideological antipathy. Its first appeal to the new administration stressed trade relations almost exclusively, in the mistaken belief that the details of the Lenin-Robins proposal, buttressed by Robins' relationship with the Republican party, and Washington Vanderlip's relationship to Harding, would finally be accepted by the United States.[97]

# 2

# Many Actors in Search of a Policy: U.S. Discussions About the Bolsheviks, 1917–1919

Here is the ever-recurring question. How shall we deal with the Bolsheviki? This particular suggestion seems to me to have something in it worth considering . . . ["the first practical step towards combatting German intrigue in Russia should be through the establishment by one of the Allies of relations with the Bolshevik *de facto* Government. . . . Should such a course be deemed advisable is not the United States, from tradition, recent entry on the scene, Latin American experience with *de facto* governments, the best suited?"][1]

In regards to this [Grant-Smith] suggestion, I do not think WE should be the ones to open intercourse with the Lenin crowd.[2]

The United States' approach toward the new Bolshevik government of Soviet Russia was fraught with contradictions. On one hand, Woodrow Wilson believed, as he told William Wiseman, Colonel House, and other personal advisors and confidants, not only that the Russian people should be left alone to work out their own salvation, but even that they should be forced to get themselves together and work it out. Only after democracy had been given a chance in Russia, and the differences "worked out," could the United States "do business" with Russia. A major problem of this approach plagued Wilson throughout his final term in the White House: what do you do with the Bolsheviks while you are waiting, and hoping, and helping, the Russian people return to their senses and "return" democracy to their country?

Wilson, his advisors, the U.S. State Department, the Allies, and the American public grappled with this slippery but most central question in the three years from the Bolshevik revolution to the election of Warren G. Harding. Because this question was difficult and unsettling and Wilson himself was often divided on what course to pursue, the struggles and divisions of those who advised him are key to understanding the American search for a consistent course and policy.

Three American assumptions—that Bolshevism would collapse, that ways must be found to keep Russia in the war, or, failing that, re-establish the Eastern front, and that democracy in Russia must be supported—remained fundamental to American policy from the March revolution at least until the end of the war with Germany in November 1918. Only the first, however, provided any reasonably clear guidance for policy—and that only in a negative fashion. Believing and hoping that the Bolsheviks would collapse certainly precluded recognizing their government officially during this first year, although even this option was briefly considered by Colonel House as part of the wide-ranging efforts to keep Russia in the war in January 1918. But even this much clarity did not help with the subtler questions concerning contact with the Bolsheviks, so long as they remained in power.

The second and third principal assumptions provided even less guidance and more confusion. The desire to preserve the Russian war effort led at times to near-*de facto* working relationships with the Bolsheviks and at times to support for efforts to overthrow them. Efforts to support Russian "democracy" developed dizzying contradictions. At times such attempts led to support for counterrevolution and at other times to restraint on intervention. They contributed to American statements of respect for the territorial integrity of Russia, and yet supported British attempts to dismember Russia and overthrow the Bolsheviks. Above all, the commitments to continue the war and to support Russian "democracy," while seemingly clear and straightforward, led to endless possibilities for misinterpretation and confusion for the large and varied number of Americans who had a role in policy formation or implementation, or who carried on the contacts with Russians in Petrograd or Moscow.[3]

## Woodrow Wilson's Advisors

Wilson received advice on policy toward the Bolsheviks from three main sources, all contributing to the confusion and contradiction of policy, who themselves were sometimes beset with contradictions. Secretary of State Robert Lansing (replaced in 1920 by Bainbridge Colby) was backed by a coterie of State Department, academic, and other "experts" on Russia. Wilson's personal friend and advisor Colonel Edward M. House had a network of governmental and private contacts and sources. British advice and policy most often reached Wilson in the person of House confidant and unofficial British ambassador Sir William Wiseman. These three groups often disagreed, and Wilson's increasingly difficult dilemmas were magnified. At times, one tendency or another would predominate. In general, Lansing and House were the most often at odds. Lansing tended to be more pragmatic in his assessment of the actual situation, quicker to recommend intervention, and less inclined to sanction dealings with the Bolsheviks on any level.[4] House was more idealistic, optimistic, anti-interventionist, and inclined to various attempts at reconciliation. British advice changed with the course of the war, the fortunes of the White Russian armies, and British public opinion, but it always remained an influential factor with both Wilson and House.[5]

## Lansing, His Advisors, and the State Department

Robert Lansing was virulently anti-Bolshevik, an attitude he had developed even before the overthrow of Aleksandr Kerensky. Only a few days after the November Revolution, Lansing confided to his diary that the United States must have nothing whatever to do with Lenin and Trotsky, and he wrote to Wilson that it would be "unwise to give recognition to Lenin, Trotsky, and their crew of radicals. We ought to sit tight and wait."[6] By December 4, he had put on paper for Wilson the outlines of a comprehensive policy of non-recognition, which Wilson declined to make official policy.[7] Lansing followed this a week later with a long letter to Wilson reiterating his opposition to the Bolsheviks, advocating "a military dictatorship backed by loyal disciplined troops," and calling on the United States to throw all of its support to General A. M. Kaledin.[8] Lansing tried again, in January 1918, to have an official statement released.[9] And by mid-1918, Lansing had become, at least in his personal correspondence, stridently caustic, calling Bolshevism "the most hideous and monstrous thing that the human mind has ever conceived," a "monster which seeks to devour civilized society and reduces mankind to the state of beasts."[10] Before he left office, in late December 1919, Lansing undertook yet again to make Wilson take a definitive anti-Bolshevik position, in a long memorandum on the Russian situation.[11]

Lansing's policy advice as Secretary of State was augmented considerably by a range of other voices within and close to the State Department. In the Department itself, Counselor Frank Polk, Assistant Secretary of State William Phillips, and head of the Russian Division Basil Miles were the most influential. Nearly every matter dealing with Russian policy received the attention of at least two of these men before it reached Lansing. This included reading of reports from abroad, as well as developing policy memoranda and personal reports for Lansing and screening mail and requests for personal interviews for those outside the Department.[12]

State Department Counselor Frank Polk was in a particularly advantageous position. Not only did he have the ear of Lansing, but he was close to Colonel House as well, and his right-hand man, Gordon Auchincloss, was House's son-in-law. Thus House (and Wilson) had back-door access to the State Department and information from Russia that did not run through Lansing, but rather through Polk and Auchincloss, a not-inconsiderable factor by the time of the Paris Peace Conference.[13]

Polk tended to play a confidential and cautious role. He did not openly contradict Lansing's policy, but his links to House made him more moderate. He did not become an advocate for any specific position on the Russian question, but he acted as a link between House and Lansing, searching for a consensus on issues of controversy.[14] He supported Lansing, however, with legal advice and precedent with regard to the non-recognition issue, and staunchly upheld the Secretary of State in his determination to withhold any acknowledgement of the Bolshevik regime. He also served as the one within the State Department who had the contacts to question the drift of policy on Russia, which became more and more evident from the summer of 1918 up to, and well into, the Paris Peace Conference.[15]

William Phillips, a career diplomat, served as Chief of the Division of Far Eastern Affairs before becoming Assistant Secretary of State, but had no first-hand knowledge or experience in Russia. Nor did he play any independent role within the State Department on policy toward the Bolsheviks. He carried out directives from Lansing and at times from Polk (when Polk was Acting Secretary of State during Lansing's sojourn at the Paris Peace Conference), and he participated in the debate within the State Department about the best policy direction following the Bolshevik revolution, siding with those who advocated some kind of public statement regarding non-recognition (the Lansing position).[16]

Crucial to the day-to-day State Department work on Russia was Basil Miles, Chief of the Division on Russian Affairs. Miles brought to the Department considerable knowledge and background in Russia, beginning as private secretary to U.S. Ambassador George Meyer in St. Petersburg in 1905 and 1906 and afterwards serving as Third Secretary in the Embassy until May 1907. Miles then left the Foreign Service for work with the U.S. Chamber of Commerce until August 1916, when he was appointed special assistant to Ambassador Francis and special envoy to the Root Commission in 1917. After the Root mission, he was brought back to the State Department as special advisor on Russian affairs.[17]

Miles, due to his background and expertise, was consulted on all matters of policy vis-à-vis Russia, and was particularly active in the development of memoranda and policy papers on the important questions of recognition and contact with the Bolsheviks. Despite his role as chief strategist for Lansing, he consistently displayed a greater degree of openness than his chief did to the question of contact, especially during the crucial period of January and February 1918, before the finalization and ratification of the Treaty of Brest Litovsk. In consecutive policy memoranda of January 28 and February 5, 1918, Miles argued that the United States should begin dealing unofficially with the Bolsheviks, as well as with every other party to the developing conflict.[18] If the United States were to refuse all contact, however, Miles agreed with Lansing that the government should make a public pronouncement of its reasons, citing the need to wait for a stable, democratic government. And finally, on February 5, Miles agreed with Lansing and issued the memorandum to American officials in Petrograd, ordering them to cease all contact with the Bolsheviks.[19]

Miles continued to coordinate State Department policy options on Russia until the fall of 1919, at times overwhelmed by the huge job of coordinating various departments of government in an effort to achieve consensus, and at times totally ignored by Wilson and House. The effort to achieve unity on the question of *de facto* relations with the Bolsheviks in the winter and spring of 1918 was so divisive and making so little progress that Lansing brought in a special consultant, Archibald Cary Coolidge, to interview the principals, review the evidence, and come in with a special report. Coolidge concluded that the task Miles was charged with was impossible for such a small staff in the face of contradictory evidence. He concluded by recommending that the United States do nothing, reasoning that "if the Bolshevik power is presently to go to pieces of itself, we may be saved the necessity of making up our minds definitely as to the truth of the evidence."[20] By the time Miles left the government, however, he had built up the Division from its initial one staff member and two secretaries to a staff of thirteen, and left it firmly on the way to controlling future United States policy toward the Bolsheviks.[21]

## Samuel N. Harper

Supplementing the information and advice that Secretary of State Lansing received from within his Department and from staff in Russia were others with knowledge of Russia, most prominent among them Samuel N. Harper of the University of Chicago. Harper emerges as a central figure in the policy debate concerning that ever-present Wilson question, "How do we deal with the Bolsheviki?" He was perhaps the first full-fledged academic expert on Russia who was also an advisor to the U.S. State Department. Knowledge of his role is tremendously aided by the fact that he was a prolific writer and correspondent, and during the first, crucial years, he continued to teach at the University of Chicago even as he was advising the State Department. He was in touch with virtually everyone who had any impact on what the United States did or was going to do in Russia.[22]

Harper's entree to the State Department and the upper echelons of policy discussion within the Wilson administration was facilitated by the standing of his patron, Charles R. Crane. Crane was a wealthy businessman who had made his fortune in plumbing fixtures, a philanthropist, and a world traveler who had a special interest in Russia, China, and the Arab world. He was a contributor to Wilson's presidential campaigns; often lent his advice, both solicited and unsolicited, to the State Department and Wilson himself; and was a member of the Root mission to Russia in the summer of 1917.[23] Crane took a special interest in the fledgling discipline of Russian studies, and began making financial contributions to the University of Chicago, which enabled Harper to carry on his dual role as specialist professor and consultant to the State Department for the rest of his career.[24]

Apart from Crane and his son Richard, who (conveniently) was Robert Lansing's personal secretary, Harper's major confidants were the permanent staff of the State Department, Basil Miles and William Phillips.[25] Although he became one of the Inquiry team that Colonel House pulled together for advance research for the Paris Peace Conference and worked through George Creel and J. T. Shotwell, he did not meet with Colonel House until mid-1918 and was never considered one of House's confidants.[26] But Harper was not firmly and unequivocally anti-Bolshevik and anti-contact as might befit a State Department advisor. Rather, he suffered with some of the same agonies and struggles over the Bolsheviks that Wilson and House experienced. Harper was at first a strong supporter of the Provisional Government, accompanying the Root Commission on its investigation in the summer of 1917, and for a time he served as both personal advisor and interpreter for both Ambassador Francis and the American Red Cross Commission.[27] Harper never lost his passion for "democracy" for Russia and for the war effort there. Harper's support for the Provisional Government often blinded him to its problems and the growing strength of the Bolsheviks during the summer and fall of 1917.[28]

Harper always opposed recognition of the Bolshevik government, agreeing with the State Department's central position from the beginning.[29] But he had mixed feelings about intervention and the possibility of working with the Bolsheviks. For a while, he tried to steer a middle course between the "recognitionists," as he called them—Raymond Robins, William C. Bullitt, and others—and the interventionists.[30] In the winter and into the spring of 1918 he favored contact with the Bolsheviks in the face of opposition to this approach within the State Department. As Harper put it in a memorandum written soon after Trotsky's successful stalling at Brest Litovsk: "we can get in contact with them without recognizing them as a government. But if we are going to 'play' them, we must be very careful to outwit them."[31] He spent a good deal of energy working to define a position on "contact" with the Bolsheviks that would put him neither in the camp of the recognitionists nor in that of the interventionists. As he wrote to Richard Crane on June 30, 1918: "I make a distinction between the three phrases, 'get into touch with,' 'cooperate with,' and 'recognize.' The second phrase, 'cooperate with' I consider synonymous with 'recognize as the de facto government.' " He favored "get in touch with."[32]

Even in 1919, he favored Wilson's Prinkipo proposal, when it was attacked by many of his friends in the State Department and in the Friends of Russia groups. He maintained contact and friendship with Raymond Robins and Thomas Thacher of the American Red Cross on their return from Russia in the summer of 1918, longer than most other prowar liberals.[33] He was also willing to correspond and even meet with those in favor of recognition, even Harold Kellock of the Soviet Russian Recognition League and Santeri Nuorteva of the Finnish Information Bureau, and to recommend such contact to others.[34] Harper moved very slowly and with much trepidation into the fully anti-Bolshevik, Red Scare mentality that gripped most of the country by the fall of 1919.[35]

Harper played a crucial role in policy debates in and out of the State Department from 1917 to 1920 because of his correspondence and contacts with almost all of the key groups and individuals.[36] He consulted part-time with the State Department from 1918 to 1922, and he kept up academic and public organization contacts as well, most notably with the Russian American Chamber of Commerce, the American Friends of Russia, and the Russian-American Economic League.[37] The League became particularly important because of its role in advocating an American economic and relief commission, which was seriously considered by Wilson and House in the summer and fall of 1918.[38] By the fall of 1918, he had become one of the most sought-after speakers and consultants on Russia in the country, and utilized his position at the University of Chicago for a wide variety of public and governmental assignments.[39] Harper viewed his role in the State Department as developing the best compendium of objective information possible on Bolshevik Russia then available in the United States, and he aimed to steer a careful line between the hysterical anti-Bolshevik press and what he saw as the equal or greater distortions of the pro-recognitionists.[40]

Harper's work on Russian-American economic issues exemplified a key dilemma American policymakers faced in 1918 and 1919. They wanted to keep open economic discussions, even with the Bolsheviks, in hopes of reaping benefits after a new, non-Bolshevik government came into office. On the other hand, they refused to actually complete any negotiations on political or economic issues with the Bolsheviks. That would have meant letting down their non-Bolshevik friends. Harper played a strong role in economic discussions, in part because of his close friendship with William Chapin Huntington, commercial attaché in Petrograd and later head of the Russian desk at the Commerce Department. Together, they developed a proposed plan for economic penetration of Russia for the long-run benefit of the United States, which involved both Bolshevik and non-Bolshevik Russia.[41] As early as March 1918, and insistently through the autumn, Harper advanced their plans in every conceivable forum, arguing repeatedly that "there will be no political order in Russia until the economic distress is relieved. And to accomplish the latter someone must help Russia get, or produce, manufactured articles. . . ."[42]

Harper also served as an important link between moderates opposed to accommodation with the Bolsheviks and conservatives pushing the Red Scare. His information for the Senate Judiciary Committee's investigation provided the detailed background and press analysis for attempts to prove that those advocating a conciliatory position toward the Bolsheviks were wrong, even liars, and to move the administration in an increasingly anti-Bolshevik direction throughout 1919 and 1920.[43]

## Colonel Edward M. House and His Influence

Colonel Edward M. House had greater access to Woodrow Wilson than any other person, at times functioning virtually as a substitute President, although his influence declined precipitously following the famous House-Wilson "break" during the Paris Peace Conference in 1919.[44] At various points in the twists and turns of the search for an American policy toward the Bolsheviks, Wilson relinquished decision-making entirely to House.[45]

House was quite careful to coordinate his thinking with the President's, however, even under such conditions. Moreover, House had his own sources in the State Department, notably his son-in-law Gordon Auchincloss and his good friend counselor Frank Polk. So he was in an excellent position to anticipate State Department thinking as well as Presidential wishes.[46]

House was a liberal whose values were similar to Wilson's, but he was much more pragmatic and inclined to compromise. He was probably the strongest administration voice consistently opposed to intervention. House was also the channel for many liberals and even radicals into the administration. He was open to discussions and correspondence with individuals such as William C. Bullitt, Lincoln Steffens, Raymond Robins, and William B. Thompson, when neither Wilson nor Lansing would see them. House also pursued several of his own initiatives on the Russian question in an effort to avoid either intervention or recognition, among them economic penetration and famine relief.

The House papers and the Wilson papers are full of the record of House's consultation with Wilson on the various policy questions connected with Russia and the Bolsheviks. Their relationship can in a very real sense be traced by following this consultation. At the time of the Russian revolution, Wilson confided in House fully and gave him tremendous responsibilities. In late October 1917, House left for Europe to represent Wilson at the Supreme War Conference of the Allies. On his departure, House expressed to his diary his own sense of the closeness of the relationship: "There is no subject too intimate to be discussed before me, there is nothing that can be thought for my comfort or pleasure that is not urged upon me."[47]

On his return from Paris, House immediately became involved in discussions with Wilson concerning Russia as he prepared his Fourteen Points speech, urging him to appeal to the Russian people and avoid hasty judgements about the Bolshevik revolution, to give instead the "broadest and friendliest expressions of sympathy and a promise of more substantial help." And House records that "there was no argument about this because our minds ran parallel, and what he wrote about Russia is I think . . . the most eloquent part of his message."[48]

In early March 1918, they still thought along parallel lines. The Congress of Soviets was about to meet in Moscow, and House thought it would be a good idea to send another reassuring message of friendship to the Russian people. Wilson responded with another such message.[49]

By June, House had determined that the best approach was a new Relief and Economic Commission for Russia, to forestall continued Allied requests for intervention. Although he got Wilson's approval for such a Commission, to be headed by Herbert Hoover, it was never constituted or dispatched, and instead Wilson eventually made his famous decision to dispatch 6,000 American soldiers to Siberia, a decision House opposed.[50] By September, when House queried Wilson about the progress regarding the economic and relief policy, Wilson intimated that it had become bogged down in the Commerce Department. House took steps through Auchincloss to get Vance McCormick and the War Trade Board involved, but the momentum of the plan had been slowed and was never to dominate American policy, soon becoming eclipsed by the difficulties of the intervention policy and the new problems raised by the end of the war.[51] House even remarked to his diary at this time that "I disagree almost entirely with the manner in which the President has handled the Russian situation" in allowing the military intervention to take precedence over economic and relief initiatives.[52]

Wilson and House remained very close, however. For the second time, Wilson sent House to Paris for consultations with the Allies preceding the Paris Peace Conference, giving him unprecedented powers of personal representation and showing every confidence in his ability to make decisions Wilson would approve of. House noted in his diary on the eve of his departure that Wilson said to him, "I have not given you any instructions because I feel you will know what to do."[53]

House successfully represented Wilson (i.e., to Wilson's satisfaction) at these meetings, and the two remained remarkably in concert early in the Paris Peace Conference in 1919. But by the time of Wilson's departure for the United States in mid-February, his relationship with House had noticeably cooled. When House suggested to Wilson that "we could button up everything during the next four weeks, [Wilson] seemed startled and even alarmed at this statement." House was forced to reassure Wilson, and this signaled the beginning of what was to become a significant loss of confidence by the President in his chief advisor, and a widening of the gap between them on all matters of substance.[54] After this point, House's efforts toward alternative Russian policies were frustrated by Wilson's preoccupation with other issues and his increasing lack of close consultation with House on Russian policy.[55]

House served Wilson in one further respect concerning Russian policy. He was a key channel to thinking and policy in Britain. House kept Wilson fully informed about the British through two unofficial sources: Sir William Wiseman, chief British intelligence agent in the United States; and William H. Buckler, aide to U.S. Ambassador Walter Page in London and source for House of information concerning Labour and Liberal opinion in Britain.[56]

House began his close relationship with Wiseman in the spring of 1917, and they jointly worked out schemes for Russia to present to their respective governments.[57] Wiseman reported directly to Foreign Minister Arthur Balfour, and thus Wilson was able to avoid the usual State Department–Foreign Ministry bureaucracy and get action on ideas directly. Likewise, Wiseman had a direct link to Wilson through House, and often met with the President when House felt it was important.[58]

House's connection with William H. Buckler provided another and quite different form of intelligence. Buckler maintained close ties to the liberal and socialist world of Britain, and provided House with information that he was unable to get through regular embassy channels. On questions of Russian policy, Buckler was able to get to House details concerning the Labour Party's attitudes and contacts, talks with Bolshevik envoy Lev Kamenev and Labour leaders, and the attitudes of the liberal and labor press to R. H. Bruce Lockhart's contacts with the Bolsheviks in Petrograd. Thus House kept informed about British approaches to the Bolsheviks in ways that were not reported through normal State Department channels.[59]

House's attitudes toward the Bolsheviks remained remarkably consistent during the less than two years following the Bolshevik revolution until he ceased to be a factor in American policy by the summer of 1919. From the beginning, he was determined that America should remain the friend of Russia and should do everything possible to keep Russia out of the arms of Germany. It was on his initiative that Wilson and Lansing were persuaded to state publicly in late November 1917 that Russia was not to be considered an enemy, despite its intimations that it would leave the war.[60] He persisted in his attempts to persuade Wilson, the State Department, and the Allies to continue their support of the Russian people, both in public statements and, if possible, militarily, in an effort to keep the Bolsheviks as far from Germany as possible during the negotiations over Brest Litovsk.[61] His concerns over Russia's falling into the German camp were so strong during this period that he went as far as to discuss privately with Balfour and Wiseman the possibility of the United States recognizing the Bolsheviks as a way to forestall German influence in Russia. He was the only top U.S. advisor to contemplate such recognition.[62]

With the failure of that strategy and the ratification of Brest Litovsk, discussions moved increasingly to various schemes of Allied intervention. House consistently opposed all such plans, including the early December efforts to assist the White forces in the Caucasus, the March push to persuade the Americans to support Japanese intervention in Siberia, the British effort in April and May to convince the United States that the Bolsheviks would consent to intervention, and the final push on a Wilson decision to intervene directly in Siberia in June and July.[63] Even after intervention had become limited U.S. policy, with the approval of forces for Murmansk and Siberia, House worked against them. With the Armistice in November, he became the foremost voice in the administration, apart from all of the military advisors, urging immediate U.S. withdrawal.[64]

Accompanying these efforts were the various schemes to work toward some kind of accommodation with the Bolsheviks in the context of the Paris Peace Conference. When Prinkipo foundered, House, with British support, took the initiative for the Bullitt mission. As it became clear that neither Wilson nor the British were prepared to push for its adoption on Bullitt's return, House turned once again to his favorite plan for Russia: food relief. He revived the ideas of mid-1918, and patched together what became known as the Hoover-Nansen plan. It was to be his last—and the United States' last—initiative on the thorny question of the Bolsheviks in the Wilson administration.[65]

Despite the often divergent advice that House and Lansing usually gave to Wilson, House respected Lansing, consulted him often,[66] and kept closely in touch with State Department thinking through House's son-in-law, Gordon Auchincloss, aide to State Department Counselor and Acting Secretary of State Frank Polk. House used Auchincloss as a private source of information in the State Department, and entrusted to him numerous special assignments.[67]

Auchincloss retained the confidence of both House and Polk, and thus facilitated easy coordination between House's policy and the State Department's.[68]

Auchincloss played a particularly important role in the preparation and implementation of the House plan for a Russian Relief Commission as an alternative to intervention in the early summer of 1918, working as a useful intermediary between Lansing, House, Polk, Herbert Hoover, and President Wilson.[69] At the time of the Paris Peace Conference, Auchincloss functioned as an aide to House and continued this role as channel for House to Polk and the State Department in Washington. Although his closeness to House endured, Auchincloss during this period became increasingly estranged from both Lansing and Wilson, losing influence on important policy questions long before House did.[70] His last role of consequence in Russia policy came with his and David Hunter Miller's work at turning the Bullitt mission into the Hoover-Nansen plan, and their revision of Bullitt's draft response to Nansen.[71]

One of Colonel House's most important roles in the Wilson administration was to serve as a channel for liberals and radicals with concerns and ideas on Russia policy. Wilson himself corresponded with a few such voices, notably Lincoln Colcord of the *Philadelphia Ledger,*[72] but House kept in contact with many more. These included Lincoln Steffens, Colcord, William C. Bullitt, Walter Lippmann, Thomas W. Lamont, Max Eastman, Albert Rhys Williams, Louis Edgar Browne, Bessie Beatty, and John Reed.[73] House was usually noncommittal in discussions with the more radical voices, but he consistently supported their right to be heard, and continued meeting with all returnees from Russia through the end of his service to the Wilson administration. Occasionally, as in the case with Colcord and William C. Bullitt, the relationship developed its own dynamic. Their suggestions and advice had their impact on House's thinking and his policy suggestions to the President.

House's relationship with Colcord went back to the earliest days of House's ties to Wilson.[74] By the time of the American entry into the war, and the March revolution in Russia, they were meeting almost daily. House would give Colcord ideas for articles and editorials for the *Public Ledger,* and Colcord would give House advice on foreign policy issues pending in the administration. Increasingly, Colcord's concerns about Russian policy came to the fore.[75]

Following the Bolshevik revolution, Colcord and House continued to meet. In the winter and spring of 1918, Colcord became a leader of a group of liberal journalists and analysts who advocated the withdrawal of Ambassador David Francis from Russia and the appointment of a special commission to open up contacts with the Bolsheviks as a way of keeping Russia in the war and maintaining American influence in an increasingly chaotic situation. House, for a time, seemed open to such a suggestion.[76] Then the moment passed, and both House's and Colcord's major concern became restraining the forces of intervention within the administration.[77]

House met William C. Bullitt when Bullitt wrote for Colcord at the *Philadelphia Public Ledger* in 1916 and 1917. Bullitt left the *Public Ledger* for a position in the State Department, on the recommendation of House, and

retained his close relationship with House from that time until Bullitt's resignation from government following his disillusionment with Wilson at the close of
the Paris Peace Conference.[78] House's close relationship with Bullitt may be
responsible for an incident in late October 1917, when the *Public Ledger*
published some details of the upcoming Allied war conference that the administration had specially requested the press not to publish. Although Lansing
and the State Department exonerated Bullitt, Wilson seemed to hold him
responsible, and commented on his youth and inexperience several times.[79]

Despite this incident, Bullitt settled into the State Department, working
primarily on analyses of German propaganda, but drawn increasingly to the
Russian question. At the time of the October revolution, he began to analyze
Soviet positions on war settlement, and added his voice to those from Russia
urging the Administration to find a way to deal with the Bolsheviks and keep
Russia in the war.[80] Throughout 1918, he peppered House with memoranda
on all phases of the situation, consistently recommending contact with the
Bolsheviks and warning against intervention. Bullitt became one of the few
administration advocates for the recommendations of Raymond Robins in the
State Department in early 1918, and his specific suggestions were often quite
close to House's own positions.[81] House rarely responded in writing to these
letters and memoranda, but he met with Bullitt frequently, and his diary
indicates that he was consistently reflecting on the same issues as Bullitt
during the same periods of time. Although their reasoning varied and Bullitt
tended to be more emotional, they usually agreed on the key issues of Russian
policy: contact with the Bolsheviks, Japanese intervention, and American
intervention. By November 1918, Bullitt had become something of a pariah in
Lansing's State Department. His incisive memorandum, "The Bolshevist
Movement in Western Europe," in which he advocated compromising with
moderate socialists to isolate the Bolsheviks, was rejected by the State Department but fit perfectly into House's own approach. House moved to see that
Bullitt was added to the staff of the peace delegation to Paris.[82]

The Committee on Public Information (Compub) functioned as yet another source of information and advice for the Wilson administration on
Russian policy, and another thread of House's personal influence. Compub
was formed in April and May of 1917, at the time of America's entry into
World War I, to serve as the first "war information office" in American
history. As George Kennan has noted, Compub was a combination public
information, censorship, and intelligence office.[83] It was headed by Woodrow
Wilson's old friend George Creel, a man who shared Wilson's own distaste for
government bureaucracy and who always had a direct line to the President.[84]

Representing Compub in Russia were two men on fire with the mission of
the United States in the war: Edgar G. Sisson and Arthur Bullard. Sisson was
appointed the head of the information office for Petrograd when it was established in October 1917, just before the Bolshevik revolution, and left Washington with what he felt were personal instructions from Wilson.[85] Bullard, a
veteran journalist and former Secretary of the Friends of Russian Freedom,
assisted Creel in the initial organization of Compub in April 1917. He at-

tempted to get on the Root mission staff but was vetoed by Lansing.[86] Finally, he left for Russia on his own in June 1917, entirely unofficially but with a personal understanding and charge fom Colonel House and, indirectly, from President Wilson.[87] Although Bullard began to work with Sisson by December, and eventually took over the Compub office from him, during the important early days after the Bolshevik revolution he functioned as Colonel House's eyes and ears in Petrograd. In Kennan's evaluation, Bullard was "the best American mind observing on the spot the course of the Russian Revolution."[88] Bullard and Sisson both ignored the usual State Department channels and reported back directly; Bullard to House and Sisson to Creel.[89]

Bullard's advice to House and Creel remained remarkably consistent, from the Bolshevik revolution to his departure from Bolshevik territory in the spring of 1918: open up contact with all elements, including the Bolsheviks, promote American interests and democratic values, and do not cut the United States off from opportunities. This was essentially the advice that House wanted to hear. As Ernest Poole was to remark later, "he [Bullard] felt strongly that the work of his group should be strictly confined to the friendly publicity campaign. He was at all times strongly against taking part in any activities against the Soviet Government."[90]

In Bullard's initial twenty-page missive to House on December 12, 1917, he argued strongly that informal contact with the Bolsheviks was essential to keeping open the possibility of influencing their conduct in negotiations with Germany and keeping Compub activities in Russia alive.[91] In his January memo on the Bolshevik movement in Russia, Bullard argued that the United States needed to maintain an openness and communication with the Bolshevik movement despite dislike for it and opposition to its aims and methods.[92] As late as March 1918, although Bullard disagreed with Raymond Robins about the question of material aid to the Bolsheviks, he still argued for contact, and cautioned against intervention.[93]

## Britain and France

American decisions about the Bolsheviks were not made only in the context of this shifting kaleidoscope of conflicting American advice. They also had to take into account the attitudes and actions of America's two major allies in World War I—the British and the French, particularly the British. Despite Woodrow Wilson's desire to preserve America's freedom of action in the Great War by entering as an "associated power" and not formally joining the alliance, and despite making both Britain and France very angry at times with his arrogance and insistence on the United States' prerogatives, Wilson consulted closely with the Allies, especially the British, on almost every decision concerning the Bolsheviks. France's role was most often played out in conjunction with, or in counterpoint to, Britain.[94] The United States most often responded to French concerns as they were reflected through British eyes and British interests.[95] The other Allies, the Italians and the Japanese, were clearly tangential to the central British-American-French discussions over Allied policy toward the Bolsheviks.[96]

The point of departure for any discussion of British or French policy was the war against Germany. The need to maintain some kind of effort in Russia against Germany persisted, in British and French eyes, even after the Armistice. But there was no agreement between France and Britain about whether the war against Germany in Russia could best be pursued by cooperating with the Bolsheviks, attempting to overthrow them, or both.[97] Moreover, as Jay Kaplan points out, Britain and France developed quite different perceptions of the threat Bolshevik Russia posed. France desired a strong Russia to serve as a balance to Germany, but was very worried about the possibility of Russian-German collaboration. Britain, on the other hand, wanted a weaker Russia, and was concerned about the international "virus" of Bolshevism. These perceptions led Britain to desire a settlement with a weakened Bolshevik state, while France was determined to remove all German and Bolshevik influence from Russia and reestablish a strong, pro-France Russia.[98]

Despite these differences that continued to surface, the Allies attempted to coordinate their policy, both before and after the Armistice. The initiative in most cases rested with Britain. Britain first proposed trying to work with the Bolsheviks to maintain the Eastern front, then to support the anti-Bolshevik forces, and finally to make peace. In no case were British initiatives fully supported by France and the United States.[99] A modified British position usually prevailed in any agreements, however, in part as the least-common-denominator between the United States and France.

## British-American Consultations

Most of the close consultation between the British and American policymakers involved three main issues: (1) the extent to which the Allies should develop some kind of contact with the Bolsheviks in the hope of working with them to some greater or lesser extent against the Germans; (2) the level of American support for, and cooperation in, intervention against the Bolsheviks, both in North Russia and in Siberia; and (3) the repeated efforts to find some formula for settling with the Bolsheviks at the time of the Paris Peace Conference. Consultation on the first two issues revolved around the William Wiseman–Colonel House connection and, in Russia, the Raymond Robins–Bruce Lockhart relationship. The third discussions were carried on primarily among Lloyd George and his secretary Philip Kerr and William C. Bullitt, William H. Buckler, and Colonel House.

The British, in the person of Ambassador Sir George Buchanan in Petrograd, were the first among the Allies to urge that some form of unofficial relations be established with the Bolsheviks. While agreeing with his American and French colleagues David Francis and Joseph Noulens that recognition was out of the question, Buchanan urged in a telegram to the Foreign Office that "we shall have to enter into unofficial relations with it as the only *de facto* authority." As Buchanan noted in his diary at the time, "we must establish some sort of contact with it for the conduct of certain current affairs."[100]

In a memorandum to the War Cabinet, Foreign Minister Arthur Balfour agreed with his Ambassador and recommended that Britain "avoid, as long as possible, an open break with this crazy system." He reasoned that a definite break in relations would endanger British subjects in Russia and could even drive Russia into the hands of Germany.[101]

The United States was at first reluctant to agree with this British position. When Cecil Spring Rice, then British ambassador to Washington, discussed the matter with Secretary Lansing, Lansing explained the American position as one of "abstention"—that even establishing *de facto* relations was going too far for the American government. Only slowly, and under pressure from Raymond Robins and Colonel House, did the State Department swing round to the British and French position.[102]

Britain soon formalized its arrangements, appointing R. H. Bruce Lockhart and according Maksim Litvinov, already residing in Britain, similar privileges in exchange.[103] These terms were explained in a note to the United States and France in early January.[104] Before long, Britain, France, and the United States had unofficial contacts in operation in Petrograd, meeting both with each other and with Foreign Commissar Trotsky: Lockhart for Britain, Jacques Sadoul for France, and Raymond Robins for the United States. In each case the relationship established was different. Only Lockhart was officially appointed and had direct access to policymakers in his government. Sadoul was attached to the French military mission, but was responsible to the chief of that mission, General Niessel, and indirectly to the French ambassador, Joseph Noulens. Robins had an informal relationship with American Ambassador David Francis and other channels through Compub staff members Bullard and Sissons, and through the Red Cross to Colonel House.[105]

By February, the pendulum had begun to swing the other way. Colonel House began to think seriously about recommending recognition of the Bolsheviks as a way to combat German influence and keep Russia in the war. Before broaching it with President Wilson and the State Department, he asked for British advice in a cable to Balfour. Both Wiseman and Balfour advised strongly against it, and House was persuaded to drop the idea in favor of the then-rather-well-developed British position of informal contact through special emissaries.[106]

From February through April, the British used their developing *modus vivendi* between Lockhart and Trotsky to try to persuade the Bolsheviks to sanction their intervention in Russia against the Germans, particularly in the north. They used the information received from Lockhart to try to persuade the United States, through Sir William Wiseman, that Trotsky was on the verge of inviting the Allies in, in the hope that the United States would join in intervention and would also reduce its opposition to Japanese intervention in Siberia.[107] Only a last-minute effort by William C. Bullitt and Colonel House changed a memo from Wilson and Lansing agreeing to Japan intervention.[108]

By July, Wilson had finally joined the British in North Russia and had issued the famous *aide-mémoire* regarding intervention. But this commitment, despite all of the efforts the British had made, fell far short of their hopes. The British believed, however, in the words of Lloyd George, that "the essential thing is that we should get movement started without delay." Perhaps a few American troops could be expanded to many more. Perhaps the restrictions placed on Americans would be lifted.[109]

The United States continued to disappoint British advocates of intervention. But after the armistice with Germany and the opening of the Paris Peace Conference, American and British views on the Bolsheviks began to coalesce once again. Pressed by the State Department to take a clear position on the Bolsheviks and further intervention after the war, President Wilson begged off, preferring to consult with the Allies. From this point on, all United States decisions regarding the Bolsheviks would be made in close consultation with Britain.[110]

## A Complicating Factor: Provisional Government Ambassador Boris Bakhmetev

No discussion of influences brought to bear on Woodrow Wilson's struggle for a policy toward the Bolsheviks can be complete without an examination of the role of the Russian Provisional Government Ambassador to the United States, Boris Bakhmetev. Bakhmetev, a liberal-minded member of the Constitutional Democratic Party, came to Washington in June 1917 as the new Ambassador to the United States. From the first days of his stay in Washington, he developed a sympathetic relationship with Assistant Secretary of State Breckinridge Long, State Department aide (and House son-in-law) Gordon Auchincloss, and, for a time, Colonel House himself. He seemed the very embodiment of Woodrow Wilson's hopes for a Democratic Russia, which the March revolution represented.[111]

House spent many hours with Bakhmetev in the summer and fall of 1917, and together they developed ideas for revising American war aims, strengthening the Allied commitment to a liberal, democratic Russia, and supporting the Provisional Government. House expressed his favorable impression of Bakhmetev in his diary, noting that they spoke "the same language."[112]

Following the Bolshevik seizure of power, Bakhmetev drew an immediate distinction between the Russian government and the Russian people, insisting that the Bolshevik regime was composed of usurpers who would soon be overthrown. He appealed to the U.S. government to continue to work with him until the restoration of democracy in Russia.[113] The State Department did not immediately respond to Bakhmetev's entreaties, and it was several weeks before he received an audience, this time with George Creel, the head of the Committee on Public Information and a personal friend of President Wilson's. Creel met with Bakhmetev about November 22, and agreed to talk to the President and use his influence to preserve Bakhmetev's position. According to Bakhmetev, Creel then met with Wilson, who assured him that he had no intention of abandoning the Provisional Government representative. A meeting was then arranged with Secretary of State Lansing, who formally assured Bakhmetev of the U.S. government's continued support.[114]

House next met with Bakhmetev on December 22, when the two discussed the broad questions of the attitude that the United States should take toward Russia. Bakhmetev urged the administration "not to abandon Russia," and suggested strongly that the President include significant reference to its support in a forthcoming message to Congress. House credited Bakhmetev at least in part for the formulation of Wilson's support for Russia in the Fourteen Points Address.[115]

As time went on, however, Bakhmetev saw House more infrequently, conducting most of his business with Breckinridge Long of the State Department and John Leffingwell of the Treasury Department. The Wilson administration developed a system for using Bakhmetev's embassy to channel funds to anti-Bolshevik forces during the next several years of civil war. Bakhmetev's role in policy discussions, particularly concerning the sensitive issue of contact with the Bolsheviks, was extremely limited. House recorded in his Diary only two meetings with Bakhmetev after December 1917: one in March 1918, in which Bakhmetev urged House and the United States to oppose Japanese intervention as being not in the interest of the Russian people, and the second in February 1919, when Bakhmetev made an attempt to give his own Prinkipo proposal to Wilson, a plan for consultation with all Russian factions except the Bolsheviks.[116]

Bakhmetev only met with Woodrow Wilson once, a formal audience for the presentation of his credentials as new Provisional Government Ambassador, on July 5, 1917. At the time the two seemed fully in concert with their visions of a liberal, democratic Russia.[117] As time passed, however, and the fortunes of the Bolsheviks grew stronger, Bakhmetev and the Provisional Government Embassy played an increasingly subsidiary role in Wilson's thinking. Bakhmetev later attributed the lack of access to the President and the infrequency of his meetings with House to influences on the President who urged him to recognize, or at least deal with, the Bolsheviks; primarily House's relationship with journalist Lincoln Steffens.[118]

Rather than a dominant influence on policy, Bakhmetev and his embassy fulfilled but one role in an ambiguous and often-contradictory policy of the Wilson administration on Russia. Bakhmetev continued to be recognized as "Ambassador of the Russian People," and his embassy was used to channel funds to assist in both covert and overt intervention. But this in no way obviates the very real openness that Colonel House and, at times, Woodrow Wilson, showed to the parallel necessity of finding a way to work with the Bolshevik government, which remained in control of Great Russia. Although Bakhmetev tried to argue in his reminiscences that Wilson's refusal to reach an accommodation with the Bolsheviks was the result of his (Bakhmetev's) continuing influence at the State Department, the story is considerably more complex than that. In a very real sense, Woodrow Wilson permitted dealings with Bolshevik Russia to go forward despite the wishes of Bakhmetev and his supporters.[119]

## Woodrow Wilson's Frustration

In nearly two years of intense consideration of the burning question of how to deal with the Bolsheviks, Woodrow Wilson's administration never effectively established a policy. The constant fluidity of the situation enabled many approaches to be tried, and gave considerable latitude to other American actors actually engaged with the Bolsheviks.[120]

Wilson at times approved of and pursued contradictory policy initiatives, or drew back from courses of action once begun. In 1918 he approved, for example, the maintenance of informal contacts with the Bolsheviks under the general supervision of Ambassador David Francis, yet he acquiesced in the recall of General William V. Judson and Raymond Robins, who had initiated and maintained such contacts.[121]

Later, early in 1919, Wilson responded to an overture by Bolshevik envoy Maksim Litvinov by dispatching William C. Buckler to Stockholm, and he set the general policy for the dispatch of House aide William C. Bullitt to Moscow to meet with Lenin. Yet on each occasion he drew back from the implications of these initiatives and did not follow up. At critical times, Wilson would pull out of discussions on policy toward the Bolsheviks, and leave the decisions up to Colonel House, Secretary Lansing, or others.[122] With the notable exceptions of the important decisions to intervene in the Russian civil war (July 1918) and to issue the Prinkipo invitation in Paris (January 1919), Wilson tended to postpone or retreat from definitive statements concerning the Bolsheviks.[123] This magnified the roles of his advisors, and their differences, and the shifting winds of American public and press opinion on this issue.

Wilson struggled with the question of what to do with the Bolsheviks from the standpoint of his own ideals and values. He tried to apply his fundamental conviction that American democracy and American free enterprise were absolutely right, not just for America, but for Russia and the world. He believed himself to be a Christian statesman on a mission to bring the American way of life to the world.[124] As John Reed, who was later to clash strongly with Wilson over his policy toward the Bolshevik revolution, perceptively observed about Wilson following a long interview with him after Reed's return from Mexico in 1914: "He seems animated by extremely simple ideals—Christianity, Liberty, and Fair Play. . . . He is very American. . . . Deep within him is a principle, or a religion, or something, upon which his whole life rests. . . . Wilson's power emanates from it. . . ."[125]

Wilson's deceptive simplicity and moral clarity go far to explain his initial success as a politician and his ability to lead through forceful persuasion. As Alexander and Juliet George have written, Wilson's moralism had its strong points in the political world:

What ever course he happened to advocate at the moment, it was not only "right" but intimately bound up with human progress in general. Arrayed on his side were "God," "progress," "the breath of fresh air," "forces of righteousness." Whereas another man might have been ruined by so many contradictions and reversals of political beliefs, Wilson escaped the usual consequences because he could convince people of his complete sincerity and of the "righteousness" of whatever position he was at the moment taking.[126]

A belief in his own "righteousness," however, did not always lead to hoped-for results, as an examination of Wilson's tenure as president of Princeton University shows. Wilson's vaunted "principles" often stood in the way of effective leadership at Princeton and showed themselves more often as intractability than as statesmanship.[127]

Moreover, the two sides of Christian moralism—a desire to do good to one's fellows, to ameliorate conflict and violence, on one hand; and the inflexibility of "righteousness" on the other, were not always compatible, either in policy application or even within the mind of Wilson himself. Wilson's press secretary, Joseph Tumulty, recalled that Wilson reflected out loud on this dichotomy shortly after he was nominated for the presidency in 1912:

> You know, Tumulty, there are two natures combined in me that every day fight for supremacy and control. On the one side, there is the Irish in me, quick, generous, impulsive, passionate, anxious always to help and to sympathize with those in distress. . . . Then, on the other side, there is the Scotch— canny, tenacious, cold and perhaps a little exclusive. I tell you dear friend, that when these two fellows get to quarreling among themselves, it is hard to act as umpire between them.[128]

These two sides of Wilson, the compromiser and the crusader, were reflected in his approach to people and politics, as well as to the world and to revolutionary challenges to his ideal world order. There was a part of him that tried to be open to the idea of revolution as a force to be accepted and incorporated into a higher consensus for society. But the crusader in Wilson, with such strong beliefs about the proper course for the world and for Russia, also saw revolution—and Bolshevism in particular—as a threatening obstacle to achieving any higher consensus on Wilson's terms. Wilson's inflexibility and uncompromising moral judgement tended to sweeping condemnation of Bolshevism, leaving his confusion and agony more in the realm of whether to best *deal with it* by force or by compromise.[129]

In order to examine in more detail Wilson's dilemmas and choices in American policy toward Bolshevik Russia, it is important first to remind ourselves of his approach and policies toward Tsarist Russia and the Provisional Government of Russia from March of 1917. For Wilson's initial, and in some cases long-term, responses to the Bolsheviks were cast squarely in the framework of his understanding and hopes for the Russia of March 1917.

Wilson knew little about the details of Russia or Russian politics prior to 1917. In general, his progressivism left him indifferent or even hostile to the

Tsarist government. The coming of World War I made him hopeful, following the lead of his advisor Colonel House and the expertise of George Kennan the elder and Samuel N. Harper, that war might topple the Tsar and bring democracy to Russia.[130]

Wilson welcomed the revolution of March 15, 1917, enthusiatically, as did most American liberals. Following the swift recommendations of Ambassador David Francis and Secretary of State Robert Lansing, Wilson recognized the Provisional Government a scant week later, the first foreign head of state to do so, and soon thereafter authorized Francis to extend American credits to the new regime.[131] Discussion of this step took place in a Cabinet meeting on the imminence of United States' entry into World War I. As George F. Kennan has pointed out, Robert Lansing led the discussion advocating the linkage of the two steps: recognition of the new government in Russia, and American entry into the World War.[132] As many historians have noted, the United States was on the verge of entering World War I regardless of the revolutionary process in Russia, but it certainly enlarged the scope and sweep of the rhetorical formulation of Woodrow Wilson's address to the Congress on April 2 to be able to link the two events.[133]

Wilson couched the language of his Declaration of War squarely in terms of the struggle between absolutism and democracy, and his major positive example was the coming of democracy to Russia. Wilson went as far as to claim that the "great, generous Russia people have been added in all their naïve majesty and might to the forces that are fighting for freedom in the world. . . . Here is a fit partner for a league of honor."[134] Wilson's linkage of his crusade for democracy in the World War and his belief that democracy had come to Russia was a fateful one. It was to color his attitude and approach to the revolutionary struggle in Russia for the rest of his presidency.[135]

The working assumptions on which the American search for a policy was based were in large measure set by the Wilson linkage of democracy, Russia, and world crusade—first for war and then for peace. The realities of the revolutionary struggle in Russia between March and November, the growth of Bolshevik support, and the increasing war weariness of the Russian people, were not factored into Wilsonian and American policy development. Instead they remained driven by the assumptions of the April 2 Declaration of War.

These several assumptions reflected, in large part, Wilson's thinking, but they were also malleable enough to permit a considerable degree of interpretation and experimentation by American officials. The first and most important assumption was the belief that the Bolshevik government could not last and that, given the chance, the Russian people would "return" to "democracy."[136] This assumption was accentuated by the ardor with which the United States greeted the overthrow of the Tsar in March, and the nearly total identification of the United States with the Provisional Government. The United States refused to grant any credence to reports from observers on the ground concerning the evolving revolutionary process, the emergence of the Soviets as a rival governing force, or the increasing inability of the Russian army to maintain any enthusiasm for fighting. Rather, as Wilson remarked both privately and publicly, the enthusiasm of the Russians for the war would improve once a bond was forged between them and the American people.[137]

This tendency to see and hear only what would fit with preconceptions of the "stirrings of Russian democracy" continued after the Bolsheviks took control. Reports from Russia showing the reality of Soviet control were discounted as self-serving, while evidence of opposition to Bolshevik rule was seized upon as proof of imminent Bolshevik collapse. Wilson himself was very slow to recognize the significance of the November revolution, writing several letters in the days immediately following the revolution that continued to discuss Russia as if the Provisional Government were still in power.[138] American reports to Washington predicted the demise of the Bolsheviks for several years running, and the *New York Times* and other leading press organs constantly made similar statements.[139]

The second major assumption was really a corollary of the first. Just as American officials hoped for and assumed the eventual collapse of Bolshevism, so they also believed and assumed that a way could be found to keep Russia in the war on the side of the Allies. This hope contributed to several quite contradictory strands of American policy. It contributed to America's refusal to accept growing evidence that the Russian people were tired of the war and that no government could long survive that did not end it.[140] Thus, the tendency to refuse to accept Bolshevik rule was intensified. At the same time, this strong desire to keep Russia in the war and the belief that it could be done led a great many Americans, especially those in Petrograd, to believe that the Bolsheviks could be persuaded to stay in the war; or at least to refuse to aid the Germans and to deliver war supplies into the hands of the Allies.[141] Finally, any American predilection toward intervention in Russia was greatly strengthened by a strong desire to preserve the Eastern front. It is an interesting consequence that the overwhelming desire of the Wilson administration to keep Russia in the war contributed both to the first informal working relationships between Americans and the Bolshevik government *and* to the American decision to intervene.[142]

Yet a third conviction helped motivate the search for an American policy. This reflected, perhaps more than the other two, Woodrow Wilson's own moral vision of American foreign policy. Increasingly, Wilson stood behind his initial inclinations, which he had first formulated in response to revolutionary upheaval in Mexico: that international intercourse was impossible with a revolutionary, non-democratic government. Just as the United States fervently welcomed the coming of democracy to Russia in March, so it viewed with increasing hostility the consolidation of Bolshevik power, believing it to be fundamentally undemocratic.[143]

Woodrow Wilson himself was never able to satisfactorily reconcile the tensions inherent in these principles. He viewed Bolshevism as fundamentally undemocratic and a direct challenge to his hopes for liberal democracy not only for Russia, but for Europe and the rest of the world as well. To recognize such a government, in Wilson's mind, would have been to deny his own deep faith in the future of the world.[144] At the same time, Wilson's belief in democracy for Russia restrained his interventionist impulses. He was never able to throw himself wholeheartedly into the massive interventionist schemes of Winston Churchill and General Ferdinand Foch of France because of a lingering conviction that they were antithetical to his belief in democracy.[145] He tried, with decreasing success, to reconcile his virulent opposition to Bolshevism with his conviction that Russia had to work out its own destiny. Ultimately, Wilson provided leadership neither for intervention nor for reconciliation. He continued to hope, at times in spite of sobering reality, that the Soviet government would collapse and a new democratic government would take its place, one that he could support and nurture.[146]

Wilson's profound belief that he knew what was right for Russia (even as he was unable to find a medium-term workable policy) had one rather important side effect. He was never really interested in hearing the unfolding story of what was really happening in Russia, especially with regard to the staying power of Bolshevism, particularly if it contradicted his own best hopes for Russian democracy. He consistently refused to meet personally with almost everyone with first-hand experience in Russia after the Bolshevik revolution. William V. Judson, William Boyce Thompson, Raymond Robins, Thomas Thacher, William C. Huntington, Ambassador David Francis, William H. Buckler, William C. Bullitt, DeWitt Clinton Poole—the major official and semi-official Americans returning from Russia with first-hand experience with the Bolshevik government—were uniformly denied a presidential hearing.[147]

The combination of Wilson's refusal to deal with the changing reality of the unfolding situation in Russia and his conviction that democracy was the soon-to-come answer brought increasing frustration to his attempts to devise a workable Russian policy in the face of Bolshevik survival. As his frustration grew, Wilson became less interested in providing strong and creative leadership on the issue, and he increasingly opted out of decisions, especially at crucial times. This was particularly true in Paris, when opportunities that existed for serious negotiations were lost because of Wilson's failure to act. This left, at many crucial junctures, decisions in the hands of advisors, or simply in a limbo of confusion.[148]

As a result, there never was an American policy for dealing with the Bolsheviks until late in Woodrow Wilson's administration, when his old friend and new Secretary of State Bainbridge Colby issued a definitive statement of non-recognition and non-intercourse. In the interim, Woodrow Wilson assumed much more the role of offstage actor in the developing story of the relationship between Americans and Bolsheviks: the blazing of new paths that only much later would become reflected in American government policy. The many Washington actors in the search for a policy about the Bolsheviks had to take a back seat to those in Petrograd and Moscow who found themselves forced to experiment with new ventures in the face of unprecedented situations and little guidance across 5,000 miles of war-torn Europe and stormy Atlantic.

# II

*Interactions in Russia,*
*1917–1918*

# 3

# Judson, Trotsky, and Bolshevik-American Military Collaboration, 1917–1918

> This is revolution, but the fact remains that the Bolsheviki have maintained themselves in power in Petrograd and Moscow and are the *de facto* government in those cities and, although there are opposition movements, Bolshevik power is undoubtedly greatest in Russia. . . . I am willing . . . to swallow pride, sacrifice dignity, and with discretion do all that is necessary to prevent Russia's becoming the ally of Germany. It is possible that, having accomplished the establishing of relations with the Soviet government, the Allied representatives could influence the terms of peace and thus preserve Russian neutrality.
> —*U. S. Ambassador David R. Francis to Secretary of State Robert Lansing, December 24, 1917*[1]

On December 1, 1917, less than a month after the Bolshevik seizure of power in Petrograd, Brigadier General William V. Judson, chief of the American Military Mission in Russia, met with Soviet Foreign Commissar Lev Trotsky in an effort to influence the terms of the Soviet armistice with Germany. This meeting marked the first substantive political or military contact between any United States official representative and responsible authorities of the new Soviet government.[2]

Although Secretary of State Robert Lansing issued subsequent orders forbidding political contact between U.S. representatives in Russia and the Bolsheviks, political, economic, and military contacts and collaboration continued despite the ban, even after the signing of the Soviet-German peace at Brest Litovsk. Judson and Trotsky's initial meeting spawned an array of efforts by others, including Chief of the American Red Cross Mission to Russia Raymond Robins, and U.S. military aides Captain E. Francis Riggs and Colonel James A. Ruggles, to work with Trotsky and the new Red Army to influence the terms of the armistice, secure Allied military aid for renewed war against Germany, deny military supplies to Germany, rebuild the Russian army, and join forces against Germany in North Russia.[3]

All of these efforts were dominated by the reality of war with Germany, for both the Americans and the Bolsheviks. While many of the discussions had broader political and economic implications, the immediate talks themselves stood or fell by the attitudes of the two sides concerning the threat and reality of German military power. This reality provided the impulse motivating Judson, Riggs, Robins, and Ruggles on the American side, and explains the extent to which U.S. Ambassador David R. Francis supported these initiatives. It also explains in large measure the willingness of Trotsky and Lenin to countenance the possibility of American and other Allied military assistance, collaboration, and even intervention. George F. Kennan has powerfully portrayed the overwhelmingly desperate Allied military situation in the winter of 1918, a key motivating force for American military representatives in Russia:

> At 4:30 A.M. on March 21, after a night of particularly ominous stillness, six thousand German guns suddenly opened up, with a deafening thunder, on the British sector of the front. The dreaded spring offensive had begun. It represented the greatest single military operation ever mounted, to that date. . . . The full weight of the attack fell on the British, already worn by years of unremitting losses, efforts and sacrifice. . . . Not until mid-June would the military situation be stabilized and the state of extreme danger overcome.
>
> Small wonder, then, that as the German offensive got under way a note of sheer desperation entered into the calculations of the British military planners at the Supreme War Council with respect to Russia and the possibilities for reviving the eastern front. The war now hung by a thread. Who knew?— perhaps the thread lay in Russia; perhaps even a token revival of resistance in the east, even the slightest diversion of German attention and resources from the western front, would spell the difference between victory and defeat. If there were even a chance that this was the case, should not every possibility, however slender and implausible, be pursued?[4]

For their part, the Bolsheviks supported Allied military collaboration as long as there was a threat of German attack. This threat remained real even after the ratification of the Brest Litovsk treaty, as German troops continued to advance slowly across the front, and only subsided markedly with the restoration of diplomatic contact between the Germans and the Bolsheviks in early May 1918.[5]

American and Bolshevik strategy in this overall context of the German threat differed, and each side responded to pressures and events from November to April. At the outset, U.S. military representatives agreed to meet with their Bolshevik counterparts for the express and limited purpose of attempting to influence the terms of the initial armistice with Germany in ways that were favorable to the Allies, particularly with respect to holding the opposing armies in place and preventing German capture of Russian military supplies.[6] In addition, the Americans hoped that the Armistice would last as long as possible without a treaty of peace being signed, not only to tie up the German forces, but to enable Bolshevik and Allied propaganda to influence the troops.[7] To act on the concern to prevent Russian war materials from falling into German hands, the Allied military attachés even took the step in December of organizing the Joint Allied Finance Committee, empowered to purchase or trade with the Russian army for military supplies that could be sent to the Western front.[8]

In the period both before and soon after the finalization of the Brest Litvosk peace, the United States maintained a slim hope that the Bolsheviks could somehow be induced or forced by the severity of the German terms or by the German army's advance to resist militarily, and that they would call on Allied assistance for such a fight. Judson, Robins, Riggs, and Ruggles all shared this hope and were able to convince Ambassador Francis of its possibility.[9]

By late March, this possibility began to recede and the American strategy began to shift in two directions: Allied assistance for the reorganization of the Red Army, in case of German attack; and persuasion of the Bolsheviks to invite the Allies to intervene in North Russia or Siberia, to fight the Germans themselves. Riggs and Ruggles, in their conversations with Trotsky, continued to believe that the Bolsheviks were sincere in their intention to build an army to resist the Germans, and so advised Ambassador Francis.[10] Francis authorized his military aides to cooperate with the French and Italians in providing assistance to Trotsky in training officers for the new army, but explained his reasoning to the State Department in quite different terms. An army "so organized," he wrote, "can by proper methods be taken from Bolshevik control and used against Germans, and even [against] its creators. . . ."[11] Riggs and Ruggles argued on similar grounds for the continuation of efforts to persuade the Bolsheviks to authorize Allied intervention against Germany. In this case, however, Francis was less accommodating, never agreeing with his military aides that Bolshevik consent to intervention was either possible or necessary, and increasingly moving toward a position recommending American intervention without Bolshevik consent.[12]

Although full-scale military collaboration was never authorized by the State Department or the War Department, actual engagement and collaboration occurred on the scene in Russia at various times over several months. Specific prohibition of military contact, although it prevented major commitment of American supplies and assistance, did little to hamper the exploration of possibilities in Russia itself, which continued clear up until a final breaking off of talks in mid-April, well after the ratification of the Bolshevik treaty with Germany.[13]

Bolshevik thinking concerning military collaboration developed at some variance with Allied plans. At the time of the Armistice, Trotsky was quite willing to hold German troops in western Russia and the Ukraine where they were more susceptible to propaganda. At this time, he still believed quite literally in the imminent outbreak of revolution among them.[14] Trotsky continued to negotiate for Allied assistance against Germany during and even after Brest Litovsk because of his own conviction that a real peace with Germany

was not only not desirable but frankly impossible, and that war would ultimately resume; in which case the Bolsheviks would need all the help they
could get.[15]

After Brest Litovsk, Trotsky was replaced by Georgi Chicherin as Foreign
Commissar, but he was almost immediately named War Commissar, and put
his energies behind the task of building the new Red Army. Bolshevik hopes
for Allied military help correspondingly shifted strategically. On one hand,
Trotsky desperately needed Allied technical assistance in the training and
even recruitment of former Tsarist army officers for the new Red Army,
whether it was to be used against Germany, against White Russian forces in
the civil war, or against an Allied intervention. That was immaterial. What
mattered was reconstructing a serious fighting force.[16]

On the other side of the continent, the Soviets became increasingly concerned by the specter of Japanese intervention in Siberia. If the Allies, and
particularly the Americans, could be induced to believe in the possible military cooperation with the Bolsheviks, perhaps they could restrain the Japanese from full-scale intervention in the Far East. This concern began to surface even before Brest Litovsk, and became a key element in all Bolshevik
interaction with American representatives from late March to July.[17] Three
factors converged in late March: the need to build up the Red Army, the
concern over Japanese intervention, and uncertainty about German intentions
in the immediate aftermath of Brest Litovsk, when diplomatic contact with
Germany was suspended and German troops continued to advance into Russia. These factors together helped produce an unprecedented openness and
friendliness in Bolshevik representatives toward the Allies. As George Kennan notes, "The Bolshevik leaders were never more cooperative, correct, and
obliging in their dealings during the last days of March and the first days of
April. . . . Trotsky and Chicherin were 'conciliatory, helpful, and frank.' "[18]

All of this should not obscure the continuing attitude of Lenin toward all
of these discussions. As John Reed noted as early as January 6, "it would be
almost impossible to convince Russia that America's object was not to force
the Russians back into the ranks of the 'imperialistic allies.' Perhaps it would
be possible to persuade them to accept American munitions, in case of war
with Germany, *'but not American military help.'* " (Reed's emphasis).[19]

Lenin himself consistently agreed with this strategy. He reluctantly voted,
in the crucial February 22 Central Committee meeting, in favor of "accepting
potatoes and arms from the Anglo-French imperialist bandits," but only if
peace with Germany could not be obtained.[20] He had no objection to
Trotsky's efforts to solicit American and Allied technical assistance in the
reformulation, recruitment, and training of a new Red Army officer corps.
But he was absolutely opposed to any possibility of a Soviet invitation to
Allied troops to intervene in Russia for any purpose, and he made that very
clear both to Trotsky and to the Allies.[21]

The key figure in initiating such discussions from the American side was
Brigadier General William V. Judson, chief of the American military mission
in Russia and military attaché to the U.S. Embassy. Judson, a military engi-

neer by profession, served five months as an observer on the Russian side of the Russo-Japanese war, and was a member of the Root mission to Russia in the summer of 1917. After this he became military attaché and chief of the military mission. Judson was, quite properly, most concerned with the Russian war effort. Because of his overwhelming concern to keep Russia in the war, he advocated Allied support for the Kornilov revolt. He followed this, after the Bolshevik revolution, by arguing in favor of a working relationship with Trotsky to prevent the Bolsheviks from cooperating with the Germans.[22] Judson's relationship with Ambassador Francis was always shaky. By the time of his departure from Russia in late January 1918, he was utterly convinced that the State Department had conspired to prevent the War Department from acting on his recommendations to develop a working relationship with the Bolsheviks.[23]

In the immediate aftermath of the revolution, Judson first ran afoul of Francis when he sent two of his aides, E. Francis Riggs and Jacob Bukowski, to meet with Trotsky to achieve assurances concerning the maintenance of the Polish military guard engaged for the protection of the embassy, and to extract a promise from the Bolsheviks assuring the safety of foreigners in the capital.[24] Francis became nervous at this official contact of the military mission with the new government, and warned Judson to do nothing that would imply, in any way, United States recognition of the new government. Judson, concerned that Francis was forbidding *all* contact and determined to exercise his own independent authority as chief of the American military mission, responded that he intended to continue with such "trivial intercourse with Smolny—on matters of telephones, guards and the like—as will enable me to secure such [military] information. . . ."[25]

The Bolsheviks had begun their attempts to contact the Allied military representatives with the Decree on Peace itself, issued the day after the Kerensky government fled Petrograd, November 8. What is often overlooked in most discussions of the Decree on Peace is that it called for negotiations, with no preconditions, with any and all of the powers then at war, and proposed an immediate three-month armistice. The Decree on Peace was, in effect, the new government's first call, not only to Germany, but to all of the Allies for negotiations.[26]

Trotsky began work as Foreign Commissar on November 20, and immediately followed up the Decree by issuing a formal announcement of it and a call for an armistice to the Allied governments on November 21 and the neutral governments on November 22.[27] None of the Allies responded directly to any of these overtures, but the Decree on Peace and the publication of the Secret Treaties (also begun November 22) created much consternation in Allied capitals. Word of all of these acts was relayed by Ambassador Francis to the U.S. State Department.[28]

In the meantime, the Soviet government took direct steps to conclude an armistice, issuing orders to the commanding Russian general at the front, Nikolai Dukhonin, to cease military operations and to contact German generals about an immediate armistice.[29] A *New York Times* report of November 21 rumored the immediate suspension of American supplies for the Russian front pending clarification of the Bolshevik government position on the war. When a copy of this report reached Judson, on November 25, he sent it with a note requesting that the chief of the Russian General Staff, Marushevski, tell him whether Russia intended to stand by its Allies against Germany and indicating that, although he did not know the truth of the story, it "correctly states the attitude of the Government of the United States."[30] The other Allied military staff, meanwhile, had separately approached Dukhonin, urging him to ignore directives from Smolny and continue the war.[31] Trotsky was incensed at both actions and responded with alacrity, calling the notes "flagrant interference in the domestic affairs of Soviet Russia."[32] Dukhonin was dismissed, and a formal protest was issued by Trotsky to the Allied governments against interference in Soviet affairs.[33]

Trotsky, in anticipation of a successful armistice with Germany at the front, made one last attempt to involve the Allies in the armistice, calling the chiefs of the military missions together on November 27 and urging them once more to join the negotiations. In this message, Trotsky noted that the Bolsheviks "did not demand a parliamentary recognition. . . . We want business negotiations. . . . Are the Allies willing to begin negotiations for immediate armistice aiming at the conclusion of peace and democratic principles? . . ."[34] In Francis' transmission of this note to the State Department, he observed, "Trotsky note . . . is presuming and insulting to Allied Governments."[35] Francis received a very prompt response from Secretary of State Lansing: "You are to make no reply to communications mentioned in your 2034 November 27th, your 2039 November 28th and 2040 November 29th, and are informed that this Government awaits further developments. No statement has been made by the President."[36]

Later that same day (November 27), Judson had a long talk with Raymond Robins, newly named head of the American Red Cross Commission to Russia. Robins assumed command from William B. Thompson, who returned to the United States via London the same day. On his departure, Thompson issued a statement to the press on behalf of the Red Cross, asserting that, notwithstanding the *New York Times* story regarding the cut-off of military supplies, shipments from the Red Cross would continue.[37]

By the time of his meeting with Robins, Judson began to have second thoughts about his earlier letter to Dukhonin, written by Major Monroe Kerth and protesting the separate armistice. Since it appeared that the Bolsheviks and Trotsky exercised military power, perhaps that was not the best way to establish a working relationship. So Judson consulted Robins, who by that time had already meet with Trotsky several times on behalf of the Red Cross.[38] Robins and Judson found themselves in very substantial agreement that an effort should be made to influence Trotsky and the Bolsheviks in the Allies' favor on the terms of the armistice agreement with Germany. Judson asked Robins to meet again with Trotsky concerning Bolshevik openness to American military suggestions. In the meantime, Judson wrote a second note to Dukonin attempting to undo the damage of Kerth's earlier message, and he asked Ambassador Francis if he could not arrange a direct meeting between himself and Trotsky to pursue the armistice conditions.[39] As Judson reflected in his diary that night, "The Bolsheviks are beginning to exhibit the only guts visible among all the different contending political elements in Russia. They are the only ones apparently who can do anything with the soldiers and if the latter are to stay in position and ever do any fighting, even defensively, it may be that it must be under the Bolsheviks."[40]

In his second, conciliatory note to Dukhonin (which essentially ended up with Trotsky), Judson practically apologized, requesting that

> nothing should be construed as indicating that my government has or may be expected to express preference for the success in Russia of any one political party or element over another. . . . There is no reason why the attitude of her Allies toward Russia or toward any important elements in Russia should be upon anything but a most friendly foundation.[41]

Before sending this second letter, Judson consulted with Francis, who, he indicated, "had no objection."[42]

Robins followed up his talk with Judson with a meeting with Alexander Gumberg, his colleague and interpreter; and Trotsky on November 30. At this meeting Robins urged Trotsky to seriously consider including some Allied provisions, such as transfer of military supplies, in the Bolshevik armistice suggestions to the Germans, and Trotsky expressed a willingness to do so, but he asked for Robins to send Judson himself for a face-to-face meeting. As Sisson later reported Robins' message to them, "The general was welcome to continue communication . . . either by letter or in person."[43]

Immediately Robins, Sisson, Judson, Wright, and Francis met concerning Trotsky's invitation and Judson's and Robins' obvious desire to meet it. Wright, Sisson, and Robins supported Judson in his argument that the Bolsheviks were the *de facto* government and almost certainly would be negotiating with Germany over the terms of an armistice. Therefore, the best thing for the Allies to do would be to attempt to influence the terms of such an armistice. The meeting ended in some confusion, with Francis giving his reluctant consent to a visit; preferably not by Judson himself, but by one of his subordinates; and that before doing so he should sound out the British and French about their positions concerning a meeting to discuss armistice terms. The British general Alfred Knox, was at first open to the idea, but was overruled by Ambassador George Buchanan. The French were opposed from the start. Judson, aware that time was of the essence, decided to proceed alone, and requested Sisson to arrange a meeting with Trotsky for his aide, Riggs. The word came back immediately. Trotsky would see only Judson. Judson again visited Francis, informing him of this fact, and received his "reluctant" consent for the visit, set for the following day, December 1.[44]

This meeting marked the first substantive political contact between any United States official representative and responsible authorities of the new Soviet government. Both Soviet and American governments viewed it as significant. Although no one in Washington had authorized the meeting, Ambassador Francis had authorized it, and he had also immediately informed the State Department of that fact. Francis wrote Lansing before the meeting that he was considering sending Judson to talk to Trotsky in order to influence conditions of the armistice, and he cabled the Secretary of State on December 1 that "Judson saw Trotsky today with my approval."[45] For their part, the Bolsheviks publicized the visit immediately, and while noting that Judson had come informally, "as the recognition of the Soviet Government had not yet taken place," "he had come in order to start relations, and to make clear certain conditions, and to clear up certain misunderstandings."[46]

Judson and Trotsky met for forty minutes. Judson pressed hard for his concerns regarding the conditions of the armistice, particularly with regard to holding troops in place on the Eastern front, and refusing to exchange prisoners immediately. In addition, Judson pressed Trotsky to prolong the armistice negotiations themselves as long as possible, not only for the general purpose of delay, but also that the Allies might either join such discussions later, or, at the least, continue to make their wishes known to the Bolsheviks regarding terms as talks unfolded. Finally, Judson discussed with Trotsky the related concern to protect Russian military supplies from the Germans, seeking means to transfer as much of them to the Allies as possible. In almost every respect, Trotsky was responsive to Judson's concerns. Trotsky told Judson "that he would be glad to have me cable to the United States that in the negotiations he would observe and endeavor to protect the interests of Russia's Allies; he further stated that the points I raised appealed to him or had already been in his mind and that the armistice commission would be given instructions in accordance therewith."[47]

Although it has often been pointed out that the practical effect of Trotsky's agreeing to Judson's suggestions was rather minimal, since the Germans had already by that time begun the process of shifting large numbers of troops to the Western front, there is every indication that Trotsky did in fact fulfill his agreements made with Judson. Certain of his suggestions were embodied verbatim in the Russian proposals in the armistice, and subsequently agreed to by the Germans; particularly the continuation of the armistice, the delay in prisoner exchange, and maintaining the status quo of the opposing armies.[48]

Almost more important to the Soviets, however, than the details of agreement on military provisions of the armistice was the political significance of the visit. Toward the end of his visit, Judson expressed the hope that formal relations could continue in order to prevent misunderstandings in the absence of an American decision to recognize the new government. He went on to say, according to Trotsky's account made public the next day, that "the time of protests and threats addressed to the Soviet Government has passed, if indeed there ever was such a time."[49] Although Judson later denied saying these exact words, he admitted that they expressed his sentiment, and that he had no problems giving that impression.[50] Ambassador Francis, however, was most upset about Trotsky's characterization, and it played a part in the subsequent State Department move to have Judson prohibited from further contact and recalled.[51] Sisson pointed out that the *Izvestia* article had another, more positive benefit, giving the United States "the only favorable press" since his arrival.[52]

Judson returned from the meeting elated that he had achieved concrete results for the allies, in the specific, short-term gains regarding terms of the armistice, as well as in the broader results that could be built on in the future. These results, he was convinced, included the following: (1) the meeting "tended to make Trotsky adopt a more uncompromising course during the negotiations, thus increasing the chances of a break"; (2) it limited "for a time, the interchange of goods (between Germany and Russia) and the release of prisoners"; and (3) it "served to establish me somewhat in Trotsky's confidence so that if necessary or advisable later he might have been willing to listen to my suggestions and advice."[53] Judson exceedingly regretted the fact that within days he received instructions to break off any such continued contact, because, as he pointed out, over the next two or three months, "the ablest Germans and Austrians were in the closest association with them."[54]

Before receiving new instructions from Washington, Judson was a blaze of activity. On December 3, he requested that Francis give him access to cable traffic between the embassy and Washington, particularly that which related to the military situation and the German-Soviet negotiations. Francis refused this request.[55] The following day Judson again discussed the situation with the British military staff, in light of his visit to Trotsky, and persuaded them to go along with his policy of "conciliating the Soviet government to a certain extent in the object of saving what is possible from the wreck."[56] And he wrote a long, detailed, and optimistic report to the War Department, proposing a whole program of aid and assistance to the Russian military, in the event of the breakdown of negotiations with Germany and the resumption of war. This program included sending American troops, American advisors, and technical support for the operation of the Russian railroads, including actual operation of them if agreed to by the Bolsheviks; massive amounts of railway material and military supplies of other character; and the creation of an American commission in Russia empowered to act in response to other Russian requests for aid.[57]

Judson discussed and prepared these requests in consultation with Raymond Robins, whom he was now working with on a daily and even hourly basis. As soon as Secretary Lansing received word of Judson's visit to Trotsky, he dispatched a telegram to Francis explicitly forbidding American representatives "all direct communication with the Bolsheviks."[58] After this time, Judson had to pursue his entire strategy through Robins, while Francis cabled Washington to determine if the prohibition against contact also applied to the Red Cross representative.[59] From this time forward, until his departure from Russia in late January, Judson relied on Robins to forward his suggestions and proposals to Trotsky and the Bolshevik government. While respecting the interdiction of his own contacts with the Bolsheviks, Judson never changed his conviction that close cooperation with Trotsky could potentially prevent a

separate peace with Germany, or at the least could appreciably aid the Allies
in terms of supplies, delays, propaganda, or prisoners.[60]

Judson and Robins were quite aware that that they operated in a never-
never land where approval for their activities might be withdrawn at any
moment. As Robins wrote to his wife Margaret on December 30,

> I, a Red Cross man, am the only person in any authority that is permitted by
> our government to have any direct intercourse with the *de facto* government
> that has complete control over three fourths of Russian territory. . . . Each
> hour I am expecting my reall for my services and at the hour that the General
> commanding the military mission of the United States and the sole military
> attaché of the American Embassy has to send all communications through me
> to the Russian government, we are expecting to be reprimanded for the only
> action between hostile bayonets and our materials in this country.[61]

Yet Judson pressed on. Following another visit by Robins to Trotsky on
December 18, receiving assurances that the provision in the armistice for non-
transfer of troops would remain in place as long as the armistice and that no
transfer of war materials would be permitted, Judson decided that he must
renew his attempts to persuade Ambassador Francis of the wisdom of their
policy.[62] On December 22 he had a long meeting with Francis in which he
implored the ambassador to join him in recommending to the United States "a
broad Russian policy." He urged the ambassador to accept the Bolsheviks as
the *de facto* government of Russia, and to do everything possible to keep them
in the war or, if that failed, to prevent the Germans from taking full advantage
of the situation. The United States "was becoming isolated," warned Judson,
and it was necessary to "pour oil on troubled waters" if the United States was
to have any hope of influencing Trotsky.[63]

Judson followed up this meeting with an immediate letter to Francis,
urging that he act immediately to recommend the new policy to Washington,
including the "[assistance] in the reorganization of all the elements of military
strength still present in Russia, in order that she may be better prepared to
continue her defense in case the present peace negotiations fail. . . . Act on
the theory that Russia is entitled to sympathy not condemnation. . . ."[64]

But Francis already had taken steps to recommend a policy in keeping
with this Judson-Robins position. On Christmas Eve he cabled Lansing, outlining the situation as he saw it and wondering whether it might not be a good
idea to establish direct contact:

> This is revolution, but the fact remains that the Bolsheviki have maintained
> themselves in power in Petrograd and Moscow and are the *de facto* govern-
> ment in those cities, and, although there are opposition movements, Bolshe-
> vik power is undoubtedly greatest in Russia. . . . I am willing . . . to swallow
> pride, sacrifice dignity, and with discretion do all that is necessary to prevent
> Russia's becoming the ally of Germany. It is possible that, having accom-
> plished the establishing of relations with the Soviet government, the Allied
> representatives could influence the terms of peace and thus preserve Russian
> neutrality.[65]

Although Lansing by this time had already taken steps to recall Judson, the various recommendations and memos from Robins, Francis, Judson, and Bullard did have an impact elsewhere in the State Department.[66] In a long memorandum on January 1, Basil Miles, the head of the Russian Division, unaware that Judson had been recalled, recommended to the Secretary of State that the military attaché be given broad authority to take independent action on military matters, including, if necessary, direct contact with Trotsky or other Bolsheviks. Although Lansing ignored this memorandum, it was sent on to Wilson and considered as part of a broader question of informal contact with the Bolsheviks.[67]

In any event, interaction went on in Petrograd. Francis also held a long meeting with Robins the day after Christmas. The next day, Judson reported to his diary after talking with Robins that "the Ambassador has at last cabled home for authority to have intercourse with the Bolshevik Government . . . [and] he has authorized Robins . . . to go to Trotsky." Judson just hoped that it was not too late.[68]

On December 31, the Russians broke off negotiations at Brest Litovsk. Trotsky told Robins that he needed assurances of Allied support in order to continue the war. Robins and Judson again met with Francis, after which the ambassador authorized them to "go to Trotsky and inform him that [the United States] would render all assistance possible."[69] This stimulated a frantic period of American effort to prevent the continuation of German-Russian negotiations and to persuade the Allied governments to offer concrete assistance for Russia to remain in the war.

On New Year's Day, 1918, William V. Judson received notice of his recall to Washington "for consultations."[70] Although this removed the military official favoring contacts with the Bolsheviks from the scene in Petrograd, it by no means stopped the consultations. These were continued, with Raymond Robins, Francis Riggs, and William Ruggles acting in place of Judson and with the approval of Ambassador Francis.

Between the receipt of his recall notice and his departure on January 23, Judson himself did not take as active a role in the frantic negotiations, but he continued to make strong recommendations on Russian policy to the War Department. Following Ambassador Francis' lone interview with Lenin on behalf of the Romanian ambassador (the Diamandi incident) on January 14, for example, Judson cabled the War Department, again urging a policy to enable such discussions to be expanded.[71] And just before his departure, Judson received a long report from Riggs that he had commissioned, including recommendations for some kind of working relationship to facilitate military discussions. Judson passed on these recommendations almost verbatim to the War Department in his final cable on the day of his departure, urging that "friendly intercourse . . . not involving recognition" be quickly established; otherwise the United States would soon become second to Germany in the Bolsheviks' considerations.[72]

Even on his way home, Judson continued to urge his recommendations on the War Department, which remained conspicuously silent in response. On

January 27, he cabled from Stockholm that "we may lose many chances to serve our own interests and thwart the enemy and our representatives may soon have to quit Russia unless we have friendly intercourse with the Bolsheviks. . . ."[73]

On his return to the United States, Judson wrote a series of three reports, in February and March, concerning his experiences and with continued recommendations in the same vein. Since he received no answers to his communications and was unable to receive a hearing before either the Secretary of War or the President, Judson, in some exasperation, wrote the Army Chief of Staff on March 14, detailing his communications since the time he was in Russia, and noting that "to practically none of my communications did I ever receive response, nor were any instructions sent for my general guidance."[74] This still elicited no response, and Judson gave up until late in 1919, when he wrote a massive synopsis of his entire experiences and received the belated thanks and apologies of the Secretary of War.[75]

Judson's recall did not make Raymond Robins or the other advocates of continued military collaboration slow their efforts. In fact, the most intense and promising discussions between the Allies, Trotsky, and Lenin occurred in the immediate aftermath of that decision. These meetings, in January and February of 1918, were spearheaded by Robins for the United States; R. H. Bruce Lockhart, special envoy for the British; and Captain Jacques Sadoul for the French, and involved political as well as military issues.[76]

On December 31, Robins returned very excited to Ambassador Francis from a long meeting with Trotsky. He reported to Francis that Trotsky was convinced of some kind of German "plot," and was ready to break off all negotiations. Trotsky asked Robins what the Americans would do if such a break came. On the strength of this, and with the support of Bullard, Sisson, Riggs, Ruggles, and Judson, Robins was able to persuade Ambassador Francis to promise American assistance and support in any resistance the Bolsheviks might mount to a German advance. Francis also agreed to seek the concurrence of the French and the British in such an effort.[77]

This agreement by the Americans and their Allied counterparts in Petrograd may well be the high-water mark of opportunity for the development of some sort of *modus operandi* for Americans and Bolsheviks in Russia. Almost everyone concerned, from President Wilson to Raymond Robins (with the conspicuous exception of Secretary of State Robert Lansing) seemed amenable to exploiting the opportunity.[78] On New Year's afternoon, Edgar Sisson attended the Central Executive Committee of the Soviets of Workers', Soldiers' and Peasants' Deputies. In his report to Francis and Robins, he stressed the readiness of the deputies to resume the war, and indicated that in his opinion an American offer of assistance might strengthen their resolve to stand against the Germans. Francis cabled Washington that he would do anything necessary to prevent a Russian peace with Germany, including offering concrete military assistance.[79]

The next day Francis even agreed to draft specific cables for Robins' use in discussions with Trotsky, promising American assistance, including supplies and munitions, credits, and technical and military advice. These cables would be sent as soon as evidence was received of the failure of the armistice and the resumption of war against Russia by Germany.[80] Although the armistice never failed entirely, its tentative character helped Robins use the cables to keep military collaboration alive. A few days later, Trotsky left for Brest Litovsk, having convinced Lenin that stalling tactics might either enable the German troops to rise up in revolution or enable the Allies to come fully to the aid of the Bolsheviks. Lenin, without the Central Committee votes necessary to put through an immediate peace, agreed to support Trotsky provisionally.[81]

Trotsky's departure to Brest Litovsk and the resumption of negotiations with Germany necessarily kept Robins' consultation on military aid suspended, awaiting a breakdown of German-Soviet negotiations. He continued wide-ranging contacts with the Bolshevik leadership, however, meeting Trotsky whenever he was in Petrograd, and Lenin on important occasions. The substance of most of these discussions was not military, however, but detailed Red Cross business, and political and economic matters (see Chapter 4). In the process, Robins did everything he could to keep the possibility of military collaboration squarely in front of the Bolsheviks and the Americans. He even went as far as to use the occasion of Judson's departure to the United States to tell Lenin and Trotsky that Judson was being sent to Washington to explain to President Wilson the best ways that the United States could be of military assistance to the Bolsheviks when war with Germany was resumed.[82]

Robins insisted, both at the time and later, that he was convinced that peace between the Bolsheviks and Germany was impossible because the two cultures were so fundamentally opposed. He was certain that eventually peace talks would break down and the Russians would turn to the Allies for assistance in building resistance against the German advance. Robins' hope was that the United States would be ready and willing to provide that assistance when the time came and would not be "beaten out" in this opportunity for influence by the British and the French.[83] Judson, in a retrospective look at Robins' efforts in this regard, even claimed that Robins "convinced the Bolshevik leaders that the Germans were asking too much, that the Bolsheviks could get better terms the longer they waited, and that the United States would assist the Bolsheviks if they came to a final falling out with the Germans."[84]

As noted previously, Robins' Allied colleagues in this search for military collaboration with the Bolsheviks against Germany were R. H. Bruce Lockhart for the British and Jacques Sadoul for the French. Lockhart arrived in Petrograd in mid-February and had his first meeting with Trotsky on February 15. From that time until mid-April he worked in full concert with Robins in pursuit of a policy of economic, political, and military collaboration with the Bolsheviks. Lockhart recommended military measures to his government in coordination with what Robins was recommending to Francis. Lockhart was convinced, from the time of his first meeting with Trotsky, that limited cooperation with the Bolsheviks was possible, noting that "the policy I advocate is one of expediency. Trotsky will cooperate with us so long as it suits him. Our attitude should be the same."[85]

While Robins and Lockhart discussed a wide variety of political, economic, and military issues with Trotsky and Lenin, Jacques Sadoul confined his efforts almost strictly to the military realm. Sadoul was a lawyer and a socialist, and was not a primary officer in the French military mission. Yet he became important by virtue of his sympathy with the Bolsheviks and his contact with Trotsky.[86] Of the three "unofficial agents," Sadoul was the most sympathetic to the Bolshevik position. And he had considerably more success in his efforts to persuade his superiors to make the requisite commitment of aid. He persuaded not only the French military mission but the French government itself to approve a policy of aid and support for the rebuilding of the Red Army, on condition that it would be used against Germany. According to Sadoul's own account, Trotsky continually requested French assistance to build up the Red Army as a fighting force against Germany.[87] From late January until early April, the French general staff prevailed in a policy debate with the Quai d'Orsay concerning the degree of cooperation to give the Bolshevik government. The collapse of Ukrainian resistance helped convince the general staff that a strong, unified Russia was still essential for France's security, and that the Bolsheviks were the most anti-German element and the group best able to unify Russia.[88]

The French tendered their official offer to the Bolsheviks on February 22, in the midst of the Soviets' walkout from the negotiations at Brest Litvosk (the famous Trotsky *démarche*), and just before the Germans halted their new offensive. Sadoul's efforts to persuade his government coincided almost exactly with his need to convince Trotsky that his representations were in fact genuine. Although clearance from the French government did not come through until February 21, Sadoul orally promised such aid to Trotsky on February 20. Trotsky, ever the sceptic, waited until a phone call from French ambassador Noulens the next day.[89] Then he brought the offer to the Bolshevik leadership.

Neither London nor Washington ever seconded the French offer. The French Embassy in Washington informed the U.S. State Department of the their decision on February 19, and asked "whether the United States will give similar instructions to the American Ambassador in Petrograd."[90] Despite Lansing's brusque, handwritten notations, "This is out of the question," and his insistence that Woodrow Wilson agreed, Ambassador Francis was never informed, and American consultations, always falling short of top-level commitment, continued.[91] Lockhart tried strenuously to get British Cabinet support, but he never overcame the distrust of Curzon, Churchill, and Bonar Law, and had only the lukewarm endorsement of Lloyd George.[92]

Despite the lack of corresponding offers from London and Washington, the Bolshevik Central Committee voted narrowly to accept the offer, aided by Lenin's vote *in absentia,* and his famous scribbled note indicating his willingness to "accept potatoes and arms from the bandits of Anglo-French imperialism."[93] This effort never got off the ground, however, because of a new German ultimatum and the Bolshevik acceptance of it on February 25. Franco-Soviet collaboration actually occurred in March, however. Trotsky requested that French officers assist in training and inspection. Such officers were actually assigned and did a few days' work in late March and early April before French policy changed, the Quai d'Orsay got its way, and French offers of military collaboration ceased.[94]

The Bolshevik decision of February 22 to accept the French offer of aid (and any accompanying British or American offers) needs further amplification. As E. H. Carr notes, the debate in the Central Committee occurred just at the time when the newly revised German terms had been received and it was still by no means clear what the Bolshevik response would be:

> Trotsky was still clutching at straws in order to avoid acceptance. It was an instructive debate, revealing a straight cleavage between "realists," who believed that the regime in its present plight, and whatever its attitude to the German terms, could not reject aid from whatever source, and "Leftists," whose revolutionary principles still forbade any partnership with capitalist powers.[95]

Bukharin led the principled leftists, who had voted for the continuation of the revolutionary war and now voted for rejecting aid from the Allies to pursue that war, because they were capitalists. Bukharin formally proposed "to enter into no kind of understandings with the French, English and American missions respecting the purchase of arms or the employment of the services of officers or engineers," but this motion was defeated. Finally, Trotsky's opposite motion, to accept aid from any source, although without political obligations, was carried by the narrow vote of 6–5 (not counting Lenin's hand-delivered note in favor).[96]

To underscore the seriousness with which possible aid from the Allies was pursued at this time, the Bolsheviks also dispatched Lev Kamenev to London and Paris to seek assistance. Although he landed in Britain on February 23, and had several unofficial discussions, he was not received by the British government and was soon deported. Paris refused him admission altogether.[97]

Despite Bolshevik acceptance, under pressure from Lenin, of the new, more onerous German peace terms on February 25, and the actual signing of the Peace of Brest Litovsk on March 3, Trotsky did not cease his efforts to get British and American assistance for possible resistance to Germany or for the rebuilding of the Red Army. Because of Raymond Robins' testimony before the United States Senate in 1919, his discussion with Trotsky of March 5, 1918, has become infamous, and perhaps has received an inordinate amount of attention and focus from historians, who at times seem to think that the possibility or failure of any *modus operandi* between the Allies and the Bolsheviks hinged on the conditions or the communications breakdown involved in this famous episode or the related talks that Lockhart held with Trotsky on the same day.[98] While this episode was only one in a series of overtures and entreaties by Trotsky to the Allies that began long before March 5 and continued into early May, it does remain a key link in a long chain of events concerning military and political collaboration possibilities in early 1918.

As Robins described the genesis of these negotiations before the Overman

Committee in 1919, he was at Smolny to see Trotsky about changing the Red
Guards on his milk supplies. Trotsky asked him, point-blank, "Do you want
to prevent the Brest peace from being ratified?" Robins replied, 'There is
nothing that I wanted to do as much as that." Trotsky said, "You can do it."
Robins laughed and replied, "You have always been against the Brest peace,
but Lenin is the other way; and frankly, Commissioner, Lenin is running this
show." According to Robins, Trotsky said, "You are mistaken. Lenine real-
izes that the threat of the German advance is so great that if he can get
economic cooperation and military support from the allies he will refuse the
Brest peace, retire, if necessary, from both Petrograd and Moscow to
Ekaterinberg, reestablish the front in the Urals, and fight with allied support
against the Germans."[99]

Robins, despite his willingness to accept Trotsky at face-value, decided
that he wanted something in writing that he could use to try to move the
American government. He asked Trotsky to put his conditions in writing—
what kind of aid would the Bolsheviks need from the Allies to refuse to rattify
the Brest peace and return to the war with Germany? The document that
Robins received was drawn as a series of questions, an inquiry of the Allies
concerning the nature and extent of aid that they would send if Russia resumed the war with Germany. As Kennan rightly points out, there was never
a promise by either Trotsky or Lenin to resume the war, only an implication
that this would be done if Allied response was satisfactory.[100] Robins later
claimed that the Bolshevik leaders also promised, if the United States would
cooperate, "that the several officers of the military missions would be permitted to act as supervisors on the frontiers to enforce the embargo against war
materials and other supplies. . . ."[101]

No specific responses were ever received to the various copies of the
question that Robins dispatched. There is evidence, however, that Trotsky's
questions were received, considered, and rejected by Wilson, Lansing, and
House. Ambassador Francis sent a copy of Robins' message and Trotsky's
questions to the State Department on March 9, and even added that Trotsky
had agreed to the supervision by America "of all shipments from Vladivostok
into Russia and a virtual control of the operations of the Siberian Railway" *if*
Japanese intervention could be forstalled.[102] Arthur Bullard argued against
any response in the following terms: "We ought to be ready to help any honest
national government. But men or money or equipment sent to the present
rulers of Russia will be used against Russians at least as much as against
Germans."[103]

Robins' conviction that Trotsky was serious is certainly credible, however,
based on both the earlier record of entreaties for Allied aid, and Trotsky's
continued unwillingness to vote for the peace, preferring to abstain on the
final vote in spite of Lenin's entreaties.

Despite Robins' lack of official response to Trotsky's questions from Washington, Ambassador Francis did more than forward the message to Washington. He acted with dispatch in favor of the requests. By this time Francis was
living in a railroad car in the provincial capital of Vologda, having fled Petro-

grad ahead of the German advance in late February. He received Robins' cable, and he also received a personal message from General Neissel, the head of the French Military Mission, delivered to him by Jacques Sadoul on March 5. Both messages urged him immediately to advance military assistance to the Bolsheviks to help resist Germany. On the strength of these entreaties, Francis dispatched his two military attachés, Colonel Ruggles and Captain Riggs, to Petrograd to confer with the French and to meet with Trotsky and others involved with the Bolshevik military, to ascertain the details of military aid desired and to offer United States' assistance. As Francis related to Niessel in his personal answer. "I desire [Ruggles] to have no hesitation to meet with Russian officials, or even with the Commissaires of the Soviet government. . . . The Allies should make every effort to assist those Russian forces which will sincerely oppose the German advance."[104]

Colonel James A. Ruggles, American military attaché since the departure of General Judson in late January, and his assistant, Captain E. Francis Riggs, were generally in accord about the need to continue General Judson's policy of keeping lines open to the Bolsheviks for possible military collaboration. Riggs, however, had been closer to Judson, had served in Russia longer, and tended to be less cautious and more friendly to Robins and Lockhart.[105] Riggs had written a long report for Judson, giving his recommendations on Russian policy before his departure, in which he urged continued work and coopera-tion with the Bolsheviks.[106]

Ruggles was more reticent than Riggs, closer to Ambassador Francis, and generally urged caution in responding to Robins, Lockhart, or Bolshevik initiatives.[107] Ruggles did, however, continue to urge in memoranda and let-ters to both the War Department and Ambassador Francis as late as May 1, 1918, that some kind of diplomatic presence by the Allies with the Bolsheviks be maintained, if only to help offset German diplomacy, and that military and commercial contact should be continued.[108] By late May, however, he had swung around to Ambassador Francis' position of urging intervention without Bolshevik consent, believing that the majority of Russian people would wel-come [it] especially if the United States participated."[109]

Ruggles and Riggs had been dispatched to Petrograd to meet with Trotsky and Bolshevik military staff even before Robins' famous meeting with Trotsky. When they arrived in Petrograd they were confronted with Robins' enthusiastic entreaties to help relay the Trotsky inquiries to Washington, but they delayed, pending their own meeting with Trotsky on March 8.[110] Ruggles and Riggs were armed with instructions from Francis authorizing them to consult with Bolshe-vik military authorities "concerning military preparations for resistance to the German advance in the event the separate peace may not be ratified . . . or in the possibility that the German advance may be resumed. . . ."[111]

Although Kennan asserts that "Ruggles and Riggs found that their task had already been largely acomplished by Robins" and that their interviews with Trotsky and Bonch-Bruevich were "inconclusive,"[112] Ruggles' cables con-cerning the meetings contained certain definitive recommendations, as do Riggs' memoranda for the files. Although Ruggles noted that it was "too early yet to judge of what can be accomplished by Bolshevik leaders," he belived that the Bolshevik intention to resist Germans was "probably sincere because based on vital interests." The "main thing," in Ruggles' view, was to prevent Allied governments from "reprisals or occupations."[113] Ruggles went on to say, in a more detailed report, that "Trotsky desires allied assistance, especially American" and that he was "now willing to reorganize army under rigid discipline, recalling Russian Government officers."[114] Riggs, in his memorandum on the Ruggles meeting with Trotsky, noted that Trotsky said "that the decision in Moscow . . . would be greatly influenced by the amount of encouragement received from the Americans" and that "foreign officers would be welcome as instructors."[115]

Francis reported on his communications with Ruggles three different times: in a short cable to the State Department on March 9, in a brief wire to Raymond Robins on March 11, and in a longer message to Secretary Lansing on March 12. While his briefer messages of the ninth and eleventh emphasize that "it is too early to judge" and "no definite program [has been] adopted,"[116] on March 12 Francis emphasized the reorganization of the Russian army, the recall of Russian officers, and the encouragement of resistance to Germany. He concluded, "I am not sanguine but not hopeless, and military attaché feels likewise."[117]

In retrospect it seems clear that although the Soviet ratification of the Brest Litovsk treaty severely restricted long-term possibilities for U.S.-Soviet military collaboration, this appeared much clearer in Washington than in Moscow and Petrograd. In fact, the treaty ratification had no immediate negative impact on discussions concerning military assistance. During the months of March and April, Robins and Trotsky continued to formulate plans for Allied assistance to the new Red Army, and Trotsky met specific Robins requests to keep raw materials and military supplies from falling into the hands of the Germans. Moreover, Riggs and Ruggles continued to meet with Trotsky, General Bonch-Bruevich, and other Red Army counterparts, in exploratory talks concerning technical assistance and training.

Riggs attended two such meetings with General Bonch-Bruevich, head of the Special Staff of the Red Army, on March 8 and March 10. In both cases, Riggs and Ruggles pushed for specific details on the form American aid might take, and what might be expected from the Russians in terms of resistance to German encroachment. Bonch-Bruevich was never able to give an unequivocal response, because a political decision had not been made, but he appointed another officer as continuing liaison, and he reiterated the Russian openness to Allied instructors.[118]

Trotsky's reasons for continuing to pursue these talks were clear. He continued to believe that the peace would not hold and that the Bolsheviks would be forced to fight for their existence. In such a case, he would need all the help he could get. On top of that, he had the responsibility of building a new Red Army out of very little, and was quite willing to give the Allies military information about the Germans, and even give them some control over training and communications if he could get expert advisors and engineers to aid in such a task.[119] As Trotsky told the American journalist Herman Bernstein in mid-March, "our party is now busily occupied with the creating of a new body for defense. . . . We invite military experts, serving the old regime. We solicit their aid because of their experience. . . . I considered the question of reorganization of the army so important that I decided to leave the post of Commissaire of Foreign Affairs."[120]

The specific requests by Trotsky for French and American staff officers to assist in training were apparently stimulated by Sadoul in a meeting with Trotsky on March 20. At this meeting, Trotsky presented an official request, in the name of Sovnarkom, for forty French officers to aid in training and organization of the army.[121] Trotsky followed up this request with a less ambitious one to the United States, in meetings with Riggs and Robins on March 19 and 21. At this time, he requested five American army officers for "inspection, drill, and equipment," and a unit of railway operating men and equipment.[122] The French accepted Trotsky's offer, and three or four officers actually began work before the program was terminated in April; but the Americans were slower to act. Riggs and Robins strongly recommended accepting the opportunity, and so advised Francis, with Riggs believing Trotsky "sincere in his plans to raise an army for defense," but Ruggles remained undecided; "not thoroughly satisfied that the new army [was] intended for German resistance."[123]

Francis himself was uncertain. His first instinct, as he put it in a cable to Lansing, was similar to Ruggles': "Highly important we know for what such army be used."[124] He then asked for advice both from Consul General Maddin Summers in Moscow and from Washington.[125]

Secretary Lansing immediately responded in negative and cynical fashion, with a counterquestion. Was there any truth to the rumor that there was some connection between the Bolshevik request and the desire of the German General Staff that Allied military personnel remain in Russia and not be directed to the Western front? What was the substance of possible collusion between the Bolsheviks and Germany?[126] Lansing might well have been influenced in his concerns by a cable from Bullard to House of a few days earlier, in which Bullard noted: "new and more conclusive evidence forwarded by courier. Germany must desire to divert Entente resources, men, money and material from western front. . . . Soviet leaders who now ask for Allied help must be suspected of acting on orders German staff."[127]

Francis, unwilling to ignore either Lansing's charges of German collusion or the pressure from Robins and Riggs, came up with a clever solution to his dilemma. He immediately requested that railway engineers be sent from the Stevens Commission (then in Harbin and Japan) to Vologda, and that Ruggles and Riggs assign military "inspectors" for use by the Red Army. But he claimed that his reasons for doing so were to prepare the groundwork for a move *against* the Bolsheviks. He explained this decision in a cable to Lansing:

French having assigned thirty-eight therefore and Italians ordered ten from Italy. Have authorized military attaché to do likewise because it is inadvisable

to refuse. . . . My main and strictly confidential reason is that army so organized can by proper methods be taken from bolshevik control and used
against Germans. . . . I am not revealing last reason to Robins or Riggs.[128]

Francis went even further in a confidential letter to Consul General Summers, stating: "I hope and expect that such army after being organized will be
more under the influence of the Allies than under Trotsky who is amenable to
flattery. . . . If the present Bolshevik leaders prove to be German agents or
under the influence of the German General Staff we can influence the army
not only against Germany but against its creators also. . . ."[129]

As it turned out, neither of Francis' orders was ever carried out. The State
Department balked at the assignment of railway experts to Vologda; stalling
while it insisted, over a month-long period, on clarifications from Francis.
Although Colonel George H. Emerson and several others were finally dispatched "for consultations" in early May, they never arrived.[130] As for the
decision to provide military "inspectors," Ruggles dragged his heels in implementing it because of his own misgivings, and demanded a direct order from
the War Department, which responded that word would be sent through the
State Department to Francis. This word did not arrive until April 5. By that
time Francis had changed his mind after consulting with the French ambassador, Noulens. Noulens and Francis agreed that any military collaboration
should be conditioned "upon Soviet acceptance of Japanese intervention,"
which effectively killed the effort.[131]

This consultation among the Allied ambassadors and military missions in
Vologda on April 2 and 3, resulting in the clarification of conditions for
continued collaboration with the Bolsheviks, came just a few days before the
long-rumored landing of Japanese troops at Vladivostok on April 5. This
event immediately shifted the attention of both the Allies and the Bolsheviks
toward intervention. Desultory conversations between the military missions,
Trotsky, and Bonch-Bruevich continued throughout April and into May, accompanied by increased political discussions among Lockhart, Chicherin,
Lenin, Robins, and Sadoul. The Allied side aimed to try to persuade the
Bolsheviks to issue an invitation for Allied intervention against Germany.
Trotsky was willing to explore this possibility in exchange for the promise of
Allied pressue to dull the effect or reduce the scope of the Japanese interven-
tion, which increasingly became the preoccupation of Bolshevik leadership.[132]

Riggs had one long conversation with Trotsky the day after the Japanese
landed, April 6. He reported that Trotsky's entire concern was the Japanese
landing. Riggs requested from the War Department some kind of statement
opposing that intervention, but also expressed the hope that perhaps a way
could be found for Trotsky to invite the Allies in to help in countering the
Japanese.[133] Riggs and Ruggles maintained their belief in the possibility of
Allied intervention with Bolshevik consent until mid-May, bolstered by Bruce
Lockhart's intensive negotiations to this effect.[134]

Before final decisions were made, Riggs wrote a long memorandum on the
Russian situation in late April, recommending negotiations for Bolshevik

consent for intervention, as well as the maintenance of liaison with the Red Army and Bolshevik diplomatic and military personnel as a way of offsetting German diplomacy. It was absolutely imperative, he argued, that the Allies, including the United States, maintain a presence in Bolshevik Russia, negotiating a *modus vivendi* that could make possible the transfer of further war matériel to Allied hands and establish the basis for "technical and commercial contact."[135]

The other American officials in Russia, however, were distinctly divided about the efficacy of this strategy. Consul General Summers absolutely opposed it; he resisted any discussions with the Bolsheviks and refused to countenance their right to speak for the Russian people. He preferred Allied intervention without invitation. Raymond Robins also opposed it, for precisely opposite reasons. He believed that *any* intervention should be resisted, regardless of its sanction, *because* the Russian people would oppose it. Ambassador Francis at first liked the idea, particularly as explained by his military attachés, but increasingly came around to Summers' position, which he recommended by early May. By this time, Lansing and Francis were seeing eye to eye. Lansing approved Francis' course, opposing substantial military aid under any conditions, but he had "no objection to military attachés' lending such assistance as you deem in accord with spirit of the Department's instructions."[136]

There was always only the slightest possibility that Lenin would countenance an invitation for Allied troops to enter Soviet Russia, under any conditions.[137] Lenin only reluctantly wrote his note agreeing to accept *aid* to fight the Germans. But nowhere can one find any evidence whatever of Lenin's even considering inviting in Allied troops, and there is plenty of evidence to the contrary. Even Trotsky's expression of interest in the idea was most carefully circumscribed, as witnessed by the three exacting conditions he laid out in a meeting with Jacques Sadoul: (1) The Allies must coordinate their actions with the Japanese. (2) Operations must remain strictly military. Political or economic interference in Russia's internal affairs must be absolutely prohibited. (3) The Japanese and the Allies must specify the concessions they required.[138]

Most evluations by scholars and students of military discussions between American and Bolshevik representatives from November 1917 to April 1918 have been influenced strongly by the comprehensive treatment found in Kennan. They tend to dismiss such discussions as illusory because of the dominant need for Russia to get out of the war and the absolute determination of Lenin to effect that exit.[139] What such evaluations overlook, however, are the subtler possibilities of limited cooperation for limited purposes, and the impact that such cooperation might have had on the subsequent development of Soviet-American relations. It is one thing to dismiss the facile observation of Raymond Robins and William V. Judson that the United States, by failing to follow up on Trotsky's famous queries of March 5, passed up an opportunity to keep Russia in the war. It is quite another proposition, however, to ignore the repeated recommendations of Riggs, Ruggles, Robins, and even Francis that the United States had positive, concrete interests to be gained by certain measures of military cooperation with Trotsky. It seemed a certainty that the Bolsheviks would quit the war with Germany. That still leaves a great amount of latitude on other questions, such as how quickly they left it, under what conditions, and how many supplies and equipment could be kept from the German army. These were all subjects open to negotiation and open to a certain degree of American influence. Moreover, the possibility of American help in the reconstruction of Russia's railroads, the development of military equipment and advice, and determination of sources of military supply cannot be discounted.

British envoy R. H. Bruce Lockhart summarized for Raymond Robins numerous concrete ways Trotsky had offered to be helpful to the Allies in the struggle against Germany: (1) Allied officers were invited to assist in the building of the new Red Army. (2) British naval officers were invited by the Bolsheviks to rebuild the Black Sea fleet. (3) British naval officers in Petrograd were provided concrete assistance. (4) The Bolsheviks initially cooperated with the Allies in the intervention in Murmansk. (5) The Czech corps began their odyssey east to Vladivostok with Bolshevik cooperation. (6) The Allies were allowed to take possession of numerous military supplies at Archangel.[140] Although Bolshevik-Allied military cooperation eventually broke down and was superseded by intervention and hostility, several of these cooperative ventures seriously impeded the German war effort in Russia and contributed to the narrow margin with which the Allies were able to turn back the German spring offensive in the West. Had the Allies availed themselves more fully of some of these opportunities, even more obstacles could have been placed in the Germans' way in the critical first months of 1918.

# 4

# Raymond Robins and Discussions on Political and Economic Cooperation 1917–1918

Our diplomacy is past speaking about. Could it be better told than in the fact, I, a Red Cross man, am the only person in any authority that is permitted by our government to have any direct intercourse with the *de facto* government that has complete control of over three fourths of Russian territory and more than five sixths of the bayonets of the Russian people. Each hour I am expecting my recall for my services. . . .

—*Raymond Robins to Wife, Margaret, December 20, 1917.*[1]

I suppose that you know Raymond Robins personally. I did not till I met him here. . . . From what I see of him here, I judge that when he fights, he does it so wholeheartedly that his opponents do not quickly forget it. And I do not suppose that there is any great cordiality towards him in the camp of the Administration. But whether or not he has been on the right side before, he has been and is on the right side here. Of all the officials of our Government, whose trail I have encountered here, he has been the most important, the most intelligent, the most singleminded in his patriotism and the most sympathetic to democracy—in short, the best American. In those qualities he has been not only pre-eminent, but—unfortunately—almost unique. . . . He has done more than any other individual here to win a little respect and trust for our country. . . .

—*Arthur Bullard to George Creel, December 9, 1917.*[2]

Colonel Robins, himself a workman by origin, was able to understand that in Russia only two things were possible: either the Soviet government or else complete chaos. He did not waver and came to the conclusion that it was necessary to give economic help to Russia for her consolidation, otherwise, in his opinion, she would be threatened with disruption at the hands of German imperialism. A believer in modern economic giants and having no faith in the strength of socialism in America, he was nevertheless a man with clear penetrative insight. . . . For him there existed two alternatives: either German capital would assist the economic reorganization of Russia, in which case American capital would lose its greatest market in the future, or on the other hand American capital would help Russia economically and thus prevent a German monopoly.

　　　　　　　　　　　—*Karl Radek, September 1918*[3]

Raymond Robins, chief of the American Red Cross mission to Russia from December 1917 until his departure in mid-May 1918, pursued an extraordinary array of contacts with Bolshevik leaders in his singleminded efforts to establish a *modus operandi* between the United States and the new Soviet government in opposition to German efforts to penetrate and control Russia. Although other official and semi-official American representatives held discussions with the Bolsheviks during this period, Robins' efforts were the dominant force, and without him very few meetings would have been held. For nearly six months, Robins was able to maintain a degree of trust of both the Bolsheviks and the official American community in Petrograd and Moscow. In fact, the diversity of people testifying to his effectiveness and integrity during these months fully supports the considered judgement of Arthur Bullard that Robins was "the most important, the most intelligent, the most singleminded in his patriotism, the most sympathetic to democracy . . . [a man] who had done more than any other American to win a little respect for our country."[4] People as diverse in their work and their judgements as Felix Dzerzhinsky, Cornelius Kelleher, Theodore Roosevelt, V. I. Lenin, Leon Trotsky, Arthur Bullard, William V. Judson, and David Francis all affirmed the integrity and intentions of Robins during his time with the Red Cross in Russia, even where they disagreed strongly concerning his objectives, effectiveness, or conclusions about the Bolshevik government.[5]

　　Robins had unprecedented access to the Bolshevik leaders during much of this time. His interpreter, Alexander Gumberg, was a Russian-American Jew whose brother was a Bolshevik and who knew Trotsky when the latter was working on the Russian paper *Novy Mir* in early 1917 in New York.[6] Gumberg helped Robins get early access to Trotsky and later to Lenin. Once the contact was established and trust developed, Robins had practically *carte blanche* access to Trotsky and Lenin. Robins' and Gumberg's papers are full of letters and notes from Trotsky and Lenin to Bolshevik functionaries, asking that one or another small favor be done or access granted for Robins or Gumberg.[7] Trotsky also saw that Robins was given access to all of the direct telephone numbers of himself, Lenin, Dzerzhinsky, Bonch-Bruevich, Y. K. Peters (Military-Revolutionary Committee) and other Bolshevik leaders.[8]

　　From January to April of 1918, the struggle for a working relationship between the United States and Bolshevik Russia revolved around Raymond Robins and his discussions with Trotsky, Lenin, and other Bolshevik leaders. This chapter looks closely at those discussions, in a broad context of negotiations with Germany, consolidation of Bolshevik power, confusion and contradiction among various American agencies in Russia, cooperation and conflict with British and French representatives, and hesitation, ambiguity, and poor communication among American leaders in Washington. This discussion concentrates on political and economic matters, although these cannot be totally separated from the military collaboration discussed in Chapter 3.

Robins' negotiations with Trotsky and Lenin can be divided into six periods for the purpose of clarity: (1) early meetings with Trotsky (and other early meetings of U.S. representatives with local Bolshevik authorities in Moscow and elsewhere) in order to assure the continued safety of Americans, American agencies, and Red Cross work following the Bolshevik seizure of power; (2) the December to early January meetings among Lenin, Trotsky, and Robins, marking the high point of Soviet-American cooperation and the greatest degree of unity in the American community regarding Robins' efforts; (3) January–February meetings, mostly with Trotsky, focused on Robins' efforts to prevent the conclusion and signing of Brest Litovsk but also dealing with other issues; (4) early economic discussions between Robins and Lenin, U.S. commercial attaché Huntington, and Bolshevik commissars Bronski and Larin; (5) March 5 to 11 discussions focused on Robins' attempt to persuade Lenin and Trotsky, and then the American government, to reach an agreement that could prevent the Bolshevik ratification of the Brest Litvosk treaty with Germany; (6) Robins' incessant "rail diplomacy" of March and April of 1918, where he shuttled between Ambassador Francis in Vologda and Bolshevik leaders in Petrograd and Moscow trying to solve a range of economic, political, and military problems but in which Japanese intervention and Soviet-American economic cooperation took center stage.

### Robins and the Red Cross Commission: Background

The definitive biography of Raymond Robins remains to be written, although a number of historians, led by George F. Kennan, William Appleman Williams, and Neil Salzman have devoted a good bit of energy to analyzing his time in Russia, from August 1917 to May 1918.[9] Before Kennan's and Williams' books in the early 1950s, the standard interpretations of Robins' discussions with the Bolsheviks rested in large measure on his own testimony before the Senate Judiciary Committee (the Overman Committee) in 1919. This interpretation, quite predictably, was divided between those who agreed with Robins that the United States had missed a great opportunity for developing an early understanding with the Bolsheviks and those who were convinced that Robins was, if not pro-Bolshevik, certainly a naïve and misguided idealist who had been hoodwinked by Lenin and Trotsky.[10]

Williams and Kennan deepened our understanding of Robins with their studies, based heavily on extensive research into the primary sources. Williams utilized Robins' and Gumberg's own family papers and personal interviews with Robins before his death. Kennan plumbed the papers of his numerous contemporaries, including Ambassador Francis, Red Cross workers Thomas Thacher and Allen Wardwell, and Arthur Bullard. But the great gulf separating two diametrically opposed interpretations persisted and perhaps even widened because of the approaches used by the two authors. Kennan, despite scrupulous fairness to Robins' motives and the most detailed accounting of his work in Russia, argued that Robins was misguided in his belief that there was any chance of Russia's remaining in the war, and even left the distinct impression that Robins was acting contrary to Ambassador Francis' best judgements and explicit instructions.[11] Williams showed quite convincingly, especially in his dissertation, Robins' broader economic and political efforts to develop some kind of *modus vivendi,* even beyond his urgent hope to keep Russia in the war. But Williams was so sure of the antipathy of the Wilson administration to Robins' efforts that they seemed doomed to him before they even began to get started.[12] Moreover, the abbreviated form of Williams' arguments as they appear in his book are imbedded firmly in his broader argument about the economic basis for America's Soviet policy. Consequently the details, subtlety, and complexity of the political struggle taking place in Russia and in Washington in early 1918 are often overlooked.[13]

A comprehensive review of Robins' own writings and those of others about him, and an analysis of his actions during those critical six months in Bolshevik Russia underlines clearly the broad and far-reaching goals he pursued in reference to American interests in Soviet Russia. Reestablishment of Russia as a fighting force, or, failing that, creation of as many obstacles to German domination of Russia as possible, were clearly uppermost in his mind. Robins firmly believed that an agreed peace between the Soviet power and German militaristic autocracy was impossible; that the two cultures were in "fundamental opposition and could not long survive contact one with the other."[14] As General William V. Judson often reiterated, one of Robins' key accomplishments was "to sow dissension between the Germans and the Russians."[15] And there were times when Robins couched nearly all of his objectives in anti-German terms.[16]

Yet to view all of Robins' work in this light is to seriously misunderstand it. It ignores Robins' own fundamental commitments to long-range Soviet-American understanding, and it undervalues several of the broader political and economic initiatives launched by Robins, Lenin, and Trotsky. It even misreads a fundamental tenet of Robins' approach to politics, particularly politics in Russia. Key for Robins was to base any strategy on a correct appraisal of the factual situation. As he himself said in February 1918,

> The allied failure in dealing with Russia since the Bolshevik Revolution has been largely due to their demand that Russia immediately present a fighting front against the Central Empires. For the time being this is impossible. . . . This is a fact situation here, and sometimes the facts change with the hours. They have to be accepted whether they accord with theories or not. The simplest of these facts, and the one that has not changed . . . is that the Bolshevik government controls Great Russia.[17]

This fact, "Bolshevik Government," was the fundamental reality for Robins. His commitment was to American interests. His time spent in Russia was an effort to advance American interests in the face of Bolshevik reality. It led him to the conclusion that every effort should be made to "work with" those in power. In the long run, he believed, that would best serve the interests of both America and Russia:

> Can we not work with this thing, and finally bring out the better purposes of these folks, who are kindly, worthy people in the main? Can we not deal with these men? . . . Let us not abandon this land, but let us work through those that are in power and have got the rifles behind them. Whatever is done in Russia for quite awhile has got to be done with these people. . . . I believe that the best answer to Bolshevik Russia is economic cooperation, food, friendliness on the part of America, the relationship that we could bring about that would help us, help Russia. . . .[18]

Before looking in detail at the negotiations that Robins and Gumberg initiated with Lenin, Trotsky, and others, it is necessary to introduce the American Red Cross Commission and to frame the context in which Robins pursued his initiatives. The American Red Cross Commission to Russia was organized in June 1917 and arrived in Russia in July. Its ostensible purpose was relief work, but several members of the commission felt responsible for other activities; in particular supporting the Provisional Government and strengthening the war effort.[19] The Commission was quasi-governmental. Although nominally independent, the Red Cross Commission to Russia had been created by a U.S. War Council decision, and it could only function with the approval of the government. Because it was wartime, all the mission members were actually commissioned as military reserve officers. As such, they were expected to share information and consult closely with the American military mission and the United States Embassy. The mission was even authorized to use military code in sending Red Cross messages.[20] Although the original chairman of the Commission was Dr. Frank G. Billings, a Chicago physician, industrialist, and financier, millionaire copper magnate William Boyce Thompson assumed control of the Commission's work soon after its arrival. Thompson asserted from the start that his mission, which he had been given from the government, was "to undertake any work which was necessary or advisable in the effort to prevent the disintegration of the Russian forces."[21] Thompson had in large measure funded the Commission out of his own pocket, and he soon decided to pour even more money into the hands of the Social Revolutionaries in an effort to prop up Aleksandr Kerensky's government.[22] These moves by Thompson soon created a split within the Commission. Billings and the "scientific group" became convinced that Thompson was determined to become heavily involved in politics, and a number of them decided to return to America by early September 1917. Before they left, Billings put Raymond Robins in charge of field work for the entire mission, leaving Thompson as chief.[23]

Raymond Robins had been appointed to the Red Cross mission at the personal insistence of Theodore Roosevelt, whom Robins had supported for President in the campaign of 1912.[24] In that campaign, Robins first attracted the ire of Woodrow Wilson. Robins was a former Bryan Democrat who switched to Roosevelt in 1912. Wilson invited him to a private luncheon in an effort to keep him in the Democratic camp because of his influence in progressive Illinois politics. As Robins put it in later years, he had the sense that Wilson felt that "I'm a tremendous person and you don't seem to appreciate it yet."[25] Wilson's antipathy increased in 1916. Robins ran for the United States Senate in Illinois on the Progressive ticket, winning enough votes to deny the election to the Democratic candidate, a personal friend of Wilson's. Robins also traveled elsewhere in the country during the campaign, speaking on behalf of Republican presidential candidate Charles Evans Hughes against Wilson.[26]

Before his political involvement in Chicago, Robins had been a miner in Montana, and before that had found his own fortune in the frozen gold fields of Alaska in the great gold rush of the 1890s. An experience in that period of his life changed him forever and goes far to explain his motivations in later years. Prospecting for gold in the fall of 1897 far up on the Yukon River, his party was trapped on an ice floe and forced to hike through Chilkoot Pass in the dead of winter.

> Halfway inland the rear half of the column crashed into each other when a man up ahead fell over exhausted. Quickly the word came back that they would wait half an hour for the man to recover. Then, with him or without, they would plod on. The shock of the decision jarred Robins. . . . It was not right, he angrily decided. At the rear of the column another man acted, saving the man and his pack. Robins decided "that man had something [he] didn't." Later, Robins asked why he did it. "I guess you'd say I was just trying to do what Christ would have done," the man replied.[27]

From that day on, Robins began to explore the dimensions of what came to be called Christian humanitarianism or the "Christian social gospel." It motivated his approach to the Bolsheviks in Russia. Most important, it helped him understand the great desire for human betterment that motivated socialism. After he made his fortune in the Alaska gold fields, he determined to devote the rest of his life to bettering the lot of humanity: one-third to bettering the economic conditions, one-third to improving government, and the last third to strengthening morality.[28] He became a lay preacher, active in speaking at Christian youth events from that time until the end of his life. He began to fight for the rights of labor, married activist Margaret Dreier, and settled into the Progressive movement in downtown Chicago.[29]

The Christian commitment never left him. It can be seen vividly in his diary from his time in Russia. Many entries include a partial prayer or reference to "God our Father." Morning entries often began, "Awake with a Purpose! To Do His Will—To Do God's Will in the Power of the Holy Spirit."[30]

Robins was a dynamic figure, a brilliant speaker, and an indefatigable worker. What characterized him most clearly was his conviction that problems must be dealt with directly; that the best way to get information was to go out and find it. He was a "hands-on" type of personality who mistrusted bureaucracies and institutions and believed instead in going right to the source of a situation. He consistently criticized those who discussed and theorized, preferring instead to evaluate situations on the spot. He called this the difference between the "indoor" or bureaucratic mind, and the "outdoor," activist mind:

> Diplomats, heads of military missions, nearly all the "intelligentsia" continued to reason and act in the Russian situation as if they were dealing with a Western Euopean country supported by a large, middle class of small property owners. This was the fatal error resulting from dealing with this original and exceptional situation from an indoor precedent horizon rather than the outdoor realities.[31]

Robins and Thompson at first regarded each other with mutual suspicion and hostility. One was a Wall Street magnate; the other a progressive from Chicago. They had clashed on several occasions in the 1912 and 1916 campaigns. Hermann Hagedorn recounts from conversations with both their initial reactions to the news that each was on the Red Cross mission. Robins, seeing Thompson's name on the list of members, exclaimed, "W. B. Thompson? . . . What's that Wall Street reactionary doing on this Mission?" When Thompson discovered Robins, his reaction was equally disdainful: "That uplifter, that troublemaker, that Roosevelt shouter? What's he doing on this Mission?"[32]

Yet the two, on the long train ride across Siberia to Petrograd in July of 1917, gradually began to fall into discussions with each other, and slowly grew to develop a mutual respect and a working relationship that was to last throughout their Russian experience and even to withstand the pressures of the Red Scare.[33]

The Red Cross mission arrived in Petrograd the first of August 1917, just after the Root mission departed. Professor Samuel Harper, who had come to Russia with the Root mission, stayed on in Petrograd as guide and interpreter for the Red Cross mission, and he and Robins struck up a strong friendship. This helps explain why, among administration and Russian experts in the United States, Harper was among the last and most reluctant to abandon Robins in the summer and fall of 1918.[34] The mission was received by Prime Minister Kerensky on August 8, and Thompson immediately took the initiative to put forth his ideas, not only for Red Cross work in Russia, but for an American effort to save Russia for the Allies. Thompson immediately subscribed 500,000 rubles to the Russian Liberty Loan, and promised Kerensky he would seek five million rubles from the J. P. Morgan syndicate and a tremendous new commitment of American government assistance.[35]

Thompson and Robins assumed the leadership of the Red Cross Commission. Numerous strategy meetings were held among Robins, Thompson, Ambassador Francis, and Kerensky. Key efforts were to reestablish the food supply, and to reinvigorate the government, the people, and the army in their fight against Germany. Robins was put in charge of field operations and sent into the countryside to see what could be done in the way of purchasing grain and assessing the needs for medicine, clothing, and milk. Thompson stayed in Petrograd to deal with the government and to lay plans for an ambitious propaganda effort.[36]

In late August, Thompson wrote to the head of the Red Cross in Washington, Henry P. Davison, and requested that he meet with President Wilson and persuade him to back a new, massive campaign to turn around the Russian war effort and strengthen popular support for the Kerensky government.[37] Wilson advised Davison that he did not feel a major new program was necessary, and even the House of Morgan declined to subscribe to the bond campaign Thompson had desired.[38] But Thompson was not deterred. He decided to proceed on his own and to continue his efforts to change the mind of his government. He ordered one million dollars of his own money transferred to the Russian Ministry of Finance and requisitioned huge sums from the Red Cross for a major new food and medicine drive.[39]

Meanwhile, Robins was working in the countryside, primarily in south Russia, in an effort to cut through the distribution problems preventing supplies of grain from reaching the cities and to purchase grain that the Red Cross needed for feeding refugees in the cities. Robins soon discovered that the Kerensky government had little authority in the countryside. Instead he was being told everywhere to deal with the local soviets of workers' and peasants' deputies. He cabled Thompson, asking him what he should do. Thompson's advice was succinct: "You were sent to get the grain. Get the grain."[40]

This experience, and Robins' later speeches to assemblies of workers and soldiers in Petrograd at the behest of Kerensky, Thompson, and Ambassador Francis, convinced Robins that the soviets were the rising power in a constantly changing Russian scene. If he were to survive, Kerensky must align himself with the soviets.[41] This conviction only deepened in the aftermath of the Kornilov coup attempt in mid-September. Thompson and Robins stood practically alone among the Allied personnel in Petrograd in their unswerving allegiance to Kerensky. Yet Robins and Thompson also saw clearly that the soviets were a force to be taken seriously. The fact that Kerensky prevailed only with major support from the soviets and from the Bolsheviks was not lost on either Robins or Thompson. Now Thompson and Robins clearly saw eye-to-eye in their analysis. This was to stand Robins in good stead in the first days after the October revolution.[42]

The defeat of Kornilov also impressed upon Robins and Thompson the fragility of Kerensky, and Thompson stepped up his efforts to get more support from Washington to supplement his personal propaganda campaign. Thompson already had involved in his plan two other influential Americans in Petrograd: Frederick M. Corse, the Petrograd manager for the New York Life Insurance Company; and H. Grosvenor Hutchins, a vice-president of the New York Bank of Commerce. The three of them informed Ambassador Francis in general terms concerning their plans, but told him no details, at his request.[43]

Hutchins headed home to New York with the mission of persuading the administration, through any and all avenues, to take the need for extra funds seriously.[44] Hutchins finally secured an appointment with Colonel House on September 22, and after talking with Creel, an appointment with President Wilson on October 23.[45] Before this meeting, Thompson had also cabled further details through the military attaché and the War Department code for Davison and House.[46]

Wilson did not accede to Thompson's requests, but he did agree with Creel that some kind of propaganda and educational effort was required in Russia, and appointed Edgar G. Sisson, former *Chicago Tribune* editor and Creel's personal choice, as special Compub agent for Russia, along with an appropriation of $250,000. Sisson met briefly with Wilson, received the distinct impression that he had been appointed as the President's personal representative, and received a copy of his orders. In this letter, Wilson said "we stand ready to render such aid as lies in our power, but I want this helpfulness based upon request and not upon offer . . . try to express the disinterested friendship that is our sole impulse. . . ."[47]

Sisson left the United States immediately, but did not arrive in Petrograd until November 25, two weeks after the Bolshevik revolution. He was to figure prominently in Raymond Robins' efforts to establish a positive relationship with the Bolsheviks, at first serving as one of his staunchest supporters. Later Sisson turned against Robins when he became convinced that Lenin and Trotsky were involved in a conspiracy with Germany against the Allies.[48]

Because of Wilson's decision to send Sisson instead of the large sums of money that Thompson needed, Thompson and Robins were forced to greatly reduce the scope of their propaganda efforts in the days leading up to November 7. Robins, now back in Petrograd, also had the distinct sense as he spoke to great crowds of workers and soldiers that the people were slipping away from Kerensky and were responding to the Bolsheviks' slogan of "Peace, Land, and Bread."[49]

Robins and Thompson made a last-ditch, unsuccessful effort to persuade the British, the French, and Kerensky to modify the government's program, primarily on the land question, in such a way that the soviets might still give it support if it came to a showdown with the Bolsheviks. The Bolshevik seizure of power arrived within days—not to the great surprise of the two of them.[50] Following the fall of the Winter Palace, Thompson sent Robins to find out the truth of rumors that Kerensky was at Gatchina, thirty miles away, and would return with an army. Robins returned exhausted, with a sobering story:

> One after the other, men began to climb out of the government trenches. Within ten minutes Robins learned that half of Kerensky's troops had gone over to the Soviet. . . . Kerensky was through, he told [Thompson]. The Soviet had all the power there was in Russia. There were only two things to do: get in touch with Lenin and Trotsky and work with them with a possibility of rebuilding the eastern front; or to pack their grips and get out as fast as they could run.[51]

Thompson did not panic, and he and Robins spent several hours thrashing out the situation. They were both convinced that, regardless of the rumors concerning German gold already swirling around Lenin and Trotsky, the Bolsheviks were in power and would be for some time. If the Red Cross activities were to continue, or they were to have even the slightest chance of saving anything from Germany, they had to at least attempt to work with them. Thompson told Robins to go to Smolny and try to see Trotsky.[52]

The deciding factor for Thompson was Robins' argument concerning the war. As he put it later, "The problems which it was apparent to me must be met in Russia were three in number: 1. How to assist Russia and keep her actively fighting in the Entente. 2. Failing in No. 1, how to prevent Russia from making a separate peace. 3. Failing in Nos. 1 and 2, how to prevent Russia from being used by Germany against the Allies."[53] But Thompson was quite aware, not only of the personal commitment he had made to Kerensky (which was common knowledge in Petrograd), but also that he needed strong support from Washington if he were to continue. As Thomas Thacher noted, "If it hadn't been Russia, everybody on the Red Cross mission, beginning with WB, would have been shot when the Bolsheviks came in. They had been fighting Lenin and Trotsky tooth and nail."[54] General Judson insisted that the Commission, especially Thompson, move its offices to the military attaché's headquarters. Thompson did move, but only for two nights.[55] But he and Robins began to formulate a new strategy, one that left Robins in Petrograd to try to unite the Americans in an effort to work with Lenin and Trotsky in every way possible against Germany, but that sent Thompson home to Washington to make the strongest possible case for the continuation of an American effort in Russia. Robins later recollected that he urged Thompson to go to Washington: "Washington must know the truth about this situation. You are the only man who knows it and it is absolutely necessary that you should interpret this situation to the governing people in the United States. You are known here, moreover, as a Wall Street man and if you stay here you are taking a perfectly needless risk."[56]

Before Thompson left, he and Robins developed a five-point program aimed at salvaging everything possible for the Allies in Russia under the Bolsheviks. This program included: (1) propaganda and revolutionary agents into Germany; (2) U.S.-Soviet cooperation in economic reorganization, salvaging Allied supplies; (3) railroad reorganization by the United States; (4) an economic commission for the purchase of raw materials; (5) Allied support for a new Russian army.[57]

On November 28, 1917, William B. Thompson left Petrograd for London and Washington, after promoting Raymond Robins to Colonel and putting him in command of the Red Cross in Russia. Remaining with Robins in Russia were four other Red Cross officers, several of whom would play key roles in the future: Allen Wardwell, Thomas Thacher, both New York lawyers; and William Webster and Heywood Hardy, detail and supply men. All the others left with Thompson for America.[58] Robins' admiration for Thompson remained. As Robins was to tell the Senate Overman Committee:

He [Thompson] had altogether the best mind in the Red Cross Mission. he thought around all of us. I bear this testimony in this presence under oath that when I lost the trail as I did lose the trail half a dozen times in that complex situation, he called me in and said, "There is the trail over there, Robins," and in every instance he was right. He had one of those perfect noses, like a pointer dog, for a scent.[59]

## First Contacts with the Bolsheviks

As he prepared to go to Smolny for his initial meeting with Trotsky on November 10, Robins realized that he would need a new interpreter. He had been using Sasha Kropotkina, introduced to him in the late summer by American commercial attaché William C. Huntington and well known and friendly to the Kerensky government.[60] Someone new seemed necessary for entrée to the Bolsheviks. Robins remembered Alexander Gumberg, a Russian Jewish expatriate from New York who had returned to Russia with the Root mission in the summer, and had been assisting various Americans with translation, guidance, and contacts ever since. Gumberg was acquainted with Trotsky from Trotsky's time with *Novy Mir* in New York, and Gumberg's brother was a Bolshevik in Petrograd, working at Smolny, the Bolshevik headquarters. Gumberg contacted Trotsky directly and arranged for a personal meeting between him and Robins. Following this meeting, Robins hired Gumberg permanently as guide and interpreter. Gumberg also worked during the early days after the Bolshevik accession to power as interpreter for Edgar G. Sisson of the Committee on Public Information. He remained with Robins throughout his stay in Russia, and returned with him to the United States in May of 1918.[61]

Gumberg's role in the negotiations between Trotsky, Lenin, and Robins has often been overlooked. Robins himself defended Gumberg strongly in his testimony to the Overman Committee, and a recent study by James K. Libby has brought out the details of Gumberg's lifelong commitment to both America and Russia.[62] Gumberg really could not be fairly categorized as a Bolshevik sympathizer. Rather, he had a deep love for two countries and two peoples, American and Russian, and devoted his life to bringing them together. As he said in a letter to Governor Goodrich of Indiana in 1921, "my only ambition is to be useful in this tremendous problem of reconciliation between Russia and the rest of the world, and particularly the United States."[63] As Louis Fischer, who knew Gumberg well, put it, "In Alex, Russia and America merged in a remarkable synthesis. . . . For many Americans, Alex was the bridge to Soviet Russia. But subsequently he helped Russia understand America. . . . His great art . . . consisted in provoking others to talk."[64]

Robins and Gumberg formed a most compatible team. Gumberg brought his knowledge of Russian and his contacts in Russian society. Robins brought his energy, his decisiveness, and his contacts with American political and financial leadership. Neither could have accomplished what he did without the other.[65] Robins in later years was quick to credit Gumberg for much of his success and contacts, noting that "whatever success I have had was due in some large measure to Gumberg."[66]

Robins and Gumberg met with Trotsky for the first time on November 10.[67] Before going to Smolny, Robins persuaded Thompson to allow him to change the guards at the Red Cross warehouse, engaging the Red Guards.[68] That there was a meeting at all was in itself rather remarkable. Robins was known at Smolny for his support of Kerensky. Were it not for Gumberg, he probably would not have gotten past the guards. Trotsky agreed to see him only reluctantly.

Once the meeting began, Robins put all his cards on the table. He immediately admitted his preference for Kerensky, but said that was over, and that "he knew a corpse when he saw it and believed that the thing to do with it was not to sit up with it but to bury it."[69] He then said to Trotsky that he would deal with whoever was in power because he wanted the Red Cross to remain in Russia and he wanted Russia to stay in the war. Robins also said that he had to have certain assurances from Trotsky to show him that the Bolsheviks indeed had the government power to give protection for the Red Cross work. Trotsky indicated his willingness to have the Red Cross continue its work, and personally authorized the fulfillment of Robins' specific requests. A thirty-two-car train of Red Cross supplies was transferred without hindrance from Petrograd to Rumania, and a shipment of four hundred thousand cans of condensed milk was moved from Murmansk to Petrograd. Trotsky's orders in these cases were honored by both the railroad and the Red Guards. It clearly appeared to Robins that the Bolsheviks were in control of the main lines of communication and government, and that at least Trotsky, the Foreign Commissar, was willing to work with Robins and had the power to have his orders carried out.[70] "I won Trotsky," Robins recalled much later, "by putting my case absolutely on the square."[71]

Robins returned to Thompson and told him of the interview, and they both agreed that the Red Cross should stay for the present and see what could be done. "Our job," Robins recalled Thompson saying, "is to prevent a separate peace and prevent raw materials from going to the central empires."[72] To test Trotsky's willingness to cooperate in this endeavor, the Red Cross leaders asked to have fifty railroad cars of supplies held at Vyborg to keep them from falling into German hands. They were held, and eventually reached Allied hands.[73]

No first-hand accounts from Trotsky or Soviet sources are yet available for these early meetings between Trotsky and Robins. But there is indirect evidence of the accuracy of Robins' accounts. Trotsky did refer to the visits on several occasions, both at public speeches, recorded by the Petrograd press, and at a meeting of the Bolshevik Central Committee on November 20 and 21. At this time he used the meetings as a way of explaining his belief that the United States, of all the Allies, would be the most open to some kind of accommodation with the Bolsheviks. "America can be tolerant," said Trotsky, "with regard to the existence of the Soviet government."[74]

Robins, as it turned out, was not the only American seeking early contact with the Bolshevik authorities for assurances in light of the recent change of power. Official U.S. consular representatives in both Petrograd and Moscow felt compelled to make representations in order to fulfill their consular responsibilities. North Winship, Consul at Petrograd, visited Trotsky on December 4 "for the purpose of making arrangements for American citizens to leave Russia." Winship, who made arrangements to visit Trotsky after consulting with Ambassador Francis and the U.S. Counselor to the Embassy, J. Butler Wright, reported that his talk with Trotsky, lasting about ten minutes, "was as friendly as his mental hostility would permit" and that procedures were worked out to permit Americans who wished to do so to depart Petrograd and Bolshevik Russia without hindrance.[75]

Likewise, in Moscow, Consul General Maddin Summers, despite his harsh antipathy to the Bolsheviks, felt compelled to make representations to the local Military Revolutionary Committee, the *de facto* government in Moscow, in order to make sure of the safety of American citizens in Moscow. As Summers explained his action to Ambassador Francis, "we have told them that we did not recognize the Government and that our representation to them was of a temporary character."[76]

Francis, however, was becoming very concerned about the increasing number of contacts of American representatives with the Bolsheviks, especially after General William V. Judson persuaded him to allow a visit to Trotsky to discuss terms of the armistice on December 1. Francis made clear to Summers, the consular staff, and all other official and semi-official American representatives that no contact with Bolshevik authorities was to take place without his permission. On December 6, Secretary Lansing, in response to Judson's visit to Trotsky, issued an edict cutting off all contact between American representatives and the Bolsheviks.[77]

Suddenly, the American community in Russia was faced with a major dilemma. Much of their work could not be carried on without such contact, however minimal. Even Summers, despite his hatred of the Bolsheviks, did not want Americans to leave Russia. He hoped that the Bolsheviks would soon be overthrown, but in the meantime, in order to counteract massive German propaganda, "every effort must be made to maintain every American agency in Russia."[78] Summers sent Vice-Consul DeWitt Clinton Poole from Moscow to Petrograd, to consult with the Embassy, military attaché and Red Cross staff about the situation.[79]

After long meetings, and encouraged by the positive response to Robins' and Judson's meetings with Trotsky, all the significant American representatives in Petrograd: Robins; Jerome Davis of the YMCA; Judson, Sisson and Bullard from Compub; Butler Wright and Norman Armour from the Embassy; and William C. Huntington, the commercial attaché, jointly agreed to recommend opening informal channels of communication with the Bolsheviks. They hoped this would lead to some kind of working arrangement to facilitate operations against Germany.[80]

Edgar Sisson, who had only arrived in Petrograd on November 25, joined

Robins as one of the most articulate spokesmen for this viewpoint. Not only had Sisson come armed with what he thought were personal instructions from President Wilson, but he was absolutely convinced that he could do none of his work without at least the tacit consent of the Bolsheviks. As he put it, "this plan required the use of the mechanical facilities wholly in the control of the Bolshevik government: telegraph agencies, printing shops and, to a lesser degree, distributing agencies."[81] Although Ambassador Francis still dissented from this view, Sisson and his colleague Arthur Bullard wrote to George Creel at the Committee on Public Information office in Washington, recommending "immediate establishment of working, informal contact with *de facto* power by official representatives."[82] Bullard praised Robins, stating taht "all of us" were in agreement on contact, and urged Colonel House and Creel to lay this out in the strongest possible terms to President Wilson.[83] Robins in the meantime wrote to his chief, Henry P. Davison, and Judson wrote in similar terms to the War College.

The American community was united on one other issue as well: the necessity of replacing Ambassador Francis with someone more reliable and with better judgement. Bullard put the situation quite succinctly in a letter to House:

> That Francis is a sick man entirely overwhelmed by the situation, that he has shown himself unamenable to the advice and urging of his civil and military advisers, that he has created hopelessly hostile relations with people where it is his obvious duty to seek cooperation—all this—is not the reason that seems most compelling to me. The old gentleman has allowed himself to get mixed up with a woman to such a degree that his position here is impossible.[84]

This woman, Mathilde de Cram, was suspected by every American who knew her of being a German spy, or at least a great risk. And yet Ambassador Francis not only allowed her the run of the embassy, he even enlisted her assistance in coding cables.[85]

Sisson's and Bullard's cables calling for informal contact with the Bolsheviks and the replacement or recall of Ambassador Francis reached Washington at the same time that Francis was calling Lansing's attention to Sisson's, Robins', and Judson's overzealous involvement in politics.[86] Sisson and Bullard were directed by the President, through Creel, to stay away from political matters, leaving them to the Embassy; and Judson was recalled.[87] Sisson and Bullard did not accede to the President's or Secretary of State's wishes. In fact, Creel encouraged them not to.[88] Sisson secured the services of Gumberg, which made coordination with Robins easy, and the two of them worked out a joint plan to get American and Bolshevik propaganda into the hands of German troops at the front. This was effected with the active cooperation of Karl Radek and Trotsky.[89]

Robins' own status remained tenuous, as Ambassador Francis sought instructions about whether the Red Cross envoy could continue to hold meetings with Trotsky. Yet Robins retained the initiative, and on his own met with

Trotsky several times between December 5 and 20, specifically to follow up Judson's initial meeting about armistice conditions.[90]

Meanwhile, William B. Thompson was in London trying to persuade British leaders to work with the Bolsheviks against Germany. This came at a most opportune time. Thompson had hoped to meet with Colonel House before he left London for Washington. Although this did not succeed, he met instead with key officials in London, including U.S. Ambassador Walter Hines Page; Lord R. D. Reading, British Ambassador to the United States; Admiral G. K. Hall, the Chief of British Naval Intelligence; Sir George Clark, the representative of Foreign Secretary Arthur Balfour; Lord Carson of the War Office; and Britain's propaganda chief, John Buchan.[91]

Finally, on December 14, Thompson and Thomas W. Lamont had a working lunch with Prime Minister David Lloyd George. Thompson presented his ideas for a new Allied plan to Lloyd George and left a proposal in writing for the Prime Minister. This plan emphasized the importance of new initiatives in Russia against Germany and the appointment of diplomatic personnel not tied to the old regime or the provisional government who would work with the Bolsheviks to deny advantages and supplies to Germany. Thompson argued that the Bolsheviks might be the key to the entire war against Germany, and that it would be much better to try to use them against Germany than to allow Germany to use them against the Allies. He also argued that the Bolsheviks, because of their fundamental weakness, needed the Allies and so might be willing to cooperate. Thompson was convinced that the Bolsheviks were not yet under Germany's sway. "At present they are nobody's Bolsheviks. Don't let us let Germany make them her Bolsheviks. Let's make them our Bolsheviks."[92] Thompson went on to urge the appointment of an informal group of new Allied agents to coordinate policy in Petrograd and to keep in unofficial contact with the Bolsheviks.[93]

Lloyd George, according to all accounts, agreed wholeheartedly with Thompson's analysis and his recommendations. Not only did he tell Thompson and Lamont to tell President Wilson and Colonel House of his strong agreement, but he promised to move immediately to appoint a British representative in Petrograd to open up channels of communication with the Bolsheviks.[94]

This move already had been under intense discussion in Whitehall for some weeks. It had first been recommended by British Ambassador to Russia George Buchanan himself, days after the revolution. It had become increasingly clear that a new appointment was needed because of Buchanan's personal ties to the Kerensky government.[95] A long memorandum by a special War Cabinet Committee headed by Milner and Balfour had been prepared on December 9, in which it was argued that it was

> to our advantage to avoid, as long as possible, an open breach with this crazy system. . . . We ought if possible not to come to an open breach with the Bolsheviks or drive them into the enemies' camp. . . . no policy would be more fatal than to give the Russians a motive for welcoming into their midst German officials and German soldiers as friends and deliverers.[96]

The War Cabinet, in a long discussion on the same day, agreed, noting that it was critical "that Russia was as helpful to us and as harmful to the enemy as possible . . . to antagonize [the Bolsheviks] needlessly would be to throw them into the arms of Germany."[97]

During these same days, Robert H. Bruce Lockhart, former British Vice-Consul in Petrograd until early September 1917, had come down to London from Scotland and was earnestly lobbying all of his contacts in government to the same end as Thompson. From November 27 to December 18, he met with politicians as diverse as Arthur Henderson, Bonar Law, and Lord Milner. Increasingly the conversation turned to the necessity of a new Allied policy toward the Bolsheviks, and the need for new British envoys to implement it. On December 21, Lockhart was summoned to Downing Street to meet Lloyd George and was appointed on the spot the head of a special British mission to establish unofficial relations with the Bolsheviks.[98] Lockhart reported later that Milner told him that Lloyd George had been "greatly impressed" by his meeting with W. B. Thompson, and that Lloyd George himself had said that he did not know whether Thompson was right about Russia, but "everyone else who has talked to me about Russia has been wrong."[99]

Thompson's and Lockhart's meetings with Lloyd George and other British officials had immediate effect. Soon after Lloyd George's meeting with Lockhart, the British Cabinet formulated a new policy with regard to these "unofficial" relations in a suggested Allied policy memorandum, agreed to by Clemenceau and Pichon, and sent immediately to House and Wilson. It became the basis on which Robins, Lockhart, and French envoy Jacques Sadoul functioned, albeit with different degrees of support and communication, for the three nations in Petrograd. This memorandum, written by Milner and Cecil, recommended that "at Petrograd we should at once get into relations with the Bolsheviki, through unofficial agents, each country as seems best to it. . . . We should represent to the Bolsheviki that we have no desire to take part in any way in the internal politics of Russia, and that any idea that we favour a counterrevolution is a profound mistake. . . ."[100]

In early January, the War Cabinet further elaborated on this policy, and the powers and responsibilities granted to Lockhart:

> Mr. Lockhart was now in the same position as that occupied by our Consul at Helsingfors, who dealt directly in a political capacity with the de facto Government of Finland. . . . Mr. Lockhart should be placed in an analogous position in regard to his dealings with the de facto Government in Petrograd. . . . By taking the step suggested, we did not either support or condemn Bolshevism as such, but merely facilitated dealings with the de facto government. . . .[101]

All of this was reported fully to Washington. In fact, Lockhart's work was reported in great detail to Colonel House through William Wiseman, sometimes the best way that Raymond Robins' work came to the White House's attention after Lockhart arrived in Petrograd. Wilson responded in a memorandum to Lansing on January 1, "This seems to me to be a sensible programme . . . and I am writing to ask your opinion as to the most feasible and least objectionable way (if there is any) in which we could establish similar unofficial relations with the Bolsheviki."[102]

Lockhart left England for Petrograd in mid-January, after first having several meetings with the unofficial Bolshevik representative in Britain, Maksim Litvinov. Litvinov functioned in England as Lockhart functioned in Petrograd: as unofficial, but nevertheless government-sanctioned, representative with diplomatic privileges. These meetings solved a major dilemma for the British government. They provided the basis on which each government's representative could be accepted, and tolerated, in the other's country for the next six months. The mutuality of the arrangement provided certain security and access guarantees not afforded Raymond Robins and the Americans in Petrograd.[103]

## Robins and Francis

Raymond Robins' work met with an obstacle. His regular meetings with Trotsky and others in the Bolshevik government since the revolution were endangered. He had already had success in securing Bolshevik consent to continue Red Cross work and to keep Russia, if not in the war, at least tilting toward the Allied side. A promising beginning came to a crossroads. After Secretary of State Lansing's December 6 prohibition of official American contacts with the Bolsheviks, Ambassador Francis tested its inclusiveness. He cabled Lansing to ask whether the prohibition applied to Robins and the Red Cross. Before an answer was received on December 22, Robins made himself the link and undertook negotiations with Trotsky on behalf of Ambassador Francis. This would put Francis in his debt and cement a working relationship enjoyed by the two men despite strong external and internal disagreement. It lasted until Robins' departure from Russia in May 1918.[104]

These quasi-official negotiations were over the Kalpashnikov affair. Their interesting details were not so important as their consequences, which provided Raymond Robins with continued contacts. In brief: Andrei Kalpashnikov was a Russian military officer in the service of the American Red Cross unit for Rumania. In 1917, before the Bolshevik revolution, he had gone to the United States on behalf of the Red Cross to raise money for ambulance equipment and, if possible, to purchase new ambulances. He made the purchase and had the ambulances shipped across the Pacific and Siberia. They were waiting in Petrograd for shipment to Rumania at the time of the Bolshevik revolution. Just before Kalpashnikov and the ambulances were to leave Petrograd for Jassy, Rumania, on December 20, he was arrested on Trotsky's orders and held under charges of a conspiracy to supply the ambulances and other equipment to the anti-Bolshevik Cossack forces on the Don River. Furthermore, and most critical for the United States, Ambassador Francis was implicated in the conspiracy.[105]

Robins went to Smolny at once to talk to Trotsky in an attempt to defuse the potential tension and remove the Embassy and the Red Cross as targets. Trotsky was furious and refused to see him unless he could show that he was officially sent by Ambassador Francis. Robins returned to the Embassy and persuaded Francis that official authorization was needed.[106]

The Embassy was armed with proof that Kalpashnikov, on inquiring with regard to the shipment of the ambulances, had been told that he must seek and receive explicit permission from the Bolshevik authorities. Robins went again to talk with Trotsky, on December 21, carrying with him the most explicit authority he was ever to receive from the United States government— an authorization from J. Butler Wright, Counselor of the Embassy, on behalf of the Ambassador—that he was "authorized to speak for the American Embassy in this connection in order to correct any misapprehension that may have arisen."[107] This time he missed Trotsky, who had already headed for the theater.[108] In an incendiary speech at the theater, Trotsky made public the entire episode, exonerating Robins but castigating Ambassador Francis and demanding an explanation. Alexander Gumberg, sent by Robins to listen, reported fully to his boss.[109]

Before Robins returned to see Trotsky on December 22, the fateful answer from Washington regarding Robins' contacts with the Bolsheviks had been received by Ambassador Francis. Robins was included in the ban on contacts. Robins asked Francis if he wished him to refrain from returning to meet with Trotsky, or did he wish him to disregard the order. As Francis testified in 1919, he told Robins, "I think it unwise for you to sever your relations abruptly and absolutely; that is, I mean to cease your visits up there. Furthermore, I want to know what they are doing, and I will stand between you and the fire."[110] Thus Robins escaped the order forbidding all other American personnel to have contact with Soviet officials. Robins' singular initiative remained the one thread of contact between American officials and the Bolshevik government in Russia. Improper as the December 22 directive made it, nonetheless Francis could not afford to let go either, and consequently defended Robins against Lansing. As it turned out, Francis forced Secretary Lansing to modify the order on December 29 and to grudgingly accept the importance of Robins' contacts.[111]

Robins had only indifferent success effecting Kalpashnikov's release (he was held until April 28), and Kalpashnikov himself claims Robins did next to nothing for him.[112] But Robins succeeded in separating himself, the American Red Cross, and the American Ambassador from the case, in the process putting himself permanently in the debt of David R. Francis. As Robins himself put it in his diary on December 24, "All clear and Trotsky is the power. . . . The blow fell on orders from America. . . . The Knight Errant . . . wins two first points. . . ."[113]

Both Francis and Robins followed the incident with efforts to have the order forbidding contacts rescinded. Robins wrote an urgent cable to his chief, Henry Davison, of the Red Cross: "Please urge upon the President the necessity of our continued intercourse with the Bolshevik government. Otherwise impossible to arrange for transportation and distribution of supplies, particularly milk. Ambassador approves this statement and has advised State Department to same effect."[114] Francis added a note to this cable, "Please note my approval as stated above." Under this guise of "distribution of supplies," Lansing responded on December 29, modifying his order, but explicitly noting that "he acts for and represents Red Cross and not Embassy."[115] By this time, however, both Francis and Robins knew otherwise. Robins had become a political operative for Ambassador Francis, empowered to talk with Lenin and Trotsky on behalf of the United States.[116]

## The Robins-Francis Relationship

Robins' relationship with U.S. Ambassador David R. Francis had been subject to a good deal of difference of opinion ever since their quite divergent testimonies concerning it to the Overman Committee in 1919. At that time, Francis attempted to distance himself from Robins, while not quite disavowing his authorization for the contact. Robins, determined to set the record straight, insisted on a second appearance before the Committee, in which he produced more documents showing the numerous times Francis had asked him to act on his behalf.[117] On this point, both George Kennan and William Appleman Williams, for completely different reasons, argue the more limited nature of the partnership. Kennan tends to paint Francis as rather cut off from most knowledge of Robins' contacts, and Williams puts Francis firmly on the side of counterrevolution, and therefore sees him only using Robins for his own purposes and for a limited period.[118]

I take exception to both Williams and Kennan. Particularly on the basis of a prolific correspondence record in the Francis papers (certainly backed by the Robins papers, and by the glimpses we have from numerous others, including Bullard, Sisson, and Wardwell), I am convinced that Francis viewed Raymond Robins' contacts with Lenin, Trotsky, Chicherin, and other Bolshevik leaders from November 1917 until May 1918 as Francis' own contacts. Robins was an extension of Francis' authority. Francis was really most anxious for Robins to continue such contacts, as they provided him with a critical source of information on the Bolsheviks and enabled him to work out, on an amicable basis, various small problems that beset the life and work of the American Embassy and consulates in Russia. Even more important, these contacts provided Francis the opportunity to press the Bolsheviks to remain in the war against Germany, or, failing that, to keep Russian resources in Allied hands. This is a major reason Francis was willing for Robins to continue to keep in contact with the Bolshevik leaders until his departure and even why, after his departure, Francis authorized Acting Consul General DeWitt Clinton Poole to take over Robins' role of contacts with the Bolsheviks.[119]

With the single, albeit conspicuous, exception of Robins' final meeting with Lenin on the Soviet economic proposal to the United States, the Francis papers support Robins' claim that he kept Francis fully informed of all his dealings with Soviet leaders. Every other meeting of substance between Robins and Lenin,

Trotsky or Chicherin is reported fully in the Francis papers, either via letter or memorandum from Robins, or via notation or family letter from Francis. Numerous indications in Francis' desk diary also attest to the very frequent personal meetings the two men had throughout the winter and spring of 1918.[120] More substantive materials concerning Robins appears in the Francis papers than does communication from Washington concerning Wilson's and Lansing's Russia policy, which may help explain why Francis appeared to waver in his recommendations concerning contact with the Bolsheviks.[121] In addition, the Francis material on Robins is at times more substantive concerning these meetings than that contained in Robins' own papers, which tend to be sketchy on many points.[122]

Another common belief about Francis is that he was cut off from information and knowledge about Soviet society and the processes of revolutionary change around him, thus somehow trapped into an unhealthy reliance on Robins and his access.[123] The materials in the Francis papers also dispute that contention. The papers are full of information from all manner of sources concerning Bolshevik government and Russian life and society, including translations of all key articles from *Pravda,* the *Bulletin* of the Bolshevik Central Executive Committee, the Council of Workers' and Soldiers' Deputies, and non-Bolshevik newspapers such as *Rodina* and the *Petrograd Echo.*[124] To what extent Francis read, absorbed, and acted on such information must be determined issue by issue, but he was by no means cut off from it, nor did he have to rely on Robins for all of his information.[125]

Contrary to Francis' own testimony before the Overman Committee or what he has written in his memoirs, Francis' letters and papers show that he was fully in touch with Robins, and in large measure supportive of Robins' contacts with the Bolsheviks, up to the very end of his stay in Russia. Only when the final quarrel between Robins and Consul General Summers threatened to boil over and Summers offered to resign did Francis begin to have second thoughts about Robins' contacts with Lenin and Chicherin, and even then he still counseled Robins and Summers to work out their differences. While the Francis papers shed light on the Robins-Summers dispute and Francis' role in trying to mediate it, and they also show Francis' basic sympathy for Summers position, they do not show any evidence of Francis' conspiring with Summers to undermine Robins, contrary to the assertions of Williams. Rather, as has been intimated elsewhere, they show Francis trying to maintain a dual policy of contact (Robins) and hostility (Summers).[126] Robins' departure and Summers' death actually made things easier for Francis. Poole took over the contact role, but without Summers' hostility or Robins' overt sympathy.[127]

## *De Facto* Relations

The period of time from the Kalpashnikov incident (December 21) and Ambassador Francis' assumption of responsibility for Raymond Robins' contacts with the Bolsheviks up through mid-January 1918 marked the time of greatest success for Robins' strategy. Not only did Robins enjoy concrete and signal victories, but his efforts enjoyed unified support from the American political and diplomatic community. In addition, official Washington grudgingly agreed to allow him to continue, and even President Wilson seriously considered adopting an official American policy very close to what Robins recommended.

Accomplishments included a number of breakthroughs. Robins successfully persuaded the Bolsheviks to treat Kalpashnikov as a lone renegade, without damaging the Red Cross or the American Embassy. Ambassador Francis promised conditional military and economic aid if Brest Litovsk talks broke down and Russia resumed war with Germany. President Wilson made some excellent statements about Russia in his famous address of January 8, and Bolshevik cooperation was secured for the massive distribution of the relevant portions of the speech in Russia. Finally, the month was capped by Robins and Gumberg's effecting the release of the Rumanian ambassador Diamandi, and engineering the first official meeting of Francis and Lenin in the process. Robins' pocket diary for January reflects his excited, upbeat mood: January 2: "Win! Agreement for cooperation." January 26: "All is clear in the heart of the situation." January 27: "Meeting with Ambassador in bed. Complete agreement."[128]

Every American agency in Russia, with the exception of the Consulate General, was recommending some kind of *de facto* relations with the Bolsheviks by the first of January 1918, and had so informed their superiors in Washington.[129] Arthur Bullard, perhaps the most influential of all Americans in Russia because of his penetrating insights and his direct influence with Colonel House, had made very clear his own conviction that Robins' approach was the only one that made sense at this time.[130] And even Ambassador Francis, shaken by the Kalpashnikov incident and excited by the possibilities Trotsky seemed to intimate of a resumption of war with Germany, began at this same time to cautiously recommend a change in the American attitude toward the Bolsheviks. As he cabled to Lansing on January 2, "Surely our interest is to prevent separate peace. . . . might consider it advisable to commit myself to recommend assistance to de facto government on condition that negotiations absolutely terminate. . . ."[131] Francis went even further in a "standby" cable which he drew up for Robins' discussions with Trotsky, promising that "if the Russian armies now under command of the peoples' commissaires commence and seriously conduct hostilities against the forces of Germany and her allies, I will recommend to my government the formal recognition of the *de facto* government of the peoples' commissaires."[132]

In a second draft standby cable, Francis also promised economic assistance, under the same conditions.[133] Francis recounted all of this in a long letter to Lansing on the same day, indicating his own excitement and optimism about the breakdown of Russian-German talks and his standby promises.[134]

At the same time, William B. Thompson and Thomas W. Lamont had arrived in Washington, fresh from their encouraging talks in Britain, including Thompson's long meeting with David Lloyd George. Thompson made a num-

ber of efforts, both directly and through other peoples, to see President
Wilson, in order to make his recommendation that the United States cooperate with the Bolsheviks against Germany, but he was never able to do so.
Nevertheless, his numerous meetings with others and the news of his recommendations added to the buildup of pressure within the administration to
develop unofficial relations. Thompson first saw George Creel, who was certain that the President would want to see Thompson. Creel told Thompson
that he fully supported the essence of the recommendations Thompson had
given Lloyd George. Creel returned from his meeting with Wilson crestfallen,
reporting that Wilson did not want to meet Thompson because since he had
spent a million dollars of his own money in Russia, he "did not care to meet
that kind of man."[135]

Thompson and Lamont were not deterred by the President's unresponsive-
ness. They met with Colonel House, Navy Secretary Josephus Daniels, Secretary of War Newton Baker, Supreme Court Justice Louis Brandeis, Herbert
Hoover, Bernard Baruch, State Department Counselor Frank Polk, and finally, Secretary of State Robert Lansing. Everywhere they urged the development of a constructive policy toward the Bolsheviks, the appointment of unofficial but high-level envoys, and the adoption of a strategy designed to deny
Russian assets to Germany.[136] Thompson also met with a number of United
States senators and gave speeches and met with the press. His views received a
very wide hearing and major publicity, with articles in the *New York World,* the
*Wall Street Journal,* the *New York Times,* and the *New Republic.*[137]

The flurry of ideas surrounding the latest events in Russia, the communications from Bullard, Sisson, and Robins, and especially Thompson's activated
connections promoted a climate in which Wilson himself had to entertain
Thompson's suggestions, despite the President's personal disdain for the magnate. On New Year's Day, 1918, Wilson, newly aware of the British move to
deputize Lockhart as their official contact with the Bolsheviks, commented on
this development with approval to Lansing, and asked him what was the
"most feasible and least objectionable way . . . in which we could establish
similar unofficial relations with the Bolsheviki."[138]

Lansing immediately advised against it, persuading the President to maintain the status quo, but urged him to make an appeal to the Russian people in
his upcoming speech to Congress on U.S. war aims.[139] Other voices were
urging a similar emphasis, including House, Sisson, and Foreign Secretary
Balfour. Sisson, in a long cable to Creel on January 3, urged, "If President will
restate anti-imperialistic war aims and democratic peace requisites of American thousand words or less. . . . I can get it fed into Germany in great quantities in German translation and can utilize Russian version potently in army
and everywhere. . . ."[140] Francis, Robins, and Bullard all could point to similar suggestions they had made in the days and weeks leading up to the Fourteen Points speech.[141]

Responding to the unified wisdom of his advisors House and Lansing,
Wilson decided to include a statement about Russia in his Fourteen Points

speech to Congress on January 8. House saw the reference both as a response to Trotsky's continual appeals to the Allies to join in general peace negotiations and as a way of responding to those voices urging Wilson to show his support for Russia.[142] While it was impossible to respond directly to Trotsky's appeal, Wilson was willing to use the public arena to communicate with the Bolsheviks concerning American hopes for Russia. Those who thought they discerned a willingness in Wilson to begin to deal with the Bolsheviks seized upon Point Six:

> The evacuation of all Russian territory and such a settlement of all questions affecting Russia as will secure the best and freest cooperation of the other nations of the world in obtaining for her an unhampered and unembarrassed opportunity for the independent determination of her own political development and national policy and assure her of a sincere welcome into the society of free nations under institutions of her own choosing; and, more than a welcome, assistance also of every kind that she may need and may herself desire. The treatment accorded Russia by her sister nations in the months to come will be the acid test of their good will, of their comprehension of her needs as distinguished from their own interests, and of their intelligent and unselfish sympathy.[143]

When he spoke of receiving Russia into the family of nations under "institutions of her own choosing" and called for the evacuation from Russian territory of all foreign troops, this can be interpreted as his implicit acknowledgement of the existence of a Russian government with the Bolsheviks in power. In addition, Wilson made specific references elsewhere in his speech to the negotiations at Brest Litovsk, and characterized the Russian representatives there as legitimate spokesmen for the Russian people.[144] These references accorded at least an inherent legitimacy to the Bolshevik government *for the moment,* and at least a stage in Russia's development of "institutions of her own choosing."

But the speech can also be interpreted as an appeal to the Russian people over the heads of their government, and a reaffirmation of Wilson's belief in and commitment to a "democratic Russia." Wilson's speech, and its emphasis on Russia, served many purposes by its deliberate ambiguity and availability for sympathetic interpretation from diverse political quarters. By this device, the President could remain the helmsman without committing himself to a particular course.

Wilson's speech was widely hailed by the entire liberal community, both those who wanted closer contacts with the Bolsheviks and those who were adamantly anti-Bolshevik. The latter included Russian Provisional Government Ambassador Bakhmetev, still a close adviser to the State Department and Colonel House on Russian policy.[145]

In Petrograd, the speech arrived on the wires on January 10. Robins and Sisson immediately saw it as a golden opportunity to solidify relationships with the Bolsheviks. Gumberg got a meeting for both of them with Lenin, and they sought to follow up on Sisson's promise to Creel to get the speech distributed all over Russia and into the German lines via the Russian troops at the front.[146]

Their January 11 meeting with Lenin may very well mark the high point of Soviet-American cooperation between 1917 and 1920. It was the first time either Sisson or Robins had met Lenin. They brought a full Russian text of the Wilson speech in with them, and, as Sisson said, "it did not take one minute to convince him that the full message should go to Trotsky [at Brest Litovsk] by direct wire. He grabbed the copy and sprinted for the telegraph office himself."[147] Lenin saw the significance of the speech for the Bolsheviks as well as for the world, and agreed immediately to Sisson's requests for wide distribution through Bolshevik channels to the army and into German lines, for which he suggested that they see Radek. Sisson quoted Lenin as considering Wilson's statements "a great step ahead toward the peace of the world," and quibbled with it only in one of its weakest sections, which was, in Sisson's opinion, the passage concerning colonialism.[148] Lenin saw the possibility of converting the abstractions of Wilson's speech into concrete policy benefiting the Soviet government. He challenged Sisson and Robins to urge their government to take the next step at this pivotal point. Lenin asked three questions for which he demanded answers from the United States: When will it be implemented? When will the United States begin negotiations? When will Wilson recognize the Soviet government?[149]

Sisson and Robins met with Radek the next day to make arrangements for sending thousands of copies of the speech in German and Russian through Russian lines into Germany.[150] The two Americans then took the speech to the major dailies to see if they would print it. *Pravda* agreed only to print excerpts, and editorialized impugning Wilson's sincerity. But *Izvestia* not only printed it in full, but in Sisson's words, "allowed us to black face the passages we desired—all clauses relating to Russia—and printed a comment that this was sincerely meant—the recognition of the idealism of the Soviets."[151] Other papers, even the anti-Bolshevik ones, also printed excerpts, although those opposed to the Soviets usually left out favorable Wilson comments about the Russian government. The *Bulletin of the Soviets* printed the entire speech and editorialized very positively, claiming a "moral victory of the peace policy of the Council of the Commissaries of the people . . . the speech of Wilson is a conscientious estimate of the activity of the Soviet government. . . . See how friendly a tone the President of the North American Republic speaks before the whole world of the actions of the Russian Workmen and Peasants' Government. . . ."[152]

The Americans also plastered Petrograd with handbills reprinting the speech in Russian in its entirety. One of them is found in the Francis Papers, with a note from embassy aide Taylor to counselor Wright, "Here is a copy of the President's speech. We are putting all our effort these 2 or 3 days in getting 500,000 of it out and effectively placed."[153]

The January 11 Lenin meeting with Robins and Sisson was highly significant for yet another reason. It cast a different light on the Soviet leader, which changed the interaction between Sisson and Robins. The two men went away from the meeting with profoundly different evaluations of the character and motivation of Lenin. Both were impressed with his decisiveness and realism. But an important difference emerged. Robins' estimation of Lenin rose, which led him toward a close cooperation with him comparable to his relationship with Trotsky. On the other hand, Sisson went away from the meeting convinced that Lenin was devious and calculating. His distrust grew. Sisson gave an example of why. When commenting on Wilson's kind words for the Russian government, Lenin exclaimed, "Yet I have been called a German spy." To Robins, it meant nothing. Sisson took it as sinister. This talk, which began a closer Robins-Lenin rapport, marked the beginning of Robins' and Sisson's falling out. It also dates the point of an intensification of Sisson's obsessive efforts to prove Lenin was in fact a German spy.[154]

Robins followed up the triumph of the Fourteen Points distribution with another solid accomplishment. He and Gumberg were instrumental in arranging a visit to Lenin both for Ambassador Francis himself and for the entire Allied diplomatic corps. This meeting could not have occurred without the newly established relationship between Lenin and Robins. Gumberg and Robins requested a meeting with Lenin to plead for the release of the Rumanian Ambassador Constantine Diamandi, seized by the Bolsheviks for anti-Soviet activities of Rumanian soldiers on the Russian-Rumanian frontier. The Rumanians had been harassing, disarming, and in some cases killing Russian troops and Bolshevik agitators engaged in propaganda work among the Rumanians.[155]

The consequence of Robins' new status with Lenin was to provide the only direct contact between Francis and Lenin. Ambassador Francis long refused to have anything directly to do with the Bolsheviks himself, remarking on more than one occasion that he "never would talk to a damned Bolshevik."[156] But the outrage to one of the ambassadorial corps was too much even for Francis' scruples, and as the dean of the corps, he agreed with Robins that he would lead the delegation. Lenin confirmed the appointment with a note to Francis, the only known direct communication between the two.[157]

Lenin received the American, French, Belgian, Chinese, Italian, and Serbian ambassadors politely, listened to their protests in silence, then responded by pointing to the extremely difficult situation Russian troops found themselves in.[158] The Serbian ambassador, Spalakovitch, could not contain his venom, and unleashed a torrent of abusive words at Lenin at one point, saying, "You snake, I grind you under my heel." Someone tried to stop the tirade, but Lenin only responded evenly, "Let him speak; at least he's saying what he thinks."[159] According to Sisson, Francis emerged from the meeting temporarily impressed, calling Lenin "an agreeable, friendly person."[160]

Lenin agreed to consider the ambassadors' complaint and left the distinct impression with Gumberg that Diamandi would be released were the Allies willing to pressure the Rumanians.[161] Following the visit, Diamandi was released, and General Judson encouraged the Rumanians to decrease their harassment of Russian troops.[162]

This crisis solidified Raymond Robins' position as the *de facto* American representative to the Bolsheviks. Now both his relationships with Trotsky and Lenin were grounded in mutual respect. Soon afterward he was given the private telephone numbers of Lenin, Trotsky, Chicherin, Bonch-Bruevich, Dzerzhinzky, and the Peter and Paul Fortress for his and Ambassador Francis' private use.[163]

Robins' perceptions of Trotsky and Lenin at this time appear in retrospect quite accurate. He recognized in Trotsky a fellow skilled speaker, but noted that he was "a sort of prima dona, mercurial, passionate, moody, the 'spoilt darling' of the Russian proletariat."[164] Yet Robins also recognized Trotsky's power, especially his ability to move people to action, and to manipulate situations in diplomacy. Most important to Robins was always Trotsky's ability to get things accomplished, which particularly impressed him in his rebuilding of the Red Army in the spring and summer of 1918.[165] Arthur Bullard commented on Trotsky and the Trotsky-Robins relationship in the following terms: "On the whole he seems fairly well disposed towards America and has a real personal regard for Col. Robins, in whom he recognizes a strong, fearless, honest man."[166]

Robins' view of Lenin, in contrast, portrayed him as

> heavy-set, deliberate, always cool . . . writer, thinker much more than orator . . . far-seeing and patient-spirited, head and shoulders above Trotsky in fundamental qualities, he is the first personality in Russian public life. . . . at all times he has presented the same steadfast, patient, utterly courageous, fanatical and confident character.[167]

Although Sisson later tried to show that the Bolsheviks had contempt for Robins and were simply using him, Bullard and other less-prejudiced observers disagree.[168] The expressions from both Lenin and Trotsky show a great deal of respect for Robins and range from private Trotsky notes of December all the way to Lenin's respectful note of May.[169] Even such an observer as Kalpashnikov, with his genuine disdain for Robins, admitted that the Bolsheviks respected the Red Cross leader.[170] After their initial meeting, Robins soon nurtured a relationship with Lenin that rivaled the one he had with Trotsky. When Robins and Gumberg had to leave their headquarters at the Savoy Hotel in Moscow in early April 1918 when it was closed, the Bolsheviks gave the Red Cross "a big old mansion that had belonged to a sugar magnate."[171] "Robins represents the liberal bourgeoisie of America," said Lenin to socialist Albert Rhys Williams before Robins left Russia. And it was for this reason that Lenin wanted to do business with him.[172]

## Struggle Against Brest Litovsk

Despite the dissolution of the Constituent Assembly by the Bolsheviks on January 18, Robins' relations with Lenin and Trotsky continued to improve throughout late January and February. The negative impact of this Bolshevik action was felt more in the United States, and in the months to come, rather than on the spot at the time. American attitudes in Petrograd at the time were relatively unaffected. Most observers commented, as did Robins, on the mild reaction of the Russian people and the strengthening of the government's authority.[173] During the period from mid-January through the ratification of the Brest Litovsk treaty in early March, Robins estimated that he saw Trotsky or Lenin three times a week, on the average. Topics of conversation ranged from milk deliveries or the danger of anarchists, to American war aims and the negotiations with Germany. Robins kept Ambassador Francis closely informed about these visits, as he had promised following the Ambassador's abrogation of the order forbidding further contact.[174] Robins was acutely aware of the importance of his role, and of his temporarily high standing with Francis and Smolny. He resolved to push his agenda hard while his influence lasted, since it might dissipate at any time. As he wrote to Margaret on January 21, "at last all have come to agree more or less with my point of view. It is, however, very late in the day."[175]

Robins struck while the iron was hot. For the first and only time he focused his efforts on a recommendation to his government for "prompt recognition of Bolshevik authority." In a January 23 memorandum to American Red Cross chief Henry Davison, Robins argued that such recognition was the only way to deter Trotsky and Lenin from a settlement with Germany.[176] Partly he was prompted by Trotsky's warnings. Before he returned to Brest Litovsk to resume interrupted negotiations on January 21, Trotsky had hinted broadly to Robins that some American recognition or aid was essential to strengthen his hand with Lenin.[177]

This Trotsky push was augmented by new requests for reciprocity in the way of passports for couriers, a Bolshevik demand Britain agreed to. It regularized the status of newly appointed envoy Bruce Lockhart and, reciprocally, the Soviet envoy in Britain, Maksim Litvinov. However, Ambassador Francis and the State Department refused. They did not ask the Bolsheviks for passports for couriers, and did not want a formal agreement on reciprocity. Instead, they incongruously demanded to be treated with all diplomatic courtesies themselves, yet they extended none.[178]

As further inducement for a last-minute settlement with the Americans, Trotsky held out the possibility that the Bolsheviks would not repudiate the Tsarist and Provisional Government's state debt. Trotsky intimated that the Bolsheviks would be willing to do this in exchange for recognition and credits.[179] Despite a more than two-week delay, from January 16 to February 3, which Raymond Robins was convinced was solely for the purpose of giving the United States a chance to respond, the decree repudiating Russia's debts was promulgated on February 3 and published widely on February 8.[180] The American government was recalcitrant at the very moment its opportunity to influence events could have been critical.

Robins' strong cable of January 23 advocating recognition was preceded by similar recommendations from many others. When it was recommended again by two different sources, U.S. chargé d'affairs Grant-Smith and president of

Harvard Charles Eliot in mid-January, Wilson pressed Lansing, noting in respect to the Grant-Smith proposal that the United States open up *de facto* relations as a way of combatting German influence, "this particular suggestion seems to me to have something in it worth considering."[181] Lansing remained obdurate, remarking to Polk, in regards to this suggestion, "I do not think WE should be the ones to open intercourse with the Lenin crowd. . . . If France or England wish to do this let them propose it."[182]

At this same time, Wilson's inclination received strong support from another quarter. Senator Robert Owen, populist Democrat from Oklahoma, member of the Democratic National Committee, and sometime Wilson supporter, wrote a cogent memorandum to Wilson and Lansing calculated to appeal to Wilson as a progressive reformer and to his desire to do something positive to help the people of Russia. Owen proposed opening up informal relations with the Bolsheviks and, in conjunction with such a move, dispatching food supplies to relieve the suffering caused by the Allied blockade of Germany, increasing the number of people in the consular service to take full advantage of commercial and relief opportunities, and establishing a regular courier service to keep closely in touch with fast-breaking events on all fronts in Russia.[183] Wilson responded very positively, and immediately wrote a note to Lansing asking him to take the suggestions seriously.[184]

Wilson's note was this time answered by Basil Miles, who responded with a memorandum opposing *de facto* recognition but agreeing that some sort of direct contact needed to be established with the Bolsheviks, and agreeing with all of the other points in Owen's memorandum.[185] Wilson apparently thought his concern had been taken care of when he dropped another note to Lansing on February 4, remarking, "As I understand it, our official representative in Petrograd is keeping in touch with the Bolshevik leaders informally. Am I not right?"[186] He was right, of course, in terms of the actual reality of the situation on the spot. He was not at the time right about State Department policy, which still officially remained the prohibition of all contacts with the Bolsheviks.

Lansing and Miles scrambled, with Miles writing a particularly obfuscating reply trying to draw a distinction between Raymond Robins' serving as a channel of information, and opening up presumably two-way communication. At the very time the State Department was responding to Wilson's inquiry, it received yet another cable from Francis in Petrograd asking for an exception to the policy of no-contact for Robins to visit Trotsky. Finally, Lansing succumbed to the pressure and authorized limited contact to be carried out on Francis' behalf, remaining clear that this was to fall far short of a working relationship. Lansing wrote Francis that the "Department approves your course and desires you gradually to keep in somewhat closer and informal touch with Bolshevik authorities using such channels as will avoid any official recognition. . . . Department's previous instructions are modified to this extent."[187]

While the State Department responded to the pressure for informal relations by only grudgingly accepting the reality of Robins' contacts with the Bolsheviks on behalf of Francis, similar recommendations to Colonel House stimulated the only serious consideration of American recognition of the Bolshevik government. Even Ambassador Francis, under pressure from Robins and Bullard, mulled over the idea in cables to Washington, saying he was "inclined to recommend simultaneous" recognition of the Bolshevik government and other non-Bolshevik forces on the Russian periphery.[188] Arthur Bullard, while not quite recommending formal recognition in a long letter to House, believing that *de facto* relations would suffice, did point out that some of the confusion over American policy would be dispelled with a recognition decision, and would put the pressure on the Bolsheviks with regard to Germany. In any case, he believed, the United States should make a clear statement one way or the other.[189] William C. Bullitt also recommended *de facto* recognition to House to two memoranda in early February.[190]

House followed up Bullard's and Bullitt's suggestions immediately. In a conversation with British agent William Wiseman on February 12, he confided that he and President Wilson had about come to the conclusion that the United States should recognize the Bolsheviks as a way of putting double pressure on Germany. Not only would it potentially move the Bolsheviks away from a final peace at Brest Litovsk, but it might also add needed encouragement to opposition forces in Germany and Austria.[191] But Balfour and Wiseman discouraged House in this course, and the idea was summarily dropped by February 27.[192]

Before Wilson's and Lansing's rejection of *de facto* relations, Robins and Gumberg used their influence and access at Smolny in two incidents in the latter days of January. During Trotsky's absence from Smolny at Brest Litovsk, Ivan Zalkind, a rather hard-line Bolshevik who showed no particular sympathy for the Americans nor had any particular liking for Robins or Gumberg, was acting Foreign Commissar. On January 30, Zalkind transmitted to the American Embassy a resolution passed earlier by a group of Petrograd anarchists, calling for the release of American labor agitators Mooney and Berkman, and threatening a demonstration at the American Embassy that very night. Francis and Robins were outraged, and Robins sent Gumberg immediately to Lenin to demand an apology from Zalkind and ask him to stop the planned demonstration. When no apology was forthcoming, even though the Bolsheviks said they would send guards to the Embassy, Robins went back with Gumberg to Lenin to again ask for an apology. Lenin asked him if it would suffice if he sent Zalkind to Switzerland.

Lenin got mileage out of his gratuitous offer. Zalkind's own memoirs and the records of the Bolshevik Central Executive Committee make it clear that the decision to reassign Zalkind to Switzerland for purposes of international political agitation had been made earlier. Only Georgi Chicherin's delayed return from England prevented its being carried out. But the effect it achieved was to convince Robins and Francis that their intervention had been decisive. The anarchist demonstration did not materialize, and Zalkind was sent to Switzerland.[193]

Later in February, Robins had a more direct impact on the fortunes of the anarchist movement. The anarchists remained strong, despite their defiance of the Bolsheviks and their constant harassment of the Allied diplomatic community. The Red Cross Rolls Royce was comandeered by a group of anarchists who forced Robins and Gumberg into the street. Robins went immediately to Smolny and demanded of Bonch-Bruevich, the Secretary of Sovnarkom (the Council of People's Commissars) that the car be returned immediately as a way of proving Bolshevik strength against the anarchists. Bonch-Bruevich sent Robins to see Dzerzhinsky at the Cheka, who promised him that something would be done in a few days. Subsequently, Dzerzhinsky coordinated massive raids on all the anarchist centers in Petrograd and returned Robins' car to him "unscratched." Robins was convinced that the timing of the raids was motivated at least in part by a desire to maintain friendly relations with him and keep open the possibility of aid from the Allies.[194]

Finally, Alexander Gumberg used his personal access to Lenin and his powers of persuasion to derail John Reed's appointment as Soviet Consul to New York.[195] Although both Robins and Sisson later claimed credit for this effort, the Gumberg papers show that Lenin's decision resulted from Gumberg's conviction that such an appointment could never be accepted by the United States and would only further set back the possibility of any recognition.[196] Reed and Robins had been close, although they disagreed, and Gumberg may well have thought he needed to act on his own.[197] Gumberg laid before Lenin a copy of Reed's "Skeleton Report" concerning his discussions of the possibilities of Soviet-American economic relations with Lunacharsky, Bonch-Bruevich, and others, in which he went as far as to claim that "a restricted capitalist state" could be created within the bounds of socialist Russia. While Lenin himself came close to advocating something like this a few years later, this breach of government confidences and speculation was too much for Lenin. He canceled Reed's appointment on the spot.[198]

On the first of February, Robins made his final break with Edgar G. Sisson. Sisson and Robins had first begun distancing themselves subsequent to their January 11 meeting with Lenin. At a long meeting of February 7, the break was completed. At this meeting they discussed at length the so-called Sisson Documents alleging a German-Bolshevik conspiracy. Certain of these documents had been rumored, and copies even passed from hand to hand in Petrograd for several months. Robins had come into possession of a rather substantial set in late January. He had these translated, and he studied them extensively, coming to the conclusion that they were forgeries. He immediately confronted Sisson with his doubts.[199] Sisson was not convinced, and neither was Ambassador Francis. Beginning in early February, both Sisson and Francis acted publicly and privately on the assumption that the documents were genuine. They branded Lenin and Trotsky as German agents who could not be trusted.[200] Arthur Bullard sided with Robins and wrote a long report to Colonel House confiding his doubts about the authenticity of the documents. Bullard's analysis proved much more accurate than Sisson's report, later published by the United States government.[201]

## Robins and Lockhart

Robins replaced his former close working relationship with Sisson with an even closer bond with R. H. Bruce Lockhart, the British envoy who arrived in Petrograd on January 30. The two were immediately compatible and began to cooperate in a sustained effort in February, March, and April to prevent the completion and ratification of the Brest Litovsk treaty. Both Robins and Lockhart tried to persuade their governments to promise aid and cooperation to the Bolsheviks. The two also worked to deny Allied and Russian assets to the Germans. Lockhart's initial impressions of Robins are worth recording:

> With his black hair and his aquiline features, he has a most striking appearance. He was an Indian chief with a Bible for his tomahawk. . . . Lenin had captured his imagination . . . of all foreigners Robins was the only man whom Lenin was always willing to see and who ever succeeded in imposing his own personality on the unemotional Bolshevik leader. . . . I liked Robins. For the next four months we were to be in daily and almost hourly contact.[202]

Robins was equally struck by Lockhart, and claimed they breakfasted together daily from the time of their first meeting until Robins' departure. Robins noted their numerous meetings in his diary.[203]

Since the efforts at military cooperation and aid have already been detailed in Chapter 3, this discussion will confine itself to Robins' and Lockhart's working relationship and the highlights of their cooperation in the pre–Brest Litovsk period. Robins immediately gave Lockhart his analysis of the situation and his conviction that resistance to Germany could still be developed by the Bolsheviks. Lockhart agreed, and urged on his government the development of a "policy of expediency" with respect to the Bolsheviks, in which he advocated strongly making an "agreement of calculation [with Trotsky] and not of love." Lockhart further noted that "cooperation is only possible if we humour him a little and avoid as far as possible all points of dispute."[204] Lockhart was joined in his assessment by Edward Birse, his commercial attaché, who reported that "Mr. Lockhart's presence in Russia is a great asset" and that he was doing "a great job."[205]

Lockhart drew in his diary excellent verbal portraits of both Trotsky and Chicherin. He also recorded receiving from Lenin a most candid assessment of the possibilities of Bolshevik-Allied cooperation. Lenin told Lockhart that he had no intention of being made a "cat's paw for the Allies." Although he was willing to risk cooperation for limited aims, Lenin did not believe that either the American or British government was equally willing.[206]

## Early Economic Discussions

Serious economic discussions between the Bolsheviks and the Americans began in February. Both Robins and Trotsky had touched on economic issues from the beginning of their dialogue, and one of W. B. Thompson's major recommendations had been the establishment of an economic commission.[207] The two Bolshevik leaders had often mentioned the desirability of American economic assistance. But the opening of meaningful discussions came in mid-February.[208]

The first of these meetings was a long discussion on February 13 between American commerical attaché William C. Huntington and Jacob Bronski, head of the Soviet Department of Trade for the ministries of Trade and Industry and Labor. The meeting was arranged by Alexander Gumberg, who accompanied Huntington.[209]

Huntington was commercial attaché in Petrograd and Moscow from mid-1916 to mid-1918 and was then assigned to Siberia. On his return to the United States in late 1918, he became head of the Russian desk at the Commerce Department. Huntington played an important role in early economic discussions with the Bolsheviks in 1918. He had expressed a willingness to talk with the Bolsheviks soon after the revolution, convinced that only such an approach would deny their assets to Germany.[210]

Huntington also served as an important link with Samuel N. Harper of the University of Chicago.[211] Several of the most important of Huntington's policy memoranda found their way to Wilson via Harper and Charles R. Crane. Huntington's strong plea for a comprehensive American plan for economic penetration of Russia, both Bolshevik and non-Bolshevik, was taken very seriously in Washington.[212]

At their first meeting, Huntington and Bronski reviewed the current state of Russian-American trade. Huntington noted that the United States still might sell basic goods to Russia, as long as payment could be arranged. He also indicated a range of Russian raw materials the United States desired. Bronski responded by stressing the Soviets' desire to trade with the United States, "but our difficulty is in arranging the credit for the interval which must elapse between the receipt of the American manufactured goods and the delivery to you of Russian raw materials."[213] Nevertheless, Bronski indicated that the Soviet government was most desirous of seeing an agreement between the United States and the Council of the Commissaries of the People, particularly concerning shoes and agricultural equipment, which were in critically short supply. Bronski brought up the availability of platinum, which the United States desired, and said that it was available for the United States to purchase at any time. He then asked for American cooperation in fixing the railroads and in assessing, enumerating, and salvaging massive amounts of goods still remaining at the ports of Vladivostok and Archangel.

Huntington promised to explore this with the U.S. Railway Commission and to take up up the other points with the American Ambassador. Huntington concluded his assessment of the meeting with his impressions of Bronski: "honest, sincere, and anti-German . . . very intelligent but quite inexperienced. . . . He is the one of the best of their men." Huntington remained dubious, however, that the Bolshevik government would last or that agreement at the top levels of the government could be achieved concerning the points proposed.[214]

Bronski apparently had other conversations with American representatives, although only cryptic references to them appear in Robins' diary and in Sisson's log. On February 10, Sisson noted "Bronski's plan for raw product monopoly to the United States."[215]

Only a few days after Huntington's conversation with Bronski on February 15, he and Henry Emery of the U.S. Railway Commission had an extensive conversation with Yuri Larin, the Bolshevik Commissar in charge of railroads. At this meeting, of which only fragmentary evidence is available in American archives, the Soviet government requested that an American expert from the U.S. Railway Commission come into the Soviet office and essentially reorganize the Russian railways and take charge of transportation throughout the country, at least until it was organized according to American standards.[216] Indications of such Soviet interest in American help for the railroads had been floated at least since Judson's meeting with Trotsky of December 1.[217] It would remain a constant subject of American-Soviet conversation until departure of American personnel in the fall of 1918.[218]

Soviet authors P. Sh. Ganelin and V. A. Shishkin, citing Soviet archives, also discuss a meeting held on February 15 between Huntington and Larin, which may or may not be the same meeting as the one discussed above. In this meeting, however, there is an emphasis on trade discussions as a priority over railroads. Larin, according to these accounts, offered to put Soviet-American trade on "a new basis" by cutting through the credit and cash tangle by proposing a type of barter system where needed goods and resources would be exchanged directly. The difference, if any, would be made up for by exclusive rights to exploit certain raw materials. This perhaps is the same reference to "raw products monopoly" earlier mentioned by Huntington.[219]

That the Bolsheviks considered these conversations crucial can be seen by the numerous references to plans for economic relations with the United States in published Soviet materials from the February 1918 period. At the time of the Bolshevik debates over accepting aid from the "Anglo-French imperialist bandits" on February 22, the protocols of the Central Committee show a spirited disagreement between Bukharin and Lenin on the desirability of improving economic relations with either or both of the imperialist coalitions. The United States was mentioned specifically, and Commissioner Larin, siding with Lenin, expressed his own belief that some kind of economic deal with the United States could be struck.[220] Larin expanded on these thoughts in published recollections later in 1918, comparing the possibility of economic relations with the United States to what had already begun to happen with Finland, "on a strictly reciprocal basis."[221]

Toward the end of February, the Bolsheviks were under tremendous pressure from Germany. Even after their capitulation to the German ultimatum, the Soviets were threatened by a continued German troop advance toward the capital. Robins encouraged Ambassador Francis to leave Petrograd, but not to abandon Russia. Francis' thinking was along the same lines. Not wishing to follow the Bolshevik leaders to Moscow, but nonetheless not desiring to leave, Francis decided to settle in Vologda, a provincial railway juncture, midway between Archangel, Petrograd, and Moscow. Francis and Robins each took credit for the decision on Vologda for himself. But there is no doubt that Robins was responsible for all of the arrangements, including personal intervention to remove a last-minute hitch in permission for the train to leave Petrograd.

It was to prove the beginning of the most ambitious diplomacy of his stay in Russia. Robins used his own personal Red Cross car to travel the rails over the next two months in a last-ditch attempt to keep the Allies and the Bolsheviks working together against German interests.[222]

## Robins' Rail Diplomacy, March–April 1918

Robins traveled the rails over these two months with the full support and knowledge both of Ambassador Francis and the Soviet government. He carried with him a pass from Ambassador Francis, "[commending] him to the courtesies of all to whom this Certificate may be presented" and requesting "that he be permitted to enter Moscow and any other city in Russia he may desire to visit."[223] But perhaps more important for his unhampered travel, he carried an order from Bonch-Bruevich that permitted him to attach his car to any train in any direction.[224] Francis' support for such a mission was indicated in his letter to Summers at the time, in which he commented, "You probably know my estimate of the bolshevik regime but I realize that the only power in Russia which can offer any resistance whatever to the German advance is the Soviet Government. When my house is on fire I don't ask the quality of the water used to extinguish the flame."[225]

Robins' first efforts centered around the famous Lenin-Trotsky document he procured in an eleventh-hour attempt to prevent the ratification of the Brest Litovsk treaty at the All-Russian Congress of Soviets on March 14. This document, handed to Robins by Trotsky after a meeting between the two on March 5, put in writing the conditions under which the Bolshevik leaders would advocate abrogation of the Brest Litovsk treaty and resumption of war against Germany. Essentially, it was an inquiry of the Allies, the United States in particular, concerning the nature and extent of aid that could be promised.[226]

It is important to note that Robins' effort was pursued jointly with R. H. Bruce Lockhart. London was sent a similar plea by Lockhart, and Lockhart's interview with Trotsky and Lenin was perhaps even more revealing than Robins'. Trotsky emphasized in this meeting that the Bolsheviks would fight if they were attacked, either by Germany or Japan, and he stressed the danger of Japanese intervention much more than he had in discussions with Robins. Moreover, Trotsky emphasized that the ratification of the Brest treaty was not the critical factor for the continuation of the war with Germany. Much more important in his mind was the development of an effective Bolshevik resistance. For that resistance, French, British, and American cooperation were actively sought.[227] British concern, however, remained a fighting front against Germany. The British claimed not to understand Trotsky's preoccupation with Japanese intervention. As Balfour wrote to Lockhart, "Why will [Trotsky] not also try a working agreement with the Japanese?"[228]

Communication of the Lenin-Trotsky questions to the American government in Washington was fraught with numerous delays and difficulties. At this point it is reasonable to suppose that the document did not arrive at the State Department before President Wilson dispatched his message to the Congress of Soviets on March 9, even though Secretary Lansing said later that this message constituted "sufficient answer" to the Soviet request for aid.[229] American Consul Tredwell in Petrograd detailed the problems of transmittal without Ambassador Francis' code, resorting finally to the military code and sending it to the War Department on March 6.[230] Ambassador Francis also cabled the State Department on March 9 about Robins' meeting with Trotsky, but without a copy of the Trotsky questions. This cable was passed to Wilson.[231] Lincoln Colcord, intimately involved in efforts to get a sympathetic message from Wilson to the Congress of Soviets, said later that no one he met with in the government, which included Lansing, Bullitt, Polk, and House, ever mentioned the Soviet request in the crucial hours during the composition of Wilson's message.[232]

Woodrow Wilson's open letter to the All-Russian Congress of Soviets meeting in Moscow on March 12 through 16, 1918, stirred tremendous interest both in Russia and in the United States. Colonel House recorded in his diary his own belief that Wilson intended it in part as a signal to the Soviet government that channels of communication between Washington and Moscow remained open.[233] Although it was addressed to "the Russian people," and stated regretfully that the United States was "unhappily not now in a position to render the direct and effective aid it would wish to render," the message "assured" the Russian people that "the whole heart of the people of the United States is with the people of Russia in the attempt to free themselves forever from autocratic government and become the masters of their own life."[234]

The Soviet Congress responded to the message, expressing "its gratitude to the American people, above all the laboring and exploited classes of the United States, for the sympathy expressed to the Russian people by President Wilson."[235] Although Ambassador Francis later reported that he knew that Zinoviev had been calling this reply "a slap in the face" of Wilson,[236] an editorial in *Izvestia* welcomed Wilson's message and found it a document of "extraordinary political importance," claiming increasing sympathy in the United States for the Soviet government. *Izvestia* noted, "With the United States we may have friction, encounters, struggle, but there can also be an agreement . . . we can come to an understanding with the United States."[237]

Ambassador Francis, in a letter to Consul General Summers, explained that Wilson's message "appeared to be favorably received by the great mass of the people in Russia," and he deemed the message "a help and not a hindrance in the present situation." Francis did note, however, the concern that he and others felt that the sending of the message to the Soviet Congress in some way recognized its existence, but he expressed the belief that such a message was not a prelude to such recognition, but rather a means of influencing the Russian people.[238] The British War Cabinet simply noted that Wilson's message "did on behalf of the United States exactly what Mr. Lockhart had urged the British Government to do."[239]

Brest Litovsk was overwhelmingly ratified by the Soviet Congress after a strong speech by Lenin concerning the Soviet people's need for peace. Raymond Robins failed to get a sufficiently positive response from the American government to Lenin's and Trotsky's questions about aid. Yet Wilson's message to the Congress kept the channels of communication open, and Robins did not cease his efforts on the rails from Moscow to Vologda to Petrograd.

Robins turned once again to concentrating his energies on building constructive relationships between the United States and the Bolsheviks. He did this in two areas: concrete military cooperation in the rebuilding of the Red Army, and a pattern of economic relations firm enough to serve as the basis of a long-term political relationship. The former failed to develop, in the face of Japanese intervention and the increasing likelihood of Britain's and the United States' joining in. Then Robins pursued the remaining issue vigorously, despite his eventual realization that he could no longer make progress in Russia, but must return to carry on the struggle in the United States.

In pursuing these twin objectives, Robins was plagued by the persistent obstacles of Japanese intervention and developing rumors of German-Bolshevik collusion. He enjoyed close collaboration with British envoy Lockhart almost to the end of his stay, and he maintained close communication, if not trust, with Ambassador Francis. Robins knew that his effectiveness depended on the tolerance, if not the active support, of his Ambassador. This led him to maintain deliberate contact, sending numerous direct cables in March and early April, keeping Francis fully informed of his discussions with the Bolsheviks, and responding promptly and efficiently to every request made of him.[240] Such communication and exchange was made possible by Lenin. Robins visited Lenin on March 13 and secured a permit for a direct wire from Moscow to Vologda. He carried on the bulk of the communication with Francis on this wire.[241] Close contact continued through the end of April, 1918. Even after Robins decided to leave in the face of imminent recall, Francis still asked him to convey messages to the Bolshevik government.[242]

Robins and Lockhart saw eye-to-eye on the need both to develop military and economic cooperation with the Bolsheviks and to forestall Japanese intervention. As Lockhart noted in his memoirs, "We succeeded in establishing a remarkably smooth cooperation. Almost to the bitter end we were in complete agreement regarding policy."[243]

At first, Lockhart thought that Robins was in the stronger position with his government, since Lockhart had to struggle to get the British Foreign Office to heed his increasingly urgent missives.[244] As time went on and the British Foreign Office became more positive, it was Lockhart who assumed the dominant role. Robins wrote to aide Allen Wardwell on April 3, "We are marking time here with the British policy now leading the play and it is our policy accepted by the British Foreign Office while we are still chasing shadows. . . ."[245]

By the end of April, Lockhart had convinced Balfour that the only chance for the British policy in Russia was to work with Trotsky, at least on a minimal level. As Balfour commented to the British ambassador to Washington, Lord Reading, regarding Trotsky, "we are obliged either to defy him, to work with him, or to do nothing. The first of these three alternatives is dangerous, and the last fatal, and we are therefore obliged to accept the second, whatever misgivings this may cause us."[246]

In fact, Robins' connection with Lockhart became the key to contact with Robins' own government. Robins was never sure how many of his recommendations ever went from Francis to Washington, and he began to rely on Lockhart's direct line to Balfour and Milner to relay recommendations via British agent William Wiseman to Colonel House. This soon became the major way that Robins' work and his recommendations were brought to the attention of the American government. Though cut off from the U.S. State Department, Robins got his point of view, strengthened by Lockhart's agreement, quickly to House.[247] Robins and Lockhart met daily for breakfast, coordinating information and strategy.[248]

The two enjoyed unprecedented access to the Bolshevik leaders during March and April of 1918. They had no difficulty getting appointments with Trotsky and Lenin, and they literally could walk in to see Foreign Commissar Chicherin and his key staff members Karakhan and Radek. They were even allowed to sit in on certain meetings of the Bolshevik Central Executive Committee and other supposedly private Bolshevik discussions.[249]

Lockhart saw clearly that the Bolsheviks were most amenable to an understanding with the Allies in March and April. They were worried about the continued pressure of Germany and the uncertainty of Allied intervention, but the question of Japanese intervention loomed as a huge obstacle to any agreement.[250] As Lockhart reflected later, "At one moment we would be reporting favourable progress with Trotsky. The next day we would be back to where we were before. The Japanese had landed troops at Vladivostok. Scowls from Trotsky. All privileges to the British stopped."[251]

Lockhart and Robins raised the issue of Japanese intervention with repeated urgency in their communications almost as soon as Lockhart arrived in early February. Both representatives constantly reiterated that any move by Japan might doom military and economic cooperation, and even their efforts to prevent the ratification of Brest Litovsk. The Bolsheviks were well aware of the debate about this possibility within Allied circles, and they were convinced that the Americans had grave doubts about the advisability of Japanese intervention. They put great stake in the ability of Robins and Lockhart to put pressure on the American and British governments to resist Japanese moves in the Far East, even informing their Siberian Soviet representatives in mid-

February of the critical need "to keep Americans informed regarding all attempts of the Japanese to get hold of our national property as well as all facts of Japanese provocation."[252]

The Bolsheviks were not mistaken regarding the pressure being exerted on the American government. President Wilson had been persuaded to write a note to the Japanese government on February 28. This note declined to participate in any intervention but left the distinct impression that the Japanese had the United States' blessing to intervene on their own.[253] The British so interpreted it, and informed Lockhart on March 6 that the Japanese might be "compelled to take action."[254] Colonel House, however, was appalled at the Wilson action. After receiving a strong complaint about it from William C. Bullitt, House pointed out to Wilson in the strongest terms how his note conflicted with all of his previous decisions to resist Allied interference in Russian affairs. It also endangered American interests in Far Eastern Russia. House persuaded Wilson to reverse himself with a note to American embassies on March 5, in which he reaffirmed the United States' opposition to any intervention in Siberia.[255] Wilson even told British ambassador Reading that one of his reasons for such a decision was a concern that any intervention "in opposition to the wishes of the Bolshevic [sic] authorities" would be absolutely counter to the American commitment to Russian democracy.[256]

Soviet concern remained intense. Trotsky and Lenin pressed the American government with inquiries relayed by Robins on March 5, asking pointedly, "what steps would the Allies take to prevent Japanese landing in Vladivostok?"[257] Trotsky stressed the same themes repeatedly in his long interview with Lockhart on March 12, warning that "if the Allies are to allow Japan to enter Siberia, the whole position is hopeless." Lockhart agreed with Trotsky about the critical importance of this matter, noting to Milner,

> My position here will be greatly weakened by [Japanese intervention]. At best the Bolsheviks will look upon me as an honest man whose opinion, however, carries no weight with his own government. At the worst, they will regard me as an agent of an anti-Socialist government who has been sent out to fool with promises of help while his Government prepares its plans for their destruction.[258]

Soviet concerns regarding Allied collusion in plans for intervention in Siberia were heightened by reports that Allied consuls in Vladivostok, including the American John Caldwell, were actively engaged in protest against Soviet institutions and the formation of a local Red Guard. The consuls were also reportedly openly conspiring against the Bolsheviks with anti-Soviet forces in the area. Chicherin in turn protested strongly, as did Trotsky, and Robins was forced to go to discuss the matter with Lenin, who was not convinced by Robins' explanations.[259]

The British War Department, furious at Wilson's March 5 reversal, was convinced that Lockhart and Robins were to blame for the final result—the refusal of the United States to countenance or support Japanese action in

Siberia. General Knox, in a long paper to the War Cabinet on March 18, charged directly, "it is believed that two individuals were largely responsible for the suicidal delay in Japanese intervention—the American 'Colonel' Robins and Mr. Lockhart."[260]

Robins and Lockhart continued to argue strongly against such intervention to their respective governments in the last days of March and the first of April, but to no avail.[261] On April 5, Japanese marines went ashore at Vladivostok. Now Lockhart and Robins received dire warnings of the severest consequences from Chicherin, who held them and their governments responsible for the Japanese action, believing that American consent had been given. Chicherin demanded of Robins "an immediate explanation of the attitude of your Government." Robins, in a long note to Ambassador Francis, warned that "we are now at most dangerous crisis in Russian situation," and urged that somehow the Japanese action be contained in order to prevent the loss of all American influence with the Bolshevik government. For the Soviet government believed, in Robins' words, "if Japanese advance, it means America has consented."[262]

Though Francis advised Robins that the "Soviet government [is] attaching undue weight to landing of Japanese," and urged him to reassure them that "there is no intention or desire on the part of any of Russia's allies to attach any of Russia's territory,"[263] even the limited nature of this landing and the lack of immediate follow-up of British or American troops failed to assuage Bolshevik fears. Lenin and Trotsky were still convinced that other Allied troops would soon follow. Robins' hopes for a far ranging military agreement with the Bolsheviks were dashed. As Robins wrote to Wardwell, "The general situation is extremely critical. . . . Refusal thus far by the Allied governments to disclaim responsibility for, or cooperation in, any hostile intervention in Siberia is rapidly crystallizing the situation adversely to American interests."[264]

Robins was practically in despair. On April 10, he had a long discussion with Chicherin and Karakhan, whom Robins found of no help, refusing to see his point about the need for continued cooperation and adamant in their outrage at Allied attitudes.[265] By the end of the month, the Bolsheviks expanded earlier charges of collusion by Allied consuls at Vladivostok into direct charges of a "conspiracy against the government of the Soviets in Siberia." For Robins, "these [were] dark days . . . conditions rotten."[266]

Robins' depression was deepened by his fears that Lockhart had begun to desert him. In mid-April, he repeatedly confided to his diary that Lockhart had begun to turn away from his previous commitment to try to reach an agreement with the Bolsheviks. By April 17, he noted in some despair, "All closing in now. Lockhart gets anti-twist from home."[267]

Robins and Lockhart also became the recipients of charges by Sisson, consul in Siberia David Macgowan, and even Ambassador Francis, that the Bolsheviks were German agents, evidenced by the ratification of Brest Litovsk.[268] One of Francis' persistent accusations, which he repeatedly quizzed Robins about, was that Austro-Hungarian prisoners being held in Russia, captured earlier in the war, were being organized and armed to join the new Bolshevik army.

When Robins raised the issue with Trotsky on March 19, Trotsky immediately requested that the United States appoint its own investigator whom Trotsky would give all facilities necessary to track down the truth of the rumors and make a report.[269]

Robins consulted with Lockhart, and they agreed to send Lockhart's military aide, Captain W. L. Hicks, and Robins' own aide, Captain William Webster. The two of them proceeded to Siberia, making numerous stops along the way, armed with documentation from Trotsky, Robins, and Lockhart. They filed a number of detailed reports, including a long summary of April 26, which showed conclusively the falsehood of the prisoner-arming reports, and also documented rather completely the increasing Soviet control of the railroad and of provincial areas such as Irkutsk.[270]

## Economic Discussions

Faced by increasingly wide obstacles, Robins still firmly persisted in trying to make progress in Soviet-American economic cooperation throughout March and April. Robins was convinced that long-range hope for Russian-American relations lay primarily in the economic sphere. He believed "that the best answer to Bolshevik Russia is economic cooperation, food, friendliness on the part of America."[271] Robins began his post–Brest Litovsk efforts with an inquiry to Francis on March 22, passing on a request from the Bolshevik government asking whether a Soviet economic commission would be received in the United States.[272] These efforts ended only with his departure to the United States on May 14, carrying a long proposal from Lenin for a full-range program for Soviet-American economic relations.[273] Robins felt so strongly about the importance of the economic program that he pressed Ambassador Francis to move to Moscow in mid-April: "Russian economic conditions force general reorganization internal economy under either German or American supervision and support. Largest economic and cultural enterprise remaining in world. Your position influence most powerful factor."[274]

In the intervening months, Robins also negotiated several concrete economic agreements with the Bolsheviks. He persuaded the Soviets to ask for, and the United States provisionally to grant, American advisors and engineers for the reorganization of their railroads. He also negotiated the United States' purchase of a large supply of Soviet platinum, and he persuaded Lenin to exempt the International Harvester Company, the Singer Sewing Machine Company, and the Westinghouse Brake Company from the provisions of the new Soviet decree nationalizing all industry. Robins' constant discussions with Lenin and other Bolshevik officials also stimulated a flurry of internal Bolshevik discussions of economic relations with the United States, which resulted in the Lenin-Robins plan, and bore fruit eventually in the mission of Ludwig C. A. K. Martens to the United States.

Trotsky's request for American railway experts already has been discussed in conjunction with military cooperation. There remain details, however, that show the economic importance of this request. Robins testified later that the Soviet request for assistance for the railways was not simply for technical assistance, but rather a proposal that the United States help reorganize the entire Russian transportation system:

> one half for transportation of wheat and meat from centers of surplus to centers of deficit in European Russia, the other half to be used for the evacuation of supplies, raw materials, and munitions from such areas as might be overrun by a German advance, and for the benefit of the Allies. According to this plan, it would serve both Russia's internal needs and the allies' war needs with Germany.[275]

Despite Ambassador Francis' statement that the "Soviet government has not specifically defined uses for railway men,"[276] there is evidence that Robins relayed such details to Francis. Francis' reluctance to cooperate with the Bolsheviks led him to delay his recommendations to the Railway Commission and the State Department. As a result, despite a formal request for six units in late March, Secretary Lansing forbade Stevens, then waiting in Japan, to send the units and test the possibility of such a cooperation.[277]

Robins was more successful in his intervention with the Bolsheviks on behalf of several American companies functioning in Soviet Russia. Among others, the International Harvester Company, the Singer Manufacturing Company, the J. M. Coates Company, the Westinghouse Brake Company, and the National City Bank all asked for Robins' assistance in their dealings with the Bolshevik government. Robins successfully persuaded Lenin at a meeting in late March to exempt International Harvester, Singer, and Westinghouse from Bolshevik provisions on nationalization of industry.[278] He also managed to get banking regulations relaxed to enable National City Bank to continue operations.[279]

The discussions and intervention on behalf of International Harvester continued throughout the spring. Following Robins' first intervention, International Harvester again contacted Robins, requesting that he smooth the way with both American and Soviet officials to enable $500,000 in U.S. parts to be imported to Russia for Harvester manufacturing. Although Robins was successful in his discussions with Bolshevik officials, American officials were noticeably more reticent. Samuel Harper and other Americans were contacted on Harvester's behalf, but it took until June to persuade the War Trade Board to issue the required licenses. The entire transaction fell through before completion when all American diplomatic contact terminated with intervention in July and August of 1918.[280]

Negotiations over the sale to the United States of a large quantity of the strategic metal platinum consumed a great deal of Robins' time and energy from mid-March until his departure. Trotsky approached Robins in the period before the ratification of Brest Litovsk when it appeared that German forces would occupy Petrograd and the Bolsheviks were making arrangements to move to Moscow. The platinum was in the possession of the Russian State

Bank and was quite a large quantity, something over 1,000 pounds. If it had fallen into German hands it could have made a major difference in the war.[281] Robins informed Francis about its availability and asked for permission to buy it.[282] Francis asked him to get details regarding quantity, price, and availability, requesting that it be delivered to Vladivostok.[283] Robins met with Soviet Trade Commissar Bronski on March 25 and obtained prices based on quotes in New York and London, with agreement about delivery and quantity.[284] Francis cabled for government authority for Stevens of the Railway Commission to spend the money and make the purchase, but the transaction was held up because of disagreement regarding method of payment and exchange.[285] Stevens finally completed the negotiations in Petrograd himself in mid-April, and the purchase was actually effected.[286]

By far the most wide-ranging and extensive discussions between Soviet and American representatives during March and April 1918, were those that centered around long-term economic relations between the two countries. They culminated in Lenin's extensive economic proposal, which he sent to the American government via Raymond Robins on his departure on May 14.[287] These discussions began even before Brest Litovsk, but they accelerated in intensity and seriousness during March and April. In addition to discussions between Robins and Lenin, there were conversations between Robins and Bronski, Robins and Trotsky, Huntington and Larin, American consul in Petrograd Roger Tredwell and Larin, and numerous discussions in various Bolshevik commissions and party bodies. All the discussions focussed on the nature and scope of desired American-Soviet trade, and the conditions and provisions necessary for it to be expanded. A specific request from the Soviet government to the United States to receive a Soviet economic trade commission in the United States to explore the dimensions of any economic agreement became the major request as early as March 22 and would remain the key request on the table until Robins' departure.[288]

The Soviet request for an economic commission was stimulated by two series of discussions, one between Consul Tredwell and Soviet Commissioner Larin on March 19, and the other an internal set of discussions in the Soviet Foreign Trade Commissariat the last two weeks of March. In his discussions with Tredwell, Larin claims to have reached an agreement in principle for the establishment of a new basis for trade relations with the United States, utilizing gold and goods as the basis for credit. On the strength of this assurance, the Foreign Trade Commissariat and Lenin agreed to forward the request for an economic commission to Robins on March 22.[289] The Soviet internal discussions regarding resumption of trade with the United States were not unknown to the Americans. *Nashe Vremya* of March 29 carried an article quoting "government sources" that so alarmed Consul General Summers that he brought it to Ambassador Francis' attention. According to the article, the Supreme Council of the National Economy had made the decision to resume trade, and it was based on an offer "from an American government official," apparently Tredwell or Robins. Summers was furious because he had never heard of the discussion, and neither had Francis.[290]

Francis also was apprised of an early-April discussion among representatives of the Commissariat of Agriculture, the Commissariat of Foreign Trade, the Moscow City Food Committee, and the Moscow Narodni Bank. According to the memorandum Francis received, the object of the April 4 meeting was "to exchange opinions regarding the question of trade with America." The Soviets decided that it was necessary to send a commission to America to explore in detail the various possibilities. The delegates were especially interested in importing agricultural machinery and implements.[291]

Robins urged the request on Ambassador Francis repeatedly throughout March and April, but received only vague responses. He held a long meeting with Lenin on April 3. The economic commission and the entire economic program with the United States was a major subject of their conversation.[292] The Japanese invasion of April 5 shifted the focus of discussions for several days, but by April 14, Robins was even more convinced that the economic plan was the only remaining option for Soviet-American cooperation. He had dinner with military attaché Riggs, Soviet general and assistant to Sovnarkom V. D. Bonch-Bruevich, and an unnamed Bolshevik engineer that evening. Their entire conversation centered around the economic plan.[293]

The next day Robins resumed advocating the economic program in communications with Francis and with Washington with increasing urgency, going as far as to warn, "unless such cooperation between governments, useful work ended May first."[294] On April 18, he noted in his diary, "plan of government for economic help American not in program." By April 20, he was almost despairing, pleading with Francis, "unless organized opposition planned, organized cooperation only alternative intelligent action. Micawber policy becoming daily more impossible. Government asks daily regarding railroad men, army instructors, economic commission, agricultural machinery, other technical experts and manufactures."[295]

By the end of April, Robins had become convinced that Francis would take no action and that the only way for such a broad-ranging economic plan to be considered would be for him (Robins) to return to the United States and argue for it. He held final conferences with Radek, Trotsky, and Lenin, and received endorsements from Ruggles and Riggs, before receiving the final plan from Lenin on May 14.[296] There is even indication in some sources, although not verified, that the Soviet government considered formally requesting the American government, through Robins, to ask the Red Cross to take over the entire food administration in Petrograd, and also to request that Robins "be appointed political advisor on economic questions from the government of the United States to the Soviet of People's Commissars."[297]

Lenin's plan for economic cooperation with the United States was developed in the Council of Export Trade in the Supreme Council of the National Economy.[298] It served as the basis for much of Raymond Robins' lobbying on his return to the United States. Robins accompanied Lenin's request to the United States for a Soviet economic commission with a request of his own that an American economic commission be appointed for immediate travel to

Soviet Russia, and empowered to negotiate and purchase all manner of required goods.[299]

## Robins Leaves Russia

Robins' decision to leave Russia was not made solely to advocate at home a change of American policy toward the Bolsheviks. At almost precisely the same time he made the decision, long-festering friction between himself and Consul General Maddin Summers came to a head. This dovetailed with the residual opposition to his efforts in the State Department, kept in check only because of Ambassador Francis' former support. As long before this as early February, President Wilson had written to Secretary Lansing, complaining about Robins:

> It is very annoying to have this man Robins, in whom I have no confidence whatever, acting as political adviser in Russia and sending his advice to private individuals. I wonder if you feel about it as I do and whether you would be willing to consult with Mr. Davison of the Red Cross with a view to having Robins reminded of his proper functions and their limitations?[300]

Robins and Summers had never seen eye-to-eye, but it was only upon the movement of the Soviet Government to Moscow that the friction escalated almost to the breaking point. Robins stayed in Moscow, Summers' own turf, and met with the Bolsheviks on a regular basis. Increasingly, the Soviet government treated Robins as their only channel to the U.S. government, even on what might normally be seen as consular matters, and Summers became more and more outspoken in his opposition. On March 25, he wrote to Francis, "I can assure you that any interference in any way here with my work will result in serious consequences," and by the next day Francis reported their open differences to Secretary Lansing.[301] A few days earlier, Robins and Summers had had a conference in an attempt to work out the basis of a better understanding, but both went away from the meeting convinced that working together was impossible.[302] Summers made his feelings known to Francis, and suggested that he was so frustrated, tired, and disgusted with Robins that he was considering requesting a State Department transfer. This possibility spurred Francis to a long series of memos, letters, and cables to Summers trying to explain the basis of his working relationship with Robins, and to urge Summers, in the strongest terms, not to request a transfer.[303] Summers by this time was convinced that Robins was practically a Bolshevik agent, and refused Francis' request that he use the direct line to Vologda that Robins had secured, warning Francis that he had "reason to believe that [Robins] had exceeded his authority in communicating to others confidential information furnished him."[304] Summers never produced any evidence of this charge, however.

Robins, meanwhile, had been confiding to his diary that his relationship with Summers had deteriorated and that he also sensed a distinct change in Francis' support for his position. As he wrote to his colleague Allen Wardwell on April 3, despite his daily correspondence with Francis, "Still I know that if he held me over a cliff and could afford to let go he would do so with a sigh of genuine relief."[305] Robins' concerns about the lack of an American response to a program of cooperation with the Soviets were now compounded by lack of support from Ambassador Francis. Two days later, Robins wrote to his Red Cross chief, Davison, for the first time openly asking to be recalled "if administration Red Cross here unsatisfactory."[306]

Summers escalated his concern in early April, noting to Francis that he was "getting rather sick of this dual situation and am anxious to put an end to it," and advising Francis that he was about to bring the entire situation to the notice of the State Department in Washington, because he "cannot for a moment consent to a purely unofficial person assuming the functions which the Department considers as pertaining to my office . . . [and I am] seriously embarrassed by the constant references in the press to Colonel Robins as the 'official representative of the United States at Moscow.' "[307]

Although Francis, in a handwritten note to both Summers and Robins, urged them to "make every effort to work harmoniously,"[308] Robins saw the handwriting on the wall, convinced now that Francis was no longer going to support him in his position. He noted to his diary on April 13 regarding Francis, "no sort of cooperation possible there"; on April 15, "there is a curious feeling of change in the air"; and on April 17, "all closing in now."[309] He reiterated in a cable to Davison of April 15 that all work should end May 1 "unless there is a change in the attitude of the government."[310]

No such change was forthcoming. On the contrary, at that very moment, actions were being taken leading to his recall. On April 19, Gordon Auchincloss recorded in his diary, "it would be a very good idea if Robins left Russia, inasmuch as his reports irritate the President a good deal."[311] Francis reported confidentially to Summers on the same date, "I was planning in my mind to find some diplomatic way to send Robins away from Moscow."[312] Summers made it clear to the State Department that either he or Robins must go; reiterating to Francis on April 23, "As you state I think the matter will come to a head in short time. If we recognize the Bolsheviks I cannot remain here and do not think that I should be asked to do so."[313] Francis, while indicating Robins' usefulness, was clearly with the Department, that should a choice have to be made, Summers should be retained and Robins recalled.[314]

Robins took steps to wrap up his work, finishing the distribution of remaining medical supplies and asking Allen Wardwell to come along with him for a series of final conferences with Bolshevik leaders. Robins advised Wardwell that there were serious differences between him, the Consulate, and the Embassy, and that it was very likely that he would be leaving shortly.[315]

Francis reassured Summers that Robins was preparing to depart, and that a last-minute flurry of rumors of his own replacement and Robins' accession to Ambassador were full of hot air. But suddenly Summers collapsed in his office and could not be revived. The medical diagnosis was heart failure due to stress. Acting Consul DeWitt Poole took over and the American community in Moscow, including Robins, gathered for Summers' funeral, even receiving condolences from Foreign Commissar Chicherin and personal words of regret from his representative Voznesenski.[316]

The American community believed that Robins was to some degree to blame for Summers' death because of the enormous buildup of stress in the month before his untimely demise.[317] But within a few days, Raymond Robins received a cable from Secretary Lansing, informing him that "under all circumstances consider desirable that you come home for consultations."[318] Robins left Moscow on May 15, after final consultation with Ambassador Francis, Lenin, and Trotsky in a private train, armed with letters and passes from Bolshevik authorities. Trotsky wrote him a long and fulsome letter of farewell, saying "you were one of the few who cared to and could impartially comprehend those immense difficulties under which the Soviet power had to labor."[319] Robins left Allen Wardwell in charge of Red Cross activities, encouraging him to work closely with Chicherin.[320]

Assessing the work of Raymond Robins in Bolshevik Russia over the six months from November 1917 to May 1918 is a most difficult task. By the normal yardstick measuring effectiveness he would have to be called a failure, because the policies he espoused were not adopted by his government, and he was ultimately recalled, later suffering a good deal of private and public misunderstanding and even abuse for his efforts.[321] And there is no denying the fact that his most fervent hope, the cooperation of the United States with the Bolsheviks in opposition to German influence in Russia, was at least a short-term failure, killed by the twin blows of the peace of Brest Litovsk and the decision by the Allies to intervene against the Bolsheviks rather than cooperate with them.

Yet his broader goals of laying the basis for Soviet-American economic cooperation as a way of strengthening overall Soviet-American relations may well be seen as the first step in what later became a modest success. Robins did manage for a period of nearly six months to "keep a foothold" with the Bolsheviks. In concert with Samuel N. Harper, it is possible to affirm that in the process "he thus did us, and Russia, a great service."[322] Except for his failed efforts at military cooperation, the rest of his program, particularly giving the Allies a fighting chance to compete with Germany for Russian economic organization, remained a live possibility after his departure. This was largely due to the cooperation with the Bolsheviks set in motion by his strenuous efforts. As he said with passion to the Overman Committee,

> I was trying to keep my feet on the ground all the time and to see facts, and not to be stampeded by rumor or the unfounded opinion of others, and I tried to serve the allied Governments and the Russian Government and people from day to day, and I am ready to meet the day of judgement on what I did. I doubtless made mistakes, as all people do. I doubtless made misjudgements. But on the whole, the history of the situation has vindicated my position.[323]

# 5

# Chicherin-Poole Discussions, May–August, 1918

Poole here returning Moscow tonight has called on Chicherin and stated pursuant to my instructions was my only authorized channel of communication with Soviet Government. Huntington, also Moscow, arrived while I was there and pursuant to my instructions is establishing relations with Russian-American Chamber of Deputies [Commerce] watching Germans and making informal acquaintance with Soviet officials.
—*Francis to Lansing, May 20, 1918*[1]

All of this was discussed in the most friendly and cordial manner and with the explicit statement on my part that I was quite without instructions from either you or the Department and was giving expression only to my personal views. The Bolshevik policy as he summed it up is to maintain equilibrium and an equal contact with the Allies and with the Germans, commercial as well as political, and to put off to the last possible moment any active military operations.
—*Poole to Francis* re *Conversation with Chicherin, May 24, 1918*[2]

The death of United States Consul General Maddin Summers and the departure to the United States of Raymond Robins presented Ambassador David Francis an opportunity to consolidate informal contacts with the Bolsheviks during the second week of May 1918. Soviet Foreign Minister Georgi Chicherin took the occasion of Summers' death to telegraph Francis directly, expressing condolences and requesting permission to attend the funeral service. Francis granted the request, and Chicherin sent Vladimir Voznesenski, Chief of the Far Eastern Division of the Foreign Commissariat, who gave a most friendly tribute to the United States.[3]

Francis asked the State Department not to replace Summers with a new Consul General unfamiliar with Russia, but rather to allow Consul DeWitt Clinton Poole to serve as Acting Consul General.[4] He then asked Poole to maintain political contacts with the Bolsheviks and encouraged him to utilize U.S. commercial attaché W. Chapin Huntington to maintain economic relations.[5]

From that time until the departure of American diplomatic personnel from Soviet Russia in August 1918, Poole and Chicherin developed a most amicable dialogue concerning every aspect of Soviet-American economic and political relations. In the course of these three months they met approximately twice weekly, and coordinated conversations among other representatives of the two governments, including Karl Radek, Lev Karakhan, P. Lebedev, Voznesenski, and Jacob Bovin on the Soviet side; and Huntington, Vice-Consul John Lehrs, and U.S. Railway Representative George Emerson on the American side.[6] Trotsky and Lenin only rarely participated in this period, as did Ambassador Francis himself. Allen Wardwell, remaining in Russia representing the Red Cross mission after the departure of Robins, confined his discussions with Bolshevik officials to concrete questions on the work of the Red Cross, and generally stayed away from broader political and economic questions.[7]

Poole reported to Francis at length on his biweekly meetings, and most of the other American-Soviet conversations were also recorded in detail on the American side. These reports, found mostly in the Francis papers, indicate the early development of a serious, businesslike relationship and paint a more positive image of the Bolsheviks and Chicherin than has generally been reflected in the prevailing literature.[8]

Most of the Chicherin-Poole discussions were dominated by the increasing specter of Allied intervention against the Bolsheviks, especially from late June to early August, but earlier meetings resolved specific consular cases and cipher access and facilitated amicable discussions of railway cooperation and economic relations. As Richard N. Debo, Chicherin's foremost Western biographer, has noted, "The American Consul General and the Soviet Foreign Commissar succeeded in placing their relations on a basis of frank candidness and respect."[9] Perhaps most extraordinary, the two agreed to enlarge the U.S. Consul's representation throughout Soviet Russia, and Chicherin acccepted the fact that such a network would be able to gather a diverse body of information for the United States, even establishing open contacts with the Bolsheviks' political and military opposition.[10]

United States' and Bolshevik objectives in carrying on these discussions differed. The United States, through Francis and Poole, wanted to keep the Bolsheviks friendly to the Allies as long as possible, especially during the critical period in the late spring and early summer when German pressure was continuing to increase and before Allied intervention was fully decided on and implemented. "Our continuing preoccupation," wrote Poole, "was to see if the Bolsheviks might not still lend a hand at least to the extent of defending Russian territory."[11] Francis, who began advocating intervention in early May, was still cognizant of the advantage of maintaining Bolshevik good will, and he advised Poole on the matter.[12] Francis also held out the hope that the Bolsheviks might be persuaded to ask for Allied intervention against the Germans. As he explained to Lansing, "I am endeavoring without encouraging hope of recognition to establish such relations with Soviet government as will prepare way for their request[ing] Allied intervention without my formally requesting same. . . ."[13]

The State Department, while agreeing that Poole maintain informal relations, was concerned lest Poole stray into all kinds of discussions apart from direct American interests, as they believed Raymond Robins had done. They therefore advised Francis on June 10 to limit Poole's discussions "to matters affecting American interests."[14]

DeWitt Clinton Poole was admirably suited for the role he was to play over the next several months. He had graduated from the University of Wisconsin and had been in the Foreign Service since 1915 and on Summers' consular staff in Moscow since August of 1917. Summers had made a special effort to get Poole, whom he assigned as head of the commercial section.[15] Poole had fulfilled his role with quiet competence. Even his mission to Rostov in December of 1917 to explore the strength and extent of anti-Bolshevik opposition there was accomplished with a high degree of professionalism. During his stay in Bolshevik Russia he did not let his own antipathy to Bolshevism get in the way of his careful fulfillment of his job and quite objective reporting of his meetings with Bolshevik leaders.[16]

For their part, Chicherin and the Bolsheviks hoped to stave off Allied intervention for as long as possible and to separate the United States from its British and French allies. While Britain and France had already made some commitment to intervention by May of 1918, the United States did not move into Siberia and the north until July. Meanwhile, the Germans continued to advance in the Ukraine and Western Russia in violation of the Brest Litovsk treaty. It was definitely in the Soviet interest to try to keep the United States friendly, even to the point of encouraging the Americans in the belief that U.S. aid might be solicited against Germany, particularly in the north. In the longer run, the Bolsheviks still hoped to finalize some kind of economic agreement with the United States similar to the one that Raymond Robins had taken to Washington with him. Chicherin was often quite frank in his discussion of Bolshevik objectives with Poole: "The Bolshevik policy as he summed it up is to maintain equilibrium and an equal contact with the Allies and with the Germans, commercial as well as political, and to put off to the last moment any active military operations."[17]

In a May 26 letter to Francis, Poole summarized Lenin's policy as resting on the need to (1) prevent intervention and (2) improve the general economic situation. Both of these objectives required the development of good relations with the United States.[18] Chicherin himself, in innumerable direct messages to the United States, and also in his reports to Soviet and Bolshevik congresses and published articles and reminiscences, supported this analysis.[19] Even after American intervention, Chicherin continued to insist that the United States be treated differently from the British and the French, because "the United States Government was compelled by its Allies to agree to participate in intervention . . . [and] its decision is not regarded by us as irrevocable."[20]

The Bolsheviks were not entirely happy with Poole, however, recognizing that his sympathies were not the same as Raymond Robins'. They knew of his role in contact with the Cossacks on the Don, and they suspected him of conspiring against them by the use of agents such as Xenophon Kalamatiano.[21] Therefore, they tried to exploit contacts with other Americans because they "most intensely wish[ed] to have another connection. . . . Nothing is more desirable to us than to get into friendly relations with the United States."[22] To this end, Radek, Karakhan, Chicherin, Lebedev, and other Bolsheviks attempted to ingratiate themselves with other Americans to have an alternative to Poole. This also explains, at least partially, the appointment of Maksim Litvinov as Bolshevik representative to the United States in early June.[23] Chicherin's effort to work with the United States even went as far as to ask for American assistance in late May to ask the government of China to admit an accredited Soviet consular representative, despite the obvious fact that the United States itself had never admitted any official Soviet representatives.[24]

One of the first issues settled by the diplomacy of Poole and Chicherin was the right of the United States to communicate with its consular representatives and the State Department by encoding its cables. In early May, when the Soviet government charged Allied representatives in Vladivostok with a conspiracy against Bolshevik control, it suspended the rights of the Allied missions to communicate with their Vladivostok representatives in code.[25] Ambassador Francis joined in a protest with the French, British, and Italian ambassadors against this prohibition, but he cautioned Poole in Moscow that the Allied representatives were walking on thin ice. If they protested too loudly, the Bolsheviks might simply ask the representatives to leave, and "a government has a perfect right to object to any representatives from a government . . . without giving reasons therefore. . . ."[26] He urged Poole to explore the matter with Chicherin but to do it delicately.

On May 24, Poole had a long talk with Chicherin, and found him quite willing to "adjust" the situation. According to Poole, Chicherin "referred to the whole business of cipher prohibition as 'stupid and unfortunate.' " Poole expressed the hope that "the exercise of a little patience and diplomacy" could put the issue in the past.[27] Francis was soon able to wire Lansing that Chicherin had issued the order that "all cipher telegrams all consuls for America or for European Russia must be sent unhindered."[28]

Soon it became clear, however, that the British and French representatives had not been granted the same privilege, and the fact of a special position for the United States began to worry both Poole and Francis. As Francis cabled Lansing, "I think acceptance of special privileges inadvisable and recommend Department so instruct Caldwell. Soviet government industriously endeavoring to create discord between Allies especially America and Japan. . . ."[29]

Yet American representatives did not reject the opportunity to continue to use cipher cables, a privilege not again withdrawn by the Bolsheviks for the duration of American diplomats' stay in Soviet Russia in 1918. In fact, in late June, when transmission delays affected American communications to the State Department, Vice-Consul John Lehrs went to Chicherin and obtained priority for American official messages, notwithstanding Francis' continued protest that Poole should "abstain from accepting from the Soviet Government any favors not extended to the other allies." In almost the same breath, however, Francis asked Poole to request that Chicherin give one of his cables "prompt transmission on the ground that it is a personal and not an official message."[30]

Before he died in May, Consul General Summers had begun the process, with State Department approval, of vastly expanding American consular representation throughout Russia. A number of new representatives were designated "vice consuls at Moscow" but stationed in provincial cities in South Russia and Siberia, primarily to gather information for Summers and to make contacts with anti-Bolshevik organizations.[31]

After Summers' death and Robins' departure, Poole brought up the activities of these new vice-consuls with Chicherin and asked that they be allowed to continue to operate, to keep him and Washington informed on conditions throughout Russia. Chicherin was concerned and upset, and shared with Poole his fear that the Cheka would think all of these consuls were engaged in espionage, but reluctantly agreed to let them proceed with their work unhindered.[32] Chicherin instead attempted to work through these various local representatives as additional channels to try to establish a working relationship with the United States. He urged local soviets to have friendly relations with the United States and thus build further pressure on Ambassador Francis and the State Department. Before long, Francis and Poole became quite aware of this tactic. Francis reported to Lansing that "as the Allied missions have friendly relations with local Soviet, central Soviet government contemplates establishing diplomatic relations throughout that channel with those missions."[33]

The Bolshevik hope to utilize any Americans to try to nudge Poole, Francis, and the State Department in the direction of a working relationship extended also to the hoped-for representatives of the American Railway Mission. Colonel George H. Emerson and six other engineers had been dispatched to Vologda for "consultations" with Ambassador Francis in early May.[34] When Poole, Huntington, and Lehrs first called on Chicherin soon after Summers' death, Chicherin confused them with Emerson and the Railway Commission, about which he inquired eagerly.[35]

Soon, Francis and Poole realized the great desire of the Soviets for assistance from the Railway Commission, and they determined to extract concessions from Chicherin as the price of the assistance. Poole suggested that, at the very least, the Bolsheviks give control in the operation of selected railroads over to the Allies, and that a major portion of the railroads in question be given over to the evacuation of Allied supplies.[36] When Francis suggested this to Lansing, however, Lansing responded with a prohibition of any communication or negotiation between the Railway Commission and the Bolsheviks. Rather, only Francis had Lansing's permission to discuss matters with Chicherin. Lansing told Francis that Siberia was awash in rumors that Emerson's trip west to confer with Francis meant that the United States had made an agreement with the Bolsheviks with regard to U.S. control and operation of the Trans-Siberian Railroad and that this was somehow a "tacit recognition of the bolshevik government."[37] Francis responded that his only desire was the "removal of supplies beyond the reach of Germans."[38] As the Czech crisis became paramount in Francis' thinking and the Allied missions prepared for intervention and departure, the whereabouts of the Emerson party soon faded from consciousness. They never arrived, deciding to remain in Siberia in light of the intervention.[39]

Chicherin's and Poole's discussions of economic relations began almost immediately following Summers' death, with an introductory meeting involving Poole, commercial attaché W. Chapin Huntington, and Vice-Consul John Lehrs with Foreign Commissar Chicherin on May 14. At this meeting, Poole introduced Huntington as the American representative "with his knowledge of Russia and Russian and his technical experience and education" who might do "much to foster the mutual economic interests of the Russian and American people." Chicherin then gave Huntington the names of a number of Bolshevik commissars active in economic fields, both foreign trade and domestic planning, for him to talk with about Soviet-American economic cooperation.[40] Francis, however, on hearing from Poole, immediately cautioned him "not to commit our Government without authority from the Department or the Embassy, to any policy presupposing formation of official relations of even a commercial character."[41]

Huntington did pursue, with Francis' blessing, the work of the Purchasing Commission. This Commission had originally been set up by the Allied military attachés to purchase as many supplies and materials needed by the Allies as possible to keep them out of the hands of the Germans. By August 1, Lieutenant P. I. Bukowski could report to Colonel Ruggles the extent of the success in such purchases: 170,000 tons of copper, lead, instruments, machinery, cartridges, guns, ammunition, and shrapnel—85% to 90% of all valuable supplies and materials in the Petrograd and Moscow areas had been made available to the Allies and kept from the Germans.[42] Primary among these strategic materials remained platinum, and Huntington continued to purchase whatever was available.[43] He also was authorized by Francis to purchase quantities of textiles, again to keep them out of German hands.[44]

Chicherin suggested that Huntington and Lehrs meet with the representatives of the Union of Cooperative Societies (Tsentrosoyuz), concerning the possibility of the United States', or some American representatives', developing direct economic relations with the Societies. Poole and Huntington considered asking the Cooperative Societies to accumulate certain Russian goods for the United States, in the hope that American ships would be able to come to one or another of the northern ports and that some kind of deal could be approved. This possibility foundered, however, on the lack of ability of Lehrs, Huntington, or even Poole to commit the United States to anything. As Poole said in some frustration to Francis, "As to the Bolsheviks, if we are to get anything out of them, you know we must be prepared to 'talk business.' "[45]

The Bolsheviks tried, in every meeting and in every conceivable forum from late May through early July, to get some kind of commitment from the

United States concerning the extent to which it was willing and able to assist Russia economically. Essentially, they used the specific ideas contained in the Lenin economic proposal given to Raymond Robins on his departure.

At every turn, Poole was unable to reply concretely. He asked Francis, "to what if any extent the U.S. is able or prepared to help in the economic field?"[46] But Francis, while insisting that Soviet requests to send an economic commission were "pending" in the State Department, also revealed the reasons for his and Lansing's reluctance to make any moves toward the establishment of serious economic relations with the Bolsheviks:

> that government has shown ignorance of all rules of commerce beside contempt for moral and commercial obligations; furthermore Lenin was shrewd enough to see that every move or relation that strengthened industrial conditions in Russia aided or added to the moral and political support of the Soviet government. . . . I am unwilling even indirectly to render assistance. . . .[47]

In early June, Chicherin and the Bolsheviks revived their request, this time in the context of the establishment of the German-Russian Economic Commission about to have its first meetings in Berlin. The Soviets offered a similar arrangement to the United States so that American capital would have every opportunity to compete with the Germans. Chicherin offered, in a meeting with Poole on June 7, to give the United States a number of specific economic concessions in the form of exclusive rights over the exploitation of certain minerals and the establishment of economic enterprises, in exchange for economic assistance. Poole replied that he saw certain technical difficulties in cooperation between capitalism and socialism and also that he was unsure of the available free capital in the United States in the wake of the war. But, as he said to Francis, he also wanted to make it absolutely clear, since "anything in the nature of a commercial agreement with the present government must be carefully avoided" that "all was not going to be clear sailing."[48]

These same proposals were floated that week in the Soviet press, in a detailed article by Karl Radek in *Izvestia,* June 5; an article in *Novaya Zhizn,* June 2; and another in *Nasha Rodina* on May 29. As *Novaya Zhizn* remarked, not only did

> the soviet power agree to give concessions to foreign capital in Russia, there is a comprehensive supplement to these principles, placing the question on very concrete ground, enumerating those branches of industry and production in which the soviet power should like to see foreign capital invested, thus presenting an actual and exact offer.[49]

But the American response remained the same. If anything, the detail and specificity of the Chicherin and Radek proposals were even more unacceptable to the United States. As Poole wrote to Francis, "These and the reported proposals to America seem to me disgusting. As I understand them, they are no more nor less a selling of their boasted socialistic principles in the hope of getting 'a mess of pottage.' "[50]

Despite this rejection, the Bolsheviks persisted in this basic offer clear to the end of U.S. diplomatic representation in Soviet Russia in 1918 and beyond. Almost on the eve of Ambassador Francis' departure from Vologda to anti-Bolshevik Archangel, Karl Radek visited the Ambassador, laying out the same proposal, granting the United States "the same concessions, privileges and advantages that it had been forced to grant to Germany in the Brest Litovsk Treaty."[51] Germany forced Russia in that treaty to cede the Ukraine, Finland, Eastern Poland, the Baltic States, and the western borderlands (Belorussia) to Germany. This included nearly one-third of Russia's arable land and up to one-half of its heavy industry. Although the treaty did not include many commercial provisions, each country was to enjoy most-favored-nation status in the other, and Russia was not permitted to restrict the export of lumber or minerals.[52] Clearly, Radek was not considering giving away great stretches of Russian land to the United States, but the Bolsheviks were serious about concessions and trading privileges.

Bolshevik efforts to come to some kind of economic understanding with the United States even extended to sending representatives to Francis and Poole claiming they were empowered to speak on behalf of either the Bolshevik government or anti-Bolshevik forces, whichever the United States wished to do business with! This particularly involved the efforts to get American food supplies into Russia in the summer of 1918. Vladimir Lebedev, former Secretary of the Navy in the Provisional Government under Kerensky, came to Vologda and met with Ambassador Francis in mid-June. He came representing the Department of Provisions of the Soviet Government and made a proposal of a trade of raw materials and supplies for foodstuffs. If the American government was unwilling or unable to respond to such a proposal if tendered by the Soviet government, he was authorized to make such a proposal from the coalition of groups opposing the Soviet government in Moscow. Francis responded that he had already made a request to his government for twenty thousand tons of flour for the benefit of the Russian people, and that he would be glad to reiterate that request, and possibly to expand it. Lebedev then asked whether he should bring a written proposal from the Soviet government he should bring a written proposal from the Soviet government or the anti-Soviet coalition. Francis asked him for a proposal from both sources, but such written proposals were never forthcoming, and the U.S. government never responded to Francis' request for flour.[53]

The Bolsheviks also tried to approach the United States government in Washington directly in the late spring, at a time when they expected Raymond Robins' influence to be at its zenith. They hoped that their proposals would be the subject of widespread consideration in the Congress and the Wilson administration. On June 5, Ambassador Francis received a cable from Foreign Minister Chicherin, announcing the appointment of Maksim Litvinov as representative in Washington. Chicherin said in his message "hopes friendship, your government will not object, our purpose closer relations, intimate friendship between our peoples."[54]

Chicherin followed this telegram with a personal visit to Poole, in which he said "that in the view of the Soviet government, their relations with Washington were of the first importance"; that "Washington had become for them indeed a more important capital than London." Chicherin went on to say that he hoped Poole would explain to the United States government how useful it would be to have a knowledgeable Bolshevik representative in Washington, familiar with the Allies and close to Bolshevik leadership. Chicherin told Poole that Litvinov was precisely such a figure. Poole went on to tell Francis that he had consulted with Lockhart about Litvinov, and that Lockhart said that he considered Litvinov "hardly a thorough going Bolshevik" who was chosen "because of his special familiarity with Anglo-Saxon countries as well as because of the fact that he is a friend of Lenin's of long standing."[55]

Litvinov later wrote to then–Soviet Ambassador to Britain I. M. Maisky concerning his own role in the appointment. Litvinov "became convinced," he wrote, "that the centre of the intervention movement was being shifted to Washington." Litvinov wrote to Lenin, indicating that he could do "more good to the Soviet Government in the U.S.A than in England." Lenin agreed and appointed him Soviet plenipotentiary in Washington.[56]

The Bolsheviks pursued the nomination aggressively. Litvinov approached the American Embassy in London, taking with him official documents showing his appointment, and applied for a visa. This was denied after a long delay on the grounds that no acknowledgement of his appointment was ever received from Washington.[57] In the meantime, Voznesenski paid another visit to Poole and informed him that he was going to Vologda and hoped to meet with Ambassador Francis to inquire about Litvinov's appointment. Poole told him that it would be some time before any answer could be expected from Washington.[58]

Francis had forwarded Chicherin's message that Litvinov had been appointed to Washington and further recommended that no action be taken, including not acknowledging its receipt. This recommendation was agreed to by the State Department, in a memorandum from Polk to Wilson, and readily accepted by Wilson.[59] No further discussion of this nomination occurred in the Wilson administration, and after several months, the Bolsheviks realized it was a dead issue. Whenever Chicherin or others raised the question with Poole during June or July, he simply said that the matter had been referred to the Department of State.[60] However open Woodrow Wilson was to unofficial channels of contact with the Bolsheviks, he was not about to receive an official Soviet representative in Washington.

In late June, relations between Chicherin and Poole were complicated not only by disagreements over transportation of the Czech corps and increasing Bolshevik uneasiness over Allied intervention, but even by a seemingly minor incident that resulted in the removal of John Lehrs, vice-consul and one of Poole's mainstays in economic and consular discussions with the Bolsheviks. Lehrs had long been involved, both under Summers and then under Poole, in detailed pursuit of consular cases involving difficulties United States citizens had with Russian authorities. Since the early spring of 1918, he had dealt with the Bary case, in which John Bary was accused of bribery and extortion. Although Bary was not exonerated, Lehrs was able to show the involvement of Soviet government officials in the matter, and was responsible for the arrest of two Soviet officials, including an agent of the Cheka.[61]

Lehrs had made a request to the Council of People's Commissars on June 1 for licenses for American consular officials to carry firearms. For some weeks he received no reply to his requests. Both Radek and Chicherin put him off when he inquired. Finally he went to see Radek on June 27, determined to force the issue. At this confrontation, Lehrs demanded the issuance of the licenses. Radek responded by saying that Dzerzhinski and the Cheka refused to issue them, claiming that the American consular representatives were counterrevolutionary. This so enraged Lehrs that he threatened to arm the consular representatives even without the required licenses, whereupon Radek calmly informed him that if he did so, they would be subject to being shot on sight by the Cheka for carrying unlicensed firearms. Lehrs responded with a counterthreat that anyone coming to take away their arms would themselves be shot. Radek answered that the entire conversation would be reported to his government, and in the midst of the exchange Lehrs walked out.[62]

Poole was able to defuse the incident only by means of a conciliatory but still defensive response to Chicherin and, more important, the reassignment of Lehrs to Ambassador Francis in Vologda, "for his personal safety." In his letter to Chicherin, Poole regretted "that Mr. Lehrs permitted himself to be provoked into an ill-considered reply, [but] at the same time [Poole made] objection to Mr. Radek's gratuitous condemnation of the American representatives in Russia as 'counter revolutionaries.' "[63]

Poole continued to assure Chicherin of his "appreciation of [his] constant friendly and courteous bearing."[64] Francis concurred with Poole's decision to remove Lehrs, but noted that "it seems now as if you and all Americans might be compelled to leave there before long."[65]

Relations between Poole and Chicherin had already been subjected to severe strain before this incident. Most difficult of all issues plaguing the relationship was the growing tension over the possibility of Allied intervention. Ambassador Francis, after several months of attempting to straddle the fence on this issue, began strongly advocating intervention, if possible with Bolshevik consent, in cables to Secretary Lansing and the State Department. In a notable cable of May 2, he placed his entire program of action and recommendations—unofficial contacts, Allied consultation, military collaboration, railway assistance, and commercial discussions with the Bolsheviks—in the context of this strategy. He again advocated a strong American attempt to get the Bolshevik leaders to request intervention against Germany, or at least not to oppose it.[66] By May 15, however, he had practically given up on the possibility of Bolshevik consent, and asserted to Poole that he didn't "think we can afford to ask their consent before we decide to intervene—they may possibly condition their consent upon our giving them moral support if not recognition, neither of which we can afford."[67]

French and British representatives in Russia likewise were moving in the direction of intervention. French general LaVergne couched his recommendation in terms of the immediate need for intervention. Each day lost, he argued, was "a threat to the success of any military operations we may eventually undertake." Lavergne believed that the Bolsheviks would reluctantly give their consent once they saw that intervention was inevitable.[68]

British representative Lockhart, the strongest proponent for the necessity for Bolshevik consent, began to shift his ground under pressure from the French and his own military. He was unable to get both the French and Americans to agree on an approach to the Bolsheviks. The Americans were reluctant to ask directly, and the French didn't want to ask at all. By May 15, he counseled Balfour, "If possible intervention should be obtained by invitation, but failing that, without." In any event, military preparations should be made as if intervention were going to occur because "intervention will not be refused when it is plain that Allies are agreed and that intervention is inevitable."[69] Lockhart based this belief on a long conversation of the same day with Trotsky, who was resigned to war with Germany. Lockhart asked him if he was ready therefore to accept Allied intervention. Trotsky responded that he was ready to discuss a joint Allied proposition. He even went so far as to tell Lockhart that if the Allies could ever agree on a joint approach, he would see Lockhart "not for half an hour but a whole day."[70]

Lockhart later insisted that some kind of arrangement with the Bolsheviks was possible clear up until late June, if the Allies had ever agreed on a policy.[71] Yet on May 25, when Lockhart visited Vologda for a consultation with Ambassador Francis, French ambassador Noulens, and Allied military representatives, it became clear that the new policy was one of intervention, with or without Bolshevik consent. Noulens was absolutely clear on the necessity for this position, and Ambassador Francis was willing to go along. Lockhart had no means of being able to show that the Bolsheviks would ever agree even if they were invited, and he was reluctant to find himself isolated, so he agreed to recommend immediate intervention to his government.[72]

Ambassador Francis' own unwillingness to directly ask Trotsky or Lenin or Chicherin to invite the Allies in was shared by the U.S. State Department and President Wilson himself. Francis was unwilling to ask the Bolsheviks for permission to intervene because if it were declined, it might commit the United States *not* to intervene, out of respect for the wishes of the government they had asked.[73] Lansing agreed with this perspective, and Wilson went even further, reiterating his own belief that Trotsky was "absolutely untrustworthy" and "the only certainty in dealing with such a man was that he would deceive you."[74] Poole put much more stock in the nebulous desires of the "Russian people," and assured Francis that if the President, before agreeing to intervention, felt the need for some kind of consent, that "everyone appears convinced that the [other sections of the population] favor direct aid from the Allies. . . . We have an invitation, necessarily more or less inarticulate, from the majority of the Russian people."[75]

Clearly, the United States' declared commitment to self-determination as a *sine qua non* of any decision on intervention did not include consulting with the existing Bolshevik government in Great Russia in the middle of 1918. It was

much easier, and more reassuring, to make assumptions about the desires of the
Russian people based on Woodrow Wilson's own conceptions of democracy.

In the midst of all of this consultation and cogitation by the Allies, Poole's
discussions with Chicherin were increasingly dominated by the threat of intervention. In a long meeting between the two of them on May 24, the bulk of
Chicherin's time was spent expressing his strong concerns about the prospects
of Allied intervention and his hope that the United States would not join what
he saw as an Anglo-French conspiracy. He also expressed concern that sentiment in favor of intervention was growing in the United States, reading Poole
a dispatch from the Washington correspondent of the Petrograd telegraph
agency. Poole responded by expressing as strongly as he could the friendly
purposes of the United States toward the integrity of Russia. But Poole never
promised Chicherin that the United States would not intervene, because its
overwhelming concern was opposition to Germany. Chicherin responded by
reiterating Bolshevik policy of avoiding as long as possible a break with either
Germany or the Allies.[76]

On May 28, the two men had another long discussion concerning intervention, this time in the wake of the arrival of the U.S.S. *Olympia* off the north
coast of Russia at Murmansk. Chicherin was convinced that this was an omen
of intervention. This time Poole told Chicherin that he believed American
policy would be based on two factors: (1) the historic reluctance of the United
States to intervene in other countries; but also (2) the "growing conviction in
the popular mind in the United States" that some kind of action against
Germany in Russia needed to be initiated to turn the tide of war. Chicherin
responded, according to Poole, by arguing, not against intervention on principle, but purely on the basis of whether it would be effective against Germany.
Thus the conviction grew among Allied personnel in Russia that the Bolsheviks would not oppose Allied intervention when it came.[77]

By early June, Poole and Francis were of the belief that nearly all Allied
representatives in Russia, including even some journalists who had previously
been opposed, were now in favor of intervention. The two men were heavily
engaged in planning for the implementation of such an intervention as soon as
the Allied governments gave the word. On June 4, for example, Francis
journeyed from Vologda to Petrograd, in part to facilitate the evacuation of
Allied stores away from the German frontier, and also to make discreet
contact with anti-Bolshevik forces in the former capital, on the assumption
that soon the Bolshevik government would collapse. Francis followed this trip
with a dispatch to the State Department, openly predicting the collapse of the
Bolshevik government and asking for permission to support a new, anti-
Bolshevik government.[78]

Just at this time, however, U.S. Consul in Archangel Felix Cole, himself
becoming aware of the increasing Allied sentiment and preparations for intervention, wrote a long and incisive memorandum recommending against it,
which Francis, Poole, and eventually the U.S. State Department felt compelled to respond to. Cole based his argument on many of the grounds Francis' and Lockhart's previous anti-intervention position had been based on:

support for the Russian people and opposition to German influence. He argued that intervention would effectively give up any chance of making progress in either area. Cole argued that "the best way to meet Germany in Russia and give her battle . . . [is] to make Russia independent of Germany by sending her . . . what she needs for her factories. . . . We can make more friends in Russia by the proper use of sugar, boots, fishnets and machinery than by 200,000 or 500,000 troops."[79]

Francis responded to Cole's arguments with a memorandum of his own on June 13. He asserted that the Bolshevik government was a "corpse that no one had the courage to bury" that had become "so putrid that it should be removed in the interest of public health."[80] Francis' response marked the first full-fledged expression of his intense anti-Bolshevism. Although he had never made a secret of his dislike of the Bolsheviks, Francis had tempered his abhorrence both in public statements and in recommendations to the State Department in the winter and spring of 1918 while it was important to explore the possibility of working with the Bolsheviks against Germany. Once that hope was gone and he had firmly committed himself to intervention, Francis no longer held his feelings in check. He favored intervention, not only to combat Germany, but to destroy the Bolsheviks.

Poole took Cole's arguments more seriously, responding in some detail himself, and asking one of his aides, Willoughby-Smith, to analyze Cole's arguments for a more considered response to the State Department. Poole, while admitting some of Cole's points, argued that Cole's memorandum was "an excellent illustration of the danger of discussing general problems from a local point of view," believing that intervention was primarily a "movement to protect Siberia against German penetration."[81] Poole used Willoughby-Smith's arguments in his memorandum to Francis of July 6. Both of the consuls hoped that Washington had made a decision without regard to Cole's arguments; which in fact proved to be the case.[82]

Meanwhile, in early June, problems associated with the movement of Czechoslovakian troops eastward on the Trans-Siberian Railroad served to provide those pressing Wilson and the U.S. administration for intervention with new justification. The Czechoslovak Corps was a separate force within the Russian army composed of two divisions of more than 70,000 Czechoslovakian soldiers. The bulk of these soldiers had deserted the Austro-Hungarian army or had been captured by Russian troops. Following the March revolution in Russia in 1917, they joined with a group of Czech volunteers in Russia to form this elite corps, which rapidly became one of the most efficient fighting units in the entire Russian army. Leaders of the movement for Czechoslovakian independence, such as Thomas J. Masaryk, finally prevailed on the Allies to permit this force to be reunited with other Czech forces fighting in France, and the Bolshevik government initially agreed with the plan for the troops to be shipped to Vladivostok on the Trans-Siberian Railroad and then sent by ship to France.[83]

Incidents between Czechoslovakian troops and Bolsheviks along the Trans-Siberian Railroad subsequently provided the immediate excuse for

Woodrow Wilson's decision to cooperate with Anglo-French and Japanese plans and authorize the sending of 6,000 American soldiers to Siberia.[84] What is more important for this discussion, however, is the character of American-Bolshevik interaction in Russia at the time of the Czech crisis, most particularly the interchange between Consul Poole and Foreign Minister Chicherin, as well as other American and Bolshevik representatives in Russia at the time.

As the Czech forces began to move east, under an order by Trotsky facilitating their passage unhindered to Vladivostok, they ran into some difficulties with local Bolshevik forces and regional soviets. The American consul in Irkutsk, Ernest L. Harris, played a positive role as intermediary between the Czechs and local government and military officials at several places on the railroad. Harris brought the two sides together for negotiations and at times suggested compromises that kept the Czechs moving with the reluctant acquiescence of the local authorities. The detailed record Harris has left of his role in these negotiations is not merely the record of the breakdown of the original agreement with Trotsky for the movement of Czech troops, but also a quite fascinating account of the respect Bolsheviks at the local level had for the integrity and fairness of American representatives.[85] The Commissar for Foreign Affairs of the Central Siberian Soviet Government, Geyzman, even went as far as to address Secretary of State Lansing concerning these negotiations, indicating his respect for the consul's work, and the Soviet's commitment to do "everything to settle without bloodshed. . . . We do all in our power to find amicable mutual understanding. . . . Czecho-Slovaks will be able without any obstacles and as quickly as possible follow to the east, and our mutual normal relations will be restored."[86]

Harris' yeoman's work and this agreement, however, ultimately did not succeed. Clashes broke out repeatedly between the Czech troops and local Bolshevik guards, encouraged by White forces opposing Bolshevik control of the railroad. Trotsky issued an order demanding the disarmament of the Czechs, which was refused, and suddenly Chicherin and Poole had a first-rate crisis on their hands.

On June 4, Poole visited Chicherin and let him know clearly the United States government's emphatic disagreement with the order disarming the Czechs, and its full concurrence with British and French determination that the Czechs should proceed unhindered to Vladivostok. He went as far as to tell Chicherin that the United States government would consider the enforcement of Trotsky's order as "an unfriendly act, hostile" to the Allies.[87]

Poole later that same day returned to see Chicherin in company with Bruce Lockhart and the Italian and French consuls general to underline the full agreement among the Allies on this matter. According to Poole's account, both Karakhan and Chicherin, who were present at this second meeting, "were plainly very much impressed by our united front and the determined tone of our protest. Chicherin said at first that disarmament was absolutely necessary and then finally suggested that some arrangement . . . might be arrived at."[88]

Lockhart's own report on the same meeting noted that "Chicherin and

Bolsheviks most anxious to avoid a conflict and avoid intervention. Lenin favours conciliation."[89] Lockhart's strong protest, however, came as a shock to Chicherin, who had counted him before this time as a friend opposed to intervention. As Lockhart had noted some weeks earlier, the Bolsheviks were worried that the Czechs "were to be the vanguard of an anti-Bolshevik intervention," and now they were sure of it. As Lockhart recorded in his memoirs, Chicherin and Karakhan were now convinced that intervention was inevitable:

> Chicherin, looking more like a drowned rat than ever, stared at us with mournful eyes. Karachan seemed stupidly bewildered. There was a painful silence. Everyone was a little nervous and none more than myself, whose conscience was not quite clear. Then Chicherin coughed. "Gentlemen," he said, "I have taken note of what you said." We shook hands awkwardly and then filed out of the room.[90]

Interestingly, Poole's strong and vigorous statement of United States policy, with Francis' full support, and his total association of the United States with British and French were not cleared with the State Department. Poole and Francis were chided for their unilateral action, since communication directly with Chicherin was only authorized in cases "directly affecting American interests." Francis, however, issued a counterprotest, defending Poole's behavior and arguing that he thought the Czechs "were American interests."[91]

Chicherin delivered a note to the British, French, American, and Italian representatives on June 13 and immediately made it public. In this note, he reiterated that the Czechs must be disarmed, but stressed that this "cannot be considered in any way as an act of hostility to the powers of the Entente." He then went on to detail the Soviet case against Czech actions along the railroad, particularly their collusion with anti-Bolshevik forces in various locales, again calling upon the Entente representatives to cooperate in this disarming of the Czechs, and not to use it as an excuse for intervention, which he deplored.[92]

Poole and Francis, however, stepped up their preparations for intervention, which they increasingly believed was imminent, and for which they ardently cabled Washington. Francis took steps to call together Allied representatives, including military ones, for an important conference in Vologda to coordinate strategy in case of intervention.[93] Poole detailed American vice-consul Jenkins to "develop contact discreetly with the anti-Bolshevik elements, as we may soon have to deal with these in a more definite way."[94]

Poole then took the extraordinary step of suggesting to consuls in Siberia that the Czechoslovakians should hold as much territory along the railroad against the Bolsheviks as possible. In any case, the Allies would be happy if the Czechoslovakians would "hold their present positions."[95] In this message, Poole exceeded any instructions from either Francis or the State Department and played a role in hastening what would become a fight of Czech soldiers against the Bolsheviks, contrary to Woodrow Wilson's stated position concerning the limitations on U.S. troops in Siberia. Francis, while realizing that Poole's message went beyond U.S. policy, supported his consul, writing him on June 20 that his "instructions were excellent" and that Francis would stand behind him in his decision.[96]

Poole also developed plans for dispatching consular agents to each projected area of military operations to serve as political agents with "the authority of carrying out a campaign of popular preparations in advance of military movements and of conciliating the people in the zone of military operations."[97] Moreover, Poole himself increasingly met with anti-Bolshevik contacts and kept Francis informed circuitously so as to stymie possible Bolshevik interception of their communication.[98] Francis sent an urgent cable to Lansing at the same time, calling "allied advance in Siberia very important if not absolutely necessary," believing that it would "be welcomed by great majority Russians especially after Allied intervention Murman[sk], Archangel."[99]

Poole and Francis received yet another communication from Chicherin on June 15, protesting "the presence of military vessels belonging to the belligerent powers in the ports of the Russian republic," including both the north and Vladivostok, and urged the United States to withdraw its ships to separate itself from what seemed to be the hostile attitude of the British and French.[100] Francis recommended that the note not be complied with, and that it not even be afforded the courtesy of a reply.[101]

The Czech crisis and the presence of warships in Russian ports seemed to the Bolsheviks to portend imminent intervention. Chicherin decided, in a last-ditch effort to avoid intervention, or at least to avoid American participation in any British-French-Japanese effort, to turn his attention from Consul Poole to Ambassador Francis. Chicherin had occasionally addressed notes to Francis, but he now began a sustained effort to involve him in personal dialogue by sending emissaries to Vologda and developing an almost frantic campaign to get him to move his headquarters to Moscow.

Chicherin dispatched Voznesenski, one of his chief aides, to Vologda to call on Francis on June 18, after first telephoning Poole to alert him. Neither Chicherin nor Voznesenski said what they desired to discuss with Francis, but it was assumed that rumors of intervention were the cause of anxiety.[102] Francis and Chicherin gave quite different accounts of this first meeting. Francis said that Voznesenski's chief message had been to personally assure the Ambassador that Chicherin's note demanding that Allied war vessels leave Russian ports was "pro forma," to which he expected no reply or action. "The notes were sent to please Germany," Voznesenski told Francis, in reply to a direct request from the new German ambassador Count Wilhelm von Mirbach. Voznesenski also told Francis that "the Bolshevik leaders had to say a great many things that they didn't mean."[103]

Francis told him that the United States would have established much closer relations with the Bolsheviks if they had shown any inclination to resist Germany.[104] Francis also stated that Voznesenski asked directly if and when Allied intervention, with United States' participation, could be expected. Francis said that he did not know. When Voznesenski told him that he wished to return the next week and have a further discussion, Francis told him that he might not be so forthcoming on the next visit: "I informed him that I would not be as candid with him again and on his return would not tell him whether I knew or not."[105]

Francis also painted Voznesenski in rather disparaging terms, calling him a "shrewd talkative little Jew" who "has the cheek of a government mule,"[106] and reported that Voznesenski felt that there was no difference between the governments of Germany and the United States, especially since the Czecho-Slovak incident.[107] Francis, in reporting the meeting to Secretary Lansing, concluded that he "cannot respect a government however which is not sincere and do not think it merits support from such a Government as ours."[108]

Chicherin, however, chose to put a different emphasis on the Voznesenski visit, at least in his communication to Francis concerning it. He stressed the importance of the meeting itself, Francis' polite reception of the Soviet envoy, and expressions of mutual respect of the two countries and their representatives, and he also noted their discussion (which Francis mentions in none of his reports) concerning the possibility of Ambassador Francis' coming to Moscow for the meeting of the upcoming All-Russian Congress of Soviets. Chicherin expressed a desire to meet with Francis on that occasion, and noted that such a trip, "even as a private citizen" would "tend to foster good relations between your government" and the Soviet government.[109]

Voznesenski did return to Vologda within a week, and he spent over an hour with Ambassador Francis on the successive days of June 28, 29 and 30, staying for nearly three hours on his final visit the evening of the thirtieth. This time there was no doubt in Francis' mind that the sole purpose of Voznesenki's visit was to try to ascertain anything he could about plans for intervention and American participation in those plans. Francis determined to deceive him as far as possible. Instead of telling him that he would not tell him even if he knew anything, he decided instead to tell him that "if it had been decided upon he did not know it," in order to help prevent what appeared to be rapid Bolshevik preparations to resist intervention.[110]

It proved a bit difficult to deceive Voznesenski, since on June 27 a number of British troops went ashore at Murmansk, accompanied by a small contingent of American Marines backed by an American naval vessel. While the rumors at Vologda flew concerning the numbers of these soldiers, ranging from a few thousand to as many as 90,000 Allied men, it was clear that something was afoot. What remained unclear to both Francis and Voznesenski was the extent of the forces and the level of American participation.[111] Chicherin made public two notes of protest to Bruce Lockhart concerning the British landing at Murmansk on June 28 and June 30, but for the moment he chose to ignore the participation of the United States.[112]

Francis' attempts to mislead Voznesenski and Chicherin occurred precisely when he was engaged in a spirited effort to convince the State Department and President Wilson of the urgent necessity for immediate intervention and while he was coordinating Allied representatives in Vologda to the same end. Practically his entire diplomatic working days were "engaged about intervention matters." He and Poole cabled the State Department directly, telling Lansing that "the situation has come to the most critical pass which has yet been experi-

enced. . . . The moment is peculiarly ripe for allied intervention."[113] Francis
also prepared a special cipher cable to be sent through Lansing to special
presidential confidants John Mott and Charles Crane, asking them to personally meet with the President and urge Allied intervention on him.[114]

By July 4, the rumors of invasion had become fact. The Allies were ashore
at Murmansk and were expected imminently in both Archangel and Siberia,
but no official American statement had yet been issued. Francis was in a
quandary and decided to use the occasion of the anniversary of American
independence to make a public address to the Russian people in Vologda.
This was a *tour de force,* calling upon all the Russian people to stand up for
their democratic rights and assuring them of the persistent friendship and
support of the United States. Moreover, Francis declared that despite pressure from Germany, he and the United States would stand with the Russian
people and remain in Vologda. This speech was well received in Vologda, with
enormous coverage by the local press.[115]

Foreign Minister Chicherin, meanwhile, took the occasion of the anniversary of American independence to address warm and conciliatory messages to
Consul Poole, Ambassador Francis, and the American people. In his message
to Poole he lauded the "revolutionary traditions of the young American democracy" and expressed the hope that "solid and intimate friendship . . .
[would] unite the peoples of our two countries." He also called upon Francis
to help in "trying to overcome the difficulties that are sometimes present."[116]
To Francis he expressed "best wishes and hope for intimate cooperation of
your people and ours" and pledged that he would work "hand in hand for
continuous friendship" of the Russian and American people.[117]

Francis was struck by the fact that Chicherin's message to him did not
mention the two governments, but referred exclusively to the Russian and
American people. He noted to Poole, "this is exactly what I have been endeavoring to bring about and it is what the bolshevik government has up to the
present time prevented." Francis asked Poole to tell Chicherin that he appreciated his message and "reciprocate the sentiments" but that he declined to do
so himself because he wished "to preserve [his] record of never having addressed Chicherin directly."[118] Poole was also touched by the personal note
Chicherin sent him, noting, "I wish that they were all like him." He thanked
Chicherin for the two messages.[119]

This exchange of friendly sentiments, however, did not obscure the march
of events toward intervention. Within days the discussion between Poole and
Chicherin returned to more of the "difficulties" that plagued the relationship.
On July 8, Poole visited Chicherin and protested the detention of 200 escaped
Italian war prisoners who desired to be repatriated to Italy. Chicherin insisted
that the Soviet government wanted the same end, but that the Italians had
gone to Archangel where the local Bolshevik authorities had proclaimed mar-
tial law in anticipation of an imminent Allied landing.[120]

Poole also noted, in a direct cable to Secretary Lansing, his conclusion that
Chicherin and Trotsky had almost totally diverged in their attitude toward the
Allies at that moment. Trotsky, convinced that intervention was already under-

way, had become "violently anti-ally" and had reportedly proposed a Bolshevik declaration of war. Chicherin, on the other hand, was increasingly conciliatory, still clinging to the hope of diverting America from an interventionary coalition. Lenin, according to this view, was undecided about the proper strategy and Poole still hoped to influence him through Chicherin. Poole also differed from Francis, believing that the Bolsheviks were not on the verge of collapse.[121]

Chicherin now turned his attention to a concentrated effort to persuade Ambassador Francis to leave Vologda and come to Moscow, where he could be better protected and subject to greater influence by the Foreign Office as well. Francis later wrote in his memoirs that this effort was directly stimulated by a German demand for his deportation following his July 4 public appeal to the Russian people. A more likely and proximate reason for the urgency of Chicherin's effort, however, was the assassination of the German ambassador, Mirbach, in Moscow on July 6 and the stepped-up activities of anti-Bolshevik Socialist-Revolutionaries and other groups around Vologda.[122]

On July 10, Chicherin telegraphed Francis, addressing him as dean of the diplomatic corps and inviting him and his Allied colleagues to Moscow, because Vologda was deemed unsafe and the Bolsheviks felt they could no longer protect the ambassadors. He then told Francis that he was sending Karl Radek to Vologda to discuss the matter with Francis in person.[123] On receipt of Chicherin's message, Francis immediately convened a meeting of the Allied ambassadors and discovered that they all had received similar messages, but that the tone of the message to the French was much stronger and more insulting. A joint response to Chicherin was developed, agreed upon, dispatched, and released to the local Vologda newspaper, *Listok,* which published the exchange as an extra. In Francis' reply on behalf of the Allies, he expressed his full confidence in the people of Vologda's ability to protect the Allied ambassadors. He studiously ignored the Bolshevik government, and rejected the request for the diplomatic corps to move to Moscow.[124]

Radek did not arrive in Vologda until July 12, just at the time when Francis was in conference with his Allied colleagues. Francis suggested that Radek meet with all of them, but both Radek and French ambassador Noulens refused categorically to appear in the same room together, so Francis agreed to meet with Radek by himself, but as dean of the diplomatic corps and thus representing all of his colleagues.[125] Bruce Lockhart has recorded his impressions of Radek at this meeting: "For this delicate task they had chosen the Bolshevik Puck, and, if his effort failed, he richly satisfied his own sense of humour. He appeared before the Ambassadors with his revolver. He argued, cajoled, and even threatened."[126]

Following his long meeting with Francis, Radek immediately telegraphed Chicherin his account of the meetings. This wire was intercepted by a British agent and provided to Ambassador Francis. Among other things, it called Francis "a stuffed shirt" and said that British commissioner Sir Francis Lindley was the "only man who has any sense." Radek also charged that Lindley considered Ambassador Noulens' behavior "childish."[127]

More important than these characterizations by Radek was the substance of the conversation between Francis and Radek, and here the two accounts substantially agree. Radek reiterated Chicherin's concern for the safety of the ambassadors, citing the fact that the Socialist-Revolutionaries had split, and that one faction was planning some kind of attack on the Allied ambassadors in order to blame it on the Germans or the Bolsheviks. Some of the Socialist-Revolutionary representatives who had fled Moscow were rumored to be heading for Vologda on such a mission. Radek offered, however, to inform his government if Francis would give him a written statement "relieving them of all responsibility for your safety." He also underlined again his and the Bolsheviks' continued respect for the American people and their "friendly relations with Russia, and said that the Bolsheviks were not willing that it should ever be said that the Soviet government had been "incapable of guaranteeing the safety of their representatives."[128]

Francis responded, both personally and in writing, to Radek. He explained to him that the Allied ambassadors' reply to Chicherin's request had already been communicated to the Foreign Minister by telegraph, and that both he and the other Allies stood by their decision to stay in Vologda, confident in the full support of the people of Vologda. He also wished to know what demands the German government had made on the Soviets in the wake of the assassination of Mirbach, believing that the request to have the Allied ambassadors move to Moscow was one of these demands. "Our going to Moscow," said Francis, "might be construed by some people as a confession that we were implicated in that dastardly act" (the assassination of Mirbach).[129] Radek promised to convey these requests to his government, and said that he would be back "when [he] received further instructions." Ambassador Francis promised to receive him at that time.[130]

Radek immediately followed his meeting with Francis with a further memorandum, even before he had received any other instructions from Chicherin. In this memo, he argued that the Bolsheviks were not trying to deceive the Allies or to cajole them into coming to Moscow for political reasons. If they wanted to break with the Allies, he said, they would not have sent a special representative to Vologda, but would rather have simply issued an ultimatum.[131]

Before Chicherin advised Radek further regarding his strategy *vis-à-vis* the Allies, another issue complicated the situation. Not only had British troops at Murmansk begun to advance toward the interior, in violation of understandings given by Lockhart to Chicherin regarding the purpose of that landing, but the British, French, and American representatives in Murmansk had signed a treaty of defense with the Murmansk Regional Soviet. This soviet had defiantly broken with the Bolsheviks after Trotsky had at first given his permission for them to seek Allied assistance against the Germans and then rescinded it. The treaty—signed July 6 by Rear Admiral Thomas Kemp, British commanding officer of Allied troops at Murmansk; French Captain Petit; and the Reverend Jesse Halsey, United States YMCA representative in Murmansk—assured Alexei Yuryev, the chairman of the Murmansk Regional

Soviet, of Allied support against both Germans and Bolsheviks. Despite the unorthodox nature of its negotiation and the rather shaky basis of U.S. representation in its signing, it was officially approved by the U.S. government in October 1918, and served as the legal basis for American intervention in the Murmansk region.[132]

Chicherin sent a protest against the United States treaty with Murmansk to Poole on July 13, and immediately made it public. Even in this note, he still insisted that the Bolsheviks put a high value on the "friendly attitude" of the United States and hoped "that the friendly American government will not continue to follow the road of violating the territorial integrity and elementary rights of the Soviet Russian Republic."[133]

The very next day, Francis received another note from Radek, giving him the response to his question about German demands, assuring Francis that the German government "has put forth only the most natural demand: the punishment of the accomplices of the crime and the strengthening of our guard of the Embassy." Radek went on to reiterate the Bolsheviks' concern for the safety of the American ambassador and their desire for him to move to Moscow. This time he emphasized "that the noncompliance with our request we will regard as an act of definite unfriendliness and animosity."[134]

On the same day, Francis received yet another telegram from Chicherin, notifying him that extra guards would be placed around the Vologda embassies for the ambassadors' protection, and reassuring him that no "command" was intended by the "invitation" to the ambassadors to move to Moscow. Chicherin went on to offer the ambassadors "beautiful villas" on the outskirts of Moscow if the ambassadors would just move.[135] Francis and his colleagues decided that no further communication was really necessary with either Radek or Chicherin, since they had several times restated their position, but Francis nonetheless sent a further telegram to Chicherin on July 15, informing Chicherin that the Allies "accept[ed]" his assurance that the guard stationed around their chanceries had their protection as its "sole aim."[136] Finally, Francis telegraphed Poole, asking him to visit Chicherin personally and complain about the "offensive" tone assumed by Radek and distinguishing between the "courteous wording" of Chicherin's telegrams and the "brusque and curt nature of Radek."[137]

Radek himself left for Moscow on July 17 and tried to see Ambassador Francis as he was leaving. Finding no one available, he left a last personal message for Francis, expressing his "deep esteem" for him and for the United States and promising him that the Commissariat would continue to communicate the strong desire of the Bolsheviks for Francis to move to Moscow. He also expressed regret that the British landing of troops at Murmansk had "interrupted" American communications with the State Department in Washington, and said that they would be restored if possible.[138]

From this moment on, Francis' strategy with regard to the Bolshevik request for him to leave Vologda for Moscow was dictated, not by concerns for his safety or any defiant "trust" in the security and friendship of the people of Vologda, but almost entirely by the timing of Allied intervention and the military situation at Archangel. On July 17, Francis received a visit in Vologda by a British captain, McGrath, who arrived the same day from Archangel. McGrath urged Francis and the other Allied chiefs to make immediate plans to leave Vologda for Archangel, because the "continued presence of the Allied Ambassadors at Vologda would embarrass and possibly hamper" the plans of the commanding British general, Ernest Poole, in the northern region. Instead, they should plan their departure so that they could arrive in Archangel at the same time as General Poole. Francis agreed, and outlined for his Allied colleagues a plan whereby they should be prepared to leave for Archangel on a moment's notice. According to this plan, the Allied envoys should not tell the Bolsheviks this until they had already departed, to keep from being taken hostage. Furthermore, they should leave a skeleton staff in Vologda to keep the embassies functioning, to give credence to their stated purpose of going to Vologda "temporarily."[139]

On July 23, Chicherin renewed the request to Francis to come immediately to Moscow. This time the message was clear and curt: "Again we tell you Vologda is unsafe. Another day may be too late. Again we invite you to Moscow." Francis replied equally briefly: "We have determined to take your advice and quit Vologda."[140] Francis deliberately did not tell Chicherin that he and the other Allied ambassadors were leaving, not for Moscow, but for Archangel.

At first the station master would not let their train depart, but instead telegraphed Moscow, which asked where the train wanted to go. When told "Archangel," Chicherin cabled, "Archangel is not a fit place for Ambassadors to live. Going to Archangel means leaving Russia." But finally, early in the morning of July 25, Francis and the other Allied ambassadors left Vologda for Archangel. Here they received the eventual protection of Allied and anti-Bolshevik forces, and after a period of time there were evacuated to London.[141]

Francis' departure was a clear sign of the impending isolation of the Bolsheviks from all Allied contact in Russia. Although Acting Consul General Poole managed to stay on for another two months, and Red Cross Representative Allen Wardwell remained until October 17, their effectiveness in any political dialogue disappeared with Francis' departure and the arrival of Allied troops in North Russia. Political contact between American and Bolshevik representatives in Russia was effectively ended until 1933, with the sole exception of the mission of United States envoy William C. Bullitt to Moscow in 1919.

Even to the end, Chicherin attempted to dissuade Francis from his course. He sent a message on July 24, almost concurrent with his reluctant approval for the departure of the train to Archangel that a "warm friendly reception awaits" should Francis change his mind and choose to come to Moscow. Chicherin insisted that "relations between our two countries are not going to be affected by an event to which we will not ascribe any political character."[142]

Chicherin also wrote a long memorandum to John Lehrs about the communication difficulties the American Embassy and Consulate had experienced because of the Allied landing at Murmansk. In this message he expressed his regret at the breakoff, but said that all Soviet communications had been disrupted, not just those to America or Britain. Wireless was the only way left to communicate between Bolshevik Russia and the West. Even this channel went through Paris. Chicherin also noted that he hoped that "Mr. Francis and the other Ambassadors . . . will return soon to Russia and to Moscow," and asked Lehrs to convey to Francis the hope in "the near future to establish with him close and friendly relations under more normal conditions."[143]

After Francis' departure to Archangel, Poole sought out Chicherin for a personal meeting to determine if the Ambassador's exit meant the breakoff of all relations between the United States and the Bolsheviks, or whether their relationship and the American consul's status in Moscow might continue. Poole expressed his concern about the insistence of the Bolsheviks on the Ambassador's departure from Vologda, and his solidarity with the British and French. Poole insisted that any rupture of the diplomatic privilege of any of the Allies would be considered an infringement on all. With regard to the impact of the departure of the ambassadors on the continued presence of the consuls in Moscow, Chicherin insisted that this "should not work any change in the relations heretofore existing between the American government and that of the Soviet Republic." Poole then informed him that as far as he was concerned, he would remain in Moscow, "as long as the Soviet authorities would permit. . . . as long as they would allow . . . a reasonable share of such facilities for communication as might exist, would afford [him] the consideration and privileges due [his position] and assure [his personal] security." Chicherin replied that "it was very much the desire of the Soviet government that our relations should continue as heretofore."[144]

Despite this expressed hope, relations between Allied representatives in Moscow and the Bolsheviks deteriorated markedly following the departure of the ambassadors to Archangel. As Bruce Lockhart noted, "The Bolsheviks rightly interpreted [the flight] as the prelude to intervention." The Bolsheviks were determined, however, that the onus for breaking relations would be on the Allies, so they tried to avoid situations that would "put the blame for any rupture of relations on the Bolsheviks."[145]

The most immediate problem threatening the continued stay of Allied representatives in Moscow was the status of military personnel in the face of hostile Allied actions against the Bolsheviks. Poole, together with Lockhart and the Consuls General of France and Italy, visited Chicherin and Karakhan on July 26 to protest the detention of a French noncommissioned officer and a French soldier as well as a number of Polish and Czech soldiers. The Allied representatives suggested, since these military personnel having no diplomatic status seemed to be a major cause of problems between the two sides, that they be immediately evacuated. In principle, Chicherin and Karakhan agreed, but they pointed out the logistical difficulties in accomplishing this. Both sides agreed on a conference of military attachés and diplomatic representatives, along with the Bolshevik commissars for Foreign Affairs and War. Also,

according to Poole, Chicherin agreed that military attachés with clear diplomatic functions did not fall in this category and were to be protected in the
same way as other diplomatic representatives.[146]

A few days later, Japanese consul general Ueda met with Karakhan, who
raised obstacles to the orderly departure of any of the military attachés.
Karakhan noted that the agreement treating them the same as diplomatic
representatives meant they could not leave until all diplomatic ties were broken.[147] On July 29, Chicherin told Poole that any departure of military personnel through Archangel was impossible because of the military situation and
would have to be indefinitely delayed.[148]

That same evening, Lenin spoke to a joint session of the Moscow soviet and
various trade unions in the city. In this important speech, he attacked the
British-French "imperialism" unmercifully, and condemned their advances
from both the north and the south, notably omitting the United States from his
tirade. This speech seemed to the Allied representatives, on hearing reports of
it, tantamount to a declaration of a state of war.[149] Although Poole's first
reaction was to ignore it, the rest of the consuls urged a protest and explanation.
Poole led his colleagues in a visit to Chicherin on July 30. Chicherin insisted that
it did not mean a state of war, but it was clear the situation was most serious.
The next day, the British landed at Onega and began bombarding the approaches to Archangel, which they occupied on August 4.[150] In the meantime,
Chicherin wrote a note to Poole, reiterating what he had said in their meeting,
but also insisting that an explanation could not be given for Lenin's statement,
since it was not meant to be made public.[151]

The news of the Allied occupation of Archangel hit Moscow like a bomb-
shell. The Allies and the Bolsheviks were both convinced that it presaged a
major attack and an Allied march on Moscow with substantial forces. Everyone prepared for the worst. The next morning, 200 Allied nationals (although
no Americans) were arrested by the Cheka. Poole again protested to Chicherin, who assured him that no diplomatic personnel would be affected, and
that Americans would be safe. Only a few hours later, and apparently without
Chicherin's knowledge, British and French consular personnel were arrested.[152] But Chicherin wrote a long, handwritten letter to Poole, almost a
personal plea for understanding. In this August 5 letter, he assured Poole that

> our people are still at peace with yours and that to enable you to continue
> acting as representative of the United States the same facilities would be
> granted you as heretofore . . . we regard you as the representative of a nation,
> which to use your own words, will undertake nothing against the Soviets if we
> retaliate with precautionary measures against the warlike measures directed
> against us. . . . We have done nothing to provoke this aggression . . . our
> people want nothing else but to remain in peace and friendship. . . .[153]

In relaying a copy of this to the State Department, Poole noted his agreement with Chicherin that "the situation is altogether anomalous and unprecedented," again stating his understanding that the Bolshevik government "[did
not] desire a state of war, and will take *de facto* measures of war only to the

extent that such measures are directed against it."[154] A few days later, Chicherin again wrote to Poole, almost plaintively, asking him if the remaining personnel from Vologda had arrived safely in Moscow. "I hope everything is all right," he said, realizing that his own control over the situation was daily shifting to the forces of the Cheka and others within the government who were determined to make strong and immediate reprisals in the face of the invasion.[155]

Poole realized that it was only a matter of time before departure was inevitable. He burned his codes, officially requested the protection of the Swedish and Norwegian legations (neutrals), and requested a train for safe passage out of Russia for all remaining American nationals. This train did not leave until August 26, and Poole himself remained in Moscow until September 20, with American Red Cross representative Allen Wardwell the last American to depart on October 17. What contact remained between Poole, Wardwell, and Chicherin in these weeks was devoted solely to the welfare of Allied nationals and their own concerns with the mounting Red Terror. The Allied landing at Archangel had effectively ended any constructive dialogue.[156]

It is important to note, however, that despite Chicherin's loss of power and influence at the end, he was able to maintain a difference in the Bolsheviks' treatment of the Americans as opposed to the British and the French. French and British diplomatic personnel were arrested, while the American compound was placed under siege but its premises were never violated. To the very end, Chicherin and the Foreign Office apparently believed that the Americans were but reluctant participants in the intervention. The Foreign Office retained enough power, even with Lenin incapacitated by the attempt on his life on August 31 and with the Cheka increasingly spreading terror, to keep Poole and other Americans safe until their final departure.[157]

The departure of Americans from Bolshevik Russia in the late summer and fall of 1918, and therefore the ultimate failure of Chicherin and Poole's attempts at a working understanding, must not overshadow what they managed to accomplish. In the face of severe difficulties and provocations both within and without, and at times almost wholly without detailed communication or support from their home governments, these two professionals carried on a serious dialogue, remarkably free of rhetoric. It was focused on concrete solutions to concrete problems, maintaining always the long-range hope for a better relationship between the peoples of their two countries. In this they were ultimately vindicated. And, had it not been for intervention, subversion, assassination, and terror, they might themselves have made the working relationship blossom.

# III

*Isolation and the Search
for Peace, 1918–1919*

# 6

# Isolation and the Struggle
# for Contact

the fundamental reason for the failure of all the attempts of the Allies to maintain working relations with the Bolshevik government [is] complete bad faith on the part of the latter. The impossibility of depending upon the accuracy of any statement of the Commissar for Foreign Affairs and the absence of any assurance that a promise once given would be fulfilled undermined the structure of even our informal relations and foredoomed to failure all attempts at practical cooperation.
—*Dewitt Clinton Poole, September 5, 1918*[1]

[It is a] misfortune that the Allies had ever broken with the Bolsheviks, as by not interfering in Russia's internal affairs they would have gained the respect of the Russian democracy and at the same time minimized the danger of bolshevism in their own countries. The extreme measures to which the bolsheviks had been forced to resort were largely the result of the consistent support accorded by the Allies to every counterrevolutionary movement in Russia.
—*Lockhart on Conversation with Karakhan, September, 1918*[2]

As for whether it would accomplish the purpose or not that isn't the argument. That can never be foretold. The workings of truth and publicity are almost too complicated to follow, even after the event; it's always difficult to say, this word did this thing. All that we can do is to speak the truth and let it go. . . .
—*Lincoln Colcord to Senator Hiram Johnson, January, 1919*[3]

The departure of American diplomatic personnel and the decision of the American government to join its British and French Allies in military operations in north Russia and Siberia put an end to serious dialogue between American and Bolshevik representatives from August until December 1918. The predominant character of what exchanges survived was mutual recrimination: from the Bolsheviks, caustic references to Allied invasion, and from the Americans, increasing horror at the excesses of the Red Terror. In the midst of the isolation and hostility, however, both sides groped toward ways to resume the interrupted discussions. In the United States, Raymond Robins tried his utmost to utilize his political contacts to persuade the administration to try his program for Russia. When that failed, he worked through senators Hiram Johnson, William Borah, and other Progressives hostile to the Wilson administration to expose the administration's Russian policy and build public support for the end of intervention and the resumption of constructive dialogue. At the same time, the Bolsheviks, led by Foreign Minister Georgi Chicherin, sporadically tempered their fear and hostility with invitations to the United States to resume discussions.

The relationship between intervention and Red Terror is a complex one, and it is too easy to agree with Lev Karakhan that "the extreme measures to which the Bolsheviks had been forced to resort were largely the result of the consistent support accorded by the Allies to every counter-revolutionary movement in Russia."[4] On the other hand, it is not fair to say, as did DeWitt Clinton Poole, that "since May the so-called Extraordinary Commission against Counter-Revolution has conducted an openly avowed campaign of Terror. . . . The assassination of Uritski and the attempt on Lenin are the results of this high tyranny."[5]

Rather, the assassinations of German ambassador Mirbach (July) and Petrograd Cheka head Uritski (August 30), the attempt on Lenin's life (August 30), the exposure of British and French efforts at subversion and counterrevolution, and the seemingly full-blown Allied invasion (July–August) created a climate that allowed the already-established Cheka to greatly accelerate its acts of terror and to unite the Bolshevik party behind this campaign. As Bruce Lockhart noted in his memoirs, the Allied intervention was a disaster partly because of its contribution to the terror: "It intensified the civil war and sent thousands of Russians to their death. Indirectly, it was responsible for the terror. Its direct effect was to provide the Bolsheviks with a cheap victory, to give them a new confidence, and to galvanize them into a strong and ruthless organism."[6]

The Cheka was established on December 20, 1917, as the Bolshevik agency to combat counterrevolution. The "Extraordinary Commission to Fight Counter-Revolution and Sabotage," as the Cheka was officially called, was put under the control of Felix Dzerzhinski.[7] While it certainly arrested, executed, and imprisoned many without trial in the first few months after its creation, the Cheka's activities were subject to considerable debate within the society and even within the Bolshevik party. It is doubtful whether "terror" is the appropriate term for its work until after the assassinations and the advent of intervention and civil war in the early fall of 1918.[8]

Opposition by the Czechs and uprisings against the Bolsheviks in Moscow, Yaroslav, and Nizhnii Novgorod signaled the first full-blown unleashing of the Cheka.[9] Dzerzhinski also gave an interview to the newspaper *Svoboda Rosii* in which he defended the Cheka, calling terror "an absolute necessity during time of revolution." He explained the Cheka's policy as a "fight against the enemies of the Soviet Government," including "political adversaries."[10]

Following the July British landing at Murmansk, the treaty between the French, the British, the Americans, and the renegade Murmansk soviet, and widespread rumors of an imminent Allied invasion at Archangel, the Bolshevik Central Executive Committee passed a stringent resolution on July 29. This resolution declared "the socialist fatherland in danger" and implemented a number of emergency measures, among them the "subjection of the bourgeoisie" to "mass terror" and the mass arming of workers, and the "straining of all efforts in the fight against the counter-revolutionary bourgeoisie."[11]

In the several weeks in August between the time of Consul Poole's decision to seek the evacuation of all American subjects and the protection of the neutral embassies and the actual departure of American nationals on August 27, American Red Cross representative Allen Wardwell made several visits to the office of Jacob Peters, the head of the local Moscow committee on counter-revolution and a close associate of Dzerzhinski. Wardwell was singularly unsuccessful in his attempts to receive any assurances regarding safety from arrest or fair treatment for either American or other Allied personnel. He also recorded his memories of the atmosphere in Peters' offices: "Horrible, gloomy, dirty place, reminded me of stories of the French Revolution." Wardwell found Peters "very disagreeable."[12]

Wardwell also met regularly with Chicherin, Karakhan, and Yakov Sverdlov, the last at that time chairman of the Bolshevik Central Executive Committee. Wardwell's relationship with Sverdlov seemed to be most positive, and he often exchanged information with the Bolshevik commissar regarding conditions of prisoners. Sverdlov, while showing concern for the situation of Allied civilians, also used these meetings to let Wardwell know that the Czechs and the anti-Bolshevik White forces were also guilty of acts of terror, sabotage, and mistreatment of women and children, asking Wardwell to use Red Cross good offices to investigate.[13] Most Americans finally departed on August 27, and Wardwell used the occasion to unleash a torrent of frustration in his diary regarding American policy, which he did not understand:

> We cannot understand just what America's attitude is. . . . The American statement . . . seems hardly frank; they say they are not in favor of intervention, but are coming in solely to protect Allied military supplies . . . and to protect the Czecho-Slovaks from the armed German and Austrian war prisoners. This is utter rot. Czechs fighting Red Army. . . . Are we going to support the Czechs . . . or are we to back down and leave the Czechs stranded, or are we trying to straddle the two questions. . . . the questions cannot be straddled. They must be met. If we are fighting these people, let's say so and get it over with. . . .[14]

Within a few days, he was grateful the Americans were safely away. On August 30, 1918, in separate actions in Petrograd and Moscow, terrorists connected with the Socialist-Revolutionary Party of the Right assassinated Uritski, the Chairman of the Petrograd Cheka, and attempted the assassination of Lenin. Within days, a wholesale Red Terror was systematically spread across the country, legalized by action of Sovnarkom, which ordered "the shooting of all persons associated with White Guard organizations, plots and conspiracies."[15]

The day after the attempt on Lenin's life, the Cheka raided the British embassy in Petrograd, killing British naval officer Cromie, who had shot a Cheka agent in the course of a struggle. On September 1, British representative Bruce Lockhart was detained by the Cheka and questioned, then released, only to be rearrested and imprisoned a few days later.[16] At the same time, the Bolsheviks accused Lockhart, French consul general Grenard, and French general Lavergne of a fantastic counterrevolutionary plot. It was alleged that they had conspired to bribe Soviet troops, assassinate Lenin, seize the government, and proclaim a military dictatorship.[17] Lockhart remained in custody until October 2, without trial, when he was exchanged for Soviet representative Maksim Litvinov, then in Britain.[18]

Although there is little doubt that the extent of the so-called Lockhart plot was generally magnified by the Cheka, the facts about French and British activities in support of counterrevolutionary attempts to overthrow the Bolsheviks remain somewhat sketchy. In a review of Western and Soviet historiography, fresh materials from British Foreign Policy archives, and some interesting notes from Soviet sources, historian Richard Debo has concluded that "If Lockhart was not involved in Reilly's scheme to overthrow the Bolshevik government, it was the only variety of conspiracy from which he abstained." Most interesting and provocative is Debo's conclusion that the "Lockhart-Reilly plot" was known to Dzerzhinski and the Cheka for several months, and may even have been "taken over" by Cheka agents for counterespionage purposes during the summer of 1918.[19]

Lockhart himself admitted, in his official report for the British Foreign Office of November 1918, that he had indeed supplied nearly one and a half million rubles in support for "the Centre," the counterrevolutionary coalition designed to bring together all forces opposing the Bolsheviks. The "Centre," with British and French help, attempted a coup at the same time that uprisings occurred in the countryside and Allied forces advanced toward Moscow from the north, south, and east.[20] Although Lockhart's *Memoirs* and *Diaries* deny any involvement in a conspiracy, his letters and papers clearly show otherwise. Lockhart began his negotiations and conversations with Boris Savinkov, the key Russian organizer of the Centre, as early as May 17. He sent details regarding his meetings of May 26, June 1, June 8, July 6, July 18, July 23, and July 25 to British foreign secretary Balfour and Lord Milner.[21] Although Balfour cautioned him on June 3 to have "nothing whatever to do with Savinkoff's plans," Lockhart persisted, arguing that he could not "leave Moscow until [he had] completed final arrangements in connection with The National Centre." In late July, he took part in a full-scale National Centre conference, to make those final arrangements for the unified action.[22] French involvement, while it has never been laid out as carefully as the new materials in the Lockart case, has been documented, not just by Lockhart's own testimony, but in memoirs and the evidence of René Marchand, French military representative.[23]

Consul Poole reported on the Bolshevik statement regarding the Lockhart conspiracy to Secretary Lansing. Poole used Chicherin's accusations against the British and the French as a means for attacking the Bolsheviks for their "complete bad faith" and said that the incident "revealed . . . the fundamental reason for the failure of all the attempts of the Allies to maintain working relations with the Bolshevik government [because it was impossible to] depend upon the accuracy of any statement of the Commissar for Foreign Affairs. . . . [This] foredoomed to failure all attempts at practical cooperation."[24]

Consul Poole and the United States government were not entirely blameless of involvement in conspiracies against the Bolsheviks. Poole already had served as a listening post for Consul General Summers with anti-Bolshevik groups in both South Russia and the Moscow area.[25] But more important, from the Bolshevik point of view, he took over a network of consuls and "information agents" scattered all over Russia following Consul General Summers' death in May of 1918. Although Foreign Minister Chicherin had reluctantly acceded to Poole's request to allow the expansion of vice-consul posts, the Bolsheviks were suspicious that some of the posts were used to gather intelligence and even to assist anti-Bolshevik forces.[26] Poole always insisted that the agents and consuls were gathering information useful for American trade and were not engaged in espionage of any kind.[27]

One of his agents, however, the Russian-American businessman Xenophon Kalamatiano, directed a whole group of other agents in information-gathering for the Consulate General, including much information concerning military movements of the Bolsheviks that could be useful both to anti-Bolshevik forces and to anti-Bolshevik conspiracies.[28] Although arrested by the Cheka and condemned to death for his alleged role in the conspiracy against the Bolshevik leadership, Kalamatiano was eventually released from prison in 1921. Evidence about his and Poole's involvement in any such conspiracy is fragmentary and inconclusive.[29]

Following the arrest of Lockhart and the "exposure" of the Anglo-French conspiracy, the Bolsheviks expanded the activities of the Cheka. The Central Executive Committee passed a resolution warning that the workers and peasants would respond to what it called the "White Terror" of its enemies "by a mass Red Terror."[30] Leonid Krasin, a Bolshevik engineer and intellectual recently returned to Moscow from Stockholm to take over the direction of the Ministry of Foreign Trade, reported his own observations on this cruel period to his wife:

> After the assassination of Uritski and the attempt on Lenin, we went through a period of so-called "Terror," one of the most disgusting acts of the neo-Bolsheviks. About six hundred to seven hundred persons were shot in Moscow and Petrograd, nine-tenths of them having been arrested quite at random or merely as suspect of belonging to the Right Wing of the S.R.'s or else of being counter revolutionaries. In the provinces this developed into a series of revolting incidents such as arrests, executions en masse, and wholesale eviction of bourgeois and educated people from their houses, leaving them homeless. I had to fight for the release of at least thirty engineers. . . . Even now not all of them have been saved. . . .[31]

Consul Poole reported his observations on the extent of the terror to Secretary Lansing in early September. In this cable, he noted that "thousands of persons have been summarily shot without even the form of trial. Many of them have no doubt been innocent of even the political views which were supposed to supply the motive of their execution." Poole closed his report with a plea for stepped-up Allied intervention, arguing that "the truly efficacious course is a rapid military advance from the north. Our present halfway action is cruel in the extreme. Our landing has set up the Bolshevik death agony. It is now our moral duty to shield the numberless innocents who are exposed to its hateful reprisals."[32]

In another report to Lansing on the same day, Poole said that he had personally talked with the Dutch minister William J. Oudendyk, who had returned from a visit to Chicherin. Poole said that he did not understand the "hesitating" policy of the United States, and recommended that Lansing should warn Chicherin that the "present lawless course cannot be continued with impunity . . . that by its present lawlessness the bolshevik government has adopted the most sure means of ending whatever hesitation may still exist at Washington." Poole went on to predict (as it turned out, quite erroneously) that "the American people, will, in the end, proceed against a treacherous and persistently lawless government in central Russia no less vigorously than they are now proceeding . . . against Germany."[33]

Before his departure on September 20, Poole followed this report on the Terror with two others, detailing continued massacres, shootings, and detentions. He also noted that he had "protested personally to Chicherin, pointing out that Bolshevik cause teeters on verge of complete moral bankruptcy," but that Chicherin had "no control and but small influence over extraordinary commission."[34] These reports moved the Secretary of State to recommend that President Wilson issue a statement to all associated and neutral governments and legations protesting the continued Terror. Wilson issued such a statement on September 21. It noted that the American government "believes that in order to check the further increase of the indiscriminate slaughter of Russian citizens all civilized nations should register their abhorrence of such barbarism," and it called on other governments to do the same.[35]

U.S. Red Cross representative Allen Wardwell also visited Chicherin to protest the Terror. His protest was so strong and uniquivocal that Chicherin felt forced to respond. Chicherin accused Wardwell not only of "displaced immixtion in the affairs of a foreign state" but blasted Wardwell's statement that he had condemned White terror as well as Red: "Where are these utterances of condemnation? When and in what form did the American Red Cross protest when the streets of Samara were filled with corpses of young workers shot in batches by America's allies?"[36]

By the time Wardwell became the last American out of Bolshevik Russia on October 17, he was thoroughly embittered by his experience and strongly anti-Bolshevik. On his way back to the United States he advised Sheldon Whitehouse, United States chargé in Stockholm, that proposed efforts to send relief supplies into Russia should not be pursued. Wardwell believed it was impossible to get supplies in without the cooperation of the Russian Red Cross, which was thoroughly under the control of the Bolsheviks. Returning to Russia to distribute such supplies "might induce the Bolsheviks to think that we do not intend to move against them and might discourage that part of the population which is anxiously hoping for us to drive out the Bolsheviks."[37]

Lansing immediately cabled his assent to this analysis, noting that the "department cannot sanction any activities, however urgent and distressing the need, which require cooperation or patronage of Bolshevik authorities."[38] United States-Bolshevik separation was complete with this decision, and would remain so for the next two months. Only the armistice with Germany in November would again raise the persistent question bedeviling Woodrow Wilson, "How do we deal with the Bolsheviks?"

### Raymond Robins, Hiram Johnson, and an Alternative Policy

Meanwhile, back in the United States, Raymond Robins had been engaged in a determined effort since his arrival in June to change American policy. Robins returned to the United States resolved to do everything he could to prevent intervention and to persuade the American administration to seriously pursue the economic opportunities offered in Lenin's comprehensive proposal.

Even on his way across Siberia to Vladivostok, Robins began to get ominous signals of the reluctance of the Administration to pursue a constructive policy. Lockhart cabled him to do "nothing against intervention" since the situation had changed.[39] On his arrival in Vladivostok, in Tokyo, and in Seattle in early June, Robins received messages from the State Department "requesting" that he say nothing about his Russian experiences until he had been debriefed in Washington.[40]

When he met William B. Thompson in Chicago, Robins enthusiastically told him that he was on his way to tell the government everything he knew and to change United States policy in Washington. Thompson cautioned him that the atmosphere had changed. "Panther," he said, "you've got something to learn. Hero in Petrograd is zero in Washington."[41]

Nor was Robins' companion, Alexander Gumberg, forgotten by those determined to slow Robins' efforts. As soon as Robins and Gumberg arrived on the East Coast, Edgar Sisson called on Gumberg and told him, in no uncertain terms, to "keep out of politics while the war lasted." As Sisson recounted, Gumberg gave that pledge. "A mighty man in Russia, he was powerless in America."[42]

Robins had been preceded to Washington by Red Cross colleagues William B. Thompson and Thomas Thacher. Although Thompson had some considerable impact on his return in December and January, by the time Thacher returned in April the mood had already begun to shift in favor of intervention, and the administration was distinctly unreceptive to Thacher. Robins had sent Thacher with letters and highest recommendations, and Thompson attempted to get him appointments with administration officials. Thacher tried to get a meeting with Wilson through sympathetic contact William Kent, a member of the U.S. Tariff Commission, but was only able to see

Secretary of State Lansing and Gordon Auchincloss, Colonel House's secretary. Auchincloss expressed his doubts about Thacher's proposals for an economic commission, and Lansing noted his own conviction that Thacher was pro-Bolshevik.[43]

Thacher did seize the opportunity, however, to make a full written report to Lansing. He also developed what later was published as a pamphlet, "Russia and the War," in which he urged American aid and cooperation "in opposing German domination and control" and detailing Soviet requests for railway, economic, and military assistance made in the winter and spring of 1918. "The opportunity is open to the Allies," argued Thacher, "with America taking the lead, to send men to Russia, who, in cooperation with the Soviet organization, will be able to control the situation [so] as to prevent German domination." Thacher's main recommendation was for an American economic commission, to be composed of "able" Americans, to be sent to Russia at once to "exercise control over the use and disposition of Russian resources which are vitally needed by Germany."[44]

Robins took almost the same approach to the administration that Thacher had taken less than a month before. His first meeting in Washington was with Secretary Lansing on June 26.[45] Robins, unlike Thacher, took care to alert some of his political contacts in advance, knowing that a political battle loomed. Robins informed his old friend, progressive Republican Senator Hiram Johnson of California, of his return. Robins asked Johnson for his assistance in cables from Vladivostok and Chicago.[46]

It was well that the Senator was prepared. So was the State Department, which was determined to stop Robins' bid to influence U.S. policy toward the Bolsheviks. Basil Miles, head of the Russian Division of the State Department, had asked Lansing a few days earlier if he might make an examination of Robins' luggage on his clearing of Customs in Seattle. The State Department wanted to see if it could find anything to link Robins to Bolshevik agitation in the United States. Lansing agreed with Miles that the search should be made and urged him "to make it thorough."[47]

At Robins' meeting with Lansing, the Red Cross chief presented the Secretary of State with his proposal (quite similar to Thacher's) for an economic commission. But, just as Robins was preparing to present Lenin's full program for economic relations, as well as other recommendations, the Secretary of State said that he had other work to do and sent Robins to see Lord Reading and Henri Bergson, the main French lobbyist for intervention.[48]

Robins tried to see President Wilson, but he was always put off, and he soon decided to concentrate his energies on the economic commission idea on the one hand, and building political support and strength in cooperation with senators Johnson and William Borah on the other.[49] At Lansing's request, Robins sent him a written memorandum entitled "American economic cooperation with Russia" on July 1. This memorandum detailed many of the suggestions embodied in Lenin's plan, but there is no evidence that Lenin's original plan was ever given by Robins to Lansing or anyone else in the administration, and there is no copy in State Department archives or Woodrow Wilson's papers. Robins' memo to Lansing focused on the positive purposes of American assistance for Russian economic reconstruction, utilizing the economic commission as the vehicle.[50] President Wilson, in a memo to Secretary Lansing on July 3, thanked Lansing for enclosing Robins' proposal, of which he said, "The suggestions are certainly much more sensible than I thought the author of them capable of. I differ from them only in practical details."[51]

Following his meetings at the State Department, Robins turned his attention to the political front. He wrote a long, fifty-four-page personal report on his Russian experiences for Senator Hiram Johnson the first week of July. He began a series of meetings with the Senator to answer his questions and persuade him to make United States policy in Russia a major preoccupation in an attempt to shape a positive administration policy.[52] Robins also spent an evening with ten senators, including Johnson, pulled together by William B. Thompson. Of these, only Johnson and William Borah of Idaho followed up with any personal interest.[53] As Johnson wrote to his daughter concerning this meeting, "It was very interesting to observe [Senator Reed] Smoot, dry as dust, hard as nails, without imagination, or vision, questioning Robins, and to hear Robins' illuminating responses. I again say to you that the views of Robins meet with scant respect here."[54]

Johnson himself was particularly struck by the fact that Robins, Thompson, and Thacher agreed so fundamentally, despite their contrasting social and class backgrounds. Johnson also remarked on the fact that it appeared that the Bolsheviks made repeated overtures to the United States to compete economically with Germany for the future development of Russia. Yet "they have been met with a stubborn obstinacy, which the man of property always exhibits, even to his own destruction, when one under him demands a little of God's blessings."[55]

Johnson, while struck by Robins' experiences and much taken with his proposals, declined to get involved in a political struggle until the shape of administration policy became clear. The Senator still hoped that constructive proposals for Russia, especially in the economic realm, would be made by Wilson.[56] This reluctance of Johnson to immediately engage the administration left Robins temporarily bereft of influential friends who could put political pressure on the administration. Robins was left to pursue his own, at times tenuous, contacts within the administration, William Kent, Samuel Harper, and Colonel House.

Robins did make headway with liberals interested in Russian policy. He had a long talk with Herbert Croly of the *New Republic,* who wrote to Robins that he was "greatly indebted" for "such a complete account."[57] This conversation was at least partly responsible for the increasingly critical tone of *New Republic* editorials concerning the administration's Russian policy. By August, the *New Republic* complained that "we have lost most of our chances of an understanding."[58]

Robins' impact even extended to the neutralization of such previously anti-Bolshevik societies as the Friends of Russian Freedom. The more cautious and open stance of this society so infuriated one of its founders, George Kennan the elder, that he severed his connection with the organization because of his belief that it had "fallen under the control of Ransome, Robbins [*sic*], and other American Bolsheviki."[59]

Robins' return to American politics, and his emphasis on economic relations in his suggestions for a new American policy toward Russia, fell squarely into an already lively debate within and close to the administration regarding Russian policy. Discussions, proposals, and counterproposals about various schemes for aid, economic penetration, or relief became the battleground on which the fight between those favoring dealing with the Bolsheviks and those desiring military intervention to oust the Bolsheviks was played out. At times the schemes under consideration required limited cooperation with the Bolsheviks with the aim of forestalling German penetration and domination of Russia. At other times the proposals were frankly anti-Bolshevik and aimed at assistance for, and economic cooperation with, non-Bolshevik parts of Russia. The power of the economic solution to an intractable problem was so strong that in its various forms it became the dominant talking point for liberals on all sides of the Wilson administration and was used by more conservative forces as well. And even later, in Paris, when schemes for negotiation and massive intervention fell apart, what remained as the only solution the Allies could unite on was another form of the relief and economic assistance plan that was so debated in 1918.[60]

One of the earlier influential pleas for an economic program was made by William C. Huntington, commercial attaché in Petrograd, soon after the Bolshevik revolution. In a long letter to Samuel N. Harper, Huntington called for the United States to act boldly with the new Bolshevik government, to seize the moment and the opportunity in competition with Trotsky: "The foreign missions here with their fear of recognizing him, and their men who have no conception of sociological problems, are making fools of themselves. Russia is out of the war; let us help her to make order. Let us feed Petrograd; let us feed Finland; let us play the game big and bold. . . ."[61]

The first public splash for the idea of a new commission for Russia to focus on relief and economic assistance was made by progressive Republican senator William Borah, in an article for the *New York Times*, "Shall We Abandon Russia?" in early December 1917. Borah neatly sidestepped the question of recognition of the Bolsheviks with his plan for economic assistance and relief to combat German influence. His idea received a tremendous response among liberals in the United States, including Colonel House and other influential voices within the Wilson administration. The League to Aid and Cooperate with Russia was formed as a result of this article, and remained the primary group in the society promoting this idea until it split between pro- and anti-intervention forces in the summer of 1918.[62]

At the same time that the League was promoting the idea of economic and relief cooperation with Russia in the spring of 1918, the "pro-recognitionists" picked up on it as well. Raymond Robins' numerous discussions with the Bolsheviks about economic and aid requirements had begun to filter back to

Washington, and his assistant, Thomas Thacher, wrote a report in April that began to be promoted among Robins' friends.[63]

House took ideas from the Thacher proposal and others from the League, the State Department, and the Department of Commerce, where Huntington had been actively promoting the idea. House then put together a plan for the President's approval: a "Commission for the Relief of Russia." This commission was to be funded out of the President's War Fund, to be headed by Herbert Hoover, and to be the United States' answer to Britain and France's constant demands for intervention in Siberia. Unlike Thacher's and Robins' schemes, the House Commission would have nothing directly to do with the Bolsheviks, and its only relationship to military intervention would be that it would be "accompanied" by some military force to protect it in its work.[64]

House cleverly built a rather unassailable coalition in favor of the plan before bringing it to Wilson. Lansing had already been thinking along these lines; Archibald Coolidge's internal evaluation of State Department Russian efforts had recommended similar action in late May, and the War Trade Board had likewise formally recommended some kind of economic or relief commission.[65] Wilson reserved judgement, however, both on the suggestion of Hoover to head it (not being willing to spare Hoover from his role as head of European relief), and on whether it would be sufficient to answer the concern of the Allies.

It was in this context, during late June and early July, that Raymond Robins presented his own plans for an economic commission to his friends close to the administration. Robins' ideas, if not the specific detail of his or Lenin's economic proposals, became part of the administration and policy debate. A detailed, unsigned, and undated memorandum incorporating many of his ideas can be found in Gordon Auchincloss' papers. This memorandum stressed the possibilities of cooperating with the Soviet government to further American economic interests, arguing that

> American business men of technical experience in economic, financial, commercial, industrial and transportation enterprises can be placed in positions of authority and influence under the Russian government, and thus enabled to effectively control, in the interest of the Allies, the use and disposition of Russian resources which would otherwise be controlled and used by Germany.[66]

This was to be done through the means of an economic commission, Robins' main idea. This commission would involve "practical men of organizing ability" who would deal with railway management, industrial and labor relations, government finances, commercial credit, manufacturing distribution, and food administration and control. The commission would also explore the immediate renewal of Russian-American trade relations.[67]

Robins' own proposal presented to Secretary Lansing on July 1, "American Economic Cooperation with Russia," focused on the economic advantages, both to the United States and to the Russian people, of an economic commission in cooperation with the Soviet government. Robins stressed that the Russian people and the Soviet government were ready to welcome American assistance in economic reconstruction and desired a strong counterweight to German influence. In addition to the tasks already mentioned by the Auchincloss memorandum, Robins' proposal stressed the need to help in the creation of a "voluntary revolutionary army" and its economic support. Robins diagnosed Russia's main economic problems as a "breakdown of the ordinary processes of distribution" rather than a lack of resources, and therefore noted how ideally suited American technical and economic assistance was to the solution of such a problem.

Robins' plans for the commission were so far-reaching and ambitious that he recognized that it could not be supervised by any of the current departments of the government. Rather, he urged that a "separate and independent department of the government" be created, headed by someone "enjoying the absolute confidence of the President, responsible only to the President."[68] Robins did not specify a budget for the Commission. He did estimate, in his report of a few days later to Hiram Johnson, that an immediate $50 million fund and a "prospective margin as high as $250 million" would be needed for the purchase and transportation of raw materials in Russia.[69]

For a short time it appeared that Robins' idea of an economic commission in cooperation with the government might be acceptable. William B. Thompson was able to arrange for him a meeting with Herbert Hoover, who would be one of the key administration figures in any such scheme, and the person Colonel House had proposed to Wilson to head any commission. Hoover and Robins clashed over their analysis of the Russian situation, but Hoover was quite taken with Robins' proposals for an economic commission. Robins may have had some influence over Hoover's willingness to let his own name be put forward for House's plan to Wilson.[70] It soon became clear, however, that Hoover's own ideas for an economic commission did not include any possibility of cooperation with the Bolshevik government or the local soviets.[71]

One of the key lobbyists for some kind of economic plan remained Samuel N. Harper, foremost American academic Russian expert. Harper ended up backing House's plan and eventually turned against Robins and his ideas. For a time immediately after Robins returned, he remained open to his old friend from common struggles in support of Kerensky.[72] When Harper first heard that Robins was coming back to the United States, in late May, he was disappointed, writing to Richard Crane that "he was just the man for the delicate and difficult job over there."[73] Harper also believed at this time that the reason Robins was returning to the United States was that "no active, constructive work" was being supported by the United States, a reason Robins himself gave.[74]

When Harper first read Thacher's long report in early June, he noted that it "reflects also the views of Raymond Robins." Harper endorsed its call to work with the local soviets, which he agreed were "going to be permanent institutions." In a letter to Walter Lippmann concerning Russian policy, Harper argued that "we must recognize that [the soviets] are the only authority over there, and that they are a real power." Harper drew the distinction between the soviets and the Bolsheviks but recognized the reality of Bolshevik power and influence within the soviets. Harper agreed with Thacher that no economic plan would succeed that did not take account of Soviet power and deal with it. This was precisely Robins' own position.[75]

Harper welcomed Robins home with a warm letter on June 15, asking for an early meeting with him. He noted that "with your help perhaps we can get something done." But he also went on to inform him, quite contrary to Robins' own inclinations, that the League to Aid and Cooperate with Russia was going to start a major publicity campaign "for public support of the President's policy to stand by Russia," which Harper indicated he supported.[76] Despite Robins' cabled response regarding his arrivals in Chicago and Washington, the two did not meet until after Robins had been through his first series of meetings with administration officials and senators. By this time both men were moving in opposite directions. Robins increasingly opposed the administration, while Harper solidified his position behind the House proposal and against any contact with either the soviets or the Bolshevik leadership. By July 15, Harper was complaining that while his time with Robins was "satisfactory," "this dear, sincere man has not the best of judgment at all times."[77] Harper maintained his respect for Robins even after this time, and admitted to Mott that perhaps he had changed his mind about Robins because he had "heard a great deal from the non-Bolsheviki recently with regard to Robins." Nevertheless, he took steps to distance himself from Robins and his circle of friends, believing that Robins had " 'used himself up,' at least for the moment."[78]

By this time, liberal opposition to Robins and his suggestions had become fierce. Herbert Carpenter, the director of the League to Aid and Cooperate with Russia, warned Harper that Robins "has certainly struck a very unpopular chord" and that "Lenine [*sic*] and Trotsky managed to successfully surround Robins with a hypnotic atmosphere which made it possible for them to use him to their advantage, rather than his obtaining any advantage through them."[79] Carpenter went on to claim a few weeks later that Robins had "convicted himself of assuming dangerous official authority and action" and that he was now surrounded by "parlor bolsheviki forces."[80]

Meanwhile, the House plan was becoming unraveled within the Administration even before final approval. Wilson balked at sending Hoover to head it, and no one could agree on other names. Wilson encouraged Secretary of Commerce William Redfield to think that he and the Commerce Department would manage the operation, with the help of the Russian-American Chamber of Commerce and in consultation with the State Department. As the bureaucracy of the Commerce Department began to work out detailed plans, Lansing became upset, complaining that State was being ignored. Wilson received many letters of advice about the commission once word of its imminent appointment leaked to the public. And the British were not at all pleased at the prospect that such an effort might be the full response of the United States to Britain's continual pleas for military support in Siberia.[81]

Wilson linked the economic commission to Siberian intervention in his

July 17 *aide-mémoire*. Various American schemes for penetration of Russia were managed, more or less badly, through the War Trade Board for the duration of American involvement in Siberia.[82] But the broader idea of economic and relief efforts as a way of dealing with the Bolsheviks in central Russia did not die with the intervention decision. House was personally upset with the President's attempt at linkage, and believed that economic assistance in Siberia would ultimately fail.[83] As the European armistice neared, voices were proposing yet again a broad plan for American assistance and economic contact for Russia, plans that were to surface at Paris in a reformulation of the original House idea.[84] As Wilson said so clearly to the Council of Four in Paris, "the only way to kill Bolshevism is to establish the frontiers and to open all the doors to commerce."[85]

Ever after Wilson's *aide-mémoire* of July 17, announcing the United States policy of limited military intervention accompanied by an economic program, primarily for Siberia, Robins still hoped that the economic commission idea might be revived within the administration. He met with Tariff Commissioner William Kent, who wrote to Wilson on behalf of Robins and his ideas, noting the numerous "constructive proposals" that Robins claimed the Bolsheviks were willing to entertain.[86]

Nothing came of this approach, however, and it soon became apparent to Robins that the idea of an economic commission was dead. Robins had failed and the administration was set on its intervention policy. The focus of debate had shifted away from any need to establish working relations with the Bolsheviks. Following the decision to intervene in Siberia, Wilson wrote to Senator James Hamilton Lewis, "I don't think you need fear any consequences of our dealing with the Bolsheviki . . . because we do not intend to deal with them. . . ."[87] Robins left Washington with William B. Thompson for a late summer vacation trip to the West, leaving Hiram Johnson and others to consider how and whether anything could be done in the Senate.[88]

### Bolshevik Overtures

Despite the withdrawal of American representatives from Bolshevik Russia, the intensification of civil war, and the unleashing of the Red Terror, Soviet foreign minister Chicherin did not stop his sporadic efforts to communicate with the United States. From August to October 1918, he probed in various ways, by inquiries to journalists, contacts with neutrals, and direct diplomatic notes, either sent by wireless or delivered by third parties.

In early August, the Bolshevik military attaché in Stockholm, Captain Stromberg, made contact with a Mr. Wyatt of the Swedish Foreign Ministry, exploring the possibility of opening up negotiations with Allied governments, including the United States. Sir Eric Howard, British representative in Stockholm, inquired of the Foreign Office whether it would serve Allied interests to pursue these conversations. Lord Hardinge noted on the request, "the days for coming to an agreement with the Bolsheviks by negotiation are passed."

Foreign Minister Balfour then sent a reply to Howard, concluding that "under existing circumstances . . . it would [not] serve any useful purpose to use Stromberg to negotiate with the Bolshevist Government but there is no objection to Mr. Wyatt obtaining from him all the information that he can."[89]

At almost the same time, Allied personnel, with the exception of Consul Poole and Red Cross chief Wardwell, began their departure from Moscow. In a long interview with Chicherin and Karakhan, Swedish consul general Widenstrom picked up a note of entreaty and a wish to negotiate and compromise, especially from discussions with Karakhan. This led him to address a special memorandum to the United States State Department concerning what he felt were the opportunities provided by the fact that the "relatively moderate" Chicherin and Karakhan were holding the upper hand in the Foreign Office. This should perhaps be exploited, he suggested, before the moment passed.[90]

On August 27, Chicherin dispatched a message to P. Berzin, the Soviet representative in Switzerland, for transmission to United States and Japanese representatives in Switzerland for communication to their governments. This message served as the Bolshevik response to an earlier Allied communication "to the Russian people" attempting to explain intervention in terms of defense of the Czechoslovakians. Chicherin responded quite politely but firmly, saying the intervention was "based on pretexts which do not correspond to the truth of events. Detachments of Czecho-Slovaks are neither menaced by Germans nor Austrians."[91]

After U.S. Consul Poole's departure in mid-September, the American Red Cross representatives Captain William Webster and Allen Wardwell made ready for their own departure. Chicherin seized the opportunity of Webster's departure to Stockholm to send a message requesting him to ask Raymond Robins to issue an invitation for a Bolshevik representative to come to the United States for direct negotiations, because "nothing is more desirable to us than to get into friendly relations with the United States." Chicherin complained about the fact that Consul Poole was the only contact, and now he, too, was gone. "We most intensely wish to have another connection," said Chicherin, and he asked Webster to seek Robins' help in soliciting an invitation.[92]

British Foreign Office archives are full of a series of wireless messages from Chicherin and others in the Foreign Office to Western news agencies, including Reuters. Most of these messages concern the "Lockhart conspiracy" and details of White atrocities in the civil war, but they also routinely include a call for armistice negotiations with all the Western powers.[93]

Finally, in early October, Chicherin conceived the idea of a long personal note to President Wilson, complaining about American participation in the intervention and trying to help explain why this was so upsetting to the Bolsheviks. This note would also contain an explicit and detailed call for peace negotiations, asking the United States what its conditions were. Chicherin and Karakhan first developed some ideas for such a note, and then consulted with Lenin. Lenin responded to their idea in some detail, leaving no doubt that what eventually was sent bore his mark. Lenin gave the following advice to the foreign commissars concerning this message:

Write it in detail, politely, but caustically, saying: in any case we consider it our duty to propose peace—even to governments of capitalists and multi-millionaires—in order to try to stop the bloodshed and to open the eyes of the peoples. . . . Do the capitalists want some of the forests in the north, part of Siberia, interest on 17 thousand millions? If so, then surely they won't make a secret of it. We propose to you: state outright, how much?[94]

Chicherin's final note, dispatched October 24, was composed out of immense frustration, not only at the refusal of the Allies to communicate, but at the impact of invasion and civil war. Yet, as it was received by Wilson, this note was perceived only as a polemic: caustic, bitter, and angry. Chicherin accused the United States President of hypocrisy and double dealing and tried to expose the contradictions between Wilson's fine-sounding phrases, quoted directly from the Fourteen Points, and his actions with regard to Bolshevik Russia. Chicherin began with a full restatement of Wilson's Point VI, reminding him of his message to the Congress of Soviets in March at the time of the Brest Litovsk negotiations. Chicherin then accused Wilson of making attempts "to create a pretext for a war between Russia and the United States" by spreading false rumors about the arming of Austro-Hungarian prisoners of war and the forced escalation of the Czechoslovakian crisis.[95]

Chicherin went on to discuss Bolshevik resistance and gains in the civil war and then issued his first plea for peace, responding directly to Wilson's plea for Germany to cease the war: "your present proposal of international negotiations for a general peace finds us alive and strong and in a position to consent in the name of Russia to take part in the negotiations." Citing Wilson's demand that Germany enter negotiations on the basis of the "evacuation of occupied territories," Chicherin pledged Bolshevik readiness to conclude an armistice on the same conditions. Therefore he requested Allied evacuation of all Russian territory.[96]

Chicherin continued by discussing Wilson's proposals for a League of Nations and the economic causes of war in an interesting preview of what would be a *tour de force* along these same lines at the Genoa Conference in 1922. Following this withering broadside against capitalism and its responsibility for war, Chicherin still insisted that the Bolsheviks "accept as a basis your proposals about international peace and about a League of Nations," stating that "we have no objection to 'an open discussion of your peace terms.' "

But at this point, Chicherin moved into high gear, in terms explicitly following Lenin's advice. He made a frank appeal to what the Bolsheviks believed were the true motivations of capitalism:

Give us precise and businesslike replies . . . precisely what tribute do the Governments of the United States, England, and France demand of the Russian people? Do they demand concessions, do they want the railways, mines, gold deposits, etc. to be handed over to them on certain conditions, or do they demand territorial concessions, some part of Siberia, or the Caucasus, or perhaps the Murmansk coast? We expect you, Mr. President, to state definitely what you and your allies demand. . . . the absence of a reply from

you will serve for us as a silent reply. The Russian people will then understand that the demands of your Government and of the Government of your
Allies are so severe and vast that you do not even want to communicate them
to the Russian government.[97]

Despite the several places in this note in which Chicherin called for negotiations, or agreed to respond to Wilson's call for general peace negotiations,
Wilson heard only the caustic and accusative tone. The President was indeed
insulted and refused to respond. It would take a much different approach, and
a considerably different tone, to once again convince the American President
that a new effort should be made to talk to the Bolsheviks.[98]

## Robins and the Sisson Documents

One other important event in this period served to illustrate the isolation of
Bolshevik Russia from the West and the extent to which public opinion had
shifted away from Raymond Robins' proposals. Yet this same event simultaneously galvanized Robins out of his depression into a last surge of activity
to change the country's mood and the administration's policies. This was the
long-awaited publication of the Sisson papers on September 15, alleging a
German-Bolshevik conspiracy.[99] Although this is not the place for an exhaustive analysis of these documents and their impact on Soviet-American relations, a few comments are perhaps needed to frame the context in which
these papers were authenticated and published by the Committee for Public
Information, with the explicit approval of President Wilson. These events
helped bring Raymond Robins out of hibernation and persuaded Hiram
Johnson to resume his inquiries into America's Russian policy in the fall of
1918.[100]

Sisson made his report to President Wilson on May 9, 1918, presenting
copies of the documents at that time and asking that they be published.[101]
Ambassador Francis had been advocating such a step since mid-February and
had used his own and State Department funds to assist in the purchase of
documents.[102] Arthur Bullard, Colonel House, and the State Department,
however, had strong doubts about both their authenticity and the advisability
of publication.[103] Moreover, British intelligence refused to be a party to any
statement concerning their authenticity, and raised many questions about the
origins of the documents and their contradictions.[104]

Nevertheless, Wilson was persuaded by George Creel to publish the documents. Creel met with Wilson in early September without the knowledge of
the State Department. Lansing, Miles, and Polk had expressed doubt about
the authenticity of the documents, and were greatly concerned about the
timing of their release, coinciding as it did with the imminent departure of
Consul Poole from Moscow. As Lansing protested to Sisson, the publication
of the documents "will not only tend to arouse bitter animosity against Mr.
Poole and the other Americans in Russia . . . but will not unlikely imperil

their lives and jeopardize further the already precarious position of the official representatives of the Allies."[105]

When House raised all of these concerns with Wilson *after* publication, Wilson said that he was "thoroughly satisfied" about the authenticity of the documents. But he admitted House's concern that it meant a "virtual declaration of war upon the Bolsheviki government."[106] There is also evidence that Wilson himself seemed quite taken with the idea that Trotsky and Lenin were German agents. He had felt this way at least since a conversation with British ambassador Reading on April 25.[107]

The resulting publication created a furor. It was accompanied by a quasi-historical analysis done by Samuel N. Harper and J. Franklin Jamieson, President of the American Historical Association.[108] Wide publicity was given to the documents. Pro-recognitionists hurried to brand them forgeries, using Robins' arguments.[109] The *Chicago Tribune* and the Associated Press tracked Robins down in Superior, Arizona, and demanded that he discuss a statement issued by Santeri Nuorteva of the Finnish Information Bureau that declared that Robins had investigated the Sisson documents and had found them absolute forgeries. Nuorteva had already written to Robins (a letter he received much later, due to his travels), pleading with him to "publicly reveal the truth." Nuorteva wrote, "If you are not moved to do so out of respect to truth itself, should not your love of the honor to your country impel you to do all in your power to save your country. . . ."[110] But Robins refused to make a statement, declaring that he was under instructions from the State Department.[111]

But the pressure on Robins to make a public statement grew. Herbert Croly, the editor of the *New Republic,* wrote Robins, asking that he help in a "careful analysis" of the Sisson documents.[112] Nuorteva was arrested by American military intelligence agents in New York City and held incommunicado for forty hours. He was then reportedly subjected to a long interrogation in which his captors attempted to make him confess that he was simply a mouthpiece for Robins. This arrest and interrogation clearly revealed the strategy of the U.S. government in dealing with Robins: tie him as directly as possible to the strongest advocates of the Soviet government in the United States, thus discrediting him. Nuorteva appealed once more for Robins to go public with the truth about the Sisson documents. Nuorteva then published the long "Open Letter to American Liberals," urging the exposure of the truth about Sisson.[113]

John Reed, who knew Robins in Russia, was arrested in New York after completing a major speech defending the Russian revolution and calling for the truth about the Sisson forgeries. He appealed to Robins to testify on his behalf, and eventually a subpoena was issued.[114] Reed's trial was postponed, and by the time Robins' testimony was desired, Robins had already given a voluminous statement of his views to the Senate's Overman Committee.[115]

But Robins received yet another subpoena from American radicals near the same time. Mollie Stiemer and several others were arrested in New York for violations of the Espionage Act because of their protests against the administration's Russian intervention. Stiemer had quoted Robins and the

Sisson documents in her speeches. Robins was ordered to appear but evaded
the subpoena. By this time Robins had decided that it was time to tell his
story. Robins agreed to testify of his own free will. Although the presiding
judge ruled his potential testimony "immaterial" and refused to let him continue, Robins was determined to press for full disclosure of his experiences.[116]

Robins' first move was to appeal to Hiram Johnson to accelerate his inquiries in the United States Senate. Johnson had defended Robins on the floor of
the Senate when he was attacked as a Bolshevik by right-wing senator Miles
Poindexter of Washington in July 1918. But Johnson was away from Washington, D.C., most of September and October, following the death of his
daughter-in-law.[117] Johnson also was reluctant to begin a wholesale attack on
administration policy while the war with Germany still raged, because of the
danger of running afoul of the Espionage Act. As he wrote to his friend and
political supporter C. K. McClatchy, publisher of the *Sacramento Bee*, in
August, "if discussed fairly, honestly and freely, [Administration Russian pol-
icy] would subject the participants to persecution under the espionage law.
The test of loyalty, according to the majority of people, is agreement with
their views. Disloyalty is disagreement with those in power."[118]

While Johnson and Robins began to prepare their approach for a major
publicity effort in the United States Senate, the administration took steps of
its own to investigate Robins and determine if he could be prosecuted under
the espionage act. The War Department began inquiries into Robins' views to
see if he could be accused of disloyalty. This inquiry found Robins "fully
patriotic, registered for draft and [ready] to go into army as private if called."
Yet because of his activities in Russia it recommended that he should not be
allowed to return to Russia, as some in the YMCA and the Red Cross were
urging him to do.[119]

The intelligence investigation gave rise to contradictory rumors about Robins. On one hand, his friends were worried about a possible indictment.
Theodore Roosevelt and Gifford Pinchot wrote Robins concerned letters of
support. Pinchot expressed the belief that "no doubt the charges will break
down."[120] On the other hand, those opposed to Robins were still preoccupied
with his potential influence. Samuel Harper wrote to William C. Huntington
not to worry about Robins, that he was "out of the running completely." And
Basil Miles wrote to United States Ambassador Francis, then in Archangel,
that he should "not be disturbed by any rumors you may hear of the influence
with the Department or with the White House, of Raymond Robins—he has
none, quite the contrary."[121]

But the administration, having deliberately cut off all avenues of influence
to those with contact and experience with the Bolshevik government, found
itself desperate for information from these same people as it began to consider
the problems of comprehensive peace in Europe. At the same time the government was investigating Robins, Colonel House's group preparing for the
Peace Conference, the "Inquiry," needed materials on Bolshevik Russia.
Through Samuel Harper, a request for Robins' complete file of *Izvestia* was
made. Manley Hudson of the Inquiry asked "if he does not want to lend it to

the Department of State can you induce him to lend it to the Inquiry, or can you induce him to lend it to the Carnegie Endowment?"[122]

Finally, in early December 1918, following the Armistice, Hiram Johnson felt he was ready to publicly confront the administration on its Russian policy. Robins prepared detailed memoranda for Johnson on a series of questions for the administration. These questions were based largely on Robins' own experiences in Russia, and backed by original documents. The documents included Lenin's and Trotsky's request for American assistance if the Brest Litovsk treaty were unratified, detailed cable traffic showing Ambassador Francis' reliance on Robins' assistance in negotiations with Lenin and Trotsky, the offer of the Soviets for American assistance in the reorganization of the Russian railroads, and other specific evidence.[123]

Johnson used these materials in a major address to the Senate on December 12. In this speech he introduced a resolution asking the Secretary of State to provide the Senate with a number of specific documents and an explanation for its Russia policy, as well as specific details concerning United States troops in Russia, their mission, and their expected date of withdrawal. Johnson denied any sympathy either for the Soviet government or for Bolshevism, but he demanded to know "what our sons are fighting for," and blamed the government, particularly the Creel Committee, for misleading the American people and withholding critical information on the possibility of negotiations with the Bolsheviks.[124]

Response to this speech was overwhelmingly positive. Johnson wrote to his son Jack the next day that he "really felt good about it after it was done . . . it was a great tribute to have these cynical old fellows, who listen to nobody but themselves generally, miss their luncheon and sit throughout the talk. . . . It has started discussion and quite a row."[125] Johnson also wrote to his conservative friend Meyer Lissner on December 18 that "the very inquiry has aroused the most intense interest [because] no one has dared to ask about it . . . indeed, during the delivery of the speech I had an attention from Senators seldom accorded. There is much more behind this Russian situation than mere horror of the Bolsheviks."[126]

Johnson was soon so overwhelmed with supportive letters from people all over the country that he was forced to develop a form letter to respond.[127] The liberal press also responded positively, with supportive editorials in *Dial*, the *New Republic*, and other journals.[128]

Johnson was unclear precisely what steps to take next. He was not sure that he should go as far as Robins wanted him to in publicly accusing the administration of duplicity. As he wrote in a long response to Theodore Roosevelt in late December, he was

> in something of a quandary in reopening the subject, which of course I shall do at the earliest possible moment. I detest Lenin and Trotsky, and abhor Bolshevism, and I will not be put in the attitude of defending one or advocating the other. And yet the facts show a moral responsibility rests on us. . . . Of course to present the documents in the case and prove these facts will

cause a shriek of dismay and denunciation of the one, who has the temerity to do it, as an anarchist and Bolshevist. I think, however, we can afford to tell the truth, even about those we abhor, and I am rather inclined to think I shall do it.[129]

Although Johnson continued to raise the issue on the Senate floor through January, he did not utilize many of the detailed charges Robins had provided him with. Some of his friends warned that he should not associate himself so closely with Robins and Robins' information. Johnson also faced a concerted administration effort to discredit both him and Raymond Robins.[130] He wrote to his brother Arch on New Year's Day, 1919, that "my difficulty is to avoid getting mixed with the Radicals, whom I detest, and all of whom are enthusiastic about my actions."[131] He also warned Raymond Robins that he was holding back on making public some of Robins' documents, stating that he was "unable to see how you can ever justify [their] disclosure."[132]

The State Department realized Johnson's strength and the potentially devastating setback to administration policy that the California senator's resolution and charges constituted. Lansing, in Paris, was so concerned that he sent Acting Secretary of State Frank Polk to see Johnson to attempt to convince him of the weakness of his case. According to Johnson, Polk said that Johnson's key evidence—the Bolshevik questions at the time of Brest Litovsk ratification—"came to them unsigned and were never seriously thought of. . . . His attitude, apparently, was that the letter was considered inconsequential and of doubtful authenticity."[133]

In an effort to mollify Johnson, Polk did offer to meet with Raymond Robins for a more extended discussion of the situation. This meeting never occurred, however, and there is reason to doubt Polk's sincerity. In a letter from Polk to Lansing a few months later, Polk gave his frank assessment of Robins, calling him "unreliable and even untruthful, although he may not be conscious of it."[134]

Some of Johnson's friends were so concerned that he might abandon the effort because of the pressure from the State Department that they implored him to continue to speak out. As Lincoln Colcord wrote on January 9,

> As for whether it would accomplish the purpose or not that isn't the argument. That can never be foretold. The workings of truth and publicity are almost too complicated to follow. . . . All that we can do is to speak the truth and let it go. . . . It is more difficult for you than it needs to be. I want to say that it is also a tremendous opportunity. The young and vital forces of the country are waiting for the word. Anything can happen; it is a time when truth and courage can come into their own.[135]

Johnson's resolution to withdraw American troops from Russia reached the Senate floor on February 10. A long, emotional debate continued for four days, with Johnson receiving bipartisan support from senators disillusioned with various aspects of the administration's foreign policy. Final votes occurred February 14. A motion to table resulted in a tie, thirty senators not voting. Vice President Marshall voted to break the tie, killing the resolution. Despite the defeat, the debate exposed deep undercurrents of unease regarding the administration's Russia policy.[136]

By mid-February, the administration and Senate were so concerned about the trend of opposition to U.S. policy that they persuaded Senator Overman to shift the focus of his Judiciary Subcommittee from German propaganda to Bolshevik propaganda. This was an open effort to smoke out and embarrass the administration's opposition and show the American people the dangers of Bolshevism. Robins testified before the Overman Committee in March and April, supported personally by Senator Hiram Johnson.[137]

Yet Raymond Robins and Hiram Johnson ultimately failed in their attempt to persuade the Administration or the country to adopt an alternative policy toward the Bolsheviks. This failure marked the end of one phase of struggle by those with direct experience with the Bolsheviks to persuade the Wilson administration to listen. A second phase came on its heels and to some degree overlapped it, and this time it involved Woodrow Wilson more directly. The Peace Conference in Paris had to turn its attention, not only to Europe, but also to Russia.

After the spring of 1919, however, Hiram Johnson did not return to the subject of Russia, but rather turned his attention to Presidential politics and the fight against the League of Nations. He never wavered in his belief that he did the right thing in demanding answers from the administration about U.S. intervention in Russia. He expressed it well in a defense of his actions to his friend Meyer Lissner in April 1919:

> Those good people to whom you talked, who said I was a damn fool, I venture to say, have no sons or relatives in north Russia. Wounded American boys there freezing to death, others fighting for weeks without the opportunities to take off their clothes, insufficiently clad, without proper rations, harshly commanded by British officers—all this has not appealed to any of these gentlemen. In what a strange atrophied condition war has left our brains. These things do affect me, Lissner, and they get under my skin, and I am glad that I am yet able to understand suffering and wrong and raise my very feeble voice to prevent them. These good people who with perfect equanimity see others' sons killed without warrant in a foreign war, under foreign commanders, abandoned, and forgotten, and deserted, by their own people, for myself, I can not understand.[138]

# 7

# Maksim Litvinov and the Bolshevik Opening to the West

We have been insistent that we would help Russia. We have said that the acid test of friendship for Russia at this time would be the course of conduct adopted by her friends. We have said we propose to serve Russia and not to use her. . . . these statements which seem to have committed this Government publicly, seem to require some definite action. 1. The President before he leaves could define our attitude toward the Bolsheviki. 2. The President before he leaves could say that, while details could be left for subsequent adjustment with other delegations, at the conference, the United States proposes to see that all Russia is heard.
> —*Basil Miles, Chief, Russia Division, State Department, December 1, 1918*[1]

I venture to appeal to your sense of justice and impartiality . . . I hope and trust, above all, that before deciding on any course of action you will give justice to the demand of *audiatur et altera pars*.
> —*Maksim Litvinov to Woodrow Wilson, December 24, 1918*[2]

Agreement with Soviet government will counteract Bolshevism by prosperity . . . the more statesmanlike and influential section of the Soviet government, Lenine [sic], Tchicherin [sic] and Litvinoff [sic], prefer to reach this millennium by slower stages. They favor an understanding with the Entente, provided that the Soviet form of government can be preserved.
> —*William H. Buckler, Notes on Conversations with Litvinov, January 14–16, 1919*[3]

Soviet Russia faced civil war, foreign invasion, and virtual isolation from the rest of the world by the fall of 1918. The Bolshevik government's response was a combination of hostility and military resistance, accompanied by a desperate bid to open peace negotiations following the conclusion of the Allies' armistice with Germany in November 1918. A new breathing space, this time from war with the Allies rather than Germany, was desperately needed. From early November until the convening of the Paris Peace Confer-

175

ence in January, the Soviet government addressed at least five specific proposals for peace to the United States and the Allies. The proposals varied in form and approach, but they uniformly called for a cessation of hostilities and a negotiation of outstanding problems between the two countries. Several of them admitted, for the first time, the Soviet government's responsibility for at least a portion of Russia's war debt, and offered to surrender Russian territory and recognize *de facto* control by other anti-Bolshevik Russian governments of certain areas, in exchange for the withdrawal of Allied forces and the lifting of the Allied military and economic blockade.

The key breakthrough came with Lenin's dispatch of Maksim Litvinov as ambassador extraordinary to the West, to Stockholm, in early December 1918. Litvinov's knowledge of Britain and the United States was immediately put to use in skillful diplomatic approaches to both, culminating in the famous Christmas Eve appeal that he addressed to President Wilson. This in turn led to the dispatch of American attaché William H. Buckler to Stockholm for the first substantive discussions between an American and Bolshevik representative since the Chicherin-Poole meetings in the spring of 1918. It also contributed to British, Canadian, and American pressure for an invitation to the Bolsheviks to present their proposals in some way to the Paris Peace Conference.

The meetings Litvinov had in Stockholm came at the eleventh hour, for already the Allied blockade and pressure on the neutrals was steadily closing off all Bolshevik avenues to the West. The blockade was ostensibly instituted against Germany, but was continued after the November Armistice on the pretext of ensuring that Germany would ratify the Versailles Treaty. As Richard Ullman points out, however, this was "patently a pretext," because there was little chance of significant helpful interchange between the Bolsheviks and the Germans. In reality, this measure was part of the war the Allies had begun to wage in the hopes of overthrowing Bolshevik power.[4]

The Allies did all they could to cut off chances for the Bolsheviks to spread propaganda in the West by pressuring the neutral countries that had established some form of relations with the Bolsheviks to break relations and expel the Bolshevik envoys. By early 1919, this policy began to bear fruit, and Bolshevik representatives were expelled from Switzerland, the Netherlands, Spain, Sweden, Norway, and Denmark. By April, the only Western representatives in Moscow were the Danish Red Cross, and no Bolshevik representatives remained in any Western countries.[5]

This final isolation necessitated a new Soviet approach to diplomacy, utilizing the Red Cross, prisoner talks, trade representatives, and broadside appeals by radio in place of traditional diplomacy. By these methods the Bolsheviks approached the United States in 1919 and 1920 following the collapse of efforts in Paris.[6] Before the closing of the Bolshevik window on the West in Stockholm, however, Maksim Litvinov most skillfully used it in December 1918 and January 1919.

Soviet foreign minister Georgi Chicherin paved the way for these discussions with a series of overtures to the Allied powers in November and the first days of December. Even before the German Armistice, Chicherin contacted the Norwegian chargé at Petrograd, asking him to act as intermediary with the United States and other Allied governments. Further, Chicherin stated that he was "willing to make more concessions, and that he particularly desires to enter into negotiations with the United States." The Norwegian government inquired of the United States whether such overtures should be explored.[7] Lansing consulted with the other Allies hurriedly, and chose to ignore the Bolshevik request, noting in a message to President Wilson, "I think you will agree with me that neither of the notes should be dignified by a formal reply." Instead, Lansing proposed a strong anti-Bolshevik statement to the President. Wilson chose to do nothing, preferring to await Allied consultations preparatory to the Paris Peace Conference.[8]

On November 8, Chicherin's approaches were followed up by a resolution passed by the All-Russian Congress of Soviets calling for immediate negotiations with all the Allied powers.[9] At the same time, R. H. Bruce Lockhart was finishing a long report to the British Foreign Office detailing his most recent conversations with Vice-Commissar Karakhan. In this report, Lockhart stated his conviction that the Bolsheviks were serious about Karakhan's apparent offer "to come to terms with the allies and make commercial concessions . . . while the question of loans might be reconsidered and a settlement arrived at. . . ." Although Lockhart argued that intervention should be continued, others in the British government were beginning to consider other options.[10]

Despite the lack of response to his earlier attempts, Chicherin tried again in early December. He sent an appeal by wireless on December 2 to the governments of Britain, France, Italy, and the United States, protesting against intervention and asking once again for an Allied response to the continued openness of the Bolsheviks to discussing peace terms. Chicherin stated that "the Russian Republic has offered peace to the Entente countries, but the governments of the latter have left this offer unanswered, their answer is the present new aggression."[11] Chicherin also took advantage of the fact that Dutch minister William Oudendyk was leaving Petrograd at the same time. The Bolshevik commissar sent the message and a further offer through Oudendyk to the Allies. No Allied response was given to this proposal either, since, in the words of the British Foreign Office, "It has been decided that it is premature to enter into relations with the Bolsheviks."[12]

Chicherin's persistent proposals to the Allied governments even in the face of rejection or dismissal created some dissension within the Bolshevik government. But Lenin backed Chicherin fully, deciding to seize the favorable opportunity provided by the Armistice to send Litvinov on a personal mission to the West for peace.[13]

Even before Litvinov's arrival and beginning of his mission in mid-December, cracks began to appear in the seemingly implacable stance of the U.S. State Department. Basil Miles, head of the Russia desk, was asked to submit his thoughts concerning approaches to take to the Russian question in preparation for the Peace Conference. His response clearly came down on the side of finding a way for all Russian voices to be heard in the Conference. "We have said that the acid test of friendship for Russia at this time would be the course of conduct adopted by her friends," wrote Miles. "The President before he leaves could say that, while details could be left for subsequent adjustment with other delegations. At the Conference, the United States proposes to see that all Russia is heard."[14] Nowhere did Miles rule out talking with the Bolsheviks. Although Woodrow Wilson did not adopt his recommendation to make a public declaration of policy, clearly the door to discussion had been opened a crack. Lenin and Litvinov were determined to try to open it further.

Litvinov had been preceded to Stockholm by V. V. Vorovski, one of the first Bolshevik emissaries abroad. Vorovski was appointed plenipotentiary in Scandinavia soon after the October revolution, and worked assiduously in Stockholm to open up contacts with Scandinavian governments and with labor representatives and the media.[15] His propaganda efforts on behalf of the Soviet government were so successful that the United States government singled him out for special efforts to get him removed and the Stockholm office shut down. U.S. Ambassador to Sweden Ira Morris met with the Swedish Minister for Foreign Affairs several times in efforts to get rid of Vorovski, pointing out "the free access which Bolsheviks in Russia have had for their propaganda in Sweden and also the ability to use Sweden for transmitting Bolshevik propaganda to the United States and the Associated Governments."[16]

The Swedish minister informed Morris on December 5 that the Swedish government had decided to take steps against the Bolsheviks in Sweden. As soon as its own representatives were all returned from Russia, Sweden expected to get rid of Vorovski and his associates.[17]

Before his departure in 1919, however, Vorovski played an important role in contacts with Americans and Britons coming in and out of Russia, and in opening the way for later substantial Scandinavian-Soviet economic contacts. The Bolsheviks expanded their Scandinavian representatives under Vorovski in the fall of 1918, appointing Dr. Jacob Soritz as chargé in Copenhagen. Soviet Russia had intended to establish a large Commercial Department in Stockholm, before the Scandinavian countries bowed to the Allied pressure and expelled the Bolshevik representatives in 1919.[18] Both Bruce Lockhart and William C. Bullitt met with Vorovski on their way to Petrograd, and were impressed with his culture, learning, and ability to compromise.[19]

Maksim I. Litvinov arrived in Stockholm in the first few days of December 1918. One of his first acts was to send notes to all Allied governments, calling for the participation of Soviet Russia in the forthcoming peace conference and offering to discuss outstanding issues with the governments in the interests of ending a state of war.[20] He also had a long interview with British journalist Arthur Ransome, correspondent for the *London Daily News*. In this interview Litvinov announced the Bolsheviks' readiness for peace, openness to compromise on the debt question, and willingness to provide substantial economic concessions to the Allies. Litvinov was provided full powers of negotiation by Lenin on December 18, and authorized to open negotiations with any of the Allied or neutral powers.[21]

Litvinov concentrated especially hard on the British during his first few weeks in Stockholm. He made indirect contact with British representative

R. H. Clive on December 4. Through an intermediary, Litvinov informed Clive that a prime reason for his mission to Stockholm was to open negotiations with the British government "with the object (1) of preventing allied intervention in Russia and (2) securing some kind of recognition." In return for this, Litvinov stated that the Bolsheviks were prepared to meet some British demands, including taking responsibility for Russia's foreign debt, releasing detained British subjects, and offering compensation for the murder of Captain Cromie, the British officer killed in the aftermath of the Mirbach assassination.[22]

The Foreign Office, however, declined to meet with Litvinov directly, fearing that it would signal a step on the road to recognition, which it was unwilling to make. Response to the overture, however, indicated the coming fissures in the British Foreign Office over policy toward the Bolsheviks. To Basil Thompson's comment, "Of course no compromise with Bolshevism is possible," Foreign Secretary Arthur Balfour responded, "I fear that we may find a compromise with Bolshevism is not only possible, but necessary." For the moment, however, the Foreign Office was content to wait, avoiding any action as long as possible.[23] Further inquiry by Clive on December 7 elicited the same response. The Foreign Office declined to authorize direct contact.[24]

In one other matter, however, the British government was willing to be conciliatory. Near the same time, Clive passed on to the Foreign Office a request of the Swedish Consul General in Moscow from Soviet Assistant Foreign Commissar Lev Karakhan for the transmittal of 3,000 rubles to Karakhan's father in Harbin. The Swedish Consul General recommended approval, noting that "Karakhan was always helpful in dealings he had with him regarding the release of British officials," and the consul thought that the British government might find that granting such a favor could be of help to "the interests of British subjects still detained." The Foreign Office reluctantly granted the request, but was careful to note that in no way did this signal a change of policy toward the Bolsheviks.[25]

On December 20, Litvinov pressed the point through journalist Arthur Ransome, who visited Clive and told him that Litvinov wanted to talk with him because he had definite proposals to present to the British government. Clive asked for permission to meet. This permission was still declined by the Foreign Office. Clive was told to send word to Litvinov to submit his proposals in writing and they would be duly considered by the British government. The Foreign Office cautioned Clive that "any recognition we give, even to the extent of considering Litivnoff proposals, will be exploited by the Bolsheviks to the full, both internally and externally, it will increase their moral strength, discourage our friends and influence the attitude of neutral neighbors."[26]

But these developments kicked off a serious discussion on policy toward the Bolsheviks in the meeting of the Imperial War Council of December 23. In these discussions, Winston Churchill, David Lloyd George, and Balfour clashed regarding the wisdom of following up Litvinov's overtures, even to the extent of considering proposals submitted in writing. Churchill was opposed to any consideration whatever, wishing instead for a forthright policy to destroy the Bolsheviks or at least to ignore them totally. Lloyd George argued for at least ascertaining what the Bolshevik proposals were. Balfour finally agreed with Lloyd George, at least in part. A Bonar Law formulation to "instruct Clive to get Litivnoff to put his terms in writing" was finally approved, with the proviso that this did not mean Clive was authorized to meet with Litvinov, only to receive his proposals in writing. This was to be absolutely unofficial and without any direct reference to the British government. In the course of the discussion, the propaganda of the Bolshevik representatives in Stockholm was also mentioned. Lloyd George's response, interestingly, was that "we had no right to complain, for we had four or five armies on their soil, which, in the course of their operations, not infrequently shot Bolsheviks."[27]

While the British were awaiting Litvinov's proposals, he addressed yet another message to all of the Allied governments, officially informing them that he had been granted authority from the Soviet government to enter into formal negotiations. Litvinov asked for a place and time for meetings with him to be set, "should their Governments reciprocate the desire of the Russian Republic of a peaceful settlement of all the outstanding questions which may give rise to a continuation of hostilities between the countries concerned."[28] To this letter, the British Foreign office simply noted that the question was receiving high-level consideration by the War Cabinet. It was also due to be discussed with the French and with President Wilson in a few days, in preliminary talks prior to the opening of the Peace Conference in Paris.[29]

Before Wilson left Washington for London, he received a long and personal appeal from Litvinov, written on Christmas Eve. In this letter, Litvinov based his remarks, not on any caustic references to Wilson's hypocrisy as Chicherin had done earlier, but squarely on the high ideals of Wilson's own thinking. Litvinov stated that Russia was prepared to enter into negotiations on the basis of what Wilson had offered to all of the belligerents in the Great War. He complimented Wilson, claiming that "the principles proclaimed by you as possible basis for settling European questions, your avowed efforts and intentions of making settlement conform to demands of justice and humanity, induce and justify me to send you this statement."[30] Litvinov went on to note, quite accurately as it turned out, that the Allied nations had "only two courses open to them: . . . open or disguised intervention . . . [or coming] to an understanding with the Soviet government." He appealed to Wilson that the former course meant only the 'prolongation of war, further embitterment of the Russian masses, intensification of internal strife, unexampled bloodshed," while the second course could mean helping Russia "regain her own sources of supply and give her technical advice how to exploit natural riches in the most effective way for the benefit of all countries." After discussing some of the tragedies the Russian people had had to deal with as a result of war and invasion he closed by appealing directly to Wilson's sense of fairness: "I venture to appeal to your sense of justice and impartiality. I hope and trust, above all, that before deciding on any course of action you will give justice to the demand of *audiatur . . . altera pars* ['let the other side be heard']."[31]

This message, by all accounts, made a strong impression on Wilson. It came to him in the context of deepening concern in the United States over continued American participation in intervention in Russia in the wake of the Armistice, sharpened by the impassioned speech on the Senate floor by Senator Hiram Johnson on December 12. "What is the policy of our nation toward Russia?" Johnson had asked.

> I do not know our policy, and I know no other man who knows our policy. I do know that we are killing Russians, and they, when they can, are killing ours, and that this we are doing upon Russian soil. . . . I warn you of the policy, which God forbid this nation ever should enter upon, of endeavoring to impose by military force upon the various peoples of the earth the kind of government we desire for them, and that they do not desire for themselves.[32]

Wilson brought Litvinov's letter with him to London, where he had consultation with Lloyd George and British political leaders, as well as an hour-long interview with the editor of the *Manchester Guardian,* C. P. Scott, on December 29. Scott spent a good portion of that hour discussing Russia with Wilson. In the course of their conversation, Wilson stated his unequivocal opposition to further intervention in the Russian civil war, and discussed with Scott the possibility of opening conversations with the Bolsheviks in order to get "much fuller information as to the facts . . . whether we recognized them formally as a *de facto* Government or not."[33]

In his discussions with Lloyd George and other British political leaders, Wilson began struggling with the question of Russia's representation in Paris. Lloyd George and Canadian prime minister Robert Borden believed it was absolutely necessary for Russia to be a part of the peace settlement.[34] While having doubts about the practicality or advisability of this, Wilson expressed a strong inclination to determine the specifics of Bolshevik peace proposals in response to Litvinov's letters. The British told Wilson that they were awaiting a written statement of Litvinov's proposals, but cautioned against any direct contact with him or other Bolshevik emissaries before fully evaluating their positions, and not without consultation with the French, Italian, and Japanese allies. Further Allied action was postponed pending these two developments.[35]

Response from the French was received on January 4. The French government was considerably upset that the British would even consider a direct contact with a Bolshevik representative, considering it "inopportune and dangerous." France hoped that the British government would "instruct its representative at Stockholm not to reply to Monsieur Litvinoff."[36]

Meanwhile, however, Wilson consulted with his intimate advisor Colonel House. House agreed with Wilson that it was crucial to get more information on the Bolshevik proposals. They decided to send House confidant William H. Buckler, an aide to the American embassy in London, to Stockholm to meet with Litvinov, hear what he had to say, and report back.[37]

Litvinov, when asked in an interview in the Swedish paper *Politiken* whether he expected an answer to his notes and letters to the Allies, responded "there is no good having too great hopes about this, but now that we have displayed to the world our willingness for peace, responsibility for continued war and bloodshed rests on the Entente."[38]

Litvinov chose not to respond to the British request for a written proposal, since British representatives were unwilling to meet with him directly. He did respond, however, to the December 30 request of respected Norwegian lawyer Ludwig Meyer for Litvinov to state the Bolshevik terms for peace. In a January 10 response, Litvinov wrote, "the only demand that Soviet Russia has put to the Allies, is that they should discontinue all direct or indirect military operations against Soviet Russia, all direct or indirect material assistance to Russian or other forces operating against the Soviet Government, and also every kind of economic warfare and boycott."[39] The Soviet government, indicated Litvinov, "would be willing to reconsider some of its decrees affecting the financial negotiations of Russia towards other countries" and "would certainly desist from carrying on any propaganda in the Allied countries." Litvinov also indicated that he was not prepared to go further on terms, because the Allies had never stated their terms, nor had they responded to the many peace overtures made by the Soviet government since the Armistice.[40]

William Buckler, the envoy chosen by Wilson and House for the most important assignment of talking with Litvinov, "was destined to become one of the world's most famous archaeologists and one of America's least known diplomatic agents."[41] Archaeology was his training and his first and last love, but he served with the Foreign Service from 1912 to 1919, first with the Austrian and Turkish divisions and then as aide to U.S. Ambassador Walter Page in London. When the United States entered the war, Buckler was officially detailed to the preparation of studies and recommendations in preparation for an eventual peace conference. His real role was confidant and informant for Colonel House on labor and liberal opinion in Britain, something Ambassador Page was notoriously poor at providing. On questions of Russian policy, Buckler was able to get to House details concerning the Labour Party's attitudes and contacts, talks between Bolshevik envoy Lev Kamenev and labor leaders, and the attitude of the liberal and labor press to R. H. Bruce Lockhart's contacts with the Bolsheviks in Petrograd. Thus House kept informed about British approaches to the Bolsheviks in ways that were not the normal State Department channels.[42]

Buckler met Maksim Litvinov in January 1918 when the latter was in residence in London as the semi-official Bolshevik representative, the counterpart of Bruce Lockhart in Petrograd. At the time, Buckler reported to House that "nobody doubts that this country will somehow enter (or perhaps was already entered) into informal relations with the Bolsheviks." He reported that such a course was favored by the liberal press, and also to some extent by the sensationalist press, such as the *Express* and the *Daily Mail*. This interest in contacts with the Bolsheviks coincided with those who believed a way had to be found to negotiate a settlement with Germany short of complete victory.[43]

By June 1918, Buckler told House, erroneously as it turned out, that "it is now understood that the Foreign Office is preparing to recognize the Soviet

Government." He was correct, however, in his assessment of the importance of new initiatives by the British in the dispatch of a special economic mission to Moscow just before intervention. Although this mission failed in the wake of intervention and isolation, it was revived a few brief months later, as the war with Germany neared an end.[44]

Although Sir William Wiseman considered Buckler "an alarmist and more or less of a Bolshevist," House valued Buckler's sources and his detailed reporting of left and liberal British opinion. House convinced Wilson that Buckler was the perfect man for the Litvinov mission, in part because he was so personally loyal to House.[45]

Wilson's and House's decision to dispatch Buckler to Stockholm marked an important departure for the United States and a breakthrough for the Bolsheviks. The British, in response to Litvinov's overtures through Ransome and Clive, had insisted that Litvinov detail his proposals in writing *before* they would agree to a face-to-face meeting. Litvinov steadfastly refused to do this, insisting that the British do him the courtesy of receiving him in person. Even in his letter to Ludwig Meyer, Litvinov would only give the barest outline of the Bolshevik terms. The Americans, convinced that understanding the Bolshevik position was important to deliberations in Paris, took the chance of offending their British and French allies and sent Buckler to Stockholm.

Buckler had discussed the possibility of such a mission with House in Paris the first few days of January. Soon after his return to London, Buckler received a telephone message through the counselor of the Embassy, Butler Wright, telling him that a decision had been made "that it was the desire of the President" that Buckler proceed to Stockholm post-haste to carry out the mission that was discussed in Paris. He was then scheduled to go from Sweden to Lausanne, Switzerland, to attend an international labor conference, before reporting back to House in Paris in late January.[46] Wilson's personal interest in Buckler's mission was evidenced by his inquiries of House and Lansing concerning Buckler's progress. Lansing reported to him on January 13 that Buckler was expected to arrive in Stockholm that day.[47]

On Buckler's arrival in Stockholm on January 13, he met with U.S. Ambassador Ira Morris and explained his mission. According to Buckler's account, Morris was "at first shocked at the bare semblance of any approach to the Soviet Government" and threatened to hold up the approach pending confirmation from Colonel House. In further discussion, however, Morris reluctantly agreed to the meetings, in part convinced by his own military attaché, Colonel Colvin, who pointed out the immense military difficulties of a considered program of intervention. Since "pursuing hostilities of unknown magnitude, with no visible army to carry them out" was so "impracticable . . . upon reflection he clearly saw the possible advantages of coming to an agreement" and concurred with Buckler that the approach to Litvinov should be pursued.[48]

It proved easy to arrange meetings with Litvinov. The two men met three times over the next three days for periods of several hours each time, on the last occasion joined by Arthur Ransome, with Litvinov's approval. No notes were kept during the meetings, but Buckler wrote down his own detailed notes immediately following each meeting. At the end of the meetings, Litvinov reviewed these notes, and "initialed them as a sign that they accurately represented his views."[49]

The meetings between Litvinov and Buckler cannot be considered "negotiations" in any true sense of the word, because Buckler was not armed with any United States proposals, nor was he empowered to even present American ideas for a settlement. He explained to Litvinov at the beginning of their discussions that he was "merely a private telephone through which he could supplement his telegram of December 24," and that he had "no authority to make proposals of any kind."[50] Litvinov complained on several occasions that he found it difficult to formulate Bolshevik proposals in the absence of anything substantive coming from Allies, and asked Buckler to make it known clearly that if discussions were to proceed any further, a list of Allied or United States demands must be submitted.

Despite this insistence on Litvinov's part, and the disparity of the positions of the two men, Litvinov did find it possible to detail in substantial measure Bolshevik proposals. Following the talks, Buckler did not confine himself in his reporting to being a simple "telephone," but took it upon himself to make definite proposals of his own to Colonel House, President Wilson, and the Peace Commission.[51]

Litvinov began his talks with Buckler by discussing Soviet concerns and attitudes toward the United States. On one hand, Litvinov said that the Russian people respected the United States and wanted to believe in President Wilson's stated "desire to help Russia." Wilson's March 1918 message to the Congress of Soviets was much applauded, because it expressed a certain recognition of Soviet power and was the only message received from a head of state. On the other hand, American participation in intervention in Archangel and Siberia "placed American motives in a bad light and suggested that the President's belief in the right of a people to regulate its own political affairs was not sincere." Moreover, Litvinov explained to Buckler, "Russians feel keenly the unfairness shown by your Government in taking their news about Russia from biased and reactionary sources, and in accepting at their face value forgeries such as the Sisson documents," without giving the Soviet government a chance to respond to the accusations and allegations.[52]

It was for this reason, Litvinov explained, that he wrote to President Wilson on December 24, believing that the Bolsheviks deserved a chance to be heard. Litvinov practically apologized for Chicherin's note of October 30, which Litvinov "regarded and still regards as a mistake," calling it "a piece of propagandist journalism, discourteous in tone and calculated rather to repel than to conciliate." On the contrary, Litvinov stated, the Bolsheviks "are genuinely anxious for real and permanent peace."[53]

Litvinov then went on to show Buckler just how devastated the Soviet government and Russian people were from the combination of the Great War, civil war, and foreign intervention, and the lengths they were willing to go to to achieve peace. He told Buckler that the Russian people "detest the military preparations and costly campaigns which have been forced on [them]." If the

Allies and the United States "really desire peace . . . they can easily have it," for the Bolsheviks were prepared "to make concessions on every point."[54]

Litvinov particularly stressed the desirability of the "economic restoration of Russia," which necessitated compromise. Litvinov refused to give details on the exact nature of compromise on the debt question, stating that he could not give them until he saw what claims the Allies would make and could respond with a specific list of resources that the Soviets were willing to make available to meet those claims. He proposed to Buckler the essence of some kind of bargain involving debt, claims, and credits, tied in with a revival of foreign trade and Bolshevik economic concessions to the United States. "These particulars could be worked out jointly by experts from both sides," stated Litvinov, and he stressed again that the "conciliatory attitude of the Soviet Government is unquestionable." Litvinov noted particularly the impossibility of getting along without "expert assistance and advice, especially in technical and financial matters, not to mention foreign machinery and manufactured imports."[55]

Litvinov next turned to the question of Bolshevik propaganda in the West, claiming that "if peace were once made, Russian propaganda would no longer menace the countries not sharing the Bolshevist doctrine." Revolutionary propaganda, he claimed, was a function of war, but it would stop when the war stopped. He did, however, admit to heavy Bolshevik propaganda in Germany, but claimed it was absolutely necessary because Germany was "Russia's most dangerous enemy" and therefore the Soviet government was "fully justified." Litvinov insisted strenuously, however, that he had not carried on revolutionary propaganda during the eight months in which he represented the Soviet government in London. Rather, he had "replied to attacks made upon his government." As for countries Russia was at peace with, Litvinov pledged that "no Russian propaganda will be attempted." If "conditions are not ripe for a revolution . . . no amount of propaganda could produce those favorable conditions."[56]

Litvinov turned his attention next to the specific conditions arising out of the end of military hostilities. He offered amnesty to all those who had taken part in attacks on the Soviet government, permitting those who wished to emigrate the possibility of doing so. With regard to the specific "governments" and territory controlled by other forces, Litvinov claimed that in South Russia, in Siberia, and at Archangel the local forces' weakness would be exposed once foreign support was suspended, and they would collapse. On the other hand, he expressed no hostility toward Finland, Poland, Sweden, or the Ukraine, offering to recognize their right to self-determination if they would cease their attacks on Soviet Russia. Litvinov refused categorically at this meeting to recognize "the purely autocratic and self-appointed regime of Kolchak in Siberia."[57]

After stressing once again that matters could not proceed further without some specific Allied response to these tentative proposals. Litvinov admitted mistakes that the Soviet government had made in the course of the revolution and civil war. He came close to apologizing for overzealous Bolshevik attacks on the intelligentsia and the peasant cooperatives and stated that all were being welcomed back now to help with reconstruction.[58]

In response to a question from Buckler concerning Russia's attitude toward the League of Nations and whether Russia would join such a League if it were created, Litvinov expressed skepticism "as to the effectiveness of such a League to prevent war, owing to the imperialistic attitude of many members of the League." But if such a League were able to prevent war "without encouraging reaction and without interfering in the internal affairs of countries," then the League would "have the support and participation of the Soviet government." Litvinov was extremely dubious, however, that such a League "will ever materialize."[59]

In the last of the three meetings between the two men, Litvinov stressed once again the openness of the Soviet government to an agreement with the United States, but said that in his mind "the real question was whether the Allies and the United States would allow the Soviet government to exist." If they would, an agreement would be quite possible to negotiate. Litvinov also urged Buckler to recommend that the Americans investigate the situation in Soviet Russia for themselves, so that they "would satisfy themselves that the Soviet Government is not a mere forcible despotism of a minority, but that it has a genuine hold on the Russian people."[60]

After this meeting, British journalist Arthur Ransome stayed on for another half-hour conversation with Litvinov and then met with Buckler. Buckler also recorded his notes on this meeting with Ransome and Ransome's assessment of the situation. Ransome had been in Moscow until August 1918 and had kept closely in touch with the Bolsheviks through contacts in Stockholm and through numerous discussions with Litvinov. Ransome concluded after meeting with Litvinov that the Bolsheviks were really serious about negotiations to stop the war. He also believed that they would be willing to compromise on territory, even perhaps being willing to give up good portions of Siberia, in exchange for peace.[61]

Ransome also told Buckler that he believed a policy of Allied intervention, even a limited one with a strong economic boycott, might eventually prevail. But the great danger in such a strategy was that it would not therefore settle the question of the government of Russia. Instead it would simply lead to further civil war and further intervention. On the other hand, if a policy of peace were pursued by the Allies, it might well lead to the gradual diminution of Soviet power and the rise of some kind of coalition government. "The more statesmanlike and intelligent Bolshevists, like Lenin, Tchitcherin, Vorovsky and Litvinov . . . favor an understanding with the Allies," said Ransome. He told Buckler that continued hostility to the Allies was only desired by the most extreme Bolsheviks. A wise Allied policy, therefore, would be to deal with the moderates now rather than have to face the extremists later. Such a decision, in Ransome's opinion, would have the effect of moving the Soviet government to the right. The end of the war would bring overwhelming problems of reconstruction, "requiring technical and financial assistance from Europe and the United States."[62]

Buckler left Stockholm for Copenhagen immediately after his meetings with Litvinov and Ransome, and found that his return trip to Paris would be delayed because of transportation difficulties in the chaos following the war. He decided at that point to send an immediate short report on his conversations to the Peace Commissioners in Paris, while indicating that he would still like the opportunity for a longer, personal report on his arrival in Paris. In this cable to Lansing and the Peace Commissioners, Buckler also stressed the importance of removing blocks to communication and negotiation with the Soviets if the United States were serious about pursuing these conversations. He noted that Litvinov had been deprived by the Swedish government of all mail privileges and wireless cipher for communication with Moscow, and that he feared expulsion from Stockholm at any time. Buckler also expressed the desire to continue the conversations with Litvinov if the U.S. had proposals to advance, and said that he would stay in Copenhagen to await further orders before returning to Paris, "in case you wish me to return to Stockholm."[63]

As for the substance of his talks with Litvinov, Buckler touched on the main points expressed in his immediate notes, but stressed that Litvinov said that the "Soviet Government was anxious for permanent peace" and that "the Soviet government is prepared to compromise on all points." Buckler also noted that "the conciliatory attitude of the Soviet Government is unquestionable," although he was not clear whether that was his own appraisal or simply his report of Litvinov's statement. Buckler also discussed in his memorandum to Lansing "Russia's great need for expert assistance and advice especially in technical and financial matters" and quoted Litvinov as saying that "if peace were made Russian Bolshevist propaganda in foreign countries would cease at once."[64]

Buckler also took the opportunity of his enforced stay in Copenhagen to cable his old friend Colonel House. In this cable he did not confine himself to a summary of the Litvinov discussions, but rather forcefully expressed his own recommendations for American policy. Following Ransome, he stated that military occupation and intervention could only succeed in the long term, if ever, and therefore it was wise to try to get a favorable peace settlement with the Bolsheviks now. It might still be possible to trade peace for territory, relying on "normal conditions as a disinfectant against bolshevism." Buckler said he was convinced

> that we can make a fair bargain regarding foreign debt and foreign interests. . . . If the allies boldly say, "We are now convinced that the Soviet Government has a firm hold on the Russian people, and will recognize it on conditions . . . we contemplate generous treatment and expect the same in return." Such an attitude will pay both in the long run and at once by strengthening the moderates . . . will drive the Soviet movement to the right.[65]

Wilson and House did not wait for Buckler's return to Paris to move on his recommendations. Wilson read parts of Buckler's cable to House to the Council of Ten on January 20, noting his conclusion that "it is possible for an agreement with Russia to be made at once, thus obviating conquest and policing," and that "we can make a fair bargain regarding foreign interests and the foreign debt if we do not greatly curtail Russian territory."[66]

Meanwhile, Buckler paced nervously in Copenhagen, waiting for a summons to Paris. In a letter to his wife, Georgina, on January 21, he worried: "no telegram today and I rather doubt if any comes tomorrow. The Russian skein is so tangled that I suppose before deciding anything, many persons must be considered."[67]

The very next day, however, Buckler received a summons to Paris, along with a request to arrange for Arthur Ransome to come as well, to help in briefing the Peace Commission delegates. Buckler's scheduled trip to Lausanne and the Labour Conference was put off, because "Russia is uppermost in their minds," as Buckler expressed to Georgina. "Thoughts of compromise must be spreading."[68]

Shortly after Buckler left Copenhagen for Paris, a letter was received for him from Litvinov, following up their conversations. In this letter, which was forwarded to Buckler in Paris, Litvinov expressed his great concern about "bitter enemies" who would try to torpedo any ideas of conversations or peace with the Bolsheviks, and urged Buckler to do his utmost to get his full report in front of President Wilson as soon as possible. Litvinov told Buckler that both French ambassador Noulens and Danish envoy Scavenius, who were deeply prejudiced against the Bolsheviks, had already made presentations to the Peace Conference, and he feared that a decision might be made even before Buckler arrived in Paris.[69] Litvinov followed up this letter with a shorter note, written the same day, noting that he expected any day to have to leave Stockholm, due to Allied pressure, and that he could be reached, if he were allowed to move to Norway, in care of Ludwig Meyer in Christiana, Norway.[70]

Buckler wrote Georgina once more en route to Paris, "thrilled to see in the papers the new olive branch held out to Russia" (the Prinkipo proposal by the Allies, calling on all Russian parties to meet). He finally arrived in Paris on January 29, where he cooled his heels waiting to be called to report to the Peace Commission. Buckler made his headquarters while in Paris with his brother-in-law, Henry White, one of the Commissioners.[71]

Buckler finally made his report to the Peace Commissioners the following day, January 30, but President Wilson was not in attendance. It was indeed fortunate for the consideration of Buckler's recommendations by the Peace Conference that he had telegraphed the substance of his report to Lansing and House earlier. By the time he had returned, the Peace Conference had moved to other issues, but his recommendations had led to Wilson's Prinkipo Island invitation, which was at that time pending. Buckler was asked to stay in Paris to consult with House, Wilson, and the Commissioners as desired, should the Prinkipo invitation lead to negotiations or conversations. Buckler believed that "the ice seems broken" and that "the British like ourselves will go to Prinkipo even if the invitation is accepted by nobody except the Soviets."[72]

The Peace Commission did send Buckler and William C. Bullitt to meet with Lloyd George's private secretary, Philip Kerr, to discuss follow-up to Buckler's meetings with Litvinov and British and American strategy in the face of a possible breakdown of Prinkipo due to French and White Russian intransigence. From this meeting Buckler came away convinced that the British were committed to talking with the Bolsheviks. The groundwork was also laid at this meeting for what became the "Bullitt Mission" to Moscow, the last American and British effort to negotiate a Bolshevik-Allied agreement.[73]

Buckler remained in Paris for a time, used by the Peace Commissioners for his ability to elicit information in interviews, but he left the Foreign Service after the collapse of the Wilson administration's efforts to get the peace treaty ratified. At this time he left public life and returned to his archaeology. Buckler's convictions that negotiation with the Bolsheviks would strengthen the moderates and isolate the extremists in the Soviet government went untested until the early 1920s.[74]

Maksim Litvinov's success in reaching Woodrow Wilson was facilitated by the President's deep concern with integrating Russia into the approaching peace conference, and also was strengthened by the tide of public opinion in the United States in the New Year, 1919. Senator Hiram Johnson's queries had struck a nerve, and the sentiment in Congress increasingly moved away from military intervention and toward some kind of accommodation, although the exact dimensions of any settlement seemed elusive. Many congressmen wanted the United States simply to stay away from Russian politics and confine its assistance to humanitarian efforts to restore the "normal conditions of life."[75] Thomas Thacher, sensing a change in the political wind in Washington and greatly encouraged by rumors emanating from Paris, wrote to Raymond Robins on January 14, urging him to become involved in a major push for a new American policy toward the Bolsheviks. Thacher wrote that all these things taken together "indicate a complete change of front which, if not too late, may mean the formulation of a policy of some wisdom."[76]

The Bolsheviks themselves tried to take direct advantage of the congressional inquiries. The Chairman of the U.S. Senate Foreign Relations Committee, Senator Gilbert Hitchcock, had tried to respond to the persistent inquiries of Hiram Johnson by making a public declaration of the reasons why American troops were in Russia. Hitchcock based his defense largely on Wilson's *aide-mémoire* of July 17 and the need to fight Germany in north Russia. But the Armistice had cast serious doubt on this rationale. Foreign Minister Chicherin sent a direct response through the Danish chargé, still in Petrograd, to Secretary Lansing and the American Commissioners in Paris. Hitchcock had claimed that one of the reasons for the continued presence of American troops in Russia was to "maintain a gateway for the arrival and departure of diplomats and other American citizens." But Chicherin noted pointedly "we think that the best way to attain that end is to enter into an agreement with our Government." Chicherin went on to reiterate the various approaches and proposals the Bolsheviks had made to the United States since the Armistice, including the Litvinov proposal to Wilson. Chicherin hoped that "the peaceful views of the able Senators will be shared by all Americans," and he again requested the United States government "kindly to make known the place and date for opening peace negotiations with our representatives."[77]

Maksim Litvinov also followed up the Hitchcock declaration with an inquiry of his own through Doctor Davidson, an intermediary in Stockholm who often provided U.S. Ambassador Ira Morris with the latest communications and intelligence from Bolshevik sources. Davidson reported a conversation with Litvinov on January 21 in which Litvinov reiterated his offer to Buckler to "compromise on all matters involving foreigners such as foreign debts and external business relations. " Davidson noted that Litvinov "seems well informed of airing that Russian affairs have had in the United States Senate."[78]

Ludwig Meyer, Litvinov's Norwegian lawyer-confidant, also did not miss the opportunity to pursue the issue. Before the United States Senate vote on Johnson's resolution to withdraw American forces, Meyer wrote directly to Johnson enclosing a copy of his letter from Litvinov on January 10, setting out some Bolshevik conditions for peace. In his letter to Johnson, Meyer hoped that Litvinov's letter "may be of some use to you."[79]

Maksim Litvinov's Christmas Eve appeal to President Wilson and the Bolshevik envoy's follow-up talks with William H. Buckler achieved at least one modest aim. They established the Bolsheviks' openness to serious negotiations with the West to end a state of war. They also placed the outlines of a possible agreement in the public eye. These conditions would be returned to many times before the United States finally negotiated an agreement establishing diplomatic recognition in 1933, with that same Maksim Litvinov. By that time, any probing of Litvinov's openness to trading territory for peace, as indicated by Buckler and Ransome, had become irrelevant, because the White armies had long since collapsed. But the other key concessions—the ending of revolutionary propaganda and Soviet responsibility for the Russian government's foreign debt—were key pieces in the eventual settlement.[80]

# 8

# Paris I
# the Prinkipo Failure

The effect of the Russian problem on the Paris Conference . . . was profound: Paris cannot be understood without Moscow. Without ever being represented at Paris at all, the Bolsheviki and Bolshevism were powerful elements at every turn. Russia played a more vital part at Paris than Prussia!

—*Ray Stannard Baker*[1]

[Russia] was the Banquo's ghost sitting at every Council Table.
—*Herbert Hoover*[2]

The Paris Peace Conference marked a watershed in American, and Allied, policy toward Bolshevik Russia. Since the Armistice had brought an end to the conventional rationale for intervention, a decision of a much more fundamental character had to be made. Would the Allies intervene massively in an effort to destroy the Bolsheviks? Or would they seek to bring them into the peace process, and come to terms with their permanence as the government of Great Russia? Bruce Lockhart, the British representative in Moscow, was released from prison and returned to Moscow in the fall of 1918. On November 1, he addressed a long policy memorandum to the Foreign Office. In this memorandum he urged massive intervention as his preferred option, but he also urged the British government to make a decision one way or another, either to eliminate the Bolshevik menace or to come to terms with it, but not equivocate or waffle between the two positions.[3]

Over the course of the long meetings in Paris during the first half of 1919, neither Britain itself nor its Allies could ever unite fully behind either policy. Neither massive intervention nor serious negotiation was ever fully pursued. The lowest common denominator, limited intervention, economic blockade, and aid for anti-Bolshevik forces, continued to be Allied policy, now stripped of much of its anti-German rationale.

The Allies tried in various ways to come to a common policy toward the

Bolsheviks and the "Russian problem," but all of the schemes developed failed for one reason or another, and none had the full support of Britain, France, and the United States necessary for its implementation. Essentially, five distinct efforts were made to break out of the partial measures that seemed to hamstring Allied approaches—three peace initiatives and two war initiatives. The first, the Anglo-American proposal to bring all the Russian factions together in a peace conference at Prince's Islands (Prinkipo) failed essentially because of French and White Russian resistance to the idea of discussions with the Bolsheviks. The second, Winston Churchill's massive intervention scheme, foundered largely on the rock of American unwillingness to commit the troops necessary, not to mention divided counsels within the British government. The secret American mission to Moscow led by William C. Bullitt brought back extremely favorable terms for peace. This mission, however, had to contend not only with French opposition, but with changed political conditions in Britain and the lack of real support from Woodrow Wilson. The Hoover-Nansen initiative for food relief tied to an armistice was fatally flawed by unequal political conditions that the Bolsheviks saw no reason to meet without equal accommodation by their enemies. And finally, the partial recognition and stepped-up assistance for Admiral Aleksandr Kolchak, the Peace Conference's desperation ploy in May and June 1919, was doomed by Kolchak's own failure to unify anti-Bolshevik forces and the growing military successes of the Red Army. This decision marked the end of active Allied consideration of negotiations with the Bolsheviks. Only after Kolchak, Denikin, and other White forces had been defeated would first Britain, then France and Italy, and finally the United States move toward accommodation and negotiation with the Bolsheviks in the 1920s.

The story of the consideration of the Russia problem at the Paris Peace Conference is certainly the best-known of all the attempts at negotiation and discussion between the Allies and the Bolsheviks between 1917 and 1920. The next three chapters will concentrate on a consideration of the failures of the three peace initiatives: Prinkipo, Bullitt, and Hoover-Nansen; attempting to focus on the Soviet-American interaction, the role of the United States, and the larger canvas of Soviet-American relations in the Lenin-Wilson years.[4]

In one sense, the United States had been preparing for Allied considerations regarding Russia in Paris practically since the Bolshevik revolution. In late 1917, Colonel House began the organization of the Inquiry, a group of experts drawn together to begin preparing background studies on every potential aspect of the forthcoming peace in Europe. Samuel N. Harper was asked to join this group to contribute research on the current situation in Russia.[5] Harper was later joined by Archibald Cary Coolidge, and Walter Lord and Samuel Eliot Morison of Harvard University. All of these men were to figure prominently in the U.S. staff on Russia and Eastern Europe in Paris.[6]

By the fall of 1918, as a German armistice loomed, questions concerning a Russia policy for Paris began to be raised with increasing frequency. Woodrow Wilson's consistent reaction to such questions was to defer any decision until the Peace Conference. Once the decision had been taken regarding limited intervention in July 1918, Wilson refused to become party to any Allied initiatives pending the peace conference. Sir William Wiseman pressed Wilson on this point in October, insistent that a political conference concerning action in Russia was imperative. Wilson responded that any definitive policy should wait until the Peace Conference. Until then, he told Wiseman,

> I believe in letting them work out their own salvation, even though they wallow in anarchy for a while. I visualize it like this: a lot of impossible folk, fighting among themselves. You cannot do business with them, so you shut them all up in a room and lock the door and tell them that when they have settled matters among themselves you will unlock the door and do business.[7]

In whatever scheme was developed, Wilson wanted to emphasize America's strengths: "idealism, men and materials," and he wished somehow to bring peace to Russia as well as Europe. He believed with Lloyd George that Europe could not be at peace if Russia were still at war.[8]

Colonel House, in preliminary discussions with the British, was quite concerned that the Russian issue could be an explosive one in Paris. He and Lloyd George privately agreed that they would try to avoid having speeches made on the issue, preferring to work quietly and privately for a solution.[9]

Secretary of State Lansing, for his part, wished that a statement of American aims with regard to Russia and the Bolsheviks would be made before Paris, as a way of clearing the air and making explicit America's repugnance of the Bolsheviks. Wilson refused to do this, despite pressure from both Lansing and Polk, who tried to convince him that "no one can take the lead so well as the President in defining the attitude of the associated Governments on this question."[10]

On board the *George Washington* en route to Paris, the staff and commissioners of the American delegation to the Peace Conference prevailed upon Wilson one evening to share his hopes, plans, and goals for negotiating the peace. In the course of that conversation, Wilson stressed the importance of a lasting peace "made on the highest principles of justice" throughout Europe as a key element in any strategy of resistance to bolshevism. He left the group with the "distinct impression . . . that he was not considering a further advance against the Bolsheviki."[11] Wilson also reportedly told Russian Prince Georgi Lvov, a leader of the anti-Bolsheviks in Paris, that Russia "should have no official representatives at the peace conference" at all, but rather that the Allies would consult with "unofficial" individuals representing different points of view.[12]

Wilson met with Lloyd George the last few days of December before arriving in Paris. At these conversations, in addition to advocating the pursuit of clarifications from Maksim Litvinov regarding Bolshevik peace proposals, Wilson made it very clear that he opposed further intervention in Russia and was looking toward early withdrawal of American troops from Russia.[13]

British consideration of an Allied policy at Paris had been under intense review since the Armistice. In the armistice agreement with Germany, the Allies had, in British eyes, made very clear their dual purpose with regard to Russia: protection from both German and Bolshevik influence.[14] The Allies completed a naval and military encirclement of Russia in addition to an economic blockade, and these were tightened as a result of the Armistice. Thus the rudiments of a *cordon sanitaire* were already in place at the time of the dicussions concerning the Peace conference, and remained in place in the absence of any agreement on policy.[15]

The British War Cabinet held its first full-scale post-Armistice discussion of Russia policy on November 14. At this meeting, the Cabinet considered a series of papers prepared by the Foreign Office and the War Office. The War Office, under Sir Henry Winston, suggested three possible courses of action: (1) the withdrawal of all troops and the buildup of an effective *cordon sanitaire;* (2) a major military effort to crush bolshevism; or (3) supply of friendly White forces to assist them against the Bolsheviks, then withdrawal of Allied troops. All of these options were hostile to the Bolsheviks, but two were potentially undoable.[16]

The War Office was inclined toward option two but could not recommend it because it did not believe that Britain had either the troops or the resources to effect it. This led Winston to option three as a less desirable, but more feasible, route.[17] The Cabinet agreed with Winston that a massive anti-Bolshevik crusade was unfeasible, and urged instead that as much aid as possible be given to "friendly forces in those regions which most closely affected the interests of the British empire." Lord Milner then articulated a principle to guide British action in Russia in the post-Armistice period: "Where there was in existence a friendly, anti-Bolshevik government which it was to our advantage to support, we should support it . . . even though it entails anti-Bolshevik action." Implicit in this principle was that the British government was bound to assist those Russians "who had remained loyal to the Allied cause."[18]

But no one was particularly happy with this policy, and hope remained that a unified Allied policy could be arrived at at the Peace Conference. As Lord Milner wrote to Russian émigré Nabokov on December 12, "We try to help, here and there, anybody who seems to be trying, with the slightest chance of success, to stem the Bolshevist tide. That is a purely opportunist policy. It is better than nothing, but it is not nearly enough. I hope that the approaching conference of the allies may enable us . . . to arrive at some more vigorous and more constructive policy."[19]

The tenor of War Cabinet conversations changed markedly in mid-December. Public opinion began to move against further intervention in the face of a coming peace conference, and questions were raised in Parliament calling for the withdrawal of British forces. The War Cabinet held a long debate on December 10 concerning the fate of British troops and British policy about Russia that reflected this pressure.[20] Following Maksim Litvinov's overtures to R. H. Clive in mid-December, debate was stimulated once again. Although the Foreign Office refused to permit Clive to open direct meetings with Litvinov, it sparked an intense discussion within the Cabinet that was to continue, in one form or another, for over a year. In some ways this argument was not resolved within the British government until the second resumption of diplomatic relations in the late 1920s.[21]

The War Cabinet debate of December 30 and 31 focused specifically on the seemingly disparate options of negotiations or full-scale intervention. The Foreign Office, led by Balfour, declined to hear Litvinov or to invite the Bolsheviks to Paris, stressing the "obligation" Britain had to its anti-Bolshevik friends. Lloyd George, supported strongly by a number of representatives from the British Empire, notably by Prime Minister Robert Borden of Canada, emphasized the critical need to move toward peace and to end the intervention. Winston Churchill, soon to become War Minister, emerged at this time as the major proponent of a strategy of massive intervention. The upshot of the Cabinet discussion was a compromise position supporting Lloyd George. This position noted the need for peace and a winding down of all intervention, but it gave way to the Foreign Office to the extent that "where there was an external aggression by the Bolsheviks against an existing Government with which we had been cooperating, we should be entitled to support that government in any manner which did not involve military intervention."[22] No immediate move was made to terminate British troop involvements in Russia, however. The Cabinet preferred to wait to see if some unified Allied position could not be agreed upon in Paris.[23]

In the course of these discussions, the Cabinet also decided to request from Litvinov his proposals in writing before deciding whether to meet with him.[24] In addition, Prime Minister Borden suggested that all the Russian factions be invited to Paris to meet with the Conference and settle their differences. Lord Robert Cecil amended this suggestion to include the element of an immediate ceasefire as a requirement for participation. Lord Milner then suggested that if the Borden-Cecil position were adopted, "there was no reason why all the governments in Russia, including even the Bolsheviks, should not be invited to the Peace Conference."[25]

Although no action was taken on this proposal at the time, Lloyd George adopted it with alacrity, and asked both the United States and France whether it could not be the basis for an Allied response to the question of Russian representation in Paris. He requested an answer to whether the following message could not be sent to all the Russian parties, including the Bolsheviks: "If the aforesaid Governments and parties will immediately suspend hostilities on all fronts for the duration of peace negotiations and then if they or any of them should desire to send representatives to Paris to discuss with Great Powers the conditions of a permanent settlement, the Great Powers would be prepared to enter on such a discussion with them."[26]

Robert Borden's role in the British initiative that led to the Prinkipo proposal often has been overlooked.[27] Yet it was his initiative Lloyd George agreed to and acted on. As Borden reflected in his memoirs,

I did not see how the war could be regarded as having terminated if we should leave the Peace Conference with five or six nations and Governments still fighting in that country; and I suggested, in lieu of forcible intervention, that the Governments of the various States in Russia should be induced to send representatives to Paris for conference with the allied and associate nations.[28]

Lloyd George's initiative caused a good deal of comment within the British Cabinet and among the Allies, some of it quite unfavorable. Milner grumbled privately, "LG has had severe attack of Bolshevism."[29] The War Office warned General Alfred Knox that the discussion concerning Russia in Paris "may be a prolonged one."[30] Wilson's press secretary Joseph Tumulty wrote Wilson, "Proposal of Lloyd George that the Russian Bolsheviki be invited to send peace delegates to Paris produced very unfavorable impression everywhere. It is denounced as amazing."[31]

Lloyd George's initiative was bobbled by the United States' State Department, magnifying the American reaction. When Acting Secretary of State Polk received the memorandum, he did nothing publicly, nor did he notify the Peace Commissioners in Paris, assuming that they were fully acquainted with the initiative. He simply commented privately to Assistant Secretary of State William Phillips, "As the Bolsheviks are sure not to pay any attention to any such appeal . . . it would not be helpful to ask Kolchak and Denikin and the others to refrain from hostilities, nothing could be accomplished, and the impression created would be bad."[32]

Polk compounded his error when he was asked by the press on January 11 about the proposal and the French response to it. (Pichon denounced it in the strongest terms—see below). Polk did not make the connection between the two, and declared that the United States "had received no proposal for the Bolsheviki to be allowed to send delegates to Paris." In an explanatory memo to Lansing, Polk assumed "full responsibility for the misunderstanding," but press interest in the story heightened in the following weeks. The *Dial* of January 25, for example, claimed the incident showed "how little our officials are to be entrusted with the formulation of any democratic foreign policy, when left unchecked or uncriticized. . . . The proposal was not communicated to the President in Paris, and if newspaper dispatches report correct, our peace delegates were astonished. . . ."[33]

In the meantime, in Paris, Foreign Minister Stephane Pichon made known in no uncertain terms France's opposition to meeting with Bolsheviks under any conditions. Pichon particularly expressed outrage that the Allies should even consider inviting the Bolsheviks to the peace conference, calling such proposals tantamount to recognizing a group of thugs and saying that "the French Government, so far as it is concerned, will make no contract with crime." Instead, Pichon said, the Allies should admit representatives of the non-Bolshevik forces to present their claims, and should continue to supply arms, money, and military support to their efforts to overthrow the Bolsheviks.[34]

This note was leaked to the Paris newspaper *L'Humanité* and published, causing an immediate sensation in Paris. Lansing and House contacted the British ambassador in Paris, Lord Derby, complaining that they were not informed. French Premier Georges Clemenceau was furious with Pichon, not because of the policy, but because he acted without the courtesy of consulting with the United States. According to Ambassador Derby, Clemenceau threatened *L'Humanité* with suppression if it published the letter, which it did anyway. (It was not suppressed.) Clemenceau also claimed that the British telegram was sent when both Balfour and Cecil were away from the Foreign Office, "at the instigation of somebody with Bolshevist tendencies." As Derby reflected, "it will indeed make a certain amount of friction between our own Government and the French government . . . [but] the publication of such an extremely confidential document is a bad augury for what will happen if the press is to be allowed to publish what it likes without censorship."[35]

The stark differences among the Allies concerning Russian representation in Paris were immediately aired at the first meeting of the Council of Ten of the Peace Conference on January 12, 1919. Pichon argued that the interests of Russia could be represented by inviting the various Russian representatives already in Paris. These "represented every shade of opinion." Lloyd George responded that "they represented every shade of opinion except the prevalent opinion in Russia. . . . The Bolshevists were the de facto government. . . . To say that we ourselves should pick the representatives of a great people was contrary to every principle for which we had fought."[36] This clash prevented any agreement concerning official Russian representation in Paris. All that could be agreed was that individuals such as those mentioned by Pichon could be heard by the conference informally.[37]

The following day, Pichon tried a new ploy. In the context of further discussion about representation of some of the smaller powers, he remarked that the question of representation of Russia had been settled the day before. The conference had agreed to hear Prince Lvov, Boris Savinkov, and other Russian represenatatives already in Paris. But Lloyd George immediately demurred, noting that they had agreed only to talk with such individuals informally and that they had reached no agreement on the representation for Russia as a whole. After further debate, the council agreed to postpone this contentious issue until after the point of a general policy vis-à-vis the various Russia questions had been discussed and determined.[38]

In the interim, the British and American positions were considerably strengthened by an important report prepared by British military representatives in Russia and shared with Wilson on January 20. This report showed the continued strength of the Soviet government as well as its serious need to make peace with the Allies. One of the conclusions drawn by this paper was that intervention, if not undertaken in a massive way, simply served to strengthen the Bolshevik government.[39] One of the staff members of the Inquiry, R. H. Lord, also prepared a background memorandum on Russia for Wilson. This memorandum tended to stress Bolshevik weakness, although it did note that "the fear of foreign intervention and of an accompanying counterrevolution is rallying many elements to the Bolshevist government."[40]

Near the same time, Consul Poole, then still in Archangel, wrote a long cable stressing the difficulties of military intervention if not accompanied by political measures. He cautioned the State Department that "there will be a reaction of disillusion and discontent" and urged "that no active Russian policy be entered upon unless we are ourselves willing and able to put it through vigorously and generously."[41]

The Allies returned to the controversial issue of Russia on January 16. Lloyd George led off the discussion with an attempt to clarify the British position, which he claimed had been severely misunderstood and misrepresented. He stated that it had never been the intent of the British government "that the Bolshevik Government should be recognized to the extent of offering them a seat at the Peace Conference." Rather, a truce had been proposed, followed by an invitation to the various would-be governments to come to Paris "to explain their position and receive from the Allies, if possible, some suggestions for the accommodation of their differences."[42]

Lloyd George said that it seemed to him there were only three possible alternatives for the governments assembled in Paris: (1) a decision that Bolshevism was such a menace that it must be totally eradicated, which meant an accelerated war at great cost of life; (2) a siege of Bolshevik Russia, which meant the responsibility of starving a huge population; or (3) a search to find some way of ending the war and accommodating Russian differences. He proposed the third alternative as the only humane and feasible choice. President Wilson strongly agreed with him, stating that the British proposal "contained the only suggestion that led anywhere. If the Bolsheviks refrained from invading Lithuania, Poland, Finland, etc., he thought we should be well advised to allow as many groups as desired to do so to send representatives to Paris. We should then try to reconcile them, both mutually and with the rest of the world."[43]

Both Wilson and Lloyd George continued to stress the need for better information on Russia. Pichon, realizing that his position was not getting across, seized on this opening and asked for the council to hear the French ambassador to Russia, Joseph Noulens, and the Danish minister, Scavenius, before making any decisions. This session was set for January 21.[44]

Lloyd George claimed later, in his memoirs, that he

> would have dealt with the Soviets as the *de facto* Government of Russia. So would President Wilson. But we both agreed that we could not carry to that extent our colleagues at the Congress, nor the public opinion of our own countries. . . . I therefore accepted as a compromise a proposal that we should proceed along the lines of inviting delegates from all the contending sections to meet the Allies at some convenient time and place.[45]

Before this meeting, both Colonel House and British foreign minister Arthur Balfour had separate meetings with Clemenceau, who was struggling to find some position he could support. In his talk with House, Clemenceau agreed that military intervention was impossible, but he could not see his way clear to an alternative. House said that they both agreed that they "should exert all the wisdom possible in order to devise some plan by which this critical and dangerous situation might be met."[46]

In his talk with Balfour, Clemenceau impressed on Balfour the absolute impossibility of France's agreeing to receiving Bolshevik representatives in Paris, being "afraid on the one hand of the results which the Bolshevist visit would produce upon the few extremists in Paris, and on the other of the effects if would have upon the great body of moderate opinion." Balfour told Lloyd George that he did not believe Clemenceau would change his views on this and that some other approach should be found.[47]

The session on January 20 began with the appearance of French ambassador Joseph Noulens. According to most reports, he was not impressive. Lloyd George noted that "he was inclined to be pompous, tendentious, and not informative" and that "he repeated the gossip and hearsay of the Parisian journals of the Extreme Right about the horrors of Bolshevism." More important, his direct experience was woefully out of date, as he had left Bolshevik Russia in February 1918. Wilson's only comment during Noulens' appearance was a question about the popularity of the Bolsheviks, to which Noulens responded that "all the well to do classes, including the richer peasants and working men, were against the Bolsheviks."[48]

Dutch minister Scavenius followed Noulens. Scavenius presented more substantive information, but was still strongly anti-Bolshevik. He stressed the desirability of military intervention, but believed that only an overwhelming Allied force would make success certain.[49]

A discussion ensued. President Wilson read the cable he had just received from William H. Buckler in Stockholm, giving the essence of the Bolshevik appeal for peace and their suggestions for compromise on the foreign debt, territory, and other issues. As Lloyd George noted, "this memorandum has a special significance," but he regretted that Litvinov "had no official position which would give his offer the status of an official pronouncement by the Bolshevik Government."[50]

The Peace Conference did not discuss the Litvinov message; they adjourned for the evening, in obvious disagreement about how to proceed on the question of Russian representation and Russian policy.[51] Lloyd George used the interim to consult with the British Empire delegation. At that meeting, although some expressed hesitancy regarding meetings with the Bolsheviks, there was real clarity that massive intervention was impossible and that some effort should be made to bring the various sides in the Russian civil war together; if not in Paris, then at some other location.[52]

The next day the Council of Ten returned once again to the question, and President Wilson suggested a modification of the original British proposal to invite all the Russian factions to Paris. Wilson "wished to suggest that the various organized groups in Russia should be asked to send representatives, not to Paris, but to some other place, such as Salonica, convenient of approach, there to meet such representatives as might be appointed by the

Allies . . . in order to see whether they could draw up a programme upon which agreement could be reached."[53]

Lloyd George immediately agreed with the suggestion, pointing out that this would keep all representatives from having to pass through Europe. They could go directly through the Black Sea. Sonino of Italy wondered why this was even necessary, since the Russian representatives were also in Paris and could be brought together in one room, except the Bolsheviks, "whom they did not wish to hear." But Lloyd George responded "that the Bolsheviks were the very people some of them wished to hear."[54]

At this point, Georges Clemenceau took the floor, noting once again that "in principle, he did not favour conversation with the Bolsheviks," primarily because "we would be raising them to our level by saying that they were worthy of entering into conversation with." But, since Bolshevism posed a very grave threat, and other solutions seemed impossible, "sometimes in politics it is necessary to hold conversations with criminals." His primary concern, he explained, was to keep Bolshevism from spreading. He believed the main way to do that was to erect as many barriers as possible.[55]

Since his colleagues seemed so keen on discussions, Clemenceau was willing to go along, especially after hearing President Wilson's suggestion of holding the meetings at a location far from Paris. Clemenceau then asked Wilson if he would draft a paper explaining the Allies' position and inviting the Russian factions to a meeting. Clemenceau suggested to Wilson "that the manifesto to Russian parties should be based solely on humanitarian grounds," stressing the threat of famine. Lloyd George, while agreeing with Clemenceau's suggestions, added that "he thought the emissaries of the Allied Powers should be able to establish an agreement if they were able to find a solution . . . they should be authorized to accept a compromise." Balfour added further that he felt a condition for the meeting should be a ceasefire by all parties. Wilson agreed, and this was added to his instructions for drawing up the statement. Finally, after some interesting sparring among the delegates about whether they thought the Bolsheviks would ever accept such an invitation, "it was agreed that President Wilson should draft a proclamation, for consideration at the next meeting, inviting all organized parties in Russia to attend a meeting to be held at some selected place, such as Salonica or Lemnos, in order to discuss with the representatives of the Allied and Associated Great Powers the means of restoring order and peace in Russia."[56]

The next day, President Wilson brought to the Council his draft text, which he had composed on his own typewriter, of a statement and invitation to the parties in the conflict in Russia. After some discussion, this was accepted basically as written. This appeal bore all the marks of Wilson's idealism. In it he claimed that the associated powers wanted only "to help the Russian people, not to hinder them," and recognized "the absolute right of the Russian people to direct their own affairs." "[The Allies] recognize the revolution without reservations, and will in no way and in no circumstances aid or give countenance to any attempt at a counterrevolution." It also pledged, somewhat disingenuously, that the Allies did not wish "to favour or assist any one of those organised groups now contending for the leadership and guidance of Russia as against the others."[57]

Wilson then got to the heart of the invitation, calling for "every organized group that is now exercising or attempting to exercise, political authority or military control anywhere in Siberia, or within the boundaries of European Russia as they stood before the war just concluded" to send three representatives to the Prince's Islands in the Sea of Marmora (nine small resort islands just a few miles from Constaninople). These representatives would confer with Allied representatives "in the freest and frankest way, with a view to ascertaining the wishes of all sections of the Russian people." One condition was placed on this invitation: "a truce of arms," that "aggressive military action cease." The invitation then promised free transit for any of the parties across the Black Sea to the Islands, and asked that all parties be at Prinkipo (as the islands were called) by February 15.[58]

This celebrated proposal was Wilson's first appeal for peace to the Bolsheviks, as well as his first effort to patch up a split between Lloyd George and Clemenceau. The genesis of the idea was not only Robert Borden's and Lloyd George's push to bring the parties to Paris, but Litvinov's appeal to *audiatur et altera pars*.[59]

Although the proposal stated that it would "be sent tonight by wireless to all interested parties," it was never formally relayed to the Bolsheviks. A number of the White governments received direct communication either from the Russian Political Conference or the French government. Wilson was' afraid that to send it to the Bolsheviks would have denoted some form of recognition. He was caught again between his two inclinations: he wanted to be fair, but he did not like the Bolsheviks.[60]

Chicherin, upon hearing of the proposal, immediately tried to ascertain its authenticity, and requested an official invitation. In a cable of January 29, Chicherin stated that his government had "not received the invitation" and felt "compelled to draw your attention to this fact in order that the absence of an answer from our side should not be a cause of misrepresentation."[61] Wilson noted in a Peace Conference session that "to send an official communication would be tantamount to a recognition of the Bolshevik government." Lloyd George said that the Bolsheviks had received their notice "like everybody else." The Bolsheviks only learned of the proposal over the radio and through the newspapers.[62]

The Bolsheviks disagreed about whether and how to respond to the Allied initiative, although it appears that Lenin favored accepting the invitation from the beginning. He informed Trotsky of the invitation by telegraph on January 24, urging him to step up his advance on Rostov, Chelabinsk, and Omsk before any truce took hold, and noting "the person to visit Wilson will, to all appearances have to be you."[63] Trotsky responded at once, promising to exert all efforts to take Rostov and the Don, but expressing no concern or hurry regarding the conference. Then he begged off, recommending that Lenin send

"Chicherin and Raokovski. They are better equipped for this; there will be no call for 'polemics' on this occasion, since everything has been made clear already."[64]

Chicherin later recalled his own discussions with Lenin when they first got word of the Prinkipo proposal. Chicherin wrote that "Lenin immediately said it was necessary to submit our own proposals to the Allied countries without waiting until we received the invitation."[65]

Chicherin began the process of consultation for the Bolshevik response. He wired V. V. Vorovski, still in Stockholm, asking his opinion of the proposal and its genuineness. Vorovski wired back his own misgivings to the Foreign Office, expressing concern about the location of the meeting: "The adoption of a lonely island as the place for a conference, far away from European political centres, can only have for its object the surrounding of it by an impenetrable secrecy or create for it a fictitious and political publicity."[66]

The next day Grigori Zinoviev gave a major speech to the Petrograd Soviet, devoting a substantial portion of it to his analysis of the Allies' moves concerning Russia in Paris. He noted a "struggle between two tendencies": that of the French, who wanted to send large numbers of troops to Russia in support of counterrevolution, and "the more moderate line of the American President Wilson." He called Prinkipo "a practical proposal" by the Americans and the British. Since "they have not got strength enough to crush us," they had "therefore to try by some means or other to draw out our fangs" and "take advantage of our weariness." Zinoviev pledged "never to trust those gentlemen" who had been trying to crush Bolshevik power, but still advised accepting the invitation to Prinkipo, in order to "expose the attempt of the French, Japanese and American imperialists." By going to Prinkipo, the Bolsheviks could "compel these gentlemen to take off their masks."[67]

This speech of Zinoviev's was important because Allied intelligence sources had reported a political struggle between Lenin and Zinoviev. According to this report, Lenin had attempted to remove Zinoviev from his powerful position in the Petrograd Soviet but had failed.[68]

The internal Bolshevik discussion about the appropriate response to the Prinkipo invitation spread even to Bolshevik contacts in the United States. Santeri Nuorteva, originally the Finnish communist representative in the United States, acting on behalf of the Finnish government during the period in 1918 when it was controlled by Bolshevik forces, visited the U.S. State Department on January 29, accompanied by Harold Kellock and Hearst lawyer McFarland. They met with Acting Secretary of State Polk. Nuorteva, claiming to represent the Soviet government in the United States, asked American assistance in transmitting a message to Lenin in support of the Bolshevik acceptance of the Prinkipo invitation. This message urged Lenin to accept "this opportunity to let the world compare your strength, aims and accomplishments with those of various Russian pretenders," claiming public opinion in the United States was "more open-minded and sympathetic than ever." "Your willingness to place your cause before the eyes of the world as compared with obvious disinclination of your opponents to do so would make a favorable impression."[69] Polk refused to make any commitment to transmit the message, telling Nuorteva only that he would send it to the delegation in Paris, who could determine the issue. Lansing and the Paris delegation took no action, and the latter never reached Lenin.[70]

Before a Bolshevik response was transmitted to the Prinkipo invitation, the American and British delegations investigated any leads that might tell them whether the Bolsheviks might accept. William H. Buckler, the Allied representative most recently in touch with the Bolshevik leadership, was asked by Philip Kerr, Lloyd George's secretary, whether he felt the Bolsheviks would agree to come to Prinkipo. He responded that he felt they might well do so, provided only that "it did not involve the abolition of their Soviet constitution, which to them was an almost sacred possession."[71]

The Bolshevik government finally responded in a wireless from Chicherin on February 4. This message accepted Wilson's invitation to meet at Prinkipo, and laid out in some detail the terms on which the Soviet government was prepared to negotiate. In this statement Moscow again offered, as in the Litvinov discussions with Buckler, to recognize and negotiate the Russian debts, to negotiate the possibility of accepting the "annexation of Russian territories by the Allied powers" and other "territorial concessions," to pledge noninterference in the internal affairs of other states, and to grant economic concessions, all in exchange for an end to the civil war and foreign intervention.[72]

The Bolsheviks apparently believed that they could afford to accept other governments' operating on Russian territory because they were convinced that such governments would rapidly collapse once foreign aid had been withdrawn. Time, Lenin and Chicherin believed, was on their side. Chicherin stressed, in this note, that

> The Russian Soviet Government attaches such great value to the conclusion of an agreement which would bring hostilities to an end, that it is ready immediately to enter into negotiations for this purpose, and even—as it has often said—to purchase such agreement at the price of important sacrifices, with the express reservation that the future development of the Soviet Republic will not be menaced. . . .[73]

Zinoviev, in a second major speech on Prinkipo to the Petrograd Soviet two days later, backed Chicherin's response, but he blamed the problem on the desperate food situation that the Bolshevik government faced. He noted that "our military situation is not bad, [but] our food situation is very bad. . . . War has exhausted all countries including our own." He also called the proposed terms an "unfavourable peace" but one that "in the course of time . . . will be profitable to us and not to our enemies" and concluded that such a peace "would not mean that we would, even for a second, stop building up our Red Army. It would mean that we would put no trust whatever in the bit of paper which we would sign."[74]

Chicherin's note, while generally well received in Bolshevik circles, did not end internal discussion of Soviet government policy toward the Allies.

While generally supported on the right and among the moderates, the leftist opposition felt it was a betrayal of the revolution, and tried to oppose it even as they had opposed the Brest Litovsk agreement. Some Bolsheviks went further than Zinoviev and complained that "it went a little too far in the way of concessions."[75] Even the critics, however, understood the necessity of seeking peace because of the extreme exhaustion of people from so many years of war and revolution. A number of leaders consistently complained to British journalist Arthur Ransome, "We cannot get things straight while we have to fight all the time."[76]

The Bolshevik Party Executive Committee met February 10 to evaluate Chicherin's action and to consider further developments. At this meeting, Chicherin reported on the general international situation and sketched in some detail the Soviet peace proposals, including the latest, without appearing too hopeful that the Prinkipo conference would ever take place, because of opposition from the French. Then Nikolai Bukharin spoke. Contrary to his position in the Brest debate, Bukharin admitted that Lenin had been right and that peace was absolutely necessary, if only to try to split American and French capital. He also praised Chicherin's note for its lack of diplomatic language and its clear and unvarnished statement of the case. "Tell us what you want," it says, "and we are ready to buy you off, in order to avoid armed conflict." He considered the note useful even if it were rejected. Maksim Litvinov stressed the possibility that Britain would side with America against France, and if that were to happen, something might be achieved. At the close of the debate, the Executive Committee unanimously approved a resolution supporting Chicherin and the Foreign Ministry's peace offensive, including the specific note in reply to Prinkipo.[77]

For the next several weeks, Allied sources in Paris continued to receive smatterings of indications that the Bolshevik leadership was divided over the advisability of making peace at Prinkipo. One intelligence report had Trotsky and the Cheka opposing the move; Trotsky believing that the Red Army was on the verge of capturing the Ukraine and turning the tide of the civil war. Lenin continued to insist that a new breathing space was necessary, however, and was able to overrule those who opposed him, pointing out the extreme economic difficulties the government faced. He said to the Moscow Soviet, according to one report, "We must have the courage to confess freely that our Communist plan is going unquestionably to smash if we do not change front."[78]

Besides the Bolshevik response, the Allies received acceptances from four other Russian governments: the Soviet Ukrainian Government, the Government of the Crimea, the Lithuanian Government, and the Provisional Government of Latvia.[79] All other Russian governments, particularly the main White governments in the civil war, refused to attend, or, in many cases, refused to reply. The responses of these governments, however, were strongly conditioned by the reactions they received to their initial astonishment at being asked to sit down with the Bolsheviks. When it was clear that the Whites would be backed in their resistance by the French, and in some cases the British (Churchill continued to give his strong support), the Russian White forces stiffened their resolve and made unequivocal public statements of opposition.[80]

John M. Thompson has argued convincingly that French opposition to Prinkipo, not White Russian recalcitrance, was the key factor in its defeat. Had the French supported the conference, their clients would have attended, albeit reluctantly.[81] The French government was bitterly opposed to Wilson's initiative, and the pro-government and anti-Bolshevik press built up to a fever pitch in its denunciations of British and American perfidy in the Prinkipo proposal. They vowed to support loyal Russian resistance to dealing with the Bolsheviks under any conditions.[82]

Although the Prinkipo initiative was a British-American one, neither government exerted strong pressure on the French or the White Russian forces to overcome their resistance. Philip Kerr indicated privately to Buckler that the British believed the Bolsheviks would accept the invitation. He also said that the British government would be willing to meet the Bolsheviks at Prinkipo even if they were the only group to come. Lloyd George expressed similar sentiments privately to American representatives. But none of this was made public, and both statements were later repudiated.[83] At the same time, War Minister Churchill was publicly promising British assistance to the anti-Bolshevik forces in their resistance.[84]

As for the United States, key participants in the delegation expressed considerable unease at Wilson's accomplishment. Colonel House had not been part of the deliberations because of illness, and he privately expressed a certain distance from the proposal, and regret that his own idea, food and economic relief, had been shunted aside.[85] Later, as the Prinkipo idea unraveled, House conveniently claimed that he had never been in favor of it in the first place.[86]

Lansing was skeptical from the start and expressed his reluctance to all concerned. He did see the impossibility of military intervention, and he explained to Polk, "in these circumstances the best and humane thing to do seemed to be to make an appeal of some sort to the warring elements to cease violence while the peace conference is in session." Lansing went along with the proposal because of his belief that it was better than Lloyd George's earlier proposal to treat with the Bolsheviks directly. As he said in a long letter to Polk, "What could we do? I have the idea even of investigating those assassins. We know enough about them already. But what other course had we but to seek to bribe them to stop murdering by suggesting an investigation on condition that they stop fighting? Will it work? I don't think so. But no one had anything better to suggest."[87]

Earlier, at a meeting of the American Commissioners, a memorandum was dicussed concerning the White forces' skepticism about Prinkipo because the Bolsheviks would not adhere to any ceasefire. Lansing "agreed heartily with the opinion expressed that the Bolsheviks would undoubtedly violate the terms of any truce."[88]

Lansing's predilections were reinforced by the strongly negative comments he received from elsewhere in the State Department. Counselor and Acting

Secretary of State Frank Polk cabled from Washington his own skepticism, while Consul Poole, in Archangel, positively blistered the wires. Poole wrote a strong letter on January 23 raising questions about the United States' entire stand vis-à-vis Russia and the Bolsheviks. He urged that, rather than holding any meetings with the Bolsheviks, a strongly worded anti-Bolshevik statement be issued "condemning the evils which it has propagated," and claiming that nothing the Bolsheviks said or did could be relied on because "their most solemn assurances can have no value."[89]

Poole followed this up a week later with a cable informing the State Department of the strongly negative sentiment both of the government and the people of the Archangel area concerning the Prinkipo proposal. He called it "morally if not practically impossible," and reported "deep and widespread feelings of injury and resentment that . . . patriotic elements should be dealt with by the Peace Conference on the same basis as the Bolsheviki. . . ."[90]

By February 4, Poole was so incensed over the issue that he tendered his resignation; personally confused, as he put it, by the "moral perplexity into which I have been thrown."[91] Only a conciliatory statement from Lansing kept him from resigning. Poole responded to Lansing with gratitude, noting that "now that you know how deeply I feel the moral issues involved in our attitude toward the Moscow government, I am happy to continue with my work, confident in your own keen appreciation of these issues. . . ."[92]

Of the American delegation, only Bullitt, Buckler, Bliss, and White strongly supported the initiative, particularly after French and White Russian opposition became clear. Henry White, despite his staunch Republicanism and his personal friendship with Henry Cabot Lodge, noted in a January 24 letter to William Phillips that "if anyone suggests the horror, as no doubt some one will, of meeting the Bolsheviks for any purpose whatever, it may interest you to know that the only alternative . . . was that a large military expedition should be sent into Russia, the greater part of which should be composed of our troops."[93] White consistently supported Prinkipo, perhaps in part because of his half-brother, William H. Buckler's, role in initiating it and his personal belief that discussions with the Bolsheviks were the only answer to Russia's travail.[94] William C. Bullitt even went so far as to suggest in a memorandum to House that the United States should withdraw its support from the Archangel government because of that government's reluctance to come to Prinkipo.[95]

American press response to Prinkipo was predictably divided between conservative and liberal, but on the whole was restrained and generally supportive, not out of any love for meetings with Bolsheviks, but more "because the Peace conference had taken some definite action with regard to Russia." As a weekly review of American opinion for the Peace Commissioners in Paris noted, "resentment at the so-called contact with crime was much less than expected."[96] As time went by, however, and no conference materialized, press opinion changed from support to ridicule, calling the conference "a fiasco" and again urging the Paris conference to take some definite action on Bolshevism.[97]

This shift coincided with two other important developments in Washington. On February 14, Senator Hiram Johnson's resolution in the United States Senate calling for the immediate withdrawal of American troops from Russia came to a vote after extended debate. It went down to defeat only after a tie was broken by the Vice President. The debate exposed deep undercurrents of unease regarding the Administration's Russia policy. The debate, however, referred only occasionally to the Prinkipo proposal, and was generally couched in terms of America's interest in bringing its boys home from Europe. Isolationist Republicans joined with anti-Wilson Democrats to support Johnson's initiative, in part because of their hatred of Wilson's approach at the Peace Conference.[98] Just a week before, on February 4, the Senate Judiciary Subcommittee investigating German propaganda shifted its attention to Bolshevism. This committee began calling witnesses in what became an extensive investigation of Bolshevik activities both in Russia and the United States and an attempt to link opposition to the Administration's Russia policy to disloyalty.[99]

Wilson did follow up within a few days of the issuance of the Prinkipo invitation by appointing two American representatives to the conference, George Herron and William Allen White.[100] White, the respected American journalist and writer, was in Paris covering the Peace Conference. He was called in by presidential aide Ray Stannard Baker at the end of January and asked whether he would be one of the American representatives. Baker told White that Professor George D. Herron had been chosen as the other.[101] White agreed with some reluctance to serve because, as he said, "I was abysmally ignorant."[102]

White also saw Colonel House, who remarked, "I'm glad you are going to take charge of this Bolshevik thing for us!" White told House that he would go to Prinkipo "only if they let all the newspapermen go who wanted to go." Here he sided with the Bolsheviks, who wanted full-scale publicity as security against the French and the French-supported Russian forces, "who do not want to confer with the Bolsheviks." House told White in this conversation that he had only two requests of the Bolsheviks: "First, that they devote their propaganda to their own country; and second, that we establish peace."[103]

White's nomination was well received, both in Paris and in the United States, but the same cannot be said for that of George Herron.[104] Herron, serving in Geneva as an embassy aide, was loosely attached to the Peace Commission. He sent many long reports to Colonel House in 1918 and 1919 on questions of prisoner release, conditions in central Europe, and conditions in Russia, drawn from his numerous contacts in the émigré community in Geneva. As William Allen White has said, Herron functioned somewhat as a "superspy" with an extensive network of contacts among Social Democrats in Germany and throughout Central Europe.[105] The general belief in the American press was that Herron served as Wilson's and House's personal eyes and ears in Geneva, even though House noted more than once, "I did not know Herron and had written to him but once and then in the most casual way."[106] Herron himself also admitted, despite his long reports and recommendations to House and Wilson, "that not in one thing during the whole course of the war or the peace contrivances did the President really do as I wanted him to, even at the time when my influence with him bulked largest."[107]

But Herron's appointment as a Prinkipo delegate released a storm of protest in the American press. The press accused Herron of Bolshevism and immorality because of his rather openly flaunted marital infidelity and his commitment to democratic socialism.[108] At first, Wilson stood behind him, noting to Lansing that he was "much the best man we could use in the circumstances and it would be most unfair now to cancel his appointment."[109] By late spring, however, Wilson had moved entirely away from him, saying in response to a query from House, "I am through with him."[110]

Herron was actually strongly anti-Bolshevik and was considered one of the anti-Bolshevik Russian forces' strongest American friends in Europe.[111] Following his appointment, Herron did his best, first in Geneva and later in Paris, to persuade the various Russian groups to agree to come to Prinkipo, arguing especially after the Bolshevik acceptance that to do otherwise would be to give a clear field to Lenin and Trotsky. Herron was convinced that the Prinkipo invitation was misunderstood by the Russians, and he tried to explain "that we were not going there to establish a final treaty of peace, but to give an open hearing to all Russian parties."[112] He had some success in his ministrations, persuading some of the Kadets; Baron von Wrangel; Nicholas Tchaikovsky, head of the North Russian Government; and representatives of the Omsk government to come to Prinkipo, if indeed it were held. But these groups noted the lack of support of French representatives for the meeting, and qualified their acceptances.[113]

Herron wrote from Geneva to House, explaining these meetings and asking if it might not be a good idea to have similar meetings in Paris to try to save the Prinkipo conference. House responded that Herron did not need to return to Paris just at that time, because the Peace Conference was again considering the Russian situation, and that he would let him know the result.[114]

House never did summon Herron back to Paris, and he only learned of the demise of the Prinkipo conference when he returned on his own to Paris on February 17. Herron came to Paris for further meetings with Russian groups with the assistance of William Allen White. Both White and Herron met several times with House but always came away unsatisfied regarding their instructions or the possibilities of Prinkipo.[115] Finally, about February 20, they "were unceremoniously informed by the chief clerk of the American Commission" that Prinkipo had been indefinitely postponed by the Peace Conference a few days before. The clerk did not bother to tell them that William C. Bullitt had already left Paris on a secret mission to the Bolsheviks.[116]

Although White Russian recalcitrance, backed by the French, killed the Prinkipo proposal, the Allies seized on the omission by the Bolsheviks of any response to the Allied call for a ceasefire as an indication of a lack of seriousness on their part, and tried to cite it later as a reason Prinkipo failed.[117] Neither the Allies nor the White Russian forces ceased fighting either, however, and Prinkipo had no mechanism whatsoever to begin or enforce a truce. When the Bolshevik failure to cease fighting was discussed at the peace conference, Balfour asked a simple, pointed question: "Had the allied troops abstained from hostilities? Or, to put the question another way, had all the Allied military operations been defensive in their character?" His questions were met with silence. Even Churchill did not attempt to defend Allied actions in this regard.[118]

The frank Bolshevik statement of terms and offers of concessions to the Allies, however, infuriated Woodrow Wilson. His response was so antagonistic that it would appear that any possible settlement at Prinkipo was doomed to fail even if all parties had sent representatives. When the debate on Russia resumed in the Council of Ten on February 14, Wilson noted "this answer was not only uncalled for, but might be thought insulting."[119] Wilson also claimed later that Lloyd George was even more insulted, stating, "We cannot let that insult go by. We are not after their money or their concessions or their territory. That is not the point. We are their friends who want to help them and must tell them so."[120]

Wilson resisted pressure from Winston Churchill and Clemenceau to drop Prinkipo entirely and instead adopt a far-reaching plan of military operations against the Bolsheviks. Churchill had been sent to Paris to represent Britain by Lloyd George who was struggling with political opposition at home.[121] Churchill had unnerved Lloyd George with a forceful advocacy of an interventionist policy against the Bolsheviks at a War Cabinet meeting on February 12. Although Lloyd George's moderate policy prevailed in this meeting, Churchill continued to badger Lloyd George until finally the Prime Minister told Churchill to go to Paris and plead his case to the other Allies, apparently hoping that Wilson would shoot down the idea for him.

Following this War Council meeting and Churchill's departure for Paris, Lloyd George wrote a long letter to his secretary, Phillip Kerr, who had remained in Paris. Lloyd George was responding to Kerr's missives of recent days concerning French intransigence over Prinkipo. Kerr wanted to know what to make of Clemenceau's entreaty that Balfour do a favor for the old man, "if he loved him." On Balfour's affirmative reply, Clemenceau asked him if he would postpone the Prinkipo question until after President Wilson left. Lloyd George put his own interpretation on this remark, telling Kerr that "the old tiger wants the grizzly bear back in the Rocky Mountains before he starts tearing up the German Hog." Lloyd George then went on to stress to Kerr in the strongest possible terms that the Russia question "should be discussed and decided one way or another before President Wilson leaves." "There is nothing worse than indecision," he said. "If Prinkipo is to be hung up then they must decide at once what the substitute is to be." Lloyd George continued to favor convening the conference, but only if there was "a fair chance of securing the attendance of the parties." He no longer was willing to meet the Bolsheviks alone because it "would answer no useful purpose." He railed at the Russian parties who refused to come, accusing them of "behaving stupidly," and blamed the French and Italians for their intransigence.[122]

Churchill appeared before the Supreme Council in special session. Both Lloyd George and Italian prime minister Orlando were absent, and Wilson was set to leave for the United States later that evening. After Balfour's introduction, Churchill claimed to represent the British Cabinet, and demanded to know what the Allied position on Russia was to be. Was the Prinkipo plan still alive or would it be dropped? He pushed very hard for a decision before Wilson's departure, since the Prinkipo meeting had been scheduled for the very next day. Up to this point, he accurately expressed the British Cabinet's and Lloyd George's own position. Churchill then detailed his own misgivings about Prinkipo, especially if it meant meeting only with the Bolsheviks, and urged a decision for stepped-up military intervention against the Bolsheviks, going considerably beyond Lloyd George's position.[123]

Both Clemenceau and Wilson refused to be pushed into an immediate decision on Prinkipo. Clemenceau was concerned because the French were awaiting an imminent formal decision from the Russian political conference in Paris against the meeting. He also stalled because he felt it would be easier to kill the project after Wilson's departure.

Wilson tried to prevent a decision because he was not yet ready to abandon Prinkipo and was opposed to massive intervention. Wilson also tried to clarify his own sense of Prinkipo, claiming that it was not to be a negotiation session at all, but rather for "fact finding."[124] Since the Bolsheviks went beyond a simple agreement and refused to participate in the ceasefire, it might be necessary "to imitate Mahomet and go to the Russian governments." Wilson went on to say that "he would be quite content that informal American representatives should meet representatives of the Bolsheviks."[125]

Churchill pressed his attack, however, asking whether the Council would authorize the raising of an army of volunteers if Prinkipo failed. Wilson, while making known his personal objection and his doubts about whether volunteers could be recruited, stated that he would leave the decision to the majority of his colleagues. The meeting broke up as Wilson left on his journey to the United States.[126]

The next day the Council of Ten returned to the question of Russia and the Prinkipo invitation, with Churchill and Balfour representing Britain, and House and Lansing the United States. Churchill pressed his position, asking the French chief of staff, General Alby, to detail the Allied military position in Russia. The picture Alby painted was bleak, and cried out for increased Allied assistance to keep friendly Russian, Baltic, and Crimean forces from being overrun by the Bolsheviks. Churchill then proposed that a new note be addressed to the Bolsheviks from the Allied governments, agreeing to come to Prinkipo only if the Soviets ceased hostilities and withdrew their troops a distance of five miles from pro-Ally forces. If this were done, the Allies would "invite" their Russian forces to do the same and the conference would commence. Otherwise, Churchill proposed, the Allies should greatly step up their military activities against the Bolsheviks. He then proposed that an Interallied Military Commission for Russia be appointed at once, consisting of the chief military representatives of the Allies, and that this commission should draw up plans for military operations in Russia "in anticipation of the Soviet Government refusing to accept the terms and continuing hostilities."[127]

As Philip Kerr pointed out in a letter to Lloyd George about this proposal, Churchill's draft "was a departure from the original Prinkipo proposition, insofar as it was addressed to the Bolshevik government alone and made it a condition of coming to Prinkipo . . . [that] it should unilaterally halt its military operations."[128]

Kerr proposed an alternative to Churchill and Balfour, which was addressed to both sides and offered to begin negotiations "provided a truce had been signed within ten days on all fronts." Balfour, however, preferred Churchill's draft, and thus it was presented to the Council. In his letter of the same day to Lloyd George, even Kerr himself seemed to come around to Churchill's point of view, "provided it is drafted in such a form as to give every inducement to the Bolsheviks to accept the armistice." Kerr rightly noted that the original proposal seemed to promise neutrality, whereas the Allies were "actually fighting side by side with Koltchak and against the Bolsheviks." Churchill's position was more honest, and might "bring the Prinkipo issue to a head one way or another." Kerr warned Lloyd George, however, that in his opinion, Churchill, by gearing up the military commission, was "bent on forcing a campaign against Bolshevik Russia by using Allied volunteers, Polish and Finnish and any other conscripts that can be got hold of, financed and equipped by the Allies. . . . I think you ought to watch the situation very carefully . . . if you do not wish to be rushed into the policy of a volunteer war against the Bolsheviks in the near future."[129]

Clemenceau, while heartily endorsing Churchill's call for a military commission and military planning, did not like the "last chance" Prinkipo proposal at all. In fact, he claimed that he was entirely opposed to the original plan and had gone along with it only "to avoid the introduction of elements of discord into the conference." Now, since the proposal had been uniformly rejected by all but the Bolsheviks, who instead "had offered the allies money," the conference "should not attempt to deceive itself," but should "say nothing" further about Prinkipo. If anything were necessary, it should be as simple as possible, and should by no means give the Bolsheviks another opportunity for dissimulation and propaganda.[130]

House, on behalf of the United States, "thought the question to be decided was how to finesse the situation against the Bolsheviks." He, too, said House, "had never been in favor of the Prinkipo proposal." Now that it had been proposed, the Allies must see it through. They would then be in a better position if eventually military operations were decided upon. In any case, House urged a few days' delay for consultation within the delegations. Balfour seconded this plea, and the conference adjourned its Russian discussion for two days, to Monday, February 17.[131]

The intervening two days were filled with intense meetings within the delegations and cables from Paris to London and Paris to Washington. Kerr followed his earlier letter to Lloyd George with another, detailing his own views on the situation. Kerr particularly made reference to Churchill's call for a military crusade, calling it "a fundamental and colossal mistake to be drawn into a war with Soviet Russia." Kerr noted that any Allied effort "to suppress

Bolshevism in Moscow by force would . . . cause grave difficulties at home, and would land us with the ultimate responsibility for the government of Russia for a considerable number of years. . . .[132] Kerr did not think it possible, however, for the British to "abandon" the pro-Ally Russians. He believed that either they must be given enough support to keep them from being overrun or, if possible, terms for them must be negotiated with the Bolsheviks. He favored the latter course, believing it still necessary "to get into relations with the Bolsheviks now," but "as one belligerent to another." He then proposed that negotiators be sent to deal with the Bolsheviks anywhere it could be arranged, "under a flag of truce or at Stockholm or Helsingfors."[133]

This simple "truce and talk" proposal was elaborated in a longer memorandum that Kerr wrote for Balfour, enclosing a copy for Lloyd George. In this proposal Kerr argued that it "would be a great mistake to break off relations with the Bolsheviks altogether." If relations were broken off, the Allies would be left with only three alternatives, all of them unpalatable: full-scale war, complete evacuation, or a continuation of just enough support for the White forces to keep them from being overrun, something everyone said they did not want to continue. In proposing immediate truce negotiations with the Bolsheviks, Kerr argued that the Bolsheviks would "rapidly decline" once they negotiated peace, because of their desperate economic situation. Furthermore, if negotiations were tried and failed due to Bolshevik intransigence, the British government would be in a much stronger position to push for full-scale intervention.[134]

There is no evidence of any immediate response by Balfour or Lloyd George to Kerr's suggestions for truce negotiations. Later discussions with House and Bullitt, and the British-American decision to send Bullitt to Moscow to talk to Lenin, certainly were prefigured in some of these proposals. Lloyd George was incensed, however, when he received Kerr's description of Churchill's plan for a military crusade. Lloyd George responded to Churchill immediately, saying that he was "very alarmed" at such a proposal. He stated bluntly that the Cabinet "never authorized [it] . . . and never contemplated anything beyond supplying . . . [the] necessary equipment" to enable anti-Bolshevik armies to hold their own. He cautioned Churchill that it was very well to prepare contingency plans, but that he also had to "ascertain the cost." According to his information, said Lloyd George, "intervention was driving the anti-Bolshevist parties in Russia into the ranks of the Bolsheviks."[135]

Lloyd George was also quoted by Lord Riddell as saying that Churchill's desire to conduct a war against the Bolsheviks "would cause a revolution! Our people would not permit it."[136] Lloyd George sent telegrams in a similar vein to both Balfour and Kerr. By a Sunday meeting of the British Empire Delegation, Kerr could report to Lloyd George that his various messages had "had their effect. The discussion showed pretty clearly that everybody was agreed that effective war against the Bolsheviks was probably impracticable because of public opinion at home, and that it was probably undesirable on its merits."[137] Kerr also told Lloyd George that he had followed his instructions and shared Lloyd George's messages with Colonel House. House agreed "except that he was opposed even to the appointment of a [military] commission of Enquiry" because it could be used, especially by the French, as "the beginning of an anti-Bolshevik War." House agreed with Kerr and Lloyd George that they should "keep in touch with the Bolsheviks with the object of gradually bringing them to terms, restoring allied influence in Russia and so composing the peace."[138]

House's consultation with Kerr reflected some of the intense work the American delegation had also done during the weekend. Gordon Auchincloss, House's aide, spent a number of hours with Sir William Wiseman, a British agent close to the American delegation. They drew up a memorandum with a plan for dealing both with Churchill and Prinkipo and drafted the "Declaration of Policy Issued in the Name of the Allied and Associated Governments." This draft declaration reiterated the main points of Prinkipo, underlined the need for hostilities to cease and *de facto* governments to remain in control, Allied subjects to be given right of free entry, amnesty to be given to political prisoners, and it promised the withdrawal of Allied troops from Russian territory as soon as possible. The draft ended with the following statement: "The Allied and Associated Governments declare that if the *de facto* Governments of Russia will sign an armistice on all fronts on the above mentioned terms, they are prepared to enter into negotiations with them at any suitable place at the earliest moment."[139]

The Auchincloss-Wiseman draft memo accompanying the declaration urged the Allies not to say that negotiations were broken off, but to "issue a statement saying that the Bolsheviks have not complied with conditions for meeting and have misinterpreted the Allies' note." Therefore, the Allies needed to issue another statement "to clear the issues." The memo then listed various responses under two headings: "What we will do if they come" and "What we will do if they don't come." Under the former, they stressed the "disinterested nature of the allies' concern for Russia" and the commitment to *de facto* control of various parts of Russia by various governments. Under the latter heading, the Allies should "conclude that Russia does not want to join in world peace" and that therefore a commitment would be made to "protect neighboring states from their TERRORIST [emphasis in the original] armies, (1) by sending forces to these states and (2) drawing an economic cordon around Russia."[140] Auchincloss and Wiseman concluded their memorandum by committing the Allies to be ready "at any time" to meet Russian delegates "when they inform us they are prepared to join with us in seeking peace and the free development of peoples." They also noted that the Soviets, in responding to the original Prinkipo proposal, had complained that it had been received only by wireless. Therefore, "care should be taken that all the Russian factions receive an identical note and in the same manner."[141]

The next morning, February 17, Auchincloss showed the memorandum to Colonel House, who urged him to share it with Lansing, Bliss, and White, and to prepare for a discussion of the Peace Commissioners that morning. This meeting of the Commissioners would ready the delegation for the resumption of discussions in the Council of Ten later in the day. The Auchincloss-

Wiseman memorandum went through numerous revisions on the way to serving as the basis for the American position.[142]

At the meeting of the American Commissioners, much of the Auchincloss draft was upheld, but the blame for the breakdown of Prinkipo was shared among "certain groups" rather than just the Bolsheviks. The Commissioners excised a major portion of Auchincloss' draft implying the threat of military action. House and Bliss vetoed this section, certain that they spoke also for the absent Woodrow Wilson. House noted in this meeting that "in his opinion Winston Churchill was attempting by degrees to lead us into a position by which we would have to commit ourselves to enter war with Russia." House was unalterably opposed to this and backed Bliss in his opposition even to constituting a military commission for contingency planning for military alternatives.[143]

As House noted in his diary, "We came to a general agreement which was quite contrary to the view of the French and Italians, and that section of the British represented by Winston Churchill." House knew, however, because of Kerr's consultation with him, that the American position fully accorded with that of Lloyd George.[144]

General Tasker Bliss's opposition to British and French military plans had been building steadily since the fall of 1918. In early September, he wrote to General Peyton March, the Chief of the General Staff, that not only should the United States not send any more troops, it should make plans to bring home the ones in North Russia and Siberia as soon as possible.[145]

After his appointment as a delegate to the Peace Conference, Bliss received many entreaties from Russians in Paris on the subject of intervention, pleading for more American support. To these overtures he uniformly explained that his own recommendation was that the United States not support an expanded Allied intervention, and he believed that Colonel House and President Woodrow Wilson stood behind him.[146] Bliss was also the recipient of entreaties from members of Congress and petitions from state legislatures.[147]

House and Wilson, despite occasional irritation with Bliss's rather plodding and scholarly ways, respected his convictions and his position. House once remarked to his daughter, Janet Auchincloss, that he considered Bliss "a very brainy man."[148] On January 6, Bliss made a special point of bringing to the President's attention a dispatch from the Archangel front pinpointing the failure of Russian troops to advance against the Bolsheviks and the "senseless" loss of life the American unit suffered in its backup role.[149]

Bliss's correspondence with Wilson during these months shows consistent and persistent recommendations against further intervention and the earliest possible withdrawal from both North Russia and Siberia. Although at times Wilson temporized, on most occasions he agreed strongly with Bliss. In an exhange in early January, for example, Bliss stressed Bolshevism's powerful social indictment of capitalism and noted the difficulty of stopping such an ideology with military force. Rather, the ignorance and hunger that fed it had to be attacked directly. This position reinforced the President's growing preference for fighting Bolshevism with food, something that later became the heart of American policy.[150]

On February 9, Bliss received a long letter from British general Sir Henry Winston concerning the need for more American troops in North Russia. Bliss recommended to President Wilson just the opposite: the preparation for evacuation of all American troops from North Russia as soon as it could be arranged.[151]

In this position Bliss was supported fully by Buckler, Bullitt, and House. Philip Kerr privately assured House that Lloyd George, contrary to Wilson's letter, fully intended to withdraw the British troops from Archangel on the first of May.[152]

Bliss was unequivocally opposed even to the creation of a military committee, feeling it would be "very unwise if anything should be done . . . which could be construed by anyone as indicating an intention on the part of the United States to take part in an intervention in Russia."[153] Bliss also fully supported giving Prinkipo a second chance, even going as far as to recommend in the meeting of the American commissioners that a financial expert, such as Norman H. Davis, be appointed to join the Prinkipo mission because of the key issues of the debt and reconstruction.[154]

Bliss had prepared for the American Commissioners a long statement of unequivocal opposition to military planning in any form, declaring categorically that the people and government of the United States would never support full-scale military operations to overthrow the Bolsheviks. Instead, the answer to Bolshevism in Europe was the relief of misery and starvation. The other Commissioners agreed with Bliss that such a statement should be read in the Peace Conference as a way of countering Churchill's project.[155] According to several eyewitnesses, however, House and Lansing declined to read the full statement, prompting Bliss to remark to Joseph C. Grew, "They lost their sand."[156]

When the Peace Conference resumed on the afternoon of February 17, Churchill's resolution calling for the military representatives to undertake such planning was postponed for delegation consultations after an acrimonious debate that was not even recorded in the minutes, and about which our knowledge is gleaned only from various participants' diaries and letters. House opposed Churchill strongly, and recorded in his diary that "it was literally Balfour and myself against Churchill, the French and the Italians."[157] Auchincloss reported that Clemenceau had made "a disagreeable speech" and that Balfour was "mad clean through."[158] Also indefinitely postponed was any follow-up statement or activity with regard to Prinkipo. No one was willing to go further in the absence of Lloyd George and Woodrow Wilson.[159]

House and Kerr immediately held a long private meeting to discuss policy moves to propose to their chiefs. House and Kerr both reported on this meeting in letters to Wilson and Lloyd George, respectively. Although in agreement on most of the basics, Kerr's letter to Lloyd George provided a fuller statement of Kerr's own views, along with his agreements with House. Both men agreed that "no foreign intervention in Soviet Russia and no foreign troops [should] be sent to aid of non-Bolshevik Russia unless volunteers choose to go of their own accord, but material assistance . . . [should] be supplied."[160] But Kerr, in his letter to Lloyd George, also stressed the importance of replacing Prinkipo, if in fact it were to be dropped, with some alternative "positive" policy. Kerr said to Lloyd George that he told House that "you felt that we ought to stand by our friends until we could bring about some reasonable settlement of the Russia problem." Kerr's own view of how to do this was that the Allies should negotiate with the Bolsheviks, "provided that they signed an armistice suspending hostilities on all fronts" and that the Allied obligation "to defend our friends . . . did not include the obligation to refuse to speak to the Bolsheviks or to conquer Bolshevik Russia on their behalf." Kerr then presented a case to Lloyd George for negotiations with the Bolsheviks for a settlement securing for Kolchak, Denikin, Archangel, and the western borderlands "the free control of their own affairs . . . while at the same time ending the war with the Bolsheviks." Kerr told Lloyd George that House agreed with this position. Kerr asked Lloyd George whether he also agreed, noting that the chief objection to it might be that it involved "meeting with the Bolsheviks."[161]

When Woodrow Wilson heard about Churchill's efforts to mount a military crusade, he responded immediately with letters to House and the Commissioners, reiterating that he "would not be in favor of any course which would not mean the earliest practicable withdrawal of military forces." Wilson warned House, "It would be fatal to be led further into the Russian chaos." He further advised House to "be very plain and decided to the effect that we are not at war with Russia and will in no circumstances that we can now foresee take part in military operations there against the Russians."[162] The Commissioners quickly reassured him that Churchill's project was dead and that there was "little danger that it will be revived again by the Conference."[163]

While this in fact turned out to be true, it was by no means sure at the time. Churchill on his return to London a few days later, argued strenuously in the War Cabinet for a revival of the idea and an endorsement by the Cabinet. Lloyd George, rather than tangle with him directly, hid behind the inability of the Allies to come to a unified decision, despite numerous attempts.[164]

Meanwhile, former U.S. Ambassador to Russia David R. Francis met with Woodrow Wilson on the boat returning from France to the United States. Francis suggested that Prinkipo be transferred to Petrograd and all Russian factions be "summoned" to work out their differences. Francis warned against any agreements with the Bolsheviks, which he believed would result in Germany's thorough domination of Russia within ten years.[165] Francis had also met earlier in Paris with General Bliss, who observed in his diary that he and General Nolan had "expected that we would get some real notion about Bolshevism" from the discussion but that they "learned absolutely nothing."[166]

On the other hand, Samuel Eliot Morison, one of the youngest staff members of the American delegation, articulated Kerr's pro-negotiation position in a long memorandum to Dr. Isaiah Bowman of the delegation's Russian and East European Division. Morison argued that the United States should negotiate with the Soviet government "at Prinkipo or elsewhere, without further delay than may be necessary to arrange a truce." Morison noted that although Prinkipo had received limited acceptance among the Russian factions, it had been accepted by the Bolsheviks, whose reply was "sufficiently conciliatory to offer a basis for a separate negotiation." Morison pointed out that it was "clearly not the fault of the Soviet Government" that the other parties had refused the invitation. Furthermore, he stated that an Allied refusal now would give the Bolsheviks ample reason for arguing that the Allies were to blame for a breakdown in discussions, especially in the face of the almost total lack of any alternative policy.[167]

Morison then detailed in convincing fashion the objections to other policies and argued that the best way to protect America's friends among the anti-Bolsheviks was to negotiate an armistice and guarantees while it was still possible. Morison acknowledged that "the difficulty of dealing with such men as the present Bolshevist leaders" was "the greatest obstacle." But he advanced the argument, then being made by the liberal press in the United States, that a "rift" was developing in the Bolshevik party between a "moderate" wing led by Lenin and Litvinov and a "more violent and intractible" sector led by Trotsky and Zinoviev. Morison believed that a conciliatory Allied response would strengthen the hand of the moderates and possibly "lead to an abandonment of terrorism."[168]

Finally, Morison believed, the moment was ripe for negotiation, because of the poor Allied military situation, coupled with the desperate Bolshevik economic condition whereby the Bolsheviks were "in a mood to make concessions." If negotiations were avoided, the Bolshevik military situation, improving daily, might lead to a capture of the Ukraine and an amelioration of their economic situation, thus making them less inclined to compromise. A golden opportunity to end the war and protect the anti-Soviet borderlands might be lost.[169]

Unbeknownst to Morison, by the time he composed this most engrossing and suggestive memorandum, William C. Bullitt had already left Paris for consultations with the British in London en route to Stockholm, Helsingfors, Petrograd, and Moscow for a top-secret mission to explore just what terms could be arranged between the Allies and Lenin.[170] Just after Bullitt was dispatched, an assassin's bullet wounded Premier Clemenceau, and the Peace Conference was paralyzed for about ten days, until his recovery and the return to Paris of Lloyd George and Woodrow Wilson. During this period, the French announced publicly that Prinkipo was a dead letter, but the American delegation continued to insist that the matter was simply postponed indefinitely.[171]

In reality, however, Prinkipo had died some weeks before, and perhaps had never had any chance at all. French hostility and White Russian recalcitrance were not all that stood against it. Woodrow Wilson and Lloyd George never believed that it was more important to talk with the Bolsheviks than to support the White Russian forces, even though they also opposed an overwhelming military crusade using Allied troops. All that kept the Prinkipo idea alive for several weeks was the determination of Philip Kerr, the strong American military opposition to expanded intervention, and the reluctance of the British and American delegations to abandon Prinkipo when there was no policy to take its place.

# 9

# Paris II:
# Bullitt's Mission to Lenin

No real peace can be established in Europe or the World until peace is made with the revolution. This proposal of the Soviet Government presents an opportunity to make peace with the revolution on a just and reasonable basis—perhaps a unique opportunity.

—*William C. Bullitt, Report to U.S. Peace Commissioners, March 28, 1919*[1]

William C. Bullitt's secret mission to Moscow in March 1919 has received a great deal of attention from historians, partly because of the focus Bullitt himself placed on it in his extensive testimony before the Senate Foreign Relations Committee in the fall of 1919.[2] Because the details of the Bullitt mission itself are well known, this treatment will place the mission in the broader context of discussions concerning the Bolsheviks in the Allied community in Paris, and debate about the mission in Moscow.

Before proceeding to a discussion of the Bullitt mission itself, it might be well to briefly consider the American Peace Commission's staffing on the Russian question, and William C. Bullitt's own role and relationship to Wilson, House, the Peace Commissioners, and staff.

Robert H. Lord, a professor of history and specialist on Poland at Harvard University, was the head of the Russian and East European Division of the Peace Commission. A member of Colonel House's Inquiry since 1917, Lord had little specialized knowledge of Russia itself and relied on other members of the Inquiry, such as Samuel N. Harper, and the staff in Paris, notably Samuel E. Morison and William C. Bullitt, to provide it.[3] Lord and the staff of his section concentrated their attention on papers and materials prepared for the Peace Conference on boundary questions, history, and trade relations, giving almost no attention whatsoever to the Russian Bolsheviks. It was assumed either that the Bolsheviks would not be in power long, or that the Peace Conference would not deal with them. The staff instead concentrated on the western borderlands and general questions concerning Great Russia historically and economically.[4]

Lord did prepare, as did all the other geographic section chiefs, a weekly report to the Peace Commissioners on the situation in Russia and Eastern Europe, which came to be increasingly dominated by news of the Bolsheviks and the civil war.[5] He also provided regular intelligence bulletins to Bullitt, whose job with the Commission in Paris was Chief of the Division of Current Intelligence Summaries.[6]

Lord's most substantive recommendations to the American Commissioners on Russia concerned backing for the requests of the Baltic states for material support and credits, and an effort to tie any extension of the Prinkipo invitation to a demand that the Bolsheviks release U.S. consul Tredwell, who had been detained in Tashkent, and U.S. intelligence agent Xenophon Kalamatiano. In both cases, the American commissioners, Colonel House, and even Secretary Lansing rejected Lord's recommendations because of broader American policy considerations. On the question of the Baltic states, despite Woodrow Wilson's fervent support for self-determination, the United States continued to support the White Russian position in favor of an undivided Great Russia. And since the Prinkipo invitation was issued to Bolsheviks and anti-Bolsheviks, it was seen as totally inappropriate to tie its continuance to a demand placed upon the Bolshevik government. Moreover, such a move would necessarily bring the United States into direct communication with the Bolsheviks, a step that was anathema to Lansing and others.[7]

The lack of attention given questions of relations with the Bolsheviks by Lord and his staff, however, did not mean that the American Commissioners and their staffs did not deal seriously with the broader questions of the United States Russian policy, and the ever-present question of how to deal with the Bolsheviks. Rather, these questions were big and constant policy questions, under attention from Bliss, Lansing, White, House, Wilson, and, increasingly as time wore on, William C. Bullitt.

Bullitt had first joined the State Department in December 1917 as an Assistant Secretary of State, recommended by Colonel House after considerable personal interchange between the two while Bullitt was a reporter for the Philadelphia *Public Ledger*. Bullitt's role with the State Department was current intelligence on and analysis of Central Europe, and he reported directly to Colonel House from the date of his appointment. His knowledge of and interest in Russia stemmed from his focus on the breakdown of order and the problems of revolution in Central Europe. He became more and more convinced as 1918 went on that the struggle there was one between the ideals and example of Lenin and those of Wilson. The old absolutist order lurked in the wings on one hand, and a complete breakdown of social order waited on the other. Bullitt wrote many persuasive memos to House giving detailed and trenchant analyses of political conditions and recommending a direct United States approach to the causes of misery and violence as a way of stemming the revolutionary tide. This was a position both House and Wilson had consider-able sympathy for.[8]

Although Bullitt was devastated when Wilson decided on limited military intervention in Russia in the summer of 1918, the approaching European armistice revived his excitement about Wilsonian idealism and peace negotia-tions, especially as it seemed that questions about the causes and conse-quences of revolution in central Europe and Russia could not be ignored in Paris. So Bullitt persuaded Colonel House to get him a position on the delega-tion, and he was appointed Chief of the Division of Current Intelligence, accompanying the President and his party to Paris late in 1918.[9]

Bullitt's official duties in Paris originally consisted of putting together a daily bulletin of up-to-the-minute news and information essential for the American Commissioners. As everyone soon became buried in paper, this was abandoned in favor of an oral briefing with each Commissioner every morning. Bullitt soon parlayed this into an eviable position at the center of a constant flow of information, in which he pursued his own interests in the liberal and revolutionary struggles of Central Europe and Russia. Bullitt kept up his relationship with Colonel House and maintained constant discussions with House's secretary Gordon Auchincloss, the various section chiefs, Press Secretary Ray Stannard Baker and delegates Henry White and Tasker Bliss. It was therefore no exaggeration to note, as did Charles Seymour, that for many staff members of the delegation Bullitt was "the most useful man at the conference."[10]

With the important exceptions of Colonel House and of course Woodrow Wilson, Bullitt probably had his hands on more information than any other American in Paris. U.S. Senator Philander Knox asked Bullitt when he testified before the Senate Foreign Relations Committee, "you were practically a clear-ing house of information for the members of the American Mission?" Bullitt responded, "That is what I was supposed to be . . . it was my duty to be in constant touch with everyone who was in the American delegation. . . ."[11]

Bullitt's ceaseless activity made him a storehouse of useful information about others' work. He was also assisted by the natural inclination of many of the young staff members in Paris to favor liberal and idealistic solutions to the problems of the Peace Conference. It is probably for this reason that skeptics and conservatives, like George H. Herron and Robert Lansing, later accused Bullitt of manipulating many of the staff to favor his "Bolshevik ideas" and an accommodation with the Soviet government. Herron groused later that "while the question of Prinkipo was held in the balance, all the voices were in favor of an agreement with the Soviet Government, and not one voice against it."[12]

Bullitt's work for the State Department on Central Europe and his interest in revolutionary movements combined to make him the Peace Commission's foremost expert on Bolshevism. His memoranda on the Bolshevik movement, with considerable detail about revolutionary activities in Hungary, Italy, Swit-zerland, Austria, and Germany, became staple briefing papers for members of the American delegation and were viewed favorably by both Lansing and

House.[13] In two comprehensive memos, Bullitt stressed that "economic disorganization and famine are the parents of Bolshevism" and urged in the strongest possible terms the mounting of a major hunger relief and economic reconstruction effort coupled with contacts and support for moderate socialists throughout Europe as the best means for countering the spread of Bolshevism.[14]

In Paris, Bullitt was at the center of the circle of staff and delegates, both British and American, who were determined that Buckler's meeting with Litvinov should be followed up with further investigations or negotiations and that the Prinkipo proposal, once tendered, should be implemented. Bullitt and House held a brainstorming session about Russia in mid-January, prior to the Prinkipo breakthrough and at a time that the French were stonewalling the invitation of various Russian governments to Paris because the Bolsheviks would have had to be included. At this meeting, the two men agreed that it would not be "desirable" to try to force the French to accept a meeting of all factions in Paris. Instead, perhaps a special American delegation should be readied for a mission to Russia to "examine conditions with a view to recommending definite action." Most appropriate for such a mission, in Bullitt's view, were Judge Learned Hand, Raymond Fosdick, and William Allen White, and possibly someone with first-hand experience with the Bolsheviks, such as Albert Rhys Williams, or "Bullitt as general bootblack."[15]

Bullitt went on to recommend a process for such a mission to approach the Bolsheviks, remarkably similar to what was used the next month by the Bullitt mission. He told House that the projected mission "should get in touch with Litvinov in Stockholm, or some other representative of the Soviet Government, to explain the purpose of the mission and to ascertain whether or not the Soviet Government will consent to admit the mission to Great Russia."[16] If a favorable answer was received, the mission could proceed directly to Petrograd. Bullitt also recommended that any Allied missions to Russia should remain independent of each other, allowing different personnel and conditions for possible British and American missions and enabling one to proceed without reference to joint Allied action. This was another important condition that eventually enabled the Bullitt mission to occur.[17]

While Prinkipo was pending, Bullitt used his influence to recommend to House and Wilson the immediate withdrawal of American troops from North Russia and the negotiation of an armistice with the Bolsheviks there, a course both General Bliss and Colonel House favored.[18] Bullitt was also sent with William H. Buckler by the Commissioners to meet with Philip Kerr to explore the next joint British-American steps on Russia. At this meeting, Kerr indicated Lloyd George's interest in getting British troops out of North Russia as well, and favored meeting with the Bolsheviks at Prinkipo or elsewhere, since a prime British objective was stopping the Russian civil war.[19]

Following Chicherin's February 4 Bolshevik response to the Prinkipo invitation, Bullitt immediately prepared a memorandum for House with suggestions about the American response. In this memorandum, Bullitt emphasized the very poor military situation for American and British troops in Archangel, the Bolshevik acceptance of the Prinkipo meeting and their willingness to negotiate an armistice (although not accepting one unilaterally), and the growing opposition in the United States to keeping American troops in Russia. All of these factors prompted him to conclude that the Allies "should offer an immediate armistice on all fronts to the Bolsheviki."[20]

Though House did not see fit to recommend this to President Wilson, much less the British and the French, Bullitt's continued stress on the importance of negotiation and direct contact with the Bolsheviks coincided with House's own concerns regarding Russia, and the apparent demise of Prinkipo. Following up Wilson's own expressed willingness to "go to Mahomet," which he had expressed in the last session of the Council of Four before his departure to the United States on February 14, House apparently received authorization from Wilson to pursue a secret exploratory mission to Moscow with the British.[21] House discussed the matter with Secretary Lansing on February 16, indicating that he had the President's approval. Lansing agreed to send Bullitt, but to gather information only. Lansing agreed, so he recorded in his diary, "to cure [Bullitt] of his Bolshevism."[22]

The next day House visited Philip Kerr and discussed with him the idea of a secret mission to Lenin to explore the possible terms the Bolsheviks might accept as preliminary to official negotiations with the Allies.[23] Kerr had written Lloyd George a few days earlier hinting that Wilson and House might propose some kind of informal mission to Lenin.[24] Later the same day, House asked Bullitt to prepare for an immediate mission to Russia.[25]

Although Bullitt's persistent advocacy of such a mission from January 19 was certainly instrumental in the final House-Lansing-Kerr decision to send him, it was by no means the first mention of the idea of an Allied commission or mission to Bolshevik Russia to gather information and engage in exploratory talks. Various proposals for such a mission had been floating around British and American government and liberal circles since soon after the Bolshevik revolution, and explicit and detailed suggestions in this direction had been made by Bullitt himself in February 1918.[26]

Ironically, as John M. Thompson points out, it may have been the conservative British publisher Lord Northcliffe, who had helped sabotage the Bullitt proposals, who renewed the idea of such a mission in House's mind in early January 1919.[27] House's secretary, Gordon Auchincloss, visited Northcliffe on January 9 and reported that Northcliffe "suggested that a commission should be sent to Russia after securing the approval of the present government."[28] Auchincloss relayed this suggestion to President Wilson at a meeting on January 13, including it as a recommendation of Colonel House's and further recommended that "the President should appoint as American members of this Commission radicals. The President said that this procedure was also in his mind."[29]

House, meanwhile, discussed the idea with Lansing, who raised it at a meeting of the American Commissioners on January 18 and indicated his opposition. Bliss was favorably disposed, especially if the French kept stonewalling efforts to bring the various Russian factions together.[30] Bullitt followed this discussion with his own long memorandum on January 19. In the meantime, Lincoln Steffens had heard about the possibility from his old friend Colonel House, and Steffens indicated in a letter to his brother-in-law that if such a mission were dispatched, he would like very much to be on it.[31]

The Council of Ten's Prinkipo breakthrough of January 21 put aside for a time the consideration of an exploratory mission to Russia. The idea came back strongly following the refusal of the White governments to come to Prinkipo and Churchill's push for major military intervention. Following House's request to Bullitt to prepare to go on February 17, he was issued a formal letter by Secretary of State Lansing, and given a letter of credentials from the Peace Commission by Joseph C. Grew. Lansing's letter "directed" Bullitt "to proceed to Russia for the purpose of studying conditions, political and economic, therein, for the benefit of the American commissioners plenipotentiary to negotiate peace."[32] Grew's letter was quite similar, differing only in that Bullitt was "authorized by the American commissioners plenipotentiary."[33]

Colonel House temporarily put Bullitt on hold, however, pending the results of House's discussions with Philip Kerr and Kerr's consultations with Lloyd George about a way to revive Prinkipo. All of these consultations were suspended when, on the morning of February 19, Premier Clemenceau was wounded in an assassination attempt. Interestingly, Clemenceau had just moved the previous evening for a recess in the Peace Conference because "he wished to devote the whole day to thought on the Russian question."[34] This event threw plans awry. Lloyd George immediately informed Kerr that any new proposals for the Peace Conference would have to be suspended indefinitely, because as long as Clemenceau was wounded, he "would simply have to hold up a finger and the whole thing would drop to the ground."[35]

Instead, House and Kerr turned back to their contingency plan . William C. Bullitt was dispatched on a secret mission to Lenin to explore the nature of terms for negotiations with the Bolsheviks. It was hoped by both key aides that Bullitt could bring back something concrete for Lloyd George, Wilson, and Clemenceau to consider on their respective returns to active discussions in Paris in a few weeks.[36]

On February 20, House told Bullitt that he should leave for Russia as soon as possible, "to attempt to obtain from the Soviet Government an exact statement of the terms on which they were ready to stop fighting. . . . The plan was to make a proposal to the Soviet Government which would certainly be accepted."[37] Bullitt spent February 20 and 21 in meetings with Lansing, House, Kerr, Balfour, and Steffens, soliciting terms for presentation to Lenin. He received outlines of acceptable terms from both House and Kerr, who made it clear that they were acting totally unofficially, but with the authorization of their respective chiefs, Wilson and Lloyd George.

House responded to a series of questions Bullitt put to him regarding terms of an armistice. First, was the United States prepared to declare an armistice on all fronts, if the Bolsheviks would stop the forward movement of their troops and do likewise? Second, would the United States demand that their French, British, Italian, and Japanese allies also accept and honor such an armistice? Third, if fighting were stopped, would the United States reestablish economic relations with European Russia, "subject only to the equitable distribution among all classes of the population of supplies and food and essential commodities?" Fourth, would the United States push for a joint statement for the total withdrawal of Allied forces from Russia, subject only to a Bolshevik assurance prohibiting retaliation against White forces? House answered in the affirmative to all four of these questions. Finally, Bullitt asked House whether a Bolshevik promise to pay all foreign debts was a necessary precondition for an armistice. House said that it was not, but that "such a statement would be extremely desirable to have."[38]

After several discussions with Philip Kerr and Sir Maurice Hankey of the British delegation, Bullitt asked Kerr to give him a sense of the kind of conditions that would be acceptable to Lloyd George, Balfour, and the British government. Kerr wrote an outline of these conditions in a letter to Bullitt, noting however that they had "no official significance and merely represent suggestions of my own opinion." This was despite the fact that Kerr told Bullitt and House personally that he had discussed the matter with Lloyd George and Balfour and that he was giving Bullitt "a fair idea of what conditions the British were ready to accept." Kerr informed Lloyd George about the project in a letter of February 18, asking for a reply by telephone. We have no record of his reply.[39]

In any event, and despite Kerr's disclaimers, the British government was intimately involved in Bullitt's mission. Bullitt used Kerr's outline for his negotiations. British military and diplomatic personnel assisted in getting the party from London to Scandinavia. As Lincoln Steffens reported, "the British paved our way. They had reserved our places on trains and boats and at the London Hotel. When we called for our tickets on the boat to Norway they were delivered to us 'all paid.' British consuls met and speeded us through Norway, Sweden, and Finland."[40]

Since the eight points of the Kerr letter became the basis of what Bullitt brought back from Lenin, it may be useful to detail them as Kerr outlined them:

    1. Hostilities to cease on all fronts.

    2. All *de facto* governments to remain in full control of the territories which they at present occupy.

    3. Railways and ports necessary to transportation between Soviet Russia and the sea to be subject to the same regulations as international railways and ports in the rest of Europe.

    4. Allied subjects to be given free right of entry and full security to enable them to enter Soviet Russia and go about their business there provided they do not interfere in politics.

    5. Amnesty to all political prisoners on both sides: full liberty to all Russians who have fought with the Allies.

    6. Trade relations to be restored between Soviet Russia and the outside world under conditions which, while respecting the sovereignty of Soviet Russia, insure that allied supplies are made available on equal terms to all classes of the Russian people.

7. All other questions connected with Russia's debt to the Allies, etc., to be considered independently after peace has been established.

8. All allied troops to be withdrawn from Russia, as soon as Russian armies above quota to be defined have been demobilized and their surplus arms surrendered or destroyed.[41]

As Kerr said later, in a post-mission explanation to the British Foreign Office, "I thought it would be a good plan to get first hand information from Russia." Bullitt and Kerr discussed, in a "perfectly unofficial manner, the possible basis of a settlement with Russia." Kerr laid out orally to Bullitt the most essential conditions from his point of view: (1) immediate ceasefire on all fronts; (2) acceptance of all existing governments in Russia as the "de facto governments of the territories they controlled"; (3) withdrawal of Allied forces from the territory of Russia simultaneously with the demobilization of the Red Army.[42]

Although Kerr emphasized in his report the "unofficial" and "personal" nature of his suggestions, Foreign Office Secretary Balfour's comments regarding Kerr's report are most pertinent: "Mr. Kerr's apologia is not very convincing . . . it strikes me that Mr. Kerr's unofficial conversations with Mr. Bullitt must have influenced the proposal which was brought away from Russia."[43]

Bullitt's pre-departure meeting with Lansing was devoted to the subject of the urgency of the release of American consul Roger Tredwell, formerly in Petrograd and most recently in Tashkent, where he had been detained by local Soviet officials. Lansing had discouraged efforts of Lord and other delegation staff to appeal to the Bolsheviks for Tredwell's release in the context of Prinkipo discussions, since that proposal had been made to all Russian governments. Now, however, Lansing urged Bullitt to make representations for Tredwell "to do everything [possible] to obtain his release."[44]

Bullitt, House, Kerr, Lansing, and Hankey did not discuss the details of Bullitt's mission with anyone else before his departure. The fact of the mission and its general outline *were* mentioned at a meeting of the American Commissioners on February 22, the very day Bullitt left Paris. Two days later, Joseph C. Grew, as Secretary of the Commissioners, issued credentials for Bullitt and wrote a memorandum to the State Department informing Polk and others of the trip. Moreover, the text of this telegram, which noted that "Bullitt will endeavor to enter into unofficial relations with some representative of the Soviet government for the purpose of obtaining permission to proceed to Petrograd" was approved by the Commissioners in their meeting of the same day.[45] Therefore, White, Bliss, and Grew knew of the trip, if not its details, contrary to their later denials.[46] Christian Herter, Grew's secretary, insisted much later that the Commissioners had been quite aware of Bullitt's mission in advance, and even that he was to do preliminary negotiations, not just gather information: "At that time, the line he should take was quite clear . . . he was sent as an emissary to prepare the way for further discussions."[47]

Both House and Bullitt believed that secrecy was of the essence in this mission. Special care was used to keep news of the mission from the press and from the French. Mission members were asked not to say goodbye to their families and friends, and to tell no one where they were going. Secretary Lansing belatedly gave a memorandum to French foreign minister Pichon at a meeting of the Council of Ten on March 15. This was just a week before Bullitt's return and only a few days before the first press leaks exposed the effort. In this memorandum, Lansing insisted that Bullitt had been sent for information purposes only, to get "recent information concerning the true situation in Petrograd and Moscow." Lansing also told Pichon that this information was needed to prepare for the resumption of discussions on Russia in the Council. Wilson, Lloyd George, and Clemenceau would be fully involved in that continued discussion.[48]

For the same reasons of secrecy, Bullitt and House chose to keep the group extremely small. Bullitt took with him only Captain W. W. Pettit, a military intelligence officer and expert on Russia, fluent in the language; his personal friend, naval clerk R. E. Lynch; and the radical journalist Lincoln Steffens. Pettit was along both as a military presence and as translator and guide. Lynch, Steffens recalled, came only to provide diversion for Bullitt. He remained in Helsinki and did not accompany the party to Russia. Steffens joined at the personal request of Colonel House, to accompany Bullitt "unofficially." Steffens was therefore "capable of official repudiation." Steffens was also chosen because he had been in Russia in 1917 and was a friend of a number of Bolsheviks. He might help provide credibility for Bullitt with the Bolshevik leadership. All negotiating was to be left to Bullitt, who was later criticized severely for not bringing either a more conservative and skeptical companion or at least someone with more diplomatic experience.[49]

Bullitt's party left Paris February 22 and London on the twenty-fifth via a British naval vessel to Christiana, Norway. Before leaving Norway, Bullitt cabled House and Grew the dates of the party's projected arrival in Stockholm and asked that U.S. Ambassador Ira Morris "communicate soon and confidentially through his private channels to Moscow Government the purpose of this party and the fact that we shall shortly be in Helsingfors and shall desire to proceed at once to Petrograd and Moscow."[50]

Lansing immediately acted on this recommendation, and cabled both the Christiana and Stockholm legations to assist the party, using their contacts with Scandinavian communists. Lansing also informed the State Department in Washington of his action.[51] By return cable, Frank Polk urged Lansing that Morris be advised to keep well out of any negotiations carried on to get the Bullitt party into Russia, for "[if] the Bolshevik government has any suspicion as to who is making the move, they will make the matter public at once as, in our opinion, it will be a very valuable bit of propaganda."[52]

The party arrived in Stockholm on March 1, and Ambassador Morris proved quite helpful. He personally involved himself in seeing to their comfort and in contacts to assist them in getting to Moscow. At the same time he managed to avoid "involving himself in relations with the Soviet Government."[53] Bullitt and Morris seemed to hit it off quite well, and Bullitt discussed his entire mission with the Ambassador, who was "very much impressed." In a long letter to House from Stockholm, Bullitt recommended that "Mr. Morris ought to be given a larger field of activity as soon as possible."[54]

Bullitt then went on to tell House that "there is every indication that Lenin is in a thoroughly conciliatory mood" and that he hoped to have a meeting with Lenin and Trotsky on March 11 or 12, after which he would immediately cable a statement of the terms they proposed. Bullitt then noted, "it looks as if my end of this job was going to be easy and as if the hardest fight would be yours in Paris to get the thing across. . . . BUT YOU HAVE GOT TO PUT IT ACROSS" (emphasis Bullitt's).[55]

Morris had indeed been most helpful. He put Bullitt and his party in the care of Karl Kilbom, a Swedish Communist with excellent ties in Bolshevik Russia, who regularly traveled back and forth between Stockholm and Petrograd. Kilbom was skeptical when first approached by Morris, especially when Morris tried to assure him that the Americans only wanted to collect information—that they were not spies. "What differentiates spying from collecting information?" countered Kilbom. Finally, however, Kilbom agreed to help. Further assistance came from an unlikely source. Herbert Hoover arranged for a visa for Kilbom to get to Helsinki, then in the hands of White forces. Kilbom then went ahead to Petrograd to arrange for reception of the party by the Bolsheviks.[56]

The Bullitt party stayed a few days in Helsinki, then set off for the border town of Terijoki alone. Before leaving Helsingfors, Bullitt again cabled House, asking that Lansing be informed that Bullitt had "reason to feel certain that [he] shall have definite proposition from the Soviet Government to transmit within a week or at most ten days."[57]

Upon crossing the border (where, as Steffens recalled, Bullitt "outdid in arrogance" a Finnish officer), Kilbom was waiting with an official Bolshevik delegation "accompanied by a brass band and cavalry troops." On the train from the border to Petrograd, Kilbom told them that he had talked on the telephone with Lenin and had met with Zinoviev, and that they would be met by Chicherin and Litvinov when they arrived.[58]

In fact, there was no greeting party at the train station, due to a mixup, but they arrived safely at their hotel in a cold, starving city in the midst of war. Steffens later recalled their first encounter with a responsible official, Zinoviev:

> Unwillingly, without greeting, he snapped one question at me in German, "Sind sie bevollmächtigt?" "No," I answered and I began to explain the preliminary nature of the mission. He would not listen. When he heard that we were not plenipotentiaries he turned away abruptly, and we never saw him again. Apparently there was some dispute among the Russians as to the purposes of the Bullitt mission and whether to deal with it.[59]

Bullitt himself picked up on this division within the Party leadership, which was a real and enduring split. As Bullitt explained in one of his reports to the Peace Commissioners,

Trotsky, the Generals and many theorists believe the Red Army should go forward everywhere until more vigorous intervention by the Entente is provoked, which they count upon to bring revolution in France and England. . . . Lenin, Tchitcherin [*sic*] and the bulk of the Communist Party on the other hand, insist that the essential problem at present is to save the proletariat of Russia . . . from starvation. . . . They advocate, therefore, the conciliation of the United States even at the cost of compromising the revolution.[60]

Chicherin, as Foreign Minister, led in the articulation of this position. Just before Bullitt's arrival in Petrograd, on March 3, Chicherin was quoted by Alfred Nagel in a long memorandum to Ambassador Morris, passed on to the State Department. In this memorandum, Nagel quoted Chicherin as saying that there were "two tendencies" among the Allies, one favoring and one opposing conciliation. Chicherin then continued to show his own position in the Soviet camp favoring conciliation by stressing his friendship with the United States and insisting that "the United States of America of all Allied powers was more friendly to Soviet Russia."[61]

Chicherin took the leadership in discussions with Bullitt, appearing at his hotel two and sometimes three times a day to hammer out the details of what would be presented to Lenin in Moscow. Once an agreement was reached, he also played an important role in keeping key members of the ministry supporting the proposal. He wrote twice, for example, to Christian Rakovski, the Soviet Minister in the Ukraine, urging him to support an agreement as a way of ending intervention: "The decision is very important. . . . If we don't try to get an agreement the policy of blockade will be pressed with vigor. They will send tanks . . . to Denikin, Kolchak, Petlura, Paderewski. . . ."[62]

Zinoviev and Trotsky remained opposed. Zinoviev had previously gone along with the conciliatory Prinkipo reply only reluctantly, and now was convinced that the Bullitt mission was another ploy. Hence he was skeptical if the mission were not empowered for actual negotiations. Trotsky, writing to Lenin on March 17, commented mostly on the general offensive of the White forces, and then noted in passing, "at this very moment America sent off its eavesdroppers to assess whether we should hold firm or not and to determine its own policy." He did not feel it worthy of any more notice, preferring to concentrate his energies on the prosecution of the war.[63]

But Lenin made his own policy, and never more than in this instance. He consulted closely with Chicherin and Litvinov during the time of Bullitt's negotiations in Petrograd and Moscow and participated personally in the drafting and revision of the proposed terms of peace eventually approved and given to Bullitt to take back to Paris. As Chicherin remarked a few years later, "Each word in our proposals to Bullitt was carefully weighed by Vladimir Ilyich."[64]

Lenin was determined to pursue a second breathing spell, even a second Brest peace if necessary, to preserve the revolution and the Bolshevik state. In the month since the expiration of Prinkipo, the Bolshevik military situation had improved only marginally, and the economic situation had markedly deteriorated. Even Bullitt himself, inclined to exaggerate the health of the Bolshevik government, was forced to remark on the terrifying human tragedy starkly put before him in Petrograd and Moscow: "Russia today is in a condition of acute economic distress . . . every man, woman and child in Moscow and Petrograd is suffering from slow starvation. . . . The entire population is exceptionally susceptible to disease. . . . Industry, except the production of munitions of war, is largely at a standstill. . . ."[65]

In a speech to a large public meeting in Petrograd on March 13, the day before he gave the final Bolshevik peace terms to Bullitt, Lenin affirmed the critical nature of the Bolshevik situation, and the humiliating need to again appeal for an unequal peace. He called Brest itself "atrocious, outrageous, humiliating," but the policy that necessitated it "entirely correct." He then said that the Bolsheviks now faced a similar crucial situation; that the Allies stood poised to crush the Soviet state. Signing a peace treaty was again the only way out.[66]

And yet, Arthur Ransome, who had two long meetings with Lenin during the crucial month of March, found him serene, even happy, in spite of bearing such a terrible burden. Ransome felt the reason was simple:

> he is the first great leader who utterly discounts the value of his own personality. . . . More than that, he believes, as a Marxist, in the movement of the masses which, with or without him, would still move. His whole faith is in the elemental forces that move people, his faith in himself is merely his belief that he justly estimates the direction of those forces. He does not believe that any man could make or stop the revolution. . . . [67]

Lenin agreed to meet with Bullitt personally, according to Swedish communist Karl Kilbom, because he was persuaded that the American wished to negotiate seriously. "There was no doubt," Kilbom wrote, "that Lenin was happy about the delegation."[68]

After Bullitt finished his preliminary meetings with Chicherin and Litvinov in Petrograd, he proceeded to Moscow for final negotiations with Lenin. Before his departure, he cabled an update on his situation to Colonel House and Secretary Lansing. In it, he predicted with confidence that he would have an agreement within a few days, saying that "both Tchicherin and Litvinov, speaking with authority, stated that the Soviet Government is most favorably disposed towards the cessation of hostilities." But Bullitt also mentioned a number of sticking points that had already cropped up. The Bolshevik leaders were concerned about the Allied difficulty of controlling the myriad groups arrayed against the Bolsheviks. They also expressed grave doubts that Britain and the United States could persuade France to accept any settlement. On the other hand, Bullitt optimistically reported that the Soviets were willing to assume responsibility for payment of the Russian foreign debt if the settlement were signed. Finally, Bullitt, worried that the Allies might already have made a decision about Russian policy in the absence of his proposals, pleaded with House and Lansing not to do anything until he was able to get them an agreement. He called for them to "suspend judgement" because he was so certain that "the Soviet Government [was] disposed to be reasonable."[69]

Bullitt arrived in Moscow on March 12, continued to meet regularly with Chicherin and Litvinov, and finally had a long meeting with Lenin on the fourteenth. At this meeting the final terms of the proposal were agreed on, which were subsequently given to Bullitt (dated March 12) with the assurance that they had been approved by the Bolshevik Central Committee.[70]

The Central Committee had discussed the proposals on two separate occasions before approving them at Lenin's request. Their discussions focused on the same issues that had dogged the discussions about the acceptance of Brest Litovsk a year earlier, particularly the need to make major concessions.[71] Bullitt convinced Lenin and Chicherin, however, that only by demonstrating that the Bolsheviks had agreed to concessions could he ever hope to persuade the French in Paris to go along with the agreement. As Chicherin wrote to Rakovski following one of the last negotiating sessions, Bullitt "does not believe that big concessions can be won for us in Paris. But he hopes to carry this proposal through."[72] In Paris, Bullitt defended the proposals by pointing out the Soviet concessions and insisting that what he had obtained was the "maximum" lengths the Soviets were willing to go to in what seemed to be an unequal accord.[73]

The final provisions of the agreement differed little from the draft points that Bullitt had brought from Philip Kerr. In some striking respects, in fact, the language agreed to was identical to what Bullitt had submitted. This is true, for example, of the Kerr Phrase, "all *de facto* governments to remain in control of territories they occupy." It may have been, not mere coincidence, but shrewd calculation on Lenin's part that this phrase—which meant the indirect acceptance of the various White governments by the Bolsheviks—was most important to the British, and the possible linchpin to potential British-American agreement with the entire accord.[74]

In fact, the Soviets did make a number of concessions. They agreed that all existing Russian governments would remain in *de facto* control of the territory they occupied at the time of the agreement, and they pledged not to "attempt to upset by force" those governments, if the Allies and the White governments would make the same pledge. This provision, if carried out, would have left the Bolsheviks in control only of central Russia, with hostile governments surrounding them. It also signified more of a concession on land by the Bolsheviks than they made to the Germans at Brest Litovsk. Had this been agreed to by the Allies, it would have meant a Bolshevik government's giving up large land areas on the western, southern, and northern Russian borderlands that had been controlled by Russia for most of the nineteenth century. Bullitt was particularly struck by the far-reaching nature of this concession, as he indicated both in his Senate testimony and, later, in an important passage in his study of Woodrow Wilson.[75]

The Bolsheviks further agreed to give a general amnesty to all political opponents, release all prisoners of war, and "recognize their responsibility for the financial obligations of the former Russian empire." Bullitt indicated later that he believed there was even room for strengthening these two provisions to the Allies' benefit, by adding some language prohibiting Soviet propaganda in the West and reserving the Allies' right to arrest and detain pro-Bolshevik political opponents.[76]

In return, the Allies had to agree to raise the economic blockade, allow the Bolsheviks free access to all Russian ports and railways, and withdraw all foreign troops from Russian territory. The Bolsheviks agreed to a ceasefire a week from the time of the acceptance by the Allies of the proposal, and indicated their willingness to come to a conference of all Russian parties and the Allies a week later.[77]

In an explanatory note in his accompanying cable, and later in his report, Bullitt noted that the Bolsheviks were very opposed to any conference's being held in Prinkipo, much preferring Norway, Finland, or even "a large ocean liner anchored off Moon Island or the Aaland Islands." The Soviet government also requested that "either the radio, or a direct telegraph wire to Moscow should be put at its disposal." The Bolsheviks were not oblivious to the fact that the Prinkipo location was isolated and access to it controlled by the Allies.[78]

The Allies were also asked to make concessions. Most notably, the agreement called for them to suspend military aid to the White forces and to agree to insist that their Russian allies honor a ceasefire. Although some observers claim that the Bolsheviks received "more than they were required to give,"[79] those who have studied this agreement in the context of the history of Soviet-American relations agree with John M. Thompson that "the Soviet leaders gave up a good deal, the terms proposed containing more concessions than the West has been able to extract from the Soviet government from that day to this [1967]."[80]

The Bolsheviks were not inclined to keep these concessions on the table indefinitely, nor were they ready to agree not to take advantage if the occasion arose. Lenin set an April 10 deadline for the West to accept the specifics of the proposal. He also told Chicherin that "if they do not accept our proposals now, they will not get such favorable terms from us the next time."[81] Also, in a conversation a year later with British journalist John Silverlight, Lenin frankly admitted that "when we proposed a treaty to Bullitt a year ago, a treaty which left tremendous amounts of territory to Denikin and Kolchak, we proposed this treaty with the knowledge that if peace were signed, those Governments could never hold out."[82]

But Lenin kept the Bullitt terms on the table through December 1919, despite the lapsing of the April 10 deadline, referring to them repeatedly.[83] He also expressed the hope, in a farewell conversation with Arthur Ransome, who left Russia with Bullitt and Steffens, that "I am sure we can come to terms, if they want to come to terms. . . . England and America would be willing, perhaps, if their hands were not tied by France."[84] This latter concern, which bothered Lenin from the outset of Prinkipo, was so strong that a separate note was handed to Bullitt by Chicherin. This note stated, "The Soviet Government is most anxious to have a semiofficial guaranty from the

American and British Governments that they will do their utmost to see to it that France lives up to the conditions of the armistice." Bullitt refused to agree that this statement become part of the official proposal, but did agree to pass on the concern to House and Wilson in Paris.[85]

Steffens met with Lenin separately, late in the same day as Bullitt, and found him "tired but hopeful."[86] Steffens and Bullitt left Moscow the very next day with the final agreement. After picking up Pettit in Petrograd they left immediately for Paris.

In Helsingfors on March 16, Bullitt cabled the essence of the terms to Wilson, House, and Lansing, asking that they be conveyed as well to Philip Kerr, but otherwise kept absolutely secret.[87] In this cable, Bullitt stressed that "the Soviet government considered itself bound to accept the proposals contained therein" and said that he "found Lenin, Tchitcherin, and Litvinov full of a sense of Russia's need for peace, and therefore, disposed to be most conciliatory." Bullitt also amplified on a number of points in the official text. He stated, for example, that the Bolsheviks agreed that the "allies and Associated countries should have the right to send inspectors into Soviet Russia to see to it that distribution of supplies was equitable." Bullitt closed his message with the belief that "there is no doubt whatever of the desire of the Soviet Government for a just and reasonable peace, or of the sincerity of this proposal, and I pray you will consider it with the deepest seriousness."[88]

In a personal follow-up cable to House the following day, also from Helsingfors, Bullitt pleaded with House to do his utmost to persuade others that the proposals should be accepted. He reiterated the importance of sharing the terms with Philip Kerr, and he asked House to wire him at Stockholm or Christiana his own view of the "possibility of acceptance" of the proposal. "If you had seen the things I have seen . . . and talked with the men I have talked with, I know that you would not rest until you had put through this peace," Bullitt wrote.[89]

Bullitt also took steps to try to establish a permanent link with Bolshevik Russia before his departure from Finland. He ordered Captain W. W. Pettit to return to Petrograd and estabish a liaison office to facilitate future contacts and negotiations and to make a more thorough report on conditions there than Bullitt had been able to do in his brief survey. Pettit asked that Sergeant Krause, from his office in Paris, be sent to Helsingfors with a courier passport, civilian clothing, and supplies to assist as a shuttle contact with Helsingfors. Bullitt cabled these requests immediately to Paris for the consideration of the Peace Commissioners.[90]

At first, the Peace Commission approved the requests, "with the exception perhaps of giving to Sergeant Krause a courier passport," which the Commissioners agreed should be done only "if absolutely necessary."[91] The very next day, however, Secretary Lansing overruled the decision of the Commission and ordered Joseph Grew, the Secretary of the Commission, to recall Pettit to Paris immediately. In seeking to carry out this order, Grew asked his personal secretary, Alexander Kirk, to consult with the other Commissioners, since the new telegrams were "contrary to the decision of the Commissioners taken yesterday." Kirk did check with the Commissioners, who reversed themselves, and Pettit was recalled.[92]

Following the receipt of these orders, Pettit returned to Helsingfors, expressing considerable disappointment with the American decision. In a letter to the Commissioners, he summarized the situation in Petrograd and noted, "The presence of some one in touch with the outside world in Petrograd appears advisable. The friendship that the Soviet Government has for the United States dictates that such a person should be an American. If the American Mission is not in a position to retain a representative in Petrograd, cannot General Churchill send an intelligence officer here?"[93]

The Commissioners had an immediate change of heart about another aspect of Bullitt's mission even before his return to Paris. On March 19, Colonel House suggested a draft telegram from the Commissioners to Bullitt in Stockholm, congratulating him on the success of his mission. At first the Commissioners simply postponed sending it until they had a chance to read all of Bullitt's cables. David Hunter Miller, one of the legal advisors to the Commission, was opposed to congratulating Bullitt, as were Lansing and White. Miller felt that "Bullitt had been completely fooled" by the clever Lenin proposal. But before this process could be completed, Colonel House himself withdrew the telegram, telling the Commissioners that the President was still considering the best approach to take to negotiations with Lenin and therefore no congratulations should be sent.[94]

Bullitt returned to Paris on March 25 and went immediately to see Colonel House. Bullitt gave House the original copy of the Bolshevik proposal, signed by Lenin and with the seal of the Commissariat of Foreign Affairs. Bullitt stressed the importance of pushing forward with an Allied response. House told Bullitt that he now saw a way out of "that vexatious problem" but only "if we can get action by the Prime Ministers and the President." Bullitt painted a stark picture of the economic crisis of Bolshevik Russia for House and urged action to relieve starvation and suffering. But House cautioned him, as a matter of political pragmatism, not to stress the privation of the Bolsheviks in his report. House was afraid, he said, that "most of the allies . . . would just as soon have the people starve as not. . . . It is fear that will bring about a Russian settlement, not pity."[95]

House called President Wilson for Bullitt, but Wilson said he had a headache and would see Bullitt the next day. House also urged Bullitt to talk to Kerr and Lloyd George in the meantime.[96]

Bullitt's stress on starvation and economic dislocation was significant for House, because it fit perfectly into his previous predilections for food relief as an antidote to Bolshevism. Even as he explored, with Orlando, Wilson, and Lloyd George, the possibility of Allied action on the basis of the Bullitt-Lenin proposals, House was developing in the back of his mind a backup proposal to revive the old food and economic relief ideas in a new form. As he noted in his diary right after talking with Bullitt, "While Bullitt was talking I was maturing plans which I will begin to put in execution tomorrow."[97]

To gauge House's specific reactions to the Bullitt-Lenin proposals, it is most helpful to examine his comments on the original proposal Bullitt left in his hands. House expressed some skepticism regarding the Bolshevik terms, noting all those provisions that would have to be brought to the attention of the Allies, and about which some might have grave reservations, particularly those that aided in the stabilization of the Bolshevik government. On the key provision of the mutual recognition of the various *de facto* governments, House noted that it would "principally" benefit the Bolsheviks. He also highlighted the provision for the removal of the economic blockade, noting that it would aid in the "stabilization" of the government. On the provision of the draft treaty giving the Bolsheviks "the right of unhindered transit on all railways and the use of all ports," House noted that this would include Poland, Finland, and the Baltics, and would be advantageous to the Bolsheviks.[98]

House also worried about the Bolshevik advantage gained by the provision of free entry into both Allied countries and the borderlands for Soviet citizens. On this later provision, House noted that in some cases such a provision contravened the laws of Allied countries and Poland. As for the provisions for reciprocal free entry into Bolshevik Russia of both nationals and officials, in House's view this was "useless to bordering countries and generally speaking to others," so long as the Bolsheviks remained in power. Most crucial of all to House, and a provision he underlined several times, was the one calling for the withdrawal of all Allied troops and the cessation of military assistance to the anti-Soviet Governments. On the draft of this provision, House wrote, "all military assistance to anti-Soviet governments to be stopped."[99]

Despite these reservations, House began exploring the possibilities of support for the Bullitt-Lenin terms the very next day in a discussion with Premier Orlando of Italy. In this discussion, House stressed the need for an armistice, said that "Russia had become orderly," and argued that the Bolsheviks would leave the other governments alone if an agreement could be reached. He also argued that the Red Army was now over one million strong, and would fight if peace were not made. It seemed to him, House said to Orlando, that it was necessary "either to reckon with the de facto government, or remain in a state of war, or semi-war." Since no government was prepared for further intervention, why should the allies not "proceed to draw up a treaty with Russia . . . practically on our own terms," and send it to Moscow? Orlando agreed with this approach and said that House could count on his support.[101]

The next day, in the Council of Four, Orlando spoke at length for the first time on Russia. He essentially reiterated the choices of negotiation or intervention, and complained that the Allies had done neither, thus leaving Russia policy in limbo.[101]

In the meantime, House pursued steps for the consideration of this policy by Lloyd George and Wilson. He telephoned the President again and found he still did not want to meet with Bullitt. In fact, Wilson did not want to have a substantive discussion about Russia even with House, because he was preoccupied with the German settlement. House therefore decided to take up the matter with Lloyd George and try to get him committed as he had Orlando.

As House recorded in his diary that night, "If peace is to come to the world, the Russian settlement must be part of it. I told Orlando, as I shall tell George, that a settlement with Russia will enable us to treat with Germany in a much more positive and satisfactory way."[102]

To move the process forward, House talked to his son-in-law and aide, Gordon Auchincloss, and his legal advisor, David Hunter Miller, and asked them to take the Bullitt-Lenin proposals and prepare a draft treaty incorporating some of the provisions. This armistice should be drawn up "to suit ourselves," in Auchincloss's words. If the terms of such a treaty could be agreed on by Wilson, Lloyd George, and Orlando, then perhaps Clemenceau would go along, and something could be sent back to the Bolsheviks for finalization.[103]

When House asked Miller to help out with the legal provisions, Miller told House that he was opposed to doing it, arguing that "you will get an agreement with these people which you will carry out and they will get something out of it, and then they will refuse to carry out their part of the agreement." Nevertheless, he and Auchincloss agreed to try to draft something.[104]

On the same day, March 26, Bullitt made a long report to the American Commissioners Bliss, White, and Lansing. House was present for part of the discussion, and Wilson was absent. The Commissioners spent most of the day with Bullitt. He went away from the meeting convinced that the Commissioners had agreed that the terms provided a basis on which to make peace.[105]

In this matter he was largely correct. Colonel House had already indicated to him his support and the steps he was taking to line up the Big Four behind the proposal. Henry White, under the influence of William H. Buckler, who had returned to Paris on March 21 and was rooming with White, was prepared to support the Bullitt terms. White wrote to his son Jack on March 21 that "we are causing inquiry to be made in Russia as to whether something is not to be done with the conservative element among the Bolsheviks . . . which desires to come to terms with the rest of the world . . . inasmuch as military expeditions are out of the questions, the only other alternative would seem to be to come to terms with them if it be possible. . . ."[106]

White went even further some days later. In another letter to Jack, he wrote, concerning the Bolsheviks, "If they are really the de facto government of Russia, it may, and probably will, be necessary for a great while for us to recognize them as such."[107]

Bliss also supported the initiative. He spoke out strongly the next day in the Council of Ten on the subject of Bolshevism, stressing the impossibility of stopping Bolshevism with military force. Bliss argued that "peace, with a determination of frontiers" and "lifting the blockade and thereby allowing the entire world to go back to work" were the only solutions.[108]

Even Secretary Lansing's first reactions in the Peace Commission were cautiously positive. He noted that Bullitt argued "that the Bolsheviks are coming to their senses and beginning to establish public order and authority among more normal lines." While noting that Bullitt was "unavoidably biased," still, he said, "it is an interesting story and furnishes much food for thought."[109]

On the strength of the initial support from the Commissioners and Colonel House and under the explicit direction of Colonel House, Bullitt prepared a declaration of policy on Russia for the Russian section to present to the Commission. The Russian section urged the Commission to adopt and recommend this statement to Wilson for immediate action. This memorandum, adopted by the Russian section, headed by R. H. Lord, and submitted to the Commissioners on March 27, was subsequently sent under cover of a supporting memorandum, from the Commission on March 31 to President Wilson. This memo is often overlooked in light of Bullitt's long written report, also submitted to the Commissioners, Secretary Lansing, and President Wilson on March 27. It may be more important, however; not only because it represented the views of both Bullitt and Lord and the rest of the Russian section, but also because there is clear evidence that it reached Wilson and may have received serious consideration, at least for a brief time.[110]

This Bullitt drafted memorandum regretted the demise of Prinkipo, although it placed no blame for its failure. It stated unequivocally that the Allies had no intention of interfering "with the solution of the political, social, or economic problems of Russia," but also that they could "have no dealings with any Russian Government which shall invade the territory of its neighbors or seek to impose its will upon other peoples by force." Rather, it was the "earnest desire of the associated peoples" to assist the people of Russia through a massive relief effort, which could not occur under conditions of war. Therefore, the declaration called for an in-place ceasefire and armistice for two weeks. During this time, all governments accepting the armistice should send representatives to a conference to discuss peace on the terms of the Lenin-Bullitt agreement (*de facto* control by the various Russian governments, free movement, rights of official representatives, political amnesty, withdrawal of Allied military forces, and cessation of military aid and lifting of the economic blockade).[111]

The cover memo for this declaration, sent by Lansing to Wilson on March 31, developed the case for an armistice even more, by claiming that the "isolation of the Russian revolution from the German and Hungarian problem" would "be of obvious military advantage." It also argued that "the Bolshevist government sincerely desires an armistice" and submitted that, were Allied representatives appointed, an armistice could be immediately arranged "under a flag of truce."[112]

The same day that Lord presented the Russian section's recommendations to the Commissioners for transmittal to the President, William C. Bullitt presented his own written and oral report. The written report consisted of the terms of proposed agreement as brought from Lenin and Chicherin, accompanied by a detailed report from Bullitt giving some of his impressions of the situation in Russia. Many of these impressions were the type of material Colonel House had urged him not to put in writing. Bullitt's report began with a discussion of Russia's "acute economic distress," pointing out the sad state of transportation, industry, and food production and distribution. But then Bullitt emphasized the "order" and control the Bolsheviks had over the revolution, claiming that "the destructive phase of the revolution is over and all the energy of the Government is turned to constructive work." Bullitt's report also claimed that the people gave "general support" to the government "in spite of their starvation" because they "lay the blame for their distress wholly on the blockade." Bullitt also noted that the leaders of the two remaining legal opposition parties—Volsky, leader of the Right Socialist–Revolutionaries; and Martov, leader of the Mensheviks— both called for an end to intervention and support for the government in order to defend the revolution against its enemies.[113]

Bullitt also argued that, although there was some difference of opinion with regard to foreign policy among the Bolsheviks, it had not become an "open breach in the ranks of the party." Lenin's policy of "conciliation of the United States even at the cost of compromising with many of the principles they hold most dear" had clear and strong support. Bullitt rightly pointed out that Lenin felt "compelled to retreat from his theoretical position all along the line" and argued that he was "ready to meet the western Governments half way." Thus the terms that Bullitt brought from Lenin represented, in Bullitt's view, this "half way position," including serious concessions and compromises by the Bolsheviks. Finally, Bullitt concluded, Lenin's government was "as moderate as any socialist government which can control Russia." The proposals presented, in Bullitt's view, "an opportunity to make peace with the revolution on a just and reasonable basis—perhaps a unique opportunity."[114]

William Pettit and Lincoln Steffens also submitted written reports on their impressions, in the form of memoranda and reports to Bullitt. Bullitt included these along with his own report in his later testimony to the Senate Foreign Relations Committee.[115] Pettit argued in a March 29 memo that he was "firmly convinced that though a majority of the population of Petrograd may not be communist, most of the intelligent citizens realize that there is no other government which can preserve order." He also stressed the friendliness of people toward the United States, in spite of "our activities during the past 18 months," and he argued that "the United States has the opportunity of demonstrating to the Russian people its friendship and cementing bonds which already exist."[116]

Pettit also reported on his time in Petrograd after Bullitt's departure, where he spent several hours with Schlovski, Chicherin's representative in Petrograd. Schlovski "was most optimistic about the situation" and was "convinced that the Paris conference will adopt a policy favorable to Russia."[117] Pettit also gave his own recommendations to Bullitt: "some sort of recognition of the present government, with the establishment of economic relations and the sending of every possible assistance to the people."[118]

Steffens wrote a long report to Bullitt, in which he began by noting that Bullitt took him along "because, you said, you thought my experience in reporting political, labor and revolutionary movements" might be of use. Steffens reflected on the mix of revolutionary temperament and caution among the Bolshevik leaders and predicted that "Lenin and his Commissaires will stand by their offer to us until Paris has answered, or until the time set for the answer—April 10th—shall have passed. . . . They are practical men. . . . They are all idealists, but they are all idealists sobered by the responsibility of power. . . . Lenin has imagination. He is an idealist, but he is a scholar too and a very grim realist."[119] Steffens went on to explain why, in his thinking, the Bolsheviks were now seriously interested in making peace:

> They think they have carried a revolution through for once to the logical conclusion. . . . They want time to go on and build it higher and better. They want to spread it all over the world, but only as it works. . . . We want to stop fighting. We know that each country must evolve its own revolution. . . . We are fighting now only in self-defense. We will stop fighting, if you will let us. . . . We need the picked organizers and the skilled workers now in the army for our shops, factories, and farms.[120]

Bullitt's long report and recommendations were not considered by the Commissioners until their meeting of April 2. By that time, Secretary Lansing had consulted with Frank Polk and others in the State Department. Lansing was now fully convinced of the folly of Bullitt's suggestions. The other Commissioners, under the impression that the whole matter was under intensive review by the President, declined to take any position.[121]

Bullitt lost no time seeking a consultation with the British. He spoke briefly with Philip Kerr immediately on his return, who arranged for him to breakfast with Lloyd George and others from the British delegation the morning of March 27, the day after his meeting with the American Commissioners. Two days earlier, Lloyd George, in his famous Fontainebleau memorandum laying out the necessity for coming to some agreement on peace with Germany, also referred to Russia and Bolshevism. His remarks seemed to indicate an openness to some kind of settlement, as he cautioned against thinking that a lasting peace with Germany was possible without dealing with Russia and Bolshevism.[122]

Bullitt breakfasted with Lloyd George, General Jan Smuts, Maurice Hankey, and Philip Kerr. He brought with him the complete official text of the proposal, shared it with them, and discussed the entire matter at some length. As Philip Kerr recalled later, "the Prime Minister cross-examined him closely in regard to conditions in Russia, and the attitude and personalities of the Bolshevik leaders."[123]

In Bullitt's account of this meeting, he said that Smuts argued that the proposal should not be allowed to lapse, "that it was of the utmost importance." But Lloyd George was consumed by the critical comments of the conservative British press, which raised the specter of an agreement with Bolshevism. "As long as the British press is doing this kind of thing how can you expect me to be sensible about Russia?" Lloyd George asked Bullitt. Lloyd George then went on to muse about the possibility of sending someone else to Moscow, "somebody who is known to the whole world as a complete conservative, in order to have the whole world believe that the report he brings out is not simply the utterance of a radical."[124]

Lloyd George then mentioned the possibility of sending Lord Lansdowne, Robert Cecil, the Marquis of Salisbury, or Smuts (who was already set for a mission to Budapest). Toward the end of the meeting, Lloyd George urged Bullitt to make his report public, in order to try to influence public opinion positively. He also told Bullitt that he would be glad to follow the lead of Colonel House, President Wilson, and the United States in pursuing the Lenin proposal; that he "would be disposed to go at least as far as we would."[125]

The next day, House had a luncheon appointment with Lloyd George for a strategy session on Russia. All Lloyd George could talk about, however, was the blowup that had just occurred between President Wilson and Clemenceau in the Council of Four. House asked Lloyd George to postpone any action on Britain's part until he (House) "could get a more matured plan for our consideration." Lloyd George agreed, and House left feeling that he was "sympathetic toward a settlement with Russia and I think will meet me halfway."[126]

But, by the time of this meeting, House had already set in motion the planning for an alternative proposal for the President's consideration. House, disturbed by the increasingly strident calls for a military crusade beginning to appear in the British press, persuaded Wickham Steed, one of the more vociferous of the editorial writers, to drop his crusade against the Bolsheviks while the Allies worked out a plan for neutral food relief coupled with a ceasefire. Gordon Auchincloss was sent to consult with Herbert Hoover on the feasibility of such an effort.[127]

Lloyd George had delegated British general Jan Smuts to Budapest on a fact-finding mission some weeks earlier. This interesting mission, which Harold Nicholson has reported on in some detail, also included, as a secret component, the exploration of whether Hungarian Bolshevik leader Béla Kun would serve as a channel for negotiations with Lenin. Smuts had written to Lloyd George on March 31 asking him if the Bolsheviks could even be asked to come to meet him at Budapest as a way to open talks. Smuts noted to Lloyd George that he felt sure that, "unless Bullitt misread the situation, [he] could make recommendations to you after a talk with the Russians which might lead to peace with Russia, and thus round off the work of the Peace Conference. And without a Russian peace the work here will be but half done. I might therefore be entrusted with the double mission."[128]

Although Lloyd George did not follow up on Smuts' suggestion, he apparently encouraged him to sound out Béla Kun about serving as a go-between. Communication between the two, however, was just as bad as between the Allies and Lenin, or worse, so nothing came of the proposal.[129]

While all this was developing, William C. Bullitt continued to push the Bolshevik proposal for ceasefire and negotiations. Bullitt met with Buckler, who a week earlier had returned from London to Paris. Buckler was very supportive and lobbied House on Bullitt's behalf, arguing that "without pacification in Russia, the Polish, Bohemian, and German problems cannot be solved. WHY [emphasis Buckler's] is it postponed?"[130]

Buckler had been asked by House to consider a special assignment to

Poland. He used the occasion to press House further on Russia policy by asking pointedly, "before climbing the Polish pyre, which may break into flames at any moment, I feel entitled to ask whether 'drift in our Russian policy' is going to continue, as it has now for two months, since I made my Stockholm report. . . ."[131] After his meetings with the British, Bullitt remained optimistic. He remarked to Buckler that he believed that "as soon as the German peace terms are settled, Woodrow Wilson will turn his mind to this Russian problem, so there is a chance of something being done ere long. . . ."[132]

Bullitt had a long talk with press secretary and Wilson confidant Ray Stannard Baker, who felt "the increasing tendency toward trying to deal with Lenin." Baker promised Bullitt to try to get publicity for his report, even asking him to draw up a press release to accompany it. But two days later, Baker had a long talk with Colonel House, who advised him to clear any press releases with Wilson. When Baker asked the President, Wilson declined to approve either the press release or the release of Bullitt's report. Baker recorded in his diary that any publication was "dangerous, unless we have taken up the policy of dealing with the Bolsheviks. No progress of any consequence today. . . . Lenin looms always on the horizon to the East."[133]

Ironically, in view of the difficulty Bullitt was having in getting action or publicity for his mission, news was by this time beginning to leak out. Most of it rebounded against the effort to open up negotiations with the Bolsheviks. Although a sympathetic article in the *New Statesman* of March 22 urged negotiations with Lenin, "who has already let it be known that he is willing to make great concessions,"[134] most of the popular British press joined the *Daily Mirror* in screaming against the rumored negotiations.[135]

The American press was split. On one hand, Wilson's press secretary Joseph Tumulty wired Wilson on April 2, "The proposed recognition of Lenine [*sic*] is causing consternation here."[136] Tumulty was referring to a blizzard of misleading press stories, beginning with the *New York Tribune* of March 24, which reported on the Bullitt mission and predicted that Wilson and Lloyd George were about to adopt recommendations favoring recognition and negotiation with Lenin. The *New York Sun* of March 28 "reported that a Russian policy was being framed 'with the greatest secrecy" by the political leaders in Paris. Both the *New York Evening Post* of March 28 and the *New York Times* of March 29 reported a rumor in Paris that Wilson had before him for consideration a note from Lenin and Trotsky requesting recognition.[137]

But most concerning to Tumulty was an article by George R. Brown, "British Favor Lenine," in the *Washington Post* of April 1. Brown reported that "Lloyd George, while opposed to Bolshevism and Lenine's methods, had decided that *de facto* recognition of Lenine and his regime was the only practical solution to the complex Russian problem." Brown stated that Wilson was the swing vote between Clemenceau and Lloyd George, and warned of the consequences of recognition. The *Washington Post* editorialized strongly against any such recognition, warning that "twisted brains in American skulls are giving Lenine aid and comfort. . . . They advocate false doctrine with glib tongues and lying hearts. They gloss over the bestiality and fiendishness of the Lenine code of war on civilization. . . .[138]

On the other hand, the Current Intelligence Division of the Peace Conference staff pointed out near the same time that America

> does not want intervention . . . she is not interested in the project of a "cordon sanitaire"; she would not countenance conciliation with Lenine and Trotsky, she is not enthusiastic on the proposition of feeding Russia, and she would feel the greatest resentment if the Soviet were officially recognized. All criticism is expressed in terms of negation, nothing constructive is offered.[139]

An editorial in the *Springfield Republican* noted that "the Allies dare not commit themselves to an avowed war on the Soviets." But the newspaper also was not enthusiastic about negotiating.[140]

A week later the negative press in the United States had pretty much died down. By April 7, nearly every major daily and news association carried the basic story of the Bullitt mission, with the fact that Bullitt had recommended a positive Allied response to Lenin's initiative. But, surprisingly,

> there has been a singular paucity to date of the warnings that might have been expected against treating with Moscow. The *New York Herald* was horrified to learn that the President was giving heed to the advice of such socialists "who had been actively advocating intercourse and compromise with the most evil destructive force the world has ever known." But so far the *Herald* is pretty much alone.[141]

The situation had not changed a week later. The staff in Paris with the responsibility of reviewing the American press for the Peace Commissioners summarized their findings as follows:

> With the exception of the *Washington Post* and a few more papers, the American press appears to be willing to take with good grace any action of the Peace Conference that gives promise of restraining Bolshevism within the Russian frontiers. . . . less opposition has been aroused than by the Prinkipo conference. . . . [America] seems ready to give consent, if not approbation, to any expedient that will meet the Bolshevik menace and establish hope again in the ability of the Peace Conference to effect a real peace.[142]

The French press, as might have been expected, was vitriolic against the Bullitt mission. Articles in the *Populaire de Nantes, Echo de Paris, Journal du Peuple,* and other journals called strongly for a "vigorous policy," and generally rejected the *cordon sanitaire* in favor of all-out war. Most felt betrayed by their British and American allies, who would dare to treat with the Bolsheviks behind their back.[143] Only *L'Humanité,* edited by the moderate Socialist deputy Cachin, urged a conciliatory policy.[144]

The Bolsheviks were only committed to agreeing to the Bullitt-Lenin terms if they were extended by the Allies before April 10. As the deadline approached, Bullitt became increasingly concerned about the lack of appreciable movement by House and Wilson. On April 2, he wrote to Colonel House, reminding him of the deadline and asking what was happening with respect to Wilson's consideration of the terms.[145] House did not respond to Bullitt directly, but within a few days House asked Bullitt's advice on the draft plan for food relief as an alternative proposal. Bullitt became acutely aware that the Lenin proposals were not going to survive, at least in their original form.[146]

Even as the House plan was being formulated, House himself expressed considerable frustration at the slowness with which the Allies were coming up with any Russian policy. House remarked to his diary on April 5,

> Nothing is being done toward settling the Russia question, which is a burning issue. Without recognizing the Soviet Government or doing anything to which the conservatives could reasonably object, an arrangement might be made now by which fighting on the Russian fronts could be immediately stopped and the advance of Bolshevism westward checked. But no one has the courage to go forward in the matter.[147]

This unwillingness to move forward on the Lenin-Bullitt proposals was also noted the same day by State Department Counselor Frank Polk in a letter to House's aide, Gordon Auchincloss. Polk said that "something should be done, and done very quickly, in regard to Russia, but I do not think I would be prepared to act on any report framed by Bullitt and Steffens after a three day's stay in Russia. . . . I should judge from the delay in any action being taken that you people in Paris share this view."[148]

During this same week, developments in Britain virtually assured that Lloyd George would back away even farther from any willingness to embrace the Bullitt proposals. On March 31, just a few days after the *Daily Mirror* and other right-wing newspapers attacked even the possibility of negotiations, George Lansbury, socialist editor of the new labor daily, *The Herald,* published a long and accurate article about the Bullitt mission. In it Lansbury challenged the British government "to take the British people into their confidence and tell us all there is to tell."[149]

The War Cabinet, with Lloyd George not in attendance, held a serious discussion on the issue that very day, considering whether "[it] was . . . possible or desirable to make terms with the Bolshevik Government, which no doubt would be glad to come to some agreement with us and to see the last of our troops. Such action, however, would run counter to the whole of our policy hitherto. . . ."[150]

Bonar Law, Chancellor of the Exchequer, argued in favor of some accommodation because of the very serious position of the British troops, but Curzon, Churchill, and others were violently opposed. In the absence of Lloyd George, no action was taken.[151]

A few days later, under pressure from Churchill, the British War Cabinet authorized the publication "Bolshevism in Russia," or what became known as the "bluebook" of Bolshevik atrocities. This was a lengthy collection of rumors, facts, overstatements, and half truths about Bolshevism.[152]

Soon the entire British House of Commons was in an anti-Bolshevik uproar, demanding explanations from Lloyd George and egged on by a series of fiery speeches from Churchill.[153] On April 9, Member of Parliament Clement Edwards moved for adjournment of the House of Commons "to call attention to alleged overtures of the Lenin government to the Peace Conference." Edwards presented a petition to the government with 200 signatures of Members of Parliament demanding explanations and urging "British plenipotentiaries to decline to agree to any such recognition" or negotiation. Home Secretary Shortt replied on the floor of the House for the Government, stating that "no such proposals had been received by our delegates at the Peace Conference."[154]

Lloyd George was forced to return to London to answer to the Commons. On April 16, in a remarkable exchange before the Commons, he disclaimed any knowledge of the Bullitt mission, stating that "we have had nothing authentic. We have had no approaches of any sort or kind . . . it is not for me to judge the value of these communications [the reported Lenin-Bullitt proposals]. If the President of the United States had attached any value to them he would have brought them before the conference, and he certainly did not."[155]

Lloyd George also stated that he had no intention of either recognizing or negotiating with the Bolsheviks, using the specter of Bolshevism in Germany as a way of helping defend his more moderate German policy that he had enunciated in the Fontainebleau memorandum. This speech was the last public mention Lloyd George would make of Russian policy until November 1919. It effectively marked the death of British support for negotiation until the demise of Kolchak and Denikin.[156]

William C. Bullitt did not take this rejection, or the refusal of Woodrow Wilson to seriously consider the proposals he brought back from Lenin, as the final answer. He continued to struggle with alternative policy formulations within the United States delegation for several more weeks before he became convinced that insurmountable obstacles had been put in his way and there was no chance of Allied negotiations with the Bolsheviks in the forseeable future. Thus, although the Bullitt mission failed, its failure must be assessed in the context of the last effort of the politicians in Paris to come to terms with the Bolsheviks: the Hoover-Nansen food relief plan.

# 10

## Paris III:
## Hoover-Nansen—The Politics
## of Food Relief

The Hoover-Nansen proposal for food relief and a Bolshevik ceasefire is usually put in the context of the demise of the Bullitt mission.[1] In reality, Colonel House began "maturing" these plans almost from the moment of his first meeting with Bullitt on his return from Moscow.[2] The concept of food relief in exchange for an end to hostilities was first formulated by House and Gordon Auchincloss in the summer of 1918 as a possible way to avoid Allied intervention and stop a developing civil war.

At the time, Herbert Hoover was suggested as the head of a Russian Relief Commission and he agreed reluctantly to serve if asked by the President.[3] This Commission was originally envisioned to work in both Bolshevik and non-Bolshevik Russia, but broke down over serious differences between pro- and anti-recognition forces close to the United States government. Instead, a version of the Commission was grafted on to the Woodrow Wilson decision to intervene in Siberia, but its scope was restricted to eastern Siberia and did not apply to European Russia under control of the Bolsheviks.[4]

One version of the original idea for Bolshevik Russia expressed the concept rather grandly:

> Through cooperation with the Soviet government American business men of technical experience in economic, financial, commercial, industrial and transportation enterprises can be placed in positions of authority and influence under the Russian government and thus enabled to effectively control, in the interest of the Allies, the use and disposition of Russian resources which would otherwise be controlled and used by Germany.[5]

The decision to intervene ended serious American discussion of economic proposals for European Russia until after the armistice. Then such discussions were revived. Former U.S. commercial attaché in Petrograd William C. Huntington wrote a long memorandum on the need for an economic plan for European Russia, in late November. Secretary of Commerce William Redfield forwarded this memorandum to President Wilson on November 22 with a supportive note. Huntington's memorandum stressed the long-term potential of a relief and economic program for combatting Bolshevism. Huntington also reminded the Secretary that "Russia holds great economic and business possibilities for the future."[6]

Near the same time, Gordon Auchincloss and Vance McCormick, the head of the War Trade Board, revived their discussions on the same subject. In commenting favorably to McCormick regarding the organization of his trade corporation for Russia, Auchincloss complained, "no one seems to be paying much attention to what is happening in European Russia and some day we are going to wake up and find we have a horrible mess on our hands, which will take us years to clean up."[7] Auchincloss also discussed relief and economic measures for Russia with William C. Bullitt in mid-December and asked Bullitt's advice about a memo on the subject for House.[8] During the same period, Cyrus McCormick wrote a letter to Wilson strongly advocating joint Allied attention to European Russia, with trade and food advanced as the answer to Bolshevism.[9]

The most fully developed preliminary plan for a ceasefire and food relief was proposed by British foreign minister Balfour after a conversation with Clemenceau in Paris early in 1919. Clemenceau refused to go along with any British plan that contemplated talking with the Bolsheviks. But Balfour found that Clemenceau was not averse to "doing something for the regions now under the Soviet government." This plan, drawn partly from conversations between Clemenceau and Wilson and amplified by Balfour, consisted of an international commission, a major program of food relief under Allied control, and an enforced ceasefire. As Balfour described it, "This scheme would seem to have the triple advantage of carrying out a humanitarian policy; of bringing us authentic information as to the internal political and economic condition of European Russia and its methods of government; and of applying a very strong inducement to the Bolshevists to modify their action in the direction of decency."[10]

Both Vance McCormick and Gordon Auchincloss continued to think through their ideas on food relief as a major component of any Allied plan for European Russia during the time the Big Four struggled with the Prinkipo proposal. McCormick dined with Lloyd George on January 30 and tried out his ideas on the Prime Minister. McCormick suggested a plan "of sending food to Petrograd with sufficient troops to protect distribution," but Lloyd George convinced him that the linking of relief with military support was impractical, and besides, it was not possible to "get Allied nations to send an army to Russia."[11]

Auchincloss' primary confidant was Sir William Wiseman. They worked together to develop the joint Allied memorandum explaining the failure of Prinkipo in mid-February and then compared ideas for follow-up in early March. Wiseman at first suggested a simple statement to the Bolsheviks that "we plan to go the limit to do everything we possibly could to feed and protect with necessary armed forces the friendly governments set up on the border of

Russia." Auchincloss suggested a more considered plan. He urged that "the Conference in Plenary Session . . . issue a statement to the peoples of the world," stressing the Allied record in relief and making a commitment to relief aid for Russia, provided the fighting stopped.[12]

The United States Peace Commissioners were also busy considering a relief proposal during the first weeks of March. On March 5, the American consul at Vyborg, Imbrie, telegraphed that deaths from starvation in Petrograd numbered 113,000 in February. Acting Secretary of State Frank Polk recommended serious consideration of a relief program, but warned that the Red Cross was inadequate for the job. Besides, it was inadvisable for the Red Cross or for any one country to have any close relationship to the Bolsheviks such a relief effort would entail.[13]

On March 20, the issue was discussed fully in a meeting of the Commissioners, who recommended that any program be a part of a full-scale Allied program for Russia. The Commissioners also were of the opinion that nothing at all could be done until the Allies agreed on an approach to the Russian problem. They advised that "the means to further the ends constituted the gravest difficulties. For instance, they would be very glad to learn how an effective armistice could be insured on all fronts, or how food and medical supplies, etc. could be distributed on a democratic basis."[14] The Commission also asked that Herbert Hoover's advice be sought. They asked whether he had come up with "any method of carrying out relief measures for Petrograd."[15]

In the meantime, Vance McCormick had intensified his consultations on this issue. Fridtjof Nansen, the well-known Norwegian polar explorer and humanitarian, had several meetings with McCormick to discuss the concept of an international relief mission for Russia. Nansen and McCormick discussed the issue on March 18 and March 21. Nansen had met both Herbert Hoover and McCormick in 1917 when he paid a visit to Washington to seek American relief for Norway.[16]

House now became centrally involved in the discussions. House was struck by William C. Bullitt's emphasis on starvation and economic chaos in the picture he painted of Bolshevik Russia. On March 27, House met with Wilson to discuss Russia. In that meeting, "the President suggested" that House talk to Hoover and Robinson of the Shipping Board "and see whether we could get ships and food to Russia in the event we wished to do so." House did contact Hoover, who indicated that the ships could be sent. House decided to involve Hoover actively in the preparation of an alternative plan, and he set Gordon Auchincloss working on such a plan immediately.[17]

Auchincloss met with Hoover and found him "strongly in favor of sending food into Russia provided the Russians keep their military forces from interfering in the states which we have set up." Hoover believed that "the distribution of food to the people of Russia will make them less eager to continue their policy of agitation." The two men struggled to reach a solution, and Hoover suggested that "we get Nansen or some neutral to start an organization for the relief of Russia."[18]

In his important position as head of all Allied relief efforts in Europe,

Hoover had met repeatedly with Clemenceau, Lloyd George, and Wilson, and had a continuing keen interest in the Russian situation. He also had stayed in touch with Russian economic relief schemes through Vance McCormick, whom he saw on a weekly basis from November 1918 through the end of the Paris Peace Conference. The frequency of his meetings with McCormick increased even more in February and March 1919.[19]

According to Hoover, President Wilson called him on March 26 and asked him to prepare a memorandum on Bolshevism and the Soviet problem.[20] In this memorandum, which Hoover sent to Wilson on March 28, the food administrator detailed his analysis of the problem and put forth his ideas for a relief effort to be headed by someone like Nansen. Hoover emphasized his strong feeling that "we cannot even remotely recognize this murderous tyranny without . . . transgressing on every National ideal of our own," but he also detailed the tremendous suffering from hunger and disease then being experienced by the people of Russia.[21]

He then called on Wilson to issue a public statement on Bolshevism, analyzing it "from its political, economic, humane, and its criminal point of view" and "showing its foolishness as a basis of economic development." Hoover asked Wilson to join with the other Allies in encouraging "some neutral of international reputation for probity and ability" to create "a second Belgian Relief commission for Russia," raising funds and food from "the northern neutrals." The Allies might even actively assist, "if [they] get assurances that the Bolsheviki will cease all militant action across certain defined boundaries and cease their subsidizing of disturbances abroad. . . ."[22]

There is no doubt that Wilson and Hoover saw eye-to-eye on the causes of Bolshevism and the best strategy for its eradication. Wilson expanded on this theme the very day of Hoover's letter, in a speech at the meeting of the Council of Four. In making clear his opposition to the use of military force against the Bolsheviks, Wilson used ideas explicated by both Hoover and Bliss on other occasions:

> To try to stop a revolutionary movement with ordinary armies is like using a broom to sweep back a great sea. . . . The sole means of acting against Bolshevism is to make its causes disappear. . . . one of the causes is uncertainty of populations about their future frontiers . . . and at the same time their distress about lack of food, transportation, and the means of work. The only way to kill Bolshevism is to establish the frontiers and to open all the doors to commerce.[23]

Meanwhile, Gordon Auchincloss was putting together a memorandum incorporating his, McCormick's, House's, and Hoover's ideas for a ceasefire and an international relief commission as an alternative to the Bullitt-Lenin negotiations. Auchincloss struggled with the practical problems of dealing with the Bolsheviks and the antipathy that the Allied leaders had to any contact whatsoever. Auchincloss met again with Hoover and House on March 29, by which time Hoover and McCormick had both met with Nansen, and persuaded the reluctant Norwegian to become involved. Overtures were also made to the Dutch and British governments. The essential elements of the plan at this point was "getting the neutrals to take the lead in feeding Russia, conditioned upon the promise that the Bolsheviki cease war on all fronts against our allies."[24]

By March 31, House, Hoover, and Auchincloss had decided that Hoover should draft a letter for Nansen to sign. Such a draft was revised by Auchincloss and House and prepared for Nansen's signature. At one point, Helmut Branting, the Swedish socialist, was also to be a part of the scheme, but House apparently decided at the last minute to stay with Nansen alone.[25]

Just before this letter was finalized and sent, William Allen White, the Kansas journalist appointed as a Prinkipo delegate by Wilson, wrote the President. White complained about the process by which he was never told about the abandonment of Prinkipo, and suggested the appointment of a new commission of inquiry for Bolshevik Russia, "a long, serious unbiased investigation by men of academic and political and military training." Wilson responded immediately to White, apologizing for his treatment and expressing interest in his suggestion, but noting that there was not time before the Peace Conference was wrapped up.[26]

Nansen's letter, sent personally to Wilson, Orlando, Clemenceau, and Lloyd George, stressed how critical famine and disease was in European Russia. Nansen then proposed "a purely humanitarian commission for the provisioning of Russia." Distribution would "be guaranteed by a commission of Norwegian, Swedish and possibly Dutch, Danish and Swiss nationalities." Such a commission, "organized upon the lines of the Belgian Relief Commission . . . would raise no question of political recognition or negotiations." Nansen closed his proposal by asking under what conditions the Allies would approve of such a commission, and whether any finances, shipping, or food and medical supplies could be provided by the United States government.[27]

The same day Nansen's letter was dispatched, Gordon Auchincloss met with David Hunter Miller for the purpose of drafting a reply on behalf of the Big Four. Before doing so, Auchincloss had lunch with Maurice Hankey of the British delegation and outlined the situation to him. Auchincloss also had meetings with Sir William Wiseman, Norman Davis, and Charles R. Crane. Meanwhile, Herbert Hoover was meeting with Henry White and the other commissioners. William H. Buckler, on overhearing Hoover, remarked to his wife, "I think this plan may go through instead of Bullitt's."[28]

The Miller-Auchincloss initial draft of a reply to Nansen welcomed the Norwegian humanitarian's proposal, but raised a series of "practical" considerations: supply, transport, and distribution. They argued that "control of transportation, so far as was necessary in the distribution of relief supplies, should be placed wholly under such a Commission" and be free entirely from Soviet government interference. Miller and Auchincloss also stressed, in the most convoluted paragraph of the letter, that no true humanitarian assistance could be granted unless "the human beings in need should themselves decide in each locality upon the method and the personnel by means of which their community is to be relieved." Of course a "cessation of hostilities" would be a precondition for any relief effort, as well as "a cessation of all troops on the Russian front." In short, the Auchincloss-Miller draft essentially demanded that the Bolsheviks unilaterally stop the civil war and withdraw their troops from the front. In return, the Allies would provide food and medicine, under control of a neutral commission. All transportation and distribution would also be under the commission's control.[29]

Miller and Auchincloss took this draft, shortened and polished it a bit for clarity, and took it immediately to Colonel House.[30] House told Auchincloss that the draft was "splendid" and that he should take it for approval to Hoover, Bullitt, and the British. Hoover also felt the letter was "splendid," and Hankey and Kerr gave their approval. Bullitt was "not at all pleased" with the draft, but, as Auchincloss noted, "I did not expect him to be."[31]

Bullitt was so upset with the draft that he took two immediate actions. He wrote a concise memorandum to Auchincloss pointing out in no uncertain terms the parts of the draft reply that were manifestly unfair to the Bolshevik government. He also composed his own draft reply in order to more fully explicate his position and argue his case with House. In his memorandum to Auchincloss, Bullitt pointed out that "the life of Russia depends upon its railroads; and your demand for control of transportation by the Commission can hardly be accepted by the Soviet Government." He also noted that Auchincloss and Miller, in their discussion of the "cessation of hostilities by Russian troops" failed "to speak of hostilities by troops of the Allied and Associated Governments," nor did it cover other nationalities fighting the Bolsheviks. The Miller-Auchincloss draft reply, according to Bullitt, said nothing about ceasing to send troops and military supplies onto Russian territory. Finally, Bullitt said, Auchincloss went "a long way towards proving Trotsky's thesis: that any armistice will simply be used by the Allies as a period in which to supply tanks, aeroplanes, gas shells, liquid fire, etc. to the various anti-Soviet governments." In short, Bullitt argued, "your armistice proposal is absolutely unfair" and would never be accepted by the Soviet government.[32]

Bullitt's alternative draft attempted to combine elements of the Lenin-Bullitt armistice negotiation proposal with the Hoover-Auchincloss relief effort, while eliminating elements unfair to the Bolsheviks. This produced a somewhat unwieldly reply calling for a complete ceasefire by all governments and all belligerents anywhere on the territory of the former Russian empire, to take effect on April 20 and extend for two weeks. Each government would then send three representatives to Christiana, Norway, for a conference, based on the eight principles Bullitt brought back from Lenin. Governments attending such a conference would assume responsibility for financial obligations of the former Russian empire. The conference would also "discuss and determine any other matter which bears upon the provisioning of Russia, the problem of establishing peace within the territory of the former Russian Empire."[33]

Bullitt integrated the provisions for food relief into the portion of the draft on the lifting of the economic blockade. In this redraft, he called for "a program of equitable distribution of supplies and utilization of transport facilities to be agreed upon by the Conference in consultation with representatives of those neutral States which are prepared to assume the responsibility for the provisioning of Russia."[34]

Bullitt was well aware of the fight he was in. He was attempting to use the vehicle of the Hoover-Nansen proposal to revive the now-desperate fortunes of the proposals he had brought back from Lenin. President Wilson was ill with a fever and flu from April 3 until April 6 and unavailable for consultation. Bullitt sought to build support for his position and to convince House of the validity of his criticisms of the Auchincloss draft. The American Commissioners had lunch with Hoover and Bullitt on April 4 to compare the two men's positions. William H. Buckler noted that Hoover argued "that food relief will quickly produce peace and it is a far easier proposal to induce the Powers to accept it."[35] Vance McCormick noted Bullitt's intense commitment to recognition and the end of the blockade. "The general impression obtained," he noted in his diary, "is that the Bolshevists are on their last legs and are ready to trade."[36]

Bullitt persuaded House not to send the Miller-Auchincloss draft to Wilson to serve as the basis of a Big Four response to Nansen, but to let him (Bullitt) take another crack at it. House agreed, but only if Bullitt stuck closely to the Miller-Auchincloss text. So Bullitt, with obvious reluctance, made what he felt were the most important changes for Soviet acceptance of the proposal. House told him that he could not mention the Bolshevik government by name. So he was forced to make reference only to the "existing *de facto* governments of Russia" in the call for adherence to the ceasefire by all parties. On the critical question of control of the railroads, Bullitt changed the Auchincloss-Miller draft by stating that "subject to the advice and supervision of the Commission, the problem of distribution should be solely under the control of the people of Russia themselves." He also changed the ceasefire provision in a fundamental way, calling for the "cessation of all hostilities" and a "complete suspension of the transfer of troops and military material of all sorts to and within these territories." On these most important questions, Bullitt was able to make only partial changes, which made it less politically unacceptable to the Bolsheviks, but by no means removed all of their concerns.[37]

On April 6, Wilson had recovered enough from his flu to meet with the Peace Commissioners and the Big Four, although he remained in bed. He also called for House to come and bring the Russia proposal. Auchincloss complained to House about the changes Bullitt had made in the proposal, claiming they "would make it impossible to send the Polish Divisions to Poland . . . and would also not require adequate control over the Russian railways for the movement of food." With a few small but significant changes however, (such as replacing "*de facto*" with "local" governments and changing "territory of the former Russian empire" to "Russia") Wilson approved and signed the letter and promised to submit it to the Council of Four for their concurrence.[38]

Auchincloss was astounded at "the casual way in which they decide these things" and did not think the British and French would agree to the proposal. Orlando and Lloyd George had no problem, however. Clemenceau delayed for more than a week after promising House and Wilson he would sign; perhaps dragging his feet until he got the French concessions on the Rhineland.[39]

Bullitt also tried once again to get action from Wilson on his original proposal from Lenin, appealing to the President to give him "fifteen minutes" to make his case in person. He received no reply.[40]

On April 9, Wilson officially brought the proposed reply to Nansen to the Council of Four. Concern was expressed in the meeting about acquiring the necessary tonnage for such a massive shipment. Hoover had asked the President to get commitments from the Allies on this, since neutral ships were insufficient. But Lloyd George questioned whether an organization could be put together to really take charge of transportation and distribution in so vast a land, or whether they were really ready to give control of that to Lenin. Wilson, however, felt that "Lenin will be only too happy to find someone to take this on." Finally, all but Clemenceau were willing to agree. He demanded more time to consider it.[41]

Since Lenin's April 10 deadline for action on his proposals was just about to expire, Bullitt demanded that the American commissioners send a telegram to Chicherin. Bullitt argued that "silence and the passing of April 10 will be interpreted as a definite rejection of the peace effort of the Soviet Government and that the Soviet Government will at once issue belligerent political statements and orders for attacks on all fronts." He urged that a message— "Action leading to food relief via neutrals likely within week"—be sent to Chicherin. The Commissioners discussed the matter and approved a revised telegram of a much more tentative nature: "individuals of neutral states are considering organization for feeding Russia. Will perhaps decide something definite within a week."[42]

American public response to the contradictory dispatches from Paris was remarkably restrained. According to the weekly review of the Current Intelligence Division of the Peace Commissioners of April 13, "America is apprehensive . . . but she seems ready to give consent, if not approbation to any expedient that will meet the Bolshevik menace and establish hope again in the ability of the Peace Conference to effect a real peace."[43]

The Big Four's reply to Nansen still had not been dispatched, because of the reluctance of Clemenceau and the French to sign the final version. Hoover, Auchincloss, and House worked to assuage French fears. House put the case to Clemenceau in a practical way, arguing that "if Russia could be opened up in some way to give the people a chance to look at conditions there, no one would desire to bring about similar conditions in their own countries."[44] In other words, House urged Clemenceau, feed Russia to prevent Bolshevism from infecting France. Hoover talked to Pichon, meanwhile, and told him categorically that he need not fear. Hoover would have no direct dealings with the Bolsheviks under this proposal. Finally the French were satisfied; Clemenceau signed the letter, and it was given to Nansen on April 17.[45]

Nansen immediately sought to dispatch the answer to the Soviets. He included with it a note to Chicherin asking to hear from him as soon as possible and reminding him that the neutral organization proposed would give its services free, but the Soviet Government would have to meet the costs of supplies and transportation not otherwise contributed. Nansen ran into all kinds of difficulties in communicating the message to Chicherin, however. Although the Big Four had signed the messge, none of their governments would allow their wireless stations to send it, because doing so would "facilitate communication with a government which was not recognized."[46] They were supported in this by the Russian political organizations in Paris, who opposed the initiative, and by conditions on the ground in Russia, where Kolchak was enjoying significant success. Nansen finally persuaded the Norwegian government to send a courier, but he was turned back by the Finns at the frontier. At last the message was wired from Berlin.[47]

President Wilson seemed quite happy with the final resolution of the vexatious Russia problem. He answered a letter from William G. Sharp, which urged some form of recognition for the Soviet regime, with the following: "I find my mind going along with yours in your comments upon the Russian situation."[48] But Herbert Hoover was disturbed that the world might get the wrong impression about the President's intentions. He drafted a statement excoriating Bolshevism in the strongest terms, which he implored House and the President to approve and make public. This memo made it clear to the world that "under the plan of a Neutral Commission for feeding Russia" there was "no intention of recognizing the men whose fingers are even today dripping with the blood of hundreds of innocent people of Odessa."[49]

House read the proposed Hoover statement the evening of April 18, was appalled, and immediately sought out Hoover the next morning, persuading him to withdraw it. Hoover, however, merely revised it to make it clearer that it was his own personal statement, and again asked House to take it to Wilson. This time Wilson, Baker, and House all tried to explain to Hoover the negative impact such a statement would have. As Baker put it, "why abuse people with whom you are about to negotiate—whom you are about to feed?"[50] House commented to his diary, "We have been trying to get this Russian matter in the shape that it now is and he has helped as much as anyone. Just as soon, however, as we have it signed by the President and three Prime Ministers, Hoover gives out a statement which would absolutely destroy any chance of its success."[51]

House told Hoover clearly that the President thought "it would be unwise to give such a statment to the press at this time . . . [even] as the expression of your own personal views." But Hoover persisted in his intent to issue a statement. He finally did make a more temperate one on April 21, to which Wilson gave his reluctant assent. This statement made it clear that the Allied proposal implied no recognition of the Bolsheviks, nor did it even mean negotiations were contemplated. It also tried to undo the Bullitt-revised Nansen statement concerning "local Russian distribution" by promising that "there shall be complete justice in distribution to all classes . . . and the guarantees of a strong neutral commission that this will be the case." Finally, quite beyond the reply to Nansen, it promised that "the Bolsheviki are to keep themselves with a certain circumscribed area, ceasing all military action and attempts at invasion." The statement kept silent about Allied or other Russian forces' willingness to abide by a ceasefire.[52]

Hoover was not the only one having second thoughts about the reply to Nansen and its troublesome implications. Winston Churchill wrote a long letter to Lloyd George on April 20, in which he noted "the armies of Koltchak [*sic*] and Denikin are not short of food . . . therefore to give food to the rest of Russia is to put the Bolsheviks on an equality with those loyal armies." Churchill also argued that it was important to maintain economic pressure on the Bolsheviks as a means to effect their overthrow. Furthermore, any such program would undoubtedly lead to "close and complicated relations with the government of Lenin and Trotsky." Any such scheme of "impartial" feeding of Russia, he concluded, "means in practice feeding Bolshevik Russia."[53]

There was also dissension in the American Commission. Bullitt continued to press for negotiation and a ceasefire, and Hoover became increasingly virulent about refusing to deal directly with the Bolsheviks. Ray Stannard Baker spoke about being "torn" on the Russian question, while Vance McCormick raised the question of whether it had been wise "to relieve Bolshevik Russia" when the State Department was proposing to recognize the Omsk government and Kolchak was winning. Gordon Auchincloss, after a discussion with Cyrus McCormick about Russia, was furious at Bullitt for his continued insistence on dealing with the Bolsheviks even in the face of Kolchak's success. Auchincloss noted to his diary, "I think we ought to get rid of Bullitt. His loose talk is doing us more harm than good."[54]

An ominous note with regard to the future of the Nansen proposal, with or without Bolshevik acceptance, was struck by Vance McCormick. After an April 24 discussion with Nansen about the difficulties he was having in conveying the Big Four terms to the Bolsheviks, McCormick remarked to his diary, "I rather hope it will be delayed as things are moving pretty fast with Kolchak government and I think some further thought should be given to recognizing Omsk government."[55]

The Paris press intensified this developing feeling. Not only did *Le Temps,* the *Echo de Paris, Opinion,* and *Débats* condemn the scheme and call for support of Kolchak, they enflamed public opinion by attacking the plan as not being Nansen's but rather a nefarious plot by American bankers to penetrate the Russian market. In a slashing editorial, *Débats* claimed that "the supplying of Russia with food is not a humanitarian work. It is exploiting humanitarian sentiments for political ends."[56]

Nansen's message to Chicherin enclosing the Big Four conditions was finally relayed to the Bolsheviks through the Norwegian legation in Berlin and the American representative in the Netherlands on May 3 and acknowledged by the Narkomindel on May 4.[57] Chicherin immediately consulted with Lenin and a reply was dispatched May 10. It was not received in Paris until May 13. In the meantime, the pressure built to drop the proposal and embrace Kolchak. McCormick tried to persuade Nansen on May 7 to withdraw the proposal in favor of one keeping silent about a ceasefire. Any mention of a ceasefire might be embarrassing to Kolchak.[58]

A proposal to strengthen the Allies' commitment to Kolchak and recognize the Omsk government came to the Council of Four on May 9, even before Chicherin's response to the Hoover-Nansen proposal was received. Although Wilson and Lloyd George were still skeptical of large-scale Allied military intervention, they were willing to entertain proposals for more direct support for Admiral Kolchak, especially in light of his military victories. Wilson relayed to the Council information from American forces in Siberia that they were increasingly forced to choose between direct support of Kolchak and abstaining completely from hostilities. Wilson tried to reiterate his conviction that the best policy was "to clear out of Russia and leave it to the Russians to fight it out among themselves." He was willing, however, to consider a stronger support for Kolchak, but only after the Allies had inquired more carefully into the nature of Kolchak's program and his commitment to elections, land reform, and democracy.[59]

Over a period of several weeks, Wilson sought to reassure himself about Kolchak and made his support conditional on a pledge from the Admiral. This pledge was made by Kolchak and received by the Council on June 5. The Council pledged its support, but stopped short of formal diplomatic recognition, on June 12. Soon thereafter, however, the importance of this action was rendered irrelevant by a reversal of Kolchak's fortunes in the civil war. By the end of June, Kolchak's march toward Moscow had been totally reversed and he was near collapse. This marked the final failure of the Russian polcy of the Paris Peace Conference.[60]

In the meantime, the Bolsheviks were seriously considering their reply to Nansen's proposal. Lenin took a personal interest in it, and addressed a long letter to Chicherin and Litvinov on May 6 giving his specific instructions for drafting a reply. In this letter he urged the two commissars to make a sharp distinction in their remarks between Nansen and the Big Three (Wilson, Lloyd George, and Clemenceau). Lenin advocated being "extremely polite to Nansen, extremely insolent to Wilson, Lloyd George and Clemenceau." He also instructed Chicherin and Litvinov to use the reply "for propaganda," since that was one of the main purposes of the Big Four's proposal. Lenin stressed the importance of fully developing the Bolshevik position because, as he said, "the Entente, while easily concealing from everyone all other documents of ours [other peace proposals] will be unable, by way of exception, to conceal precisely this reply."[61]

Lenin then developed the importance of drawing a distinction between the humanitarian nature of Nansen's original proposal, which he believed should be accepted, and the political conditions that had been added by the Allies, which should be completely rejected. "All thanks and complements to Nansen personally," he said. "Appoint a time and a place for the talks" to work out the details. "But if a truce, then this is politics." Lenin believed that any truce must be separated. The Bolsheviks were in favor of *negotiations* for a truce, as they had stated repeatedly, but they would not unilaterally accept a truce under the guise of a humanitarian proposal. Further, Lenin said, the negotiations must be with the Allies themselves, those who continued the war in their support for Kolchak and Denikin.[62]

Chicherin's answer to Nansen, dated May 10, took Lenin's advice seriously. Chicherin sharply distinguished between Nansen's original humanitarian proposal and the revised political approach of the Big Four, welcoming the first and rejecting the second. Chicherin still kept open the willingness of the Bolshevik government to negotiate an end to hostilities at a peace conference, but not as a condition to moving forward with the food relief effort. Chicherin also took pains to point out, from the Bolshevik standpoint, the cause of the misery of the Russian people and the continuation of the war, which he laid clearly at the feet of the Allies and their Russian protégés. "We are in position to discuss cessation of hostilities only if we discuss the whole problem of our relations to our adversaries, that is in the first place to the Associated Governments," he wrote. He also promised Nansen that the Bolsheviks were perfectly prepared to pay for food and medical supplies, and asked Nansen to set a time and a place to discuss the details of such a relief effort. Chicherin insisted, however, that any discussions concerning truce, ceasefire, or other political issues must be left to a peace conference.[63]

Nansen's immediate inclination was to proceed with a meeting to discuss the relief plan with the Bolsheviks, probably in Stockholm. He noted this on a copy of the Bolshevik reply, which he sent via the Danish chargé to the State Department on May 14.[64] Herbert Hoover, however, consulted with Robert Cecil, French representative Clementel, and Italian professor Attolico, who were appointed as a committee to advise the Supreme Council concerning follow-up to the Nansen proposal. They agreed that Hoover should immediately tell Nansen not to arrange any meeting with the Bolsheviks "until the whole matter has been given further consideration by the governments here."[65]

Cecil then drafted a memorandum for the Council of Four on the larger issues. He claimed that Lenin's reply amounted to nothing more than the following: "I shall be very glad to accept supplies but not to cease from fighting, though I would be prepared to enter into negotiations for a general Russian peace." Cecil also said that it was now time for the associated governments "to make up their minds what is to be their policy in Russia." He argued that there were only two courses of action: (1) "smash the Bolsheviks" or (2) define fighting lines and then ask each side to retire ten kilometers and refrain from hostilities. All those who refused would be denied any kind of aid or assistance. As Cecil rightly pointed out, "what is not defensible is a combination of the two: suggestion that Lenin must cease fighting while we are supplying arms and equipment to Denikin and Kolchak." This, he believed, was a bankrupt policy that simply spread "the belief that the Associated Powers cannot be trusted."[66]

Between the time of the report of the Hoover-Cecil committee and consideration of the Soviet response in the Council of Ten on May 20, reactions and rumors abounded in the American community in Paris. Vance McCormick reported a "hot discussion" on Russia with Thomas Lamont, Gordon Auchincloss, Jack Carter, and a Mrs. Corbin. Despite Gordon Auchincloss' dislike of Bullitt, McCormick reported, "he has been somewhat influenced. . . . Says he is down on Bolshevism, but doesn't want to have anything to do with Kolchak."[67] Auchincloss met with Hoover about the Bolsheviks' reply the next day and wrongly considered it "a rejection of the proposition."[68]

When the Council of Four met about the proposal on May 20, the same disagreements and inability to come to a decision on policy plagued them. Clemenceau insisted that no food relief could be supported unless the Bolsheviks agreed to a ceasefire. President Wilson pointed out that Lenin's argument "was that the price the Allied and Associate Powers were trying to exact for food was that their enemies should beat the Bolsheviks by compelling the latter to stop fighting." Clemenceau insisted that Lenin's word could not be trusted even if he agreed to stop fighting. Finally, the Big Four washed their hands of the proposal and let it lapse. Wilson concluded that "he did not feel the same chagrin that he had formerly felt at having no policy in regard to Russia. It had been impossible to have a policy."[69]

Even before the final action of the Council of Four concerning the Hoover-Nansen proposals, William C. Bullitt decided he had had enough. His extreme disappointment over Wilson's Russian policy was not actually what caused his public resignation from the American Commission, but rather the terms of the treaty of peace itself. After reading it through in one sitting, he decided that the number of instances where reality did not meet ideals were too many, and he could no longer continue to work for something that fell so far short of what he thought Wilson and House stood for.[70]

Wilson's failure in the "acid test" of Russian policy also was a factor. Bullitt mentioned it in his personal letter to Wilson that accompanied his more formal letter of resignation on May 17. "Russia, 'the acid test of good will,' for me as for you, has not even been understood," Bullitt said. He expressed more sorrow than anger at Wilson, criticizing him mostly for not taking his fight more to the public, sorry that he "had so little faith in the millions of men, like myself, in every nation, who had faith in you."[71]

Bullitt also wrote an accompanying note to House, urging him to bring his letter to the attention of the President and hoping that "you will agree that I am right in acting on my conviction." He hoped that their warm personal relationship might continue.[72]

Bullitt's resignation had an immediate impact in the American Commission. Bullitt called a protest meeting of the Commission staff, where he demanded mass resignations. Nine other young staff members of the Commission offered their resignations, but most were persuaded to stay on after they voiced their objections to the treaty.[73] Of those involved in Russian policy, both Samuel Eliot Morison and Adolph A. Berle sympathized with Bullitt and offered their resignations, but they were persuaded by R. H. Lord to stay. Berle later recollected a dinner at the Crillon Hotel following the protest: "Some of us had resigned, or decided to; others had not . . . the table decorations . . . were yellow jonquils and red roses. Bullitt, over coffee, tossed the yellow jonquils to the people who had not resigned and the red roses to the people who had."[74] William H. Buckler, while not resigning immediately, was thoroughly disillusioned by his experience on the Russia issue. He refused to take the Polish post offered him by the State Department, and soon left it to return, for the balance of his life, to archaeology.[75]

Others close to Bullitt and the Commission were not so charitable. Frank Polk, on hearing of Bullitt's decision, sent the following cable to Gordon Auchincloss: "How about Bullitt? A spanking seems desirable."[76] Both Henry White and Tasker Bliss, miffed at their lack of knowledge of Bullitt's mission both before and after, later denied that they had any advance knowledge whatsoever or that Bullitt was privy to important information within the Commission.[77]

Only Bullitt's testimony before the Senate Foreign Relations Committee in September 1919 and the resultant outcry it engendered marked the end of the Bullitt story. The testimony itself is well known, and continues to provide, in many cases, the detailed record of the Bullitt mission, and of the Russia question in Paris as well.[78] Although it reflects Bullitt's personal point of view and is limited by his understanding of various parts of the story, its solid reliance on documents in Bullitt's own possession kept it remarkably accurate on the points where Bullitt had a personal involvement. Without it, it is doubtful that the course of discussions with Lenin could be followed, or the struggle in Paris over the terms of the Hoover-Nansen proposal.

Bullitt's testimony created an uproar in the United States both for his revelations of Lansing's opposition to the treaty and the details of the mission to Russia. It received headline coverage in all the newspapers. Some, such as the New York *Daily News* of September 19, even took the time to cover the details of the Russian mission fully, and on successive days. It also provided fresh evidence for the liberal journals to raise questions about America's Russian policy, although they made scant headway in a climate dominated by an increasing Red Scare. The *New Republic,* after detailing Bullitt's evidence, concluded that "on the basis of this offer there could have been peace in Russia—and a peace which protected all of the various governmental groups now supported by the Allies. But at the moment of Mr. Bullitt's return from Moscow Kolchak began to show signs of success—and the offer that could have brought peace was tucked away in the files of the Hotel Crillon."[79]

Assistant Secretary of State William Phillips was so worried about the impact of Bullitt's testimony that he summarized and paraphrased it in some detail in a series of cables to Counselor Polk, then in Paris, and asked him to attempt to verify its accuracy.[80] Gordon Auchincloss cabled Colonel House, imploring him "to counteract Bullitt's misstatements," while Phillips urged Secretary of State Lansing, then on vacation in New England, to do likewise. House and Lansing were crucial to Bullitt's believability . As Phillips said in his cable to Lansing, "Everyone here that I have seen, including pretty nearly all the representatives of the press feel that Bullitt's act is wholly contemptible yet there is no one who can come out and brand his conduct as it should be branded except you who were his chief."[81]

But neither House nor Lansing was willing to be drawn into the controversy. House's first response, based "exclusively on accounts published here and State Department communiqué," was that he could not dispute Bullitt's testimony. He asked Auchincloss to send him anything that he thought was inaccurate. After receiving a longer Auchincloss letter, in which Auchincloss had to admit that "the only reflection on you was the fact that you had trusted him," House responded that "I do not want to get into the controversy unnecessarily. . . . He is practically right in his statements except that he does not give the whole story." After listening to Lloyd George privately excoriate Bullitt and authorize the British to issue an absolute denial, House recorded in his diary, "Candor compels me to record that in my opinion Bullitt told the truth."[82]

Lansing, while ranting privately at Bullitt's "despicable conduct" and accusing him of gathering information "in order to be revenged for our failure to accept his report on Russia," refused to issue a public statement. He admitted that there was "just enough truth in his statement to make it difficult. . . . Rather than make such an explanation I determined the best course was to make no comment."[83]

The accuracy of Bullitt's testimony became widely accepted since it was never disputed by anyone in a position to know. As Henry Cabot Lodge warned his old friend Henry White, who had written to the Senator from Paris trying to downplay or deny Bullitt's statements, "I am sending you by this mail a copy of Bullitt's testimony. You had better read it before you say that it amounts to nothing. He was fortified by papers at every stage."[84]

William H. Buckler, observing the controversy from Paris, most acutely summed up the impact of the entire affair, especially as it would have a lasting negative effect on William C. Bullitt. "Bullitt's statements are practically irrefutable," he wrote to his wife, Georgina, "but when a man violates confidences to that extent he must expect to be called 'liar.' It is a way of making a sensation which one can employ only ONCE [emphasis Buckler's] in one's career."[85]

Bullitt himself was well aware of the effect that such exposure of confidences, even if true, would have on his own life and career. He gave the fullest explanation of his reasons to his friend and distant relative, Nancy Astor, early in 1920. Bullitt stressed in this letter the importance, for his own integrity, of telling the full story of his Moscow mission:

> Dear Nancy:
>      . . . I am not at all surprised that you were horrified at my testimony. Yet I am certain that if you had been in my place you would have done just what I did—only more. . . . I had a definite choice: Either I could take refuge behind "I have forgotten" and "I have not the documents" or I could speak the truth, and the whole truth. I knew well that if I did give a full account of the Russian business I should be hated bitterly by three fourths of the persons who had called themselves my friends. I knew that I should throw away any chance for a normal, advancing, political career—such as most of your friends will have. . . .[86]

Bullitt also believed that full and complete testimony about his negotiations with Lenin might help end the civil war and the economic blockade, therefore saving many lives and much misery in Soviet Russia. He closed his letter to Nancy Astor by stressing this point:

> I knew also that, if I skimmed, my testimony would have no effect whatsoever in helping to end the murder by starvation and disease of the millions of Russians, who were being killed by the blockade—conducted by your government and assented to by mine. I thought that if I told the full truth, sparing no one—least of all, my own self—I might hasten the lifting of the blockade. . . . I believe the blockade will be lifted and that peace will be made with Russia a little sooner because I let go the whole truth to the Senate. Therefore the dowagers and diplomats who are mewing for my blood do not disturb me.[87]

The Bolsheviks also took the opportunity of Bullitt's resignation and the publicity it engendered to make public their own assessments of the Bullitt mission and the Russian policy of the Paris Peace Conference. In an article on May 22, 1919, in *Ekonomicheskaia Zhizn,* Chicherin gave an account of the Bullitt mission. In this article, Chicherin outlined briefly and accurately the circumstances of Bullitt's mission to Moscow, claiming that Bullitt brought an offer "from President Wilson . . . with the knowledge of Lloyd George." After agreeing to changes from Lenin, Bullitt took the proposal back to Paris, where it was "frustrated by the stubbornness of the bloodthirsty Clemenceau." Chicherin then lambasted the Nansen plan as a "shrewd plan" for "sending in a certain amount of food into Russia under conditions that the workers and soldiers of Russia be disarmed and delivered to the mercy of the Kolchaks and the Denikins." Chicherin then revealed that the secret police had decided, in view of Bullitt's resignation and subsequent publicity, to publish the proposed agreement the next day, so that it would "be clear finally to the whole world as to who really was prepared to meet all offers leading toward the discontinuance of military operations and as to who, on the other hand, having refused to consider these offers, is responsible for the continuation of bloodshed."[88] Substantial quotations from Chicherin's article and the Bullitt-Lenin terms were also broadcast by radio and picked up in the West by the Shatzap radio station. They then made their way eventually back to Samuel N. Harper, who was analyzing the Bolshevik press and statements for the State Department.[89]

*Pravda*'s publication of the full Lenin-Bullitt terms led to the first long and accurate article in the Western press explicating these terms. An article by Isaac Don Levine, datelined Petrograd, May 26, 1919, was published in the *Chicago Daily News* of June 5, 1919. This article accurately reviewed the terms and the conditions of the Bullitt mission given him by Bolshevik sources.[90] Levine also told U.S. chargé Wheeler in Stockholm on his way out of Russia that "the Bolsheviks have been completely disillusioned by the Peace terms as to the possible ambitions of the United States which they now believe to be as imperial as any other nation. The Bolsheviks feel that they were "sold on the Bullitt Mission concerning which nothing has come."[91]

Lenin himself amplified on the Bullitt mission and the Soviet attitude in a long interview of July 20, 1919, subsequently published in the *Chicago Daily News* and many other American newspapers, and reprinted in Russian in the July 25 issue of *Pradva.* In "Answers to an American Journalist's Questions," he noted that

> we have, on many occasions, given a precise, clear and written exposition of the terms upon which we agree to conclude peace with Kolchak, Denikin, and Mannerheim—for instance to Bullitt who conducted negotiations with us (and with me personally in Moscow) on behalf of the United States Government, in a letter to Nansen, etc. It is not our fault that the governments of the United States and other countries are afraid to publish those documents in full and that they hide the truth from the people.[92]

Lenin always insisted that Bullitt spoke officially for the United States government. Lenin often accused him and the United States of not living up to their obligations, especially when Westerners criticized the Bolsheviks for not carrying out their international obligations.[93]

The six-month Allied search in Paris for a formula for peace in European Russia failed. Each approach—Prinkipo, Bullitt, Hoover-Nansen—was linked to the others, yet each was burdened with certain unique handicaps. Some reasons for failure are obvious. In the case of Prinkipo, the refusal of the White Russian forces to negotiate with the Bolsheviks and the support the French gave them in this refusal doomed the initiative in the absence of the Allies' willingness to threaten either the French or their Russian clients. In the case of the Bullitt mission, Bullitt's own enthusiasm for the Bolsheviks and the lack of strong British or American government support for the mission at its outset doubtless played a major role in its demise. As for Hoover-Nansen, its conditions of unilateral ceasefire and outside control of Russian communication and transportation were clearly unacceptable to the Bolsheviks, even after these terms were softened by Bullitt's editing.

But other, deeper factors were perhaps more important in the overall failure of these and all other efforts at negotiation. Most fundamental was the fact that serious negotiations with the Bolsheviks would have required a basic shift in the way the Allied governments thought about the Russian problem. Serious negotiations would have signified, as the French readily perceived, tacit acceptance of the Bolshevik government. And that fact would have signified a withholding of support for the most basic aim of the White forces, the overthrow of the Bolsheviks, and a certain capitulation of the hope that a democratic Russia could be reconstituted. This fundamental shift of position was very long in coming for the Allies. Other conditions in the winter and spring of 1919 simply made it impossible. Although seemingly in favor of negotiations, neither Wilson nor Lloyd George could never bring himself to make such a fundamental shift.

With this in mind, it is easier to see why other factors had such an influence on Lloyd George and Wilson. These factors included the predominance of the German question, the unalterable opposition of the French to accommodation with either Germany or Russia, British politics, and near-hysteria over Bolshevism in Europe and, to a lesser degree, in the United States.

The German issue was of course key for the Paris Peace Conference. Bullitt returned to Paris from Moscow at the time of probably the greatest crisis of the entire conference. Allied unity was being severely tested because of the great difference between France's security needs and British and American desires to reintegrate Germany in the European system. The search to find a formula to make peace with Germany became paramount during this period, and the problem of Russia receded. Lloyd George was so concerned that the French demands over Germany should be resisted that, in his famous Fontainebleau memorandum, he raised the specter of Bolshevism in Germany should Allied terms be too severe. Lloyd George thus used the danger of Bolshevism as a way to get the French to relent, even as he secretly explored the possibility of negotiating with the Bolsheviks! Wilson shared Lloyd George's preoccupation with Germany and refused to distract himself by having any long discussions with House, Bullitt, or Lansing on Russia. In what Ray Stannard Baker has called "the Dark Period," Wilson was distraught over the conference's breaking up because of Clemenceau's unreasonable demands for French security.[94]

The French position on negotiations had remained constant from the time the French general staff, soon after Brest Litovsk, had decided that the reconstitution of the Eastern front with Bolshevik aid was impossible. French security needs had to be met through the destruction of Bolshevik power, the reconstruction of a strong Russia in hands friendly to France, and the buildup of the Eastern European alliance system. France never relented in its firm opposition to negotiations with Moscow, with the exception of Clemenceau's reluctant and lukewarm agreement on Prinkipo and the Nansen proposal. Despite these concessions, France took steps, at the very same time, to increase its support for the White forces and to reassure them that they would never be abandoned by France. Instead, they would be supported if they chose to resist negotiations with the Bolsheviks.[95]

As Kalervo Hovi points out, the reason for France's position is much easier to understand than the often contradictory British and American policies. France was steadfast in its refusal to negotiate because it "did not have any reason to change its attitude toward the Soviet government." That is, the reasons that helped in the development of French policy toward the Bolsheviks at the time of Brest Litovsk had not changed in the intervening months. France's security needs, if anything, depended even more on the *barrière de l'est* and the *cordon sanitaire*.[96]

On top of all of this came politics, both external and internal. On one hand, as Arno Mayer has convincingly shown, the "parties of order" underwent a powerful resurgence throughout Western Europe in the period following the Armistice. This meant increasing conservative and right-wing pressure on all the leading statesmen.[97] At the same time, revolutions in Hungary and Bavaria heightened fears of the seemingly relentless tide of Bolshevism. This reality only added fuel to the right-wing attacks on accommodation with Germans or Bolshevism (and often they were linked together). Lloyd George was especially pressured and vulnerable because of his call for leniency to Germany and leaks of the British role in reviving Prinkipo by sending Bullitt to Moscow. Woodrow Wilson came under increasing attack from conservatives at home as well.[98]

The specter of Bolshevism the British conservatives used to undermine Lloyd George's willingness to negotiate was not an illusion. Revolutions in Hungary (March 22) and Bavaria (April 5) and the meeting of the Third Bolshevik International in Moscow (March 19) coincided with a major upsurge in labor unrest throughout Europe. Although direct Soviet support for most of this activity was minimal, several Soviet actions served to keep the theory of direct Soviet control over these disparate events alive. The Soviets gave verbal support to the uprisings. They also offered food to revolutionary Germany, and Karl Radek was dispatched to Berlin to work with the local revolutionaries. A portion of the Red Army even began to move in the direction of Hungary.[99]

The collapse of imperial Germany had brought an upsurge of revolutionary activity throughout Central Europe: Germany, Austria, Hungary, and Italy. The Bolsheviks, desperate to stave off Allied intervention in the civil war, hoped that the new unrest meant help for their precarious position and the fulfillment of their dreams for world revolution. They were anxious to contact the new revolutionary movements and to render aid if possible. They also wished to reconstitute the old Socialist International movement, this time along Communist lines. But Lenin was most desirous of exploring the peace proposals with the Allies early in 1919. He waited to issue the call to the Third International until late in January, when he had received no response to Litvinov's and Chicherin's peace proposals of December and January. Ironically, the Prinkipo proposal was received just after the invitation to the Third International was published in *Pravda* on January 25.[100]

Hopes for revolution rose and fell rapidly in 1919. The German revolution was suppressed in January; the first Congress of the Comintern was held in March; the Bavarian Soviet collapsed in May; and the Hungarian Soviet Republic died in August. The juxtaposition of these events has led a number of historians to ascribe to Bolshevik planning and direction these attempts at Communist insurgency in Central Europe.[101] Others, however, including the historians who have studied the specific revolutions in depth, do not find this correlation. On the contrary, in the words of F. L. Carsten, "although the Bolshevik revolution evoked widespread sympathy among the working classes it found few emulators."[102] Historians of the Comintern Franz Borkenau and James Hulse find little direct relation between the formation of the Comintern and the development of revolutionary movements in Germany and Hungary. If anything, the correlation was a negative one. The Comintern's birth coincided with the decline of revolution in Europe rather than its rise.[103]

Yet there was another, perhaps more important reason for the establishment of the Comintern. As one authority has noted, "the third international became from the very outset an instrument upon which Soviet diplomacy relied to safeguard the integrity of the Soviet State."[104] If movements in Central Europe could become active in support of the Bolsheviks, they might hinder their governments from making war on the Soviet state. From the outset, therefore, the Comintern was seen in part as a defensive organ, to help stave off counterrevolution and intervention.[105]

Historians of the early Comintern generally agree that the overall effort to spread revolution in Central Europe failed.[106] Moreover, the actual involvement of the Bolsheviks in most of the uprisings has been greatly overstated.[107] Only in Hungary, because of Béla Kun's stay in Russia as a prisoner of war, can a strong case be made for Soviet influence and involvement. Even there, contact between Kun and Lenin was almost entirely one-sided. Kun appealed for help to Lenin and got platitudinous replies and no support.[108]

In the final analysis, it remains almost impossible to definitively determine the reasons for the failure of leaders in Paris to successfully find a way to include Russia in the peace process. It was almost certainly not as simple as blaming the failure, as many have, on Wilson's "one track mind."[109] Nor is it completely fair to leave the responsibility, as the Bolsheviks have, to the "bloodthirsty Clemenceau." But, for whatever reasons, the Bullitt-Lenin proposals failed, despite the fact, as Louis Fischer and several others have noted, that they "offered advantages to the capitalist world which exceed by far anything that has been wrenched from the Bolsheviks from that day to this."[110] Lenin and the Bolsheviks were willing to give up their western borderlands—nearly one-third of their best agricultural land—in exchange for peace, and to negotiate a debt settlement in exchange for recognition by the United States. By the time the United States was finally interested in recognition and the debt, the western borderlands were no longer negotiable.

# IV

*Economic Overtures
and Response, 1919–1920*

# 11

# The Bolsheviks and Economic Diplomacy, 1919–1920

> We well understand the tactics which we all the time have been pursuing with respect to the U.S.—namely, in all matters that the U.S. remains the capitalist country in which there is hope for breaking through the blockade.
> —*Martens to Chicherin, August 1919*[1]

> We are decidedly for an economic understanding with America—with all countries but especially with America.
> —*Lenin, October 1919*[2]

> Exchange of goods is the only means of exerting pressure on governments for obtaining political relations.
> —*Litvinov to Chicherin, August 1920*[3]

With the collapse of the Bullitt mission and the close of the Paris Peace Conference. Lenin and the Bolsheviks intensified their efforts to achieve a breakthrough with the United States. But now they shifted to a concentration on a predominantly economic strategy. Ludwig C. A. K. Martens had been appointed in January 1919 as the representative of the People's Commissariat for Foreign Affairs for the purpose of economic and diplomatic contact in New York. He attempted to present his credentials to the State Department in late March, at nearly the time the Bullitt proposals were pending.[4] Following a rebuff by the State Department, Martens devoted almost his entire attention to contacts with American businessmen. Bolshevik attempts to reach the United States State Department during the remainder of 1919 and 1920 were limited to occasional press interviews, radio, and written appeals. The waning months of the Wilson administration only strengthened this Bolshevik tendency to emphasize economic approaches, as the Soviets devoted their attention to preparation for what they believed would be a new Republican administration, motivated by the primacy of economic considerations.[5]

Lenin persisted in the belief that some kind of working relationship with the United States could be effected by economic incentives and negotiation.

His strategy for a breakthrough with the United States depended on a skillful integration of economic and political approaches designed to exploit every opening and seize any opportunity to break down capitalist and governmental resistance to contacts and weaken the interventionist forces.[6] Although political goals included diplomatic recognition in the long run, in the short run the more pragmatic aims of a working relationship and the reduction of U.S. assistance to counterrevolution predominated. In either case, Lenin believed that economic ties would assist political breakthroughs. This idea was given currency in 1919 by the fact that the Allies maintained the blockade against Bolshevik Russia. Throughout 1919, the Bolsheviks and their supporters stressed the necessity to lift the blockade for economic reasons, but the political benefits were always well understood. Bolshevik appeals to the capitalist workers in these months combined calls for an end to intervention with a demand to lift the blockade.[7]

By 1920, the Martens mission's experience with American businessmen had replaced the blockade as the economic talking point for Bolshevik appeals. In one of the major Bolshevik peace initiatives of this period, relayed through the Foreign Minister of the Swedish government in February 1920, Chicherin stressed in detail Martens' successful contacts with "American commerce and industry" and talked of the "gigantic role" the United States could play in reconstruction. He then concluded with an appeal for negotiations.[8]

Once economic contacts, however tenuous, were established, they could be used for political purposes. All of the individual business contacts could be encouraged to press the host government, and trade representatives could be employed for the same purpose. The period from 1919 to 1920 represents the fullest development yet of the Bolshevik economic strategy toward the West in general and the United States in particular. By this time, the Bolsheviks already had substantial experience in similar approaches to the Dutch, the Swedes, the Norwegians, the Danes, and the Germans, and were engaged in very intensive negotiations with the British. By August 1920, Maksim Litvinov could confidently say to Chicherin that trade was the "only means of exerting pressure on governments."[9]

This chapter deals with Bolshevik efforts to achieve an economic breakthrough with the United States during 1919–1920. The centerpiece of this strategy remained the Martens mission in New York, but it was accompanied by attempts to engage and then control Tsentrosoyuz, the Russian union of cooperatives, and various Western contacts through the Commissariat of Foreign Trade, both of which overlapped with the Martens mission.[10] (The American response to the Bolshevik initiatives will be detailed in Chapter 12)

The Bolshevik economic approach to the United States following the European armistice was originally predicated on the prompt lifting of the Allied blockade and the revival of substantial United States–Soviet trade, either through the medium of the Russian cooperative unions, which were being brought under the control of the Bolsheviks, or through the Commissariat of Foreign Trade, or both. All foreign trade had been nationalized by the decree of Sovnarkom of April 22, 1918, but the Russian cooperatives had been allowed to continue their trade, in part because it was convenient, especially in the West, and the Bolsheviks hoped to take control of the entire cooperative movement. Although this was accomplished by late 1918 in Moscow itself, the co-op representatives abroad resisted coming under Bolshevik control in many cases, and persisted in maintaining contact with non-Bolshevik Russia. Although some tried to remain "neutral" in the civil war, quite quickly most were faced with the choice of siding with the Bolsheviks or opposing them. The great majority continued their work in the West through trade with the shrinking lands of non-Bolshevik Russia.[11]

The Supreme Council on the National Economy (VSNKh), in a series of decisions in anticipation of the Armistice, outlined a plan for the appointment of a foreign trade delegation to the United States. This delegation was to be billed as a Tsentrosoyuz delegation, but was to include representatives of the Commissariat of Foreign Trade and VSNKh itself, and both A. M. Berkenheim, the President of Tsentrosoyuz; and L. B. Krasin, Foreign Trade Commissar. The VSNKh representatives were included, according to the agreement, "for information, control, and the directing of relations with America."[12] This plan was concluded as an agreement between VSNKh and Tsentrosoyuz for the "implementation of the mission of VSNKh for foreign markets."[13]

The delegation was directed to visit a number of European countries before its departure to the United States, and to establish, where possible, permanent trade offices. The delegation was also charged, under authority of the decree nationalizing foreign trade, with a number of specific, concrete purchases for Soviet Russia, for which 100 million rubles was authorized by VSNKh on November 14, 1918: instruments, trucks, rubber, sugar, skins, shoes, and tea. The delegation was also ordered to explore the possibility of purchasing cotton, tractors, farm machinery, machinery for industry and textiles, and others.[14]

Under the leadership of Tsentrosoyuz president Berkenheim, this delegation attempted to leave Soviet Russia for Western Europe and the United States. On approaching the Finnish border in late November, only the representatives of Tsentrosoyuz, led by Berkenheim, were allowed to cross. Krasin, Kamenev, and Larin, representing VSNKh and the Foreign Trade Commissariat, were turned back.[15] Berkenheim proceeded to establish Tsentrosoyuz offices in Copenhagen, Stockholm, and London before proceeding to New York in March 1919.[16]

In the meantime, the Soviet government appointed Martens as its representative in New York, and attempted to use Litvinov, Krasin, and Vorovski to open up direct contacts with both government representatives and businesses in Scandinavia and get various government contracts through the Commissariat of Foreign Trade. The Soviet government attempted in various ways over the next several years to regain control over Tsentrosoyuz representatives abroad. Until that occurred, it disavowed their trading activities.[17] The Bolsheviks eventually used Tsentrosoyuz as a cover for trade negotiations with the British, appointing Maksim Litvinov as the head of a Tsentrosoyuz delegation for preliminary discussions in Copenhagen. Krasin and Kamenev were then sent to

London for actual negotiations resulting in the Anglo-Soviet trade agreement of 1921.

Although the same strategy was attempted in approaches to the United States, it never resulted in serious negotiations. Though the United States supported the end of the economic blockade, it took the position that trade with Russia was strictly the risk of the individual business. The American government refused to get involved in negotiations, despite the fact that the Supreme Council of the Allies, acting on behalf of Britain, France, and the United States, "authorized representatives to meet M. Krassin [*sic*] and the Russian Trade Delegation now at Copenhagen with a view to the immediate restarting of trade relations between Russia and other countries through the intermediary of the cooperative organizations."[18]

Martens' credentials, whether as representative of Narkomindel, Tsentrosoyuz, or the Commissariat of Foreign Trade, were ignored, while Berkenheim successfully continued to present himself as the Tsentrosoyuz representative in New York, despite Bolshevik hostility.[19] No other Bolshevik representatives were ever given visas for the United States, despite Krasin's and Litvinov's attempts.[20]

Leonid Krasin had joined the Presidium of the Supreme Economic Council in September 1918, and for all intents and purposes took over the organization of foreign trade, although he did not receive the title of "People's Commissar of Foreign Trade" until November.[21] Krasin was a trained engineer and sometime businessman, who always approached problems in a non-rhetorical manner, "entering immediately into the technical and commercial questions . . . in a concise and businesslike manner."[22]

Krasin argued within the Politburo in favor of expanding trade with the West, particularly Germany, and in favor of utilizing Tsentrosoyuz as a way of getting a trading foot in the door of reluctant former enemies such as Britain and the United States.[23] He and Lenin agreed on most issues, including the use of Tsentrosoyuz, but it appears that Lenin put a higher priority on overtures to the United States than Krasin did, who believed in devoting most energy to the development of German commercial ties.[24] Krasin also believed that most of his energy should be put in attempts to lure the larger corporations and trusts into some kind of relationship to the Bolsheviks. Lenin was forced to remind him on several occasions not to overlook the small firms, cautioning him in March 1920, "Go after the little bird."[25] On broader arguments within the Politburo regarding the entire trade and commercial policy toward the West, however, Lenin, Krasin, Chicherin, and Litvinov were fully in accord, often siding against those who wished to phase out or downplay this aspect of Bolshevik foreign policy.[26]

### The Martens Bureau and Its Background

The establishment in early 1919 of the Soviet Russian Information Bureau, as Martens' agency was called, had several American antecedents. Immediately following the Bolshevik revolution, an American group, Friends of the Russian Revolution, was formed to support Soviet demands for an immediate, unconditional peace. This group dissolved by the time of Brest Litovsk.[27]

Early in 1918 the first group specifically organized to spread news and information about the Bolshevik revolution was formed by individuals active in the left wing of the American Socialist Party. This group, the American Bolshevik Information Bureau, was spearheaded by Louis Fraina, but also included Nicholas Hourwich of the Russian Socialist Federation and Ludwig C. A. K. Martens of the "New York Section of the Russian Bolsheviki."[28] Fraina attempted to send a telegram to the Bolshevik leadership informing them of the new organization and expressing the "solidarity" of American workers with the Russian proletariat. He also said that they had "taken steps to organize red guards." This telegram was never dispatched. It was held by the United States Chief Censor and then confiscated.[29]

Of more lasting importance to the efforts of the Bolsheviks to establish contact and openings in the United States was the work of a Finnish émigré, Santeri Nuorteva. Nuorteva, originally a teacher of history and languages in Finland, joined the Finnish Socialist Party near the turn of the century and was elected representative to the Finnish Parliament following the revolution of 1905. Nuorteva was imprisoned by the Tsarist police for six months in 1909 for writing an article in a Finnish newspaper critical of the regime. Under pressure from the Tsarist police, he emigrated to the United States in 1911, where he became active in the Finnish Socialist Federation and the American Socialist Party. Following the Bolshevik revolution, Nuorteva sided with the left wing and soon became an influential advocate for the Soviet regime.[30]

The Bolshevik revolution came to Finland on January 27, 1918. On February 19, Nuorteva was asked by Yrjo Sirola, head of the Finnish Red Revolutionary Government, to be its representative in the United States. Before the Finnish White forces overwhelmed the Reds in April, Nuorteva had already established (in March) a Finnish Information Bureau. He used this bureau throughout 1918 to further the Bolshevik cause, not only in Finland, but in Soviet Russia as well.[31]

Nuorteva was a skillful publicist and managed to get the accounts of the White Finnish government in New York banks frozen for a time. He also successfully used the argument that the White government was an ally of Germany and a defender of German interests. He received audiences with many prominent Americans to give the Finnish socialist side of the war in Finland. He managed to get the ear of Samuel Eliot Morison, the young Harvard historian who was working on the question of Finland for Colonel House's Inquiry in preparation for the Peace Conference. In a series of eight letters between March 1918 and January 1919, Nuorteva managed to persuade Morison that Germany was using Finland for its own purposes and that the aspirations of Finnish workers and peasants could not be met under the White government.[32]

As Nuorteva pursued the cause of Finland, he consistently used his opportunities to further the possibilities of American consideration of Soviet recognition or aid. This was taken seriously by Colonel House and others in the spring and summer of 1918.[33] In particular, Nuorteva's efforts to persuade the American government that some contact needed to be established with the Bolsheviks made headway with Felix Frankfurter and William C. Bullitt. In an April 22 letter to Lincoln Steffens, Nuorteva's aide Harold Kellock noted that Frankfurter had asked for Nuorteva to develop a detailed brief setting forth concrete recommendations "as to what the U.S. government should do to get into closer touch with Russia." Kellock noted in passing, "we seem to be drawn in more and more as semi-official representatives of the whole Russian situation."[34]

These discussions with Frankfurter and Bullitt in late April spurred Nuorteva and Kellock to feverish activity in May. Nuorteva attempted to persuade Samuel Harper and Herbert Porter of the League to Aid Russia that no United States program of assistance to the Russian people could ignore the Bolsheviks, and that some sort of tacit recognition was necessary if the Russian people were to be helped.[35] Nuorteva's arguments were persuasive and sophisticated and came just at the time that a serious debate about United States policy toward Russia was occurring among Wilson's liberal advisors. Nuorteva's essential point was that "any aid offered to Russia on the part of the Allies, if it is to have the confidence of the Russian people, must be unequivocally in sympathy with, or at least not in active opposition to the will of the Russian people, as expressed by the Soviets."[36] This was close to the thinking of Raymond Robins, Colonel House, Senator Owen, Senator Borah, Felix Frankfurter, William C. Bullitt, and other liberals close to the administration.[37] Harper took Nuorteva's arguments very seriously, noting in a letter to E. C. Porter, the Executive Secretary of the American-Russian Chamber of Commerce, "I do not think we can ignore such letters as this one, and urge that you as well as Carpenter see the man."[38]

Despite this interest, and the wavering possibility of the League to Aid Russia's calling for some kind of understanding with the Bolsheviks, no real action was forthcoming from those close to the administration. So Nuorteva and Kellock moved in the direction of a public campaign and a new organization. A blizzard of letters and telephone calls to American socialists, liberals, and friends of Russia prepared the way for a massive rally in Madison Square Garden June 11 and the announcement of the formation of the Soviet Russian Recognition League.[39]

This League was the immediate predecessor of the Soviet Russian Information Bureau. Its founding officers were Alexander Trachtenburg, a well-known Russian émigré radical active in the left wing of the Socialist Party; Nuorteva; Gregory Weinstein of *Novy Mir;* Harold Kellock; and Yuri Lomonosov, representative of the Russian Railway Mission to the United States, appointed by the Provisional Russian Government.[40] The purpose of the League, as enunciated in one of its pledge forms distributed at the Madison Square Garden rally, was to bring "the true facts about Russia before the people of the United States, and by all lawful and orderly means to urge the necessity of formal and friendly relations between the United States and Russia, as she is represented by the Government of the Soviets."[41]

The rally at Madison Square Garden was a huge success and created something of a sensation because of the public appearance of Lomonosov. Yuri Lomonosov was a railway expert, engineer, and former professor at the Institute of Transport in Petrograd. At the New York rally, Lomonosov made it clear that he remained a Menshevik, not a Bolshevik, but he also said that he was opposed to intervention and in favor of recognition of the Bolshevik government by the United States. He felt this was the best way to aid in the economic reconstruction of Russia. Although the Soviets might "not be to the liking of some," Lomonosov declared, "there is one advantage the Soviet Government has: it really exists. We must begin negotiations either in Moscow or in Washington as to the extent, character and conditions of the necessary help. . . ."[42]

Lomonosov was removed immediately from his post by Provisional Government Ambassador Boris Bakhmetev. Although he tried to fight legally to preserve his position, he was forcibly removed from his office by U.S. Department of Justice officials in July 1918. Lomonosov successfully managed to keep most of his papers, however, and was reappointed to his previous position by Martens in the new Soviet Russian Information Bureau in March 1919. After several frustrating months making grandiose plans for United States assistance to Russian railways that could never be effected due to resistance of the United States government, Lomonosov returned to Moscow in early 1920 and subsequently headed up a Soviet technical and trading mission to Berlin.[43]

Lomonosov was not the only former Provisional Government representative to be attracted to the new Soviet Russian Recognition League and its successor, Martens' bureau. Nicholas Goldenweiser, the representative of the All-Russian Zemsky Union (the representatives of rural towns and cooperatives), shifted his allegiance soon after the announcement of the Bureau's existence.[44]

The Madison Square Garden rally kicked off a successful organizing period for the Soviet Russian Recognition League. Although pressure was put on Lomonosov to persuade him not to make public appearances, momentum was maintained up through Wilson's decision to intervene in Siberia in late July.[45] Kellock and Nuorteva continued their correspondence with Harper, Steffens, and Bullitt and were even asked by Colonel House to suggest names for the potential commission to Russia. They recommended Raymond Robins and Lincoln Steffens.[46]

Nuorteva was extremely busy speaking in various cities around the country, where local chapters of the Soviet Russian Recognition League were formed. Nuorteva's and Lomonosov's speeches were widely circulated. In early July, Kellock was optimistic, believing that "we are really cleverer than they are and we are going to see the game to a finish." At the same time, he noted that "we have a big struggle ahead of us. The reactionary press is lined up solidly against Russia. The odds against recognition are heavy, and sometimes we get terribly discouraged."[47]

By September, Kellock and Nuorteva were definitely on the defensive. They were forced to respond sharply to Sisson's charges of German-Bolshevik collusion. They had to fight a rearguard action just to keep their former liberal friends from deserting them. Nuorteva wrote a long piece, "An Open Letter to American Liberals," published by the New York Socialist Society in September. Here he once again defended the legitimacy of the Bolshevik regime against pro-German charges.[48]

The Sisson charges stimulated Nuorteva to address another communication to the Wilson administration. On September 13, he wrote a long letter to Wilson himself in which he offered to act as a mediator between the United States and Soviet Russia. Nuorteva called on the United States to let the Soviets know "just what they expect that Government to do in order to avoid friction."[49]

Nuorteva and Kellock next seized on the Armistice as a new chance for the Soviet cause in the United States and revived their Washington contacts in November and December. New letters were written to Samuel Morison, Louis Brandeis, Felix Frankfurter, Amos Pinchot, and others with ties to the administration.[50]

Finally, on January 2, 1919, Ludwig C. A. K. Martens was appointed Representative of the People's Commissariat of Foreign Affairs in the United States by Bolshevik foreign minister Georgi Chicherin. Martens set about immediately to reorganize the Soviet Russian Recognition League as the Soviet Russian Information Bureau and to concentrate his energies in the direction of commercial contacts with American business. Only secondarily did he focus on the longer-range hope for recognition and diplomatic exchange.[51] As Martens said when he was called before the U.S. Senate Committee on Foreign Relations, "The chief purpose of my mission in the United States has been and is the reestablishment of economic intercourse between Russia and the United States."[52]

Martens was born and raised in Russia by German parents long resident in Russia but never naturalized. He was educated in Russian technical schools and trained as an engineer. He became active in the Russian revolutionary movement in 1905 and 1906, when he was imprisoned for three years and then deported to Germany, where he was forced to serve in the German armed forces. He emigrated to the United States in 1916 and continued his revolutionary activities, working actively with *Novy Mir* and the left wing of the American Socialist Party. Following the March revolution, he received his Russian citizenship from the Provisional Government, and was among the founders of the Soviet Russian Recognition League. When he received his appointment as Bolshevik representative, he was working as an engineer and administrator with Weinberg and Posner, a New York machinery firm.[53]

Martens took on Nuorteva as secretary for his new bureau almost immediately, and the latter wasted no time in seeking to influence events in both Washington and Paris. Utilizing his friend Granville McFarland, the Hearst representative in Washington, Nuorteva arranged a meeting for himself and Harold Kellock with Frank Polk, Acting Secretary of State while Secretary Lansing was in Paris. At this meeting, Nuorteva claimed to represent the Soviet government and urged the United States government to negotiate with the Bolsheviks. He also stated that the Soviet government was prepared to assume the old debts of the previous Russian governments. In addition, Nuorteva asked the State Department to relay a message to Lenin, urging him and the Bolsheviks to agree to come to Prinkipo to meet with the Allies. Polk commented in his memorandum to Lansing and House that "we do not know whether he has any authority whatever. . . . He is considered dangerous agitator but has so far kept within the law. Apparently he is being very well advised."[54]

Martens officially informed the State Department of his own presence by sending his credentials on March 19, along with a detailed memorandum, signed by himself and Nuorteva, requesting negotiations with the United States. Martens particularly stressed trade and economic affairs, noting that

> many branches of [Russian] industry, however, have not so far been able to recuperate, because of lack of raw material and lack of machinery. The needs of such industries offer a wide field for business transaction with Russia by other countries. . . . I am empowered by my Government to negotiate for the speedy opening of commercial relations for the mutual benefit of Russia and America, and I shall be glad to discuss details at the earliest opportunity.[55]

The State Department ignored Martens. He then sent a further letter to Lansing on March 31, asking what was the attitude of the U.S. government toward his presence in the United States, and even offering to leave if the government did not want him and did not "consider favorably the establishment of friendly relations with the government of Russia."[56] This time Lansing sent the Martens correspondence to Wilson, asking for his views on the matter.[57] By the time Wilson responded, Frank Polk and others in the State Department had recommended not responding to Martens' request for negotiations. Moreover, they were intensely exploring the grounds on which Martens might be forced to leave the country.[58]

But Martens had no intention of leaving quietly. One of his first actions, following his letter to the State Department, was a public request and letter to Boris Bakhmetev, ambassador of the Provisional Government (and still recognized by the United States), demanding that he turn over all assets of the Russian government under his possession or control.[59] Martens received no answer to this letter.

While the State Department ignored him, he set to work to establish the basis for extensive Soviet-American trade. The Soviet Russian Information Bureau was organized quite carefully, encompassing at least fifty individuals, thirty-five of them full-time paid staff, and seven departments, and occupying a floor and a half in the Tower Building, 110 West Fortieth Street, Manhattan. Many American socialists of various stripes went to work for the bureau.

Nuorteva was secretary and head of the diplomatic department. Gregory Weinstein, formerly of *Novy Mir,* was office manager. Abraham A. Heller, businessman and socialist, served as head of the Commercial Section. Evans Clark, former research director for several New York socialist aldermen, was publicity director. Arthur Adams served as director of Technical Department; William Malisoff, Director of the Education Department; Leo Huebsch, Director of the Medical Department; Morris Hilquit, legal advisor; Julius Hammer, head of the Accounting Department; Isaac Hourwich, the Director of Economics and Statistics Department; and Yuri Lomonosov, Railway Advisor.[60]

Soon the Bureau was overwhelmed by applications from socialists and sympathizers who volunteered their services. Some better-known radicals were bemused by the job's being entrusted to the quiet and unobtrusive Martens, who, it is true, seemed to be on working terms with most of the factions of the New York socialist community. As John Reed wrote to Louise Bryant soon after the Martens bureau was organized, "Do you remember Martens—a rather nice, blond, square faced Russian who used to go around with Lore, Fraina, etc.? Well, he has been appointed representative in the United States by the Soviet Government. . . . It is kicking up quite a fuss around here."[61]

The fuss was not limited to the radical community. Soon after the *New York Times* announced Martens' existence, the Union League of New York compiled a careful "intelligence report" from its Bolshevist Study Committee and sent it to British agent and House confidant Sir William Wiseman. This report protested that "the Union League resents the action of the Russian Soviet Republic in establishing a mission in the United States, and calls upon the Government to take immediate action to prevent its activities."[62]

From the beginning, Martens was determined to put the major emphasis of the bureau on commercial contacts with American businessmen. The commercial section was the largest, with seven permanent staff members, and substantial portions of both Martens' and Nuorteva's time were also spent in discussions and contacts with businessmen, and publicity and interpretation of those contacts. Even staff members such as Yuri Lomonosov spent part of their time cultivating commercial contacts.[63] From the substantial records of Martens' work found both in the captured records of his office in the Lusk Committee archives in New York State and in the reports and letters to Krasin, Chicherin, and others that Martens sent back to Moscow, it is quite clear that Martens believed his main task to be the establishment of economic contacts with American businessmen. These contacts could then be useful in furthering diplomatic overtures and political work, but that remained clearly secondary. As for the propaganda and organizing work of American Bolsheviks, Martens insisted on staying removed from all American domestic radical squabbles. For this stance he sometimes incurred the wrath of the left wing of American socialists, but he was always upheld by Moscow.[64]

Martens, Heller, and Nuorteva began the process of contacting American businessmen with the very announcement of the opening of their office. They issued an open invitation to businesses to come in to see them to discuss purchasing agreements and contracts on the basis of a purported $200 million in Western currency on deposit in banks in Western Europe and the United States.[65] Although there is no evidence proving deposits of $200 million, financial records indicate that several hundred thousand dollars were on deposit in Martens' name in two New York City banks, providing ample support for the Bureau's operations.[66]

The initial response of New York businesses was sufficiently encouraging not only to provide crowded offices and full schedules for Martens, Nuorteva, and Heller in the first weeks following the opening of the Bureau, but to alarm the American Russian Chamber of Commerce, the State Department, and the Russia Desk at the U.S. Commerce Department. These three agencies were forced to respond to a flood of inquiries from businesses about the possibility of doing trade with Russia, the legitimacy of Martens and company, and the like.[67] One letter from an American businessman to W. C. Huntington, former American commercial attaché of the American Embassy and in 1919 head of the Russia desk at the U.S. Department of Commerce, expressed a common view:

> Do you see any harm . . . if I should get in touch with these people who have so much money at their disposal, if it is true, and try to do some business? The aim of every businessman is to improve his financial standing and you who always, since the first day I had the privilege of meeting you, assisted me I feel will not blame me for endeavoring to make money. . . .[68]

Huntington noted to Harper in a cover letter enclosing this, "You would be surprised to know how seriously a lot of our people have taken the preposterous proposal of this man. . . ."[69]

Huntington discussed the situation with E. C. Porter of the American-Russian Chamber of Commerce and Samuel N. Harper. They agreed that the Martens approach was a serious threat, particularly in light of the fact that the Bullitt mission in Paris was pending at the time. Steps should be taken immediately to discourage U.S. business interest. As Porter noted in a long memorandum to Huntington, "Selfish interests through large financial groups might . . . result in a tendency to get behind this movement. . . . The situation is worth while watching closely for it might develop into something that would gain a good deal of headway with extremely unfortunate results."[70]

Huntington drafted, for Porter and the American-Russian Chamber of Commerce's use, a letter, "Russian Warning to American Business Men." This flyer, sent out widely in April to businesses in the New York and Chicago areas, warned against the "temptation to obtain some temporary commercial profit and advantage," and claimed not only that the Bolshevik government was unrepresentative of, and "bitterly hated" by, the Russian people, but that it was on its last legs and soon to be replaced by the Omsk government, then awaiting recognition by the United States. "Any transactions," it warned, "therefore can be only of the most temporary character, and payments made by it must be made in stolen gold or stolen goods." The warning was signed by the American-Russian Chamber of Commerce and by six other organizations of White Russians in the United States.[71]

Huntington and Harper also made sure that the U.S. State Department issued a public warning, and began to respond strongly to inquiries as well. Acting Secretary of State Frank Polk, in a letter to Mark Prentiss of the Council on Foreign Relations, pointedly noted that the State Department had "not received nor recognized Mr. Martens in any representative capacity" and had "no authentic evidence" that he was who he claimed to be. Polk went on to warn Prentiss that any businessmen contacting or making deals with Martens were doing so completely at their own risk, in light of the continuing Allied blockade, and that no export permits would be issued.[72] Huntington also began making public speeches. In a major speech at the dinner of the Council on Foreign Relations in New York, he warned his audience in the strongest terms "against entering into relations with Ludwig Martens and the Bolshevik 'commercial' representatives."[73]

Despite these warnings and Huntington's initial belief that "New York is recovering from its flurry" and that "no important firms had ever entertained serious thought of doing business with Ludwig Martens,"[74] the flood of businessmen to Martens' office continued. Nuorteva, Heller, and Lomonosov attended a major foreign trade convention in Chicago in late April. Afterwards, Nuorteva reported that they were "swamped with visitors" for two days, "mostly representatives of firms all of whom were impressed with the possibility of trade with Russia."[75] After this convention, Harper complained to Huntington that "a great many businessmen here in Chicago went around to see Mr. Heller. One told me that he had a most interesting talk with him and had promised to send all his price lists and other pamphlets."[76] Heller and Martens told businesses they met with that, upon signing a proposed contract, they were "prepared to deposit full amount of contract price in New York banks and will make payment on shipment of 10% or other comparatively small proportion of goods called for by the contract."[77]

Heller was an indefatigable salesman for Russian commercial interests, claiming "an export-import business of between one and five billion dollars a year awaits the resumption of friendly relations between the United States and Russia," including millions of pounds of flax and hemp, large quantities of furs, bristles, hides, and platinum, and "almost unlimited supplies of timber." In return, the Soviet government was prepared to purchase millions of dollars' worth of railroad equipment, agricultural implements, boots and shoes, foodstuffs, cotton, textiles, paper, and rubber goods.[78]

Heller and Martens claimed repeatedly that they had been in serious contact with over 1,500 American firms who were considering entering into trade with Bolshevik Russia.[79] Although the Lusk Committee files yield a seventeen-page single-spaced list of American firms with addresses, and there is evidence that each had been mailed a form letter by Heller, there is no evidence that such a high number of firms seriously considered doing business.[80]

There is, however, plenty of evidence that more than a handful of American firms (I counted ninety-five), including some large and significant ones, entered into serious discussions, negotiations, or correspondence indicating their intention to enter into a contract.[81] These include such firms as Marathon Tire and Rubber, Old Reliable Motor Truck Corporation, Weinberg Shoe Company, Rand McNally and Company, Baugh Chemical Company, Mathieson Alkali Works, Armour and Company Meat Products, APEX Spark Plugs, Grant Steel Company, Graselli Chemical, National Merchandise Company, Swift and Company, Cudahy and Company, Kimball Glass, Jones and Laughlin Steel, International Paper, and Scott Paper.[82] This evidence, and more extensive records of conversations and preliminary contracts in a number of cases, blatantly contradicts the statement of Lusk Committee general counsel Archibald Stevenson. Stevenson claimed in public testimony that "a careful search of the files was made and there is no indication that any commercial transaction was being consummated."[83]

Contracts were signed, subject only to the receipt of export licenses, with Robinson Machinery Corporation (for bristle processing and manufacturing), Bates Machine and Tractor Company (tractor shipment), Sullivan Mathieson Company, G. Flory Machine Company, Weinberg and Posner Engineering firm, Lane Berlow (shoes), Hartmann and Company (underwear and hosiery), Kempsmith Manufacturing (milling machines), F. Mayer (boots and shoes), Milwaukee Shaper (shapers), Steel Sole Shoe Company (shoes), and Lehigh Machine Company (printing presses).[84] In addition to these confirmations, a complete contract between the National Storage Company of Indianapolis and the Russian Soviet Government was signed on September 16, 1919, for $8.6 million worth of meats, to be shipped by first-class steamer to Petrograd or Reval. Heller also discussed in general terms tentative contracts for 440,000 pairs of boots, shoes, tea, underwear, milling machines, and machine tools, some of which were probably included in the previously named contracts.[85]

The tentative contract with Robinson Machinery corporation for bristle processing and brush manufacturing machinery is particularly noteworthy because of the extensive accompanying material found in the Central State Archive of the National Economy in Moscow. A long report on the bristle trade in North America provided a careful analysis of the market, showing the rise in imports of bristles from Russia from 1910 to 1917, and the huge market remaining. This report also contained a detailed discussion of different kinds of bristles, including those in Russia, and analyzed solidity, elasticity, texture, prices, and various kinds of manufacturing machinery.[86]

Some of the contracts were placed, not directly with the firms noted, but rather with brokers or agents. As Heller noted in a report to Martens, "such agents can do a great deal of work among manufacturers without immediate or direct cost to the bureau. These agents can likewise reach certain interests which the Bureau directly cannot do for obvious reasons."[87]

Heller and his co-workers also had conversations with major firms that never resulted in contracts because of the firms' desire to receive assurances from the State Department concerning export licenses. These included International Harvester, Rockefeller and Company, and others.[88]

Most interesting and extensive among these conversations were those with Henry Ford and Company. Martens first wrote to Ford on April 9, 1919, accompanying his note with a cable from Heller asking whether Ford was interested in selling cars and tractors to Soviet Russia. In Martens' personal letter, he said that he sought a meeting with Ford, "not about trade in the narrow sense alone," but about "all the aspects of our aspirations."[89]

Ford responded by sending a representative, Ernest Kanseler, to meet with Heller at the Ritz Carlton in New York. At this meeting, Kanseler expressed an interest in selling Ford tractors to Soviet Russia and felt that there should be no difficulty in securing export licenses. Ford was not prepared to do anything concrete until a go-ahead was given by the State Department.[90]

Although Kanseler indicated at this meeting that he did not think an interview between Martens and Ford himself would be "opportune," he invited the Bureau to visit the Ford plant at Dearborn.[91] Martens, however, persisted in his effort to develop a relationship with Ford, writing him a follow-up letter on April 21, again asking for a discussion of something other "than the purely commercial interests your firm may have. . . . We believe we could make you understand that Soviet Russia is inaugurating methods of industrial efficiency compatible with the interests of humanity."[92]

E. O. Liebold, general secretary to Ford, did agree to see Nuorteva in late April in Detroit. At this meeting, Liebold and E. L. Sorensen, the head of the Ford Tractor Division, told Nuorteva that Ford was "very interested in sending tractors to Russian peasants and sending them at the lowest possible price," but that they had already reached an agreement for such a supply with Sergei Batovin, who represented "45 banks and steamship companies in Russia." When Nuorteva convinced Sorensen that Batolin had no such contacts, and that any substantial business in tractors with Russia must be done through the Soviet Russian Information Bureau, Sorensen agreed to a meeting with Martens in August.[93]

In a long letter to Soviet Foreign Minister Chicherin, Martens described this "most satisfactory meeting." Sorensen not only offered to sell tractors to Soviet Russia, subject only to an export permit, but he pledged to write a letter to the State Department officially asking for such a permit. Martens noted that he hoped this would really lead to something because he believed that Ford tractors were "ideal machines for communal farms." Ford was willing, initially, to sell 10,000 at a cost of only $750 each. Martens also urged Chicherin to seek permission for the Bureau to purchase Ford cars and trucks as well.[94]

Occasionally Nuorteva or Heller was given the opportunity of appealing to a whole group of American firms at the same time through invitations to speak at various trade conventions. On June 4, Nuorteva was invited to speak at the Convention of the Knit Goods Manufacturers Association in Philadelphia. In this speech, he appealed for the industrial needs of Soviet Russia and discussed Russia as a vast market of unlimited potential for American goods. Nuorteva claimed that Russia "is not only ready to absorb products but that she is able to make better terms of payment than could be obtained anywhere else." He called on American businessmen to base their decisions on the pure fact that "European Russia needs hundreds of millions of dollars of manufactured goods" and that Russia was most eager to buy these from America.[95]

Closely related to the trade initiatives of the Martens bureau were the technical and engineering contacts Martens worked on personally. Martens wrote a number of letters in May 1919 in his quest to identify scientific, engineering, and technical personnel who would be interested in helping Soviet Russia. This help included the possibility of their returning to Russia to assist with economic reconstruction. One of these feelers was a letter from Martens to technical institutes and engineering schools in the United States. The letter asked the schools about the possibility of placing Russians then in the United States in these institutes for training prior to their return to assist in the reconstruction of Russia: "Among the occupations which are much needed in Russia at present and with which we are anxious to supply Soviet Russia are: engineers, mechanics, artisans, accountants, executives, agricultural experts, also all branches of medical and surgical instruction."[96]

Martens also wrote letters to any individuals whose names he could get from the various Russian-language federations in the United States, asking those with technical backgrounds to consider returning to Russia to help with reconstruction.[97] He also induced the secretary of the Russian Communist Federation in the United States to send a circular asking for an inventory of the skills of all of the Federation's members and asking for volunteers to return to Soviet Russia for assistance with reconstruction.[98]

All of these requests led to an outpouring of volunteers and offers of assistance. Engineers and technicians wrote offering their services.[99] In a long report to Krasin and Chicherin, Martens discussed the tremendous outpouring of interest, the organization of the Society for Technical Aid for Soviet Russia, and his plans for a conference in September.[100]

This conference, held September 30, was by all accounts a success. Groups of individuals pledged to return to Russia. The organization began an ambitious program of soliciting all manner of technical aid and assistance. Plans were prepared to establish workshops and areas for stockpiling tools and materials along with specialists and trainers to accompany them. Martens' various appeals even resulted in the contribution of agricultural machines, cars, boots, tools, and lathes to Soviet Russia. Shipment awaited only a means of transport.[101]

In addition to discussions with individual firms with the intent of signing contracts or agreements in principle, the Commercial Department concentrated its energies on the broader aspects of contacts with American firms. As Heller explained in a memorandum to Martens, he was working to create "an organization of responsible American manufacturers and businessmen for the purpose of helping in the work."[102]

The Bureau called a meeting of businessmen at the Civic Club on May 6 "for the purpose of getting advice and counsel relative to the work of the department and for the formation of voluntary advisory committees on purchases" for different classes of goods.[103] At this meeting, a stimulating exchange of views was held regarding the purposes of such advisory committees. One of the businessmen present, John Block, "urged the necessity of making the American public demand recognition of the Russian Soviet Government." But others, including Ludwig London and Martens himself, "emphasized the necessity of sticking to the commercial and making every effort to reach the businessmen." Others "deprecated the use of the Soviet government to propagate socialism in the United States" and urged "rigid conformity" to the business field.[104]

Martens was asked directly by the Lusk Committee whether the Commercial Department suggested to businessmen that they urge the recognition of Soviet Russia. Martens gave a flat no and instead said that the commercial department "suggests to businessmen to ask the State Department for export licenses."[105]

This statement is fully supported by the evidence that exists in files both in the Lusk Committee and in Moscow archives, and in evidence given to the Senate Foreign Relations Committee. In the latter records, letters from the American Milling Company, the Garford Motor Company, the Duplex Truck Company, the Ellis Motor Car Company, the Automatic Button Company, the Kimble Glass Company, and others were sent to Martens and his staff explaining that the U.S. War Trade Board had responded to their inquiries that no export permits were being issued for Soviet Russia.[106] One letter from APEX Chemical to Heller went considerably further in soliciting the support of a congressman. This letter stated in part, "We have the assurance of representative Oscar R. Luhring of this, the First District of Indiana, that everything possible will be done to permit shipment of our goods. He has promised to enlist the aid of other representatives and senators in Washington along this line."[107]

Although most of the contact with Washington representatives was made by American businesses, often at the instigation of Heller or Nuorteva, the Soviet Bureau was not reluctant to respond directly to requests for information on their trade and publicity activities. Heller, responding to a request from Congressman James P. Mulvihill of New York, wrote a long and detailed letter in May 1919, outlining the entire program of the Bureau with an emphasis on its work in establishing "friendly relations between the United States and Russia to get for Russia the benefit of America's productive ability and for America the benefit of the Russian market." Heller was careful not to ask Mulvihill or the American government for recognition or even for a lifting of the blockade, pointedly noting that "the Russian Soviet Government Bureau does not interfere in American affairs." Instead, this task was left up to American businessmen.[108]

Many of the businesses that seriously discussed agreements with Martens did contact either the State Department or their Congressmen, but most apparently did not strongly advocate the lifting of the blockade or anything approaching official recognition. Rather, as Arthur Bullard, chief of the Russia Division of the State Department, testified to the House Foreign Affairs Committee, "a large number of them have come with the idea that the State

Department could guarantee these contracts. They came and said, 'If we sign these contracts, will we get our money?' "[109]

One idea briefly considered by Martens, but not forwarded in its complete form to the Bolshevik leadership, was an extensive plan for the appointment of a number of Soviet consuls and vice-consuls throughout the United States, in New York, Chicago, San Francisco, Pittsburgh, Cleveland, Detroit, and Seattle. Martens hoped to be able to propose this plan at some stage of negotiations with the United States State Department. These never materialized.[110]

The Commercial Department of the Soviet Bureau also explored the possibility of persuading a group of American businessmen to form a new, large conglomerate exclusively for the purpose of trading with Soviet Russia. Heller and Nuorteva convinced former senator Thomas Martin of New Jersey to pull together the resources and the contacts to organize a company to specialize in binder-twine machinery and manufacture. According to Heller, Martin was "willing to form a company to trade with Russia on the basis of a definite order of considerable magnitude to be placed with them by us in order to attract some of the leading financial and business interests." The sums discussed approached $200 million and would have included a wide range of agricultural material and machinery. "In return," Heller said, "this company will undertake to use its best offices to bring about the lifting of the blockade and look after the shipping of the ordered materials. . . ."[111]

Nuorteva supported this proposal, and urged Martens to persuade the Bolshevik leadership to make the commitment of funds "as a necessary initial cost of breaking the blockade." Nuorteva noted that there had been some hesitancy in previous discussions in recommending such a major commitment to an American project. The Central Committee of the Bolshevik Party was divided on whether Germany or the United States should be given priority in commercial approaches. Lenin sided with Litvinov in pressing the United States' case, but Krasin and Chicherin made the case for Germany and apparently won the vote in the Central Committee. Nevertheless, Nuorteva said, "there is still left a very great field for American exports to Russia and we should utilize the offer made by the Martin combination . . . [because] the political effects of such transactions will be of great advantage to Soviet Russia."[112] Although Martens supported this proposal, it was not adopted by Krasin.

Heller also explored the possibility of transacting business with a group called the Russian-Baltic Company as soon as peace was concluded with Estonia. This would enable the Soviet Bureau to use Estonia to ship products to Petrograd and avoid the blockade. This possibility never reached fruition because of Soviet concerns about the permanence of the Russian-Baltic Company.[113]

The frustration of Martens and his colleagues with the blockade led to other interesting ideas for ways to get United States goods to Russia and return Russian goods to the United States. On May 9, 1919, Heller went across town to visit with A. M. Berkenheim, the Vice-President of Tsentrosoyuz and the U.S. representative of the Russian Cooperative Unions. Although Heller insisted at the outset that he went only "to get acquainted" and "to get what information he had to give on Russia," the two men soon explored the possibility of working together. Berkenheim insisted to Heller that he was neutral on questions of politics, and that he was committed only to maintaining and serving the network of Russian cooperatives. The two men discussed the differences between their approaches and their contacts. Berkenheim suggested that, since the Martens bureau had contact with large industrial firms, it should concentrate on supplying Russia with items "that would help in industrial development," while the cooperatives should concentrate on agricultural products and agricultural machinery. The two men parted amicably, promising to keep each other informed about Russian conditions.[114]

Nuorteva met with Berkenheim later in the summer and turned the conversation in a more political direction. Berkenheim had just returned from a meeting in Washington with several officials of the Wilson administration and told Nuorteva that he had received permission to dispatch steamers to Petrograd full of merchandise "consigned to cooperative stores on Soviet territory." Nuorteva saw an opportunity to break the blockade. While believing that Berkenheim and the cooperative movement had received this permission "with some more or less tacit understanding that his cooperatives might serve as a wedge between Russian workers and the Soviet government," nevertheless "Soviet Russia has nothing to lose by having the cooperatives send the goods" because once they had arrived it could turn them to its own advantage. To Nuorteva, the possibilities were exciting. Such a shipment could be "the first actual step in breaking the blockade." It could be the "entering wedge" for the Soviet Bureau's own direct shipments. In fact, he argued to Martens and Krasin, "If we only had a few million dollars at our disposal at this moment the best thing we could do would be to buy a shipload of goods, charter an American steamer and challenge the blockade."[115] Although Martens passed on the entire memorandum to Krasin, the suggestions were not pursued.

The lack of positive response by Krasin, Chicherin, and the Bolshevik leadership to many of these suggestions from Martens and Nuorteva illustrates some of the problems plaguing the Martens bureau. Communication with Moscow was extremely irregular and frustrating for all concerned. It was carried out almost entirely by courier. Letters, reports, and even money were conveyed by courier, but on a very irregular and totally unreliable basis.[116] Martens testified that a total of eight different men served as couriers, although he refused to identify them. Only one has been identified from other sources. This man was Jacob Nosovitsky, apparently one of Martens' major couriers and an active member of the Russian Communist Federation in the United States.[117]

Occasionally a courier would be stopped and his materials confiscated, as in the celebrated case of Carl Sandburg. Sandburg carried correspondence and $10,000 in Swedish bank drafts for Santeri Nuorteva, but was detained by the United States Justice Department upon his entry into the United States. Despite inquiries and protests, this money was never recovered by the Bureau.[118]

Most of the surviving correspondence was from the Martens bureau to Krasin and Chicherin, with few responses from the Bolshevik leadership extant. In his letters, Martens frequently complained about this situation. In one letter of July 1919, he noted repeatedly that he had received no instructions or communications from Moscow. "We have written you many times, but have received from you not one word," he wrote.[119] When Krasin, Litvinov, or Chicherin did respond, it was often long delayed and sometimes long out of date and irrelevant to Martens' current situation.[120]

Early in 1920, when Litvinov resided in Copenhagen and Krasin and Kamenev arrived in London to negotiate a trade agreement with Britain, the courier system was supplemented by direct mail. Even after Krasin and Kamenev were readily available by post, they did not correspond frequently with Martens. A Krasin missive of August 26, 1920, was so happily received by Martens that he wrote responses on September 3, September 14, and September 23—without receiving anything further in response.[121]

Chicherin, seeing the opportunity the London office provided, encouraged Krasin and Kamenev to correspond more frequently with Martens, in part to keep him fully informed of Soviet developments. Chicherin cabled Kamenev in August 1920, "How is it that having the opportunity of telegraphing America, we avail ourselves so little of it for sending information to Martens? He is editing a splendid special edition [publication] devoted to Soviet Russia and is obliged to pick up crumbs from the bourgeois press. Is it not possible to send him once or twice weekly information by telegraph . . . ?"[122]

In addition to the frustration of indirect communication, there is evidence that Krasin in particular, and sometimes Chicherin and Litvinov, disagreed with Martens' approach. Krasin questioned several of the tentative contracts signed by Martens with American firms, requesting sharply that he not commit the Bolshevik government to *anything* until the blockade was lifted. Krasin also disagreed with Nuorteva's suggestion that the Bureau cooperate in any way with Berkenheim and the New York office of Tsentrosoyuz.[123] Litvinov complained that Martens, while doing a good job, had poor political judgement and was constantly misleading the Bolshevik leadership about the possibilities of imminent and widespread trade with the United States, and of diplomatic recognition as well.[124]

Martens and Chicherin agreed on the reason for Martens' appointment as Soviet representative, however. In perhaps the clearest exchange between the two men, Martens wrote to Chicherin in August 1919 that the Foreign Commissariat's letter of the past April did not come as a surprise to him: "We well understand the tactics which we all the time have been pursuing with respect to the U.S.—namely, in all matters that the U.S. remains the capitalist country in which there is hope for breaking through the blockade."[125]

Once Krasin was in London, he began his own direct contacts with representatives of American firms, preferring to control things directly as Foreign Trade Commissar. This further complicated things for Martens. In the summer of 1920, Krasin had a long meeting with a representative of the U.S. Chamber of Commerce on the possibilities of Soviet-American trade.[126] He also held a long discussion with the director of the Standard Oil Company, who was interested in a contract for fuel oil and petrol for steamers in the Black Sea. Krasin promised oil products if Standard could persuade the American government to abstain from helping the Poles in the Soviet-Polish war and would allow the export of locomotives and other railroad equipment desperately needed by the Soviets.[127] A contract for the locomotives and other equipment was signed with the American Corporation in June and approved personally by Lenin. Lenin stipulated a number of detailed changes, particularly commission charges and a requirement for the exchange of goods at the port of Petrograd.[128]

Despite Krasin's and Litvinov's reservations about Martens, Lenin never wavered in his support for his American representative's strategy for pursuit of an economic and political understanding with the United States. Although there is no record of any Martens–Lenin correspondence during the time Martens was in the United States, Lenin's public statements during this period and his comments to Krasin, Litvinov, and Chicherin continued to support Martens' approach.[129]

Once Martens was forced to return to Moscow following his threatened deportation early in 1921, many of his proposals, particularly in the technical and engineering field, were followed up personally by Lenin. In February 1921, soon after Martens returned to Moscow, Lenin wrote a letter to assist Martens in carrying through with his proposals for technical and scientific assistance from the United States. Martens was put in charge of a project placing and assisting American workers who had returned to Russia. Lenin's letter asked that a tour of plants and factories be arranged for Martens and some of the American workers, and emphasized that "great care must be taken."[130]

Lenin continued his interest and support for the American workers in Russia through two letters to Martens of June 21 and June 27, 1921. On June 21, he explained to Martens that the details on the American workers needed to be sent through the Council of Labor and Defense and that he would support a major proposal if the United States could provide food supplies, clothing, and implements of labor for two years. He then gave advice to Martens about the drafting of his resolution, and said that he would "support the project in every way."[131]

In his June 27 letter, Lenin detailed his ideas for the organization of a garment factory staffed by American workers. He emphasized in his letter the need to "eliminate all red tape in obtaining all the necessary materials. . . . Please help the group of workers to obtain housing. . . . The factory must be built and run within the shortest possible time. The carelessness and red tape in this whole business is outrageous."[132] In 1922, Lenin, at Martens' insistence, wrote an effusive letter of thanks to Martens' creation, the Society for Technical Aid for Soviet Russia. In this letter he thanked them for the work of their members at state farms, industrial enterprises, and mines.[133] Martens also put Lenin in touch with American electrical engineer Charles Steinmetz, whom Lenin corresponded with concerning his dream for the electrification of Soviet Russia.[134]

Martens later recollected his long meeting with Lenin on his return from the United States. He wrote: "Lenin asked a great many questions during our talk. He had a wonderful way of asking questions and was just as skilled a listener." Martens said that Lenin asked many questions about the labor movement in the United States, about the possibilities of economic and technical assistance from the United States, and about other projects Martens had worked on during his years as Soviet representative. Lenin also expressed his full backing for Martens' goal of establishing full trade relations with the United States.[135]

With the exception of his letters to the State Department sending his credentials and announcing his existence and his occasional public speeches, Ludwig Martens stayed quite clear of political and diplomatic discussions. He left this part of the work of the Bureau almost exclusively in Nuorteva's hands. Even in his long letters to Chicherin, Martens spent the bulk of his time discussing the details of his economic, commercial, and technical plans and accomplishments, and made only passing references to political matters. He preferred to enclose memos from Nuorteva dealing with politics.[136]

In retrospect this was an excellent decision on Martens' part. By all accounts, Nuorteva was a shrewd, skilled, and sophisticated political and diplomatic strategist, knowledgeable about American politics and fully conversant with the details of Soviet Russia's situation. Tributes to Nuorteva's political skills have been recorded by two of his opponents, State Department Russia experts Samuel N. Harper and Felix Cole. Harper, in a letter to E. C. Porter in May 1919, spoke of Nuorteva as "a man of unusual ability [who] should, in my opinion, be handled very carefully."[137] Cole, in a 1920 letter to new Secretary of State Bainbridge Colby, spoke of Nuorteva as the "brains of Martens office" and "a very able and shrewd man."[138]

In a major speech on June 16, 1919, Nuorteva compared Soviet Russia's position facing hostility and nonrecognition with the young American Republic's facing a skeptical and hostile Europe in the late 1770s. Nuorteva insisted that

> There is nothing unusual . . . about the existence here of an official representative of a Government that has not yet been recognized by your government. When the American republic was established it sent representatives, among others Benjamin Franklin, to France and England to present the cause of the new republic. . . . Every country has the right to establish such institutions within their own confines as they think best. . . . America should be the last one to deny this right to Russia. . . .[139]

Nuorteva used his position as "secretary" of the Bureau and editor of the Bureau's publication, *Soviet Russia,* to serve as perhaps the number-one spokesman on behalf of Soviet Russia in the United States during 1919 and early 1920 when he left for Canada, England, and eventually Russia. Nuorteva began his information and publicity by giving out typewritten statements. In February 1919, he began a printed bulletin, the *Bulletin* of the Soviet Information Bureau. He was editor of the weekly *Soviet Russia,* which began publication in June 1919, and soon developed a circulation of 25,000. The organ became an influential source of information about the Soviet government, and a voice for normalization of relations with the United States.[140]

Nuorteva did not neglect to continue to cultivate the Washington contacts that he had made as director of the Finnish Information Bureau in 1918. After a long trip to Washington in May 1919, he reported to Martens about his various meetings with such individuals as Congressman Stephen Porter of Pittsburgh; Acting Secretary of State Polk; Russian specialist Basil Miles; Eugene Meyer, President of the War Finance Corporation; Clarence Wooley of the War Trade Board, and Justice Louis Brandeis.[141]

Polk was invited to a meeting with Nuorteva by Congressman Porter. Afterward, he complained that he had ended up in the same room with Nuorteva under false pretenses, but he did stay in the meeting. Polk insisted that any decisions concerning a new U.S. Russian policy would be made in Paris. He also admitted, according to Nuorteva, that "the State Department had received a great number of requests from all parts of the country to permit trade with Russia." As for the others Nuorteva met with, they were "sympathetic . . . but still hoping for some kind of liberal solution." Nuorteva believed they were essentially waiting to see what happened to Kolchak.[142]

Nuorteva took another trip to Washington in late July, visiting with several senators, including Henry Cabot Lodge, Chairman of the Foreign Relations Committee. Nuorteva reported in this instance that, although ignorance concerning Soviet Russia was still widespread, the "absolute hostility of previous months was considerably changed." Nuorteva spent most of his time talking with Lodge about the debt question, and impressed on him that it could not be settled except through negotiation, which would require at least implicit recognition of Soviet authorities.[143]

Nuorteva went on in this same report to give Martens a long analysis of the political standing of Soviet Russia in the United States, concentrating on the key question of the lifting of the blockade. Nuorteva cited the success of the Red Army against Kolchak as having influenced the American public, noting that conservative newspapers, such as the *Springfield Republican,* the *Chicago Daily News,* and the *Philadelphia Ledger,* "repeatedly point out the futility of counterrevolutionary attempts in Russia and the necessity of dealing with Russia as she actually is." Nuorteva also took issue with Maksim Litvinov's observation that the United States "had identified herself with all the moves of the imperialists against Soviet Russia."[144] While agreeing with the substance of Litvinov's remark, Nuorteva insisted that "American representatives still retain an attitude of reluctance." Nuorteva pointed out that "the paramount demand of the lifting of the blockade against Russia has been supported by the American delegates at Paris."[145]

Even Secretary Lansing had come around to the opinion that the blockade should be abandoned. Nuorteva cited a conversation that William C.

Pettit, Bullitt's attaché, had with Lansing in which Lansing said that "the best thing that could be done in respect to Russia would be to let goods enter Petrograd."[146]

Nuorteva also used the argument that the blockade was breaking down, as goods were reaching Russia from Germany, Poland, Estonia, and Finland. Moreover, Norwegian, Danish, and Swedish firms were preparing to send ships to Petrograd. All this, he argued, tended to put pressure on British and American merchants to demand that the blockade be lifted.[147] On the other hand, the opposition to the Versailles peace treaty, in Nuorteva's view, could have a negative effect on efforts to lift the blockade. If it were not ratified by the United States Senate, he predicted, "war measures including the necessity of obtaining licenses for export will remain and may be utilized in maintaining the Russian blockade."[148]

Nuorteva also undertook in this same extensive political report to propose a novel solution to the sticky problem of Russia's foreign debt. He referred to Litvinov's rather offhand suggestion that the Soviet government would be willing to grant American concessions up to the amount of the Russian foreign debt. Nuorteva seized on this idea, and said that if this suggestion were publicized, it could also be advantageous to the United States, as its indebtedness to Allied countries "could be liquidated by cancelling their indebtedness to America." Nuorteva urged that this proposition be taken with absolute seriousness, arguing that "it will create quite a sensation if it were made known here."[149]

Toward the end of 1919, Nuorteva took the lead in early negotiations concerning food and medical supplies to Soviet Russia, which various American relief organizations, led by the Quakers, were proposing. Nuorteva received assurances from several shipping companies that they would take the risk of setting out toward the Baltic with supplies only if they were paid in advance for the shipping costs. Lacking cash reserves, Nuorteva proposed to the Bolshevik government that the Quakers provide them, but nothing immediately resulted from these discussions.[150]

The final diplomatic task entrusted to Nuorteva was to follow up on overtures Martens had made to the Canadian government to open a Soviet-Canadian trade bureau. Martens had taken this initiative to expand Canadian-Soviet trade (since Canada dropped all restrictions on trade at the time of the lifting of the Allied blockade), and, perhaps more important, to serve as another political wedge in the multifaceted strategy to put pressure on the U.S. government. Martens had received a letter from George Foster, of the Department of Trade and Commerce of Canada, in May 1920, informing him that there was no legal reason why Soviet Russia could not purchase Canadian goods and have them shipped to Russia.[151] Martens raised the possibility of using the Canadian opening as a way of breaking through to the United States in a letter to Krasin of June 21, and sent Nuorteva to Ottawa to explore it.[152]

John Cooper, Director of the Bureau of Information of Canada, followed up George Foster's letter and specifically invited Martens to open a commercial bureau in Ottawa. He did advise Martens, however, that the question of a general office with an official representative "should not be raised at the present moment."[153] Questions were raised in Parliament about Nuorteva's presence, and opposition to Canadian-Soviet trade seemed to make it necessary to assume a lower profile.[154]

Nuorteva left Canada for England, where he intended to work for Krasin at the Soviet trade delegation office. Nuorteva and Krasin did not get along, however, and Scotland Yard soon arrested Nuorteva on grounds of domestic subversion, demanding his deportation. He arrived in Russia in August 1920 and was given a post in the Commissariat for Foreign Affairs dealing with English-speaking countries.[155]

Meanwhile, Martens wrote another letter to Krasin advising him of the letter from Cooper and relating a conversation he had had with the Canadian firm of Boyer and Sloan that gave the same message. Martens again asked Krasin for Soviet authorization to open a Canadian bureau.[156]

Krasin apparently responded to Martens, and not positively, even though we have no record of his letter or cable. Martens sent a series of cables to Krasin in London on August 30, September 3, September 14, and September 23, attempting to answer his objections. On August 30 he related an offer of a $2 million shipment of important milling machines financed and backed by the Canadian government to be ready at Reval in two weeks' time.[157] In his September 3 telegram, Martens took pains to assure Krasin that he understood the Soviet financial situation, in the face of what seemed to be Krasin's criticism that Martens placed too high a priority on the American market. Martens argued with Krasin that the Canadian bureau was important not only to open up Canada but because of the United States. Martens made almost the same argument in his cable of September 14.[158] The stress Martens gave this argument appears to reflect Krasin's commitment to Germany and Britain as the primary Soviet trading partners. In addition, it should be remembered that Krasin twice tried to get into the United States as part of Tsentrosoyuz delegations and was twice turned down by U.S. officials.[159]

On September 23, Martens was forced to write Krasin once again, this time to deny an article in the *Montreal Gazette* about the imminent opening of a Soviet commercial bureau in Canada. This article was apparently stimulated by the presence of Nuorteva in Ottawa and Montreal. Martens apologized, and concluded that the decision on the Canadian bureau rested with Krasin. He would await this decision. The go-ahead was never given, and over the next few months Martens was forced to make preparations for his departure from the United States, which came early in 1921.[160]

The chief charge against Martens and the Soviet Bureau used by his critics and the committees investigating him was that of "Bolshevik propaganda," the planning and fomenting of communist revolution in the United States. Although I will give major consideration to the investigations related to Martens in Chapter 11, it is worth examining the question of propaganda at this time. Both the Lusk Committee and the Moses Committee (U.S. Senate Foreign Relations Subcommittee) accused Martens and his bureau of improper political propaganda, primarily through their acceptance of invitations to speak before socialist bodies and other groups in the United States. Although the two committees, in their detailed questioning of Martens and their entry into the record of correspondence and the texts of speeches, tried to show Martens as intent on fomenting a Bolshevik revolution in the United States, they fell far short of that aim. They certainly showed substantial contact between socialist organizations and Martens, yet most of the speeches and correspondence simply showed what Martens openly avowed: the wish of the Soviet Bureau to open up trade and diplomatic relations with the United States.[161]

In most cases, in fact, Martens' speeches specifically disavowed any intent to interfere with domestic American politics. Martens' speech at Madison Square Garden on June 18, 1919, is a good example. This speech occurred immediately after the raid of the agents of the Lusk Committee on his office, and many of his files were confiscated. But he insisted in the speech that he was only interested in establishing good relations between Soviet Russia and the United States and that he did not want "in any way to interfere in the internal affairs" of the United States.[162]

Martens and Nuorteva also were careful to keep *Soviet Russia* from engaging in propaganda or support for Communist activities in the United States. The editorials of *Soviet Russia* constantly insisted that the "only aim of this publication is to do away with such prejudice which stands in the way of the establishment of relations between Soviet Russia and the United States."[163]

After first trying to insist that Martens' speeches themselves interfered in American affairs, both the Lusk Committee and the Moses Committee shifted ground and accused Martens of associating with organizations that advocated the downfall of the United States government. The committees cited speeches of others at rallies where Martens was present or referred to the avowed intent of organizations that corresponded with Martens. Martens' defense of this was clear and simple. He reiterated that he was not to be held responsible for what others said but rather for what *he* said and did, stating, "all I did was to associate with those people who were expressing sympathy toward Russia."[164]

Martens pointed out that he and his associates gladly accepted speaking engagements from any organization that wished to hear them, and that in addition to socialist organizations, they had spoken before the League of Free Nations Association, the American Academy of Political and Social Science, the Knit Goods Manufacturers Association, several church forums, the *Dial* forum, and a number of open community forums.[165] Martens also argued that letters to him from Chicherin had specifically instructed him that funds for the operation of the Soviet Bureau were not to be used for any purpose involving interference in the internal affairs of the United States.[166]

The best evidence of Martens' studious refusal to engage in activities in support of Socialist or Communist Party work in the United States comes from the various contacts he had with Socialist factions and groups in the United States and their frustration with Martens for his insistence on sticking narrowly to his work of promoting the cause of Soviet Russia and Soviet-American relations. In one letter to Cleveland Socialists, Nuorteva refused to get drawn into disputes between factions of the party, saying, "I am interested in presenting the case of the Russian Soviets and in nothing else."[167] In a speech before the Detroit convention of the Russian Communist Federation, Martens pointedly emphasized his responsibility to Soviet Russia and his refusal to subject his activities to their control. He even gave the Federation a lecture on the necessity for their movement to "develop in accordance with the will of the American workers themselves."[168] Three old Russian New York Socialists, interviewed in the 1970s by Soviet journalist Andronov, remembered Martens as "handsome, highly educated, unaffected," and absolutely unwilling to become involved in the Russian Federation's political fights.[169]

The Russian Federation did its best to bring Martens and his associates under its control. Nicholas Hourwich of *Novy Mir* instructed Martens that "the center of his attention, the compass directing his activity here into proper channels, should serve the interests of the revolutionary Socialist movement of the American proletariat . . . the left or Bolshevik wing of the American Socialist Party."[170] But Martens refused to take orders from the Russian Federation or Hourwich. Eventually Martens procured a letter from the Communist International, ruling that his office was not to be controlled by, or subordinate to, any "local organizations," but was to take orders only from Moscow.[171] Hourwich, furious that Martens refused to become involved in the organizing struggles of the American left wing, initiated a campaign for the recall of Martens, denouncing him as "counter revolutionary" and "bourgeois." Martens, in a public response to the campaign, simply reiterated that he had "nothing to do with any political party in the United States and cannot be expected to take sides."[172]

Perhaps symbolic of this campaign and of the inability of the left wing to understand and support Martens' mission was another curious incident. Nuorteva had given the English translation of the pamphlet "One Year of Proletarian Dictatorship," a tract describing the accomplishments of Soviet Russia, to the publishing committee of the left wing of the Socialist Party. After more than three months' delay, he had to ask for it back because they were so reluctant to publish it.[173]

All of the above factors made it hard for both the Lusk and the Moses committees to prove their case that Martens was centrally involved in a conspiracy to promote a communist revolution in the United States. The Lusk Committee admitted Martens' difficulties with the Russian Federation and even noted that Martens' "activities in this country have been carried on with great skill and judgment," and that it was "necessary for him to appear to be conducting his propaganda and regulating his conduct in accordance with the laws of this land."[174]

Even such an observer as Samuel N. Harper, in a letter to J. Edgar Hoover of the fledgling Federal Bureau of Investigation, was forced to conclude that Martens might well be carrying out Soviet policy *against* overt attempts to encourage revolution. Harper wrote that it might be Lenin's policy to

> cut out Bolshevik propaganda in America, in order not to arouse suspicion of business men with whom they wish to enter into business. Lenin is a great

tactician, one of the cleverest in operation today. If he can get American manufactured goods, and American capital and enterprises, he can hold on in Russia, he will therefore sacrifice his principles for the moment, and in line with this tactic might very possibly have instructed Martens to work against active Bolshevik propaganda in the United States. . . .[175]

The various Bolshevik efforts to establish serious economic relations with the United States in 1919 and 1920, led by the Martens mission, have often been obscured by the Red Scare and the political climate of this period. This is unfortunate, because the careful and persistent contacts and negotiations Martens, Heller, and Nuorteva conducted with a wide range of American businesses did much to allay the suspicions of at least a sector of American capitalism. They also did much to lay the groundwork for the breakthroughs in Soviet-American trade under the New Economic Policy of the Soviet government.

These discussions also continued the story of the efforts begun by Raymond Robins and William C. Huntington in 1918. Soviets and Americans insisted on pursuing discussions on the spot, whether in Moscow or New York, that put into practical form their belief that a working relationship must be developed between the two countries, regardless of the formal policies of either of their governments.

# 12

# The United States Responds: Red Scare and Definitive Policy, 1919–1920

Speaking of Bolshevism, the President said, "No, I am not afraid of Bolshevism in America. It makes no appeal to the educated man. . . . Russia should be left to settle her own affairs in her own way as long as she does not become a menace to others."
—*Woodrow Wilson, December 1918*[1]

In reply to your letter of October 20, 1919, concerning the so-called blockade of Petrograd, I beg to inform you that, so far as the United States is concerned, no blockade exists. It is the present policy of this Government, however, to refuse export licenses for shipments to Russian territory under Bolshevik control and to refuse clearance papers to American vessels seeking to depart for Petrograd, the only remaining Bolshevik port.
—*State Department Counselor Frank Polk, November 1919*[2]

It is not possible for the Government of the United States to recognize the present rulers of Russia as a government with which the relations common to friendly governments can be maintained. . . . the existing regime in Russia is based upon the negation of every principle of honor and good faith and every usage and convention underlying the whole structure of international law, the negation, in short, of every principle upon which it is possible to base harmonious and trustful relations, either of nations or individuals. . . . We cannot recognize, hold official relations with, or give friendly reception to the agents of a government which is determined and bound to conspire against our institutions. . . .
—*Secretary of State Bainbridge Colby, August 1920*[3]

The Bolshevik economic initiatives of 1919 and 1920, despite initial receptivity by American businesses, met increasing hostility and a worsening political and economic climate in the United States. The United States' response to Martens and his mission became caught up in the anti-radical hysteria that became known as the Red Scare. The Bolsheviks' efforts to trade with the United States were continually stymied by the refusal of the United States government to lift the economic restrictions on such trade, even after the Allies had officially lifted the blockade imposed during the war. The Red Scare poisoned the political climate, and several government investigations launched as a part of it included serious harassment of the Martens bureau, leading eventually to a deportation order against Martens at the very end of 1920 and his departure from the United States early in 1921.[4]

Definitive U.S. government response took some time to develop, in part because of differences of opinion about how to respond and in part because of both the personal ambivalence of Woodrow Wilson and then his collapse in the fall of 1919. It was not until Wilson's close friend Bainbridge Colby took over as Secretary of State in the spring of 1920 that consideration of a specific and detailed policy statement against the Bolsheviks received attention in the State Department. The final statement, known as the Colby note, skillfully utilized public fear of Bolshevism in the United States to condemn Bolshevism in Russia in such an unqualified manner that it served as a policy statement of both non-recognition and non-intercourse for three successive Republican administrations in the 1920s.

## The Developing Red Scare

Public concern and excitement about Bolshevism in the United States was given a substantial boost by the Bolshevik Propaganda Hearings conducted by a subcommittee of the Committee on the Judiciary of the United States Senate, chaired by Senator Lee Overman of North Carolina, from February 11 to March 10, 1919.[5] The Overman Committee, as it came to be called, consisted of Overman, and Senators William H. King of Utah, Josiah Wolcott of Delaware, Knute Nelson of Minnesota, and Thomas Sterling of South Dakota. The committee was originally convened in late 1918 to explore pro-German propaganda and activities of the United States Brewers Association. The Senate, through Senate Resolution 439 on February 4, extended its authority "to inquire concerning any efforts being made to propagate in this country the principles of any party exercising or claiming to exercise authority in Russia . . . and further, to inquire into any effort to incite the overthrow of the Government of this country or all government by force. . . ."[6]

Reputed links between pro-German propaganda and Bolshevik propaganda had been made by the U.S. government and those hostile to the Bolsheviks almost from the first days following the Bolshevik revolution. The publication of the Sisson documents by the Wilson administration in September 1918, purporting to prove a German-Bolshevik conspiracy, was perhaps only the most celebrated of such efforts to that time.

Senator Hiram Johnson, progressive Republican from California, had questioned the Administration's Russian policy and introduced a Senate resolution that called for the withdrawal of American troops in December 1918. In the furor over that debate, Johnson was called both Bolshevik and pro-German. In a letter to his daughter in January 1919, Johnson complained about this linkage and noted that "our President thought it essential to twist to his own purposes the Bolshevik shibboleth . . . the Wilsonian mode of government . . . is suppression, repression, and oppression; to stifle any criticism; to denounce as pro-German and disloyal any individual who makes a legitimate, embarrassing inquiry."[7]

The Overman Committee made its case for the connection by citing testimony given in its hearings on the German brewing industry by Thomas J. Tunney, police inspector from New York City; and Archibald Stevenson, New York State Attorney General. Tunney and Stevenson linked their investigation of Emma Goldman, Alexander Berkman, and other Socialists who opposed U.S. involvement in World War I with the Bolshevik calls for peace and revolution.[8]

The Overman Committee then proceeded to call a succession of witnesses drawn from the anti-Bolshevik Russian community and government experts on Bolshevik Russia, including William Chapin Huntington; Samuel N. Harper; Methodist missionary George A. Simons; Louis Marshall, president of the American Jewish Committee; and others. Their testimony painted a bleak picture of Bolshevik Russia and tried to tie Bolshevik proclamations on world revolution to domestic unrest in the United States, and to firmly cement the link to Germany.[9]

The Committee asked President Wilson if it could have access to all the consular records of the State Department bearing on the Bolsheviks. He reluctantly agreed, but said that there was little in them of any use to the committee, since it was his understanding that they were investigating Bolshevik propaganda in the United States, not abroad. Wilson also cautioned the committee not to receive hearsay testimony, but this piece of advice fell on deaf ears.[10]

No consular records were included in the published record of the Committee Hearings, and no senior State Department or White House officials testified. Instead, the Committee developed its case with the aid of former United States representatives in Russia: William C. Huntington, Samuel N. Harper, and former ambassador David Francis. Harper was asked to bring with him "full Russian Bolshevik and radical data."[11]

In his testimony Harper tried to develop his own background and the background of the Russian revolution, including knowledge gained from his own experiences in the period of time before the Bolsheviks came into power. The Committee, however, kept pushing him to comment on the situation in the United States. This frustrated Harper. Asked to discuss Bolshevism in the United States, Harper compared it to Bolshevism in Russia before November 1917 and said there was "confusion of mind about how to solve many problems." He also refused to be led into a statement on Bolshevik propaganda in the United States, insisting that he had "not heard any preaching of the doctrine of the Bolsheviki, the overthrow of the Government in America."[12] The Committee also tried to get Harper to link all the radical groups in the United States to the Bolsheviks because they all used the red flag. He refused to be drawn into the generalization, insisting that they were different and that "many men are socialists who are not Bolsheviki."[13]

Senator Nelson tried his best to get Huntington to admit that the Bolsheviks' aim was "to help Germany and Austria win the fight," but Huntington insisted that the Bolsheviks were "a group of fanatics who have their own game to play." Huntington did develop evidence about the Red Terror for the Committee, but he followed Harper in refusing to link all American radicals directly to the Bolsheviks.[14]

Only the Russian émigrés were willing to make statements directly linking American radicals to Russian Bolsheviks or to agree with the Committee's prompting. Halfway through the Committee's hearings, very little direct evidence of Bolshevik control of radical activities in the United States had been heard. Several witnesses, most notably Roger E. Simmons, formerly of the Commerce Department staff in Russia, and William E. Welsh of the Petrograd staff of the National City Bank of New York, accused other Americans who had been in Russia, such as Albert Rhys Williams, John Reed, and Raymond Robins, of conducting Bolshevik propaganda in the United States.[15]

These charges, as well as the concern of the Wilson administration and liberals in Congress that the Committee was engaged in judgement based on hearsay, caused Overman and his committee to devote the last several weeks of the hearings to testimony from a number of prominent American radicals who had been in Russia under the Bolsheviks. These included Albert Rhys Williams, Louise Bryant, John Reed, correspondent Bessie Beatty, Quaker relief worker Frank Keddie, and Raymond Robins.[16] Senator Hiram Johnson had personally talked at length with Overman and other senators in an attempt to get Robins, in particular, heard by the Committee.[17] Johnson also helped in the effort to persuade the committee to call Quaker Frank Keddie.[18]

From the Overman Committee's stated interest in developing the details of Bolshevik propaganda in the United States and in convincing the American people not only of the threat from Bolshevism but of its perfidy toward the United States, the move to call radicals who had been in Bolshevik Russia was a mixed blessing. Albert Rhys Williams proudly told of his role in the early Bolshevik Bureau of Revolutionary Propaganda. John Reed was happy to discuss the allocation of two million rubles to "the international revolutionary movement." But the radicals provided remarkably little information about any "German-Bolshevik conspiracy" and almost nothing in the way of detailed strategy for undermining the government of the United States.[19] Williams and Keddie even confidently asserted that the Soviet government should be not called a "Bolshevik government" at all, but one of "soviets," a grassroots democratic movement. And Williams, on the basis of his own experience in the Bureau of Revolutionary Propaganda, insisted that very little attempt had been made to influence the radical movement in the United States because of the strong conviction that the revolution would occur first in Western Europe.[20]

But most problematic of all from the Committee's standpoint was the testimony of Raymond Robins. Robins denounced Bolshevism as a menace to the world and insisted he would fight it in the United States. But he eloquently defended his own efforts to establish contact with the Bolsheviks and gave a ringing defense of the proper way to oppose Bolshevik philosophy:

> I think that if we answer to whatever there is of economic wrong in our own situation . . . we can meet and answer the agitation and unrest. . . . I would never expect, sirs, to suppress the desire for a better human life . . . no matter how ill founded in political fact and experience, with force. The only answer for the desire for a better human life is a better human life.[21]

Despite the paucity of evidence linking the Bolshevik leadership with radical activities in the United States, the sensational testimony of Reed, Bryant, Williams, Robins, and others added fuel to the growing belief in the American society that a Bolshevik threat existed within its own borders. This was especially true since the hearings coincided perfectly with the first meeting of the Comintern, a short-lived Soviet revolution in Bavaria, and the triumph of Bolsheviks in Hungary.[22]

As for Raymond Robins, he left the Committee a famous man, but with equal parts of American public opinion arrayed firmly for and against him. On one hand, he received a tremendous flood of requests for speaking engagements from all across the country, and took the opportunity of his Senate testimony to end his self-imposed public silence on the question of American policy toward Russia.[23] He gave a number of speeches and also wrote up his account of his time in Russia, explaining where American policy went wrong, in a series of articles in the *Metropolitan Magazine* (June–October 1919) and an abridged version in the *Chicago Daily News,* April 1919.[24] Robins also was active early in 1919 assisting other early victims of the developing Red Scare. He gave a long deposition in April in the trial of a public school teacher in New York City accused of subversion.[25]

But Robins' enemies were also at work, and he became an early target of those determined to expose Bolshevism in the United States. After a speech he gave in New York in early March, the New York Police Department contacted the American Red Cross asking for background information on Robins. Not only did the Red Cross provide it, but it contacted the Military Intelligence Division of the War Department and requested that it begin surveillance of Robins and his activities.[26]

The State Department also got into the act, soliciting information from those who had known Robins concerning his activities in Russia. Harris, United States Consul in Irkutsk, replied on March 29, stating that Robins "deliberately misstated the facts concerning Russia at that time, and he has been doing it ever since. . . . In my judgement Robbins [*sic*] is the type of man who would play the role of a Lenin or Trotsky in America if conditions were favorable."[27] Samuel Harper and William C. Huntington were pressed into service to respond to those who were swayed by Robins' appeals, pointing out the danger in Robins' statements and approach. In one letter to

Harper, the writer confessed that Robins "quite persuaded me that the allies were fools not to recognize that the Bolsheviki were in the saddle and that they should be negotiated with with the purpose of inducing them to do as much harm to Germany as possible." He then appealed to Harper to "set [the writer] straight."[28]

The President of the Privy Council of Ottawa, Canada, consulted Huntington about Robins after he was under pressure from his colleagues to invite Robins to a major civic event to present his ideas on Russia. Huntington cautioned that Robins was "too close" to the Bolshevik leaders to have the proper perspective and that the Bolsheviks "captivated him." He also expressed the concern that "three out of four of Mr. Robins' statements were interesting and pretty well true, but the fourth one [was] absolutely inaccurate."[29]

Robins was the subject of investigations by both the Military Intelligence Division and the Federal Bureau of Investigation of the Justice Department. By the spring of 1920, he despaired at changing the Administration's Russian policy and gradually abandoned his public appearances. Instead, he reentered Republican politics, working to try to secure the Republican 1920 Presidential nomination for Senator Hiram Johnson. When Warren G. Harding was nominated instead, Robins attempted to get a pledge from him to change U.S. policy toward Russia under a new administration. Robins thought he had a pledge, but Harding later backed away, deferring to his Secretary of State, Charles Evans Hughes.[30]

The conclusion of the hearings of the Overman Committee in March 1919 coincided with a series of events, including the opening of the Martens bureau, the meeting of the Comintern in Moscow, and the huge Seattle general strike, which heightened American concerns about Bolshevism and revolution in society. The resulting public hysteria, harassment of all manner of radicals and social reformers, government surveillance and investigations, the passage of legislation curbing civil liberties, and the mass arrests and eventual deportations of Russians in the United States have become known as the Red Scare. It is not possible in the context of this study to fully detail the background, causes, or consequences of the many interacting forces making up this social phenomenon. This chapter will instead attempt to highlight those events with particular bearing on the course of Bolshevik-American interaction in 1919 and 1920, and seek to determine in what ways the Red Scare affected key people active in the struggle for a Bolshevik-American working relationship.[31]

Robert K. Murray has identified a number of factors that came together to prepare the ground for the Red Scare in postwar American society. The first was the economic situation of returning G.I.'s, the peacetime reconversion, the lifting of wartime controls, and spiraling inflation. This was exacerbated by a proliferation of labor unrest, including some of the biggest industrial actions and general strikes in United States history, coupled with intransigent industrial leadership determined to return to the prewar status quo.[32]

A second basic reason why the Red Scare took hold easily, in Murray's view, has to do with American disillusionment with Progressivism and reform in the wake of Woodrow Wilson's World War I crusade. In addition, the war had firmly established the principle of absolute loyalty and equated dissent with treason. This made it easy to shift from demanding loyalty against German subversion to loyalty against Bolshevism.[33]

Finally, the staying power of the Bolshevik revolution increasingly gave heart to disparate groups of American radicals and socialists, who heightened their calls for major change in American society, using the opportunities provided by the spreading strikes. Theodore Draper, in commenting on the apparent disparity between the low organizing ebb of the American Communists at the beginning of 1919 and their excitement and optimism, gave most of the credit to the continued survival of the Bolshevik revolution: "By all normal standards, the syndicalists and Socialists of the Left Wing should have been shrouded in gloom at the end of the war. Yet the reverse was true. The Left Wing was filled with boundless hopes and intoxicating dreams. The revolution was never closer, never more inevitable. For all this, the Bolshevik revolution was responsible."[34]

## Discrediting Martens and the Russian Soviet Bureau

Ludwig C. A. K. Martens and the Soviet Russian Bureau became publicly known when Martens officially opened his offices in New York City and sent his credentials to the State Department on March 19, 1919.[35] Although the State Department refused to respond or acknowledge Martens and studiously ignored him publicly, it took him very seriously and set in motion a process designed to investigate, expose, and either jail or deport him. Assistant Secretary of State Philips, in a cable to Lansing enclosing Martens' memorandum and credentials, asked for advice on how best to proceed. He told Lansing that the State Department was initiating inquiries about Martens' activities and background because his communication put in sharp relief

> the question of the attitude which this Government should assume towards a regime whose constitution . . . stipulates, that among its fundamental tasks are the securing of the victory of socialism in this country, the abolition of private property, the repudiation of foreign obligations, and the complete elimination of whole classes from all share in Government.[36]

In the meantime, E. C. Porter of the American-Russian Chamber of Commerce; William Chapin Huntington, the head of the Russia desk at the Commerce Department; and Russia specialist and State Department consultant Samuel N. Harper were exchanging worried letters and initiating their own inquiries. American businessmen were bombarding them with queries regarding Martens' invitation for trade with U.S. firms. Porter, in answer to Huntington's request for information, responded almost immediately with a letter giving a few details about Martens and cautioning that "the stimulation of business interests in regard to the resumption of trade with Russia, even though it involves some sort of negotiation with the Soviet government is, of course, Bolshevik propaganda." He went on to urge Huntington to watch the situation very closely, "for it might develop into something that would gain a good deal of headway with extremely unfortunate results."[37] Porter then asked Harper to be in touch with his contacts in Washington to see what could be done to derail Martens.[38]

Both Huntington and Harper were immediately in touch with the State Department. Huntington, after detailing the facts as he understood them, warned Phillips that "the favorite thesis of Lenin is the blind selfishness of capitalists, and he seems to know how to utilize it." He then concluded, "You will pardon my vehemence in this matter, but it seems to me highly serious."[39]

Following a second communication from Martens to the State Department on March 31, Harper was confident enough in the response of the Department to write a note to his desk man Allen Carter. In this note Harper reminded Carter that Nuorteva should also be checked: "Trust that Martens will get no answer to his last communication to Department. If he is sent out, Nuorteva must also go, otherwise nothing has been accomplished."[40]

But the New York anti-Bolshevik Russian community was taking no chances. The Committee on Bolshevism of the Union League Club of New York prepared a special report on Martens for Sir William Wiseman, British agent in the United States. This report appealed to Wiseman to convey it in the strongest terms to Colonel House. The Club was afraid that House was succumbing to Bolshevik peace proposals. "The presence in this country of the mission," stated the report, "makes us inquire whether it is possible that the Russian Soviet Republic can have received encouragement with respect to recognition, which has warranted their establishing a bureau here." The Committee on Bolshevism went on to ask the U.S. Government in the strongest terms "to take immediate action to prevent [Martens'] activities."[41]

Martens' move to claim Russian government funds held by Provisional Government Ambassador Bakhmetev created another furor, incensing several prominent members of the New York bar who demanded to know "why it is possible for the representative of a government America is fighting to be free to defend that cause in the States." In response, however, John L. O'Brien, special assistant to the U.S. Attorney General, declined to take any action because "no state of war existed" between the United States and Russia.[42]

The Commerce Department did prevail upon the State Department to issue a statement disclaiming any knowledge of Martens and insisting that "the only Russian representative recognized by the United States is Bakhmeteff." Huntington then issued, in the name of the State Department, a long list of queries for American businessmen who might want to trade with the Soviets, ending with "5) What should be the American business attitude toward the Allied blockade which today forbids in principle free trading with enemies against whom our armies are defending themselves in Russia?" The American-Russian Chamber of Commerce packaged these statements in a flyer, "Russian Warning to American Business Men," and distributed it widely throughout the New

York business community. In this "Russian warning," the Chamber cautioned that the "so-called Soviet Government . . . not only is not representative, but is bitterly hated by the vast majority of the Russian people. . . . It need scarcely be pointed out what the attitude of Russians will be in the future toward parties entering into commercial relations with the criminal plunderers of their land and property."[43]

By June 5, Acting Secretary of State Polk was prepared to give a summary of information and intelligence gathered on Martens in a memo to Lansing and the Peace Commissioners in Paris. Polk asked for authority "to secure deportation of Martens as an undesirable alien and enemy citizen, authority for deportation to include other alien assistants, including Santeri Nuorteva."[44] Polk's memo and request were discussed in the Commission on June 14. Woodrow Wilson expressed his belief that Martens, "though pestiferous, has done nothing so far that we can allege to be illegal." He therefore cautioned against going forward too fast. The Commissioners, after reviewing the evidence, agreed with the President, and instructed Lansing to so instruct Polk.[45]

The State Department, initially dismayed, immediately moved to press its case further with the President, stressing Martens' purported German citizenship. Finally the President relented, stating that "if Martens is a German subject and can be legitimately deported," he would have no objection, but he hoped "the evidence is in fact complete."[46] Basil Miles, head of the State Department's Russia desk, prepared a long memorandum detailing the evidence proving Martens' alien citizenship and the case for his deportation. In this memo, Miles cited a Military Intelligence Division report calling the Martens bureau "the largest and most dangerous propaganda undertaking thus far started by Lenin's party in any country outside of Russia" and called for his arrest, internment, and deportation.[47]

By this time, the most serious effort to expose and undermine Martens' work was fully underway. On June 12, 1919, agents and operatives representing the Joint Legislative Committee Investigating Seditious Activities of the State of New York raided the headquarters of the Russian Soviet Bureau and confiscated great numbers of papers and records. The Lusk Committee, as it came to be called after its chairman, State Senator Clayton Lusk, had come into existence by virtue of a joint resolution in March 1919. This resolution called for an investigation by the State Legislature into subversive activities in the State of New York, "to investigate the scope, tendencies, and ramifications of such seditious activities." The Special Committee was given the power to compel witnesses and the right to employ counsel and other staff. It was also given $30,000 for its work.[48]

The resolution authorizing the creation of the committee specifically referred to the hearings of the Overman Committee and the need to follow up some of the allegations in those hearings. In particular, the Lusk Committee was struck by the evidence before the Overman Committee concerning Russian radicals on the East Side of New York City, and their alleged intimate connections to Trotsky and Lenin.[49]

Other events in January and February in New York City also prepared the groundwork for the creation of the Lusk Committee. A teacher of European history at Commercial High School in Brooklyn, during a discussion of French-Russian relations, was asked by one of his students "whether we were getting the truth about Russia." The teacher, Benjamin Glassberg, said "we probably were not" and read Senator Hiram Johnson's Senate resolution of December 1918 demanding answers from the Wilson administration. Three days later, he was suspended from school without pay, without a hearing, and without any charges pressed against him. The *New York Times* reported his suspension as being accomplished because he had uttered Bolshevik doctrines in the classroom.[50] A few days later, Archibald Stevenson, Secretary of the Union League of New York , testified before the Overman Committee's first hearings, on German brewery propaganda, that he had evidence that the Bolsheviks, on behalf of German interests, were conducting propaganda schools in New York City and were infiltrating the schools with pro-Bolshevik doctrines.[51]

The Lusk Committee conceived of its mandate in the broadest possible terms. After conferences between Senator Lusk and New York Attorney General Charles D. Newton, the Committee decided not to engage its own chief counsel; instead, Newton agreed to serve in this role. Archibald Stevenson of the Union Club was engaged as associate counsel. But Newton's personal involvement brought the entire resources of the Justice Department of the State of New York and its special agents into the service of the Lusk Committee. Newton and Lusk decided to organize a special secret force of agents to collect intelligence, and a staff of translators was employed to facilitate the examination of Russian-language materials. Special agents and the New York City police were used for periodic raids on various organizations under investigation, and public hearings in New York, Buffalo, Utica, and Rochester were held over the course of 1919 and 1920. Although the legislature had only appropriated $30,000 for the functioning of the committee, it somehow managed to utilize several hundred uniformed police in its raids and at various times employed over one thousand investigators and translators.[52]

Lawrence Chamberlin has pointed out that the "methods employed by the Lusk Committee were more extreme than those of any other legislative investigating agency" he was aware of. It made no distinction between legislative investigative functions, the police power of the executive, or the judicial functions of a court.[53] Lusk, in his opening statement at the first of the committee's public hearings, explained the need for the committee to discover the nature and activities of various radicals in their midst. He then indicated further steps the committee was prepared to take:

> If . . . this movement is seditious, if it aims at the unlawful, violent, and forcible overthrow of our institutions, if its purpose is to violently destroy the Constitution . . . then the committee will make such further investigation and take such action, both preventive and constructive as seems necessary for

the protection of our institutions and the persons and property of the citizens of the state.[54]

The Lusk Committee lost no time putting a force of its agents to work gathering intelligence on Martens bureau personnel. A "list of suspects" was developed that named virtually all the major personnel of the bureau, including Martens, Weinstein, Hourwich, Nuorteva, Heller, Clark, Gitlow, John Reed (presumably because of his well-known and short-lived appointment as Soviet Consul), and Carl Sandburg. Noted next to Reed's name on the list was the comment, "covered by the State Police."[55]

The investigation records of the Lusk Committee on the Martens bureau contain reports of agents sent to follow each of the "suspects." These agents reported in sometimes hilarious and ridiculous detail their quarry's daily movements. Receiving particularly heavy attention were Martens, Weinstein, Hourwich, and Charles Recht, Martens' attorney. Very little substantive evidence was developed by these agents, however, as they reported only on movements and meetings and overheard few conversations.[56]

Occasionally, however, the agents of the Committee produced what they claimed to be transcripts of meetings, apparently through overhearing conversations from other offices. One undated memo claims to be the transcript of two conversations between Max Eastman, editor of the *Liberator;* Nicholas Hourwich; Nuorteva; and Martens regarding Industrial Workers of the World activities and plans for organizing a strike in Winnipeg. On close examination of the second of these transcripts, however, the "Ludwig" whom the agents thought to be Martens was in reality Ludwig London of the *Liberator.* Despite the transcripts naming Nuorteva, there was no statement made by him and no evidence that he attended the meeting.[57]

The only evidence in the investigation files purporting to prove the Soviet Russian Bureau's involvement in planning and fomenting radical activities in the United States is another investigative memo—notes on a May meeting involving Eastman, John Reed, Hourwich, Ludwig London, and Samuel Glaser, again at the *Liberator* offices. In this meeting a letter from Eugene Debs of April 1 was read and discussed. A long disputation concerning plans for the strike movement occurred. In response to Reed's question about sufficient finances for the coming year, Eastman responded that large contributions were expected, including one from "the embassy," which was "prepared to contribute a good round sum about the first of July."[58] The financial records of the Martens bureau, seized by the Lusk Committee, showed no such contribution, although many of the transactions of the bureau were made in cash, including payment of salaries to staff.[59]

If the surveillance of the staff of the Martens bureau was singularly unrewarding for the Lusk Committee, the same could not be said for its surprise raid. The June 12 visit to Martens headquarters, the first raid conducted by the Lusk Committee, was carried out by New York State troopers and private agents under authority of a broad search warrant issued by the New York City magistrate. Not only was the office swept clean of all papers, including financial records and diplomatic correspondence, but all staff on the premises, including Martens himself, were taken into custody and escorted under guard to the Committee, then meeting in public session at New York's City Hall. The Committee promptly went into executive session and tried, without a great deal of success, to compel testimony from Martens and Heller, the two senior staff in custody. Heller tried to talk with the committee about his commercial responsibilities, but all the committee was interested in were his connections to the Socialist Party. Martens refused, under a claim of diplomatic immunity, to give testimony, but agreed to return voluntarily to the committee to discuss what he insisted were his open, above-board, public efforts to establish economic and diplomatic ties to the United States on behalf of Soviet Russia.[60]

Martens and his bureau immediately went to court to have the search warrant quashed, on the grounds that it was overly broad. Martens also entered a claim of diplomatic immunity. While this was eventually denied, the Lusk Committee returned a large number of papers to Martens, including his diplomatic file, with the understanding that he would bring such papers with him when he testified before the committee. The Committee then prepared a much more specific subpoena for Martens' testimony, indicating in some detail the papers it required.[61]

The lack of legal authority and hard evidence did not stop Lusk and Stevenson, however, from immediately going public with sweeping charges against the Martens bureau. They garnered sensational headlines with their claims of a Bolshevik conspiracy against American institutions. Citing no specific evidence, they insisted not only that there was an integral link between Martens and American radicals, but that Martens was the "American Lenin." They claimed that funding for all stripes of left-wing socialists came from Moscow and the Comintern through Martens, and that his bureau served as a clearing house for plans for strikes and other efforts to paralyze the government and society of the United States.[62]

Both Martens and the Soviet government reacted immediately to the raid and the charges. Martens protested that the raid and his arrest were an "outrage" and an "insult to the people of Russia," and continued to claim that his activities were legal and protected by his diplomatic immunity.[63] *Soviet Russia* printed an article, "The Lusk-Stevenson 'Investigation' " which responded directly, and with some reserve, to the Committee's charges of subversion and propaganda. This article pointed out again the nature of the bureau's work, and stressed that members of the bureau were happy to associate with any group that desired to understand Soviet Russia and work for better Soviet-American relations. The article also complained that members of the bureau were not allowed to testify in the public sessions of the committee, being heard only in executive session, and so could not counter some of the more outrageous charges Stevenson and Lusk put forward.[64]

One of the few public events sponsored by the Martens bureau, a mass meeting at Madison Square Garden, was organized June 20 to protest the raid and demand U.S. recognition of Soviet Russia. Although nominally under the auspices of the Russian Socialist Federations, all expenses were paid by the Martens bureau, and a full report on the rally was sent by courier to Chicherin.[65]

Soviet Foreign Minister Chicherin issued a formal protest to the State Department on June 24, sent via the United States legation in Stockholm. He reacted "with indignation" to the "surprising and unjustified" arrest and compared the treatment of Martens with what he claimed was the "utmost courtesy" diplomatic and consular personnel of the United States had been treated with in Russia from the time of the Bolshevik revolution up until their departure in August 1918. Chicherin went on to hint that the Soviet government hoped it would not "be compelled reluctantly" to take reprisals against American citizens in Soviet Russia.[66]

This brought an immediate response from Acting Secretary of State Phillips, who cabled Wheeler to "inform proper Swedish authorities" that Martens had not been arrested, nor did the United States "contemplate any action against law abiding Russian citizens in this country." He went on to deny Martens' diplomatic status, however, and to note his German citizenship. Phillips also noted "with grave concern" the reprisal threats, and warned that "such a course . . . would be certain to arouse in the United States an overwhelming public sentiment of indignation against the authorities. . . ."[67]

Chicherin responded some days later in rather mild fashion, noting "with satisfaction" assurances of the American government that Martens had not been arrested and stating that the Soviet government was "glad to be relieved of the necessity of making reprisals." Chicherin took the opportunity, however, to insist that Martens was a Soviet citizen and not German, and, moreover, an officially appointed representative of the Narkomindel in the United States.[68]

Martens wrote to Chicherin in detail about the Lusk Committee activities, not only the raid on the bureau but also the subsequent June 24 raid against the socialist Rand School and follow-up efforts against other radical groups, including the IWW. Martens also explained to Chicherin that counsel to the bureau had inquired of the U.S. Justice Department how it could get a ruling on the question of diplomatic status. According to this report, the Justice Department had advised Martens to do nothing until the Lusk hearings were over, and then to concentrate his attention on the State Department, because no U.S. court would rule in Martens' favor in the absence of some kind of recognition of his status by the Department of State. Martens then appealed to Chicherin for further instructions in dealing with all of these matters, complaining that he had written many letters but had received "not one word" since his credentials.[69]

An intense legal wrangle ensued over the search warrant the Lusk Committee used for the raid on the Martens bureau. Martens initially refused to testify under the order, claiming it was too broadly drawn. Subsequently, the Lusk Committee obtained a subpoena for Martens to appear before the committee and to "produce check books, bank books, books of account, both of [himself] and of the Soviet Bureau . . . and also all documents, letters and other papers sent by you and your Bureau to Soviet Russia, as well as copies of letters, documents, and other papers sent by you and your bureau to Soviet Russia since January 1, 1919."[70]

Martens, under advice of counsel, submitted to the committee all the financial records requested, but refused to provide any of the correspondence between himself, his bureau, and Soviet Russia on the grounds that this correspondence was protected under diplomatic privilege. Only the "State Department of the United States Government," argued Martens, should have jurisdiction over the question of diplomatic privilege. Martens again refused to testify under the order of the subpoena, but he agreed to give testimony to the committee voluntarily.[71]

In his testimony to the Lusk Committee on November 15 and November 26, 1919, Martens was asked very little about the actual activities of his bureau, particularly in the commercial and diplomatic areas. Instead, he was grilled on his own background, his views and knowledge of the Russian Communist Party and the American Communist Party, and his relationships with socialist organizations and his public speeches. He was quizzed in detail also about the personnel of the Bureau and their backgrounds, and the financial records and financial base of the operation, which he freely admitted was financed largely from funds provided by the Soviet Russian government. He also stated that he communicated with his government by courier. He declined, under repeated questioning, to identify any couriers or to divulge anything that passed between him and his government, under a claim of diplomatic immunity, even when he was charged directly with contempt by the Committee and threatened with legal proceedings.[72]

In Santeri Nuorteva's appearance before the Committee on December 12, he was intensively questioned about diplomatic records of the Bureau, which a subsequent search of the offices by Lusk agents had failed to unearth. Nuorteva admitted that he knew where they were, but declined to divulge them. He, too, was declared in contempt.[73]

The Committee then procured "show cause orders" for both Martens and Nuorteva, prior to seeking warrants for their arrest, in order to compel both men to appear again and produce the diplomatic records. When agents of the Committee attempted to serve these orders, they found both Martens and Nuorteva gone from New York City and outside the jurisdiction of the Committee. Neither could be served.[74]

The Lusk Committee eventually wrapped up its work in the spring of 1920 by issuing a massive four-volume report of more than four thousand pages. This report was an unwieldy collection of documents of all kinds, consisting more of appendices and illustrative material than a committee report or extracts from the hearings. Most of the report consisted of reprints of radical newspapers and pamphlets, and translations of Soviet documents. By this means, the committee hoped to persuade the public of the nature of the communist threat and radical subversion in their midst. Most of the committee's alleged links between American radicals, Soviet Russia, and plans to overthrow the government of the United States could not be proven. The coverage of the Martens bureau in the Committee's report was remarkably skimpy, largely ignoring much of the voluminous documentation of its commercial, diplomatic, and educational activities that its agents had seized. Instead, the committee attempted to show the subversive nature of the Martens bureau and its ties to American communists and radicals. The committee conveniently ignored Martens' refusal to become involved in the disputes or planning of the various parties and his insistence on sticking to economic and diplomatic work on behalf of Soviet Russia, even in the face of radical criticism.[75]

## Investigations by Palmer, Hoover, and Harper

In the meantime, the U.S. Justice Department, under pressure from senators, congressmen, public opinion, and the publicity of the Overman and Lusk committee hearings, began to move increasingly in the direction of investigation and harassment of "subversive radicals," especially aliens. Before 1919, Thomas W. Gregory, the U.S. Attorney General, had pursued investigations and prosecutions under the Wartime Espionage Act of 1917 and its companion Sedition Act of 1918, and had jailed many leading socialists and pacifists.[76]

Gregory, however, engaged in a running dialogue with American liberal supporters of the more famous of those indicted or prosecuted, such as the socialists Norman Thomas and Eugene Debs. Woodrow Wilson's own liberalism restrained Gregory from a wholesale assault, especially as the armistice with Germany became an accomplished fact. Indeed, strong campaigns were begun for amnesty for political prisoners who were in U.S. jails as a result of their opposition to the war. Although Wilson and Gregory refused to declare blanket amnesty, feeling it premature, they did take the time to examine a number of cases individually, considering pardons or commutations of sentences.[77]

The year 1919 brought increasing pressure from the Congress on the Justice Department to expand its investigations, surveillance, and prosecutions of alleged subversive radicals. Large public meetings called for a change in United States policy toward the Bolsheviks and stepped-up plans for revolution in the United States. The United States Senate, in a resolution on February 5, demanded that the Attorney General "enforce the laws of the United States" and investigate and prosecute those involved in two large radical Washington gatherings of February 2 and 3. Gregory responded that he had already initiated investigations, that he had "rather full stenographic notes of all that occurred," and that he would "take such action as in [his] judgement was warranted."[78]

This response did not satisfy many of the senators, and helped to stimulate the expansion of the Overman Committee's hearings into an investigation of Bolshevik propaganda, as well as to increase the pressure on the Wilson administration to appoint an Attorney General as Gregory's successor who would investigate and attack subversive radicals.

Wilson's press secretary, Joesph Tumulty, had been recommending as the new Attorney General the dynamic Alien Property Custodian, Pennsylvania lawyer and banker Alexander Mitchell Palmer. Tumulty told Wilson on February 1 that Palmer was "young, militant, progressive and fearless, as shown by recent investigations."[79] Wilson had resisted the appointment, in part because Attorney General Gregory and Colonel E. M. House did not regard Palmer highly and proposed other candidates. Tumulty, supported by some well-placed senators and the Wilson designee for new Democratic National Chairman, Cummings, persisted, however, and pressed his case on Wilson's return to the United States from Paris in late February 1919. Wilson, unaccompanied by House, finally agreed, writing the next day to Gregory that "my mind comes back to Mitchell Palmer . . . on the whole he is my most available man."[80]

Palmer's appointment as Attorney General was sent to the United States Senate on February 27, and he was confirmed with very little difficulty, assuming office in March.[81] At first, Palmer continued Gregory's policies of caution and circumspection in dealing with postwar cases of alleged subversion under the Espionage and Sedition Acts. He continued Gregory's case-by-case amnesty review of individuals imprisoned during the war, but refused to recommend clemency for the most famous of such prisoners, Eugene Debs.[82] He dampened talk of large-scale roundups of subversives, and affirmed one of Gregory's last acts, the cutting of ties between the Justice Department and the semi-vigilante group, the American Protective League. Palmer declared that "espionage conducted by private individuals or organizations is entirely at variance with our theories of government. . . ."[83]

But the pressure on Palmer to abandon his cautious stance and the restrained approach of his predecessor escalated in the spring of 1919. Not only had the Overman Committee concluded its sensational hearings, but the dock workers' strike in Seattle had spread to become a general strike. The mayor of Seattle, Ole Hanson, after the strike had been forcibly suppressed, toured the country explaining how to stop a Bolshevik revolution in other cities.[84]

But the crowning blow, as far as the Attorney General was concerned, was the wave of riots and bombing throughout the United States on May Day, 1919, and again on June 2. The concern over May Day was galvanized by a number of crude bombs that were delivered to the homes of several senators and other public figures active in the crusade against Bolshevism. They were followed by massive radical parades, especially in New York, Cleveland, Chicago, and Detroit, which led to riots and street fights between demonstrators, police, and citizens opposed to the marches. Finally, on June 2, another series of bombings of public figures occurred, including an attack on Palmer and his family. Though no one was hurt, the bomb exploded, causing some damage and certainly shaking Palmer's equilibrium.[85]

Palmer immediately took steps to reorganize the Bureau of Investigation of the Justice Department, appointing Raymond T. Flynn to head it up. Palmer, Flynn, and his assistants Garvan and J. Edgar Hoover, held an all-day conference on June 17, according to the *Washington Post,* to discuss the bombings and plan strategy to deal with subversive radicals in the United States. A few days earlier, Palmer asked Congress for an extra $500,000 to supplement the $1.5 million earlier requested in the Department's budget for investigations and prosecutions under the Espionage and Sedition Acts. By early August, Palmer had further solidified his strategy by setting up a new division within the Bureau, to be called the "general intelligence" or anti-radical division. To this post he appointed the young and dedicated J. Edgar Hoover, and charged him with "the responsibility of gathering and coordinating all information concerning domestic radical activity."[86]

At the same meeting on June 17, Palmer and his colleagues decided on their major strategy for dealing with domestic radicals: mass roundups and deportation of all aliens. This strategy, however, did not result in any public action until November. It took some time for plans to be made and groups and individuals to be identified. In addition, initial discussions with those responsible for Immigration and Deportation at the Labor Department were disappointing to Palmer's colleagues because of the refusal of the Department to cooperate in issuing blanket warrants. This refusal required every case to be substantiated and developed on its merits. Finally, a predicted massive outpouring of radical activity on July 4 never materialized, causing Palmer to question the decision.[87]

Public pressure continued to build for swift and comprehensive action against domestic radicals. With Woodrow Wilson incapacitated by a stroke in the fall of 1919, most of the pressure was directed at Palmer, who also had been approached as a potential Presidential candidate for 1920.[88] After first trying some prosecutions under other authority, he finally resolved that the immigration laws offered the best chance of success, and he procured arrest warrants from the Labor Department for specific members of the Union of Russian Workers whose names had been provided by Justice Department and military intelligence agents. On November 7, 1919, Justice Department agents invaded meetings of the Union in twelve cities, arresting thousands of people, far beyond those named in the warrants.[89]

This was the first of what became known as the Palmer Raids, which included later raids on the Communist Party, the Communist Labor Party, and other radical offices and meeting places, and then a massive nationwide sweep on January 2, 1920. In all of these cases, according to later investigations, civil liberties were violated and families were separated. Prisoners were held incommunicado for long periods and deprived of all rights, subjected at times to police brutality and housed in substandard conditions.[90]

Most of the thousands seized in these roundups were never deported or otherwise prosecuted, because of the nearly total lack of evidence against them. A group of 249, however, was eventually deported purely on the basis of their association with groups alleged to be engaged in activities detrimental to the United States, but mostly because they were Russian. This group of 249 was sent back to Russia via Finland, in a U.S. Army transport vessel, the *Buford*. This took place in December 1919 and was highly publicized, in part because the group included such famous names as Emma Goldman and Alexander Berkman.[91]

Soviet representative Ludwig Martens issued a protest to the State Department, condemning the arrests of Russian citizens, and suggesting that the U.S. government, instead of deporting such persons, "permit the Soviet Government through its representatives in the United States to be allowed to arrange their departure." Martens also attempted on numerous occasions, without success, to be received personally at the State Department to make his protest.[92]

In the meantime, Palmer aide J. Edgar Hoover had established close relationships with Archibald Stevenson of the Lusk Committee, U.S. military intelligence agents, and Samuel N. Harper, the State Department's foremost authority on Bolshevism.[93] Harper was working half-time for the State Department keeping the Department up to date regarding Bolshevik activities in Soviet Russia and plans and contacts around the world.[94]

Harper had begun to turn his attention to a careful study of Bolshevism in Soviet Russia early in 1919, after he testified before the Overman Committee and found himself appalled at the ignorance of the senators about Russia and about Bolshevik doctrine. He resolved at that time to devote all of his spare energies to "counteract Bolshevist propaganda." As he said in a letter to his patron, Charles R. Crane, "the best way to counteract it, in my mind, is to give wider publicity to certain indisputable facts with regard to conditions in Russia."[95] He asked the State Department why more information in its possession was not being made public, to counteract Raymond Robins' and Hiram Johnson's efforts to bring an end to intervention and effect recognition. Harper requested that the texts of certain proposals from the Bolsheviks be made public so they could be interpreted and exposed.[96]

This letter precipitated an exchange by both letter and telephone with Basil Miles and Frank Polk, and resulted in a long visit by Harper to Washington. Miles sent him a bunch of Bolshevik press that had been obtained through Scandinavian and Estonian channels, and asked whether he could analyze such materials on a regular basis for the State Department. Harper had some doubts, based largely on the scope and demands of what he was being asked to do, since he still wanted to maintain half-time work as a professor at the University of Chicago. But he eventually agreed, in the hope that some of his work would eventually be published and help to expose the real aims and strategy of Bolshevik Russia to the American people.[97] On March 15, 1919, he was appointed a half-time special assistant in the State Department, at a salary of $3,500, to work with the newly established Russia Division as a researcher and interpreter of whatever materials could be obtained from Bolshevik Russia.[98]

As Harper later described his role, he was to study "mainly public documents, and was to have access to strictly diplomatic material only where the latter contained information which could be made public." As Harper recollected, however,

> as the regular staff came to know me better and to see that I had no intention of getting "scoops" out of official material . . . I had placed on my desk more and more diplomatic dispatches. . . . My job was primarily to collect and

translate the most important of the Soviet decrees and laws, and the speeches
and writings of the Soviet leaders which shed light on the aims and methods
of Soviet legislation. . . . My idea . . . was to establish as far as possible the
documentation on Sovietism. . . .[99]

In addition to this work (which will be discussed more fully below),
Harper soon made contact with J. Edgar Hoover and began to assist him in his
investigations of American radicals with ties to Bolshevik Russia. Harper
discussed this contact with Hoover in his memoirs, but cast it in the most
favorable light, claiming that he was "obliged [to] constantly combat conclusions not supported by the documents" and insisting that he was "careful not
to have any connection with the work of detecting alleged underground activities of alleged Moscow agents."[100]

The evidence in Harper's papers tells a somewhat different story. Harper
cooperated closely with Hoover in the investigations of Ludwig Martens,
Albert Rhys Williams, and journalist Isaac Don Levine. He also provided
support and assistance in the discrediting of Raymond Robins and William C.
Bullitt undertaken by the State Department with the assistance of Military
Intelligence and the Justice Department.[101] He did express his concerns about
the shoddy methods used by Hoover and his agents, and he remained deter-
mined that his memoranda not be taken out of the context he provided. But
Harper never quit providing information, and he was instrumental in the cases
Hoover developed against both Martens and Levine.[102]

Harper's work with Hoover was not his first collaboration with intelligence-
gathering on Americans friendly to the Bolsheviks. In the spring of 1918, he
provided correspondence he had received from Santeri Nuorteva advocating
recognition of Soviet Russia to military intelligence agents in Chicago.[103]

Harper had a long-standing relationship with Raymond Robins. It took
some time after Robins' return in the summer of 1918 before Harper dis-
tanced himself from Robins' recommendations. As Harper began his work for
the State Department, he was consulted regarding Robins' statements and
publications, and he learned about the increasing campaign of surveillance
and discreditation directed at Robins. Harper was quick to point out what he
felt were Robins' deliberate misstatements, but he was reluctant to get involved in a campaign of harassment and intimidation. He continued to insist
that the best way to deal with Robins was for the State Department to issue a
full and explicit statement providing evidence against some of his claims concerning proposals from Trotsky and Lenin. The Department consistently declined to provide such documentation.[104]

Isaac Don Levine was a *Chicago Daily News* writer who wrote a series of
highly detailed reports in the spring and summer of 1919, publicizing the
Bullitt mission and Soviet overtures to the United States.[105] On his return to
the United States, his papers were seized. Found among them were copies of
confidential dispatches to the American ambassador to Sweden, Ira Morris,
from a Dr. Davidson, as well as huge quantities of newspapers, periodicals,
and books published in Russian, which Levine had authorization to purchase

for the New York Public Library. The State Department was most incensed at Levine's discussion of the Bullitt mission and the alleged terms provided by the Allies to Lenin, insisting that the proposals were all Lenin's and had no official authorization from either the United States or Britain. Harper and Carter were also outraged at Levine's use of confidential diplomatic dispatches and were determined to prepare a case against him for the Justice Department to prosecute.[106]

After DeWitt Clinton Poole took over from Basil Miles as the head of the Russia desk in the State Department in late 1919, however, he expressed skepticism of the Department's case against Levine, and asked for more hard evidence to be developed. When Carter pressed Harper for more involvement with military intelligence in digging up additional dirt on Levine, Harper backed off. He wrote to Carter with increasing concern that he was becoming involved in an area of investigation he felt uncomfortable about. "You are trying to bring me into this to an extent that worries me," he wrote Carter. "The State Department is going to get into hot water if it is not careful." The entire matter was finally dropped in June of 1920.[107]

Harper was not so reticent with regard to Bullitt himself. He urged in the strongest terms that the Department of State not only respond to Bullitt's testimony before the Senate Foreign Relations Committee, but that some way be found to expose Bullitt and discredit him, perhaps by developing alleged links between him and "international finance." In a rambling letter to Carter, Harper noted that "Bullitt . . . has never earned enough to keep up the menage he runs . . . he has been an out and out dilettante." After alluding to Bullitt's Jewish background, Harper urged further investigation. His suggestions in this case were not pursued by the Department, which felt that a low profile was the best response to Bullitt's revelations.[108]

For a time Harper was preoccupied by the idea of an international German-Jewish-Bolshevik conspiracy. He worked feverishly to try to firm up the evidence provided by the Sisson papers and also passed on rumors and tidbits of information he picked up from Charles R. Crane and others. These rumors intimated that Colonel House was Jewish and that Wilson and Lloyd George developed their peace proposals in Paris after consultation with Jewish financiers and other advisors. Harper worried, however, about putting some of these concerns down on paper, and requested that Carter destroy his letter or send it back to him immediately, so there would be no record in Washington of his concerns.[109]

Harper also provided material to Hoover and the Justice Department on Albert Rhys Williams, a Boston clergyman and socialist who had been in Russia during the first months of the Bolshevik revolution. Williams had worked with Boris Reinstein in the Soviet Bureau of International Propaganda and had returned to the United States and become extremely active with John Reed, Louise Bryant, and others in speaking and writing about his experiences.[110] Harper gathered all the materials the State Department had concerning Williams, most of which had been confiscated by U.S. Customs on Williams' return from Russia in 1918. Although Harper prepared a memorandum on this case, he expressed his own opinion to Allen Carter that even "the official passes and signed orders do not prove anything that ARW has not admitted under oath to the Overman Committee. . . ." Allen Carter disagreed with Harper, stating that the documents proved that Williams advocated the Soviet form of government in the United States, particularly in some of his speeches. After making copies, Carter turned over all of the materials to Hoover at the Justice Department, although the case was never prepared for prosecution.[111]

Ludwig Martens had left New York in the fall of 1919 to escape being compelled by the Lusk Committee to reveal diplomatic correspondence and the identity of couriers. He had gone to Washington, D. C., and agreed to testify about his activities to a subcommittee of the Senate Foreign Relations Committee, chaired by Senator George H. Moses, in the hopes of establishing the diplomatic nature of his mission. Martens even issued a public statement in advance of the hearings, welcoming "the action of the United States Senate in ordering an investigation by the Committee on Foreign Relations of all Russian agencies in America." Martens hoped to have a chance to fully present his case and also that the American people would "be able to form an opinion of the real nature of reactionary counter-revolutionary factions contending against the Soviet Republic."[112]

Immediately prior to Martens' appearing before the Committee, the Soviet envoy again issued a public statement in order to respond to rumors that the Justice Department planned to arrest him. Martens offered to cooperate with the Senate Foreign Relations Committee completely, "to furnish [it] with the most complete data and all other information about all [his] activities." Martens went on to state what he would attempt to prove in the hearings. He claimed that

> [his] work in the United States has strictly confined itself to the presentation
> of arguments in favor of the establishment of friendly relations between the
> United States and Russia, and there has been no interference whatsoever . . .
> in the internal affairs of the United States. . . . In the end it will be absolutely
> necessary for the two countries to resume friendly relations."[113]

The Moses Committee began hearings on January 12, 1920, under the authority of Senate Resolution 263. The Committee closely tied its work to that of the Lusk Committee. It was empowered to investigate

> the status of said Martens; what alleged government or power in Europe he
> represents; what if any recognition of any kind has been accorded him by this
> Government, whether or not he is an alien enemy; what propaganda, if any, he
> is carrying on for the overthrow of governments . . . [and any other informa-
> tion about his activities or anything else to do with] Russian propaganda.[114]

From the beginning, the three efforts of the Lusk Committee, the Justice Department, and the Senate Foreign Relations (Moses) sub-committee were intimately linked. The Senate resolution creating the Moses subcommittee had been introduced by Senator King of Utah soon after the Lusk Committee raid on Martens' office. When he introduced the resolution, he also made public letters to Attorney General Palmer and Secretary of Labor William B. Wilson in which he demanded the deportation of Martens as an enemy alien.[115] The Moses Committee tried to get Archibald Stevenson, the Lusk Committee associate counsel, to serve as its counsel, but Senator William Borah, the one skeptic on the Foreign Relations subcommittee, blocked that move. They next explored the possibility of retaining a Captain Trevor, also connected with the Lusk Committee, but he declined to serve. Trevor did, however, agree to work with the Moses Committee informally, and provided an invaluable link with the Lusk Committee investigations.[116] Senator Moses actually asked Hoover if he would serve as the Foreign Relations sub-Committee's counsel, but the Justice Department decided that would be too obvious. Finally, Wade H. Ellis, former Assistant to the U.S. Attorney General, and Attorney General of Ohio, was engaged as counsel.[117]

Hoover and the Justice Department consulted closely with Moses and Ellis, in the development of the case. Hoover's primary job was to prepare the Justice Department's case against Martens and to place him under arrest just as soon as he finished testifying before the Moses Committee. Hoover enlisted Harper's assistance to follow the committee testimony and to provide evidence linking Martens to Bolshevik proclamations fomenting international communist revolution.[118]

Harper had no difficulty providing Hoover with memoranda developing the details of Russian Bolshevism and plans for world revolution. It proved a bit harder to develop a direct case against Martens, and Harper tried various approaches. Harper's first reaction to claims that Martens was a longtime member of the Russian Communist Party and a close associate of Lenin and Trotsky was to discount his importance because he had never heard of him. "Martens is a very insignificant second rate man," Harper wrote to Hoover on November 18, "and I cannot imagine Lenin cooperating with him."[119] Harper's initial tactic was to try to minimize Martens' importance and keep the publicity down. He even wrote to his friend Frederick Dixon, editor of the *Christian Science Monitor,* on November 26, asking that he quit running so much information about Martens, feeling that publicity without careful interpretation would play into Martens' hands.[120]

Harper did not see any major problem in making the Justice Department's case, however. Martens had admitted that he was a Communist, and in Harper's mind, that meant plotting world revolution. At first, Harper did not find credible Martens' statements that he actively discouraged Bolshevik propaganda in the United States. But later Harper tried to explain to Hoover that Lenin might very well adopt such a tactic in order to establish economic relations with the United States.[121]

Hoover did not appreciate Harper's complex distinctions, and he asked him for memoranda dealing with Communist plans for world revolution that he could use in his brief against Martens. By January 1920, Harper had given much material to Hoover, including press releases and exhibits having to do with the Comintern, the Soviet Communist Party, and world revolution. Harper was frustrated with Hoover's preparations, because some of Hoover's promises to use Harper's material publicly were not being kept. Harper was also concerned that Hoover seemed unable to provide any evidence of Martens' personal connections to any of the world-revolution-planning Harper kept reading about in Bolshevik newspapers. Harper wrote to Carter in the State Department expressing his concerns: "I rather dread the attempt by Hoover to get [Martens], for I do not believe he will be able to prove on him. . . . Martens either does not receive newspapers from Soviet Russia, or will pretend not to have read any of the parts thereof pertaining to general politics. And you cannot make him say that he did."[122]

Hoover was not limited to the information provided by Harper as he made his case. Military intelligence agents provided information, as did agents of the Lusk Committee and those of Hoover's own fledgling operation. For domestic intelligence Harper relied particularly on military intelligence agents. He struck up a close relationship with Brigadier General C. E. Nolan, the Director of the Military Intelligence Division (MID), who provided weekly situation reviews to Hoover as well as files and regular surveillance reports on Martens and his actions and speeches, and meetings he attended. One of the new charges Hoover attempted to add to his brief on Martens was that of stimulating black agitation and race riots. These had broken out in the fall of 1919 and intensified in 1920. In one report provided Hoover by Nolan, a meeting planning a "Negro uprising" sent a courier to meet with Martens in Washington to ask him for money. A month or so later this rather tenuous report had become "evidence . . . showing that Martens has been spending a lot of money to bring about a nationwide uprising among the Negroes in America." Hoover attempted to get further evidence that would stand up legally, but the MID was unable to provide it.[123]

Harper followed the Senate Foreign Relations sub-Committee (Moses Committee) hearing on Martens quite closely and with mounting frustration. His worst fear—that the appearance of Martens before the Senate committee would "play right into their hands"—seemed to be coming true.[124] Martens, advised by skillful counsel Senator Thomas Hardwick of Georgia and supported in his efforts to tell his story by Senator Borah and often by committee chairman Moses as well, was able to fully develop his own account of his activities in the United States. He placed heavy stress on commercial contacts and the diplomatic character of his work. Early on in the hearings, he introduced evidence of the official character of his mission, including letters from Chicherin and an affadavit concerning his Soviet Russian citizenship.[125] Martens also made extensive statements pledging "no interference in U.S. affairs," and provided substantial evidence proving the interest of U.S. companies in trade with Soviet Russia and the legitimate activities of the Commercial Bureau.[126] Martens was even able to devote considerable attention to a recitation of Soviet peace proposals sent to the United States since the Bullitt mission.[127]

Most infuriating to Harper, however, were the attempts of the Committee to pin Martens down concerning his alleged involvement in propaganda to foment a Communist revolution in the United States. Not only did Martens deny the allegations, he accused the United States of being involved in a conspiracy to overthrow the Soviet government in 1918, when Acting Consul DeWitt Clinton Poole hosted a meeting of French, British, and Russian agents implicated in counterrevolutionary activities. The State Department refused to respond to these allegations by Martens for fear that the committee would demand documents State did not want to release. Martens' charges stood unrebutted, which took some of the sting out of accusations of his involvement in United States activities. As Harper lamented, "Here again there can be no answer, no debate between Martens on one hand, and . . . ourselves on the other, before the Senate. So M. gains his point, he makes the statements, which get the publicity. . . ."[128]

Harper was also concerned that his materials and advice were not being utilized properly by Hoover. Hoover and the Justice Department would not agree to any release of Harper's materials to the press while the Senate was holding its hearings, since the Senate subpoena on Martens was served prior to the Justice Department's initiating deportation proceedings. Hoover and his colleagues wanted to keep the entire case against Martens secret until the appropriate time. Harper meticulously revised Hoover's brief against Martens and cautioned him not to use certain materials that "showed controversy between editors of Soviet newspapers and those of the Communist Party newspapers," because it would undermine the case Hoover was trying to make to show complete control by the Party.[129]

Harper also complained that the Hoover brief against Martens, as well as the Foreign Relations Committee's case, was weak on "the main point of interest to the Senate, namely world revolution." He worked to try to document more evidence of a direct connection between Comintern and Soviet statements and the activities and speeches of Martens.[130]

Harper's patience with Hoover's delays and tactics almost reached the breaking point. At one point he complained to Carter, "I hate to waste any more time over this matter," and stated that he would do "nothing more for Hoover without specific orders from Poole" because he could not "afford the risk of trying to cooperate further with Hoover." But staff in the Russia department, concerned over this rift, soon came to his assistance. Felix Cole and Carter held a meeting with Hoover in which he agreed to a more careful communication and response to Harper. Harper continued to cooperate, providing advice regarding the course of the Moses Committee hearings, and to respond to specific requests from Carter and Hoover on background points concerning Martens.[131]

Hoover also finally responded to Harper's persistent concern about the importance of educating the American people about "the real purposes of the Communistic movement." He promised Harper to make his materials public just as soon as the Senate hearings were over. He also urged Harper to continue to work with the Department of State to release more materials directly and to provide background briefings for the press, who were taking a much greater interest in the entire matter. Hoover became increasingly hopeful that the tide was turning against Martens.[132]

Harper, however, remained pessimistic. At one point in the midst of the hearings, he complained to Carter, "Martens has the best of lawyers working day and night, while the Senators just drop in to the meeting without any preparations, trusting to their wits, of which they have very few, and thus playing right into M's hands."[133]

In early February, 1920, he was near despair. Harper wrote a long letter to Carter, convinced that "there is absolutely nothing for us to do. . . . We must just lie low, and let things take their course . . . [at the moment] Martens cannot be touched, for immediately any move against him would be interpreted by the country as effort of Administration to cover up its tracks and prevent further disclosures."[134] Carter responded by sharing his own concerns. He wrote Harper that it was possible, following the hearings, that the Justice Department would not proceed with its case against Martens.[135]

Carter need not have been so pessimistic. Immediately after the Moses Committee completed its hearings on March 29, it proceeded to draft its report, which was issued on April 14. This report concluded by finding that "Martens' activities here have been of a nature to render him more suitable for investigation and action by the Department of Justice than by the committee of the Senate."[136] The Justice Department moved immediately to charge Martens with being an enemy alien and to bring his case before the Department of Labor for deportation proceedings.[137]

The Moses Committee report attempted to establish the basis for the Justice Department case against Martens. It asserted that "the committee found no means to ascertain Martens' real mission in the United States," but concluded that "the entire fabric of trade negotiations which Martens unrolled was part of an ingenious scheme of propaganda to create sympathy, based upon cupidity, for the Russian Soviets and to produce by indirect means the admission of Soviet Russia into the companionship of international relations."[138] The report concentrated primarily on Martens' propaganda and his association with American Communists and Soviet Russian authorities. It declared his claims of Russian citizenship false, concluding that "Martens has no status whatever in this country in any diplomatic or other governmental representative quality." It therefore asserted that he was "a German subject, and in consequence an alien enemy."[139]

Hoover was convinced that "neither Martens nor his associates have any inkling of the basis of the deportation case" against them. But considerable publicity had already begun to leak out concerning the case, and Martens and his legal counsel took steps to prepare their response.[140] The basis of the case had been set as far back as June 1919. Both the Lusk Committee hearings and Basil Miles' memorandum in the State Department had attacked Martens as an enemy alien engaged in subversive propaganda.[141]

By early March 1920, even before the completion of the Moses hearings, Washington was alive with "the growing belief . . . that the Department of

Justice intends shortly to arrest and cause the deportation of" Martens. In an article in *The Nation,* Lincoln Colcord published late January and February correspondence between attorney John Milholland and Labor Secretary William B. Wilson. Milholland questioned recent Labor Department rulings ordering deportation of American alien members of the Communist Party because the party was "a revolutionary party seeking to conquer and destroy the state in open combat." Milholland then stated that he understood a warrant had been issued for Martens' arrest and deportation. Martens was not a member of the American Communist Party, but rather of the Russian. It appeared to Milholland that, were Martens deported, Wilson would "be in the position of having ruled against the admission into America of any member of the dominant political party in Russia; in other words, the responsibility . . . of decision in an important phase of American foreign policy."[142]

Martens' status as a diplomatic representative, an "enemy" alien, and a member of the Communist Party were the key issues of contention. They became the crux of the Labor Department's response to the Justice Department's brief against Martens.

Martens, to shore up his claim for diplomatic status, wrote another letter to the Secretary of State on March 31. He referred to his letter of more than a year before presenting his credentials, and stressed the "strictly lawful and proper" activities of his mission since that time. Martens said that the purpose of this mission was the "attainment of friendly diplomatic and economic relations between the United States and Russia."[143]

Martens also went again to the press and reiterated his activities and his testimony before the Moses and Lusk committees. He then stated that he now believed that he had been "sufficiently investigated." Martens appealed to the State Department "to learn if there is any use in persisting in my mission."[144] Martens even attempted, without success, to get a personal meeting for either himself or Santeri Nuorteva (at that time in London) with new Secretary of State Bainbridge Colby, through the intervention of Lincoln Colcord, who promised "no publicity will be given the call."[145]

Martens also sought to gather further evidence beyond his Foreign Ministry credentials to prove his diplomatic status. Kenneth Durant of his Bureau wrote Alexander Gumberg, asking him if in his knowledge *Izvestia* or other Russian newspapers had carried the announcement of Martens' appointment. Durant also wrote William C. Bullitt asking if on his mission any mention of Martens and his appointment was made. "Could you testify from your own knowledge," asked Durant, "that he was regarded as the accredited representative of the Soviet government?"[146] There is no record of answers to either of these letters.

Meanwhile, the Justice Department prepared its case, soliciting a memorandum from the State Department that affirmed the right of State "to determine when a so-called foreign government shall be recognized." The memorandum reaffirmed the State Department's recognition of the Provisional Government and its ambassador Boris Bakhmetev. Moreover, the memorandum noted that the United States government "has refused to receive or recognize Mr. Martens . . . [who] is not an accredited official of a foreign government."[147]

The Martens case was dealt with in the Department of Labor by Assistant Secretary Louis F. Post. Post had been in charge of immigration matters since March 6, 1920, and was acting Secretary of Labor for a period in the spring and summer of 1920 due to the incapacitation through illness of Secretary William B. Wilson. Post had already proven an impediment to the Justice Department's hopes for broad and sweeping deportation orders for Russian aliens arrested in the raids of November and January. He was equally cautious and circumspect in the Martens case. Hoover and the Justice Department had wanted to arrest Martens in spectacular fashion using massive publicity and wished to detain him for questioning prior to his hearing at the Labor Department. Post, however, forbade such tactics, and made sure that Senator Moses alerted him as soon as Martens was released from Senate custody. Post then arranged for Martens and his attorney to appear in his office at the Labor Department, where Martens was served with the warrant and immediately released in the custody of his attorney pending an immigration hearing.[148]

This hearing was held before Secretary of Labor Wilson, who had resumed his duties in July 1920. The record of the hearing was not made public. Wilson issued his decision on December 15, ordering Martens' deportation on the grounds that he was "an alien, a citizen of Russia, and that he entertains a belief and is a member of or affiliated with an organization that entertains a belief in, teaches or advocates the overthrow by force or violence of the government of the United States." Wilson found no evidence, however, "that Martens personally made any direct statement of a belief in the use of force or violence" for such overthrow, nor that he personally distributed propaganda advocating the use of force, or did anything else unlawful as an individual.[149]

When the Soviet government responded to this order by recalling Martens, the Secretary of Labor rescinded his deportation order, allowing Martens to depart freely. Wilson did this deliberately in order that, were there ever a change of policy by the U.S. State Department regarding Soviet Russia, there would be no "diplomatic embarrassment in the practical adjustment of relations between the two countries."[150] Before his departure, Martens appointed Charles Recht as "the attorney of the Russian Soviet Federal Socialist Republic" in the United States, and gave him the responsibility of representing indigent Russian aliens who continued to fight deportation orders arising out of the Palmer Raids.[151]

## Decline of the Red Scare

Martens' departure occurred in an atmosphere quite different from the full-blown hysteria that greeted his public appearances before the Lusk and Moses committees. After Palmer's famous raids, the American people began to regain their equilibrium. They grew tired of trying to find Bolshevik plots.

Louis Post and the Department of Labor's careful scrutiny of deportation cases certainly contributed to the cooling of passions, but so did Attorney General Palmer himself. His claims regarding the Bolsheviks became more extravagant in inverse proportion to the seriousness of actual events. Sure that May Day 1920 was going to be a repeat of riots and bombings, perhaps even an attempted take-over of state and national governments, Palmer sounded the alarm. When little or nothing happened, more voices began to be heard questioning his tactics and practices.[152]

Even Samuel N. Harper became increasingly uneasy with the methods of the Justice Department, especially in the wake of the Palmer Raids. Harper continued to believe in his efforts to expose Russian Bolshevik strategy, but he began also to protest privately to the State Department and to Hoover about the Attorney General's methods. He complained to Carter following one long memo, "this Bolshevism is getting me bad, and I am getting worried over it. . . ."[153] In a letter to Hoover, he complained that "perhaps I go around in the wrong crowd, but I have found only definite and even bitter condemnation of the raids. . . . I am much worried over this reaction."[154] Later he complained again to Carter "against the frankly propaganda activities of the Department of Justice." By April 1920, Harper began to demand proof of Attorney General Palmer's statements alleging direct connections between the strike movement and the Russian Communist Party.[155]

Harper's unease with his role was particularly apparent whenever he corresponded with other academics, when he often deliberately misstated his involvement in activities with the Justice Department. In a letter to Professor Victor West of Standard University, for example, he said that he had "taken on a purely technical job for the State Department, that of reading the Bolshevist newspapers."[156]

In April 1920, the Rules Committee of the U.S. House of Representatives, acting on a motion for Louis F. Post's impeachment, called Post to testify. The Rules Committee acted after receiving numerous complaints from Hoover, Palmer, and others that Post was allowing dangerous radicals to go free. Palmer had even complained darkly in a Cabinet meeting that Post was something of a Bolshevik himself and should be removed from office. A campaign was organized by those who wanted to get rid of him.[157]

But when Post did appear before the Rules Committee, he completely disarmed them. His command of the deportation cases, his knowledge of immigration law, and his calm and rational demeanor persuaded the committee that perhaps it was Palmer and his methods that should be investigated, rather than Post. The move for impeachment disappeared.[158]

When Palmer's hysterical charges concerning May Day led to nothing, he was brought back before the Rules Committee to answer charges that Post had made about his illegal tactics and questionable practices.[159] By this time, numerous newspapers had begun to turn against Palmer, and even substantial members of the legal profession began to have their doubts. A prestigious group, led by Felix Frankfurter and Zechariah Chafee, professors at Harvard Law School, joined a careful and clear investigation of the excesses of the

Palmer Raids. This study was prepared by the National Popular Government League and the National Civil Liberties Bureau with the help of Post's attorney in the impeachment hearings. The study, and the prestige of those who supported it, had a powerful effect on public opinion, which turned rapidly against Palmer.[160]

## Woodrow Wilson's Attitudes Toward the Red Scare and Bolshevism in the United States

Before turning to an examination of United States policy toward Soviet Russia in the changing atmosphere of late 1919 and 1920, it might well be asked what were Woodrow Wilson's attitudes and policies toward the Red Scare and the Martens deportation. An answer to this question is by no means easy. Wilson was caught in his own ambivalence about how to deal with the Bolsheviks, and his preoccupation with ratification of the Peace Treaty and the League of Nations. This, together with his physical collapse in the fall of 1919, left his thinking more fragmentary on this issue than perhaps any other connected with Russia and Bolshevism.

One of Wilson's earliest comments about American Bolshevism came in a letter Jean Jusserand, the French ambassador to Washington, sent to his chief, Foreign Minister Pichon, in the fall of 1918. Based on a conversation with Wilson, this letter discussed Wilson's knowledge of the IWW and other American radical organizations that were, in Wilson's mind, related to the Bolsheviks. Wilson told Jusserand that "the danger of conflagrations and revolutions menaces all organized states if the necessary precautions are not taken in time to assure the maintenance of order and the triumph of law. . . . I hope that, as for us, we will have done what is necessary in time. . . ."[161] Wilson also expressed his concern to British agent William Wiseman a few weeks later. In this conversation he noted that there were "symptoms of [Bolshevism] in this country—symptoms that are apparent although not yet dangerous."[162]

On the other hand, during this same period Wilson cautioned both his Postmaster General, Albert Burleson; and his Attorney General, Thomas Gregory, not to go too far in suppressing those sympathetic to socialism in the United States. Although the Wartime Espionage and Alien Acts gave the Postmaster General broad authority to control publications through suppression of mailing rights, Wilson repeatedly intervened on behalf of various publications in defense of their rights. In a letter to Burleson on September 18, Wilson insisted that "men like [socialist Norman] Thomas" be treated "with all possible consideration, for I know they are absolutely sincere and I would not like to see this publication held up unless there is a very clear case indeed."[163]

Likewise, in a letter to his Attorney General, Wilson urged that he intervene in a case in the Pacific Northwest. In this case, in Wilson's opinion, "prejudice is working . . . against men who are perfectly innocent of any kind of disloyalty. . . ."[164]

Wilson explicated this calm approach of restraint in dealing with Bolshevism in the United States in an interview with Frank Worthington, the Deputy Chief Censor of the United States, the last day of 1918. Wilson was in London on his way to the Paris Peace Conference. In this interview, Wilson developed his views on Bolshevism and how to combat it. He told Worthington,

> No, I am not afraid of Bolshevism in America. It makes no appeal to the educated man. Moreover, it must be remembered that Bolshevism is no new thing. The present state of Russia is very much the same as that of France during the revolution. . . . My own feeling is that Russia should be left to settle her own affairs in her own way as long as she does not become a menace to others. . . . Things must run their course, and it is for this reason that I am so much in favor of free speech.. . . .[165]

The end of the war brought calls from many of the President's liberal supporters for a general amnesty for all those imprisoned under the Espionage and Sedition Acts, a cessation of interference with publications, and a general relaxation of wartime curbs on civil liberties.[166] Wilson refused to issue a general amnesty, but he did caution Postmaster Burleson, "I cannot believe that it would be wise to do any more suppressing. We must meet these poisons in some other way." Wilson repeatedly questioned the Attorney General on whether pardons might be issued in various individual cases, and he urged the Overman Committee, just beginning its hearings into Bolshevik propaganda, not to accept hearsay testimony.[167]

In remarks to the Democratic National Committee during this same period, Wilson emphasized the necessity of strong government and "the essential integrity" of those governing as bulwarks against Bolshevism. He also showed some sympathy for what he believed were the underlying causes of Bolshevism. As Wilson told the Committee,

> No man in his senses would think that a lot of local soviets could really run a government, but some of them are in a temper to have anything rather than the kind of thing they have been having; and they say to themselves: "Well, this may be bad, but it is at least better and more immediately in touch with us than the other, and we will try it and see whether we cannot work something out of it."[168]

Wilson also remarked in a subsequent discussion with his advisors that the "theory" of Bolshevism "had some advantages, but the trouble was that an attempt was being made to accomplish it in the wrong way."[169]

Wilson was consulted by the State Department concerning the case of Ludwig Martens in June of 1919, when a case was made for Martens' deportation by Basil Miles and Frank Polk. At first the President indicated caution and reluctance to proceed with further investigation, writing to Lansing, "Apparently Martens, though pestiferous, has so far done nothing that we can allege to be illegal. . . . In these days of international complications it is wise to go carefully in a case like this." He then asked for Lansing and the Peace Commissioners' advice. The Commissioners had nothing further to add, supporting the President; but Lansing pressed the State Department's case, particularly the evidence that seemed to indicate Martens' German citizenship. Finally Wilson responded on that point: "Of course if Mertens [*sic*] is a German subject and can be legitimately deported, I have no objection because such grounds would be abundant, but I hope the evidence is in fact complete."[170]

Although Alexander Mitchell Palmer had not been President Wilson's first choice to succeed Thomas Gregory as Attorney General, Wilson had appointed him under pressure from Tumulty and others in the Democratic Party. Wilson made the appointment when he was in the United States during a break in the Peace Conference in late February 1919.[171] After the early June bombings, in which Palmer's own house was hit, Wilson responded with outrage and sympathy.[172] Wilson also consistently supported Palmer's refusal to bend to considerable liberal pressure to recommend the release of Eugene V. Debs. Wilson insisted to the end of his presidency that to do so would be a mistake.[173]

In August of 1919, Secretary of State Lansing and Press Secretary Joseph Tumulty increased the pressure on Wilson to make a definitive statement against Bolshevism, both in Russia and in the United States. Lansing wrote Wilson on August 7, urging him to "make a frank declaration against the Bolshevist doctrines which are certainly extending far beyond the confines of Russia."[174] Lansing enclosed with his letter a long memorandum from his head of the Russian Division, De Witt Clinton Poole, entitled, "Memorandum Concerning the Purposes of the Bolsheviki Especially with Respect to a World Revolution." In this memorandum, Poole argued that the activities of the Bolsheviks "aim to subvert the Government of the United States," and he cited many statements of the Comintern to support his contention.[175] Wilson returned this Poole memorandum to Lansing and responded to his letter on August 14, noting that "perhaps I shall have an opportunity in a Labor Day Proclamation to warn the country against Bolshevism in some way that may attract attention."[176]

Tumulty followed up Lansing's efforts with a letter of his own, impressing on Wilson the political importance of making a strong statement against Bolshevism and enclosing his own copy of Poole's memorandum. Tumulty also urged him to take seriously two letters from M. A. Matthews and W. A. Hines, detailing the "Bolshevist-Zionist conspiracy" led by Soviet "intelligence agents" Nuorteva and Martens, who were bent on destroying American institutions.[177]

Wilson did make a statement on Labor Day in which he cautioned American workers against fomenting revolution, but he stopped short of the definitive proclamation against Bolshevism being urged on him by Lansing and Tumulty. Perhaps Samuel Harper understood the President best, when he wrote to Allen Carter on August 17, "The President knows the political situation, and is a good politician; therefore he will not risk issuing a condemnation of the Bolsheviki unless he has the goods on them. . . ."[178]

But on Wilson's Western whistle-stop speaking tour of August and September 1919 in support of the League of Nations, he gave full vent to his frustrations and contributed to the mounting wave of hysteria over Bolshevism in the United States. He warned the American people about Bolshevik agents; he cautioned about those who would try to convert them to Communism; and he increasingly accused those who were opposed to the League of Nations of Bolshevism, or at least of being "unwilling dupes" of the Bolshevists. In one practically hysterical speech, in Kansas City, Missouri, on September 6, he railed at Bolshevists and their supporters in terminology that would have made Mitchell Palmer proud. In this speech, Wilson made explicit links between Russian Bolshevism and American radicalism. "If we do not want minority government in Russia, we must see that we do not have it in the United States," proclaimed Wilson. "If you do not want little groups of selfish men to plot the future of Europe, we must not allow little groups of selfish men to plot the future of America."[179]

A few days later, in Minneapolis, he said much the same thing, warning that the United States "must absolutely lock the door" against the Bolsheviks.[180] On the same trip, in Billings, Montana, on September 11, Wilson warned against the "poison . . . running in the veins of the world" and the "apostles of Lenin in our midst."[181] At Coeur d'Alene, Idaho, the next day, Wilson specifically linked the Boston police strike to Bolshevism, and he echoed the charge in Seattle a few days later.[182]

But on that same trip, while speaking in Pueblo, Colorado, Wilson was stricken with a debilitating stroke that paralyzed one side of his body. Although he partially recovered, he remained incapacitated and largely out of policy decisions and public view until April 1920. It was during this period of incapacitation that the worst excesses of the Red Scare occurred.

On his return to Cabinet meetings on April 14, Wilson joined those who were beginning to raise questions about Palmer's methods, telling the Attorney General "not to let the country see red."[183] By August, Wilson had dropped his linkage of domestic unrest to Bolshevism almost entirely, confining his comments about the Soviets to the Russian and European context.[184]

## The State Department, Russia Policy, and the Allied Blockade

In the meantime, others in the U. S. government, particularly in the Russia section of the State Department, had accelerated the process of policy formation that finally culminated in the definitive statement against the Bolsheviks, the Colby note of August 1920. Secretary of State Lansing had proposed a strong, anti-Bolshevik public statement as far back as December 1917, but others in the administration, and sometimes President Wilson himself, had always managed to delay or prevent its issuance, pending clarification of events, discussions in Paris, or other developments.[185]

Samuel N. Harper's attachment to the State Department's Russian section in the spring of 1919 and, soon after, DeWitt Clinton Poole's accession as the head of an enlarged department, resulted in more attention being given to the study of Bolshevik materials. The Russian section worked to build a careful, methodical case against Bolshevism that could serve to back up any definitive policy or public statement and tip the balance against the more cautious approach of Colonel House or Woodrow Wilson himself. Harper at one point urged his colleagues in the State Department Allen Carter and Poole not to push for a strong statement against the Bolsheviks, until full documentation of the Red Terror and the nature of the regime and its threat to the United States could be put together:

> The President knows the political situation, and is a good politician. . . . Therefore he will not risk issuing a condemnation of the Bolsheviki, unless he has the goods on them. . . . The goods are the statements of the Bolsheviki themselves. Any statement now, unless strongly backed up by documents, would not meet the demands of the liberal, to say nothing of the radical, elements of the country.[186]

Harper and the Russian section also got burned a few times in mid-1919 by liberal press skepticism when the Overman Committee or some of its witnesses tried to use some of Harper's translations out of context or without documenting them adequately. As a result, Harper resolved to proceed deliberately, and to resist publication of any partial materials.[187]

Harper completed a draft of a report for publication that he sent to the State Department in August 1919, but disagreement over its use delayed its release until late October.[188] Finally, his first efforts were issued by the State Department as "Memorandum on Certain Aspects of the Bolshevist Movement in Russia" on October 27, and published by the United States Senate in January 1920. This report concentrated largely on the question of the Red Terror, documenting the Cheka and its excesses. It was drawn from materials collected in the summer and fall of 1918 and backed up by Western observers still in Moscow. This document also discussed the undemocratic nature of the regime and its utter disregard for fundamental standards of human rights. It did not, however, make the case that many senators and others wanted tying Bolsheviks to American radicals.[189]

Poole and Carter also did their best to draw Harper into policy development and discussions within the Department as various efforts were made to draft acceptable proposals for the Secretary of State and the President. Harper, although he consulted about Martens, Bullitt, and others, demurred on the bigger questions, requesting Carter "to keep me out of these questions of policy."[190] Harper wanted to stick to research and reports, analyzing newspapers, cables, military intelligence reports, interviews, Bolshevik decrees, and other original documents.[191]

American consideration of a comprehensive policy on Soviet Russia was complicated by discussions among the Allies in the wake of the Paris Peace Conference and the Allies' inability to implement a unified strategy, with the exception of the continued economic blockade. Although the Allies agreed to lift the blockade against Germany, effective on Germany's ratification of the Peace Treaty, the Council of Four stipulated that this would not affect the blockade of Bolshevik Russia.[192]

While Woodrow Wilson participated in this decision, he and others in the United States delegation soon began asking questions about the legal basis for such a decision, insisting that, once peace had been declared, the United States could not participate in a blockade of a country it was not at war with.[193] Instead, each country should be "on its own" to trade or not to trade, as it saw fit. But no announcement regarding the lifting of any restrictions should be made. Over the course of the last half of 1919, the American position on the continued Allied economic blockade of Soviet Russia remained the way Wilson had expressed it: oppose any blockade in principle, but cooperate with it in practice. The result was that the United States became an obstacle to an effective, unified Allied plan to continue strong economic sanctions against Soviet Russia, helping in this way to break down such sanctions by the end of 1919. On the other hand, it refused to drop its own trade barriers to enable any trade to take place, a policy it maintained until well after the Allied blockade was officially lifted.[194]

The United States insistence on the illegality of a blockade in discussions with its Allied partners was strengthened by Woodrow Wilson's own position (and his departure from Paris in the summer of 1919), and by the fact that of the remaining Peace Commissioners, General Tasker Bliss was put in charge of all matters dealing with Russia. Not only was Bliss firmly opposed to Allied intervention, he was also skeptical of any campaigns, economic or military, against Bolshevism, and insisted on restating President Wilson's position against the blockade on every occasion.[195]

Bliss was assisted in this vigilance by Commissioner Henry White, who happened to be at an Allied meeting in mid-July in which the question of restrictions on neutrals' trading with Soviet Russia arose. The government of Sweden asked whether it could proceed to trade with Russia. The British and French representatives tried to insist that no trade could go forward without permission from the local Allied naval command. White refused to go along with this restriction, believing it was out of keeping with the earlier decision to lift the blockade. Instead, he queried the State Department and Wilson. In response, Wilson stuck by his previous position, insisting that "a blockade before a state of war exists is out of the question."[196]

When White communicated this position to what was now the Council of Five (Britain, France, United States, Italy, and Japan), Clemenceau was delegated to appeal to Wilson to change his mind, on the basis of a distinction British Foreign Secretary Balfour had attempted to draw between warfare and belligerency. Balfour pointed out that Allied soldiers, particularly British soldiers, were being killed in Bolshevik Russia and that the Allies had the right to defend them through economic means. Wilson responded by insisting that a blockade was not possible, but neatly sidestepped the issue of whether the British could "employ war measures to prevent the importation of munitions and food supplies into the portion of Russia now in the hands of the Bolsheviks." Wilson essentially agreed that such "war measures" could be employed, while he refused to sanction a full-scale blockade.[197]

By November 1919, the State Department had no qualms in making public Wilson's policy that no blockade in fact existed, at least as far as the United States was concerned. On the other hand, no export licenses or clearance papers were issued to any firm or trader for any port in Bolshevik Russia. Frank Polk wrote a public letter to Senator James W. Wadsworth, who had inquired about the American position with regard to the blockade. In this letter Polk insisted that "no blockade exists," but that the restrictions on trade with Bolshevik territory would be maintained because "it is the declared purpose of the Bolsheviks in Russia to carry revolution throughout the world."[198]

Soon after this time, rumors abounded that the blockade was soon to be lifted, and perhaps the Allies would even establish diplomatic relations with Soviet Russia. Lloyd George gave his famous Guildhall speech of November 8, calling for a change of policy toward the Bolsheviks and the inclusion of Soviet Russia in the world economy. The U.S. State Department soon found itself forced to deny rumors to the effect that the United States government contemplated "a compromise with the Russian Bolshevik Government."[199]

Following the announcement of the Supreme Economic Council early in 1920 that the blockade would be lifted and that trade would be resumed with Bolshevik Russia through the medium of Tsentrosoyuz, Secretary Lansing and others in the State Department sought immediately to differentiate the United States' position from that of the other Allies. While agreeing that restrictions on trade would eventually have to be lifted, the United States did not do so immediately, insisting that it was reviewing its policy. Moreover, it refused to accept the British position that negotiations could be carried on with the Russian co-ops without dealing with the Bolshevik government. As Secretary Lansing wrote to his friend Charles Valentine, "I do not believe that it can be done and keep the goods out of the hands of the Bolshevik authorities. Unless they work out some way of trading with the people in Russia without dealing with the Bolshevists I do not see any reason for changing our present policy of refusing licenses. . . ."[200]

Lansing and others made it known in no uncertain terms to the British their fear that negotiating with Tsentrosoyuz representatives was tantamount to dealing with the Bolsheviks, but also that it was really a preliminary step to dealing directly with the Soviet government, which the United States insisted strenuously must be avoided.[201] By March 6, the State Department had put together a formal reaction to the Supreme Economic Council's decision. Insisting that "a natural prelude to the reopening of trade with the regions under Soviet control would be the reestablishment of relations with the Soviet Government," the State Department stated that it could not renew even informal relations with the Bolsheviks because it "has not received substantial evidence that the good faith of the Soviet regime has been sufficiently established." On the other hand, the State Department admitted that the trade restrictions themselves could not long be maintained and signaled its willingness to remove them "soon."[201]

The Supreme Economic Council's decision also set off a series of discussions among American businesses, including some, like National City Bank President Frank Vanderlip, who had resisted earlier efforts by the Martens bureau. A group of Scandinavian businessmen, led by V. O. Phillipsen of Copenhagen, organized a conference on Russian trade in the spring of 1920 and urged Vanderlip and other members of the New York Chamber of Commerce to join them. The Chamber expressed interest and appointed a committee of five, including Vanderlip, to represent it *if* the State Department gave its consent. Vanderlip sought Polk's advice, which was negative, and then was reluctantly forced to decline the offer. Clearly, however, the pressure on the administration to join the rest of the Allies in lifting the restrictions on Russian trade was building.[203]

Nevertheless, the State Department was so set on its policy of nonintercourse that it refused to allow the Ambassador to Great Britain, Norman Davis, to attend meetings of the Permanent Committee of the Supreme Economic Council in London. Questions of implementing Russian trade were to be discussed at these meetings, and the State Department feared that Krasin and other Bolshevik representatives in London might be present and Davis would be forced to acknowledge them.[204]

The State Department also strongly admonished its representative in Riga, John Gade, for informal inquiries he made of the Soviet commercial representative in Reval because of the publicity given them in an article in *Pravda*. In an interview, which Gade later denied giving, he was purported to have said, "We have cursed Russia, we have hated Russia, we have been fighting Russia, but the deuce, we have forgotten to study Russia. . . . in order to study Russia, in order to watch with our own eyes, it is necessary for us to come into closer contact."[205]

The State Department, with Wilson's concurrence, also refused in March to appoint an American delegate, even unofficially, to the proposed League of Nations Commission to explore conditions in Russia. This commission was slated to focus its investigations on trade and economic matters. In its refusal, State reiterated its concern that the United States was not a member of the League, and that even economic "exploration" might lead to trade, which could be but the preliminary to some kind of official relations.[206]

By late June the U.S. government's "intent" to raise the restrictions on trade approached reality. Wilson determined that such restrictions could not be maintained and instructed the State Department to prepare for an announcement. Any such action, in Wilson's view, "must not be interpreted as a recognition of any existing Russian faction or of the Soviet Regime." Anyone who wanted to trade with Russia was required to so "on their own responsibility and at their own risk." The United States government intended to do nothing to assist or aid in such trade. This announcement, however, was not projected to include "the withdrawal of the present restrictions against communication with and travel in Russia . . . to prevent the spread of Bolshevist propaganda."[207]

On July 8, 1920, the restrictions on trade with Bolshevik Russia were officially removed by the Department of State, with the exception of any restrictions that pertained to the "shipment of materials susceptible of immediate use for war purposes." The State Department clarified within days that this included railway material.[208] All diplomatic and consular officers were informed in a long memorandum of July 27, in which State made it abundantly clear that this step was not preliminary to any dealings with the Bolsheviks. In fact, it argued that it had "endeavored to forestall any possible misconstruction of its action" and ordered its personnel to "take no action which, officially or unoffically, directly or indirectly, assists or facilitates commercial or other dealings between American citizens . . . and any persons, interests, or institutions domiciled within that part of Russia now under the control of the so-called Bolshevist authorities."[209]

## The Development of the Colby Note

Within weeks, the State Department strengthened this understanding of its action by issuing a comprehensive policy statement against the Bolshevik government. The immediate origins of this statement, the Colby note, can be found in the continuing legacy of Secretary Robert Lansing. Lansing resigned as Secretary of State under pressure in January 1920, but before he left, he drew up a long policy memorandum on Russia for President Wilson. In this memorandum, Lansing urged once again, in the strongest possible terms, that a long-overdue definitive policy against the Bolsheviks be adopted by the United States government. He recommended that the Bolshevik government continue to be isolated, and that the United States hold open the possibility of economic aid, humanitarian aid, and trade to non-Bolshevik areas, hoping that this would serve as an incentive in the continued struggle of the Russian people against the Bolsheviks. Although outside military aid seemed to have failed, economic assistance might still aid the White forces.[210]

In response to those within the government who were arguing that perhaps the time had come to reestablish contact with the Bolsheviks in light of the lifting of the blockade and the moves in the Bolsheviks' direction by Lloyd George and others, Lansing was adamant and uncompromising. In a long memorandum to all the legations in Europe that might be approached by Bolshevik representatives, Lansing emphasized "the futility of endeavoring to arrive at a satisfactory understanding with [the Bolsheviks]. Their ultimate purposes are inimical to all established Governments, and any seeming compromise which they may make . . . is vitiated by their avowed opportunism."[211] Lansing followed his plea to Wilson and his circular missive to American representatives abroad with another letter to Wilson. In this letter he reiterated his December statement and warned against the British position, which seemed to be tilting in the Bolsheviks' direction.[212]

Lansing had demonstrated his personal hatred of Bolshevism and the Soviet government on numerous occasions since 1917. An entry in his diary in 1919, however, best illustrates the depth of that commitment and his sense of what he thought he was fighting in the word "Bolshevik." In this entry, he wrote a fable reflecting on what he felt had happened in the attempts in Paris to bring peace to the world, entitling it "The Dove's Birthday Party":

> The dove once gave a Birthday party and many birds came with much flapping of wings, when they were assembled they congratulated the dove on its narrow escape from some fierce Dogs and also they said many nice things about the day. Then the birds began to discuss giving a life insurance policy to the dove for a birthday present. During the discussion, disputes arose about other things, and soon the whole party was scolding and quarreling and pecking at their neighbors. Meanwhile the poor dove was forgotten, and when the insurance policy was ready to be presented the birds looked for the dove and found only a heap of bloody feathers, for a foul vulture had swooped down, while the quarrels were going on, and tore the poor thing to pieces. Moral: the Dove of Peace may escape from the dogs of war only to be devoured by the Bolshevik vulture.[213]

Lansing's anti-Bolshevik legacy was, of course, amply represented in a State Department Russian Division headed by DeWitt Clinton Poole and with the continuous assistance of Samuel N. Harper. But the impetus for the Colby note, and its actual drafting, came from outside the Department. John Spargo, an American socialist with a strong anti-Bolshevik bias and a proclivity for writing long memoranda to the State Department, wrote the memorandum the note was based on. Spargo seized the opportunity of the accession of Bainbridge Colby as Secretary of State to renew his persistent campaign for a stronger American statement against the Bolsheviks.[214]

Spargo had corresponded with Wilson in August 1919, but had not managed to convince him of the necessity for a strong statement at that time.[215] Spargo, an acquaintance of Harper's, saw that Colby was much closer to President Wilson than Lansing had been. Here was an opportunity to push the issue. He addressed a long letter to Colby soon after his selection, even before his confirmation by the U.S. Senate, and presented him with a number of ideas for a comprehensive U.S. statement on Russia. Spargo also enclosed a copy of his new book, *Russia as an American Problem*.[216]

Spargo also took steps to encourage his friends and allies who shared his perspective to write to the new Secretary of State, impressing upon him the urgency of immediate action, especially in light of the seeming capitulation of the British to Bolshevik entreaties. Provisional Government Ambassador Boris Bakhmetev reiterated his own reasons that such a statement ought to be made. Bahkmetev particularly stressed the territorial integrity of Russia and the hope for a future democratic Russia.[217] Samuel Gompers, head of the American Federation of Labor and an old foe of the Bolsheviks, addressed a series of questions to Colby regarding American policy that intended to draw out the new Secretary of State in defense of a position of non-recognition and a maintenance of trade barriers against the Bolsheviks. Colby responded as Gompers had hoped, and he sent a copy of his response to President Wilson in early June. Colby emphasized the dangers of Bolshevism, stressing earlier arguments given him by Lansing and Spargo.[218]

Colby also proceeded to ask the Russian desk of the State Department to prepare for him a review of the relations of the United States with Russia since 1917. Colby also requested a draft "as to the present attitude of the United States toward those now in control of so-called Soviet Russia."[219] At the same time, Colby solicited from John Spargo his own draft of such a policy statement.[220]

The draft of the Russia desk, apparently composed by Samuel Harper, stressed the historical record since the Bolshevik revolution. This statement claimed that "earnest efforts were made by American Consuls and Allied representatives in Russia and Siberia to prevent a break . . . but the Bolsheviks did not want peace, declared open hostility to all existing governments, and committed act after act which could be described only as war against their former allies."[221]

Spargo, enclosing a long draft statement of the complete case against the Bolsheviks, wrote an accompanying letter to Colby. Here Spargo stressed that a "general statement of our policy—perhaps in the form of a general letter of instructions to all our diplomatic and consular representatives and agents— would [seem] to be imperatively indicated by the circumstances."[222] Not only was such a statement required by the international situation, according to Spargo, but it would be good politics in the presidential campaign of 1920. In addition, Spargo argued, "it would have the effect of placing before Mr. Harding—in the event of his election—a *fait accompli* not to be lightly or easily undone or reversed." It was the opportunity for Bainbridge Colby to put his personal, and perhaps permanent, stamp on American policy toward Russia.[223]

The immediate situation calling for the views of the United States government was the end of Soviet Russia's war with Poland, and the involvement of the Allies, particularly Britain and France, who had backed the Poles, in any peace settlement. Other governments were querying the United States about its attitude toward the settlement and its willingness to be involved in the negotiations. To deal with these inquiries, Colby wrote a letter to United States legations in England, Paris, Rome, and Warsaw, setting forth the policy of the United States. In this memo, he touched upon several of the themes that were later fully developed in the Colby note. While the U.S. Government was "in sympathy with arrangements for an armistice between Poland and Soviet Russia," Colby wrote, it did not "see its way clear to participating in plans extending the armistice negotiations into a general European conference which could involve recognition of the soviet regime and a settlement of long-standing Russian problems." The State Department, Colby emphasized, was "averse to any dealings with the Soviet regime beyond the most narrow boundaries to which a discussion of an armistice can be confined."[224]

In response to this memorandum, Norman H. Davis, United States Ambassador to Britain, wrote Colby concerning a conversation he had with the Secretary of the Italian Embassy. Italy was particularly anxious that the United States issue some kind of definitive statement. The Italian government was under great pressure to go along with British policy and wanted to know the U.S. position. Davis explained the Italian position to Colby in the following terms: "He intimated that his Government would not only welcome a statement of our views but would be glad to cooperate because he was satisfied that the views of his own Government were that the situation in Europe could not be solved without the moral influence of this government."[225] Davis assured the Italian envoy "that we have little or no confidence in the wisdom of negotiating with the Bolsheviks or the possibility of making any agreements with them which can be depended on." He then recommended to Colby that this opportunity to issue a comprehensive statement be exploited.[226]

Davis also wrote an additional letter to Colby, setting out his own views on what such a statement should contain. In this letter, Davis stressed American opposition to the dismemberment of Russia and urged that "we must reiterate as strongly as possible the reasons of our refusal to negotiate with or in any way recognize the Soviets." Davis went on to urge that a major point be made of the undemocratic nature of the Bolshevik regime. He closed by insisting that "it is utterly impossible for two systems based on such diametrically opposed principles to work in peace and harmony," a phrase Colby soon adopted as his own.[227]

Colby took the Spargo draft, made some changes and additions, including the Davis phrase about "diametrically opposed principles," and sent it to Woodrow Wilson. Colby proposed to Wilson that the statement be issued immediately in response to the Italians' request for a clarification of the American government's position. In his covering note to Wilson, Colby noted that the draft had "one outstanding weakness: it is impossible to say what we will DO [emphasis Colby's], if anything." He also apologized to Wilson for its length. Wilson returned it to him the same day with a handwritten note at the bottom. "Thank you. This seems to me excellent and sufficient."[228]

The final note, issued the next day and made public immediately, was indeed a full and comprehensive statement of the United States' position in opposition to dealings with Bolshevik Russia. It developed three reasons at some length: the undemocratic nature of the Bolshevik regime (its lack of representation of the Russian people); the connections of Soviet Russia with the Comintern and its campaign "against our institutions"; and the "outlaw" character of the Bolshevik regime, the "negation of every principle upon which it is possible to base harmonious and trustful relations." All of these charges were criticisms that would continue to underlie American distrust of Soviet Russia for administrations, and even generations, well into the future.[229]

Colby received immediate and positive encouragement for this statement from all those who had stimulated it. Arthur Bullard, who assumed responsibility for the Russian Division from Felix Cole on August 11, wrote a congratulatory note to Colby the same day, assuring him that he had "not read anything for a long time which has put so much heart into me as this correspondence," for which he gave Colby his "enthusiastic support."[230] John Spargo also wrote immediately to Colby, thanking him for his "splendid" note and his "wise and just appreciation of the interests of Russia," and called the note Colby's "great triumph."[231]

This was not the end of the Colby-Spargo relationship, by any means. Spargo continued to write to Colby about Russian affairs, making suggestions about programs of action and other matters right up to the end of Colby's tenure as Secretary of State.[232] Moreover, a few years later, Spargo offered to write the sketch of Colby as Secretary of State for Samuel F. Bemis' series of portraits of United States Secretaries of State. In this short volume, Spargo praised Colby's Russian policy in the highest terms and defended it from his critics.

Spargo also detailed in this book, for the first time publicly, one of his later suggestions to Colby that was never implemented. This "bold and comprehensive plan" was to enlist the Prime Minister of Sweden, Hjalmar Branting, to appeal to the Soviet government "in carefully prepared terms of genuine friendship and devotion to the aims and ideals of the Russian Revolution." Branting was to outline a "comprehensive program including the voluntary liquidation of the dictatorship," the re-establishment of the Constituent Assembly, and representative Soviets. If the Soviets responded positively, the United States would agree to recognize the Soviet government and also would cancel the debt and offer a generous program of economic assistance. Although Spargo insisted that Wilson approved this effort, Branting refused to become involved, and the proposal died.[233]

Colby's files contain a large number of congratulatory letters and telegrams, with few if any in opposition to his note.[234] Norman H. Davis, in London, did immediate surveys of the British, French, and Italian press to summarize their reactions for President Wilson and the Secretary of State. He called the French press "entirely favorable." The Italian press, however, called the note a "complete change of front," and pointed out its divergence from Prinkipo. The British tried to ignore the note as much as possible and downplayed its importance because of the American decision to remain aloof from the European system after Versailles. The British government refused to comment specifically.[235]

The Soviet government at first had difficulty in responding because of a distinct inability to get hold of a full copy of the note, relying only on press reports. Chicherin wired Kamenev in London asking for the full text. If this could not be obtained through regular public sources, Chicherin wrote, perhaps Kamenev could even request a copy from official American sources, pointing out "the importance for us to learn the real attitude of America, in order to establish our own attitude."[236]

Chicherin apparently did obtain a full text of the note, for he responded in a long letter to all Russian representatives abroad on September 10. This letter was relayed through neutral channels to the U.S. State Department. In this note, Chicherin refuted Colby's argument point by point but continued to hold open the possibility, in fact the necessity, of eventual negotiations and friendly relations with the United States:

> Mr. Colby is profoundly mistaken in assuming that only if Russia has a capitalist regime can normal relations exist between Russia and the United States. . . . in the interests of both Russia and the United States, in spite of the difference in their social and political systems, proper and loyal relations of a peaceful and friendly character . . . [should] be established. . . .[237]

# CONCLUSION

# Interaction and Exploration

This book has examined the struggle to confront the problems and issues of revolution in Russia during a world war, with a particular focus on the possibilities of, and efforts to, effect a working relationship between the United States and Bolshevik Russia from 1917 to 1920. Although none of these efforts resulted in a clear and uncluttered path toward full or lasting cooperation, this period of mutual exploration, testing, and probing kept open the possibility of constructive dialogue in the years immediately following the Bolshevik seizure of power. In fact, it was only with the dénouement of these efforts in the Colby note of August 1920 that the political and diplomatic—but not economic—interchange was cut off and the United States government was set against the Bolsheviks for the next decade.

This study reveals a surprising number of agreements between the two sides. These include continued operation of the American Red Cross in Soviet Russia, the transfer of war matériel from the Russian army to the American, the sale of strategic supplies of platinum from the Bolsheviks to the United States, the exemption of a number of United States corporations from Bolshevik nationalization decrees, Soviet agreement to the enlargement of the U.S. consular corps in Russia, and the signing of nearly one hundred provisional trade contracts between the Soviet government and American firms.

Even more significant than these agreements were the substantive discussions of political and economic relations, which foreshadowed later agreements reached in 1933 and were built upon in subsequent years. Detailed discussions of Soviet-American trade possibilities were held between Bolshevik foreign trade representatives Jacob Bronski and Yuri Larin and American commercial attaché William C. Huntington as early as February 1918. These talks formed the basis for the comprehensive proposal on Soviet-American economic relations that V. I. Lenin gave to Raymond Robins of the American Red Cross for transmission to the Wilson administration in May 1918. Although the American government did not respond, Soviet representative Ludwig C. A. K. Martens translated many of these ideas into reality in his negotiations with American firms in 1919 and 1920, laying the groundwork for the substantial Soviet-American trade of the 1920s. Moreover, the serious political negotiations between William H. Buckler and Maksim Litvinov and between William C. Bullitt and V. I. Lenin covered every major issue of controversy between the two governments, including foreign debt, revolutionary propaganda, and western borders.

But even more important than specific agreements is the fact that Americans and Bolsheviks, on behalf of their societies and often their governments, carried on an unprecedented array of interactions at a time of great uncertainty and in the face of official government-to-government hostility. This was on-the-spot diplomacy in Petrograd, Moscow, Stockholm, Paris, and New York. These encounters struggled with problems of military supplies, Red Cross medical aid, currency exchange, and contracts for goods. Soviet and American representatives also talked about the future, often with very poor instructions from their governments. Their attempts to forge agreements for the end of a state of war and the renewal of constructive relationships, both economic and political, laid the groundwork for future diplomatic breakthroughs.

Vladimir Lenin articulated a policy toward the United States from 1917 to 1920 that laid out a consistent strategy for Bolshevik representatives to follow and at the same time was dependent on shifting opportunities that presented themselves. This policy was firmly grounded in an increasing realization that the world proletarian revolution was not imminent, and that it was absolutely necessary, for Bolshevik survival, to deal constructively with Russia's former allies, Britain, France, and the United States. Within this policy framework, Lenin led in the development of a specific strategy for the United States, forthrightly embracing and incorporating his own peculiar respect for American exceptionalism. In particular, Lenin was convinced that economic ties would lead eventually to a political and diplomatic breakthrough.

This strategy singled out the United States for preferential treatment among the Allies, on the assumption that the United States be the first capitalist state to recognize the Soviets, but also in the confirmed belief that serious economic contacts could be productively developed. Other Bolsheviks in the leadership disagreed with Lenin at various times regarding both this overall policy and its detail, with Zinoviev, Bukharin, and at times Trotsky breaking with his analysis. But Lenin's commitment to such a strategy survived, prevailed, and dominated Bolshevik thinking about the United States during his lifetime. Such a strategy began to be developed by Lenin and others in the Supreme Council of the National Economy as early as February 1918 and found full enunciation in Bolshevik proposals to Raymond Robins in the spring of 1918. The Martens mission of 1919–1920 was a full-scale effort to pursue economic contacts for diplomatic purposes and resulted, from the Bolshevik perspective, in substantial benefits.

After nearly three years of intense consideration of the burning question of "How shall we deal with the Bolsheviki?" Woodrow Wilson's administration only established a policy toward the end of 1920. The constant fluidity of the situation enabled many approaches to be tried and gave considerable latitude to other American actors actually engaged with the Bolsheviks. This confusion reflected the contradictory assumptions, thoughts, and policies of Woodrow Wilson and his advisors, which remained in tension between a commitment to a "democratic" Russia and a flickering willingness to talk to the Bolsheviks. Shifting decisions provided elusive opportunities, some of which held great hope for the development of alternative politics. At several points Wilson and his closest advisor, Colonel Edward M. House, seriously considered *de facto* recognition and at other times gave their blessing to Raymond Robins, DeWitt Clinton Poole, William C. Bullitt, and others who were determined to keep channels of communication open, both during the war with Germany and after the Armistice.

Historians of Woodrow Wilson's policy toward the Bolsheviks have argued about the extent to which Wilson was driven by anti-Bolshevism, economic self-interest, or idealistic internationalism. This study contends that such a stark choice presents the issue within the wrong framework. Rather, Wilson's vacillating and contradictory policy at times displayed receptivity to evolving opportunities. Wilson was willing to explore nuanced approaches whose outcomes were by no means predetermined. Most fundamentally, Wilson himself was caught in a struggle between his anti-Bolshevik inclinations and the necessity to find a way to "do business" with the new Soviet government. This same dilemma bedeviled his advisors, his British allies, and the public at large. The story of Woodrow Wilson's Bolshevik policy is therefore not simply one of clear and unfettered implementation of policy motivated by either anti-Bolshevik conspiracy or idealistic self-determination. It instead reflects a complex and contradictory debate between the forces—and this includes forces within Woodrow Wilson—that would strangle Bolshevism and those that would find a way to deal with it. Each stage of the debate in itself reveals the different mixes of these contradictory aspects. But it is only in looking at the entire Wilson experience with the Bolsheviks that the mosaic of possibility, explored and rejected, fully reveals itself to provide the complex whole.

Yet a concentration on all of the details of the efforts of representatives of the United States and Bolshevik Russia to maintain communication and develop a serious relationship in these first years must not obscure the larger significance of this complex and subtle story. Despite intense efforts by Secretary of State Robert Lansing and others in the United States State Department, Woodrow Wilson did not issue an uncompromising denunciation of the Bolsheviks in December 1917. Nor did V. I. Lenin countenance his friend Grigori Zinoviev's desire to attack the United States at every opportunity. Instead, the first three years of the relationship between the United States and Soviet Russia can best be characterized as a probing search for a means of coexistence, in the face of the apparent impossibility of each other's imminent demise. This fact is often lost in the recital of accusations of American perfidy and collaboration in conspiracies to bring down Bolshevik power or in defenses of Woodrow Wilson's high-minded desires for a "democratic" Russia.

Judson met with Trotsky. Robins and Lenin did forge a serious and productive relationship over the course of six intensive months, with the acquiescence of the United States government. Larin, Bronski, and Huntington did carry on serious economic discussions. Chicherin and Poole did conduct a professional diplomatic dialogue. Maksim Litvinov did persuade President Wilson to send Buckler to Stockholm, and Buckler's careful reports helped bring about a serious effort for peace between the Bolsheviks and their former allies. Finally, Martens' careful overtures to American firms resulted, not in an increase in Bolshevik propaganda in the United States, but in a chorus of demands to allow American-Soviet trade to resume. All of these individual efforts had their effect. They did not result in immediate rapprochement between Bolshevilk Russia and the United States, but they kept a chaotic situation fluid and open to possibility.

Three years of probing resulted in a considerable body of experience amassed through direct contact between the two countries' representatives, even in the face of mutual denunciation. A remarkable number of American and Soviet representatives insisted on solving, in the most pragmatic fashion, problems between them. In the process they forged constructive personal and governmental relationships. The informality of these contacts and their often-unofficial nature should not obscure their very real importance. Far from a state of isolation and complete hostility, United States—Bolshevik relations in the Wilson-Lenin years were marked by a considerable degree of mutual accommodation. Proponents of constructive relations in both Soviet Russia and the United States succeeded in restoring contact when it was broken and in keeping alive the idea that their opposite number had to be dealt with, even when it was distasteful or flew in the face of popular prejudice.

This persistence allowed the introduction of the idea that Soviet-American relations could be something other than hysterical accusations hurled against capitalism and Communism. Several speculative questions present themelves that suggest research and comparative analysis for the future. Could the Roosevelt-Litvinov agreements have been negotiated without the experience of William C. Bullitt and Maksim Litvinov at an earlier stage of contact? Did the fact that the U.S. War Department and the Red Army had conducted amicable discussions in 1918 help the pragmatic working relationship developed between generals Dwight D. Eisenhower and Yuri Zhukov during World War II? Did the persistent belief of both American and Soviet representatives that constructive economic ties could be built between the two countries help in the eventual diplomatic breakthrough?

Finally, perhaps it is not stretching a point to remind ourselves that the complex mixture of fear and hostility, curiosity and respect, and even the realization of common humanity that characterizes any full accounting of the history of Soviet-American relations, did not emerge fully developed. Nor was it simply the climactic result of a post–World War II clash. It is instead the product of a longer maturation. The beginnings can be found perhaps earlier than November 7, 1917. But the first three tumultous years were formative in Soviet and American efforts to define national attitudes toward each other. Constructive possibilities, some of which came to fruition, have never been far away; just hidden from direct view.

# NOTES

## Abbreviations

| | |
|---|---|
| NAP | Norman Armour Papers, Princeton University |
| GA | Gordon Auchincloss Papers, Yale University |
| TB | Tasker Bliss Papers, Library of Congress |
| WEB | William E. Borah Papers, Library of Congress |
| LEB | Louis Edgar Browne Papers, Hoover Institution |
| WHB | William H. Buckler Papers, Yale University |
| AB | Arthur Bullard Papers, Princeton University |
| WCB | William C. Bullitt Papers, Yale University (microfilm) |
| BC | Bainbridge Colby Papers, Library of Congress |
| C&P | C. K. Cumming and Walter W. Pettit, eds., *Russian-American Relations, 1917–1920* (New York, 1920) |
| ND | Norman H. Davis Papers, Library of Congress |
| *FRUS* | *Papers Relating to the Foreign Relations of the United States* |
| DRF | David R. Francis Papers, Missouri State Historical Society |
| LG | David Lloyd George Papers, House of Lords Records Office |
| AG | Alexander Gumberg Papers, State Historical Society of Wisconsin |
| SH | Samuel Harper Papers, University of Chicago |
| ELH | Ernest L. Harris Papers, Hoover Institution |
| GDH | George D. Herron Papers, Hoover Institution |
| HH | Herbert Hoover Papers, Hoover Institution |
| EMH | Edward M. House Papers, Yale University |
| HJ | Hiram Johnson Papers, University of California, Berkeley |
| WVJ | William V. Judson Papers, Newberry Library, Chicago |
| GK | George F. Kennan Private Papers |
| HK | Harold Kellock Papers, Hoover Institution |
| RLLC | Robert L. Lansing Papers, Library of Congress |
| RLP | Robert L. Lansing Papers, Princeton University |
| ML | Maurice Laserson Papers, Hoover Institution |
| BL(H) | R. H. Bruce Lockhart Papers, Hoover Institution |
| Lusk | Records of the Joint Legislative Committee for the Investigation of Seditious Activities [Lusk Committee], State Library and Archives of the State of New York |

| | |
|---|---|
| FM | Frank Mason Papers, Hoover Institution |
| VAM(O) | Viscount Alfred Milner Papers, Oxford University |
| VM(D) | Vance McCormick Diaries, Hoover Institution |
| VM | Vance McCormick Papers, Yale University |
| NA | National Archives |
| NAM | Political Relations, United States and Russia, 1910–1929 (National Archives Microfilm) |
| PRO | Public Record Office, Great Britain (Kew) |
| AVP | Arkhiv Vneshnei Politiki, Moscow |
| *DVP* | *Dokumenty Vneshnei Politiki* |
| FP | Frank Polk Papers, Yale University |
| DCP | DeWitt Clinton Poole Papers, Wisconsin State Historical Society |
| POM | DeWitt Clinton Poole Oral Memoir, Columbia University |
| *BP* | U.S. Congress, Senate. *Bolshevik Propaganda.* Hearings before a Subcommittee of the Committee on the Judiciary 65th Congress, 3rd session, Washington, D.C., 1919 |
| MR | Max Rabinoff Papers, Hoover Institution |
| JR | John Reed Papers, Harvard University |
| EFR | E. Francis Riggs Papers, Columbia University |
| RR | Raymond Robins Papers, Wisconsin State Historical Society |
| HHWT | Hermann Hagedorn/William B. Thompson Papers, Library of Congress |
| TsGANKh | Tsentralnyi Gosudarstvennyi Arkhiv Narodnogo Khozhiaistvo [Central Government Archive of the National Economy], Moscow |
| FV | Frank Vanderlip Papers, Columbia University |
| AW | Allen Wardwell Papers, Columbia University |
| HW | Henry White Papers, Library of Congress |
| PWW | Arthur S. Link, ed. *The Papers of Woodrow Wilson,* 66 vols to date (Princeton, 1966–) |
| WWLC | Woodrow Wilson Papers, Library of Congress |
| WBW | William B. Wiseman papers, Yale University |

## Introduction

1. RR, reel 4.

2. Telephone conversation between Valentin Zorin, Chief of Foreign Department of Petrograd Soviet, and Soviet Foreign Minister Georgi Chicherin, September 30, 1918, U.S. War Department intercepts, GK.

3. This is a perfect description of Raymond Robins' initiatives. He exceeded his authority, was backed up by his ambassador, and then the U.S. State Department was persuaded to change its instructions.

4. Woodrow Wilson to Robert Lansing, enclosing Grant-Smith (chargé in Copenhagen) to Lansing, 1/20/18, PWW 46:45–46.

5. Lansing's suggestion of a definitive statement against the Bolsheviks was not adopted by Wilson, and the decision to intervene only suspended contact rather than ending it. Wilson met with Lansing a number of times on the non-recognition issue. Lansing noted on the original copy of his long memorandum on non-recognition, December 4, 1917, "President did not use it." RLP, B3. Wilson's *aide-mémoire* on intervention was issued 7/17/18. FRUS 1918, Russia, II:262–263.

6. The ratification of the Brest Litovsk treaty ended this consideration. For

House's consultations with the British, See House to Balfour, 2/14/18, EMH, B14, f288.

7. See Lockhart to FO 3/11/18, VAM (O) B364 (B); *Rodina*, 4/30/18 DRF, B33–56; *Novaya Zhizn*, 6/2/18.

8. This is particularly true of the correspondence between Raymond Robins and David Francis and between DeWitt Clinton Poole and Francis in DRF; the correspondence of William H. Buckler in the WHB, the WVJ; RR and AG; the Ludwig Martens materials in Lusk; and the newly available Martens-Chicherin correspondence in TsGANKh. Western researchers have only begun to examine newly available former Soviet Foreign Ministry Archives and Communist Party archives, both opened in the wake of the collapse of the Soviet Union in early 1992. It will take some time to determine the extent of new archival information bearing on Soviet-American relations in the Lenin period. For the latest developments on access to former Soviet archives, particularly those related to Soviet foreign policy, see the Cold War International History Project *Bulletin* No. 1 (Spring 1992), Woodrow Wilson Center, Washington, D.C.; and also Patricia Kennedy Grimsted, "Beyond Perestroika: Soviet Area Archives after the August Coup," IREX special report, March 1992.

9. Princeton, 1956–1958. I appreciate George F. Kennan's assistance, encouragement, and access to considerable personal notes on unfinished volumes of his work.

10 New York, 1967. Mayer does not, however, treat other discussions between the two parties outside the context of Paris.

11. In this connection, see particularly Christopher Lasch, *The American Liberals and the Russian Revolution* (New York, 1962).

12. Neil Salzman, *Reform and Revolution: The Life and Times of Raymond Robins* (Kent, Ohio, 1991).

13. William Appleman Williams, "Raymond Robins and Russian American Relations, 1917–1938" (Ph.D. diss., University of Wisconsin, 1950) a good portion of which (but without such extensive references) can be found in his *American-Russian Relations 1781–1947* (New York and Toronto, 1952); James K. Libby, *Alexander Gumberg and Soviet-American Relations, 1917–1933* (Lexington, 1977); Anne Vincent Meiburger, *Efforts of Raymond Robins toward the Recognition of Soviet Russia, 1917–1933* (Washington, D.C., 1958).

14. Teddy J. Uldricks, *Diplomacy and Ideology: The Origins of Soviet Foreign Policy, 1917–1930* (London and Beverly Hills, 1979), and idem, "Russia and Europe: Diplomacy, Revolution and Economic Development in the 1920s," *International History Review*, I (June, 1979); Richard K. Debo, *Revolution and Survival: the Foreign Policy of Soviet Russia, 1917–1918* (Toronto, 1979), and idem, "George Chicherin: Soviet Russia's Second Foreign Commissar" (Ph.D. diss., University of Nebraska, 1964); Hugh Daniel Phillips, *Between the Revolution and the West: A Political Biography of Maksim M. Litvinov* (Boulder, Colo., 1992). Debo's latest work, *Survival and Consolidation: The Foreign Policy of Soviet Russia, 1918–1921* (Montreal, 1992), was received too late for review.

15. Richard H. Ullman, *Anglo-Soviet Relations, 1917–1921*, 3 vols. (Princeton, 1961–1972).

16. Louis K. Fischer, *The Soviets in World Affairs: A History of the Relations between the Soviet Union and the Rest of the World, 1917–1929*, 2 vols (Princeton, 1951).

## Chapter 1

1. Unsigned article, *Rodina*, April 30, 1918, DRF, B33–56.

2. Louise Bryant cable to Internews *re* interview with Lenin, 10/13/20, FM, B2.

3. These dual tactics of appeals both to governments and to people took form right from the beginning, in the Decree on Peace. Lenin's note to Chicherin and Karakhan in October 1918, in which he urged them to appeal for peace to the government "to open the eyes of the peoples" only makes it explicit. Lenin to G. V. Chicherin and L. M. Karakhan, 10/10/18, *Collected Works* (4th ed.) 44:152. See also Lenin's "Letter to American workers," 8/20/18, in which he noted that "help from you will probably not come soon." *Sochineniia* (5th ed.) 28:74. For an excellent analysis of Lenin's hopes for public pressure in the West helping to limit intervention, see John M. Thompson, "Lenin's Analysis of Intervention," *American Slavic and East European Review,* Vol. XVII, No. 2 (April, 1958): 151–160.

4. For the best account of Soviet-American relations of the 1920s, see Joan Hoff Wilson, *Ideology and Economics* (Columbia, Mo., 1974).

5. Louise Bryant interview, 10/13/20, FM, B2.

6. See, for example, Lenin to Chicherin and Karakhan, 10/10/18, *Collected Works* (4th ed.) 44:152; Poole to Francis, 5/26/18, DRF, B33–56; William C. Bullitt, "Proposed statement to Press on Russia," April, 1919, HW, B52; Alan Wardwell's impressions of Lenin, 6/13/18, AW; Robins' long report to Johnson, 6/12/18, HJ, III:12.

7. Robins report to Johnson, 6/12/18, HJ III:12.

8. For a useful chronological summary of Lenin's foreign policy activity, see Mikhail Trush, *Vneshnepoliticheskaia deiatel'nost V. I. Lenina, 1917–1920, den za denem* (Moscow, 1963), passim. For a short English summary, see the series "Lenin's Foreign Policy Activity" in the 1968–69 issues of *International Affairs* (Moscow). For new essays on Soviet relations with the west, especially Scandinavia, see John Hiden and Aleksandr Loit, *Contact or Isolation? Soviet-Western Relations in the Interwar Period* (Stockholm, 1991).

9. See, for example, his classic "Imperialism," *Collected Works* (4th ed), particularly 22:195–210.

10. See the illuminating discussion in Debo, *Revolution and Survival,* 13.

11. See Robert C. Tucker, "Autocrats and Oligarchs," in Ivo J. Lederer, ed., *Russian Foreign Policy: Essays in Historical Perspective* (New Haven, 1962), 179; Uldricks, *Diplomacy and Ideology,* 174–175; Debo, "Chicherin," 191–192. The most famous of these instances was, of course, Brest Litovsk.

12. See Uldricks, *Diplomacy and Ideology;* Debo, "Chicherin," M. P. Iroshnikov, "Iz istorii organizatsii narodnogo komissariata inostrannikh del," *Istoriia SSSR* #1 (1964): 105–116.

13. Debo, "Chicherin," 107; Adam Ulam, *The Bolsheviks* (New York, 1984), 493, 503.

14. See Robert D. Warth, *Soviet Russia in World Politics* (New York, 1963), 103; Leonard Schapiro, *The Communist Party of the Soviet Union* (New York, 1971), 196; Tucker, "Autocrats and Oligarchs," 181; Uldricks, *Diplomacy and Ideology,* 117–120.

15. T. H. Rigby, *Lenin's Government, Sovnarkom, 1917–1922* (Cambridge, England, 1979), 47, 56, 65–66. The foremost Soviet scholar of Lenin and Sovnarkom, M. P. Iroshnikov, agrees with Rigby. See Iroshnikov, *Predsedatl' soveta narodnikh komissarov Vl. Ul'ianov-lenin, ocherki gosudarstvennoi deiatel'nosti v 1917–1918 gg* (Leningrad, 1974). Bonch-Bruevich, Lenin's secretary in Sovnarkom, lends added weight to this position in his reminiscences. See V. D. Bonch-Bruevich, *Vospominania o Lenine* (Moscow, 1963).

16. See, for example, Franz Borkenau, *World Communism: A History of the Communist International* (Ann Arbor, 1962); James W. Hulse, *The Forming of The Communist International* (Stanford, 1964); Bronko Lazitch and Milorad Drachkovitch, *Lenin and the Comintern* (Stanford, 1972).

17. See Borkenau, *World Communism,* 12; Hulse, *Forming,* 33; Lazitch and Drachkovitch, *Lenin and the Comintern,* 206; Ulam, *Bolsheviks,* 493.

18. See Trotsky's description of this in *Proletarskaia revoliutsiia,* No. 10 (1922): 57–61; *Mezhdunarodnaia Zhizn,* No. 15 (133) (1922.)

19. See Decree of Sovnarkom, December 26, 1917, in Jane Degras, ed., *Soviet Documents on Foreign Policy* (London, 1952), I:22. For discussions of the Bureau of Revolutionary Propaganda, see L. I. Trofimova, "Pervie Shagi Sovetsoi diplomatii," *Novaia i Noveishiaia Istoriia,* No. 16 (1971): 37–52; M. P. Iroshnikov, "Iz Istorii organizatsii narodnogo komissariata inostrahnikh del," *Istoriia SSSR,* No. 1 (1964): 112–114.

20. Appeal for the formation of the Communist International, 1/24/19, Degras, *Soviet Documents* I:136–137.

21. See Eugene Magerovsky, "The People's Commissariat of Foreign Affairs, 1917–1946" (Ph.D. diss., Columbia University, 1975), 142.

22. Ulam, *The Bolsheviks,* 493. See also Warren Lerner, "Poland in 1920: A Case Study in Foreign Policy Decision Making under Lenin," *South Atlantic Quarterly* 72 (Summer, 1973): 406–414; Piotr Wandycz, *Soviet-Polish Relations, 1917–1921* (Cambridge, England, 1969), chap. 9; Norman Davies, "The Missing Revolutionary War: The Polish Campaign and the Retreat from Revolution in Soviet Russia, 1919–1921," *Soviet Studies,* No. 2 (April, 1975): 78–195; Uldricks, "Russia and Europe," 59–60.

23. Louis Fischer, *The Life of Lenin* (New York, 1964), 528–529.

24. Theodore H. Von Laue, "Soviet Diplomacy: G. V. Chicherin, 1918–1930," in Gordon Craig and Felix Gilbert, *The Diplomats* (New York, 1963), 280.

25. Robert M. Slusser, "The Role of the Foreign Ministry," in Lederer, *Russian Foreign Policy,* 213; Lazitch and Drachkovitch, *Lenin and the Comintern,* 38–39; Schapiro, *Communist Party,* 196–197; Warth, *Soviet Russia,* 103; Vernon Aspaturian, *Process and Power in Soviet Foreign Policy* (Boston, 1971), 224.

26. See Magerovsky, "People's Commissariat," 71–72; Uldricks, *Diplomacy and Ideology,* 122–23. See also Teddy Uldricks, "The Soviet Diplomatic Corps in the Cicerin Era," *Jahrbücher für Gershichte Ost Europas* 23, No. 2 (1975), 213–224.

27. Magerovsky, "People's Commissariat," 16; Rigby, *Sovnarkom,* 47; Uldricks, "Cicerin Era," 215.

28. Lenin, 12/31/22, *Collected Works* (4th ed.) 45:361.

29. Magerovsky, "People's Commissariat," 71–72; Uldricks, "Development of Soviet Diplomatic Corps," 263.

30. *Novaya Zhizn,* 3/29/18, DRF, B33–56.

31. See Bullitt's proposed statement to the press, 4/4/19, HW, B52; and Chicherin as quoted by Alfred Nagel to Ambassador Morris of Sweden, 3/3/19, HW B40.

32. L. Trotsky, *Moia zhizn* (Berlin, 1930) II:62–64. Trotsky says, however, that someone else quoted him, although he agreed with the sentiments. Later, he admits to having greatly overstated the case. See Trotsky, *Sochineniia* (Moscow, 1925), Vol. III, Part II, 99; and Isaac Deutscher, *The Prophet Armed, Trotsky, 1879–1921* (New York, 1954), 327.

33. For accounts of these first days at the Narkomindel, see I. Zalkind, "N.K.I.D. v semnadsotom godu," *Mezhdunarodniaia Zhizn,* No. 10 (1921): 12; *DVP* I:85; *Mezhdunarodniaia Zhizn,* No. 15 (1922): 51–52; M. P. Iroshnikov, "Iz Istorii . . .", 107–109; L. Trotsky, "Vospominania ob oktiabskom perevorote," *Proletarskiaia revoliutsiia,* No. 10 (1922): 58–61.

34. For vivid accounts of the damage Zalkind did to relations with the Allies, see Kennan, *Soviet-American Relations* I:335–341, 401–408.

35. Deutscher, *Prophet Armed,* 395–398.

36. See Isaac Deutscher, *The Prophet Unarmed, Trotsky, 1921–1929* (New York, 1959), 56.

37. See Trotsky speech before Central Executive Committee 11/24/17, as translated by American Embassy and summarized by Francis, PWW 45:119–121.

38. See Judson Diary, 12/4/17, WVJ; Arthur Bullard, memo on Bolshevist movement in Russia, 1/23/18, AB, B13; Samuel N. Harper to Richard Crane, 2/22/18, SH, B5; Lindley for Lockhart to Milner, 2/22/18, VAM 364 (B); Balfour to Lockhart, 3/6/18, WBW, B9, F227; Lockhart to Foreign Office, 3/12/18, VAM 364 (B); Balfour to Lansing, 4/18/18, PWW 47:367.

39. Balfour to Reading, enclosed in Reading to Lansing, 4/29/18, FRUS, 1918, Russia, II:148–149.

40. Debo, "Chicherin," 98; idem, *Revolution and Survival,* 61, 85–86.

41. The first full-scale treatment of Chicherin and his policies is the unpublished dissertation by Richard K. Debo, "Georgiy Chicherin: Soviet Russia's Second Foreign Commissar" (Ph.D. diss., University of Nebraska, 1964). There is no satisfactory published bibliography. Timothy O'Connor's new study, *Diplomacy and Revolution: G. V. Chicherin and Soviet Foreign Affairs, 1918–1930* (Ames, Iowa, 1988), develops new material on Chicherin's revolutionary development, but adds little on his diplomacy. See also sketches by Von Laue in Slusser, "Role of Foreign Ministry" 213–217; Richard K. Debo, "The Making of a Bolshevik: Georgii Chicherin in England, 1914–1918," *Slavic Review* XXV, No. 4 (December, 1966): 651–662; I. M. Maiski, "Diplomats of the Lenin School: Georgi Chicherin," *New Times* (Moscow), No. 44 (1967): 10–13; E. M. Chossudovsky, *Chicherin and the Evolution of Soviet Foreign Policy and Diplomacy* (Geneva, 1973); I. M. Maisky, *Journey into the Past,* (London, 1962), 70–79; Louis Fischer, *Men and Politics: An Autobiography* (New York, 1941), 141–146. In Russian, see L. I. Trofimova, "Stranitsa diplomaticheskoi deiatel'nosti G. V. Chicherina," *Voprosy Istorii,* No. 2 (1973): 114–123; C. Zarnitski, A. Sergeev, *Chicherin* (Moscow, 1975); I. M. Gorokhov, L. Zamiatin, I. Zemskov, *G. V. Chicherin: diplomat leninskoi schkoli* (Moscow, 1966); C. Dmitrievski, *Sovetskie Portreti* (Paris, 1932), 228–240; A. O. Chubarian, *Diplomati Leninskoi Schkoli* (Moscow, 1982), 26–55.

42. Debo, "Chicherin," 100.

43. Debo, "Chicherin," 160–161; Magerovsky, "People's Commissariat," 86, 142.

44. On Chicherin's career, see especially Debo, "Chicherin," 1–91; and *idem,* "The Making of a Bolshevik," passim. References to his work habits and eccentricities are numerous. See particularly Louis Fischer, *Men and Politics,* 141–146; and S. Dmitrievski (Chicherin's former secretary in the Narmomindel), *Sovietskie Portrety,* 229–240. Chicherin's conversion to Marxism is detailed in a short article by G. Kizelshtein, "Muchitel'no zazhdu visoku Tseli" (iz arkhiva G. V. Chicherina)," *Ogonek,* No. 48 (1963), 18, with quotations from the Chicherin family archive, fond 1030, Saltykov Schedrin Library, Leningrad.

45. For more details on Chicherin's relationship with Lenin, see Debo, "Chicherin," 107; Uldricks, *Diplomacy and Ideology,* 30; Trofimova, "Stranitsa diplomaticheskoi deiatel'nosti G. V. Chicherina," especially 114, 116.

46. G. V. Chicherin, "Lenin i vneshniaia politika," *Mirovaia politika v 1924 godu* (Moscow, 1924), 3. This article is reprinted, with some omissions having to do with relations with Germany, in *Vospominania o V. I. Lenine,* (Moscow, 1984), 490–497 and *Voprosy Istorii #3* (1957): 20–25.

47. Lenin to A. A. Joffe, 7/1/18, *Collected Works* (4th ed.) 50:111.

48. Lenin to Béla Kun, late July 1919, Lenin, *Collected Works* (4th ed.) 44:271;

Lenin to Yelena Stasova, March 1920, *Collected Works* (4th ed.) 44:365. For an outside observer's confirmation of Lenin's close relationship with and support for Chicherin, see Lockhart to Balfour, 11/7/18, BL(H), B5, Russia 1918.

49. See Chicherin's discussion of this in *Two Years of Foreign Policy* (New York, 1920), 18.

50. Lenin to Chicherin, January, 1922, *Collected Works* (4th ed.) 54:1346–1347.

51. See Von Laue, "Chicherin," 264; Uldricks, *Diplomacy and Ideology,* 88–89.

52. Chicherin, *Two Years of Foreign Policy,* 18, 28. Both Debo and Kennan believe that the Chicherin-Poole relationship was essentially the only pragmatic, mutually beneficial one in the early attempts at *modus operandi*. See Kennan, *Soviet-American Relations,* II, 302, Debo, "Chicherin," 124–125.

53. No modern Western scholarly biography of Litvinov exists. The latest study is an excellent monograph by Hugh Daniel Phillips, *Between the Revolution and the West: a Political Biography of Maksim M. Litvinov* (Boulder, Colo., 1992). Arthur Upham Pope's *Maxim Litvinoff* (New York, 1943) is nonscholarly, and based largely on contemporary sources and interviews. The first Soviet biography, N. Kornev, *Litvinov* (Moscow, 1936) is a Stalinist paean. Soviet scholar Z. S. Sheinis completed a biography of Litvinov in the late 1960s, based on Soviet Foreign Ministry and Party archives. Long denied publication, it has just been published as *Maksim M. Litvinov: Revoliutsioner, diplomat, chelovek* (Moscow, 1989) in English as *Maksim Litvinov* (Moscow, 1990). Better material exists on Litvinov's earlier career, in exile and as *de facto* representative to Britain in 1917 and 1918. See particularly Hugh Daniel Phillips, "From a Bolshevik to a British Subject: The Early Years of Maksim M. Litvinov," *Slavic Review* 48, No. 3 (Fall, 1989), 388–398; Richard K. Debo, "Litivnov and Kamenev," passim; M. P. Iroshnikov, "iz istorii . . . ," 114–116; and Maisky, *Journey* 53–69. Tatiana Litvinov's reminiscences, "Vstrechi i rasulki," *Novy Mir* No. 7 (1966): 235–250, deal almost exclusively with Litvinov's exile in Britain, 1916–1918.

54. See R. H. Bruce Lockhart, *Memoirs of a British Agent* (London, 1933), 200–202; and Maisky, *Journey,* 64–66 (for Litvinov's own recollections of this meeting). For more details of this period of Litvinov's work and the relationship to Lockhart, see Debo, "Litvinov and Kamenev," passim.

55. For further discussion of this episode, see Chapter 6.

56. Buckler notes on meetings with Litvinov, 1/16/19, WHB, B6, f9; Litvinov to Wilson, 12/24/18; Degras, *Soviet Documents,* 129–132.

57. Virtually all Soviet representatives, American representatives, and outside observers support this observation of a Bolshevik strategy of preferential treatment toward the United States.

58. Trotsky speech before the Central Executive Committee of the Soviet, summarized and translated by U.S. Embassy, Petrograd, PWW 45:119–121.

59. Morris (Sweden) to Lansing, 12/1/17, FRUS, 1918 (Russia), I, 227–278.

60. Francis to Lansing, *re* Trotsky speech, 12/1/17, FRUS, 1918, Russia, I, 275.

61. "For More Realism," *Izvestia,* 3/16/18, LEB, B2.

62. Interview with Lunacharsky in Petrograd *Novaya Zhizn,* 3/29/18, U.S. Embassy translation, 4/1/18, DRF, B33–56.

63. Browne memo, 5/2/18, LEB, B2.

64. "Diplomats at the crossroads," *Novaya Zhizn,* 6/2/18, DRF, B33–56.

65. Poole to Francis, 7/23/18, DRF, B34–56; Francis to Poole, 7/14/18, DRF, B34–56.

66. Chicherin in *Izvestia*, 9/3/18, translated by U.S. Consul and enclosed in Poole to Lansing, 9/5/18, FRUS, 1918, Russia, I, 581–586. This attitude of Chicherin's at the time of the breakup of the Allies in Moscow is confirmed by other sources, including Charles Stephenson Smith of the Associated Press (see George F. Kennan, Conversation with Charles Stephenson Smith, 9/29/54, GK).

67. See Lockhart, *Diaries,* 45. For Lenin's detailed instructions to Chicherin, see Lenin to Karakhan, October 10, 1918, *Collected Works* (4th ed.) 44:152. Chicherin's final note to Wilson, however, was not without overtures to the United States. For the full text, see Degras, *Soviet Documents,* 112–120.

68. Chicherin, *Two Years of Soviet Foreign Policy,* 10–17.

69. See FRUS, 1919, Russia, 186–187; FRUS, 1920, III, 670–675.

70. U.S. military intelligence translation of telegraphic conversation between Zorin and Chicherin, 9/30/18, GK.

71. Chicherin note, 2/4/19, FRUS, 1919, Russia, 39–42; and Chicherin, quoted by Alfred Nagel to Ambassador Morris of Sweden, to Ammission, 3/3/19, HW, B40.

72. R. H. Lord to Bullitt, weekly summary of Russia and Rumania, 4/27/19, HW, B42.

73. Chicherin to Mason, telegram, 5/18/20, FM, B1.

74. Address from the All-Russian Central Executive Committee of the Soviets to the United States Congress and President Harding, 3/20/21, Degras, *Soviet Documents,* 244–45.

75. For an excellent analysis of Lenin's strategy to weaken intervention, see John M. Thompson, "Lenin's Analysis of Intervention," *American Slavic and East European Review,* XVII, No. 2 (April, 1958): 151–160. See also Lockhart's clear conclusion that a key element in the Bolshevik strategy vis-à-vis the Allies was to detach America from intervention. Lockhart to Balfour, 11/7/18, BL (H) B5, Russia, 1918. On Lenin's strength in seeing and exploiting openings, see Chubarian, "u istokov leninskoi vneshnei politiki," 39–55.

76. See Chicherin's response to Prinkipo, Feb. 4, 1919, and the long note to Wilson proposing peace, October 24, 1918, for particularly astute mixing of political and economic elements.

77. See editorial in *Rodina,* 4/30/18, U.S. Embassy translation, DRF, B33–56.

78. "Markings on P.V. Bukharsev's telegram concerning the agreement with the American Corporation and an instruction to the Secretary," 6/19/20, Lenin *Collected Works* (4th ed.) 44:389.

79. Lenin to Chicherin and Litvinov, 5/7/19, Lenin, *Collected Works* (4th ed.) 44:224–226.

80. Litvinov to Chicherin, 8/26/20, British secret service intercept, LG, F/9/2/42. On the use of foreign trade representatives, prisoner-of-war negotiators, and "humanitarian" representatives for political negotiations during the almost total breakoff of contact with the West during 1919 and early 1920, see Uldricks, "Development of Soviet Diplomatic Corps," 100–108.

81. See for example, M. L. Trush's statement, "after the signing of the Brest Peace Treaty the Soviet government began devising plans for the development of commercial and economic relations with capitalist countries." *Soviet Foreign Policy: The Early Years,* 82.

82. See Trotsky speech to Grenadier regiment, 12/13/17, DRF, B29–56.

83. John Reed, "Skeleton Report," 1/6/18, JR, 2:113 A.

84. For details on these discussions, see Gvishiani, 35–45, quoting from AVP. For

an American perspective, see Harper Memoir material, notes on meeting at City Club with Lomonosov, 2/7/18, SH.

85. Ludmilla Gvishiani, *Sovetskaia Rossiia i SshA, 1917–1920* (Moscow, 1970), 148.

86. See Samuel Harper to Richard Crane, 2/22/18, SH, B5.

87. *Congressional Record,* 1/29/19, p. 2,263. See also Robins testimony, BP, 800–801.

88. See discussions by Ganelin, *Sovetsko-Amerikanskie otnosheniia,* 156–158; and Shishkin, "Oktiabskaiia Revoliutsiia i economicheskie otnosheniia," 8–18, utilizing new information from TsGANKh, fond 413, and Tsentralnyi Gosudarstvennyi Arkhiv Oktiabskoi Revoliutsii (TsGAOR), fond 1525.

89. Lenin to Robins, 5/14/18, with accompanying plan for Soviet-American economic relations, Lenin *Collected Works* (4th ed.) 44:87; C&P, 204–212.

90. McCallister to International Harvester, 4/18/18, NA, RG 59: 861.00/1646. For the Soviet decree, see Degras, *Soviet Documents* I, 71.

91. Poole to Francis w/ John Lehrs report, 6/5/18, NAM, reel 3. Also see Ganelin, *Sovetsko-Amerikanskie otnosheniia,* 158, quoting Tsentralnyi Gosudarstvennyi Istoricheskii Arkhiv (TsGIA) Leningrad, fond 150.

92. Chicherin to Wilson, 10/24/18, Degras, *Soviet Documents,* 118–119. See also Lockhart on conversation with Karakhan, 11/7/18, BL (H), B5.

93. Litvinov to Wilson, 12/24/18, Degras, *Soviet Documents,* 131. M. E. Sonkin, *Okno vo vneshnii mir: ekonomicheskie svyasay sovetskogo gosudarstva 1917–1921 gg.* (Moscow, 1964), 122, emphasizes particularly Litvinov's economic concerns, and includes citations in support from TsGANKh, fond 413.

94. Litvinov and Vorovski to Meyer, 1/10/19, C&P, 274. For similar statements, see Chicherin reply *re* Prinkipo, 2/4/19, Degras, *Soviet Documents,* 138, offering concessions; Buckler report on meetings with Litvinov, 1/16/19, WHB; Lenin-Bullitt Proposal, 3/12/19, Degras, *Soviet Documents,* 148, with particular emphasis on normal trade relations and the flow of food supplies.

95. Nuorteva and Martens to Lansing, 3/25/19, EMH, B207. See also Committee of The Union League of New York, intelligence report to Sir William Wiseman, 4/11/19, WBW, B9, f211.

96. Lenin answers to questions put by *Chicago Daily News* correspondent, 10/5/19, Lenin, *Collected Works* (4th ed.) 30:50–51; talk with Lincoln Eyre, 2/21/20, *Collected Works* (4th ed.) 30:446–451.

97. All Russian Central Executive Committee to Harding, 3/20/21, Degras, *Soviet Documents,* 244–245.

## Chapter 2

1. Wilson to Lansing, enclosing Grant-Smith (chargé in Copenhagen) to Lansing, 1/20/18, PWW 46:45–46.

2. Lansing to Polk, 1/21/18, RLP, B4.

3. The numerous American actors in Russia, led by General William V. Judson, Chief of the American Red Cross Raymond Robins, and Ambassador David Francis, were often more important in the actual decisions concerning discussions with the Bolsheviks than were their superiors in Washington. Discussion of those principals, their roles, and their interaction with Washington will take place in the context of those discussions, in Chapters 3, 4, and 5.

4. Lansing was one of the few Wilson advisors who were openly skeptical of the

glowingly optimistic accounts brought back by the Root mission, for example. See "Memorandum on the Russian Situation," 8/9/17, RLP, Box 2: I.

5. Secretary of War Newton Baker's and his military advisors' role was limited to advice on the military efficacy of intervention, which they consistently opposed. Only in Paris did they play any role in contacts with the Bolsheviks. For Baker's advice and overall role in Russia policy, see Frederick Palmer, *Newton Baker: America at War* (New York, 1931) II:313–321. See also Baker to Wilson, 3/3/19, PWW 55:399–403. For the role of Chief of Staff Peyton March, see Peyton C. March, *The Nation at War* (Garden City, N.Y., 1934), 113–146. On General Tasker Bliss and his role in Paris, see Chapter 8.

6. Robert Lansing, *War Memoirs of Robert Lansing, Secretary of State* (Indianapolis, 1935), 341.

7. Wilson met with Lansing several times about this matter. Lansing noted on the original copy of his long memorandum, "President did not use it." RLP, B3. There is a dispute about whether Wilson agreed with Lansing in his condemnation of the Bolsheviks and simply chose to delay issuing a definitive statement, or whether he disagreed with Lansing's early and strident anti-Bolshevism. Unterberger, "Woodrow Wilson and the Russian Revolution," 52, argues the latter. Kennan (*Soviet-American Relations* I, 157–58), following Lansing's own interpretation (*War Memoirs*, 345), agrees with the former.

8. Lansing to Wilson, 12/10/17, RLP B3, Wilson, while refusing to go that far, did agree with a Lansing formulation of encouraging the British and French to bankroll Kaledin. Lansing to London for Crosby with a WW note, "This has my entire approval." PWW 45:274–275.

9. "Memorandum on Nonrecognition of a Russian Government," 1/6/18, RLP, B4; Lansing to Wilson, 1/10/18, PWW 45:562–565.

10. "Memorandum on Absolutism and Bolshevism," 10/26/18, RLP, B2: I.

11. Lansing, 8-page policy memorandum to Wilson, 12/3/19, FRUS, 1920, III, 436–444.

12. See Williams, "Robins," 78–80. Williams, both in this dissertation and in his book *Russian-American Relations 1781–1947,* argues that Polk, Phillips, and Miles were crucial in the development and implementation of U.S. policy toward Soviet Russia in the Wilson administration. While I would agree that they played an important role, to emphasize it unduly would be to ignore the often-considerable influence of Colonel House and through him a number of liberals and even radicals, and also to discount the conflicting views of Woodrow Wilson himself.

13. For examples of Polk's utilizing this double channel of influence, see Polk to Lansing, 4/16/19, FP, B9, F310; Polk to Auchincloss, 4/5/19, FP, B1, F21; Polk to Auchincloss, 12/1/17, FP, B1, F16; Auchincloss diary, 6/13/18, GA, B2, f 21, p.13; Edward M. House diary, 7/19/18, 8/15/17, 9/11/17, EMH.

14. A good example of this is the role that Polk played in developing the policy statement, in the aftermath of the intervention decision, in a way that would satisfy House, Wilson, and Lansing. See House diary, 7/19/18, EMH.

15. For example, note Polk's letter to Auchincloss, 2/18/19, FP, B1, F 20.

16. Phillips to Lansing, 12/3/17, RLP, B3.

17. Register of the Department of State, 12/19/17, (Washington, D.C., 1918), 121, 128–129; Lansing date book, 10/15/17, RLP, B3.

18. NA, RG 59: 861.00/1048 1/2, 861.01/14 1/2.

19. *Ibid.*

20. Coolidge to Lansing, confidential report, 5/20/18, RLP, B4.

21. Polk to Auchincloss, 2/18/19, FP, B1, F20; Miles to Francis, 11/1/18, DRF, B35–56; Miles to Lansing, 6/2/19, RLLC, Vol. 43.

22. The outlines of Harper's career as expert and advisor and finally staffer in the State Department in these years can be traced in his memoirs, *The Russia I Believe In* (Chicago, 1945), but the memoirs leave out much, and also distort occasionally. Harper's voluminous personal papers (79 boxes and over 40,000 pages) remain the only detailed record of his extensive contacts and significant political impact.

23. Harper notes in his memoirs that Crane took 23 separate trips to Russia from 1890 to 1930. (Harper, *The Russia I Believe In,* 6.) For an example of the kind of letters Crane wrote to Wilson, see Crane to Wilson, 7/9/18, PWW 48:570–573. For Lansing's regard for and utilization of Crane's advice, see Lansing, *War Memoirs,* 331–332.

24. Harper was first introduced to Crane as a student of eighteen in 1900, and Crane had much to do with Harper's decision to enter the field of Russian studies. Some of his education was financed by Crane and Crane's subsidy of the University of Chicago began early in 1917. (Harper, *The Russia I Believe In,* 9–10; Roger Williams to Henry P. Judson, 2/14/17, SH, B3.)

25. See Richard Crane to Harper, 3/15/17, and 5/22/17, SH, B3; and Harper to Crane, 6/30/18, SH, B5.

26. For details on Harper's rather desultory work with the Inquiry, see J. T. Shotwell to Harper, "Plan for Work," 11/30/17, SH, B4; Harper to President Henry Pratt Judson, University of Chicago, 12/14/17, SH, B4; Harper to Shotwell, 1/30/18, SH, B4; Shotwell to Harper, 8/19/18, SH, B5.

27. Harper to his brother Paul, 8/12/17, SH, B4.

28. See Harper to Crane, 4/12/17, SH, B3.

29. See Harper to Phillips, 12/14/17, SH, B4.

30. For a fully developed statement of Harper's thinking on the differences between recognitionists and interventionists, and his role in 1918, see Draft Memoirs, SH, B76. For Harper's early position against intervention, see Harper to Crane, 3/23/18, SH, B5.

31. "The Bolsheviki and Peace," 3-page draft memorandum, February 1918, SH, B54. See also Harper to Lippmann, 1/18/18, SH, B4. See also materials in "Russian docket," memoir materials, and Harper papers, including extensive notes of meetings in February 1918, where he called for a more active ambassador and agreed with Bullard's and Robins' position on "contact." By July 1918, he had resolutely turned against the Bolsheviks, while holding on to the possibility of cooperating with the soviets, believing that they still maintained a democratic composition and that the Bolsheviks could be opposed from within the soviets themselves. See Harper to Carpenter, 6/10/18, Harper to Walter Lippmann, 6/11/18, Harper to Crane, 6/11/18, all SH, B5.

32. Harper to Richard Crane, 6/30/18, SH, B5.

33. See Harper to Carpenter, 6/10/18, SH, B5. Harper was still urging Carpenter to see Robins as late as June 24, 1918 (Harper to Carpenter, 6/24/18, SH, B5).

34. See Nuorteva to Harper, 5/9/18, SH, B5; Harper to Nuorteva, 5/12/18, SH, B5; Harper to Porter, 5/11/18, SH B5; Kellock to Harper, 6/28/18, SH, B5.

35. See Chapter 12.

36. Harper began his informal contacts with the State Department as early as 1916, and was solicited for his analysis of the March revolution by Secretary of State Lansing. See F. H. Sterling to Harper, 12/12/16, SH, B3; Richard Crane to Harper, 3/15/17, SH, B3.

37. For details on these relationships, see Harper to Herbert L. Carpenter of the Russian-American Economic League, 6/5/18; Harper to Carpenter, 6/10/18; Harper to Porter, 9/16/18; all SH, B5.

38. For evidence of House contacts with Carpenter, see House diary entries, 5/14/18, 4/23/18, and 10/2/18, EMH.

39. See Harper to Huntington, 10/4/18, SH, B5, for Harper's assessment of his hard-won credibility.

40. See draft memoir material on Harper's thinking with regard to the State Department position, SH, B76.

41. For Harper's reflections on his relationship with Huntington, see draft memoirs, SH, B76. For examples of the closeness of their friendship, see Huntington to Harper, 5/17/19, SH, B6.

42. Harper to Charles R. Crane, 3/23/18, SH, B5.

43. Harper's private letters and memoranda in late 1919 became increasingly hysterical and strident, even getting caught up in gossip and speculation regarding a Bolshevik-Jewish conspiracy's influence on Lloyd George, Wilson, and House through Louis Brandeis. See Harper to Carter, 11/18/19, SH, B7.

44. Interpretations of the reasons for this break abound. It will be further discussed in the context of Russian policy in Paris, Chapters 8, 9, and 10.

45. Most famous was his decision to wash his hands of the Bullitt mission, and to leave any follow-up to House (see Chapter 9).

46. As House noted in his diary, Wilson was not fully cognizant of how closely House kept in touch with the State Department: House diary, 2/1/18, 6/8/18, EMH.

47. House diary, 10/24/17, EMH.

48. House Diary, 1/9/18, EMH.

49. House to Wilson, 3/10/18, EMH, B121, with handwritten note by House: "He did this."

50. See House to Wilson, 6/4/18, EMH, B121; House to Wilson, 6/13/18, EMH, B121; House to Wilson, 6/21/18, EMH, B121; Wilson to House, 7/8/18, EMH, B121.

51. See House diary, 9/24/18, 9/28/18; EMH.

52. House diary, 9/20/18, EMH.

53. House diary, 10/14/18, EMH.

54. Although Ray Stannard Baker was still to remark in his diary as late as March 28, "He [House] is the only man who keeps closely in touch with the President." From Baker diary, 3/28/19, PWW 56:338.

55. House diary, 2/14/19, EMH; Lansing's notes, "The President's Return to Paris," 3/16/19, RLP, B2, Vol. II; House diary, 3/22/19, Vol. 15, pp. 106–107.

56. For important accounts of Wiseman's role, see W. B. Fowler, *British-American Relations, 1917–1918: The Role of Sir William Wiseman* (Princeton, 1969); and Richard H. Ullman, *Anglo-Soviet Relations, 1917–1921,* 3 vols. (Princeton, 1961–1968). Most important for documenting Wiseman's relationship to House and Wilson are Wiseman's own papers (WBW). Buckler's correspondence to House can be found in both EMH and WHB.

57. See House diary, 5/15/17, 5/18/17, 5/23/17, 5/30/17, 2/2/18, EMH.

58. By the end of 1917, House felt that he had enormous influence with the British government through Wiseman. And, on Wilson's part, Wiseman's discretion and intelligence had broken through a general Wilson tendency to avoid consultation with the Allies and inform them only after an American decision. See House diary, 12/18/17, EMH. By the summer of 1918, however, even the most vigorous of House's attempts to get Wilson to consult with the British on American intentions on intervention were

in vain. Wilson's decision was made, then announced to the British, French, and Japanese. See House diary, 7/9/18, EMH.

59. Although Buckler's reports to House regarding British Labour and Liberal press were richest between late 1916 and August 1917 (when Ambassador Page requested that Buckler cease his confidential correspondence), a more limited version resumed in late 1917 and continued throughout 1918. See Buckler to House, 1/10/18, WHB, B5, f11; Buckler to House, 6/10/18, WHB, B5, f12; Buckler to House, 2/22/18, WHB, B5, f8.

60. House to Wilson and Lansing, 11/28/17, EMH, B121.

61. See House Diary, 1/2/18, EMH.

62. House to Balfour, 2/14/18, EMH, B10, f288.

63. House to Secretary of State, as recorded in Auchincloss diary, 12/1/17, GA, B2, f15; House diary, 3/3/18, EMH; House diary, 3/11/18, EMH; House diary, 4/24/18, EMH; House to Wilson, 6/21/18, EMH, B121; House diary, 6/27/18, EMH.

64. See Bullitt's memo to House on withdrawal from Archangel, with note from House to Wilson in support, 1/30/19, EMH, B21.

65. For detailed discussion of House's role in these initiatives in Paris, see Chapters 8, 9, and 10. Note particularly House diary, 3/27/19, in the aftermath of the Bullitt mission, where House muses, "I am trying to think something out that is workable. It is very difficult because no one wants to deal with such as Lenine and Trotsky" (EMH).

66. See House diary, 2/9/18, EMH.

67. Auchincloss functioned, for example, as the private audience for Provisional Government Ambassador Bakhmetev. See House diary, 8/19/17, EMH. He also often interviewed returnees from Russia for House, such as Red Cross staffer Thomas Thacher. Auchincloss diary, 5/28/18, GA, B2, f20, p. 30.

68. House even notes in his diary that Polk found Auchincloss more useful than Phillips, the first Assistant Secretary of State. House diary, 8/15/17, EMH.

69. See House to Wilson, 6/13/18, EMH, B121, f4285; Auchincloss diary, 6/13/18, GA, B2, f21, pp. 11–14; Auchincloss to Wilson, 6/13/18, GA, B8, f207; Auchincloss diary, 7/8/18, GA, B2, f22, pp. 6–7.

70. See Lansing's disdain for Auchincloss in his notes, "impressions as to the present situation," 3/20/19, RLP, B2, Vol. II. For Wilson, see the diary of Dr. Grayson, 4/7/19, PWW 57:62, 66; and diary of Dr. Grayson, 4/19/19, PWW 57:477.

71. Auchincloss diary, 3/29/19, 4/1/19, 4/4/19, GA, B3, F32, pp. 481, 488, 495–496.

72. See Colcord to Wilson, 12/3/17, PWW 45:191–193; Wilson to Colcord, 12/6/17, PWW 45:222; Colcord to Wilson, 12/8/17, PWW 45:250–253; Colcord to Wilson, 7/7/18, PWW 48:546–549; Wilson to Colcord, 7/9/18, PWW 48:557–559.

73. For Steffens, see Steffens to House, 2/5/18, EMH, B106; Steffens to House, 4/29/18, EMH, B106; Steffens to House, 5/8/18, EMH, B106; House to Steffens, 5/14/18, EMH, B106; House to Steffens, 6/24/19, EMH, B106. On Colcord, see particularly Colcord to House, 3/8/19, EMH, B29; and House to Colcord, 4/3/19, EMH, B29. On Eastman, see House diary, 9/26/17, EMH. On Lippmann, House diary, 9/22/17, EMH. On Lamont, see Lamont to House, 1/2/18, EMH, B182. On Williams, see House diary, 9/12/18, EMH; and House diary, 6/12/18, EMH. On Browne, see House diary, 6/26/18, EMH. On Beatty, see House diary, 3/2/18, EMH. House did not actually see Reed, but he kept closely in touch with Reed's recommendations through Bullitt and Steffens. See Bullitt to House, 5/20/18, EMH B21, f679; and Steffens to House, 2/1/18, EMH, B106, F3656.

74. Alexander George and Juliette L. George, *Woodrow Wilson and Colonel House* (New York, 1964), 191.

75. House diary, 5/22/17, EMH.

76. Colcord to House, 3/13/18, EMH, B29, f906; House diary, 3/14/18 and 4/29/18, EMH.

77. House diary, 6/26/18, and 8/6/18, EMH.

78. See House diary, 7/25/17, and 8/12/17, EMH.

79. Lansing to Tumulty, 11/6/17, PWW 44:524; Wilson to Herbert Bruce Brougham, 10/30/17, PWW 44:473.

80. For details of Bullitt's early career, see Beatrice K. Farnsworth, *William C. Bullitt and the Soviet Union* (Bloomington, Indiana, 1967), 1–29.

81. Bullitt to House, 2/3/18, EMH, B21, F 678; Bullitt to House, 2/7/18, EMH, B21, f676; Bullitt to Polk, 3/2/18, PWW 46:510–513; Bullitt to House, May 20, 1918, EMH, B21, f679; Bullitt to House, 6/24/18, EMH, B21, f679; Bullitt to House, 9/20/18, EMH, B21, f680; Bullitt to House, 9/24/18, EMH, B21, f680.

82. See Lansing to Wilson, 11/9/18, PWW 53:6.

83. Kennan, *Soviet-American Relations* I, 45–46. For the definitive story of the Committee on Public Information, see James R. Mock and Cedric Larson, *Words That Won the War: The Story of the Committee on Public Information, 1917–1919* (Princeton, 1939). Mock and Larson do not detail fully, however, Compub's work in Russia before and after the Bolshevik revolution. That story is best told in Kennan, I.

84. Kennan, *Soviet-American Relations* I, 46.

85. These "personal instructions" were in the form of a letter from Wilson to Sisson in the usual high-flown Wilson idealism, drafted by Creel for Wilson's signature. See Creel to Wilson and Wilson to Sisson, 10/24/17, PWW 44:434–435.

86. See Creel to Wilson, 5/10/17, AB, B1; Wilson to Lansing, 5/14/17, AB, B1; Wilson to Creel, 5/14/17, AB, B1.

87. See Lansing date book, 5/21/17, RLP, B3. See also corroborating evidence of Ernest Poole, memoir material, n.d. AB, B1.

88. Kennan, *Soviet-American Relations* I, 49. See also Bullard to House, 12/12/17, EMH, B21, F671. For details on both Bullard and Sisson, see Kennan, *Soviet-American Relations* I, 48–52.

89. Sisson's disdain for Ambassador Francis and State Department channels became so blatant that he had to be cautioned by Creel several times "to maintain the most friendly relations with the Ambassador." See Creel to Wilson, 12/27/17, PWW 45:367–368; Creel to Wilson, 1/15/18, PWW 45:596. For Bullard-House correspondence, see Bullard to House, 12/12/17, EMH, B21, f671; House to Bullard, 2/3/18, AB, B19; Bullard to House, 2/5/18, AB, B19; Bullard to House, 3/17/18, AB, B19.

90. Ernest Poole memorandum on Bullard, n.d., AB, B1.

91. Bullard to House, 12/12/17, EMH, B21, f671.

92. "Memo on the Bolshevist Movement in Russia," 40-page memo, January 1918 (n.d.), AB, B13.

93. Bullard to House, 3/17/18, AB, B19.

94. In fact, although Secretary of State Lansing met regularly with French Ambassador J. J. Jusserand concerning Allied policy toward Russia, the only French representative to meet with Wilson (until Paris) concerning Russian policy was Henri Bergson, who tried several times to convince Wilson of the necessity of intervention. See Bergson notebooks on meeting with Wilson, 7/25/18, PWW 49:94–95; and House diary, 6/13/18, EMH.

95. Both the American and British public and private papers support this point. British archives contain many references to French-British discussions of policy toward the Bolsheviks, but most references to the Americans are in terms of British-American discussions. Even though France was Russia's major prewar ally, British-French discussions concerning the Bolsheviks were always initiated by the British. The British achives consistently show France's having a veto over Allied policy. This conclusion is supported by Lloyd C. Gardner's discussion of Anglo-American policy toward Russia in *Safe for Democracy: The Anglo-American Response to Revolution, 1913–1923* (New York, 1984), 124–202.

96. The Italians tended to agree with the French that the destruction of Bolshevism was desirable, but they were unwilling to commit any Italian resources to see it accomplished, and were only a minor factor in deliberations. The Japanese, while central players in the discussions and decisions over intervention in Siberia, had little role in broader Allied policy toward Petrograd and Moscow. See Thompson, 60.

97. See Louis Fischer, *The Soviets in World Affairs* (Princeton, 1951) I:96; Thompson, *Russia, Bolshevism, and Versailles*, 381.

98. Jay L. Kaplan, "France's Road to Genoa: Strategic, Economic, and Ideological Factors in French Foreign Policy, 1921–1922" (Ph.D. diss., Columbia University, 1974), 54. For a penetrating analysis, see Kalervo Hovi, *The Emergence of the New French Eastern European Alliance Policy, 1917–1919* (Turku, Finland, 1975), passim.

99. See Ullman, *Anglo-Soviet Relations,* I, vii.

100. Buchanan to FO, 11/16/17, WBW, B10, f259; Buchanan diary, 11/20/17, *My Mission to Russia,* 220.

101. "Notes on the Present Russian situation," 12/9/17, printed in Lloyd George, *War Memoirs,* II, 1,545–1,547.

102. Spring Rice to Foreign Office, 12/27/17, PWW 45:369–370. See also Lady Algernon Gordon-Lenox, ed., *The Diary of Lord Bertie of Thame* (London, 1924), 227.

103. For details of British discussions with Lockhart concerning this mission, see diary of Lord Milner, 12/21/17, VAM (O).

104. Spring Rice to Secretary of State, 1/9/18, FRUS, 1918, Russia, I, 337.

105. The full story of informal contact is told in Chapters 3, 4, and 5.

106. House to Balfour, 2/14/18, EMH, B10, f288; Wiseman to Drummond, 2/27/18, PWW 46:485.

107. See Wiseman to Drummond, 3/14/18, PWW 47:35–36; paraphrase of telegram, Balfour to Reading (to House via Wiseman), 4/29/18, EMH, B10, f289; Reading to Eric Drummond, 3/27/18, PWW 47:171; Reading to Balfour, 4/25/18, PWW 47:441; Wiseman to House, 5/1/18, PWW 47:503; Lansing to Wilson, *re* discussion with Reading, 5/11/18, PWW 47:605.

108. It did not help the British cause, of course, to have Trotsky, in the aftermath of the confusion in Murmansk (where the Murmansk Soviet first invited the Allies in, then had the Bolsheviks sever relations), come out strongly against any intervention, giving orders to "resist all invasions." See Reading to Balfour, 4/7/18, PWW 47:281.

109. Lloyd George to Reading, 7/10/18, PWW 48:587–589.

110. See Wiseman memorandum on interview with Wilson, 10/16/18, PWW 51: 350–351; Polk to Lansing, 1/6/19, PWW 53:627; Lansing to Wilson, 1/9/19, PWW 53: 706.

111. No full treatment of Bakhmetev and the important role of the Provisional Government Embassy in Washington exists. Linda Killen has examined Bakhmetev's relationship to Wilson and House in a 1978 article, "The Search for a Democratic

Russia: Bakhmetev and the United States," *Diplomatic History* II, No. 3 (Summer, 1978): 237–256. Bakhmetev's role in American plans for intervention has been discussed by Robert J. Maddox, "Woodrow Wilson, the Russian Embassy and Siberian Intervention," *Pacific Historical Review* XXVI (1967): 435–448. Neither, however, fully explores the subtleties or contradictions of the Administration's increasingly strained relationship with Bakhmetev in 1918–1919.

112. House diary, 8/19/17, EMH. See also House diary, 7/22/17, and 9/29/17, EMH.

113. See Boris Bakhmetev, oral memoirs, Columbia University oral history office, 344.

114. Bakhmetev, oral memoirs, 345–349, 350–351; Bakhmetev to Lansing, 11/24/17, NA, RG59, 701.6111/199.

115. House diary, 12/22/17, EMH. It should not be forgotten, however, that various other influences were also at work on House and Wilson. At this early stage it was quite possible for Wilson to reconcile those who wanted to keep the door open to the Bolsheviks and those who wished to overthrow them.

116. House diary, 3/2/18, and 2/19/19, EMH.

117. NA, RG 59, 701.6111/174.

118. Bakhmetev, oral memoirs, 328; Steffens, *The Autobiography of Lincoln Steffens* (New York, 1931) II:770. For the decline in Bakhmetev's influence in 1919–1920, see Killen, "The Search for a Democratic Russia," 248–253.

119. Bakhmetev, oral memoirs, 406–407.

120. Although the decisions to intervene in Siberia and the North were major decisions by Wilson (particularly Siberian intervention), they are not most directly the subject of this study. Moreover, those decisions were not primarily framed by the question of how to deal with the Bolsheviki.

121. For Wilson's views on informal contact, see Wilson to Lansing, 1/1/18, PWW 45:417; Wilson to Lansing, 2/4/18, PWW 46:233; and Lansing to Francis, 2/14/18, FRUS, Russia, 1918, I:381.

122. For a discussion of the Buckler and Bullitt missions and Wilson's role, see Chapters 7 and 9.

123. Even as late as August 1919, when his advisors were pushing him, in the midst of the growing Red Scare, to issue a strong statement against the Bolsheviks, Wilson hesitated to make a definitive statement. See Samuel N. Harper to Carter, 8/17/19, SH, B7.

124. N. Gordon Levin, *Woodrow Wilson and World Politics* (New York, 1980) has convincingly developed this theme, drawing strongly from Wilson's speeches, writings, and biography. Levin defines this approach of Wilson's to the world as "American liberal exceptionalism" after Louis Hartz, *The Liberal Tradition in America*. See Levin, op. cit., 2–10, 13–19.

125. John Reed to Joseph Tumulty, 6/30/14, PWW 30:231–236.

126. George and George, *Wilson and House* 108. For a discussion of Wilson's family and religious background and the development of his moral principles, see pp. 3–33.

127. George and George, *Wilson and House*, 34–52. Ray Stannard Baker has also discussed, in his memoirs, the negative impacts of Wilson's stand on "principles," which he pursued to the detriment of others and his own health. Grayson, *Woodrow Wilson: An Intimate Memoir*, 111.

128. Joseph Tumulty, *Woodrow Wilson as I Know Him* (London, 1922), 457.

129. On this point, see William Appleman Williams, *Russian-American Relations,*

*1781–1947.* Lloyd C. Gardner has argued that the British-American strategy for Russia, while fraught with contradictions, was ultimately in favor of intervention and against accommodation with the Bolsheviks. (See for example, Gardner, *Safe for Democracy,* 192, passim.) His argument, however, and Williams' and Gordon Levin's, consistently undervalues the ambiguity of Wilson's often contradictory decisions of 1918–1919.

130. Wilson favored U.S. abrogation of the Russian-American Commercial Treaty of 1832 in 1911 as a way of showing American displeasure with anti-Jewish and anti-democratic tendencies of the Tsarist government, and he appointed obscure politicians with no knowledge of Russia as U.S. ambassadors. See Link, PWW 6:259–260; Harley Notter, *The Origins of the Foreign Policy of Woodrow Wilson* (Baltimore, 1937), 614; and Christopher Lasch, *The American Liberals and the Russian Revolution* (New York, 1962), 1–26.

131. See David Francis to Secretary of State, 3/18/17, FRUS, 1918, Russia, I, 6; Francis to Secretary of State, 3/22/17, FRUS, 1918, Russia, I, 13. Various authorizations on credits began April 3. See FRUS, 1918, Russia, I, 17–28.

132. Kennan, *Soviet-American Relations,* I, 14–16, based on Lansing memorandum, 3/20/17, RLLC.

133. See, for example, John Lewis Gaddis, *Russia, the Soviet Union, and the United States,* 54–55.

134. FRUS, 1917, Supplement I, The World War, p. 200.

135. Considering the sweeping claims Wilson made for the coming of democracy in Russia with the March revolution, he spent remarkably little time or energy between March and November following events in Russia. With the exception of the consideration and appointment of the Root Commission in April and meetings with Creel and Edgar Sisson prior to Sisson's appointment as Compub representative in Russia in October, Wilson's papers show little presidential preoccupation with the shifting fortunes of the Provisional Government. See PWW, vols. 41–45.

136. Witness Wilson's letter to Frank Clark of November 13, 1917, in which he said, "Russia, like France in a past century, will no doubt have to go through deep waters but she will come out upon firm land on the other side." PWW 45:39.

137. See Ray Stannard Baker, *Woodrow Wilson, Life and Letters* (New York, 1939) 7:320. It was not the case in these months that American officials in Washington were not getting indications of the difficulties of the Provisional Government or growing signs of Bolshevik power. On the contrary, many reports, especially from consular staff such as North Winship, consul at Petrograd, accurately reflected the true situation. These reports, however, were largely ignored; officials preferring self-serving statements about the triumph of Russian democracy. See FRUS, 1918, Russia, I, 1–186.

138. See especially Wilson to Charles Edward Russell, 11/10/17, PWW 44:557–558; and speech to AFL in Buffalo, 11/12/17, PWW 45:14.

139. See particularly Walter Lippmann and Charles Merz, "A Test of the News," *New Republic,* XXIII (supplement to August 4, 1920), 14; and Lasch, *American Liberals,* 118–124. Cabinet meetings of the Wilson Cabinet in the aftermath of the Revolution showed most members believing in the imminent collapse of the new Government, with only occasional dissenters, notably Franklin K. Lane. See *Diary of Josephus Daniels,* 11/30/17, 12/11/17.

140. It should be noted that Wilson himself questioned this assumption several times, and at least privately worried that the March revolution might lead Russians to

question their participation in the war. Wilson's concerns, however, were always assuaged by the State Department. See Link, *Wilson*, V, 410.

141. Raymond Robins of the American Red Cross, Arthur Bullard and Edgar Sisson of the Committee on Public Information, YMCA representatives, Chief of the American Military Mission General William V. Judson, and even Ambassador David Francis, all shared, to one degree or another, in this effort, even up to and after the ratification of the Treaty of Brest Litovsk. For a full discussion, see Chapters 3 and 4.

142. This led most directly to an American and British effort, largely led by British envoy R. H. Bruce Lockhart, to persuade the Bolsheviks to approve of Allied intervention. It should be noted, however, that both Raymond Robins and Woodrow Wilson, for totally different reasons, expressed considerable skepticism about this course of action; Wilson, because he did not trust the Bolsheviks, and Robins, because he did not believe by this time that intervention would help in fighting Germany. For Wilson's attitude on invited intervention, see PWW 48:133–134.

143. Reed to Tumulty, 6/30/14, PWW 30:236.

144. Particularly in Paris, Wilson often saw his whole life's work in terms of a struggle with Bolshevism. Witness Grayson's efforts to get Wilson to rest. The President answered, "Give me time. We are running a race with Bolshevism and the world is on fire." Grayson, *Wilson*, 85.

145. See, for example, Wilson's very strongly worded letter to House on February 23, 1919, stating in no uncertain terms his opposition to Churchill's schemes. PWW 55:229–230.

146. An excellent example of this rather desperate struggle to combine all of these assumptions into one policy is Wilson's famous *aide-mémoire* justifying limited American intervention in Siberia, in which he makes a strong argument as to why military intervention is unjustified, and then explains why it is necessary. PWW 48:640–643.

147. Felix Frankfurter, in a conversation with George F. Kennan in 1956, said he believed that Wilson's refusal to meet with those who had first-hand experience was due to Wilson's desire to develop policy with as few contradictory inputs as possible. (George F. Kennan, conversation with Felix Frankfurter, 10/10/56, GK). Wilson did not see Ambassador Francis either in Washington or when he was in London in December 1918. See Wilson to Francis and Francis to Wilson, 12/27/18, DRF, B35–56.

148. On Paris, see Chapters 8, 9, and 10.

## Chapter 3

1. RLP.

2. Diary of William V. Judson, WVJ; Francis to Lansing, 11/28/17, FRUS, 1918, Russia, I, 252–253; Francis to Lansing, 12/1/17, DRF, B28–56; statement by People's Commissariat of Foreign Affairs regarding Judson-Trotsky meeting, *Izvestia*, 12/2/17, translated in C&P, 55.

3. The discussions on military collaboration often overlapped with political and economic discussions, especially in the many talks initiated by Raymond Robins. For purposes of clarity, the Robins-Trotsky-Lenin political talks will be considered in Chapter 4.

4. Kennan, *Soviet-American Relations*, II, 4.

5. *Ibid.*, 127.

6. Francis to Lansing, 11/28/17, FRUS, 1918, Russia, I, 252–253; Judson to Francis *re* visit with Trotsky, 12/26/17, WVJ.

7. Bullard to House, 12/13/17, EMH, B21, F671. It should not be forgotten in this

connection that Sisson, Bullard, and the Committee on Public Information staff in Russia took advantage of every opportunity of cooperating with the Bolshevik propaganda arm in jointly distributing propaganda to the German troops at the front designed to undermine their fighting ability and morale.

8. Judson to Warcolstaff (U.S. Army War College Staff), 12/25/17, WVJ.

9. See Judson diary, 12/17/17, WVJ; Judson telegram to Warcolstaff, 12/31/17, WVJ; Robins report to Johnson, 6/12/18, HJ III:12; Ruggles to Francis, 3/8/18, DRF, B32–56; Francis to Lansing, 11/28/17, FRUS, 1918, Russia, I, 252–253.

10. Francis to Summers, 3/21/18, DRF, B32–56.

11. Francis to Secretary of State, 3/26/18, FRUS, 1918, Russia, I, 487–488.

12. Francis to Sec. of State, 5/2/18, DRF, B33–56.

13. Secretary of State to Francis, 4/5/18, FRUS, 1918, Russia, I, 495.

14. See Carr, *Bolshevik Revolution*, III, 29–32.

15. See numerous instances of this from Trotsky's discussions with Robins and Judson, particularly *Izvestia*, 12/2/17, on Judson-Trotsky visit; S. Lemel (Sisson) to Creel, 12/5/17, RLP, B3; Lockhart to Foreign Office, 3/12/18, VAM(O), 364(B); note from Soviet Government, Trotsky to Robins, 3/5/18, C&P, 81–82.

16. See interview by *Petrograd Echo* with Trotsky, as translated by American Embassy, 3/16/18, DRF, B15–32.

17. See Ruggles to Francis, 3/8/18, DRF, B32–56; *Petrograd Echo*, 3/16/18, DRF, B32–56.

18. Kennan, *Soviet-American Relations*, II, 108–109.

19. John Reed, "Skeleton Report" 1/6/18, JR, P2, A113.

20. Lenin, *Collected Works* (4th ed.) 44:67.

21. See Kennan, *Soviet-American Relations*, II, 132–133. See also A. O. Chubarian, *V. I. Lenin i formirovanie sovetskoi vneshnei politiki*, 169–177.

22. For background on Judson, see Kennan, *Soviet-American Relations*, I, 41–43; Williams, "Robins," 52, 60. Earliest reference to Judson's appointment as military attaché is found in Francis' appointment calendar, 6/27/17, DRF, B28–56. The detailed story of Judson's experiences with the Bolsheviks and his voluminous recommendations to the War Department and Ambassador Francis are found in WVJ. These papers show quite convincingly Judson's overwhelming preoccupation with winning World War I and the almost total lack of instructions from the U.S. War Department during the entire time of his stay in Russia.

23. Mott to Judson, 9/25/17, WVJ.

24. Francis to Morris, 11/13/17, FRUS, 1918, Russia, I, 235; Judson diary, 11/14/17–11/16/17, WVJ.

25. Judson to Francis, 11/19/17, DRF, B28–56. Francis admitted later that he did authorize Judson to get guards for the Embassy. See Francis, *Russia from the American Embassy*, 208–210.

26. C&P, 41–43; Degras, *Soviet Documents*, 1–3.

27. Degras, *Soviet Documents*, 4; C&P, 44–45.

28. Francis to Lansing, FRUS, 1918, Russia, I, 248.

29. James Bunyan and H. H. Fisher, eds., *The Bolshevik Revolution, 1917–1918, Documents and Materials* (Stanford, 1934), 244.

30. C&P, 47–48; *New York Times*, November 1, 1917; Bunyan and Fisher, *Bolshevik Revolution*, 244–246.

31. Chiefs of British, Rumanian, Italian, Japanese, French, and Serbian military missions, to Dukhonin, 11/23/17, Bunyan and Fisher, *Bolshevik Revolution*, 245; C&P, 49–50.

32. Bunyan and Fisher, *Bolshevik Revolution,* 245–246.

33. *Ibid.;* Degras, *Soviet Documents,* 10.

34. Trotsky to Allied military missions, 11/27/17, FRUS, 1918, Russia, I, 250.

35. FRUS, 1918, Russia, I, 251.

36. Lansing to Francis, 12/1/17, DRF, B29–56.

37. Thompson's statement to the press, 11/27/17, C&P, 48.

38. For details on these meetings, see Chapter 4.

39. Judson to War College, 11/27/17, WVJ; Judson to Trotsky, 11/27/17, RR; Judson diary, 11/27/17, WVJ.

40. Judson diary, 11/27/17, WVJ.

41. Judson to Dukhonin, 11/28/17, C&P, 48–49.

42. Judson diary, 11/27/17, WVJ.

43. Sisson, *100 Red Days,* 75. See also extract from a speech by Trotsky at Petrograd Soviet, 11/30/17, Degras, *Soviet Documents,* 12–14; Robins' testimony, 3/6/19, BP3:787–789.

44. Judson diary, 11/30/17, WVJ; Judson to Francis, 12/26/17, WVJ; Francis to Lansing, 12/1/17, DRF, B28–56.

45. Francis to Lansing, 11/28/17, FRUS, 1918, Russia, I, 252–253; Francis to Lansing, 12/1/17, FRUS, 1918, Russia, I, 279.

46. Statement by People's Commissariat of Foreign Affairs regarding Judson's visit, *Izvestia,* 12/2/17, C&P, 55.

47. Judson's telegram to Warcolstaff, 12/1/17, WVJ. See also Judson diary, 12/1/17; and Judson to Francis, 12/26/17, both WVJ.

48. For text of Armistice agreement, see Wheeler-Bennett, *Brest-Litovsk,* 379–384. See also Trotsky, *Sochineniia,* (Moscow, 1925) III:197; and Bullard to House, 12/12/17, EMH, B21, f671.

49. C&P, 55.

50. Judson to Warcolstaff, 12/2/17, WVJ; Judson draft report on Russian experiences, n.d. [late 1918] WVJ.

51. Francis to Lansing, 3/20/18, DRF, B32–56.

52. S. Lemel [Sisson] to Creel, 12/5/17, RLP, B3.

53. Draft Judson report on Russia, n.d., [late 1918], WVJ.

54. *Ibid.* See also Judson to Burleson, 4/10/19, WVJ.

55. Francis to Judson, 12/3/17, WVJ.

56. Judson diary, 12/4/17, WVJ.

57. Judson to Warcolstaff, 12/6/17, WVJ.

58. Secretary of State to Francis, 12/6/17, FRUS, 1918, Russia, I, 289.

59. Francis to Department of State, 12/12/17, FRUS, 1918, Russia, I, 301.

60. For Judson's appreciation of and support for Robins' continued efforts in this direction, see Judson's report to the War Department, 6/18/19, WVJ; draft Judson report, [late 1918,], WVJ; Judson to Burleson, 4/10/19, WVJ. For Robins' reciprocation, see Robins to Margaret, 12/20/18, RR; and Robins to Judson, 3/20/19, WVJ.

61. Robins to Margaret, 12/20/17, RR. See also Robins' report to Johnson, June 1918, HJ.

62. Judson diary, 12/18/17, WVJ.

63. Judson diary, 12/23/17, WVJ.

64. Judson and Kerth to Francis, 12/26/17, WVJ.

65. Francis to Lansing, 12/24/17, RLP.

66. Lansing discussed the recall of Judson as early as December 6 with Secretary of War Baker, and a few days later with President Wilson. Judson received notice of the

need to return home "for consultations" on January 1. (Lansing Desk Calendar, 12/6/17, 12/9/17, RLP; Judson diary, 1/1/18, WVJ.)

67. Miles to Lansing, NA RG 59:861.00/935 1/2.

68. Judson diary, 12/27/17, WVJ.

69. Francis to Lansing, 1/1/18, DRF; Judson diary, 12/31/17, WVJ; Judson to War College, 12/31/17, WVJ.

70. Judson diary, 1/1/18, WVJ.

71. Judson diary, 1/14/18, WVJ.

72. Judson to Riggs, 1/18/18, WVJ; Riggs, "Report for General Judson on the situation in Russia and what can be done to improve it," 1/22/18, WVJ; Judson to War College, 1/23/18, WVJ.

73. Judson to Warcolstaff, 1/27/18, WVJ.

74. Judson to Acting Chief of Staff, 3/14/18, WVJ. For reports, see Judson to Acting Chief of Staff, 2/26/18, PWW 46:533–536; Judson to Chief of Staff, 3/4/18, PWW 46:537–540; Judson to Acting Chief of Staff, 3/14/18, WVJ.

75. Judson, report to Secretary of War, 6/18/19, WVJ.

76. The diplomatic context and specific economic and political issues involved in these meetings will be explored fully in Chapter 4.

77. Judson to Warcolstaff, 12/31/17, WVJ; Judson diary, 12/31/17, WVJ; Francis to Lansing, 1/1/18, DRF, B36–52.

78. The political implications and possibilities will be fully explored in Chapter 4.

79. Sisson, *100 Red Days,* 196; Judson diary, 1/1/18, WVJ; Francis to Lansing, 1/1/18, DRF, B32–56.

80. Robins to Francis, 1/2/18, RR; Francis to Robins, 1/2/18, RR; Francis to Lansing, 1/2/18, DRF, B32–56.

81. For the drama of this story, see Carr, *Bolshevik Revolution,* III, 35–37; Trotsky, *Moia Zhizn* (Berlin, 1930) II:363; Deutscher, *The Prophet Armed,* 374–376.

82. Judson to Burleson, 4/10/19, WVJ; Judson's report to the Secretary of War, 6/18/19, WVJ; Judson diary, 1/23/18, WVJ.

83. Robins' report to Johnson, 6/12/18, HJ III:12.

84. Judson's report to Secretary of War, 6/18/19, WVJ.

85. Lockhart to Balfour, 2/16/18, VAM(O). For the most detailed account of Lockhart and the Bolsheviks, see Ullman, *Anglo-Soviet Relations,* I, 62–128.

86. For detail on Sadoul's background and role, see Kennan, *Soviet-American Relations,* I, 381–384.

87. Jacques Sadoul, *Notes sur la revolution bolchevique* (Paris, 1922), 202.

88. Michael J. Carley, "The Origins of the French Intervention in the Russian Civil War, January–May, 1918: A Reappraisal," *Journal of Modern History* 48 (September, 1976): 417; Kalervo Hovi, *Cordon Sanitaire or Barrière de L'Est:, The Emergence of the New French Eastern European Alliance Policy, 1917–1919* (Turku, Finland, 1975), 89.

89. Sadoul, *Notes,* 241–243.; Joseph Noulens, *Mon ambassade en Russie Sovietique, 1917–1919* (Paris, 1933) I:223.

90. Phillips to Secretary of State regarding conversation with the French Embassy, 2/19/18, FRUS, 1918, Russia, I, 383.

91. *Ibid.* It is worth noting that Lansing provides the only evidence of Wilson's concurrence, and that this decision had little effect on military collaboration in Russia.

92. See Ullman, *Anglo-Soviet Relations,* I, 62–128.

93. Lenin to the CC of the RSDLP(b), 2/22/18, Lenin, *Collected Works* (4th ed.)

44:67. See also Ullman, *Anglo-Soviet Relations,* I, 76; Hovi, *Cordon Sanitaire or Barrière de l'Est,* 93.

94. Carley, "Origins," 420–421; Carr, *Bolshevik Revolution,* III:49; Sadoul, *Notes* 274.

95. Carr, *Bolshevik Revolution,* III:45.

96. The debate can be found in *Protokoly Tsentral'nogo Komiteta RSDRP* (1929), 243–246. On Bukharin's role, see Stephen Cohen, *Bukharin and the Bolshevik Revolution* (New York, 1980), 63–69; and Leonard Schapiro, *The Communist Party of the Soviet Union* (New York, 1971), 185–189.

97. See Carr, *Bolshevik Revolution,* 44; Wheeler-Bennett, *Brest-Litovsk,* 284–286. Additional evidence for Trotsky's eagerness for Allied aid in resistance to Germany at this time can be found in his appeal to the Murmansk Soviet to resist the advance of the Germans and to "accept any and all assistance from the Allied missions," (3/1/18) in Kennan, *Soviet-American Relations,* II, 31. The full story of the Murmansk incident, which is beyond the scope of this discussion, can be found in Kennan, *Soviet-American Relations,* II, 31–57.

98. See Kennan, *Soviet-American Relations,* I, 495–499, in which he emphasizes that the document in question never "committed the Bolsheviks to anything." Similar overemphasis on this event was given by Robins himself in his testimony (U.S. Senate Documents, 66th Congress, first session, 1919, IV, 800–801); and by numerous historians, among them Lasch, *American Liberals,* 84–94 and Ullman, *Anglo-Soviet Relations,* I, 124–127.

99. BP IV, 800–801.

100. C&P, 81–82; Bunyan and Fisher, *Bolshevik Revolution,* 535–537; *Congressional Record* 1/29/19, p. 2,336.

101. Robins report, copy to Johnson, 12/5/18, HJ III:12.

102. Francis to State Department, 3/9/18, C&P, 84–85; Lansing to Wilson, 3/9/18, RLP.

103. Bullard to House, 3/7/18, EMH, B21, F672.

104. Francis to Neissel, 3/5/18, DRF, B32–56.

105. Judson diary, 1/14/18, WVJ. See also George F. Kennan's notes on conversation with Norman Armour, 11/3/53, GK.

106. Riggs to Judson, 1/22/18, WVJ; Riggs's note for files on military situation, 1/28/18, EFR.

107. See Francis to Lansing, 3/22/18, FRUS, 1918, Russia, I, 485; Bullard to House, 3/7/18, EMH, B21, F672.

108. Ruggles to MilStaff, 5/1/18, DRF, B33–56.

109. Ruggles to MilStaff, in Lansing to Wilson, 5/21/18, PWW 48:96.

110. See Kennan, *Soviet-American Relations,* I, 499–500. Kennan also believes (but cites little evidence) that Ruggles delayed because of resentment against Robins' and Lockhart's own free-wheeling diplomacy.

111. Francis to Ruggles, 3/5/18, DRF, B33–56.

112. Kennan, *Soviet-American Relations,* I, 496, 506.

113. Ruggles to Francis, 3/8/18, DRF, B32–56.

114. Ruggles to MilStaff, 3/8/18, copy, GK.

115. Riggs, military note, "Interview of Colonel Ruggles with Mr. Trotsky (Captain Riggs and Captain Sadoul present)," 3/8/18, EFR.

116. Francis to State Department, 3/9/18, C&P, 85–86; Francis to Robins, 3/11/18, C&P, 96.

117. Francis to Lansing, 3/12/18, FRUS, 1918, Russia, I, 396.
118. E. Francis Riggs, "Interviews with Bontch-Bruievitch," 3/8/18, and 3/10/18, EFR.
119. Lockhart to Foreign Office, 3/12/18, VAM(O) 364 (B).
120. Trotsky interview by Herman Bernstein, *Petrograd Echo,* 3/16/18, as translated by American Embassy, DRF, B33–56.
121. Sadoul, *Notes,* 274.
122. Robins to Francis, 3/19/18; 3/20/18; 3/22/18; C&P, 104–106; Francis to Lansing, 3/20/18, FRUS, 1918, Russia, I, 483; Robins diary, 3/18/18, RR, B42.
123. Francis to Lansing, 3/22/18, FRUS, 1918, Russia, I, 485; Francis to Summers, 3/21/18, DRF, B32–56.
124. Francis to Lansing, 3/20/18, FRUS, 1918, Russia, I, 483.
125. Francis to Summers, 3/21/18, DRF, B32–56; Francis to Lansing, 3/21/18, DRF, B32–56.
126. Lansing to Francis, March 23, 1918, FRUS, 1918, I, 486.
127. Bullard to House, 3/17/18, EMH, B21, F672.
128. Francis to Lansing 3/26/18, DRF, B32–56. Order for railroad engineers to come to Vologda in FRUS, 1918, Russia, III, 225.
129. Francis to Summers, 3/27/18, DRF, B32–56.
130. For exchange of cables, see FRUS, 1918, Russia, III, 225–227.
131. Francis to Robins, 3/28/18, C&P, 119; Francis to State Department, 3/31/18, FRUS, 1918, Russia, I, 491; State Department to Francis, 4/5/18, FRUS, 1918, Russia, I, 491, 495.
132. Political discussions concerning intervention are covered in Chapters 4 and 5.
133. Riggs to War Department, in Poole to Lansing, 4/6/18, FRUS, 1918, Russia, II, 104–105.
134. See Balfour to Lockhart, 4/30/18, VAM(O) 364 (B); Francis to Lansing, 5/2/18, DRF, B33–56; Balfour to Reading, 5/15/18, PWW 48:100.
135. E. Francis Riggs, "The Russian Situation," 4/25/18, EFR.
136. Lansing to Francis, 5/2/18, FRUS, 1918, Russia, I, 517–518. Francis to Lansing, 4/5/18, FRUS, 1918, Russia, III, 228.
137. See Kennan, *Soviet-American Relations,* II, 132–133.
138. Sadoul, *Notes* 284–285.
139. See, for example, Ullman, *Anglo-Soviet Relations,* I, 128–166; Ulam, *Expansion and Coexistence,* 68–70; Carr, *Bolshevik Revolution,* III, 43–50.
140. Lockhart to Robins, 5/5/18, C&P, 203.

## Chapter 4

1. Raymond Robins to wife, Margaret, 12/20/17, RR, reel 3.
2. Bullard to Creel, 12/9/17, AB, B14.
3. Karl Radek, introduction to Arthur Ransome's "Letter to America," September 1918, SH, B65.
4. Bullard to Creel, 12/9/17, AB. George Kennan's evaluation of Arthur Bullard's observations should not be forgotten in this context: "Bullard's was the best American mind observing on the spot the course of the Russian Revolution." (Kennan, *Soviet-American Relations,* I, 49).
5. See Roosevelt to Robins, 1/14/18, *Letters of Theodore Roosevelt,* Elting T. Morison et. al., eds. (Cambridge, Mass., 1951–1954) 8:1271; Cornelius Kelleher to Herman Hagedorn, 2/4/21, HHWT, B18; Felix Dzerzhinsky recalled in Kalpashnikov, *A Prisoner of Trotsky's,* p. 19.

6. Kennan, *Soviet-American Relations,* I, 65–66. The best study of Gumberg and his important role is James K. Libby, *Alexander Gumberg and Soviet-American Relations, 1917–1933* (Lexington, 1977).

7. See Bonch-Bruevich to Robins and Dzerzhinsky to Robins, April 1918; Trotsky to Gumberg (undated) regarding typewriter; Trotsky note regarding Soviet newspapers to Gumberg; Uritski certificate of access for Gumberg; Trotsky note for Gumberg regarding "necessary information"; Dzerzhinsky note for Gumberg; Trotsky note of December 8, 1917, admitting Gumberg and Robins to Alexandrinski Theatre; letter from Lenin to Axelrod, April 27, 1918, asking that information be made available to Gumberg—all in AG. It should be noted in this connection that not until 1921 were stenographers required to record all of Lenin's personal meetings. The record provided by Robins and Gumberg, therefore, is the only record extant of many of these meetings with Lenin.

8. Robins to Francis, 2/7/18, DRF, B32–56.

9. George F. Kennan, *Soviet-American Relations, 1917–1920,* 2 vols. (Princeton, 1956–1958). William Appleman Williams, *Russian-American Relations, 1781–1947* (Toronto, 1952). Williams' Ph.D. diss., "Raymond Robins and Soviet-American Relations, 1917–1939" (University of Wisconsin, 1950) is actually the most complete account of Robins' Russian experiences available, and contains a great deal more substantial information than his book, especially about Robins' early life. Neil V. Salzman's *Reform and Revolution: The Life and Times of Raymond Robins* (Kent State University Press, 1991) is a detailed biography, based on thorough use of Robins' family papers, including previously unavailable papers of Robins' sister, Elizabeth. While he adds rich detail to our understanding of Robins' motivations, background, and emotional state, Salzman does not go beyond Williams' or Kennan's work on Robins in Russia, and he seriously misrepresents the relationship between Francis and Robins because he neglected to use the Francis papers. William Hard's *Raymond Robins' Own Story* (New York, 1920), while based on Hard's discussions with Robins, is quite anecdotal and often unreliable.

10. Hard, *Robins, passim;* Frederick Schuman, *American Policy Toward Russia since 1917* (New York, 1923); and Louis Fischer, *The Soviets in World Affairs,* can certainly be put in the former category, as can Herman Hagedorn's biography of William P. Thompson, *The Magnate* (New York, 1935). The two standard early histories of the Bolshevik revolution, William Henry Chamberlin's *The Russian Revolution* (New York, 1935), and E. H. Carr's *The Bolshevik Revolution, 1917–1923* (New York, 1953) generally side with Carr, as do the standard early works on American foreign policy in the period, such as Ray Stannard Baker's *Woodrow Wilson: Life and Letters.*

11. See Kennan, *Soviet-American Relations,* II, 233–244.

12. See Williams, "Robins," 109–113, 122, 145–151.

13. Williams, *Russian-American Relations, 1781–1947,* passim.

14. Robins' report to Johnson, 6/12/18, HJ III:12.

15. Judson to Burleson, 4/10/19, WVJ.

16. See for example, his testimony to the Overman Committee where he said, "It was perfectly apparent, Senators, that the German program in Russia was to drive the Allies out. They wanted to get the Allies out and stop all idea of economic cooperation with America." (BP, 794).

17. Interview, L. E. Browne with Robins, February 1918, HJ III:12.

18. Robins to Overman Committee, BP, 783, 857.

19. Hagedorn interview with Robins, 1/31/31, HHWT, B21.

20. Judson to Burleson 4/10/19, WVJ; Col. William S. Graves to the Chief, War College Division, Office of the Chief of Staff, 10/17/17, GK.

21. Undated, unsigned memorandum by Thompson, HHWT, B21.

22. Henry P. Davison, Chairman of the American Red Cross during World War I, wrote his own book, *The American Red Cross in the Great War* (New York, 1919). There is not one word in it about William Boyce Thompson or Raymond Robins in the chapter on Russia. For more information on the genesis of the Red Cross in Russia, see Kennan, *Soviet-American Relations,* I, 52–62, Hagedorn, *The Magnate,* 182–223, and Claude E. Fike, "The Influence of the Creel Committee and the American Red Cross on Russian-American Relations, 1917–1919," *Journal of Modern History,* XXXI (June 1959), 93–109.

23. Robins to Margaret, 8/23/17, RR, reel 2; Robins diary, 9/6/17, RR, B42.

24. See Roosevelt to Robins, 6/10/17, RR, reel 2; Davison to Theodore Roosevelt, 6/13/17, RR, reel 2; H. P. Davison to Robins, 6/23/17, RR, reel 2.; TR to Robins, 6/28/ 17, RR, reel 2. Robins was also encouraged to join the mission by, among others, Senator Hiram Johnson of California and Assistant Secretary of Labor Louis F. Post, both of whom would later be of critical importance to Robins when he returned to the United States.

25. Robins to William Appleman Williams, 8/1/49, quoted in Williams, "Robins," 27.

26. For this episode, based on conversations, family papers, and newspaper accounts, see Williams, "Robins," 30–32.

27. Robins, conversation with Williams, 7/28/49, Williams, "Robins," 13.

28. Williams, "Robins," 17.

29. For this period of Robins' life, see Williams, 17–34; and also M. E. Dreier, *Margaret Dreier Robins. Her Life, Letters and Work* (New York, 1950), Chapters 4, 5, 6.

30. Robins diary, 9/17/17, RR, B42.

31. Robins to Johnson, 7/5/18, HJ III:12. See also George F. Kennan, conversation with William Chapin Huntington, 11/17/53, GK.

32. Hagedorn, *The Magnate,* 184–185.

33. See Robins diary, July 1917, RR, B42. See also Bessie Beatty to Robins, 6/22/ 18, on Thompson's support for Robins' position on Russia, RR, reel 4.

34. See Robins to Margaret, 8/7/17, RR, reel 2.

35. Thompson to Kerensky, 8/10/17, HHWT, B-4; Kerensky to Thompson, 8/11/ 17, HHWT.

36. Robins, "Extracts from letters of Raymond Robins," August 14–27, 1917, Theodore Roosevelt Papers, as cited in Williams, "Robins," 55.

37. Billings to Davison, 8/28/17, NA RG 59:811.142/2325.

38. Davison to Billings, 9/7/17, NA RG 59:811.142/2343; J. P. Morgan to Lansing, 8/23/17, NA RG 59:861.51/198.

39. Thompson to Morgan, 8/31/17, HHWT, B-4; Thompson to Morrow, 8/31/17, HHWT, B-4; Thompson to Davison, 9/15/17, HHWT.

40. Robins, report to Johnson, 7/5/18, HJ III:12; Thompson memo, HHWT, B5.

41. Hagedorn interview with Robins, HHWT, B21; Robins' report to Johnson, 7/5/ 18, HJ III:12.

42. Hagedorn, *The Magnate,* 214; Robins testimony, BP 768–69; Robins to Hagedorn, 1/31/31, HHWT; Bullard to Creel, 12/9/17, AB, B14.

43. Francis to Lansing, 10/26/17, RLP, B3; F. M. Corse, report of the Commission to Russia, memo to ARC and Creel, 10/22/17, HHWT, B21.

44. Hagedorn, 41; Hagedorn interview with Thacher, 6/1/32, HHWT, B21.

45. House diary, 9/22/17, EMH; Creel to Wilson, 10/12/17, PWW 44:367; Thompson, "Memo on the Russian Period," HHWT, B4.

46. Thompson to Davison, 10/8/17, GK; Creel to Wilson, 10/22/17, PWW 44:424.

47. Wilson to Sisson, 10/24/17, PWW 44:435–436; Creel to Wilson, 10/24/17, PWW 44:434; Wilson to Thompson, 10/24/17, HHWT, B4.

48. Report of Edgar Sisson on the installation of the Committee on Public Information service in Russia, 5/29/18, BP.

49. Thompson to Hutchins, 11/5/17, HHWT, B4; William V. Judson, "Report of Certain Events in Russia, 1917 to 1918," 6/6/19, WVJ, B8; Robins to Johnson, 7/5/18, HJ III:12.

50. Hagedorn, *The Magnate,* 231–237.

51. Hagedorn interview with Robins, 1/31/31, HHWT, B 22. See also BP, 782.

52. Hagedorn, 242–43.

53. Thompson, "Memo on the Russian situation," [1918,] HHWT, B5.

54. Hagedorn interview with Thacher, 3/13/31, HHWT, B21.

55. Hagedorn interview with Thacher, 6/1/32, HHWT, B21.

56. Robins interview with Hagedorn, 1/31/31, HHWT, B21; BP, 801.

57. Robins to Johnson, 7/5/18, HJ III:12. For a parallel statement, see Thompson, "Memo on Russia," HHWT, B-5.

58. Robins to Margaret, 11/20/17, RR, reel 3; Sisson, *100 Red Days,* 36–37; Thacher to Hagedorn, 6/1/32, HHWT, B4.

59. BP, 802.

60. Kennan conversation with Huntington, 11/17/53, GK.

61. See Charles Edward Russell to John Frank Stevens, 6/26/17, RR, reel 2; Charles Stephenson Smith to Melville Stone (Associated Press), 5/14/18, RR, reel 4. For evidence of Gumberg's access to Trotsky, see various passes and notes from Trotsky to Gumberg, AG.

62. BP, 887; Libby, *Gumberg,* passim. Libby's book develops little new information for the Robins story. Its major contribution is in detailing Gumberg's role, often quite independent of Robins, in advocating U.S. recognition of Soviet Russia and facilitating U.S.-Soviet trade in the 1920s.

63. Gumberg to Goodrich, 12/26/21, AG.

64. Louis Fischer, *Men and Politics,* 211–213.

65. As Libby notes, "He did not desire to Americanize Russia or to Bolshevize America. In this characteristic he was unusual among those who sought to influence Soviet-American relations." (Libby, *Gumberg,* ix).

66. Williams' conversation with Robins, 8/3/50, in Williams, "Robins," 85.

67. Although this was certainly the first formal meeting with Trotsky, Robins' diary contains a cryptic notation, "Miss Beatty, Ransome and Williams and Gumberg and Trotski and home at 2 a.m." in its entry of 10/2/17, indicating that Robins may have met Trotsky in the company of a group of radical Americans before the Bolshevik revolution. RR, B42.

68. Thompson, "Memo on the Russian Period," HHWT, B4.

69. Hagedorn, *The Magnate,* 243; BP, 784.

70. Robins testimony, BP, 783–784; Hagedorn, *The Magnate* 242–244.

71. Williams, conversation with Robins, 8/1/49, Williams, "Robins," 85.

72. Robins' interview with Hagedorn, 1/31/31, HHWT, B22.

73. Robins, testimony, BP, 784.

74. Trotsky at Central Executive Committee, 11/20–21/17, Degras, *Soviet Documents,* I, 6–7. See also account of U.S. Embassy, 12/12/17, NAM, reel 3.

75. Winship to Sec. of State, 12/8/17, NAM, reel 3.

76. Summers to Francis, 11/30/17, DRF, B28–56.

77. Lansing to Francis, 12/6/17, FRUS, 1918, Russia, I, 289. Lansing enlarged on this prohibition in a similar memorandum to all U.S. representatives in Russia, 12/18/17, FRUS, 1918, Russia, II, 9.

78. Summers to Lansing, 11/17/17, FRUS, 1918, Russia, I, 235.

79. Sisson, *100 Red Days,* 87.

80. See Lansing to Mott, 12/7/17, enclosing Davis to Mott, FRUS, 1918, Russia, I, 289; Bullard to House, 12/12/17, EMH, B21; Huntington to Harper, 11/27/17, SH, B4.

81. Report of Edgar Sisson on the installation of the Committee on Public Information service in Russia, 5/29/18, AB, B14.

82. Sisson, *100 Red Days,* 87–89.

83. Bullard to Creel, 12/9/17, AB, B14; and Bullard to House, 12/12/17, EMH, B21 and AB, B19.

84. Bullard to House, 12/12/17, EMH, B21, F671.

85. Bullard to House, 12/20/17, AB, B14.

86. For the best summary of the arguments by Bullard, Sisson, Robins, and Judson, see S. Lemel (Sisson) to Creel via Tredwell to Lansing, 12/5/17, RLP, B3, printed in PWW 45:216–217.

87. Creel to Wilson, 12/27/17, PWW 45:367–368; Sisson, *100 Red Days,* 88–90; Judson diary, 1/1/18, WVJ.

88. Creel had not only written Sisson on December 3, urging him to "coordinate all American agencies in Russia," Creel to Sisson, 12/3/17, Sisson, *100 Red Days,* 88–90, but even wrote a clarifying letter to Sisson after the President's order, essentially telling him to ignore it (Creel to Sisson, 1/21/18, Sisson, *100 Red Days,* 94).

89. "Memo of Agreement between Edgar Sisson and Alexander Gumberg," AG; Sisson, *100 Red Days,* 95; BP, 566–572; Judson diary, 11/27/17, WVJ; Bullard to House, 12/13/17, EMH, B21.

90. Robins diary, 12/7/17, RR, B42; Robins to Margaret, 12/20/17, RR, reel 3; Judson diary, 12/18/17, WVJ; Francis to SD, 12/12/17, NAM, reel 3.

91. Thomas W. Lamont to House, 1/2/18, EMH, B182.

92. Hagedorn interview with Lamont, 6/4/32, HHWT, B21; Lamont speech, 12/6/28, HHWT, B21; Lamont to House, 1/2/18, EMH, B182; Thompson to Lloyd George, 12/1/17, HHWT, B4; Lamont to Wilson, 1/9/18, PWW 45:547–548.

93. Lamont to House, 1/2/18, EMH, B182.

94. Thompson to Lloyd George, 12/1/17, HHWT, B21; Lamont to House, 1/2/18, EMH, B182; Hagedorn interview with Lamont, 6/4/32, HHWT, B21; Lamont to Wilson, 1/9/18, PWW 45:548.

95. Buchanan, *My Mission to Russia,* entries for 11/20/17; 12/3/17; 12/4/17; 12/7/17; Buchanan to FO, 11/16/17, WBW, B9; Francis to Lansing, 11/30/17, FRUS, 1918, Russia, I, 274.

96. "Notes on the Present Russian situation," 12/9/17, LG, F104, WC295 (appendix).

97. War Cabinet minutes and discussion, 12/9/17, LG, F104, WC 295 (15).

98. Lockhart, *Memoirs of a British Agent,* 197–201.

99. Robins interview with Hagedorn, 6/20/31, HHWT, B21; Lockhart, *Memoirs,* 200.

100. "Memo on Suggested Policy in Russia," 12/22/17, LG, F104, WC306 (appendix).

101. War Cabinet minutes, 1/8/18, LG, F104, WC340 (7).

102. Wilson to Lansing, 1/1/18, PWW 45:417.

103. On the Lockhart-Litvinov discussions, see Lockhart, *Memoirs,* 201–205. On the reporting on Lockhart's work to Washington, see Reading to Balfour, 5/12/18, VAM(O) MSS, Milner, 141.

104. Francis to SD, 12/12/17, FRUS, 1918, Russia, I, 301; Lansing to Francis, 12/20/17, FRUS, 1918, Russia, I, 319.

105. This short account of the background of the Kalpashnikov incident is drawn from Kennan's exhaustive account, *Soviet-American Relations* I, 191–218; and the account of Sisson, *100 Red Days* 144–166.

106. Robins diary, 12/21/17, RR, B42; Wardwell diary, 12/21/17, AW.

107. Wright to Robins, 12/21/17, RR, reel 3.

108. Wardwell diary, 12/21/17, AW.

109. Sisson, *100 Red Days,* 152; Trotsky pass for theater for Gumberg, AG; Robins diary, 12/21/17; Kalpashnikov, *A Prisoner of Trotsky,* 75.

110. Francis testimony, BP, 956.

111. Lansing to Francis, 12/29/17, FRUS, 1918, Russia, III, 106. Francis tried to claim in his testimony before the Overman Committee (BP, 965) that Robins had pushed him into taking this position, but Robins documented that Francis had taken the initiative (BP, 1,000). Francis also proudly claimed the credit in 1/31/18 letters to Davison and his son Perry (Francis to Davison, 1/31/18, DRF, B31–56; Francis to Perry, 1/31/18, DRF, B31–56).

112. Kalpashnikov, *A Prisoner of Trotsky,* 156.

113. Robins diary, 12/24/17, RR, B42. See also Wardwell diary, 12/24/17, AW.

114. Robins to Davison, 12/27/17, in Francis to Lansing, FRUS, 1918, Russia, III, 106.

115. Lansing to Francis, 12/29/17, FRUS, 1918, Russia, III, 106. It was not until February 9 that Lansing grudgingly recommended to Wilson that Francis be explicitly authorized to use Robins for political communication with the Bolsheviks, which Wilson approved on February 12. See Lansing to Wilson, 2/9/18, PWW 46:299–300 (with notation, "approved by President," 2/12/18).

116. This was admitted by Francis himself as early as January 2, in his cable to Lansing regarding political and military questions, including influencing the Armistice. "Am using Robins in these matters. Do you understand and approve?" 1/2/18, FRUS, 1918, Russia, I, 421–422.

117. For Francis testimony, see BP, 956–965. For Robins rejoinder, see BP, 1,008–1,019, particularly 1,015. Robins in his testimony notes quite correctly that Francis was asking him to make inquiries of Chicherin as late as April 28, just days before his departure.

118. See Williams, "Robins," 105–138; Kennan, *Soviet-American Relations,* I, 378–396.

119. Francis, a businessman and former Governor of Missouri, had a priority on winning the war against Germany, and viewed all questions with that goal in mind. See Kennan interview with Norman Armour, 3/9/55, GK.

120. Francis' appointment book notes 18 meetings with Robins in January 1918 alone. DRF, B30–56.

121. Francis was not close to Wilson, and carried on his correspondence with Lansing through normal State Department channels. See Francis to John F. Lee, 8/25/16, DRF, B20–56.

122. Robins' personal diary is very condensed and often simply notes meetings without getting into any detail. RR, B42.

123. These accounts cite Francis' lack of experience and detailed knowledge of events in a fast-changing situation. This impression is enhanced by Francis' own Memoirs, *Russia from the American Embassy* (New York, 1921).

124. Voluminous material of this kind can be found in every box of the Francis papers (DRF) for the time he was in Russia.

125. Particularly Francis' letters to his son, Perry, his wife, Jane, and various business associates show a Francis fully aware of the developing revolutionary situation and American contact with, and plotting against, the Bolsheviks.

126. As Allen Wardwell put it, "the Ambassador more or less wobbled between the two, using Colonel Robins as his go-between to the Bolshevik government" (Wardwell diary, 5/10/18, AW).

127. Williams, "Robins," 123–124.

128. Robins pocket-diary entries, 1/2/18; 1/26/18; 1/27/18, RR, B42.

129. For a summary of these arguments, see S. Lemel (Sisson) to Creel via Tredwell to Lansing, 12/5/17, PWW 45:216–217.

130. Bullard to Creel, 12/9/17, AB, B14; Bullard to House, 12/12/17, EMH, B21.

131. Francis to Lansing, 1/2/18, FRUS, 1918, Russia, I, 421–422.

132. "Suggested communication to the Commissar for Foreign Affairs" Francis prepared for Robins, 1/2/18, BP, 1009.

133. *Ibid.,* 1010.

134. Francis to Lansing, 1/2/18, RLP, B4.

135. Hagedorn interview with Lamont, 6/4/32, HHWT, B21.

136. Thompson to Davison, 12/31/17, RR, reel 3; Bullard to House, 12/12/17, EMH, B21; Lamont to House, 1/2/18, EMH, B182; diary of Josephus Daniels, 1/4/18, PWW 45:474–475; Thompson to Wilson, 1/3/18, PWW 45:441–442, 442–447; Thompson to Wilson and Wilson to Lamont, declining a meeting, 1/31/18, PWW 46:179–180; Lamont speech, 12/6/28, HHWT, B21; Hagedorn interview with Margaret Biddle, 10/23/31, HHWT, B21; Hagedorn interview with Robins, 1/31/31, HHWT, B21.

137. *New York World,* 1/10/18; *New York World,* 1/13/18; *Wall Street Journal,* 1/18/18; *New York Times,* 1/27/18; all in HHWT, B21; *New Republic,* 1/19/18.

138. Wilson to Lansing, 1/1/18, PWW 45:417.

139. Lansing to Wilson, Lansing, RLP, B4.

140. Sisson to Creel, 1/3/18, C&P, 67.

141. Advocates of unofficial relations with the Bolsheviks all subsequently claimed credit for moving Wilson in the direction of the references made in the Fourteen Points speech. Colcord, Robins, Sisson, Bullard, House, and Ambassador Francis all were sure their recommendations were determinative. See Bullard to Summers, 1/24/18, AB, B14.

142. See Auchincloss diary, 1/3/18, GA, regarding his discussions with House. Lansing also believed that Wilson was responding, at least in part, to Trotsky's appeals. See Lansing draft "Memoirs," RLP.

143. Wilson, speech to Congress, 1/8/18, PWW 45:534–539.

144. *Ibid.*

145. See Lasch, *American Liberals,* 85, for coverage of liberal press and public opinion. See also a letter from Wilson to Steffens on January 15, in which Wilson thanks Steffens for his support. *The Letters of Lincoln Steffens* (New York, 1938) I:417.

146. Robins diary, 1/10/18, RR, B42; Sisson, *100 Red Days,* 206–209.

147. Sisson, *100 Red Days,* 208.

148. *Ibid.,* 209.

149. *Ibid.* See also Judson to War College, 1/13/18, WVJ, B4.

150. Sisson, *100 Red Days,* 100–101.

151. *Ibid.,* 209.

152. American Embassy translation, Bulletin of the Soviets of Workers, Soldiers, and Peasants Deputies, 1/12/18, DRF, B31–56.

153. DRF, B34–56, 1917, misc.

154. Sisson, *100 Red Days,* 209, 213–214.

155. For a detailed account, see Kennan, *Soviet-American Relations,* I, 430–442, who relies heavily on the account of French ambassador Noulens.

156. Sisson, *100 Red Days,* 29.

157. Lenin to Francis, 1/14/18, DRF, B31–56.

158. The former dean of the diplomatic corps in Petrograd, British ambassador George Buchanan, had recently left for London, and as a result, no British representative was present.

159. Kennan conversation with Armour, 11/3/53, GK.

160. Sisson, *100 Red Days,* 223.

161. See Judson to Warcolstaff, 1/14/18; undated MS page by Francis in memoir materials, DRF, B34–56.

162. Judson diary, 1/15/18, WVJ. An early Soviet account of this meeting, by Trotsky's assistant Ivan Zalkind emphasized that the Western ambassadors were forced to come to Smolny, (*Mezhdunarodnaia Zhizn,* No. 10 (Moscow, 1927), 18–19.

163. Robins to Francis, 2/7/18, DRF, B32–56.

164. Robins to Johnson, 7/5/18, HJ, III:12.

165. BP, 786–787.

166. Bullard, "Memo on the Bolshevist Movement in Russia," 1/23/18, AB, B13.

167. Robins to Johnson, 7/5/18, HJ III:12.

168. See Sisson, *100 Red Days,* 303–305.

169. Trotsky to Robins, 12/14/17, RR, reel 3; Lenin to Robins, 5/14/18, C&P.

170. Kalpashnikov, *A Prisoner of Trotsky,* 19.

171. Kennan conversation with Charles Stephenson Smith, 9/29/54, GK.

172. Albert Rhys Williams, *Lenin: The Man and His Work* (New York, 1919), 97.

173. See Robins diary, 1/18–23/18 for his reaction (RR, B42).

174. Both the Francis and Robins papers are full of the exchange of correspondence between the two men, and references to their frequent person-to-person meetings.

175. Robins to Margaret, 1/21/18, RR, reel 3.

176. Robins to Davison, via Francis, 1/23/18, RLP, B4.

177. Francis to SD, 1/26/18, NAM, reel 3.

178. Francis to Perry, 1/18/18, DRF, B31–56; Francis to Ira Morris, Stockholm, 1/31/18, DRF, B31–56.

179. Francis to SD, 1/26/18, NAM, reel 3; Sisson, *100 Red Days,* 253.

180. C&P, 77–78.

181. Wilson to Lansing, 1/20/18, enclosing Grant-Smith to Lansing, 1/15/18, PWW 46:45–46; Charles W. Eliot to Wilson, 1/17/18, PWW 46:22–23.

182. Lansing to Polk, 1/21/18, RLP, B4.

183. Owen to Wilson and Lansing, 1/22/18, PWW 46:89.

184. Wilson to Lansing, 1/24/18, PWW 46:88–89; Wilson to Owen, 1/24/18, PWW 46:88.

185. Miles memorandum, NA, RG 59:861.00, 1048 1/2.

186. Wilson to Lansing, 2/4/18, PWW 46:233.

187. Lansing to Francis, 2/14/18, FRUS, 1918, Russia, I, 381. For Francis' cable, see Francis to Lansing, 2/5/18, FRUS, 1918, Russia, I, 369.

188. Francis to Lansing, 1/9/18, FRUS, 1918, Russia, I, 336; Francis to Lansing, 12/24/17, FRUS, 1918, Russia, I, 325.

189. Bullard to House, 1/23/18, AB, B13.

190. Bullitt to House, 2/3/18, EMH, B21; Bullitt to House, 2/7/18, EMH, B21.

191. Wiseman to Reading, 2/12/18, Reading to Wiseman, 2/13/18, WBW; Wiseman to Drummond, 2/19/18, PWW 46:389. There is no reference in House's diary to this conversation, nor anything further in Wilson's papers.

192. Wiseman to Drummond, 2/27/18, WBW. As for the relationship between these actions and Bolshevik-German negotiations at Brest Litovsk, this was still in the period when negotiations had been broken off. The Bolsheviks had finally decided to capitulate by February 24, but no peace had been signed, and this decision would not have been known in Washington or London by February 27. See Kennan, *Soviet-Amerian Relations,* I, 370–371.

193. James G. Bailey (Secretary of the U.S. Embassy), affadavit to Robins, 1/30/18, DRF, B31–56; Robins pocket-diary, 1/29–30/18, RR, B42; Francis to Perry, 1/31/18, DRF, B31–56; Lindley to FO, 2/4/18, PRO, FO 371/13312/10058; Zalkind, "Vospominaniia," *Mezhdunarodnaia Zhizn* (1927), 17–19; Robins to Johnson, 6/12/18, HJ III:12.

194. Robins to Francis, 2/13/18, DRF, B32–56; Robins to Johnson, 6/12/18, HJ III:12; BP, 798–799.

195. Chicherin to U.S. Embassy, 1/30/18, DRF, B31–56.

196. Gumberg, letter to his brother, 2/5/19, AG; Sisson, *100 Red Days,* 259; Robins to Johnson, 7/5/18, HJ III:12, Francis to Lansing, 1/31/18, FRUS, 1918, Russia, I, 363.

197. Robins had even loaned Reed money, and had numerous meetings with him. See Reed to Robins, 1/11/18, RR, reel 3; Robins diary, 10/5/17, RR, B42.

198. Gumberg letter to brother, 2/5/19, AG; Reed, "Skeleton Report," 1/6/18, JR. The fact of Lenin's unhappiness with Reed over this incident should not obscure the importance of these very early trial balloons on economic relations with the United States. Kennan too easily dismisses this Reed document as propaganda (Kennan, *Soviet-American Relations,* I, 409). On the contrary, these discussions fit perfectly into a developing Lenin strategy to appeal to the United States on economic grounds.

199. Robins pocket-diary, 2/1, 2, 7/18, RR, B42; Francis to Sec of State, 2/18/18, DRF, B32–56; Sisson, *100 Red Days,* 213–215, 298. Robins had expressed his doubts to the American community as early as December 26, on the basis of scattered documents and rumors. See Judson diary, 12/26/17, WVJ.

200. Francis to Lansing, 3/20/18, DRF, B32–56; Francis to Summers, 3/27/18, DRF, B32–56; Kennan, conversation with Armour, 11/3/53, GK.

201. "Memorandum from Arthur Bullard to Colonel House on German Gold," 2/20/18, AB. For Sisson's own account, see Sisson, *100 Red Days,* 356–375.

202. Lockhart, *Memoirs of a British Agent,* 222–223.

203. Robins pocket-diary, 2/12/18, 2/15/18, 2/17/18, 2/20/18, RR, B42.

204. Lockhart to Foreign Office, 2/16/18, PRO, FO 371/3299, file 1869, no. 31645.

205. Birse to Foreign Office, PRO, FO 371/3299, file 1869, no. 60381.

206. Lockhart to FO, 3/12/18, VAM(O), 364(B). Lockhart on Chicherin: see Lockhart, *Memoirs,* 220–221. On Trotsky, see Lockhart, *Memoirs,* 226–227.

207. Thompson to Davison, 12/31/17, RR, reel 3.

208. On early mention of economic issues, see Robins testimony, BP 784–785.

209. Huntington, "Conversation with Bronsky," 2/13/18, DRF, B32–56.

210. Huntington to Harper, 11/27/17, SH, B4.

211. Huntington was a student of Harper's in Chicago and maintained a regular correspondence both when he was in Russia and afterwards. This correspondence is the best source of information on Huntington's attitudes toward the Bolsheviks as well as on his interaction with Radek, Voznesenski, Chicherin, and others on economic issues. SH, B4 and 5.

212. Huntington to Harper, 11/27/17. SH, B4; Harper to Phillips, 1/2/18, SH, B4; Harper to Huntington, 1/4/18, SH, B4; Harper to Huntington, 10/4/18, SH, B5; Huntington in Redfield to Wilson, 11/22/18, PWW 53:169–180. See also Kennan notes on conversations with Huntington, 11/17/53, GK, and Armour, 11/3/53, GK.

213. Huntington, "Conversation with Bronsky," 2/13/18, DRF, B32–56.

214. *Ibid.*

215. Sisson, *100 Red Days,* 302; Robins diary, 2/16/18, RR, B42. The intense interest of Bronsky in the economic relationship continued as late as July 1918. In a conversation with Captain Webster of the Red Cross staff in Petrograd, Bronsky stressed the need for an economic agreement with the United States (Webster to Wardwell, 7/5/18, AW).

216. Thomas Thacher, "Russia and the War," 6/4/18, DRF, B33–56; Sisson, *100 Red Days,* 323.

217. See, for example, the discussion in the *Bulletin of the Soviets,* 12/13/17, DRF, B29–56.

218. Gvishiani, *Sovetskaia rossiia i SShA,* 34–35, 40–45 citing AVP, f129.

219. Ganelin, *Sovetsko-Amerikanskie otnosheniia,* 150–151, citing archival materials from *Tsentral'nyi gosudarstvennyi istoricheskii arkhiv,* (TsGIA), f1525; V. A. Shishkin, *Sovetskoe gosudarstvo i stranii zapada v 1917–1923 gg* (Leningrad, 1969), 71.

220. *Protokoli tsentralnogo komiteta RSDP(B)* (Moscow, 1929), avgust 1917– fevral 1918, pp. 206–208.

221. Yuri Larin, *Narodnoe khozhiaistvo,* No. 11, (1918), 20. On Finnish-Soviet relations, see Max Engman, "Aspects of Finnish-Soviet Relations, 1918–1920," in Hiden and Loit, *Contact or Isolation,* 57–74.

222. See Francis to Lansing, 3/20/18, DRF, B32–56; Robins to Johnson, 7/5/18, HJ III:12; Lenin to Vologda Soviet, requesting "the greatest cooperation to the representatives and members of the American Embassy," Gumberg English translation, 2/28/18, HJ III:12; Robins to Lenin, 2/28/18, DRF, B32–56; Lenin to Robins, 2/28/18, DRF, B32–56.

223. Francis certificate, 3/10/18, C&P, 95.

224. AG; See also Francis to Summers, 3/10/18, DRF, B32–56.

225. Francis to Summers, 3/10/18, DRF, B32–56.

226. C&P, 81–82; Bunyan and Fisher, 535–537.

227. Lockhart to Balfour, 3/5/18, DRF, B32–56; Lockhart to FO, 3/12/18, VAM(O), 364 B; R. H. Bruce Lockhart, *The Diaries of Sir Robert Bruce Lockhart, 1915–1938* (London, 1973), March 4, 11, 12, 13, 14, 15, 1918.

228. Balfour to Lockhart, 3/6/18, WBW, B9.

229. Lansing to Francis, 3/19/18, FRUS, 1918, Russia, I, 402.

230. Tredwell to Wright, 3/6/18, DRF, B32–56. Tredwell's letter is substantially supported by the sketchy information in Robins' own pocket-diary relating his frustration at transmission (see Robins diary 3/5/18, 3/6/18, 3/7/18, 3/8/18 RR, B42.)

231. Francis to SD, 3/9/18, C&P, 84–85; Lansing to Wilson, 3/9/18, RLP.

232. Colcord to Robins, 2/5/19 RR, reel 5, with substantial excerpts from Colcord's journal of March 9, 10, 11, and 16, 1918.

233. House diary, 3/11/18. See also Sidney Mezes to House, 3/12/18, PWW 47:12.

234. Wilson to Congress of Soviets, 3/9/18, C&P, 87.

235. Bunyan and Fisher, 538.

236. Francis to Lansing, FRUS, 1918, Russia, I, 486.

237. *Izvestia*, March 26, 1918.

238. Francis to Summers, 3/21/18, DRF, B32–56.

239. War Cabinet Minutes WC 364 (10), LG F104.

240. The record of Francis-Robins cables in the mid-March-to-late-April period is a staggering array of information, and our major source concerning Robins' work in this period. Much of it is printed in C&P 105–190, but additional cables can be found in the RR, reel 4, and DRF, B32–56.

241. Robins diary, 3/13/18, RR, B42. For confirming Francis evidence, see Francis to Lansing, 3/20/18, DRF, B32–56; and Francis to Perry, 3/17/18, DRF, B32–56.

242. Francis to Robins, 4/29/18, BP, 1,015.

243. Lockhart, *Memoirs,* 247. This is confirmed by a negative source, British general Knox, who on March 18 complained to the War Department concerning the closeness of their relationship. (Knox to War Department, "Delay in the East," 3/18/18, VAM(O), 364(B).

244. Note Lockhart to Balfour, 3/18/18, VAM(O) 364(B) in which Lockhart claims, "His ambassador is supporting him to the utmost and I am glad to say with considerable effect in Washington."

245. Robins to Wardwell, 4/3/18, RR, reel 4.

246. Balfour to Reading, in Reading to Lansing, 4/29/18, FRUS, 1918, Russia, II, 149.

247. See Lockhart to Balfour, 4/12/18, VAM(O), 364 B; Balfour to Reading, 4/29/18, EMH, B10.

248. Robins diary, 4/20/18, RR, B42; Lockhart, *Memoirs,* 256.

249. Lockhart, *Memoirs,* 256; Robins diary, 4/16/18, RR, B42.

250. Lockhart, *Memoirs,* 250, 253–54.

251. *Ibid.,* 271.

252. Lenin to Siberia Soviet representatives (Gumberg translation), 2/22/18, RR, reel 3.

253. Wilson to Japanese government, 3/1/18, PWW 46:498–499.

254. Balfour to Lockhart, 3/6/18, VAM(O), 364 B.

255. Bullitt to Wilson, 3/3/18, PWW 46:510–513. House to Wilson, 3/3/18, PWW 46:518–519; Auchincloss diary, 3/3/18, GA; Wilson to U.S. Embassies, 3/5/18, FRUS, 1918, Russia, II, 67.

256. Notes for a cable from the Ambassador to the FO, 3/9/18, PWW 46:590–591.

257. Trotsky to Robins for U.S. government, 3/5/18, C&P, 81–82.

258. Lockhart to FO, 3/13/18, VAM(O), 364 B.

259. Chicherin to Robins, 3/9/18, C&P, 87; Francis to Lansing, 3/10/18, FRUS, 1918, Russia, II, 74–75; Francis to Summers, 3/10/18, DRF, B32–56; Robins diary, 3/1/18, RR, B42. Ironically, Francis did not receive word of Wilson's earlier "hands-off" note on Japanese intervention until March 15, at which point he was thoroughly confused regarding American policy. See Francis to Robins, 3/15/18, C&P, 98–99.

260. Knox to War Cabinet, 3/18/18, VAM(O), 364 (B).

261. See particularly Robins to Francis, 4/1/18, DRF, B32–56.

262. Chicherin to Robins, 4/6/18, DRF, B33–56; Francis to Robins, 4/6/18, C&P, 134–135; Robins Diary, 4/5/18, RR, B42.

263. Francis to Robins, 4/7/18, C&P, 135–136.

264. Robins to Wardwell, 4/9/18, RR, reel 4; Robins correspondence, AW.

265. Robins diary, 4/10/18, RR, B42. See also note from Chicherin to Allied representatives on the landing at Vladivostok, 4/6/18, Degras, *Soviet Documents*, 68–69.

266. Chicherin to Robins, 4/25/18, C&P, 197–198, also enclosed in Francis to Lansing, 4/26/18, FRUS, 1918, Russia, II, 139; Gumberg's handwritten English translation of note in AG; Robins diary, 4/29/18, RR, B42; Lockhart to Balfour, 4/28/18, VAM(O), MS Milner 141.

267. Robins diary, 4/17/18, 4/9/18, 4/16/18, RR, B42.

268. See Francis to Summers, 3/27/18, DRF, B32–56.

269. Francis to Robins, 3/19/18, C&P, 104–105; Robins to Francis, 3/19/18, DRF, B32–56; Robins to Francis (II), 3/19/18, C&P, 104.

270. See Robins to Francis, 3/21/18, Robins to Francis, 3/22/18, C&P, 108–109; Robins to Francis, 3/27/18, C&P, 116; Robins to Francis, 4/20/18, C&P, 153–154; Chicherin to Robins, 3/21/18, Francis to Summers, 4/13/18, DRF, B33–56; Webster's and Hicks' reports, including their final report of 4/26/18, are found in C&P, 165–187.

271. BP, 856. See also Radek on Robins, in introduction to Ransome's "Letter to America," SH, B65.

272. Robins to Francis, 3/22/18, C&P, 108.

273. Lenin to Robins, 5/14/18, C&P, 204–212.

274. Robins to Francis, 4/18/18, RR, reel 4.

275. Robins to Johnson, 12/4/18, HJ III:12.

276. Francis to Lansing, 4/5/18, FRUS, 1918, Russia, III, 227.

277. Undated, unsigned memo in GA, B9, f225; Robins report to Johnson, 6/12/18, HJ III:12; Francis to Lansing, 3/23/18, FRUS, 1918, Russia, III, 225; Lansing to Stevens via Moser, 3/26/18, FRUS, 1918, Russia, III, 226; Francis to Lansing, 3/29/18, FRUS, 1918, Russia, III, 226–227; Lansing to Francis, 4/2/18, FRUS, 1918, Russia, III, 227; Francis to Lansing, 4/5/18, FRUS, 1918, Russia, III, 227; Robins to Francis, 4/11/18, C&P, 140. Gvishiani, *Sovetskaia rossiia i SShA,* 62–63, citing AVP, f 129, notes a letter from Chicherin to George Emerson of the Railway Commission, about the possibility of this assistance.

278. BP, 813–814; Robins to Francis, 4/17/18, C&P, 149; McAllister (International Harvester in Russia) to Robins, 4/4/18, RR, reel 4. For more on International Harvester, see Katherine A. S. Siegel, "International Harvester and the Bolshevik Revolution," unpublished paper, Society for Historians of American Foreign Relations, June 1992.

279. BP, 814.

280. McAllister to Robins, 4/4/18, RR, reel 4; Perkins (International Harvester) to Harper, 4/18/18, SH, B5; Francis to Poole, 6/18/18, DRF, B33–56.

281. Undated memo, GA, B9.

282. Robins to Francis, 3/22/18, C&P, 109.

283. Francis to Robins, 3/23/18, C&P, 111.

284. Robins to Francis, 3/25/18, C&P, 114.

285. Francis to Robins, 3/26/18, C&P, 114; Francis to Robins, 3/31/18, C&P, 123–124; Francis to Robins, 4/2/18, C&P, 130; Robins to Francis, 4/4/18, C&P, 131.

286. Francis to Robins, 4/9/18, C&P, 138; Francis to Robins, 4/19/18, C&P, 152.

287. For full proposal, see C&P, 204–212.

288. Robins to Francis, 3/22/18, C&P, 108–109; Robins to Sec. of State, 7/1/18, C&P, 212–219.

289. *Narodnoe Khozhiaistvo*, No. 11, (1918): 20; Shishkin, *Sovetskoi gosudarstvo i stranni zapada,* 70–72, citing TsGANKh, f484.

290. Summers to Francis, 3/30/18, enclosing translation of article from *Nashe Vremia,* 3/29/18, DRF, B32–56.

291. Memorandum of unknown origins, 4/8/18, DRF, B33–56. Knowledge of the Soviet decision to send such a commission to the U.S. also reached the British FO, which inquired of Washington whether it would be received. The SD responded that it had never heard of such a request. Woodhouse to FO, 4/18/18, PRO, FO 371/3327, 68689.

292. Robins to Francis, 4/4/18, C&P, 130–131; Robins diary, 4/3/18, RR, B42.

293. Robins diary, April 14, 1918, RR, B42.

294. Robins to Francis, 4/15/18, C&P, 146–47; Robins to Davison 4/14/18, RR, reel 4.

295. Robins diary, 4/18/18, RR, B42; Robins to Francis, 4/20/18, C&P, 152.

296. Robins diary, 4/27/18, RR, B42; Ruggles to Milstaff, 5/1/18, advocating "commercial contact," DRF, B33–56; Lenin to Robins, 5/14/18, C&P, 204; Robins to Lenin, 4/25/18, RR, reel 4.

297. Undated memo in GA, B9, f225; undated memo in LEB, B2.

298. Lenin to Robins, 5/14/18, Lenin, *Collected Works* (4th ed.) 44:87. See also Shishkin, "Oktiab'skaia Revol'iutsia," 13–17.

299. For details of Robins' plan for an American economic commission to Russia, see Robins' report to Lansing, 7/1/18, C&P, 212–219; Robins to Johnson, 6/12/18, HJ III:12; Unsigned memo, GA, B9, f225.

300. Wilson to Lansing, 2/4/18, RLP, B4.

301. Summers to Francis, 3/25/18, DRF, B32–56; Francis to Lansing, 3/26/18, DRF, B32–56.

302. Robins diary, 3/20/18, RR, B42.

303. Summers to Francis, 3/25/18, DRF, B32–56; Francis to Summers, 3/27/18, DRF, B32–56.

304. Summers to Francis, 3/29/18, DRF, B32–56.

305. Robins to Wardwell, 4/3/18, RR, reel 4; Robins Correspondence, AW.

306. Robins to Davison, 4/5/18, RR, reel 4.

307. Summers to Francis, 4/3/18, DRF, B33–56; Summers to Francis, 4/11/18, DRF, B33–56.

308. Francis to Summers and Robins, 4/15/18, DRF, B33–56.

309. Robins diary, 4/13/18, RR, B42; Robins diary, 4/15/18, RR, B42; Robins diary, 4/17/18, RR, B42.

310. Robins to Davison, 4/15/18, in Robins to Francis, 4/15/18, C&P, 145–146.

311. Auchincloss diary, 4/19/18, GA, B2, f19.

312. Francis to Summers, 4/19/18, DRF, B33–56.

313. Summers to Francis, 4/23/18, DRF, B33–56.

314. Francis to Lansing, 4/20/18, DRF, B33–56.

315. Robins to Wardwell, 4/22/18, RR, reel 4; Robins diary, 4/27/18, RR, B42; Robins to Wardwell, 5/3/18, RR, reel 4; Robins to Chicherin, 5/5/18, RR, reel 4; Wardwell to Robins, 5/6/18, RR, reel 4.

316. Summers to Francis, 4/25/18, DRF, B33–56; Francis to Summers, 4/27/18, DRF, B33–56; Summers to Francis, 4/30/18, DRF, B33–56; Robins to Francis, 4/27/18, DRF, B33–56; Robins to Francis, 4/26/18, DRF, B33–56; Summers to Francis, 4/30/18, and Summers to Francis, 5/1/18, DRF, B33–56; Summers to Francis, 5/3/18, DRF, B33–56; Francis to Summers, 5/3/18, DRF, B33–56; Robins diary, 5/5–9/18, RR, B42; Voznesenski speech, DRF, B33. Robins' reaction, see diary, 5/8/18, RR, B42.

317. See Kennan, conversation with Smith, 9/29/54, GK; Armour to Williams, 6/

16/50, NAP; Wardrop to FO, 5/13/18, PRO, FO 371/3331, #89567; Bullard to Poole, 5/6/18, AB, B15; Kennan conversation with Armour, 6/3/57, GK.

318. Lansing to Robins, 5/9/18, C&P, 204.

319. Trotsky to Robins, 5/13/18, AG; Francis to Poole, 5/15/18, DRF, B33–56; Francis to Scidmore, Morris, & Reinsch, 5/15/18, DRF, B33–56; Francis to Lansing, 5/16/18, PWW 48:141–143.

320. Robins diary, May 8 and 10/18, RR, B42; Wardwell diary, 5/10–11/18, AW.

321. See Chapters 7 and 11 for this story.

322. Harper to Mott, 7/23/18, SH, B5.

323. Robins testimony, BP, 832.

## *Chapter 5*

1. Francis to Lansing, 5/20/18, FRUS, 1918, Russia, I, 536–537.

2. Poole to Francis, 5/24/18, DRF, B33–56.

3. Francis to SD, 5/11/18, PWW 48:113; Chicherin to Francis, 5/9/18, DRF, B33–56; Wardrop to FO, 5/8/18, PRO, FO 371/3330/84597.

4. Francis to SD, 5/11/18, PWW 48:113.

5. Francis to Lansing, 5/20/18, FRUS, 1918, Russia, I, 536–537.

6. Poole to Francis, 5/14/18, DRF, B33–56. See also DeWitt Clinton Poole to Demaree Bess, 6/11/51, GK.

7. See Wardwell diary, 5/11/18–8/12/18, particularly 5/11, 5/13, 6/5, 6/13, 6/29, 7/5, 7/17, 8/6, 8/12—AW.

8. For these reports, see Poole to Francis, 5/14, 5/24, 5/26, 5/28, 5/30, 5/31, 6/1, 6/3, 6/5, 6/7, 6/15, 6/18, 1918—DRF, B33–56.

9. Debo, "Chicherin," 124.

10. Poole to Francis, 5/24/18, DRF, B33–56; POM, 209–210.

11. Poole to Bess, 6/11/51, GK.

12. Francis to SD, 5/11/18, PWW 48:113; Francis to Huntington, 5/20/18, DRF, B33–56.

13. Francis to Lansing, 5/20/18, FRUS, 1918, Russia, I, 536–537.

14. Polk to Francis, 6/10/18, FRUS, 1918, Russia, II, 201.

15. POM, 85–87; Summers to Francis, 8/17/17, DRF, B27–56.

16. For Poole's reports on his South Russia trip, see DRF, B28–56, and POM, 87–91.

17. Poole to Francis, 5/24/18, DRF, B33–56. See also Lockhart to Balfour, 5/1/18, VAM(O), 364(B).

18. Poole to Francis, 5/26/18, DRF, B33–56.

19. Chicherin, "Two Years of Foreign Policy," "Chetyre Kongressa," *Vestnik narodnogo komissariata inostrannykh del* (Moscow, 1919); "Lenin i vneshnaia politika," *Mirovaia politika v 1924 g* (Moscow, 1925).

20. Chicherin in *Izvestia,* 9/3/18, quoted in Poole to Lansing, 9/5/18, FRUS, 1918, Russia, I, 586.

21. For a discussion of Poole's role in covert action, see Chapter 6.

22. U.S. War Department intercept, Chicherin to V. Zorin, Chief of Foreign Department of Petrograd Soviet, 9/30/18, GK.

23. See Kennan conversation with Smith, 9/29/54, GK; Sisson, *100 Red Days,* 100–101, 198; Lockhart on Karakhan and Radek, Lockhart, *Memoirs,* 312.

24. For this curious episode, see Chicherin to Francis, 5/12/18; Francis to Poole, 5/21/18, DRF, B33–56.

25. Reading to Balfour, 5/6/18, PWW 47:544.

26. Francis to Poole, 5/15/18, DRF, B33–56.

27. Poole to Francis, 5/24/18, DRF, B33–56.

28. Francis to Lansing, 5/27/18, FRUS, 1918, Russia, I, 543–544.

29. Francis to Lansing, 5/28/18, FRUS, 1918, Russia, I, 545.

30. Poole to Francis, 6/21/18, DRF, B33–56; Francis to Poole, 6/28/18, DRF, B33–56.

31. Summers to Francis, 4/10/18, DRF, B33–56.

32. POM II, 209–210, 218; Poole to Francis, 5/24/18, DRF, B33–56.

33. Francis to Lansing, 5/18/18, FRUS, 1918, Russia, I, 535. See also Francis to Lansing, 5/28/18, FRUS, 1918, Russia, I, 544–545; Francis memorandum as basis for statement to press, 5/29/18, DRF, B33–56.

34. See FRUS, Russia, 1918, III, 225–227, for exchange of cables between Francis and State Department concerning these engineers, whom Francis originally wanted for assistance to the Bolsheviks to remove supplies and materials away from the route of the German advance.

35. Poole to Francis, 5/14/18, DRF, B33–56.

36. Francis to Poole, 5/15/18, DRF, B33–56; Poole to Francis, 5/26/18, DRF, B33–56; Poole to Francis, 5/24/18, DRF, B33–56.

37. Lansing to Francis, 6/1/18, DRF, B33–56.

38. Francis to Lansing, 6/12/18, DRF, B33–56.

39. See Lehrs to Poole, 6/13/18, DRF, B33–56.

40. Poole to Francis, 5/14/18, DRF, B33–56. See also Ganelin, *Sovetsko-Ameri-kanskie otnosheniia,* 199, who cites materials in TsGIA SSSR, f150, on this meeting and Lehrs' later meeting with Tsentrosoyuz representatives.

41. Francis to Poole, 5/15/18, DRF, B33–56.

42. *Ibid.;* Bukowski to Ruggles, 10/5/18, EFR.

43. Poole to Francis, 5/28/18, DRF, B33–56.

44. Francis to Poole, 6/13/18, DRF, B33–56.

45. Poole to Francis, 5/26/18, DRF, B33–56; Poole to Francis, enclosing Lehrs' memorandum of meeting with Union of Cooperative Societies, 6/5/18, NAM, reel 3. See also Ganelin, *Sovetsko-Amerikanskie otnosheniia,* 199, citing materials from Tsentral'nyi gosudarstvenni istoricheskii arkhiv [Leningrad].

46. Poole to Francis, 5/26/18, DRF, B33–56.

47. Francis to Poole, 5/29/18, DRF, B33–56.

48. Poole to Francis, 6/7/18, DRF, B33–56.

49. "Diplomats at the Crossroads," *Novaia Zhizn,* 6/2/18, DRF, B33–56. See also *Nasha Rodina,* 5/29/18, DRF, B33–56.

50. Poole to Francis, 6/7/18, DRF, B33–56.

51. Francis testimony, BP, 966. See also Lockhart memo on conversation with Karakhan, 11/7/18, BL(H), B5; Radek introduction to Ransome's "Letter to America," 9/18, SH, B65.

52. Wheeler-Bennett, *Brest Litovsk,* 273–275.

53. Francis to Poole, 6/19/18, DRF, B33–56; Francis testimony, BP, 969.

54. Chicherin to Francis, 6/5/18, NAM, reel 3; FRUS, 1918, Russia, I, 551.

55. Poole to Francis, 6/5/18, NAM, reel 3, file of D. C. Poole.

56. Maisky, *Journey,* 67.

57. *Ibid.*

58. Poole to Francis, 6/7/18, DRF, B33–56.

59. Polk to Wilson, 6/8/18, PWW 48:264; Wilson to Polk, 6/10/18, PWW 48:276.

60. Francis to Poole, 7/3/18, DRF, B34–56.
61. Summers to Francis, enclosing Lehrs to Summers, 4/19/18, DRF, B33–56; Poole to Francis, 6/7/18, DRF, B33–56; b256; Poole to Francis, 7/1/18, DRF, B34–56.
62. See the different but compatible versions by Lehrs and Radek: Lehrs to Poole, 6/29/18, DRF B34–56; Chicherin to Poole, 6/28/18, enclosing Radek to Chicherin, 6/27/18, DRF, B34–56.
63. Poole to Chicherin, 7/1/18, DRF, B34–56.
64. Poole to Chicherin, 7/1/18, DRF, B34–56; Poole to Francis, 7/1/18, DRF, B34–56.
65. Francis to Poole, 7/3/18, DRF, B34–56.
66. Francis to Sec. of State, 5/2/18, DRF, B33–56.
67. Francis to Poole, 5/15/18, DRF, B33–56.
68. Poole to Francis, 5/13/18 *re* LaVergne, DRF, B33–56.
69. Lockhart to Balfour in Lansing to Wilson, 5/15/18, PWW 48:101–102.
70. Lockhart, *Diaries,* 5/15/18, p. 36.
71. Lockhart, *Memoirs,* 271.
72. *Ibid.,* 282–285.
73. Francis to Lansing, 5/20/18, FRUS, 1918, Russia, I, 536–537.
74. Lansing to Wilson, 5/16/18, PWW 48:38; Reading to Balfour *re* conversation with Wilson, 5/23/18, PWW 48:133–134.
75. Poole to Francis, 5/13/18, DRF, B33–56.
76. Poole to Francis, 5/24/18, DRF, B33–56.
77. Poole to Francis, 5/28/18, DRF, B33–56.
78. Polk to Wilson, 6/6/18, enclosing Francis to SD, 6/3/18, PWW 48:277–278; Poole to Francis, 6/3/18, DRF, B33–56; Francis to son Perry, 6/4/18, DRF, B33–56.
79. Cole to Francis, 6/1/18, FRUS, 1918, Russia, II, 477–484.
80. Francis to Cole, 6/13/18, DRF, B33–56.
81. Poole to Smith, 6/25/18, DRF, B34–56; Willoughby Smith to Poole, 7/3/18, DRF, B34–56.
82. Poole to Francis, 7/6/18, DRF, B34–56.
83. For background on the Czechoslovak corps, see Kennan, *Soviet-American Relations,* II, 136–165, 277–321; and Betty Unterberger, *The United States, Revolutionary Russia and the Rise of Czechoslovakia* (Chapel Hill, 1989), 133–215.
84. Wilson's decision was made July 6, 1918, and announced to the Allies and U.S. representatives abroad July 17. For Lansing's memorandum on the decision, see PWW 48:542–543. Wilson's *aide-mémoire* is in PWW 48:639–640. For the controversy, see Kennan, *Soviet-American Relations,* II, 381–404; Betty Unterberger, *America's Siberian Expedition,* 67–68; John A. White, *The Siberian Intervention* (Princeton, 1950), 227–255; Christopher Lasch, "American Intervention in Russia: A Reinterpretation," *Political Science Quarterly,* LXVII (June, 1962), 217–223; William Appleman Williams, "American Intervention in Russia, 1917–1920," *Studies on the Left,* Vol. 3, No. 4 (Fall, 1963): 24–48; and Part II in Vol. 4, No. 1 (Winter, 1964) :39–57.
85. See ELH, B1.
86. Commissar for Foreign Affairs of the Central Siberian Soviet Geyzman to Sec. of State, 6/9/18, FRUS, 1918, Russia, II, 196–197.
87. Poole to Francis, 6/5/18, DRF, B33–56.
88. *Ibid.*
89. Lockhart to Balfour, 6/6/18, VAM, 365(C). See also Lockhart, *Diaries,* June 4, 1918, p. 37.

90. Lockhart, *Memoirs,* 285–287.

91. Francis to Poole, 6/18/18, DRF, B33–56; Francis to Poole, 6/20/18, DRF, B33–56; Poole to Francis, 6/21/18, DRF, B33–56.

92. People's Commissariat of Foreign Affairs to Allied representatives, 6/13/18, C&P, 224–226.

93. Francis to Poole, 6/10/18, DRF, B33–56.

94. Poole to Francis, 6/13/18, DRF, B33–56.

95. Poole to Consul in Samara, 6/18/18, DRF, B33–56; Poole to Francis, 6/21/18, DRF, B33–56.

96. Francis to Poole, 6/20/18, DRF, B33–56.

97. Poole to Francis, 6/16/18, DRF, B33–56.

98. A good example was Francis' letter to Poole of June 13, "I received your confidential letter of yesterday just delivered by Mr. Trapagen who has given me the name of the man you were afraid to commit to writing and from whom you obtained the confidential information" (DRF, B33–56).

99. Francis to Lansing, 6/15/18, DRF, B33–56.

100. Francis to Lansing, containing Chicherin to Poole, 6/15–16/18, FRUS, 1918, Russia, II, 486.

101. Francis to Lansing, 6/20/18, DRF, B33–56; Francis to Perry, 6/20/18, DRF, B33–56.

102. Poole to Francis, 6/16/18, DRF, B33–56; Francis to Poole, 6/18/18, DRF, B33–56.

103. Francis to Poole, 6/19/18, DRF, B33–56.

104. Francis to Poole, 6/19/18, DRF, B33–56; Francis to Lansing, 6/20/18, DRF, B33–56.

105. Francis to Perry, 6/23/18, DRF, B33–56.

106. Francis to Perry, 6/23/18, DRF, B33–56; Francis to U.S. Ambassador to Sweden Ira Morris, 7/4/18, DRF, B34–56.

107. Francis to Poole, 6/19/18, DRF, B33–56.

108. Francis to Lansing, 6/20/18, DRF, B33–56.

109. Chicherin to Francis, 6/25/18, DRF, B33–56.

110. Francis to Poole, 7/1/18, DRF, B34–56.

111. Francis to Poole, 7/1/18, DRF, B34–56.

112. Chicherin to Lockhart, 6/28/18, and Chicherin to Lockhart, 6/30/18, C&P, 226–228.

113. Poole to Lansing, 6/30/18, FRUS, 1918, Russia, II, 236–239; Francis to Perry, 6/30/18, DRF, B33–56.

114. Francis to Poole, 6/28/18, DRF, B33–56.

115. For local press coverage, see DRF, B34–56.

116. Chicherin to Poole, 7/14/18, DRF, B34–56.

117. Francis to Poole, 7/5/18, enclosing Chicherin to Francis, 7/4/18, DRF, B34–56.

118. Francis to Poole, 7/5/18, DRF, B34–56.

119. Poole to Francis, 7/5/18, DRF, B34–56; Poole to Francis, 7/9/18, DRF, B34–56.

120. Poole to Francis, 7/9/18, DRF, B34–56.

121. Poole to Lansing, 7/12/18, FRUS, 1918, Russia, I, 620.

122. David R. Francis, *Russia from the American Embassy,* (New York, 1921), 245–247; Francis testimony, BP, 947; Radek to Francis, 7/14/18, DRF, B30–56.

123. Chicherin to Francis, 7/10/18, DRF, B30–56; Francis testimony, BP, 947.

124. John Lehrs, "Memorandum of events in Vologda transpiring between Sunday July 7th, the date of the receipt of the news of the assassination of the German Ambassador Count Mirbach, and Monday, July 15, 1918," DCP.

125. Francis' testimony, BP, 947; Lehrs, 6–7, DCP.

126. Lockhart, *Memoirs,* 304–305.

127. *Ibid.,* 305; complete text in GK.

128. Radek to Francis, July 12, 1918, two different messages, one presented at the time of the meeting, one sent after the meeting, DRF, B30–56; Radek to Chicherin, GK.

129. Lehrs, 6–7, DCP; Francis to Radek, 7/12/18, DRF, B30–56.

130. Radek-Francis exchange, as recorded by Johnson, 7/12/18, DRF, B30–56.

131. Radek to Francis, 7/12/18, DRF, B30–56.

132. For the text of this treaty, see FRUS, 1918, Russia, II, 492–495. For Lansing's official approval, see FRUS, 1918, Russia, II, 556–557.

133. Chicherin to Poole, 7/13/18, C&P, 229–230; Lehrs, 7, DCP.

134. Radek to Francis, 7/14/18, DRF, B30–56; Lehrs, 8, DCP.

135. Chicherin to Francis, 7/14/18, DRF, B30–56; Lehrs, 8–9, DCP; Radek to Francis, 7/15/18, DRF, B30–56.

136. Lehrs, 10, DCP.

137. *Ibid.,* 11.

138. Radek to Francis, 7/17/18, DRF, B30–56. A full Russian-language version of communications among Chicherin, Radek, and Francis can be found in "Ofitsial'naia perepiska" (Vologda, 1918).

139. Francis to Poole, 7/19/18, DRF, B30–56.

140. Chicherin to Francis, 7/23/18, DRF, B30–56; Francis to Chicherin, 7/24/18, DRF, B30–56.

141. Francis testimony, BP, 948–949.

142. Chicherin to Francis, 7/24/18, FRUS, 1918, Russia, I, 637.

143. Chicherin to Lehrs, 7/24/18, DRF, B30–56.

144. Poole memorandum on meeting with Chicherin, 7/24/18, GK.

145. Lockhart, *Memoirs,* 306.

146. Poole memorandum, 7/26/18, NAM, reel 3.

147. Lehrs memorandum for Poole, 7/31/18, GK.

148. Poole to Lansing, 7/29/18, FRUS, 1918, Russia, I, 648.

149. Lenin, *Sochineniia* (5th ed.) 28:1–13.

150. POM; Chicherin, "Two Years of Foreign Policy."

151. Chicherin to Poole, 8/2/18, DCP.

152. POM.

153. Chicherin to Poole, 8/5/18, FRUS, 1918, Russia, I, 659–660.

154. Poole to Lansing, 8/5/18, FRUS, 1918, Russia, I, 642–643.

155. Chicherin to Poole, 8/8/18, GK.

156. For the story of these last days, see Kennan, *Soviet-American Relations,* II, 457–469.

157. In addition to Kennan's account, see Wardwell diary, 8/8–10/17/18, AW; POM; and Lockhart, *Memoirs,* 305–343; and *idem, Diaries,* 38–40. For further evidence of the special efforts the Bolsheviks made to profess their special friendship to the Americans, see Webster's account of the mass meeting in Petrograd in early August, where Trotsky and others "expressed considerable friendliness towards Americans" even as they condemned intervention and the British-French "imperialist plot." Webster to Wardwell, 8/5/18, AW.

## Chapter 6

1. Poole to Lansing, 9/5/18, FRUS, 1918, Russia, I, 581–582.
2. Lockhart on conversation with Karakhan, to FO, 11/7/18, BL(H), B5, Russia, 1918.
3. Colcord to Johnson, 1/9/19, HJ III:29.
4. Karakhan conversation with Lockhart, 9/18, Lockhart to FO; 11/7/18, BL(H), B56.
5. Poole to Lansing, 9/3/18, FRUS, 1918, Russia, I, 681–682.
6. Lockhart, *Memoirs,* 311. Most standard accounts of the Cheka and Red Terror agree. See, for example, Bunyan and Fisher, *Bolshevik Revolution* I, 574–585; *ibid.,* II, 138–151, 227–267; Xenia Eudin Papers on the Red Terror, 1918–1921, Hoover Institution, B7, f7–8; "Reign of Terror in Russia," Sergei Melgunov Papers, Hoover Institution, B4; and "Memorandum on Certain Aspects of the Bolshevist Movement in Russia," 10/19, RLP, B5.
7. James Bunyan, *Intervention, Civil War, and Communism* (Baltimore, 1936), 226–227. For an excellent discussion of Dzerzhinski and the Cheka, see Leonard David Gerson, "The Shield and the Sword: Felix Dzerzhinski and the Establishment of the Soviet Secret Police" (Ph.D. diss. George Washington University, 1973).
8. Despite the discrepancy between Latsis' estimate of 22 executions by the Cheka during its first six months and Melgunov's of 884, either figure is much lower than the many thousands executed between July 1918 and January 1919. See Bunyan and Fisher, *Bolshevik Revolution,* I, 574; and Chamberlin, *Russian Revolution,* II, 75. On the press and Bolshevik party debate concerning the Cheka, see Bunyan and Fisher, *Bolshevik Revolution,* 579–585; and Melgunov Papers, B1, f6.
9. Bunyan and Fisher, *Bolshevik Revolution,* 227–228.
10. *Svoboda Rosii,* No. 43, 6/9/18, p. 3, as translated by Bunyan and Fisher, *Bolshevik Revolution,* 227.
11. Bunyan, *Intervention, Civil War,* 138–139.
12. Wardwell diary, 8/12, 8/13/18, AW.
13. Wardwell diary, 8/26/18, AW.
14. Wardwell diary, 8/27/18, AW.
15. Bunyan, *Intervention, Civil War,* 236–239.
16. *Ibid.,* 144–45; Lockhart, *Diaries,* 8/31–9/1–2–3–4/18, pp. 40–41.
17. *Izvestia,* 9/3/18, as printed in Bunyan and Fisher, *Bolshevik Revolution,* 145–46; and C&P, 252–253.
18. For the best account of Lockhart's imprisonment, see Lockhart, *Diaries,* 41–46. See also his *Memoirs of a British Agent,* 308–313. Perhaps the most interesting thing to come out of Lockhart's detention, was his extensive conversations with Bolshevik Commissar Lev Karakhan, in which Karakhan detailed the Bolshevik strategy for detaching the United States from the Allied coalition. See Lockhart to Secretary of State for Foreign Affairs, 11/7/18, RL(H)B5.
19. Richard K. Debo, "Lockhart Plot or Dzerzhinski Plot?" *Journal of Modern History* XLIII, No. 3 (September 1971): 438–439. For Chicherin's early account, in which he largely blames the British involvement on Reilly, see *Two Years of Foreign Policy,* 19.
20. Lockhart report to FO, 11/7/18, PRO, FO 371/3368/190442.
21. Lockhart to Balfour, 5/17/18, VAM(O), MS Milner 142; Lockhart to Balfour, 6/1/18, VAM(O), MS Milner, 142; Lockhart to Balfour, 6/8/18, VAM(O), MS Milner, 142; Lockhart to Balfour, 7/6/18, VAM(O), MS 141, Lockart to Milner, 7/18/18,

VAM(O), 365(C); Lockhart to Balfour, 7/16/18, VAM(O), 365 (C); Lockhart to Balfour, 7/23/18, VAM(O), 365(C); Lockhart to Balfour, 7/25/18, VAM(O), 365(C). For Lockhart's rather bland denial, see *Memoirs,* 291–292, and *Diaries,* 9/3/18.

22. Balfour to Lockhart, 6/3/18, VAM(O), MS 142; Lockhart to Milner, 7/18/18, VAM, 365(C); Lockhart to Balfour, 7/23/18, VAM, 365(C)

23. Lockhart, *Memoirs,* 270–271, 312–313; René Marchand, "Assistance given to the Socialist Revolutionaries by the French Diplomatic Corps in Moscow," in Eudin Papers, Hoover Institution, Box 5; René Marchand, *Allied Agents in Soviet Russia* (London, 1918).

24. Poole to Lansing, 9/5/18, FRUS, 1918, Russia, I, 581–582.

25. Poole's trip to South Russia early in 1918 is described in Kennan, *Soviet-American Relations,* I, 180–183.

26. See Chapter 5 for the discussions between Poole and Chicherin about the expansion of the consul network.

27. POM, 208–209.

28. While David A. Langbart, "Spare No Expense: The Department of State and the Search for Information about Bolshevik Russia, November 1917–September 1918," *Intelligence and National Security* (April, 1989), 316–334, insists that the information-gathering was never directed against the Bolsheviks, David Foglesong, in his Ph.D. dissertation, "America's Secret War Against Bolshevism: United States Intervention in the Russian Civil War, 1917–1920," (University of California, Berkeley, 1991), has examined all of the evidence, including Soviet and British intelligence, and American archives, and concludes that much of Kalamatiano's work was military intelligence. I appreciate Mr. Foglesong's making his manuscript available to me.

29. Soviet charges that Kalamatiano was involved in the British-French conspiracy are backed by little firm evidence. The indictment mostly rests on Kalamatiano's attendance at the famous August 25 meeting in Poole's office, where Kalamatiano, French Consul General Grenard, French agent de Vertement, French journalist René Marchand, and British agent Sidney Reilly met to exchange information and coordinate plans. Marchand's charges that this meeting planned the attack on the Bolsheviks noticeably omit Poole and Kalamatiano from direct culpability, as did Sidney Reilly's own account. See Marchand, *Allied Agents,* and Sidney Reilly, *Sidney Reilly, Britain's Master Spy* (London, 1933), 14. For a full review, see David Foglesong, "Xenophon Kalamatiano: An American Spy in Soviet Russia?" *Intelligence and National Security.* 6:1 (1991), 54–95.

30. *Izvestia,* 9/3/18, in C&P, 250–251.

31. Leonid Krasin to Lubov Krasin, 9/23/18, in Lubov Krassin, *Leonid Krassin: His Life and Work* (London, 1929), 98.

32. Poole to Lansing, 9/3/18, FRUS, 1918, Russia, I, 681–682.

33. Poole to Lansing, 9/3/18, FRUS, 1918, Russia, I, 662–663. For Oudendyk's role, see William J. Oudendyk, *Ways and Byways in Diplomacy* (London, 1939), 276–311.

34. Poole to Lansing, 9/9/18, FRUS, 1918, Russia, I, 685. Even as he left, however, Poole was aware of the Bolshevik preference for the United States, remarking in a last letter to Wardwell that he took "great comfort in Sverdloff's friendship . . . and in [his] own good standing with the B's. . . ." (Poole to Wardwell, AW.)

35. Lansing to Wilson, 9/18/18, PWW 51:61–62; Wilson to Lansing, 9/20/18, PWW 51:78; note from American government to Associated and neutral governments, 9/21/18, C&P, 256.

36. Chicherin to Wardwell, 9/11/18, misc. MSS, Hoover Institution. For the development of Wardwell's anti-Bolshevik feelings, see his diary, 8/8 to 10/17/18, AW.

37. Whitehouse to Lansing *re* conversation with Wardwell, 10/29/18, FRUS, 1918, Russia, III, 160.

38. Lansing to Whitehouse, 10/31/18, FRUS, 1918, Russia, III, 160.

39. Francis to Poole, 6/18/18, DRF, B33–56.

40. Hard, *Robins*, 215–217; Francis to Consul at Vladivostok, 5/25/18, NA, RG84. That Robins took this prohibition of public statements seriously is confirmed, not only by the testimony of his friends, but by his own rejection of speaking engagements. See Robins to Lucius Teter, 7/16/18, RR, reel 2; Robins to Mrs. George Reinecke, 7/16/18, RR, reel 4.

41. Hagedorn, 272; Hagedorn interview with Robins, 2/1/31, HHWT, B21.

42. Sisson, *100 Red Days*, 95.

43. Robins to Margaret, 4/14/18, RR, reel 4; Kent to Wilson, 5/22/18, enclosed in Wilson to Lansing, 5/23/18, RLP; Lansing diary, RLP; Auchincloss diary, 5/29/18, GA, Box 2, folder 20, p. 30.

44. Thomas D. Thacher, "Russia and the War," 6/4/18, DRF, B33–56.

45. Lansing desk diary, 6/26/18, RLLC.

46. Hiram Johnson to Amy Johnson, 6/22/18, *Diary Letters of Hiram Johnson, II*. Robins had been sporadically in touch with Johnson, and held long meetings with him before departing for Russia in the summer of 1917. See Robins to Johnson, 6/26/17, RR, reel 2.

47. Lansing desk diary, 6/21/18, RLLC.

48. Robins to Bessie Beatty, 6/27/18, RR, reel 4; Robins to Hagedorn, 2/1/31, HHWT; Williams conversation with Robins, 8/5/49, Williams, "Raymond Robins," 155–156. Arthur Link *et al.* dispute Kennan's contention that Wilson never did Robins the courtesy of "receiving him and permitting him to present his views in person" (Kennan, *Soviet American Relations,* II, 230–231) by claiming that "there is no evidence that Robins or any friend of Robins asked Wilson to grant him an interview at this time" (PWW 48:489–491, footnote). While the latter may be strictly true, this does not invalidate Kennan's conclusion.

49. Robins expressed his own doubts about a meeting with Wilson in a letter to Bessie Beatty: "I have not seen the President and I have no expectation of being asked to do so." (Robins to Bessie Beatty, 6/27/18, RR, reel 4.)

50. "American Economic Cooperation with Russia," Robins to Sec. of State, 7/1/18, C&P, 212–219; also found in Lansing to Wilson, 7/2/18, PWW 48:489–491.

51. Wilson to Lansing, 7/3/18, PWW 48:489–491. The editors of PWW note that there "is no solid evidence that Robins presented or read Lenin's offer of economic cooperation with the United States to Lansing" (PWW 48:489), but it is quite clear that Robins' memo embodying many of the same ideas *was* enclosed.

52. Robins report to Johnson, 7/4/18, HJ III:12.

53. Harper reported from his own sources at this meeting that "Robins certainly got a few knocks in the Senate." (Harper to William Porter, 7/17/18, SH).

54. Hiram Johnson to Amy Johnson, 7/20/18, *Diary Letters of Hiram Johnson, II*.

55. Johnson to Amy Johnson, 7/8/18, *Diary Letters of Hiram Johnson, II*.

56. Johnson to Robins, 7/24/18, RR, reel 4.

57. Croly to Robins, 7/16/18, RR, reel 4.

58. Editorial, *New Republic* 16, No. 197 (8/10/18).

59. Kennan to Lansing, 8/20/18, RLP B4.

60. See Chapter 10 for a discussion of the Hoover-Nansen relief scheme, developed in Paris.

61. Huntington to Harper, 11/27/17,SH, B4.

62. *New York Times,* 12/2/17. See also Kennan notes on conversation with Herbert Carpenter (first executive director of the League), 11/30/56, GK.

63. Thomas Thacher, "Memo on the Russian Situation," 4/12/18, TB.

64. House to Wilson, 6/13/18, EMH, B121; House diary, 6/13/18, EMH; Polk to Wilson, 6/13/18, FP; Lansing to Wilson, 6/13/18, PWW 48:305–306.

65. Archibald Cary Coolidge, "Report on American Relations with Russia since the Triumph of the Bolsheviki," 5/20/18, RLP, B4; Thomas Chadbourne, War Trade Board, to Auchincloss, 6/7/18, GA, B9, f223; Redfield to Wilson, 6/8/18, EMH, B121; Auchincloss diary, 6/13/18, GA, B2, f21; Wilson to Redfield, 6/13/18, EMH, B121.

66. Undated and unsigned memorandum, "before armistice," GA, B9, f225.

67. *Ibid.* This memo also discusses U.S. firms Singer, International Harvester, and J. M. Coates, and includes similar detail on railway experts found in Lenin's memorandum.

68. Robins, "American Economic Cooperation with Russia," 7/1/18, C&P, 212–219.

69. Robins to Johnson, 7/4/18, HJ III:12.

70. Thacher to Hagedorn, 6/1/32, HHWT; Williams conversation with Robins, 7/27/49, Williams, "Robins," 157.

71. House to Wilson, 6/13/18, EMH, B121; House to Wilson, 6/21/18, EMH, B121.

72. Williams oversimplifies a complex situation when he says that Harper "exercised all his talents and influence against Robins" and "spent a good portion of the summer of 1918 following him around in a perpetual counterattack" (Williams, "Robins," 158).

73. Harper to Richard Crane, 5/30/18, SH, B5.

74. Harper to Archibald Cary Coolidge, 6/8/18, SH, B5.

75. Harper to Lippman, 6/11/18, SH, B5.

76. Harper to Robins, 6/15/18, SH, B5.

77. Harper to Walter Rogers, 7/15/18, SH, B5. Robins to Harper cable, 6/20/18, RR, reel 4.

78. Harper to Mott, 7/23/18, SH, B5.

79. Carpenter to Harper, 7/26/18, SH, B5.

80. Carpenter to Harper, 8/12/18, SH, B5.

81. House diary, 6/17/18, EMH; Wilson to Redfield, 6/27/18, and Redfield to Wilson, 7/9/18, EMH, B121; Lansing to Wilson, 6/29/18, PWW 48:465–466; Baruch to Wilson, 7/13/18, and Wilson to Baruch, 7/15/18, PWW 48:606–607, 611; Wilson to House, 7/8/18, EMH, B121, F4285. Wiseman to Drummond, 6/14/18, PWW 48:315–316.

82. Wilson *aide-mémoire,* 7/17/18, PWW 48:640–643; Mott to Wilson, 7/24/18, PWW 49:77–79; House diary, 8/17/18, Vol. 14, EMH; House diary, 8/20/18, EMH; Lansing to Wilson, 8/22/18, PWW 49:320–323; House diary, 9/24/18, EMH; Harper to Huntington, 10/28/18, SH; McCormick to Auchincloss, 11/4/18, GA, B6, f131.

83. House Diary, 8/17/18, EMH.

84. *New Republic* XVII, No. 210 (11/9/18); Huntington memo in Redfield to Wilson, 11/22/18, PWW 53:169–180.

85. Wilson in Council of Four, 3/28/19, Mantoux notes, PWW 56:328–329.

86. Kent to Wilson, 7/22/18, PWW 49:54–55.

87. Wilson to Lewis, 7/24/18, PWW 49:74.

88. Thacher to Robins, 8/28/18, RR, reel 4; Williams, "Robins," 166–167. For the unraveling of House's plan for an economic commission, see Huntington memo in Redfield to Wilson, 11/22/18, PWW 53:169–180.

89. Sir Eric Howard, Stockholm, to FO, and FO response, 8/2/18, PRO, FO 371/3300, file 1869, 134474.

90. Widenstrom to Swedish FO, copy to U.S. legation at Stockholm, 8/4/18, NAM, reel 3, 101.

91. Chicherin to Berzin, Soviet representative in Switzerland, transmitted by Stovall to Lansing, 8/27/18, FRUS, 1918, Russia, II, 359.

92. U.S. War Department intercept, conversation between Chicherin and Zorin, Chief of Foreign Department of Petrograd Soviet, 9/30/18, GK.

93. PRO, FO 371/3343/167993.

94. Lenin to Chicherin and Karakhan, 10/10/18, Lenin, *Collected Works* (4th ed.) 44:152. See also Mikhail Trush, *Vneshnepoliticheskaia deyatel'nost V. I. Lenina, 1917–1920, den' za dnyom* (Moscow, 1963), 215–216.

95. Chicherin to Wilson, 10/24/18, PWW 51:508–510, 555–561.

96. *Ibid.*

97. *Ibid.*

98. See Litvinov to Wilson, 12/24/18, Degras, *Soviet Documents*, 129–132. Litvinov, in his subsequent discussions with Buckler, apologized for Chicherin's diatribe, calling it "a piece of propagandist journalism, discourteous in tone and calculated rather to repel than to conciliate." (Buckler notes on meetings with Litvinov, 1/16/19, WHB, B6, f9.)

99. *The German-Bolshevik Conspiracy, War Information Series, No. 2 (October, 1918)* (Washington: Committee on Public Information, George Creel Chairman, 1918).

100. For what remains the most exhaustive analysis of these documents, casting extensive doubt on their authenticity, see George F. Kennan, "The Sisson Documents," *Journal of Modern History*, XXVIII, No. 2 (June, 1956), 130ff. See also Helena M. Stone, "Another Look at the Sisson Forgeries and Their Background," *Soviet Studies* XXXVII (January, 1985): 90–103.

101. Sisson, *100 Red Days*, 366–367.

102. Francis to SD, 2/13/18, PWW 46:341–42; "Sisson Documents file," GK.

103. See particularly Bullard's long memorandum to House, 12/12/17, EMH, B21, F671; Bullard to House, 3/7/18, EMH, B21, F672.

104. See Lockhart to Balfour, 5/8/18, PWW 48:41. By early October, the British were becoming definitive. Auchincloss, reporting a conversation with Wiseman, noted that "the English experts and authorities had gone over carefully the Sisson Papers and had come to the definite conclusion that they were forgeries" (Auchincloss to Lansing in Lansing to Wilson, 10/4/18, PWW 51:246–247). See also Wiseman to Drummond, 10/5/18, PWW 51:252.

105. Lansing to Sisson, 9/14/18, PWW 51:3–4.

106. House diary, 9/24/18, EMH. See also Bullitt to House, 9/24/18, EMH, B21, f680.

107. Reading to Balfour *re* interview with Wilson, 4/25/18, PWW 47:440–441.

108. Harper's and Jamieson's analysis of the documents did not claim they were all authentic and cast doubt on many specific documents. But the overall import was to frame the documents in historical legitimacy. This misuse of historical analysis for

political purposes continued to bother Harper in the future, as he searched for more evidence to justify his conclusions. See *German-Bolshevik Conspiracy,* 29–30; Harper, *The Russia I Believe In,* 112.

109. See Norman Thomas, "The Acid Test of Our Democracy," *The World Tomorrow* (September, 1918); *Dial* (various issues in September, October, November, December, 1918).

110. Nuorteva to Robins, 9/16/18, RR, reel 4.

111. Margaret to Robins, 9/22/18; Robins to *Chicago Tribune,* 9/22/18; Robins to Associated Press, 9/22/18; *Spokane Review* (AP Story), 9/24/18, all HHWT, B21.

112. Croly to Margaret Robins, 9/22/18, RR, reel 4.

113. Nuorteva statement, 9/18, RR, reel 4; Nuorteva to Robins, 10/7/18, RR, reel 4; Santeri Nuorteva, "Open Letter to American Liberals," *Class Struggle,* 9–10/18.

114. Reed to Margaret Robins, enclosing Reed to Raymond Robins, 9/15/18, RR, reel 4; subpoena for Robins, 10/14/18, RR, reel 4.

115. See Chapter 11.

116. Stiemer and the others were given heavy sentences. See *New York Times,* 10/18, 19, 22, 24, 26, 28, 1918, and Robins conversation with Williams, 8/5/49, Williams, "Robins," 169.

117. Burke, introduction to *Diary Letters of Hiram Johnson* I:28–29. For Johnson's speech defending Robins, see *Congressional Record,* 7/16/18, p. 9,056.

118. Johnson to C. K. McClatchy, 8/13/18, HJ III:1.

119. Kennan notes on War Department intelligence inquiry on Robins, 11/5, 14/18, GK.

120. Gifford Pinchot to Robins, 10/17/18, RR, reel 4.

121. Harper to Huntington, 10/11/18, SH, B6; Miles to Francis, 11/1/18, DRF, B35–56.

122. Hudson to Harper, 10/18/18, SH, B6; Landfield to Harper, 10/16/18, SH, B6.

123. "Memorandum concerning interrogatories upon our Russian Policy," 12/4/18, Robins to Johnson, HJ III:12; Robins to Johnson, 12/3/18, HJ III:68.

124. Johnson, speech on the Senate floor, 12/12/18, *Congressional Record,* 12/12/18, 342–347. For a draft of this speech and Johnson's notes, see HJ III:12.

125. Johnson to Jack Johnson, 12/13/18, *Diary Letters of Hiram Johnson,* II.

126. Johnson to Meyer Lissner, 12/18/18, HJ III:2.

127. See Johnson to J. O. McBierney, 12/23/18. Ninety-four similar letters can be found in the January 1919 file in HJ III:2. Johnson took note of this positive response in the *Congressional Record* of 1/9/19.

128. *Dial,* 12/14/18; *New Republic,* 2/8/19, Vol. 18, No. 223.

129. Johnson to Theodore Roosevelt, 12/27/18, HJ III:2.

130. On the pressure on Johnson to desist, see Arthur De Witt, "Hiram W. Johnson and American Foreign Policy, 1917–1941" (Ph.D. diss., University of Arizona, 1972), 77. For administration pressure, see Emery (Division of Foreign Intelligence) to Polk, 1/25/19, FP, B33, f706; Harper to Charles Crane, 1/19/19, SH, B6; and Harper to Jamieson, 1/25/19, SH, B6; Polk to Ammission, 1/24/19, HW, B39.

131. Johnson to Arch Johnson, 1/1/19, *Diary Letters of Hiram Johnson,* III.

132. Johnson to Robins, 1/15/19, RR, reel 5.

133. Johnson to Robins, 2/1/19, RR, reel 5; Polk to Ammission, 1/24/19, HW, B39.

134. Polk to Lansing, 4/26/19, FP, B9, F310.

135. Colcord to Johnson, 1/9/19, HJ III:29.

136. *Congressional Record,* 65th Congress, 3rd Session, 2/14/19. See also House to Wilson, 2/17/19, PWW 55:203–204; and Bullitt to House, 2/11/19, EMH, B21, f682.

137. BP, 3:465–723.

138. Johnson to Lissner, 4/11/19, HJ III:2.

## Chapter 7

1. NAM, reel 2.

2. Degras, *Soviet Documents,* 132.

3. Buckler notes on conversation with Litvinov, 1/14–16/19, WHB, B6, f8.

4. Ullman, *Anglo-Soviet Relations,* II, 287.

5. Debo, "Chicherin," 146.

6. Bolshevik approaches to the U.S. through the Red Cross persisted in the period following the departure of Wardwell in October 1918. Successive overtures through Wardwell and Webster in Sweden the end of October, Robins in early December, and Magnuson in late December led to nothing. See Whitehouse to Lansing, 10/29, 31/18, FRUS, 1918, Russia, III, 160; Robins to Johnson, 12/4/18, HJ III:12; Magnuson to Thompson, 12/21/18, HJ III:68.

7. Legation at Christiana to SD, 11/5/18, NAM, 3, #126; copy of telegram from Norwegian legation at Petrograd to Norwegian FO, 11/6/18, NAM, 3, #127. See also DVP, I, 549.

8. *I Documenti Diplomatici Italiene,* Series VI, Volume I, Italian State Printing Office (Rome, 1955), 7, 29, 58, 68, 188, as cited by Debo, "Chicherin," 138; Lansing to Wilson, 11/21/18, PWW 53:151–153.

9. DVP I: 557–558.

10. Lockhart to Balfour, 11/7/18, BL(H), B5.

11. Chicherin to Allied governments, 12/2/18, C&P, 268–270.

12. British FO comments on Chicherin proposal, 12/4/18, PRO, FO 371/3345.

13. Chicherin, "Lenin and Foreign Policy," *Mirovaia Politika v 1924 godu,* 7; Chicherin, "Two Years of Foreign Policy," 29.

14. Miles memorandum on Russia policy, 12/2/18, NAM, reel 2.

15. L. I. Trofimova, "Pervie shagi sovetskoi diplomati," 43–45.

16. Morris to Lansing, 12/5/18, FRUS, 1918, Russia, I, 730.

17. *Ibid.*

18. Paget, Brit. rep., Copenhagen to FO, 9/21/18, PRO, FO 371/3343/165707.

19. Lockhart to Milner, 1/24/18, VAM(O), B355 (Letters, 1918); N. Liubimov, "O V. V. Vorovskom," *Voprosy Istorii* 1971 (No. 10), 138–144.

20. DVP II:626–627.

21. Chicherin, "The Foreign Policy of Soviet Russia," 2–3.

22. Clive to FO, 12/4/18, PRO, FO 371/3345.

23. FO comments on Clive's report, 12/6/18, PRO, FO 371/3345.

24. Clive to FO and FO response, 12/7/18, PRO, FO 371/3345/20254.

25. Clive to FO and FO response, 12/5/18, PRO, FO 371/3349/200672.

26. Clive to FO, 12/20/18, PRO, FO 371/3346; FO response, 12/22/18, PRO, FO, 371/3346/ 210041.

27. Imperial War Cabinet discussion, 12/23/18, LG, F117, IWC 45.

28. Morris to Polk, 12/24/18, FRUS 1919, Russia, 1–2.

29. Clive to FO, 12/24/18, FO office notes, 12/25/18, PRO, FO 371/3346/211538.

30. Litvinov to Wilson, 12/24/18, PWW 53:492–494.

31. *Ibid.*

32. Johnson, speech on Senate floor, 12/12/18, EMH, B29, f908. For evidence of the impact on Wilson, see Polk to Lansing, 1/6/19, PWW 53:628; and Polk to Lansing in Lansing to Wilson, 1/11/19, PWW 54:83–84.

33. *Political Diaries of C. P. Scott 1911–1928,* ed. Trevor Wilson (London, 1970), 364–365.

34. For a full discussion, see Chapter 8.

35. Imperial War Cabinet Minutes, 12/30/18, PWW 53:561.

36. Brit. rep. to France Derby to FO, 1/4/19, VAM(O), B143.

37. House diary, 1/1/19, PWW 53:588.

38. Clive to FO, 12/29/18, PRO, FO 371/3346.

39. Litvinov and Vorovski to Meyer, 1/10/19, C&P, 274–276; Degras, *Soviet Documents,* 133–135.

40. *Ibid.*

41. William Charles Dunning, "The Diplomatic Career of William Hepburn Buckler" (M.A. thesis, George Washington University, 1957), WHB, B7, f12.

42. Although Buckler's reports to House on British Labour and Liberal press were richest from late 1916 to August 1917, a more limited version resumed in late 1917 and continued throughout 1918. See Buckler to House, 1/10/18, WHB, B5, f11; Buckler to House, 6/10/18, WHB, B5, f12; Buckler to House, 2/22/18, WHB, B5, f8.

43. Buckler to House, 1/15/18, WHB, B5, f8; Buckler to House, 1/22/18, WHB, B5, f8.

44. Buckler to House, 6/10/18, WHB, B5, f12.

45. Wiseman to Arthur Murray, 9/14/18, PWW 51:10; House diary, 1/1/19, EMH.

46. Harrison to Grew, 1/9/19, FRUS, 1919, Russia, 4.

47. Lansing to Wilson, 1/13/19, PWW 54:54.

48. Buckler notes on conversations with Litvinov, in memorandum to House, 1/29/19, EMH, B207, f2/795.

49. Buckler to House *re* conversations with Litvinov, 1/29/19, EMH, B2, f2/795. Soviet sources do not dispute this and invariably use the Buckler reports as their source. See for example, Chicherin, "Chetyre Kongressa"; Gvishiani, *Sovietskaia rossiia i SShA,* 198; and I. M. Krasnov, "Missiia W. Bullitta i Sovetsuyu Rosiyu i beseda L. Steffensa s V. I. Leninim," *Novaia i noveishaia istoriia* 2, (1970): 149. Thus, although we do not have Soviet notes or minutes to compare with Buckler's, we have perhaps the only instance of an agreed-upon record of conversations between the two sides in this period.

50. Buckler notes on meetings with Litvinov, 1/16/19, WHB, B6, f9.

51. Buckler notes on meetings with Litvinov, 1/16/19, WHB, B6, f9. See also Buckler's recommendations to House, 1/29/19, EMH, B2, f2/795; and Buckler to Lansing and *Ammission,* 1/18/19, HW, B38.

52. Buckler notes on meetings with Litvinov, 1/16/19, WHB, B6, f9.

53. *Ibid.*

54. *Ibid.*

55. *Ibid.*

56. *Ibid.*

57. *Ibid.*

58. *Ibid.*

59. *Ibid.*

60. Buckler's notes on Litvinov meetings, 1/14–16/19, copy to House, 1/29/19, EMH, B207, f2/795. With the exception of a section regarding the last meeting with Litvinov, Buckler's notes in WHB, and the report to House in EMH are identical. A copy of Buckler's notes can also be found in RLLC without comment from Lansing.

61. Buckler memorandum on conversation with Ransome, 1/16/19, EMH, B207, f2/795.

62. *Ibid.*
63. Buckler to Lansing, 1/18/19, PWW 54:135–138.
64. *Ibid.*
65. Buckler to House, 1/19/19, HW, B38.
66. Hankey notes on Wilson's report to the Council of Ten, 1/20/19, PWW 54:180–181.
67. Buckler to GGB, 1/21/19, WHB, B1, f19.
68. Buckler to GGB, 1/22/19, on train from Copenhagen, WHB, B1, f19.
69. Litvinov to Buckler, 1/24/19, HW, B39.
70. Litvinov to Buckler via Osborne, 1/24/19, HW, B39.
71. Buckler to GGB, 1/27/19, WHB, B1, f19; Buckler to GGB, 1/29/19, WHB, B1, f19.
72. Buckler to GGB, 1/30/19, 1/31/19, WHB, B1, f19.
73. See Chapter 9.
74. Henry White to Jack White, 3/6/19, 3/21/19, 4/8/19, HW. B10.
75. Polk to Lansing, 1/6/19, PWW 53:628; Polk to Lansing, 1/11/19, PWW 54:83–84; Polk to Ammission, 1/11/19, HW, B38. The State Department's concern regarding congressional inquiries continued unabated throughout January. See Polk to Ammission, 1/24/19, HW , B39; Polk to Lansing, 1/24/19, PWW 54:259.
76. Thacher to Robins, 1/14/19, RR, reel 5.
77. Hitchcock speech in *Congressional Record,* 1/9/19, Vol. 57, Pt. 2, p. 1,161. Also FRUS, 1919, Russia, 8; Chicherin to State Department via Danish chargé, 1/12/19, in Polk to Ammission, 1/18/19, HW, B38.
78. Morris to Ammission, 1/21/19, HW, B39; FRUS, 1919, Russia, 26–27.
79. Meyer to Johnson, 2/7/19, HJ III:12.
80. A careful comparison of the Litvinov terms as revealed to Buckler and the Roosevelt-Litvinov agreement for U.S. recognition of the U.S.S.R. in 1933 is striking. For the details of the Roosevelt-Litvinov agreement, see Litvinov to Soviet Foreign Ministry, 11/8/33, DVP, XVI, 609–610; and Litvinov to Roosevelt, 11/16/33, FRUS, Soviet Union, 29.

## Chapter 8

1. Baker, *Woodrow Wilson and World Settlement,* II, 64.
2. Herbert Hoover, *Memoirs: Years of Adventure, 1874–1920* (New York, 1952), 411.
3. Lockhart to FO, 11/1/18, BL(H), B5.
4. Detailed consideration of the two war initiatives: Churchill's intervention scheme and the increased assistance to Kolchak, will be limited and considered only in the context of the peace initiatives.
5. J. T. Shotwell to Samuel N. Harper, "Plan for Work," 11/30/17, SH, B4; Harper to Judson, explaining his Inquiry work, 12/14/17, SH, B4.
6. Harper to Shotwell, 1/30/18, SH, B4; Shotwell to Harper, 8/19/18, SH, B5; Morison to Reed, 5/20/18, JR, 3.
7. Wiseman memorandum *re* interview with Wilson, 10/16/18, PWW 51:350–351.
8. Huntington memo in Redfield to Wilson, 11/22/18, PWW 53:169–180.
9. House diary, 11/27/18, EMH.
10. Polk to Lansing, 1/6/19, PWW 53:627; Lansing to Wilson, 1/9/19, PWW 53:706; Bliss to Baker, 1/11/19, PWW 53:719.
11. Bullitt diary notes, 12/10/18, EMH, B21, f681. Also found in PWW 53:352.
12. British military intelligence memo, 12/14/18, VAM, B143.

13. Imperial War Cabinet Minutes, 12/30/18, PWW 53:560.
14. See Arno Mayer, *Politics and Diplomacy of Peacemaking* (London, 1968), 286.
15. *Ibid.,* 343.
16. War Cabinet Minutes, 11/14/18, LG, WC 502.
17. *Ibid.*
18. *Ibid.*
19. Milner to Nabokov, 12/22/18, VAM, MS English History, C696.
20. War Cabinet Minutes WC 511, 12/10/18, LG, F105.
21. See Chapter 7 for discussion of the Litivinov-Clive exchange.
22. Imperial War Cabinet Minutes, December 30, 1918, LG.
23. *Ibid.*
24. Although Thompson *Russia, Bolshevism, and Versailles,* (90) cites Borden's *Memoirs,* II, 886, as noting the War Cabinet decided "to enter into formal negotiations with an alleged Bolshevik representative to hear his proposals," the War Cabinet Minutes themselves show the decision to be for a request for proposals in writing (see Imperial War Cabinet discussion, 12/23/18, LG F117 IWC 45).
25. Imperial War Cabinet Minutes, 12/30/18, LG, F117. A substantial excerpt from these minutes can be found in PWW 53:568.
26. Balfour to Derby, 1/2/19, PWW 53:591.
27. For the latest in a long list of historians who ignore him, see Arthur Walworth, *Wilson and His Peacemakers* (New York, 1986), 128–129.
28. Robert Laird Borden, *Memoirs,* (Toronto, 1938) 890, *re* 12/30 Imperial War Cabinet Meeting. See also Robert Craig Brown, *Robert Laird Borden, A Biography* (Toronto, 1975) II:148–49.
29. Alfred Milner to Violet Milner, 1/2/19, Violet Milner Papers, VM 30, FC 110/72, Oxford University Library.
30. War Office to Knox, 1/7/19, VAM, B143.
31. Tumulty to Wilson, 1/13/19, PWW 54:53–54.
32. Polk to Phillips, 1/3/19, FP, B33, f706.
33. Lansing first heard about the proposal by reading it in the Paris press. Lansing to Polk, 1/11/19, PWW 53: 718–719; Polk to Lansing, 1/12/19, PWW 54:27; *Dial,* 1/25/19, copy in FP, B33, F706.
34. Pichon to British government, 1/5/19, C&P, 280–281.
35. Diary of Lord Derby, 1/11/19, PWW 53:721–723. For a review of the French press and this incident, see George B. Noble, *Policies and Opinions at Paris,* 1919 (New York 1935), 273–275.
36. Hankey notes of the Council of Ten, 1/12/19, PWW 54:21–22.
37. *Ibid.*
38. Hankey minutes of Council of Ten, 1/13/19, PWW 54:43–47.
39. "Appreciation of the Internal Situation in Russia," 1/12/19, LG; Balfour to Wilson, 1/20/19, PWW 54:173–174.
40. R. H. Lord memo on the Bolsheviki, in Harrison to Wilson, 1/16/19, PWW 54:91–95.
41. Poole to Polk, 1/12/19, FRUS, 1919, Russia, 32.
42. Hankey's notes on the Meeting of the Council of Ten, 1/16/19, PWW 54:99–103.
43. *Ibid.*
44. Hankey notes on Council of Ten, 1/16/19, PWW 54:103; Lloyd George, *Memoirs of the Peace Conference,* 222.
45. Lloyd George, *Memoirs of the Peace Conference,* 217–222.

46. House diary, 1/18/19, EMH.

47. Balfour to Lloyd George, 1/19/19, LG, F/3/4/7.

48. Lloyd George, *Memoirs of the Peace Conference,* 222; Hankey notes of meeting of Council of Ten, 1/20/19, PWW 54:155–156.

49. Lloyd George, *Memoirs,* 222–224.

50. *Ibid.,* 225–226.

51. Wilson's reading of the memorandum from Buckler regarding Litvinov's proposals was not the only input the Bolsheviks made in the peace conference deliberations at this time. Litvinov sent a follow-up memorandum via Danish chargé Nordlien to Lansing on January 16, reiterating his commitment to negotiation and stating, "It lies therefore with you, and not with us, if such a settlement has not yet been arranged." (Nordlien to Lansing, 1/16/19, FP, B33, f706.)

52. Lloyd George, *Memoirs,* 226–232.

53. Hankey's notes of the meetings of the Council of Ten, 1/21/19, PWW 54:181–182.

54. *Ibid.*

55. *Ibid,* 181–188.

56. *Ibid.*

57. Prinkipo invitation, from Mantoux notes of conversations of the Council of Ten, 1/22/19, FRUS, 1919, Russia, 30–31.

58. *Ibid.*

59. Litvinov to Wilson, 12/24/18, PWW 53:494.

60. Hankey minutes of the Council of Ten, 2/1/19, PWW 54:415–416.

61. Chicherin to Wilson, 1/29/19, PWW 54:345–346.

62. C&P, 297–98; FRUS, 1919, Paris, III, 835. Hankey minutes of Council of Ten, 2/1/19, PWW 54:415–416.

63. Lenin to Trotsky, 1/24/19, Jan Meijer, ed., *The Trotsky Papers* (The Hague, 1964) I:259–261.

64. Trotsky to Lenin, 1/25/19, *ibid.,* I:261–263.

65. Georgi Chicherin, "Lenin i vneshnaia politika," *Mirovaia politika v 1924 godu,* 8.

66. Vorovski to FO, British intercept, 1/26/19, in Wiseman, "Notes on the Russian situation," WBW, B9, f211.; V. V. Vorovski, *Stat'i i materiali po voprosam vneshnei politiki* (Moscow, 1959), 17, citing Arkhiv IML, fond Vorovskovo, d. 29; DVP, II:41–42.

67. Zinoviev speech to Petrograd Soviet, 1/27/19, NAM, reel 4, #140.

68. Negative intelligence bulletin, American Commission to Negotiate Peace, 1/22/19, HW, B39, PC Correspondence.

69. Nuorteva to Lenin (never transmitted), 1/29/19, in Polk to American Commission to Negotiate Peace, FRUS, 1919, Russia, 36.

70. Polk to Lansing, 1/29/19, EMH, B207, f2/802; covering note for files by Polk, 1/29/19, FP, B40, f47; Polk to Ammission, 1/29/19, FRUS, 1919, Russia, 36.

71. Buckler to Peace Commissioners, 1/31/19, HW, B39.

72. Chicherin reply to Prinkipo proposal, 2/4/19, FRUS, 1919, Russia, 39–42.

73. *Ibid.* See also Chicherin, "The Foreign Policy of Soviet Russia," report to Seventh Congress of Soviets, 5–6.

74. Zinoviev, speech to Petrograd Soviet, *Severnaya Kommuna,* 2/6/19, translation by Samuel N. Harper, SH, B67.

75. Ransome, reporting on domestic reponse to Chicherin's Prinkipo letter, *Russia in 1919* (New York, 1919), 48

76. *Ibid.*, 49.

77. Ransome details this debate, *Russia in 1919,* 49–61.

78. "Bolshevik aims and Bolshevik ideals," Lockhart memorandum, exact date and source unknown, RL(H), B5; Lenin, *Sochinenia* (5th ed.) 24:116; Lord to Bullitt, weekly intelligence summary, Russia and Rumanian section, 2/28/19, HW, B39; Morris (Stockholm) to Ammission, reporting on Dr. Davidson report, 2/13/19, HW, B39.

79. C&P, 303–307.

80. Thompson, *Russia, Bolshevism, and Versailles,* 119–127, details the multi-layered White Russian response to Prinkipo and notes that most of the public statements were saved until after the Bolshevik response. For various Russian government replies, see "Notes on the Russian situation," WBW, B9, f211.

81. Thompson, *Russia, Bolshevism, and Versailles,* 119–127.

82. Noble, *Policies and Opinions at Paris,* 280–284; and Mayer, *Politics and Diplomacy of Peacemaking,* 440–442, detail the French press's vehement reaction.

83. Buckler to American Commissioners, 1/31/19, HW, B39; Minutes of Daily Meetings of Commissioners, 1/31/19, FRUS, PPC, 1919, XI, 5–6; Minutes of American Commissioners, 2/1/19, TB, B265; VM(D), 1/30/19.

84. Ullman, *Anglo-Soviet Relations,* II, 121–128.

85. Wiseman diary, 1/22/19, WBW; Auchincloss diary, 1/20–21/19, GA.

86. House comments in Council of Ten, 2/16/19, Mantoux notes, FRUS, 1919, Russia, 64.

87. Lansing to Polk, 2/11/19, FP, B9, f308.

88. Minutes of daily meetings of Commissioners, 2/6/19, FRUS, PPC, 1919, XI, p. 21.

89. Poole to Ammission, 1/23/19, HW, B39.

90. Poole to Polk, 1/30/19, FRUS, 1919, Russia, 37. A later recollection by Poole's aide Inman painted this picture of the antipathy Prinkipo aroused in Archangel: "When I arrived in December President Wilson's picture was in every shop. America was supreme, though England was hated. The day after the invitation to Prinkipo all the pictures disappeared." Notes on statement from Mr. Inman, 4/8/19, TB, B357.

91. Poole to Polk, 2/4/19, FRUS 1919, Russia, 42–43.

92. Poole to Lansing, 2/11/19, RLLC, Vol. 41.

93. White to Phillips, 1/24/19, quoted in Allan Nevins, *Henry White: Thirty Years of American Diplomacy* (New York, 1930), 366.

94. See White to Jack White, 3/6/19, and 3/21/19, HW, B10.

95. Bullitt to House, 1/30/19, House Papers, B21, F682. Although House passed this memo on to Wilson with a note, "This is worth considering, you may wish to take it up with L. G. this morning," most of the memorandum dealt with the decision on withdrawal of American and British troops from Archangel.

96. Weekly review, American sector, 1/26/19, HW, B39. An editorial in the *New Republic* remarked, "it remains to be seen whether a policy of conciliation is still possible." *New Republic* XVII, No. 221 (1/25/19).

97. Weekly review, American section, Current Intelligence Division, 2/2/19, HW, B39.

98. *Congressional Record,* 65th Congress, 3rd Session, 3334–3421. See also House to Wilson, 2/17/19, PWW 55:203–204; and Bullitt to House 2/11/19, EMH, B21, f682. For administration concern about this debate, see Polk to Ammission, 1/24/19, HW, B39; and Polk to Auchincloss, 2/18/19, FP, B1, f20.

99. For a full discussion of the Overman Committee Hearings, see Chapter 12.

100. The Council of Ten authorized up to three representatives for each of the

Russian groups and two for each of the Allies. (Minutes of the Council of Ten, 1/23/19, PWW 54:218–219.) British representatives chosen included Prime Minister Robert Borden of Canada, who was picked to convene the conference. See Brown, *Borden,* 149; Borden, *Memoirs,* 904.

101. Later the American commissioners also appointed Livingston Phelps as diplomatic secretary to White and Herron. See Minutes of Meetings of Commissioners, 2/10/19, FRUS, PPC, 1919, XI:27–28.

102. William Allen White, *Autobiography of William Allen White* (New York, 1946), 560.

103. White to Sallie Lindsay White, February 9, 1919, *Selected Letters of William Allen White, 1899–1943,* Walter Johnson, ed. (New York, 1947), 197.

104. On the general enthusiasm for White, see Lord to Bullitt, 1/29/19, WCB.

105. White, *Autobiography,* 561.

106. House diary, 6/8/18, EMH.

107. Herron to White, 4/17/20, GDH, Vol. X.

108. See Mitchell Briggs, *George D. Herron and the European Settlement* (New York, 1971), 141–142, which cites a selection of the press in a long footnote.

109. Wilson to Lansing, 2/14/19, PWW 55:185.

110. House diary, 5/12/19, EMH.

111. Briggs, *Herron,* 142–146. See also the numerous appeals and records of discussions Herron had with various anti-Bolshevik forces and representatives in Switzerland, WDH, Doc. XXV.

112. Herron to House, 2/13/19, EMH, B59, f1849.

113. Tchaikowsky also met with Henry White on February 12, complaining that he was being "ordered" to go to Prinkipo (White memo of conversation with Tchaikowsky, 2/12/19, TB, B357).

114. Herron to House, 2/13/19, WDH, B4, Vol. X; House to Herron, 2/16/19, WDH, Ser. 1, Vol. X.; Herron to *New Republic,* 12/3/19, WDH, B4, Vol. X. For Tchaikowsky's conditional acceptance, see C&P, 305.

115. See House diary, 2/8/19, 2/18/19, 3/1/19, EMH.

116. Herron, "Defeat in the Victory," 221, WDH. White later noted that Wilson had been surprised and annoyed by the way Herron's appointment had been received in the United States. "Why he did not sense it in advance, Heaven only knows." White, *Autobiography,* 561.

117. The Big Four statement of May 26 that "this proposal . . . broke down through the refusal of the Soviet government to accept the fundamental condition of suspending hostilities" (FRUS, PPC, 1919, VI:35) became the basis of a whole range of inaccurate history blaming the Bolsheviks for the demise of Prinkipo. See, for example, Seymour, *Intimate Papers,* IV, 347.

118. Lord Hankey, *The Supreme Council at the Paris Peace Conference,* (London, 1963), 70. The reference to a ceasefire in the Prinkipo proposal was simply that there be "a truce of arms amongst the parties invited" (C&P, 298).

119. FRUS, PPC, 1919, III: 1042. After his return to Washington, Wilson told the Democratic National Committee that the Bolsheviks had accepted the Prinkipo invitation "but had accepted in a way that was studiously insulting" (Tumulty, *Wilson,* 375).

120. Tumulty, *Wilson,* 375.

121. For the House of Commons debate, see Great Britain, House of Commons, *Debates,* fifth series, CXII, cols. 189–98.

122. Lloyd George to Kerr, 2/12/19, LG, F89/2/8.

123. Hankey notes on Supreme War Council meeting, 2/14/19, PWW 55:178–183.

124. Wilson and the American delegation had been moving in this direction for some days. The Commissioners on February 12 "felt it was going a little too far to state that the meeting at Prinkipo was destined to provide for the settlement of just such problems as this . . . [and] further objected to calling the meeting at Prinkipo a conference. . . ." (Minutes of Meetings of Commissioners 2/12/19, FRUS, PPC, 1919, XI:32–33.

125. FRUS, PPC, III:1,041–1,043.

126. *Ibid.* Also found in PWW 55:181–183.

127. Council of Ten Minutes, 2/15/19, FRUS, Paris, 1919, IV:13–14; draft resolution in regard to Russian policy, 2/15/19, EMH, B207, f2/810.

128. Kerr to Lloyd George, 2/15/19, LG F89/2/16.

129. *Ibid.*

130. Mantoux notes on Council of Ten, 2/15/19, FRUS, 1919, Russia, 63–65.

131. *Ibid., 64.*

132. Kerr to Lloyd George, 2/16/19, LG, F/89/2/17.

133. *Ibid.*

134. Kerr to Balfour, 2/16/19, LG, F89/2/17

135. Lloyd George to Churchill, 2/16/19, LG, F/8/3/18

136. Lord Riddell, *Lord Riddell's Intimate Diary of the Peace Conference and After* (London, 1933), 21.

137. Kerr to Lloyd George, 2/16/19, LG, F89/2/21.

138. *Ibid.*

139. Wiseman/Auchincloss, "Notes on the Russian Situation," WBW, B9, F211.

140. *Ibid.*

141. Wiseman/Auchincloss, "Notes," WBW, B9, F211; Auchincloss diary, 2/16/19, GA, B2, f30, pp. 386–388.

142. Auchincloss diary, 2/17/19, GA, B2, f30, pp, 387–388.

143. Minutes of the American Commissioners, 2/17/19, TB, B265.

144. House diary, 2/17/19, EMH; Minutes of the American Commissioners, 2/17/19, TB, B265. A slightly less complete version of these minutes can be found in FRUS, PPC, 1919, XI:43.

145. Bliss to March, 9/3/18, PWW 49:530.

146. Bliss diary, 12/22/18, TB, B244.

147. See Bliss diary, 1/7/19, regarding meeting with Senator Owen, TB, B244; memorial from Wisconsin legislature, 5/6/19 TB, B357.

148. Bullitt diary notes, 12/18, 1/19, EMH, B21, f681, p. 1; House diary, 12/16/18, EMH.

149. Bliss memo to Wilson and Peace Commissioners, 1/6/19, TB, B247.

150. Bliss diary, 1/7/19, TB, B244.

151. Bliss diary, 2/9/19, TB, B244.

152. Bullitt to House with House note to Wilson regarding discussing the matter with Lloyd George, 1/30/19, EMH, B21, F682.

153. Bliss to House, 2/17/19, TB, B247, general correspondence.

154. Minutes of Daily Meetings of Commissioners, 2/16/19, FRUS, PPC, 1919, XI:42.

155. FRUS, PPC, 1919, XI:44; American Commissioners' Minutes, 2/17/19, TB, B385; Bliss to House, 2/17/19, TB, B247.

156. Joseph C. Grew, *Turbulent Era* (Boston, 1952) I:378.

157. House diary, 2/17/19, EMH.

158. Auchincloss diary, 2/17/19, GA.

159. Lansing to Wilson, 2/17/19, PWW 55:202–203; Wilson to American Commissioners, 2/19/19, PWW 55:208; Kerr to Lloyd George, 2/18/19, LG, F89/2/23.

160. House to Wilson, 2/19/19, PWW 55:233.

161. Kerr to Lloyd George, 2/18/19, LG, F89/2/23.

162. Wilson to American Commissioners, 2/19/19, PWW 55:208; Wilson to House, 2/23/19, PWW 55:229–230.

163. American Commissioners to Wilson, 2/23/19, PWW 55:232.

164. WC 535 (5), 2/24/19, Bonar Law Papers, House of Lords Records Office, War Cabinet Papers, 1918–1919.

165. Francis to Lansing, House, Bliss, and White, 2/23/19, PWW 55:234–235. See also Francis to Ammission, 2/23/19, DRF, B36–56. Francis apparently still believed that Lenin was a German agent, even after the Armistice.

166. Bliss diary, 2/3/19, TB, B244.

167. Morison to Bowman, copy to House, 2/24/19, EMH, B207, f2/800.

168. *Ibid.*

169. *Ibid.*

170. Bullitt received his commission February 18 and arrived in London February 22, reaching Moscow March 8.

171. Minutes of American Commissioners, 2/28/19, TB, B265.

## *Chapter 9*

1. William C. Bullitt, "Report to the President and the American Commissioners Plenipotentiary to Negotiate Peace," March 28, 1919, in *The Bullitt Mission to Russia,* Testimony before the Committee on Foreign Relations, United States Senate (New York: B. W. Huebsch, 1919), 54. (Hereafter, *Bullitt Mission.*)

2. For treatments of the Bullitt mission, see Beatrice Farnsworth, *William C. Bullitt and the Soviet Union* (Bloomington, 1967), 32–53; Mayer, *Politics and Diplomacy of Peacemaking,* 450–487; Levin, *Woodrow Wilson and World Politics,* 212–219; and George F. Kennan, *Russia and the West under Lenin and Stalin* (Boston, 1960), 130–135. For Bullitt's testimony, see *Bullitt Mission.*

3. For Lord's appointment, see Mezes to Lansing, 11/9/18, RLLC, Vol. 39. For a discussion of the Russian section of the Inquiry, see Lawrence E. Gelfand, *The Inquiry* (New Haven, 1963), 55–57, 210–215.

4. See, for example, Robert H. Lord, "Special Report on Western Russia and Poland"; Clive Day, "Russian Commercial Relations, 1918" (all historical, pre-Bolshevik); P. W. Siliesson, "Historical Notes on Russia," American Peace Commission Papers, Library of Congress, Box 28.

5. See Lord, weekly reports to Peace Commissioners, TB, B357.

6. See Lord to Bullitt reports, 1/19–4/19, TB, B357.

7. On the Baltic question, see Information Memorandum No. 21, Peace Commissioner minutes, 2/20/19, TB, B265. The Tredwell-Kalamatiano discussion can be found in Minutes of the Commissioners, 2/6/19, TB, B265.

8. For detailed discussions of Bullitt-House relationship and Bullitt's work on Central Europe in 1918, see Will Brownell and Richard N. Billings, *So Close to Greatness: A Biography of William C. Bullitt* (New York, 1988), 64–70; and Farnsworth, *Bullitt* 13–31. Farnsworth argues that Bullitt's emotional nature caused him to get swept up in pro-Bolshevik euphoria even before his trip to Moscow, and that this distorted his judgement and his analysis both of Central Europe and of Russia. This case is weak, however, before the Bullitt mission. Far from what Farnsworth called

Bullitt's "gratuitous suggestions" (p. 19), Bullitt's position on the necessity for exploring contacts with the Bolsheviks in 1918 was shared at times by House, Woodrow
Wilson, and others influential in the administration.

9. Orville H. Bullitt, *For The President: Personal and Secret* (Boston, 1972), 3;
Bullitt, *Bullitt Mission,* 3.

10. Charles Seymour, *Letters from the Paris Peace Conference* (New Haven and
London, 1965), 78–79.

11. Bullitt testimony, *Bullitt Mission,* 3–4. As an example of Bullitt's numerous
discussions with Auchincloss, see Auchincloss diary, 12/15/18, GA, B2, f28, pp. 186–
187. For Bullitt's relationship to Bliss, see Bliss diary, 12/27/18, TB, B244.

12. Herron to *New Republic,* 12/3/19, GDH, B4, Vol. X.

13. Lansing to Wilson, enclosing Bullitt memo, 11/17/18, PWW 51:622–623; Bullitt to Lansing, 11/2/18, PWW 51:563–568.

14. Bullitt to Lansing, 11/2/18, PWW 51:563–568; Bullitt to Lansing, 11/8/18,
PWW 53:6–9.

15. Bullitt to House, 1/19/19, EMH, B21, f681.

16. Bullitt to House, 1/19/19, EMH, B 21, f681.

17. *Ibid.*

18. Bullitt to House with note from House to Wilson, 1/30/19, EMH, B21, f682.

19. Buckler to American Commissioners, 1/31/19, HW, B38.

20. Bullitt to House, 2/11/19, EMH, B21, f682.

21. No direct evidence of Wilson's explicit authorization of the Bullitt mission
exists, but Wilson never denied advance knowledge of the mission, and House and
Auchincloss both indicate in their diaries general discussions with the President about
a secret American-British mission to explore conditions in Russia. See House diary, 2/
14/19, EMH; Auchincloss diary, 2/14/19, GA.

22. Lansing desk diary, 2/16/19, RLP.

23. Kerr to Lloyd George, 2/18/19, LG, F/89/2/23.

24. Kerr to Lloyd George, 2/15/19, LG, F89/2/16

25. Bullitt datebook, 2/17/19, WCB.

26. See Bullitt to House, 2/3/18, EMH B21, f678. Others floating similar ideas
included Hoover; Sidney Mezes, head of the Inquiry; Steffens; Colcord; and Harper.
See, for example, Colcord to House, 3/13/18, EMH, B29, f906.

27. Thompson, *Russia, Bolshevism, and Versailles,* 149–150.

28. Auchincloss diary, 1/9/19, GA.

29. Auchincloss diary, 1/13/19, GA.

30. Lansing desk diary, 1/18/19, RLP; Bliss diary, 1/19/19, TB, B65.

31. Steffens to Allen Suggett, 1/14/19, *The Letters of Lincoln Steffens* (New York,
1938) I:457; *Autobiography of Lincoln Steffens* (New York, 1931), 790.

32. Lansing to Bullitt, 2/18/19, *Bullitt Mission,* 4.

33. Grew to Bullitt, 2/18/19, *Bullitt Mission,* 5.

34. FRUS, PPC, IV:53–54, 56.

35. *Bullitt Mission,* 34.

36. Bullitt datebook, 2/20/19, WCB; *Bullitt Mission,* 34.

37. *Bullitt Mission,* 34.

38. *Bullitt Mission,* 34–35.

39. Kerr to Lloyd George, 2/18/19, LG, F/89/2/16; memo by Kerr (n.d.), LG, F/89/
2/17.

40. Steffens, *Autobiography,* 722.

41. Kerr to Bullitt, 2/21/19, *Bullitt Mission,* 36–37.

42. Kerr to Undersecretary of State for Foreign Affairs, 7/11/19, PRO, FO 371/4002A.

43. Balfour handwritten comments on Kerr's memo regarding Bullitt, 7/21/19, PRO, FO 371/4002A.

44. *Bullitt Mission,* 33; Minutes of American Commissioners, 2/6/19, TB, B265; Lansing to Polk, 2/8/19, FRUS, 1919, Russia, 170.

45. Minutes of the Daily Meetings of the Commissioners Plenipotentiary, 2/24/19, FRUS, PPC, XI:74.

46. FRUS, PPC, XI:70—71; FRUS, 1919, Russia, 74. After Bullitt's testimony to the Foreign Relations Committee, White and Bliss insisted on their total ignorance in advance of the mission (White and Bliss to Grew, 11/19/19, TB, B247).

47. Herter to Mordecai Rosenfield, 3/2/51, GK.

48. Lansing to Pichon, 3/15/19, TB, B246.

49. *Bullitt Mission,* 36; Steffens, *Autobiography,* 791–792.

50. Bullitt to House and Grew, 2/25/19, EMH, B21, f682.

51. Lansing to Polk, 2/26/19, FRUS, 1919, Russia, 75.

52. Polk to Lansing cable, 2/27/19, FP, B40, f49.

53. Bullitt to Ammission, 3/4/19, HW, B40.

54. Bullitt to House from Stockholm, 3/4/19, EMH, B21, f683.

55. *Ibid.*

56. Brownell and Billings, *Bullitt,* 83–84; based on Karl Kilbom, *Memoirs.*

57. Bullitt to Ammission, Helsingfors, 3/8/19, EMH, B21, f683. Lansing relayed this information to Polk, 3/10/19, FRUS, 1919, Russia, 76.

58. Brownell and Billings, *Bullitt,* 83–84, quoting from Karl Kilbom, *Memoirs.*

59. Steffens, *Autobiography,* 792–793.

60. Bullitt draft report, early April 1919, HW, B52.

61. Chicherin quoted by Nagel to Morris and Ammission, 3/3/19, HW, B40.

62. Chicherin to Rakovsky, March 1919, as quoted from Rakovsky's files by Louis Fischer, *Men and Politics* (New York, 1941), 132.

63. Trotsky to Lenin, 3/17/19, *Trotsky Papers,* 303–305.

64. Chicherin, "Lenin i vneshnaia politika," *Mirovaia politika v 1924 godu,* 8. See also M. L. Trush, *Sovetskaia vneshnaiapolitika i diplomatia v trudakh V. I. Lenina* (Moscow, 1977), 106. No Soviet archival materials concerning the Bullitt negotiations were available to Western researchers before 1992, and I was forced to document the Soviet thinking from published documents, Lenin speeches, and memoirs. When Beatrice Farnsworth sought archival materials for her study of Bullitt in the 1960s, she was told that "a search in the Central State Archive had been made but that no such material could be found." (Farnsworth, 182.) On a research trip to Moscow in April 1989, I was told that all materials connected with the Bullitt mission and all other materials involving Lenin were in the *Tsentral'nyi partinyi arkhiv instituta Marksizma-Leninizma pri Tsentral'nom komitete KPSS (TsPA IML)* [Central Party Archive of the Institute of Marxism-Leninism of the Central Committee of the Communist Party of the USSR], that specific application would have to be made to those archives for particular materials, and that access for a Western researcher was highly unlikely. In the wake of political changes in 1991, however, these materials may soon be made available, if they in fact exist.

65. *Bullitt Mission,* 49.

66. Lenin, *Sochineniia* (5th ed.), XXIV:59–60.

67. Ransome, *Russia in 1919,* 122–23.

68. Kilbom, *Memoirs,* quoted in Brownell and Billings, *Bullitt,* 87.

69. Bullitt to Lansing and House, 3/11/19, EMH, B21, f683.

70. Text, Degras, *Soviet Documents,* I, 147–150; *DVP,* II, 91–95, and *Bullitt Mission,* 39–43.

71. Lenin, *Sochineniia* (5th ed.), 38:520, 526.

72. Chicherin to Rakovski, quoted in Fischer, *Men and Politics,* 132.

73. FRUS, 1919, Russia, 78. See also *Bullitt Mission,* 45.

74. See Kerr draft, Lenin draft, and Bullitt report on this point (above).

75. *Bullitt Mission,* 54; William C. Bullitt and Sigmund Freud, *Thomas Woodrow Wilson* (Boston, 1967), 253–254.

76. Bullitt report to Ammission, 3/16/19, FRUS, 1919, Russia, 89.

77. Degras, *Soviet Documents,* 147–150; DVP, II, 91–95.

78. Bullitt to Wilson, Lansing and House, 3/16/19, WBW, B9, f211; EMH, B207, f2/810, p. 15.

79. See, for example, Lasch, *American Liberals,* 191.

80. Thompson, *Russia, Bolshevism, and Versailles,* 167. See also Kennan, *Russia and the West,* 131–133.

81. Chicherin, *Vospominania o V. I. Lenine,* III, 488.

82. Quoted in Orville Bullitt, *For the President,* 9; Lenin, *Sochineniia* (5th ed.), XXIV:603.

83. See Lenin's response to UPI questions, 7/20/19; interview with the *Chicago Daily News,* 10/5/19; and report to the Executive Committee of the Seventh Congress of Soviets, 12/5/19; all in V. I. Lenin, *On Peaceful Coexistence* (Moscow, 1967), 36–37, 42, 46.

84. Ransome, *Russia in 1919,* 225.

85. *Bullitt Mission,* 44.

86. Steffens report to Bullitt, *Bullitt Mission.*

87. Bullitt to Wilson, Lansing and House, 3/16/19, WBW, B9, f211; and EMH, B21, f683. Now printed in PWW 55: 540–545. This long telegram contains no significant differences from the complete text Bullitt carried with him to Paris.

88. Bullitt to House, Wilson, and Ammission, 3/16/19, WBW, B9, F211.

89. Bullitt to Ammission, personal for House, 3/17/19, EMH B21, F683.

90. Bullitt to Ammission, undated (received 3/18/19), RLLC, B313.

91. Minutes of American Commissioners, 3/20/19, TB, B265.

92. Grew to Kirk, 3/21/19, RLLC, Vol. 42; Commission to Negotiate Peace to Haynes, 3/22/19, FRUS, 1919, Russia, 85; Lansing to Polk, 3/22/19, PWW 56:183.

93. Pettit to Ammission, 3/29/19, HW, B41, PC files.

94. Minutes of the American Commissioners, 3/20/19, TB, B265.

95. House diary, 3/25/19, EMH.

96. House diary, 3/26/19, EMH.

97. House diary, 3/25/19, EMH.

98. House notes on Lenin/Bullitt proposal, 3/25/19, EMH, B207, F2/810.

99. *Ibid.*

100. House diary, 3/26/19, EMH.

101. Orlando on Russia policy, Mantoux notes, Council of Four, 3/27/19, PWW 56:329.

102. House diary, 3/26/19, EMH.

103. House diary, 3/26/19, EMH; Auchincloss diary, 3/26/19, GA, B3, f32, p. 471.

104. David Hunter Miller, *Diary,* 3/26/19, I:204, 206.

105. Bullitt, *Bullitt Mission,* 65.

106. White to Jack White, 3/21/19, HW, B10.

107. White to Jack White, 4/2/19, HW, B10.

108. Bliss comments, 3/27/19, Mantoux notes, PWW 56: 327–328.

109. Lansing to Richard Crane, 3/26/19, RLP, B5.

110. Russian Section to the Commission to Negotiate Peace, 3/27/19, "A Proposed Declaration of Policy to Be Issued in the Name of the Associated Governments, and an Offer of an Armistice," relayed to Wilson from Lansing and the Commissioners, 3/31/19, PWW 56:466–468. The editors of PWW point out that this document, unlike the Bullitt report of the same date, can be found in the Wilson papers, and the cover memorandum from Lansing was initialed by him. Moreover, Wilson had a great deal of respect for Lord, the head of the Russian section. On the other hand, the memo bears no marks that Wilson actually read it. Wilson did write to Lansing on April 1, noting, "I think the settlement suggested by you and our colleagues in this matter is the right and necessary one," seeming to indicate that Wilson for a day or two was leaning in the direction of an armistice and *de facto* recognition (PWW 56:512–513).

111. *Bullitt Mission*, 69–73; PWW 56:466–468.

112. Lansing and Peace Comm. to Wilson, 3/31/19, PWW 56:466–468.

113. Bullitt report to Wilson and Commissioners, 3/27/19, *Bullitt Mission*, 49–64.

114. *Ibid.*

115. See *Bullitt Mission*, 111–145.

116. Pettit to Bullitt and Ammission, 3/29/19, HW, B41, PC files; Pettit report to Bullitt, 4/4/19, NAM, reel 4, 150.

117. Pettit to Bullitt, 4/5/19, HW, B41, PC files.

118. *Bullitt Mission*, 134.

119. Steffens to Bullitt, 4/2/19, FP, B33, f680.

120. Steffens to Bullitt, 4/2/19, FP, B33, f680; *Bullitt Mission*, 124–127.

121. Minutes, Daily Meetings of the Commissioners, 4/2/19, TB, B265.

122. Lloyd George Fontainebleau memorandum, 3/25/19, PWW 56:265.

123. Kerr to Undersecretary for Foreign Affairs, 7/11/19, FO 371/4002A; *British Documents on Foreign Affairs,* 1st Series, 3:425–426.

124. Bullitt, "Breakfast with Lloyd George," *Bullitt Mission*, 66–67.

125. *Ibid.*

126. House diary, 3/28/19, EMH.

127. Auchincloss diary, 3/28/19, GA, B3, f32, p. 477.

128. Smuts to Lloyd George, 3/31/19, LG, F/45/9/31. See also Harold Nicholson, *Peacemaking, 1919* (London, 1933), 292–308.

129. Lenin at one point even urged Béla Kun "to make the fullest possible use of every opportunity to obtain a temporary armistice or peace, in order to give the people a breathing space" (British intercept, 6/19/19, Thwaites to Lloyd George, LG F/46/10/5).

130. Buckler to House, 3/25/19, WHB, B1, f7.

131. Buckler to House, 3/27/19, WHB, B1, f7. See also Buckler to GGB, 3/29/19, WHB, B2, f20.

132. Buckler to GGB, 3/31/19, WHB, B2, f20.

133. Diary of Ray Stannard Baker, 3/27/19, 3/29/19, PWW 56:338, 425.

134. C. Sharp, "Comments," *New Statesman,* 3/22/19, enclosed in Buckler to House, 3/25/19, WHB, B1, f7.

135. *Bullitt Mission*, 66–67.

136. Tumulty to Wilson, 4/2/19, PWW 56:551.

137. Editors, PWW on press coverage, PWW 56:551–552.

138. *Ibid.*

139. Current Intelligence Div., Am. Sec., weekly rev., 3/30/19, HW, B41.

140. Tumulty to Wilson, 3/30/19, PWW 56:435–436.

141. Current Intelligence Div., Am. Sec., weekly rev., 4/7/19, HW, B41.

142. *Ibid.,* 4/13/19, HW, B41.

143. Noble, *Policies and Opinions,* 288–289.

144. Cachin to Peace Commission, 3/28/19, PWW 56:386–387.

145. Bullitt to House, 4/2/19, EMH, B21, f683.

146. Auchincloss diary, 4/4/19, GA, B3, f32; Bullitt to Auchincloss, 4/4/19, Miller, *Diary,* VII:435–436; Bullitt to House, 4/6/19, EMH, B21, f683.

147. House diary, 4/5/19, EMH; published in PWW 57:34–35.

148. Polk to Auchincloss, 4/5/19, FP, B1, f21.

149. Lansbury, *The Herald,* 3/31/19, quoted in Davis to Wilson, 3/31/19, PWW 56:473.

150. War Cabinet Minutes, WC552(3) 31, 3/31/19; BL69.

151. *Ibid.*

152. Copies of the blue book were sent immediately to the U.S. delegation. See Wright to White, 4/6/19, HW, B52.

153. See Ullmann, *Anglo-Soviet Relations,* II, 144–152, for detailed discussion.

154. Curzon to Lloyd George, 4/9/19, LG F/12/1/14; Curzon to Lloyd George 4/10/19, LG F/12/1/14.

155. Quoted in Lasch, *American Liberals,* 201. See also Bullitt to Wilson, 4/18/19, PWW 57:459–460.

156. See Ullman, *Anglo-Soviet Relations,* II, 156–157; and Thompson, *Russia, Bolshevism, and Versailles,* 245–246.

## *Chapter 10*

1. See Baker, *Wilson,* II, 407–408.

2. House diary, 3/25/19, EMH.

3. House diary, 6/17/18, EMH.

4. For more details of the discussions among Hoover, House, Auchincloss, and Wilson regarding the "Russian Relief Commission," see HH, B313; Auchincloss diary, 6/13/18, GA, B2, f21; House to Wilson, 6/13/18, EMH, B121, f4285; Auchincloss to Wilson, 6/13/18, GA, B8, f207; Lansing desk diary, 6/13/18, RLP; House to Wilson, June 21, 1918, EMH, B121, f4285; HHWT, B21.

5. Undated, unsigned memo, "before Armistice," GA, B9, f225.

6. Huntington memo in Redfield to Wilson, 11/22/18, PWW 53:169–180.

7. Auchincloss to McCormick, 11/28/18, GA, B6, f131.

8. Auchincloss diary, December 15, 1918, GA, B2, f28.

9. Cyrus McCormick to Wilson, 11/29/18, SH, B6, f7.

10. Balfour to Lloyd George, 1/19/19, LG, F/3/4/7.

11. VMD, 1/30/19.

12. Auchincloss diary, 3/7/19, GA, B3, f31. For earlier Auchincloss-Wiseman collaboration, see Auchincloss diary, 2/16/19, GA, B2, f30.

13. Grew to Hoover, 3/25/19, HH, B316.

14. Minutes of American Commissioners, 3/20/19, TB, B265.

15. Minutes of American Commissioners, 3/20/19, TB, B265; Grew to Hoover, 3/25/19, HH, B316; Ammission to Polk, 3/24/19, FRUS, 1919, Russia, 100.

16. VMD, 3/18/19, and 3/21/19.

17. House diary, 3/27/19, EMH.

18. Auchincloss diary, 3/27/19, GA, B3, f32.

19. Hoover's appointment calendar records 22 meetings with McCormick between 2/1 and 4/1/19 (HH, B1).

20. Herbert Hoover, *Ordeal of Woodrow Wilson,* 117.

21. Hoover to Wilson, 3/28/19, HH, B8.

22. *Ibid.* This letter is also found in EMH, B61, f1927; and in Francis William O'Brien, ed., *Two Peacemakers in Paris: The Hoover-Wilson Post-Armistice Letters, 1918–1920* (College Station, Tex., 1978), 86–90.

23. Wilson speech, Mantoux notes, Council of Four, 3/28/19, PWW 56:328–329.

24. House diary, 3/29/19, EMH; Auchincloss diary, 3/28–29/19, GA, B3, f32; McCormick remarked in his diary concerning Nansen: "I believe he is the man to start a satisfactory neutral relief to aid Russia without recognizing Bolshevist Government" (VMD, 3/29/19).

25. Auchincloss diary, 3/31–4/1/19, GA, B3, f32.

26. White to Wilson and Wilson to White, 4/2/19, PWW 56:544–545.

27. Nansen to Wilson, 4/3/19, C&P, 329–330; FRUS, 1919, Russia, 102.

28. Auchincloss diary, 4/3/19, GA, B3, f32; Buckler to GGB, 4/3/19, WHB, B2, f20.

29. Miller and Auchincloss draft of note from Big Four to Nansen, April 4, 1919, Miller *Diary,* VII:430–432.

30. This is the draft in FRUS, 1919, Russia, 103–104; and Miller *Diary,* VII:433–434. It does not differ substantially from the first draft, but reads more clearly.

31. Auchincloss diary, 4/4/19, GA, B3, f32.

32. Bullitt to Auchincloss, 4/4/19, Miller, *Diary,* VII:435–436.

33. Draft reply from Big Four to Nansen (Bullitt), 4/4/19, Miller, *Diary,* VII:437–439. Also printed in FRUS, 1919, Russia, 104–106.

34. *Ibid.*

35. Buckler to GGB, 4/4/19, WHB, B2, f20.

36. VMD, 4/6/19.

37. Redraft by Bullitt of Miller-Auchincloss proposed reply by Big Four to Nansen, 4/6/19, Miller, *Diary,* VII:440–441.

38. Bullitt understood the political importance of these changes, and complained later that these had "made it even worse and even more indefinite, so that the Soviet Government could not possibly conceive it as a genuine peace proposition" (*Bullitt Mission,* 89).

39. Auchincloss diary, 4/6/19, GA, B3, f32; House diary, 4/6/19, EMH. The second Bullitt draft and the Wilson-approved version can be compared in PWW 57:93–94.

40. *Bullitt Mission,* 90.

41. Mantoux minutes, Council of Four, 4/9/19, PWW 57:165; Hoover to Wilson, 4/9/19, PWW 57:161; Hoover to Wilson, 4/9/19, HH, B9; Buckler to GGB, 4/7, 4/8/19, WHB, B2, f20.

42. *Bullitt Mission,* 90–93; minutes of Commissioners, 4/10/19, TB, B265.

43. Current Intelligence Div., Am. Sec. weekly review, 4/13/19, HW, B41.

44. House diary, 4/14/19, EMH.

45. House diary, 4/14/19, EMH; VMD, 4/14/19; Auchincloss diary, 4/16/19, GA, B3, f33; House diary, 4/16–17/19, EMH.

46. For the U.S. delegation debate, see Minutes of Commissioners, 4/19/19, TB, B265.

47. Fridtjof Nansen, *Russia and Peace* (London, 1923), 26–28; Nansen to Wilson, Nansen to Lenin with enclosures, 4/17/19, PWW 57:437–440.

48. W. G. Sharp to Wilson, 4/18/19, Wilson to W. G. Sharp, 4/21/19, PWW 56:512–513. See also Wilson's gracious response to Nansen, 4/18/19, PWW 57:456.

49. Draft Hoover memo to House, 4/18/19, EMH, B61, f1927.

50. Diary of Ray Stannard Baker, 4/19/19, PWW 57:508.

51. House diary, 4/19/19, EMH.

52. Hoover statement, 4/21/19, HH, B9; House to Hoover, 4/20/19, EMH, B61, f19/727; Wilson to Hoover, 4/23/19, HH, B9.

53. Churchill to Lloyd George, 4/20/19, LG, F/8/3/41.

54. Baker diary, 4/19/19, PWW 57:508–509; VMD, 4/21/19; Auchincloss diary, 4/23/19, GA, B3, f33.

55. VMD, 4/24/19.

56. Noble, *Policies and Opinions,* 290–291.

57. Hoover *Memoirs,* 418; Nansen, *Russia and Peace,* 28; Chicherin, "Foreign Policy of Soviet Russia," 7.

58. VMD, 5/2/19, 5/7/19; Buckler to GGB, 5/7/19, WHB, B2, f21.

59. Council of Four, 5/9/19, FRUS, 1919, PPC, V:528–529.

60. See Council of Four, 5/19/19, FRUS, 1919, PPC, V:725; Council of Four to Kolchak, 5/26/19, FRUS, 1919, PPC, VI:73–75; Kolchak to Supreme Council, 6/4/19, FRUS, 1919, PPC VI:321–323; Supreme Council to Kolchak, 6/12/19, FRUS, 1919, PPC, VI:356.

61. Lenin to Chicherin and Litvinov, May 6, 1919, Lenin, *Collected Works* (4th ed.) 44:225–226; *Sochineniia* (5th ed.) 50:304–306.

62. *Ibid.*

63. Chicherin to Nansen, 5/10/19, EMH, B 208j, F2/807.

64. Nansen note on Chicherin to Nansen to SD, 5/14/19, FRUS, 1919, Russia, 111–115.

65. Hoover to Nansen, in Cecil to Hankey, 5/16/19, FRUS, 1919, Russia, 115.

66. Cecil and Hoover to Council of Four, 5/16/19, FRUS, 1919, Russia, 116–117.

67. VMD, 5/14/19.

68. Auchincloss diary, 5/15/19, GA, B3, f34.

69. Minutes, Council of Four, 5/20/19, FRUS, PPC, 1919, V:734–735.

70. Bullitt to Wilson, PWW 59:232–233.

71. *Ibid.*

72. Bullitt to House, 5/17/19, EMH, B21, f683. House did respond positively, asking Bullitt to meet with him in June, when they talked the whole thing through. Later House also remained supportive, noting in his diary following Bullitt's testimony to the Senate in September, "candor compels me to record that in my opinion Bullitt told the truth" (House diary, 9/15/19, EMH).

73. Bullitt's resignation itself was immediately accepted, without comment, by Lansing. Lansing to Wilson, 5/20/19, PWW 59:314.

74. Berle to Sinclair, 12/27/39, as quoted in Brownell and Billings. *Bullitt,* 94.

75. Morison to Grew, 5/13/19, TB, B247; HW, B42; Buckler to GGB, 9/23/19, WHB, B2, f23.

76. Polk to Auchincloss, 5/24/19, recorded in Auchincloss diary, 5/26/19, GA, B3, f34.

77. See White to Henry Cabot Lodge, 9/17/19, in Nevins, *Henry White,* 463; Bliss and White to Grew, 11/19/19, TB, B247.

78. *Bullitt Mission* is simply a republication, verbatim, of Bullitt's testimony before the Senate Foreign Relations Committee.

79. *New Republic* XX, No. 255(9/24/19): 213. One of the most detailed accounts was published in the *New York Daily News,* 9/19/19.

80. Phillips to Polk, 9/16/19, FP, B40, f54.

81. Phillips to Lansing, 9/14/19, RLLC; Auchincloss to House, 9/13/19, EMH, B7, f210.

82. House diary, 9/15/19, EMH; House to Auchincloss (cable), 9/15/19, EMH, B7, f210; House to Auchincloss (letter), 9/15/19, EMH, B7, f210; Auchincloss to House (letter), 9/15/19, EMH, B7, f210.

83. Lansing to Phillips, 9/16/19, RLP, B5; Lansing to Davis, 9/21/19, RLP, B5; Lansing to Polk, 10/1/19, FP, B9, f315.

84. Lodge to White, 10/2/19, Lodge Papers, quoted in Farnsworth, *Bullitt,* 65.

85. Buckler to GGB, 9/18,20/19, WHB, B2, f23.

86. Bullitt to Lady Nancy Astor, 1/17/20, WCB.

87. *Ibid.*

88. Chicherin, *Ekonomicheskaya Zhizn,* 5/22/19, Eng. trans. in SH, B67.

89. Review of information from Russia and foreign press and wireless from Shatzap, 6/1/19, SH, B6.

90. See SH, B51, for this story.

91. Unsigned memorandum on Levine, 6/19/19, FP, B33, f684.

92. Lenin, *Collected Works* (4th ed.) 29:517. In a State Dept. analysis of this and other Soviet statements and details on the Bullitt Mission in 9/19, the author (Harper?) acknowledged that there was no publication of the Bullitt terms in the Soviet press before the *Pravda* issuance on May 23 ("Memorandum for Secretary of State, 'Alleged Bullitt Mission' September 1919," SH, B51).

93. See, for example, his statements to Louise Bryant, 10/13/20, FM, B2.

94. Baker, *Woodrow Wilson and World Settlement* II:1–4.

95. The best explication of the French position throughout this period is Kalervo Hovi, *Emergence,* passim.

96. Hovi, *Emergence,* 167.

97. See Mayer, *Politics and Diplomacy of Peacemaking,* 604–673.

98. The best discussion of the British pressure on Lloyd George is found in Ullmann, *Anglo-Soviet Relations,* II, 144–157.

99. Mayer, *Politics and Diplomacy of Peacemaking,* 9.

100. Thompson, *Russia, Bolshevism, and Versailles,* 118.

101. See for example Michael Florinsky, *World Revolution and the USSR* (New York, 1933), 48; Broncho Lazitch and Milorad Drachkovitch, *Lenin and the Comintern* (Stanford, 1972), 90.

102. F. L. Carsten, *Revolution in Central Europe* (Berkeley and Los Angeles, 1972), 17.

103. James W. Hulse, *The Forming of the Communist International* (Stanford, 1964), 77; Franz Borkenau, *World Communism: A History of the Communist International* (Ann Arbor, 1962), 416.

104. Merle Fainsod, *International Socialism and the World War* (Cambridge, 1935), 203.

105. Mayer, *Politics and Diplomacy of Peacemaking,* 240; Debo, "Chicherin," 383. See also Alexander Dallin, "The Use of International Movements," in Ivo J. Lederer, ed., *Russian Foreign Policy: Essays in Historical Perspective* (New Haven, 1962), 321.

106. Borkenau, *World Communism,* 414; Hulse, *Communist International,* 201; Barrington Moore, Jr., *Soviet Politics: The Dilemma of Power* (New York, 1965), 201;

Uldricks, "Russia and Europe," 59; Albert S. Lindemann, *The Red Years: European Socialism Versus Bolshevism, 1919–1921* (Berkeley, 1974), 290.

107. For details on Germany, see E. H. Carr, *German-Soviet Relations Between the Two World Wars* (Baltimore, 1951), 65–95; Warren Lerner, *Karl Radek: The Last Internationalist* (Stanford, 1970), 78–90; Debo, "Chicherin," 387–398; Lindemann, *Red Years*, 35–44. On the short-lived Bavarian revolution, see Carsten, *Revolution,* 222–223; Werner T. Angress, *Stillborn Revolution: The Communist Bid for Power in Germany, 1921–1923* (New York, 1963), 36; and especially Allan Mitchell, *Revolution in Bavaria, 1918–1919: The Eisner Regime and the Soviet Republic* (Princeton, 1965), 128–142, 310–327.

108. On the revolution in Hungary, see Rudolf L. Tokes, *Béla Kun and the Hungarian Soviet Republic* (New York, 1967); Ferenc Tibor Zsuppan, "The Early Activities of the Hungarian Communist Party, 1918–1919," *Slavonic and East European Review,* XLIII, No. 101 (1965): 314–334; and David T. Cattell, "The Hungarian Revolution of 1919 and the Reorganization of the Comintern in 1920," *Journal of Central European Affairs* XI (January–April, 1951): 27–38.

109. The original source of this oft-quoted saying was probably Colonel House, who wrote in his diary that he could not "get action from the President on more than one thing at a time. He seems utterly incapable of taking up more than one serious matter at once" (House diary, 5/19/17, EMH).

110. Fischer, *Soviets in World Affairs,* I, 169. Similar statements have been made by Thompson, *Russia, Bolshevism, and Versailles,* 167; and Kennan, *Russia and the West,* 132.

## Chapter 11

1. Martens to Chicherin, 8/7/19, TsGANKh f413, op. 3, del. 515, l. 17.

2. V. I. Lenin, answers to questions put by a *Chicago Daily News* correspondent, October 5, 1919, *Collected Works* (4th ed.) 30:51.

3. Litvinov to Chicherin, 8/26/20, British intercept, LG, F/9/2/42.

4. Nuorteva and Martens to Lansing, 3/25/19, EMH, B207.

5. See first Soviet appeal to Harding, 3/20/21, Degras, *Soviet Documents,* 244–245.

6. Lenin was sometimes opposed in this strategy by Bukharin and others. See Chubarian, "U istokov leninskoi vneshnei politiki," 39–55.

7. See "Chicherin to Workers of the Entente Countries," in Lord to Bullitt, weekly intelligence summary, 4/27/19, HW, B42.

8. Chicherin to Sec. of State, in Minister in Sweden (Morris) to Acting Sec. of State, 2/25/20, FRUS, 1920, III:447.

9. Litvinov to Chicherin, 8/26/20, British intercept., LG, F/9/2/42. On the use of foreign trade representatives, prisoner of war negotiators, and "humanitarian" representatives for political negotiations during 1919 and 1920, see Uldricks, "Diplomatic Corps," 100–108. See also Engman, "Finnish-Soviet Relations," in Hiden and Loit, *Contact or Isolation?*

10. Martens was appointed, in addition to his primary credentials, representative of Tsentrosoyuz and the Foreign Trade Commissariat, but the Bolsheviks also tried other approaches through these organizations independently of Martens.

11. Decree nationalizing foreign trade, 4/22/18, Degras, *Soviet Documents,* I, 71–72. The fascinating story of the Russian cooperative movement abroad can be found in TsGANKh, f. 484, op. 7. The background of Tsentrosoyuz in Russia during World

War I is detailed in Alexis Antiserov and Eugene M. Kayden, *The Cooperative Movement in Russia During the War* (Yale, 1929), especially 194–231.

12. TsGANKh, f. 3984, op. 1, d. 10.
13. TsGANKh, f. 3984, op. 1, d. 10, l. 42.
14. TsGANKh, f. 413, op. 3, d. 98.
15. *Ibid.*
16. TsGANKh, f. 484, op. 7.
17. For a very clear statement of government policy in this matter, see *Soviet Russia,* March 27, 1920. Moscow Narodnyi Bank, the bank the cooperatives kept their money in, was not nationalized until March 11, 1920, by decree of Sovnarkom. See Antsiferov and Kayden, *Cooperative Movement,* 351–352.
18. Supreme Council telegram, 4/26/20, LG.
19. Berkenheim successfully negotiated contracts for Tsentrosoyuz with the U.S. War Department for surplus goods and offered to assist Hoover and Nansen with their plan for feeding Russia. See Polk to Ammission, 4/19/19, PWW 57:512. Martens first attempted to win Berkenheim over, and then ignored him. See Nuorteva to Martens, 8/7/19, TsGANKh, f. 413, del. 515, l. 22.
20. The attempt to get Krasin to the United States to head the trade office was never entirely abandoned. Martens came up with one scheme to smuggle him aboard an American steamship in Petrograd. See Martens to Krasin, 9/23/19, TsGANKh, f. 413, op. 13, del. 515, l. 9.
21. See Krasin to Lubov Krasin, 9/7/18, in Lubov Krasin, *Krassin,* 95–96. See also *Vneshniaia torgovlia, SSSR 1918–1940 gg.* (Moscow, 1960), 45.
22. Laserson reflections on meeting with Krasin, 12/18, ML, B2.
23. Max Rabinoff, "Web of My Life," 229–230, on meetings with Krasin, 4/18/20 in Copenhagen, MR.
24. See Leeper comments on report of Seventh Congress of Soviets, 3/10/20, PRO, FO 371/4387.
25. Lenin to Krasin, 3/16/20, *Collected Works* (4th ed.) 44:358.
26. See PRO, FO 371/4032, for comments on the Seventh Congress of Soviets and the dissent by Bukharin and others.
27. Draper, *Roots of American Communism,* 107.
28. *New York Call,* February 2, 1918.
29. Fraina to Bolshevik leadership, 2/3/18, Lusk, L0038.
30. Details on Nuorteva can be found in Auvo Koistianen, "Santeri Nuorteva and the Origins of Soviet-American Relations," *American Studies in Scandinavia* (1972) 15: 1–14. Koistianen has also written a longer biographical study of Nuorteva in Finnish, *Santeri Nuorteva—kansainvalinen suomalainen* (Helskinki, 1985). Records of Nuorteva's work as representative of the Finnish Red Government are found in Lusk, L0033, Finnish Information Bureau. Koistianen has also studied "Red Finns" in America in *The Forging of Finnish-American Communism, 1917–1924* (Turku, Finland), 1978.
31. Nuorteva testimony, 12/12/19, Lusk L0037. As Nuorteva told the Lusk Committee, "From the very outset I gave information not only about Finland but about Russia as well" (p. 1,538). See also Nuorteva to the Bolshevik government of Finland, 4/18, Lusk L0033, B11, F11.
32. Morison to Nuorteva, 3/27/18; Nuorteva to Morison, 4/3/18; Morison to Nuorteva 4/7/18; Nuorteva to Morison, 4/12/18; Morison to Nuorteva, 4/23/18; Nuorteva to Morison, 4/29/18; Morison to Nuorteva, 11/22/18; Nuorteva to Morison, 1/22/19; all Lusk L0033, B11.

33. The Finnish Information Bureau files, Lusk, are full of Nuorteva's correspondence with Bullitt, House, Johnson, Borah, Felix Frankfurter, Louis Brandeis, Newton Baker, and others.

34. Kellock to Steffens, 4/22/18, HK.

35. Nuorteva to Harper, 5/9/18, SH, B5.

36. *Ibid.*

37. Nuorteva to Borah, 5/8/18, WEB, B62; Borah to Nuorteva, 5/10/18, WEB, B62; Nuorteva to Frankfurter, 5/4/18; and Frankfurter to Nuorteva, 5/8/18, both in Lusk L0033, B11.

38. Harper to Porter, 5/11/18, SH, B5. Harper responded to Nuorteva in a friendly, noncommittal fashion (Harper to Nuorteva, 5/12/18, SH, B5).

39. For copies of this correspondence, see Lusk L0033, B11 and HJ III:12.

40. Lusk L0033, "Russian Soviet Recognition League," B11; Nuorteva, *Avtobiographia,* quoted in Koistianen, "Nuorteva and Origins," 6; Kellock to Robins, 6/27/18, RR, reel 4.

41. Form dated 6/11/18, Lusk, L0033, B11.

42. Lomonosov speech, Madison Square Garden, 6/11/18, "Lomonosov file," Lusk, L0033; Berg to Lomonosov inviting him to speak, 6/6/18, Lusk, L0033 B11. See also *New York Times,* 6/11, 6/13, 6/16, 1918.

43. Lomonosov file, Lusk, L0033. For confirmation of Lomonosov's friendliness to Martens, see Porter to Harper, 3/27/19, SH, B6.

44. Nicholas Goldenweiser to Martens, 3/31/19, Lusk L0038.

45. On Lomonosov's situation, see Kellock to Nuorteva, 8/1/18, Lusk L0033, B11

46. Kellock to Harper, 6/28/18, SH, B5; Kellock to Steffens, 7/2/18, Lusk L0033.

47. Kellock to Steffens, 7/2/18, Lusk, L0033. For Nuorteva speeches, see *New York Call,* 7/29, 8/1, 8/4, 1918.

48. Lusk, L0033, B11.

49. Nuorteva to Wilson, 9/13/18, NAM reel 3, #121. For a longer statement of his position, see Nuorteva's "Open Letter to American Liberals," *Class Struggle* (Sept.–Oct. 1918), Lusk L0036.

50. Nuorteva to Brandeis, 11/19/18, HJ III:12; Morison to Nuorteva, 11/22/18, Lusk, L0033, B11; Pinchot to Nuorteva, 11/22/18, Lusk, L0033, B11.

51. Western historiography on the Martens mission is particularly thin. There are no full-length studies or biographies, and most coverage of the mission is in the context of the Red Scare (see Chap. 12). Even specialized studies of U.S.-Soviet relations refer only briefly to Martens and do not explore his mission in any detail. Soviet studies of Martens are more numerous, but they are episodic, and based largely on his reminiscences and unattributed material from U.S. investigative hearings of the Red Scare. See G. Evgenev and B. Shapik, *Revoliyutsioner, Diplomat, Uchonii* (Moscow, 1960); G. E. Reikhberg and B. S. Shapik, *Delo Martensa* (Moscow, 1966); and G. E. Reikhberg and B. S. Shapik, "Amerikanskie senatorii sudiyat sovetskogo predstavitelya," *Istoriia SSSR* (1963), 2:81–89.

52. Martens testimony, *Russian Propaganda: Hearing before a Subcommittee of the Committee on Foreign Relations, United States Senate, Sixty-Sixth Congress, Second Session* (Washington, 1920), 54. Martens credentials: Chicherin to Martens, 1/2/19, Lusk, L0032. Printed in C&P, 320.

53. Details of Martens' early life drawn from Decision by the Secretary of Labor in the case of LCAK Martens, 12/15/20, SH, B51; Martens testimony, Lusk Committee, 11/15, 26/19, Lusk L0026, and Senate Foreign Relations Committee (Moses Subcommittee), *Russian Propaganda,* 54.

54. Polk to Lansing, 1/29/19, FP, B40, f47.
55. C&P, 320–329. Also printed in FRUS, 1919, Russia, 133, 134–141.
56. EMH, B297, f2/802.
57. Lansing to Wilson, 4/2/19, PWW 56:548–551.
58. See Chapter 12.
59. Martens to Bakhmetev, 4/10/19, misc. MSS, Hoover Institution. See also Martens' testimony, *Russian Propaganda,* 37.
60. List of employees and salaries, Russian Soviet Bureau, Lusk, L0032. See also Martens testimony, *Russian Propaganda,* 41–43; Martens testimony, *Hearings of the Joint Legislative Committee Investigating Seditious Activities,* [Lusk Committee] (Albany, 1919), 1,138; Lusk, L0033; testimony of Bobroff, *Conditions in Russia,* Hearings before Committee on Foreign Affairs, House of Representatives, 66th Congress, Third Session, January 27–March 1, 1921, (Washington, 1921), 40.
61. Reed to Bryant, 3/21/19, JR. For evidence of offers of assistance, see employment application file, Lusk, L0032.
62. Intelligence report to Wiseman, Bolshevist study committee, Union League of New York, 4/11/19, WBW, B9, f211.
63. Lomonosov attended a Foreign Trade Conference in Chicago and wrote a report to Martens on the orders he generated. Lomonosov to Martens, 10/10/19, Lusk L0032.
64. The captured records of the Soviet Russian Information Bureau, Lusk, include detailed records of contacts and discussions with American businessmen, internal memoranda and reports from section heads, and evidence of the unhappiness of many American socialists with Martens. Correspondence and memoranda preserved in TsGANKh include letters from Martens to Krasin detailing Martens' work on trade questions and contacts with American firms and responding to Krasin's concerns about his work, and several letters to and from Martens and Chicherin dealing with the relationship between economic contacts and political goals. The most powerful evidence of Martens' insistence on economic contacts as opposed to political work, and the best testimony to his refusal to become involved in the differences between American Bolsheviks was the virulence with which some members of that movement condemned his strategy and attempted, without success, to get him under their control. The left wing of the New York Socialist Party even started a campaign to have him recalled. See Hourwich, "The Problems of the Soviet Representative," *Revolutionary Age,* Vol. I, No. 27 (April 19, 1919). Martens, in response to this campaign, simply commented, "I have nothing to do with any political party in the United States and cannot be expected to take sides." (*New York Tribune,* June 3, 1919.)
65. See *Weekly Bulletin,* Soviet Information Bureau, 3/24/19, and press release, 3/19/19, Lusk L0033.
66. Lusk, L0033. Harper noted, with some chagrin, his own evaluation of their solvency. "Without question they can raise enough money to make up the amount they promised to spend here in the United States," (Harper to Porter, 4/14/19, SH, B6). The importance of gold in Bolshevik efforts at trade with the West is detailed in Christine A. White, " 'Riches Have Wings': The Use of Russian Gold in Soviet Foreign Trade, 1918–1922," in Hiden and Loit, *Contact or Isolation?,* 117–136.
67. See form letter, pamphlet, sample contracts, and calling cards, Commercial Department, Lusk, L0032. Regarding the initial response of U.S. businessmen, see Bobroff testimony, *Conditions in Russia,* 40; and "Bolshevik Office Here Crowded with U.S. Businessmen," *New York Tribune,* 5/8/19.

68. New York businessmen (unidentified) to Huntington, 3/25/19, excerpted in Huntington to Harper, 4/11/19, SH, B6.

69. Huntington to Harper, 4/11/19, SH, B6.

70. Porter to Huntington, 3/22/19, SH, B6.

71. "Russian Warning to American Business Men," 4/22/19, SH, B6.

72. Polk to Mark Prentiss, Council on Foreign Relations, 4/22/19, SH, B51.

73. Huntington to Harper, 5/7/19, SH, B6; Huntington to Russian-American Chamber of Commerce, 5/14/19, TsGANKh, f. 413, op. 3, del. 515.

74. Huntington to Harper, 5/7/19, SH, B6.

75. Nuorteva to Martens, 4/29/19, Lusk, L0032.

76. Harper to Huntington, 5/2/19, SH, B6.

77. Polk to Ammission, 6/5/19, FRUS, 1919, Russia, 144–145.

78. Heller statement, 2/16/20, *Soviet Russia,* 2/21/20.

79. See, for example, Heller testimony, 6/12/19, Lusk, L0026.

80. Lists, Commercial Department, Lusk, L0032.

81. Commercial Department, correspondence, Lusk, L0032.

82. *Ibid.*

83. Stevenson testimony, 6/26/19, Lusk, L0026

84. Krasin to Martens, 10/29/19, confirming contracts, TsGANKh, f. 413, op. 3, del. 515. Robinson bristle machinery contract in TsGANKh f. 413, op. 2, del. 310. See also *Russian Propaganda,* 71.

85. National Storage Company contract, TsGANKh, f. 413, op. 13, del. 515, ll.10–15. Tentative contracts, Heller to Martens, 8/7/19, TsGANKh, f. 413, del. 515, l. 18; *Russian Propaganda,* 72–73.

86. TsGANKh, f. 413, op. 2, del. 310.

87. Heller to Martens, 8/7/19, TsGANKh, f. 413, del. 515, l. 18.

88. Heller Testimony, 6/12/19, Lusk, L0026. See also note, Huntington to Harper, undated, SH, B6.

89. Martens to Ford, 4/9/19, Lusk, L0026. For more on Ford and Russia, see Christine White, "Ford in Russia: In Pursuit of the Chimeral Market," *Business History* XXVIII, No. 4 (October, 1986): 7–104.

90. Heller on meeting with Kanseler, 4/12/19, Commercial Dept Corres, Lusk, L0032.

91. *Ibid.*

92. Martens to Ford, 4/21/19, Lusk, L0026

93. Campbell for Liebold, to Nuorteva, 4/25/19, Lusk, L0026. Nuorteva to Martens, 4/29/19, Commercial Dept. Memos and Notes, Lusk, L0032.

94. Martens to Chicherin, 8/13/19, TsGANKh, f. 413, op. 3, del. 515, l. 16

95. Nuorteva speech, 6/4/19, *Soviet Russia,* 6/14/19.

96. TsGANKh, f. 413, del. 515, l. 37–38.

97. Martens form letter, 5/10/19, TsGANKh, f. 413, op. 3, del. 515, l. 36.

98. TsGANKh, f. 413, del. 515, l. 39.

99. See letters to Clark in testimony, 6/26/19, Lusk, L0026, 236–266.

100. Martens to Krasin and Chicherin, 8/6/19, TsGANKh, f. 413, del. 515, l. 30.

101. See Lusk files, L0038, B2; *Pravda* article, 6/9/20; NAM, reel 5.

102. Heller to Martens, 8/7/19, TsGANKh, f. 413, del. 515, l. 18.

103. Report of meeting at Civic Club, 5/6/19, in Finch to Stevenson, 7/25/19, Lusk, L0038.

104. *Ibid.*

105. Martens testimony, 12/11/19, Lusk, L0026, 1,437–1,440.

106. *Russian Propaganda*, 450–452.

107. APEX to Heller, 6/11/19, Commercial Dept. Corres., Lusk, L0032

108. Heller to Mulvihill, 5/19/19, NAM, reel 4, #154.

109. Bullard testimony, *Conditions in Russia*, 100.

110. "Material on the development of Russian consuls in America," 6/19, Lusk, L0039.

111. Heller to Martens, 8/7/19, TsGANKh, f. 413, del. 515, l. 18.

112. Nuorteva to Martens, 8/7/19, TsGANKh, f. 413, del. 515, ll. 26–28. Internal Bolshevik discussions concerning a German or an American orientation were a constant preoccupation from 1918 to 1920. On the German overtures, see Carr, *Bolshevik Revolution,* III:331–33.

113. Heller to Martens, 8/7/19, TsGANKh, f. 413, del. 515, ll. 18–20.

114. Heller notes of interview with Berkenheim, 5/9/19, Commercial Dept. memoranda and notes, Lusk, L0032.

115. Nuorteva to Martens, 8/7/19, TsGANKh, f. 413, del. 515, ll. 22–24.

116. Martens testimony, 11/25/19, Lusk, L0026, 1,160–1,161. Despite considerable effort, further details of the courier system were not uncovered by Lusk or military agents. See Lusk investigation files, L0038, B4.

117. Draper, *Roots of American Communism,* 227.

118. Finnish Information Bureau files, Lusk, L0033. For more on couriers, see White, "Riches Have Wings," *passim;* and Roy Talbert, *Negative Intelligence.*

119. Martens to Chicherin, 7/24/19, TsGANKh, f. 413, op. 3, del. 515, l. 31.

120. See Martens to Chicherin, 8/7/19, responding to Litvinov letter of May, TsGANKh, f. 413, del. 515.

121. TsGANKh, f. 413, op. 2, del. 396.

122. Chicherin to Kamenev, 8/31/20, LG, F/9/2/42.

123. Krasin to Martens, 8/26/20, TsGANKh, f. 413, op. 2, del. 396.

124. Bloomfield to Poole *re* interview with Litvinov, 10/31/22, NAM, reel 2.

125. Martens to Chicherin, 8/7/19, TsGANKh, f. 413, op. 3., del. 515.

126. Chicherin to Kamenev, 8/31/20, intercept 003933, LG, F203/1/10.

127. Krasin to Chicherin, wireless intercept, 5/29/20, LG F/58/1/13.

128. Agreement with the American Corporation with Lenin's changes, 6/19/20, Lenin, *Collected Works* (4th ed.) 44:389.

129. See "Lenin's Answers to Questions Put by a *Chicago Daily News* Correspondent," 10/5/19, Lenin, *Collected Works* (4th ed.) 30:51; Lenin's letter to American workers, 9/23/19, *Collected Works* (4th ed.) 30:39; Lenin's talk with Lincoln Eyre, *The World,* 2/21/20, *Collected Works* (4th ed.) 30:451.

130. Lenin to Gorbunov, 2/21/21, Lenin, *Collected Works* (4th ed.) 44:540.

131. Lenin to Martens, 6/21/21, *Collected Works* (4th ed.) 44:542.

132. Lenin to Martens, 6/27/21, *Collected Works* (4th ed.) 44:543.

133. Lenin to the Society for Technical Aid for Soviet Russia, 10/20/22, *Collected Works* (4th ed.) 33:381.

134. Steinmetz to Lenin, 2/16/22; Lenin to Steinmetz, 4/10/22, *Collected Works* (4th ed.) 44:582–583.

135. Ludwig C. A. K. Martens, "Vospominania o V. I. Lenine," *Istoricheskii Arkhiv* 5 (Sentiabr–Oktiabr, 1958): 146–150.

136. Martens to Chicherin, 8/13/19, TsGANKh, f. 413, op. 3, del. 515, l. 16.

137. Harper to Porter, 5/8/19, SH, B6

138. Cole to Colby, 4/29/20, BC, B2.

139. Nuorteva speech, New York, 6/16/19, Lusk, L0032.

140. See first issue of *Soviet Russia,* 6/7/19; Nuorteva to Martens, report on *Soviet Russia,* 8/7/19, TsGANKh, f. 413, op. 3, del. 515, l. 29; U.S. Consul at Vyborg to Sec. of State, 3/16/21, SH, B38. See also *Revolutionary Radicalism* I:634, on the predecessors to *Soviet Russia.*

141. Nuorteva to Martens, 5/19/19, Lusk, L0032.

142. *Ibid.*

143. Nuorteva to Martens, 8/7/19, TsGANKh, f. 413, op 3, del 515, l.28.

144. Nuorteva, citing Litvinov to Martens, 5/24/19, in Nuorteva to Martens, 8/7/19, TsGANKh, f. 413, op. 3, del. 515, l. 22.

145. Nuorteva to Martens, 8/7/19, TsGANKh, f. 413, op. 3, del. 515, l. 22.

146. *Ibid.*

147. *Ibid.*

148. *Ibid.,* ll. 27–30.

149. *Ibid.,* l. 28.

150. Martens to Krasin, 9/23/19, TsGANKh, f. 413, op. 3, del. 515, l. 9; Nuorteva to Louise Bryant, 10/18/19, JR, 3.

151. Foster to Martens, 5/27/20, TsGANKh, f. 413, op. 2, del. 396.

152. Martens to Krasin, 6/21/20, TsGANKh, f. 413, op. 2, del. 396, l. 7; Nuorteva, *Avtobiografija,* in Koistianen, "Nuorteva and Origins," 10.

153. Cooper to Martens, 6/30/20, TsGANKh, f. 413, op. 2, del. 396.

154. Koistianen, "Turbulent Times: The Last Years of Santeri Nuorteva in America, 1918–1920," *Finnish Americana* III (1980): 43–50.

155. *Ibid.*

156. Martens to Krasin, 6/30/20, TsGANKh, f. 413, op. 2, del. 396, l. 6.

157. Martens to Krasin, 8/30/20, TsGANKh, f. 413, op. 2, del. 396, l. 4.

158. Martens to Krasin, 9/14/20, TsGANKh, f. 413, op. 2, del. 396, l. 2.

159. TsGANKh, f. 413, op. 2, del. 396, l. 5.

160. Martens to Krasin, 9/23/20, TsGANKh, f. 413, op. 2, del. 396, l. 9.

161. See *Revolutionary Radicalism,* 644–655; *Russian Propaganda,* 231–239, 320–322.

162. *Russian Propaganda,* 231–32. See also Martens speech in New York, 3/27/19; or speech at the *Dial* dinner, 5/22/19, *Russian Propaganda,* 232–235.

163. *Soviet Russia,* Vol. I, No. 1 (6/7/19).

164. *Russian Propaganda,* 239; *Revolutionary Radicalism* I:644–645.

165. *Soviet Russia,* 6/28/19, p. 3.

166. *Russian Propaganda,* 47.

167. *Soviet Russia,* 7/5/19.

168. Martens speech, 8/24/19, *Russian Propaganda,* 321–322.

169. *New Times* (Moscow), #17 (1970): 29–30.

170. Nicholas Hourwich, "Problems of the Soviet Representative," *Revolutionary Age* (4/19/19), 6.

171. Hourwich, "Problems," 6; *Current History* (2/20), 303–304; Chicherin to Martens, 8/30/19, TsGANKh, f. 413, op. 2, del. 396.

172. *New York Tribune,* 6/3/19.

173. Nuorteva to Martens, 8/7/19, TsGANKh, f. 413, op. 3, del. 515, l. 29.

174. *Revolutionary Radicalism* I:645.

175. Harper to J. Edgar Hoover, 11/18/19, SH, B7.

## Chapter 12

1. Wilson in interview with Frank Worthington, Deputy Chief Censor of the United States, in Bell to Winslow, 12/31/18, PWW 53:573–575.

2. Polk to Senator James W. Wadsworth, 11/1/19, FRUS, 1919, Russia, 161.

3. Colby, note to Italian Ambassador, 8/10/20, FRUS, 1920, III:463–468.

4. Of the major government operations against radicals in 1919 and 1920 (Overman Committee, Lusk Committee, U.S. Justice Department, U.S. Military Intelligence, Moses Committee, U.S. Department of Labor), only the Overman Committee did not concern itself with Martens directly, largely because its hearings convened before the public announcement of the Martens bureau.

5. *Bolshevik Propaganda, Hearings before a Subcommittee of the Committee on the Judiciary United States Senate,* 65th Congress, February 11, 1919, to March 10, 1919 (Washington, D.C., 1919). Hereafter referred to as BP.

6. BP, 6.

7. Johnson to Amy Johnson, 1/12/19, *Diary Letters of Hiram Johnson,* Vol. 1.

8. BP, 6–36.

9. See BP, particularly testimony by Huntington, 67–88; Harper, 88–109; Emons, 141–162; Bernstein, 383–416; and Hurban, 447–661.

10. Wilson news conference, 2/27/19, PWW 55:298–299.

11. Overman to Harper, telegram, 2/7/19, SH, B6.

12. BP, 99.

13. *Ibid.,* 100–101.

14. *Ibid.,* 47–48, 82–86.

15. *Ibid.,* 141–162, 267–292.

16. For this testimony, see BP, 466–896.

17. Johnson to Robins, 2/24/19, RR, reel 5.

18. Robert Dunn to Johnson, 2/20/19, HJ III:12.

19. BP, 563, 657, 677.

20. *Ibid.,* 689.

21. BP, 865, 878.

22. See Chapter 10.

23. See RR, reel 5, for the crush of speaking requests.

24. See Robins, "Social Control in Russia Today," *Annals of the American Philosophical Society,* 84:3 (July 1919), 127–144. The *Metropolitan* articles eventually appeared in book form, William Hard's *Raymond Robins' Own Story* (New York, 1920), which purported to be the truth of Robins' time in Russia but distorted a number of episodes, including Robins' own testimony to the Overman committee.

25. RR, reel 6.

26. Kennan personal notes on files of MID in War Department, GK.

27. Harris to SD, relayed by Phillips to Ammission, 3/29/19, HW B41.

28. Thomas Reed Powell to Harper, 4/4/19, SH, B6.

29. Huntington to M. W. Rowell, Privy Council, Ottawa, 4/24/19, SH, B27.

30. See Williams, "Raymond Robins," passim, for the story of Robins, Harding, and the 1920s.

31. The literature on the Red Scare is thin, and recent studies in particular are scarce. The best single volume remains Robert K. Murray, *Red Scare: A Study in National Hysteria* (Minneapolis, 1955), despite the many years since its publication. Murray's study, however, is broad and episodic, and lacks the detailed penetration specific monographs provide. Stanley Coben's "A Study in Nativism: The American

Red Scare of 1919–1920," *Political Science Quarterly* LXXIX (March 1964): 52–75 remains a compelling essay, ascribing the Red Scare largely to nativism and downplaying fear of Bolshevism as a central factor. The best study of nativism in its broad context is John Higham's *Strangers in the Land* (New York, 1970). Stanley Coben's *Alexander Mitchell Palmer: Politician* (New York, 1963) provides essential biographical background on the Attorney General of the Palmer Raids. William Preston, *Aliens and Dissenters: Federal Suppression of Radicals, 1903–1933* (Cambridge, Mass., 1963), places the Red Scare in a broader context of repression in the first decades of the twentieth century. For details on American Communists and their relationship to Soviet Russia, see Theodore Draper, *The Roots of American Communism* (New York, 1957), and Philip S. Foner, *The Bolshevik Revolution: Its Impact on American Radicals, Liberals, and Labor* (New York, 1970). Peter Filene, *Americans and the Soviet Experiment, 1917–1933* (Cambridge, Mass., 1967) provides a superb look into public opinion. Julian F. Jaffe, *Crusade Against Radicalism: New York During the Red Scare* (Port Washington, N.Y., 1972), examines the impact on New York State. Zosa Szajkowski, *Jews, Wars, and Communism,* Vol. II, *The Impact of the 1919–20 Red Scare on American Jewish Life* (New York, 1974), examines the persecution of radical Jews in New York in some detail, but provides little new information on the relationship of the Red Scare to early Soviet-American relations. Roy Talbert, *Negative Intelligence* (Jackson, Miss., 1991), is a solid look at the role of the MID and other intelligence agencies.

32. Murray, *Red Scare,* 5–11.

33. *Ibid.,* 82–104. See also H. C. Peterson and Gilbert C. Fite, *Opponents of War* (Madison, 1957), *passim.*

34. Draper, *Roots of American Communism,* 105. For more details on American radicals, their response to the Bolsheviks, and their utilization of the strikes, see Murray, *Red Scare,* 33–66.

35. See press release, 3/19/19, Lusk, L0033; *New York Times,* 3/21/19; and Martens to Sec. of State, 3/18/19, FRUS, 1919, Russia, 134–141.

36. Phillips to Lansing, enclosing Nuorteva and Martens to Lansing, 3/25/19, EMH, B207, f2/802.

37. Porter to Huntington, 3/22/19, SH, B6.

38. Porter to Harper, 3/27/19, SH, B6.

39. Huntington to Phillips, 3/29/19, SH, B6.

40. Harper to Carter, 4/3/19 (handwritten note: "destroy this sheet"), SH, B6.

41. Committee on Bolshevism, Union League Club, N.Y.C., report to Wiseman, 4/11/19, WBW, B9, f211.

42. Current Intelligence Division, American Section, PPC, 4/13/19, HW B41.

43. "Russian Warning to American Businessmen," 4/22/19, SH, B6. Huntington questions, TsGANKh, f. 413, del. 515, ll. 32–34. SD statement, Lansing to Polk, 4/17/19, FRUS, 1919, Russia, 143.

44. Polk to Ammission, 6/5/19, FRUS, 1919, Russia, 144–145.

45. Minutes of Daily Meetings of Commissioners, 6/14/19, TB, B265.

46. Ammission to Acting Sec. of State (Polk), 6/18/19, FRUS, 1919, Russia, 146.

47. Miles memorandum, 6/24/19, FRUS, 1919, Russia, 146–148.

48. Concurrent resolution of the New York State Legislature, authorizing the Joint Committee to Investigate Subversive Activities, March 1919, in Lawrence H. Chamberlain, *Loyalty and Legislative Action* (Ithaca, N.Y., 1951), Appendix I, 223–224. The best overview of the Lusk Committee and its work can be found in Chapter One of this book. See also Patricia Wesson Wingo, "Clayton R. Lusk: A Study of Patriotism in New York Politics, 1919–1923," Ph.D. diss., Univ. of Georgia, 1966.

49. See *Revolutionary Radicalism,* passim; BP, passim; *New York Times,* 2/14/19.

50. Benjamin Glassberg to Johnson, 2/16/19, HJ III:12; *New York Times,* 1/19/19. *The New York Call* 4/7/19, noted that another Washington school teacher was suspended "for praising the present Russian government."

51. *Brewing and Liquor Interests and German Propaganda,* Hearings of the Senate Judiciary Committee subcommittee, 1918–1919 (Washington, D.C., 1919).

52. Chamberlin, *Loyalty and Legislative Action,* 12–14.

53. *Ibid.,* 14.

54. *New York Times,* 6/4/19.

55. Russian Soviet Bureau investigation file, Lusk, L0038, B4, F-14.

56. *Ibid.,* B4.

57. *Ibid.*

58. *Ibid.,* notes on a meeting in May, 1919.

59. Russian Soviet Bureau administrative files, Lusk, L0038.

60. Lusk Committee Executive session, 6/12/19, Lusk, L0026; *New York Times,* 6/13/19. See also Chamberlin, *Loyalty and Legislative Action,* 18–20, 24.

61. Russian Soviet Bureau legal file, Lusk, L0026.

62. *New York Times,* 6/19/19; *Los Angeles Times,* 6/19/19.

63. *New York Tribune,* 6/19/19.

64. "The Lusk-Stevenson 'Investigation,' " *Soviet Russia,* 7/5/19.

65. Lusk, L0027; TsGANKh, f. 413, op. 3, del. 515.

66. Chicherin to SD via chargé in Sweden (Wheeler) to Polk, 6/24/19, FRUS, 1919, Russia, 148.

67. Acting Sec. of State Phillips to chargé in Sweden (Wheeler), 7/1/19, FRUS, 1919, Russia, 149.

68. Chicherin to Lomonosov, in chargé to Sweden (Wheeler) to Acting Sec. of State (Phillips), 7/14/19, FRUS, 1919, Russia, 188–189.

69. Martens to Chicherin, 7/24/19, TsGANKh, f. 413, op. 3, del. 515, l. 31. The Lusk raids on the Rand School were the most thorough of all of the Committee's work, impounding tons of papers, pamphlets, files, and other materials, and were the centerpiece of the Committee's case on subversive propaganda. See Chamberlin, *Loyalty and Legislative Action,* 24–34.

70. Russian Soviet Bureau, legal files, Lusk, L0037.

71. "Statement by Russian Soviet Government Bureau, November 15, 1919," *Soviet Russia,* 11/22/19.

72. Martens testimony, 11/15/19; 11/26/19; Lusk, L0026.

73. Nuorteva testiony, 12/12/19, Lusk, L0037.

74. Lusk Committee legal files, 12/31/19, Lusk, L0037.

75. *Revolutionary Radicalism,* 4 vols., passim. See in particular Tables of Contents of Vols. I and II. See also Chamberlin, *Loyalty and Legislative Action,* 34–38. Robert K. Murray, by not consulting the Lusk files on the Martens bureau, has fallen into the trap of accepting the Committee's linkage of Martens and American radicals. Murray's statements (p. 47), (*Red Scare*) were based on the Lusk Committee report and have become the standard historical interpretation, leaving the impression that Martens was strongly involved in organizing, funding, and directing the American radical movement during his stay in New York. Some important standard accounts of Soviet-American relations or Soviet foreign policy, such as Gaddis, *Russia, the Soviet Union, and the United States;* Kennan, *Russia and the West;* and Ulam, *Expansion and Coexistence;* ignore Martens and his mission entirely.

76. For the full story of wartime repression, harassment, and prosecution of social-

ists, radicals, and pacifists, see H. C. Peterson and Gilbert C. Fite, *Opponents of War* (Madison, 1957); and Harry Scheiber, *The Wilson Administration and Civil Liberties, 1917–1921* (Ithaca, 1960).

77. See, for example, Gregory to Wilson, 10/18/18, PWW 51:376–380; Gregory to Wilson, 11/9/18, PWW 53:12–13.

78. "Bolshevist Propaganda in Washington," letter from the Attorney General, 2/11/19, U.S. Sen. Doc. No. 386, 65th Congress, 3rd Session. See also *Washington Post,* 2/6/19, for strong criticism of Gregory's slowness in moving against the radicals.

79. Tumulty to Wilson, 2/1/19, PWW 54:428–430.

80. Wilson to Gregory, 2/27/19, PWW 55:292. For the full story of the struggle for Palmer's appointment, see Coben, *Palmer,* 150–154.

81. Diary of Dr. Grayson, 2/27/19, PWW 55:294–295; Palmer to Wilson, 2/28/19, PWW 55:339.

82. Wilson to Tumulty, 3/26/19, PWW 56:310; Tumulty to Wilson, 4/4/19, PWW 56:618.

83. *New York Times,* 4/1/19.

82. "The Fighting Mayor Who Would Banish Fear," *Current Opinion* LXVI, (April 1919): 226.

85. For a good summary of these events, see Murray, *Red Scare,* 67–81. More detail on Palmer's reaction is in Coben, *Palmer,* 203–210.

86. David Williams, "The Bureau of Investigation and Its Critics, 1919–1921: The Origins of Federal Political Surveillance," *Journal of American History* 68 (1981): 560–579; Murray, *Red Scare,* 193; *Washington Post,* 6/19/19; Coben, *Palmer,* 211–213.

87. Coben, *Palmer,* 211–213; Louis F. Post, *The Deportations Delirium of 1920* (Chicago, 1923), 56–58.

88. Coben, *Palmer,* 213–216.

89. Coben, *Palmer,* 218–220; Post, *Deportations Delirium,* 56–76.

90. Constantine M. Panunzio, *The Deportation Cases of 1919–1920* (New York, 1921). For an excellent account of the raids, see Robert W. Dunn, ed., *The Palmer Raids* (New York, 1948).

91. See "Shipping Lenine's Friends to Him," *Literary Digest* (January 3, 1920). The State Department had first explored the possibility of sending the group back to Russia via Riga, but could not arrange it. See Lansing to Commissioner at Riga, Gade, 12/11/19, FRUS, 1920, III:690.

92. Martens to Sec. of State, 11/15/19, NAM. For Martens' attempts to reach the Secretary of State, see Poole to Phillips, 11/21/19, and Kirk to Poole, 11/21/19, RLLC, Vol. 49. Martens also wrote a letter of reference for Goldman and Berkman to assist them in Moscow. See Martens to Goldman, December 12, 1919, Emma Goldman Papers, University of California, Berkeley. I am indebted to Candace Falk for bringing this letter to my attention.

93. During the Lusk investigations, the Justice Department began its own investigation of Martens, including a lengthy personal interview he submitted to willingly (see Nuorteva to Heller, 4/28/19, Lusk, L0032).

94. See Lusk, L0039, for correspondence between Hoover and Stevenson. For a sample of Hoover's correspondence with Military Intelligence, see the microfilm collection, *Federal Surveillance of AfroAmericans, 1917–1925.* (Frederick, Maryland, 1986), reels 17 and 22. For more details on Hoover's early anti-radical investigations, see Richard Gid Powers, *Secrecy and Power* (New York, 1987), 95–101; and Athan Theoharis and John Stuart Cox, *The Boss* (Philadelphia, 1988).

95. Harper to Crane, 1/19/19, SH, B6.

96. Harper to Richard Crane, 2/14/19, SH, B6.

97. Miles to Harper, 3/4/19, SH, B6; Harper to Miles, 3/8/19, SH, B6. See also draft Harper memoirs, SH, B76.

98. Polk to Harper, 3/15/19, SH, B6.

99. Harper draft memoirs, SH, B76.

100. Harper, *The Russia I Believe In,* 129.

101. In addition to correspondence and memoranda provided by Harper, the specific cases are listed in a December 1919 memorandum written by Harper and sent to SD desk staffer Allen Carter (Memorandum, 12/10/19, SH, B6).

102. For Harper correspondence with Hoover, see SH, B7. For the Levine case, see Boxes 8 and 51. For the Martens case, see Boxes 6 and 7.

103. Melvin B. Ericson, War Department, Chicago, to Harper, 5/28/18, SH, B5.

104. Harper to Carter, 6/6/19, SH, B7; Carter to Harper, 6/30/19, SH, B7; Harper to Victor J. West, Stanford University, 3/5/20, SH, B7.

105. *Chicago Daily News,* 4/25/19, 5/26/19, 6/5/19, 6/9/19.

106. Carter to Harper, 8/14/19, SH, B7; Harper memo on Levine case, n.d., SH, B51; Memo re Levine story on Bullitt, n.d., SH, B51.

107. Carter to Harper, 6/6/20, SH, B8; Carter to Harper, 11/26/19, SH, B7; Harper to Carter, [February 1920], SH, B7.

108. Harper to Carter, August [n.d.], 1919, SH, B63.

109. Harper to Carter, 11/18/19, SH, B7.

110. For Williams' own accounts of his time in Bolshevik Russia, see Albert Rhys Williams, *Through the Russian Revolution* (New York, 1921); and his testimony before the Overman Committee, BP.

111. Harper to Carter, [late January, 1920]; SH, B7; Carter to Harper, 2/3/20, SH, B7; Carter to Harper, 2/7/20, SH, B7.

112. Statement of the Russian Soviet Government Bureau, 12/23/19, *Soviet Russia* (1/3/20).

113. Public statement by Martens, 1/10/20, *Soviet Russia,* (1/17/20).

114. *Russian Propaganda,* Hearing before a Subcommittee of the Committee on Foreign Relations, United States Senate, Sixty-Sixth Congress, Second Session (Washington, D.C., 1920), 3.

115. *New York Tribune,* 6/14/19; Lusk, L0035.

116. *Russian Propaganda,* 1.

117. Hoover to Harper, 1/20/20, SH, B7; Memorandum of interview, Hoover, Cole and Carter, 1/23/20, SH, B7.

118. Harper to Hoover, 11/8/19, SH, B7; Hoover to Harper, 1/20/20, SH, B7.

119. Harper to Hoover, 11/18/19, SH, B7.

120. Harper to Dixon, 11/26/19, SH, B7.

121. Harper to Hoover, 11/18/19, SH, B7.

122. Harper to Carter, n.d. [January, 1920], SH, B7; Hoover to Harper, 1/7/20, SH, B6; Harper to Hoover, 1/11/20, SH, B7.

123. MID confidential situation survey, 11/12/19, *Federal Surveillance* (microfilm), reel 17; Weekly Situation Review, 1/14/20; and Hoover to Nolan, 9/23/20, reel 22.

124. Harper to Hoover, 1/11/20, SH, B7.

125. *Russian Propaganda,* 8–16.

126. *Russian Propaganda,* 47, 68–83, 450–456.

127. *Russian Propaganda,* 108–110.

128. Harper to Carter, [January 1920], SH, B7. Martens' testimony is in *Russian Propaganda,* 349–386.

129. Harper to Hoover, 1/11/20, SH, B7; Harper to Poole, 1/12/20, SH, B7; Carter to Harper, 1/13/20, SH, B7; Hoover to Harper, 1/20/20, SH B7.

130. Harper to Carter, [January 1920], SH, B7.

131. Harper to Carter memo, [January 1920] SH, B7; Carter to Harper, 1/19/20, SH, B7; Harper to Hoover, 1/23/20, SH, B7; memorandum of interview, Hoover, Cole, and Carter, 1/23/20, SH, B7.

132. Hoover to Harper, 1/31/20, SH, B7; Carter to Harper, 2/7/20, SH, B7.

133. Harper to Carter, [January 1920], SH, B7.

134. Harper to Carter, [January–February 1920], SH, B7.

135. Carter to Harper, 2/7/20, SH, B7.

136. *Russian Propaganda,* 15.

137. The Justice Department asked the Labor Department for a warrant for Martens' arrest in December 1919, which was issued, but the Committee subpoena reached Martens first. The State Department charged later that Martens was shielded by Lincoln Colcord, who "invited" the Senate subpoena server to visit Martens in his apartment. Cole to Colby, 4/29/20, BC, B2.

138. *Russian Propaganda,* 4, 6–7.

139. *Ibid.,* 14–15.

140. Memorandum of interview, Hoover, Cole, and Carter, 1/23/20, SH, B7.

141. Miles memorandum, 6/24/19, FRUS, 1919, Russia, 146–148.

142. John L. Milholland to Secretary of Labor W. B. Wilson, 2/25/20, in Lincoln Colcord, "Martens and Our Foreign Policy," *The Nation,* (3/13/20).

143. Martens to Secretary of State, 3/31/20, FRUS, 1920, III, 455–457.

144. Martens press statement, 3/31/20, *Soviet Russia,* 4/10/20.

145. Note for Colby regarding Colcord visit, 4/29/20, BC, B2.

146. Durant to Bullitt, 4/7/20, EMH, gen. corres., f45; Durant to Gumberg, 4/3/20, AG.

147. State Dept. to Justice Dept., 4/6/20, FRUS, 1920, III, 457–461.

148. Post, *Deportations Delirium,* 283–290.

149. "Decision of the Secretary of Labor in the Case of Ludwig C. A. K. Martens," 12/15/20. *Monthly Labor Review,* Bureau of Labor Statistics, XII, January–June 1921 (Washington, D.C., 1922).

150. Post, *Deportations Delirium,* 291–292.

151. For a good account of the decline of the Red Scare, see Murray, *Red Scare,* 263–279.

152. Martens to Recht, 1/18/21, NAM, reel 4.

153. Harper to Carter, [late January 1920], B7.

154. Harper to Hoover, 1/23/20, SH, B7.

155. Harper to Carter, 3/9/20, SH, B7; Harper to Carter, 4/20/20, SH, B7.

156. Harper to West, 3/5/20, SH, B7.

157. *Cabinet Diaries of Josephus Daniels,* 4/14/20, p. 518.

158. U.S. House of Representatives, Committee on Rules, *Investigation of Administration of Louis F. Post, Assistant Secretary of Labor, in the Matter of Deportation of Aliens,* Hearings, 66th Congress, 2nd Session (Washington, D.C., 1920).

159. U.S. House of Representatives, Committee on Rules, *Attorney-General A. Mitchell Palmer on Charges Made against Department of Justice by Louis F. Post and Others,* Hearings, 66th Congress, 2nd Session (Washington, D.C., 1920).

160. National Popular Government League, *To the American People: Report upon the Illegal Practices of the Department of Justice* (Washington, D.C., 1920).

161. Jusserand to Pichon, 9/12/18, PWW 49:538–539.

162. Wiseman on interview with Wilson, 10/16/18, PWW 51:347–348.
163. Wilson to Burleson, 9/16/18, PWW 51:12.
164. Wilson to Thomas Watt Gregory, 10/7/18, PWW 51:257.
165. Bell to Winslow, 12/31/18, PWW 53:573–575.
166. See for example, Malone to Wilson, 2/28/19, PWW 55:337–338.
167. Wilson to Burleson, 2/28/19, PWW 55:327; Gregory to Wilson, 3/1/19, PWW 55:346–347; Wilson to Palmer, 3/12/19, PWW 55:482–483. On the Overman Committee, see presidential news conference, 2/27/19, PWW 55:298–299.
168. Wilson to Democratic National Committee, 2/28/19, PWW 55:314.
169. Diary of Dr. Grayson, 3/10/19, PWW 55:471–472.
170. Basil Miles memo on Martens, 6/24/19, FRUS, 1919, Russia, 146–148; Wilson to Lansing, 6/12/19, PWW 60:484; Lansing to Wilson, 6/14/19, PWW 60:566–567; Wilson to Lansing, 6/17/19, PWW 60:641.
171. For an interesting personal account of the circumstances of this appointment, see diary of Dr. Grayson, 6/4/19, PWW 60:114–117.
172. Wilson to Palmer, 6/4/19, PWW 60, 145; diary of Dr. Grayson, 6/4/19, PWW 60:114–115.
173. See, for example, Robert Lansing's desk diary, 11/7/19, RLLC.
174. Lansing to Wilson, 8/7/19, PWW 62:203.
175. Poole memorandum, enclosed in Lansing to Wilson, PWW 62:203–205.
176. Wilson to Lansing, 8/14/19, PWW 62:255.
177. Tumulty to Wilson, 8/28/19, Woodrow Wilson Papers (Library of Congress microfilm), Series 2, reel 104; M. A. Matthews to Wilson, 8/20/19, *ibid.*
178. Harper to Carter, 8/17/19, SH, B7. An interesting footnote can be found in Wilson's response to an invitation by playwright Thomas Dixon to attend the opening of his new play *The Red Dawn: A Drama of Revolution*, which attempted, in Dixon's words, "to defend American Ideals against Red Communism." Wilson replied "Not on your life! . . . I would not go to see a serious play, no matter how fine, which dealt with the critical matters now daily pressing upon my judgment as matters of policy, for anything in the world." (Dixon to Wilson, 7/23/19; Wilson to Dixon 8/2/19, PWW 62:115.)
179. Ray Stannard Baker and William Dodd, eds., *Woodrow Wilson, War and Peace* (New York, 1927) II:10; PWW 63:70.
180. *Ibid.*, II:70.
181. *Ibid.*, II:108.
182. *Ibid.*, II:144, 193.
183. *The Cabinet Diaries of Josephus Daniels*, 4/14/20, p. 518; PWW 65:186–188. The editors of PWW note in this context that "there is no evidence that Wilson knew anything about the Palmer raids prior to this Cabinet meeting" (PWW 65:188 n6).
184. Wilson letters to American Legion, August 1920, Wilson Papers (Library of Congress Microfilm), Series 3, reel 158.
185. Lansing's proposed statement, 12/4/17, RLLP, B3.
186. Harper to Carter, 8/17/19, SH, B7.
187. See Harper to Huntington, 4/7/19, SH, B6. This was at the heart of the argument Harper had with J. Edgar Hoover. Hoover wanted to use pieces of Harper's material out of context and with inadequate documentation, for sensational publicity.
188. See Carter to Harper, 8/14/19, SH, B7; Harper to Carter, 8/17/19, SH, B7; Harper to Poole, 10/4/19, SH, B7.
189. U.S. State Department, "Memorandum on Certain Aspects of the Bolshevist

Movement in Russia," 10/27/19, published as *Bolshevist Movement in Russia,* Senate Document No. 172, 66th Congress, 2nd Session, 1/5/20.

190. Harper to Carter, 11/29/19, SH, B7.

191. Memo on research work, Harper to Carter, 12/10/19, SH, B6.

192. Council of Four, 5/9/19, FRUS, PPC, 5:521–522.

193. Council of Four, 6/17/19, FRUS, PPC, 5:530–532.

194. See Norman H. Gaworek, "From Blockade to Trade: Allied Economic Warfare Against Soviet Russia, June 1919 to January 1920," *Jahrbücher für Geschichte Osteuropas* 23 (1975): 39–69.

195. See Minutes of Commissioners, 7/1/19, TB, B265; Bliss to wife, Nellie, 7/17/19, TB, B244.

196. White to Sec. of State for Wilson, 7/15/19, HW, B42; PWW 61:482–83; Polk to White for Wilson, 7/18/19, FRUS, 1919, Russia, 153.

197. Wilson to Ammission via Lansing, 8/2/19, FRUS, 1919, Russia, 155–156; Clemenceau to Wilson, via White to Sec. of State, 7/27/19, FRUS, 1919, Russia, 154–155; White to Polk, 7/26/19, FRUS, 1919, Russia, 153–154.

198. Polk to Wadsworth, 11/1/19, FRUS, 1919, Russia, 161.

199. Chargé in Sweden (Wheeler) to Secretary of State, 11/18/19, FRUS, 1919, Russia, 123.

200. Lansing to Charles Valentine, 1/22/20, RLP, B5.

201. See British ambassador in Washington Lindsay's reports to FO regarding American reaction, 1/29/20, PRO, FO 371/4032.

202. Acting Secretary of State Frank Polk to U.S. ambassador in France (Wallace), 3/6/20, FRUS, 1920, III:703–704.

203. Vanderlip to Polk, 2/19/20, FV, B-1–8; Vanderlip to Colonel Phillipsen, 3/27/20, FV, B-2–5.

204. Davis to Sec. of State, 5/19/20, FRUS, 1920, III:711; Consul General at London (Skinner) to Sec. of State, 6/25/20, FRUS, 1920, III:716; Acting Sec. of State to Consul General at London, 6/25/20, FRUS, 1920, III:716. Woodrow Wilson also kept to this policy as late as a May 4 Cabinet meeting, fearful that opening trade would lead to diplomatic contact (PWW 65:247).

205. Bolshevik wireless, 4/7/20, NAM, reel 4; SD to Gade, 4/9/20, *ibid.*

206. Davis to Acting Sec. of State, 2/27/20, FRUS, 1920, III:448; Polk to Wilson, 3/10/20, PWW 65:77–78; Polk to Davis, 3/12/20, FRUS, 1920, III:450; Colby to chargé in London (Wright), 3/27/20, FRUS, 1920, III:455.

207. Wilson to Davis, 6/23/20, PWW 65:445; Davis to Wilson 6/24/20, PWW 65:455–56; Davis to Colby, 6/25/20, ND, B8; Acting Sec. of State to Ambassador to Great Britain, 6/24/20, FRUS, 1920, III:715–716. Even Boris Bakhmetev went along with a policy of trade without recognition. See Bakhmetev to Francis, 5/8/20, BB.

208. Official SD release, 7/8/20, ND, B27; Davis to U.S. ambassador in France (Wallace), 7/7/20, FRUS, 1920, III:717; Colby to minister in Denmark (Grew), 7/17/20, FRUS, 1920, III:718. Interestingly, Woodrow Wilson himself edited the final note, changing "Bolshevist" to "Soviet" Russia (Wilson to Davis 7/3/20, PWW 65:492.)

209. Department of State to all diplomatic and consular officers, 7/27/20, FRUS, 1920, III:718–719. This clearly ruled out any official American dealings with either Tsentrosoyuz or the Commissariat for Foreign Trade.

210. Lansing to Wilson, 12/3/19, FRUS, 1920, III:436–444; Lansing to Valentine, 1/22/20, RLP, B5.

211. Lansing to ambassador in Great Britain (Davis), legations at Warsaw, Prague, Helsingfors, 1/8/20, FRUS, 1920, III:444–445.

212. Lansing to Wilson, 1/20/20, WWLC, Series 2, reel 106.
213. Lansing diary, 4/11/19, RLP, B8.
214. For Spargo's involvement in Russian policy, see Ronald Radosh, "John Spargo and Wilson's Russian Policy, 1920," *Journal of American History* LII (December 1965): 548–560. Radosh argues that Spargo and Colby simply "gave expression to and codified the *existing* American policy toward Soviet Russia" (p. 559). As this study has argued throughout, there are many reasons why Wilson declined to make a public statement against the Bolsheviks until 1920. It is an oversimplification to claim, as Radosh does, that the Colby note was existing American policy since December 1917. See also Linda Killen, "Dusting Off an Old Document: Colby's 1920 Russian Policy Revisited," *Society for Historians of American Foreign Relations Newsletter* 22 (June 1991): 32–41.
215. Wilson to Spargo, 8/29/19, WWLC, Series 3, reel 158.
216. Spargo to Colby, 2/28/20, BC, B2.
217. Bakhmetev to Polk, 3/22/20, FRUS, 1920, III:451; Bakhmetev to Spargo, 3/24/20, BB. Bakhmetev had advocated that a comprehensive policy be issued as early as March 1919, in a post-Prinkipo memo to House (Bakhmetev to House, 3/11/19, BB).
218. Gompers to Colby, 6/8/20; Colby to Wilson, 6/11/20; Colby to Gompers, 6/11/20, BC, B3A.
219. "Draft of Statement on Relations of the United States with Russia," Russia desk to Colby, [June–July 1920], SH, B63.
220. Spargo to Colby, 7/31/20, BC, B3A.
221. "Draft of statement," SH, B63.
222. Spargo to Colby, 7/31/20, BC, B3A.
223. Spargo to Colby, 7/31/20, BC, B3A. See also Daniel M. Smith, *Aftermath of War: Bainbridge Colby and Wilsonian Diplomacy, 1920–1921* (Philadelphia, 1970), 55–74.
224. Colby to London, Paris, Warsaw, Rome, 8/2/20, BC, B3A.
225. Davis to Colby, conversation with secretary of Italian embassy, 8/5/20, BC, B3A.
226. *Ibid.*
227. Davis to Colby, 8/7/20, ND, B8.
228. Colby to Wilson, with draft, 8/9/20, BC, B3A.
229. Colby to the Italian ambassador, 8/10/20, BC, B8. Printed in FRUS, 1920, III:463–468.
230. Bullard to Colby, August 11, 1920, Colby Papers, Box 3A; Bullard Papers, Box 18.
231. Spargo to Colby, 8/14/20, BC, B3A.
232. See memoranda, BC, B3A.
233. Spargo, "Bainbridge Colby," in Samuel F. Bemis, ed., *American Secretaries of State, and Their Diplomacy* (New York, 1927–1929) X:206–208. For the full plan, see BC, B3A.
234. BC, B3A.
235. Davis to Colby and Wilson, 8/26/20, ND, B67.
236. Chicherin to Kamenev, 8/29–31/20, British wireless intercept 003993, LG, F 203/1/10. Another version is in SH, B65.
237. Chicherin to Russian representatives abroad, 9/10/20, Degras, *Soviet Documents*, 210–211. This note was relayed via Martens to the U.S. SD, 10/4/20, FRUS, 1920, III:474–478.

# INDEX